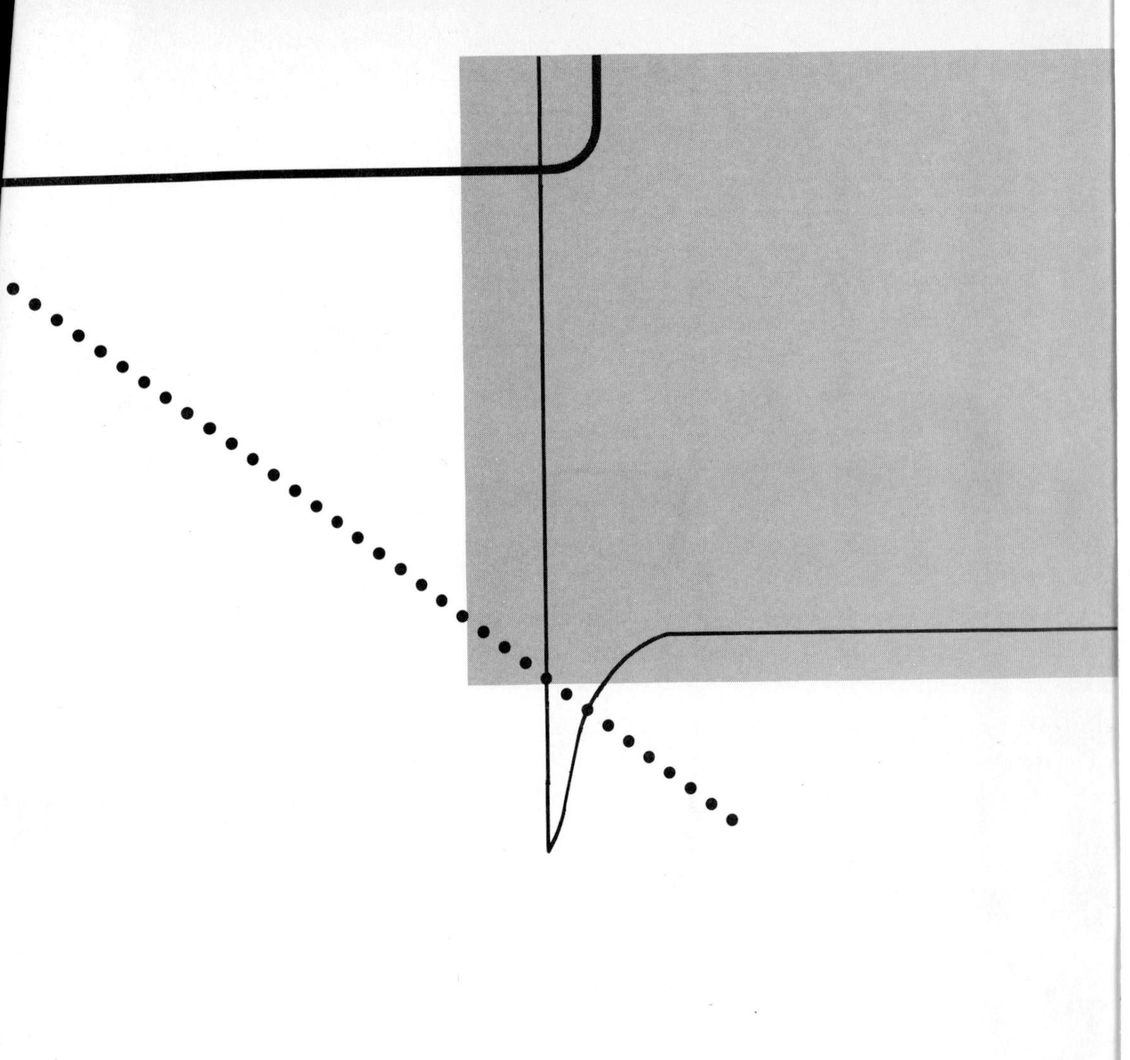

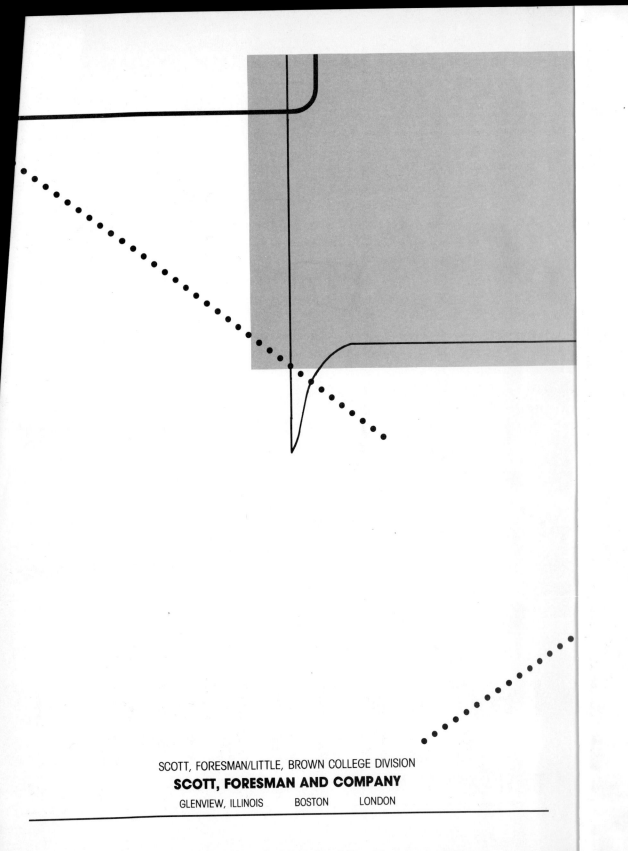

SCOTT, FORESMAN/LITTLE, BROWN COLLEGE DIVISION
SCOTT, FORESMAN AND COMPANY
GLENVIEW, ILLINOIS BOSTON LONDON

INTERNATIONAL ECONOMICS

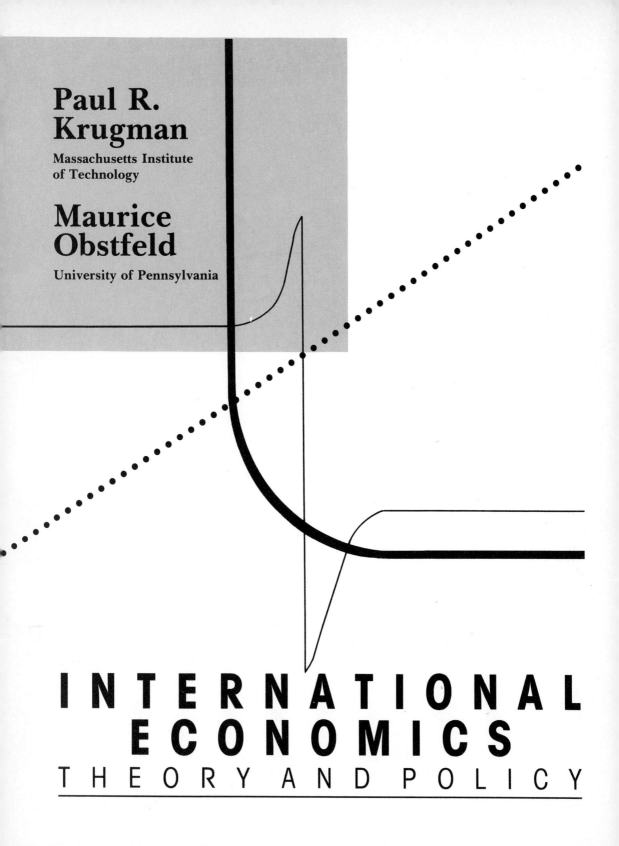

Paul R. Krugman
Massachusetts Institute of Technology

Maurice Obstfeld
University of Pennsylvania

INTERNATIONAL ECONOMICS

THEORY AND POLICY

Library of Congress Cataloging-in-Publication Data

Krugman, Paul R.
International economics.

Includes index.
1. International economic relations. 2. International finance. I. Obstfeld, Maurice. II. Title.
HF1411.K74 1987 337 87-17229
ISBN 0-673-39733-5

5 6 7 8 9 10—RRC—93 92 91 90 89

Printed in the United States of America

PREFACE

The years since 1970 have brought a steady sequence of upheavals in economic relations among countries. The fixed dollar-exchange rates of the Bretton Woods system have been abandoned in favor of a managed float; a booming international capital market has not only forged new links among the world's financial centers but also raised new unease about global financial stability; newly industrializing developing countries have seized from developed countries a significant share of the world market for manufactured exports; and most recently, macroeconomic imbalances, combined with structural shifts in trade patterns, have generated political pressures that gravely threaten the open international trading system built up so painstakingly after World War II. Even in the United States, which is more self-sufficient than nations with smaller economies, problems in international economic policy have assumed primacy and moved decisively to the newspapers' front pages.

Recent general developments in the world economy raise subjects that have preoccupied international economists for more than two centuries, such as the nature of the international adjustment mechanism and the merits of free trade compared with protection. As always in international economics, however, the interplay of events and ideas has led to new modes of analysis. Three notable examples of recent progress are the asset-market approach to exchange rates; new theories of foreign trade based on increasing returns and market structure rather than the traditional foundation of comparative advantage; and the intertemporal analysis of international capital flows, which has been useful both in refining the concept of "external balance" and in examining the determinants of developing-country borrowing and default.

The idea of writing this book came out of our experience in teaching international economics to undergraduates and business students over the past ten years. We perceived two main challenges in teaching. The first was to communicate to students the exciting intellectual advances in this dynamic field. The second was to show how international economic theory has traditionally been shaped by the need to understand the changing world economy and analyze actual problems in international economic policy.

We found that published textbooks did not adequately meet these challenges. Too often, international economics textbooks confront students with a bewildering array of special models and assumptions from which basic lessons are difficult to extract. Because many of these special models are outmoded, students are left puzzled about the real-world relevance of the analysis. As a result, current textbooks typically leave a gap between the somewhat antiquated material to be covered in class and the exciting issues that dominate current research and policy debates. This gap has widened dramatically as the importance of international economic problems—and enrollments in international economics courses—have grown.

This book is our attempt to provide an up-to-date and understandable analytical framework for illuminating current events and bringing the excitement of international economics into the classroom. In analyzing both the real and the monetary sides of the subject, our approach has been to build up, step by step, a simple, unified framework for communicating the grand traditional insights as well as the newest findings and approaches. To help the student grasp and retain the underlying logic of international economics, we motivate the theoretical development at each stage by real-world data or policy questions.

PLACE OF THIS BOOK IN THE ECONOMICS CURRICULUM

Students assimilate international economics most readily when it is presented as a method of analysis vitally linked to events in the world economy, rather than as a body of abstract theorems about abstract models. Our goal has therefore been to stress concepts and their applications rather than theoretical formalism. Accordingly, the book does not presuppose an extensive background in economics. Students who have had a course in economic principles will find the book accessible, but students who have taken further courses in microeconomics or macroeconomics will find an abundant supply of new material. Specialized chapter appendixes and mathematical postscripts are included to challenge the most advanced students.

We follow the standard practice of dividing the book into two halves, devoted to trade and to monetary questions. Although the trade and monetary portions of international economics are often treated as unrelated subjects, even within one textbook, similar themes and methods recur in both subfields. One example is the idea of gains from trade, which is important in understanding the effects of free trade in assets as well as free trade in goods. International borrowing and lending provide another example. The process by which countries trade present for future consumption is best understood in terms of comparative advantage (which is why we introduce it in the book's first half), but the resulting insights deepen understanding of the external macroeconomic problems of developing and developed economies alike. We have made it a point to illuminate connections between the trade and monetary areas when they arise.

At the same time, we have made sure that the book's two halves are completely self-contained. Thus, a one-semester course on trade theory can be based on Chapters 2 through 11 and a one-semester course on international monetary economics can be based on Chapters 12 through 21. If you adopt the book for a full-year course covering both subjects, however, you will find a treatment that does not leave students wondering why the principles underlying their work on trade theory have been discarded over the winter break.

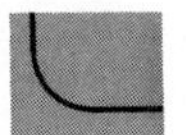

DISTINCTIVE FEATURES OF *INTERNATIONAL ECONOMICS: THEORY AND POLICY*

This book covers the most important recent developments in international economics without shortchanging the enduring theoretical and historical insights that have traditionally formed the core of the subject. We have achieved this comprehensiveness by stressing how recent theories have evolved from earlier findings in response to an evolving world economy. Both the real trade portion of the book (Chapters 2 through 11) and the monetary portion (Chapters 12 through 21) are divided into six chapters focused on theory, followed by four chapters applying the theory to major policy questions, past and current.

In Chapter 1 we describe in some detail how we address the major themes of international economics. Here we emphasize several of the newer topics that previous textbook authors failed to treat in a systematic way.

ASSET-MARKET APPROACH TO EXCHANGE-RATE DETERMINATION

The modern foreign exchange market and the determination of exchange rates by national interest rates and expectations are at the center of our account of open-economy macroeconomics. The main ingredient of the macroeconomic model we develop is the interest parity relation (augmented later by risk premiums). Among the topics we address using the model are exchange-rate "overshooting"; behavior of real exchange rates; balance of payments crises under fixed exchange rates; and causes and effects of central-bank intervention in the foreign exchange market.

INCREASING RETURNS AND MARKET STRUCTURE

After discussing the role of comparative advantage in promoting trade and gains from trade, we move to the frontier of recent research (in Chapter 6) by explaining how increasing returns and product differentiation affect trade and welfare. The models explored in this discussion capture significant aspects of reality, such as shifts in international patterns of manufacturing trade and intra-industry trade. The models show too that mutually beneficial trade need not be based on comparative advantage.

WORLD CAPITAL MARKET AND DEVELOPING-COUNTRY DEBT

Chapter 20 takes up the specific macroeconomic problems of developing countries, emphasizing the debt problem. The chapter provides an introductory view of the global capital market by placing in historical perspective the interactions among developing-country borrowers, money-center banks, and international financial institutions such as the International Monetary Fund. A teachable model of sovereign default offers students a structured approach to a problem vaguely treated in other textbooks despite its central position on the international financial scene since 1982. A broader discussion of the world capital market is given in Chapter 21, taking up the welfare implications of international portfolio diversification as well as recent problems in prudential supervision of offshore financial activities.

POLITICS OF TRADE POLICY AND INDUSTRIAL POLICY

Starting in Chapter 3, we stress the effect of trade on income distribution as the key political factor behind restrictions on free trade. This emphasis makes it clear to students why the prescriptions of the standard welfare analysis of trade policy seldom prevail in practice. Chapter 11 is focused on the currently popular notion that governments should adopt "industrial policies" aimed at encouraging sectors of the economy seen as crucial. The chapter also includes a discussion of strategic trade policy based on simple ideas from game theory.

INTERNATIONAL MACROECONOMIC POLICY COORDINATION

Our discussion of international monetary experience (Chapters 18 and 19) stresses the theme that different exchange-rate systems have led to different *policy coordination* problems for their members. Just as the competitive currency depreciations of the interwar years showed how beggar-thy-neighbor policies can be self-defeating, the current float challenges national policy makers to recognize their interdependence and formulate policies cooperatively. Chapter 19 has a detailed discussion of this very topical problem in the current system.

INTERNATIONAL FACTOR MOVEMENTS

In Chapter 7 we emphasize the potential substitutability of international trade and international movements of factors of production. A feature in the chapter is our analysis of international borrowing and lending as *intertemporal trade,* that is, the exchange of present consumption for future consumption. We draw on the results of this analysis in the book's second half to throw light on the macroeconomic implications of the current account.

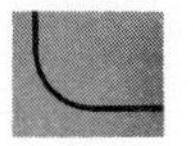

LEARNING FEATURES

This book incorporates a number of special learning features that will maintain students' interest in the presentation and help them master its lessons.

CASE STUDIES

Theoretical discussions are often accompanied by case studies that perform the threefold role of reinforcing material covered earlier, illustrating its applicability in the real world, and providing historical information.

SPECIAL BOXES

Less central topics that nonetheless offer particularly vivid illustrations of points made in the text are treated in boxes. Among these are the political backdrops to Ricardo's and Hume's theories (pp. 59 and 508); the relation between inflation and interest rates in Argentina (p. 373); and Korea's growth into a major exporter of manufactures (p. 237).

CAPTIONED DIAGRAMS

The roughly 200 diagrams are accompanied by descriptive captions that reinforce the discussion in the text and will help the student in reviewing the material.

SUMMARY AND KEY TERMS

Each chapter closes with a summary recapitulating the major points. Key terms or phrases appear in boldface type when they are introduced in the chapter and are listed at the end of each chapter. To further aid review of the material, key terms are italicized when they appear in the chapter summary, and the pages on which the terms are defined are listed in boldface type in the index.

PROBLEMS

Each chapter is followed by problems intended to test and solidify students' comprehension. The problems range from routine computational drills to "big-picture" questions suitable for classroom discussion. In many problems we ask students to apply what they've learned to real-world data or policy issues.

FURTHER READING

For instructors who prefer to supplement the textbook with outside readings, and for students who wish to probe more deeply on their own, each chapter has an annotated bibliography that includes established classics as well as up-to-date examinations of recent issues.

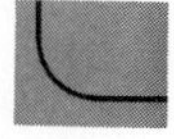

INSTRUCTOR'S MANUAL

International Economics: Theory and Policy is accompanied by an Instructor's Manual written by Michael W. Klein of Clark University. The manual includes chapter overviews, answers to the end-of-chapter problems, and suggestions for classroom presentation of the book's contents.

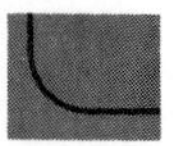

ACKNOWLEDGMENTS

Many people have contributed to the completion of this book. Jane Tufts, the book's development editor, made critical suggestions at every stage in this project. Her contribution is impossible to overestimate. Denise Clinton, economics editor, spared no effort in making sure that we produced the best book possible on schedule. The indispensable help and moral support that Jane and Denise gave so generously is acknowledged with deep gratitude. Book editor Victoria Keirnan brought order out of chaos and transformed our word-processed chapters and hand-scrawled diagrams into this finished product.

The book also reflects the distinctive input of Will Ethridge, who guided the project through its initial stages. We owe special thanks to George Lobell, the matchmaker who brought the authors of this book together.

Several colleagues used draft chapters in their courses and offered valuable suggestions. Robert Cumby of New York University's Graduate School of Business Administration gave us detailed comments that were always useful and sometimes led us to reorganize entire chapters. We also thank Alberto Giovannini and Frederic Mishkin of Columbia University's Graduate School of Business, Michael Klein of Clark University, and Torsten Persson of the Institute for International Economic Studies (Stockholm), for their advice and criticism.

Additional helpful comments were received from these reviewers: Leonardo Auernheimer, Texas A & M University; Bradley Billings, Georgetown University; Willem Buiter, Yale University; John Burkett, University of Rhode Island; Jim Cassing, University of Pittsburgh; Judy Cox, University of Washington; Amy Dalton, Virginia Commonwealth University; Alan Deardorff, University of Michigan; Sebastian Edwards, University of California—Los Angeles; David Feldman, Colgate University; John Flanders, Central Methodist College; Kenneth Judd, Northwestern University; Ki Hoon Kim, Central Connecticut State College; Peter Kressler, Glassboro State University; Nancy Marion, Dartmouth College; Keith E. Maskus, University of Colorado—Boulder; Donald L. McCrickard, University of North Carolina—Greensboro; Sean Nolan, Boston University; Arvind Panagariya, University of Maryland; Charles P. Staelin, Smith College; Edward Tower, Duke University; Ernst Weber, California State University—Northridge.

A final word of thanks goes to M. I. T. graduate student Huntley Schaller, who cheerfully shouldered the unappealing task of helping us check galleys. The remaining errors, which are fewer than they would otherwise have been, should be blamed on the authors alone.

CONTENTS

1 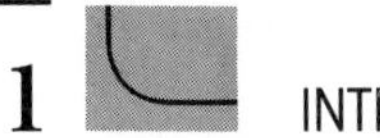 INTRODUCTION 1

PART ONE · INTERNATIONAL TRADE THEORY 11

2 LABOR PRODUCTIVITY AND COMPARATIVE ADVANTAGE: THE RICARDIAN MODEL 13

*will appear in all subsequent chapters

7 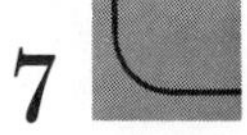

INTERNATIONAL FACTOR MOVEMENTS 148

PART TWO · INTERNATIONAL TRADE POLICY 171

8

THE INSTRUMENTS OF TRADE POLICY 173

10 TRADE POLICY IN DEVELOPING COUNTRIES 229

11 INDUSTRIAL POLICY IN ADVANCED COUNTRIES 253

13 EXCHANGE RATES AND THE FOREIGN-EXCHANGE MARKET: AN ASSET APPROACH 306

14 MONEY, INTEREST RATES, AND EXCHANGE RATES 342

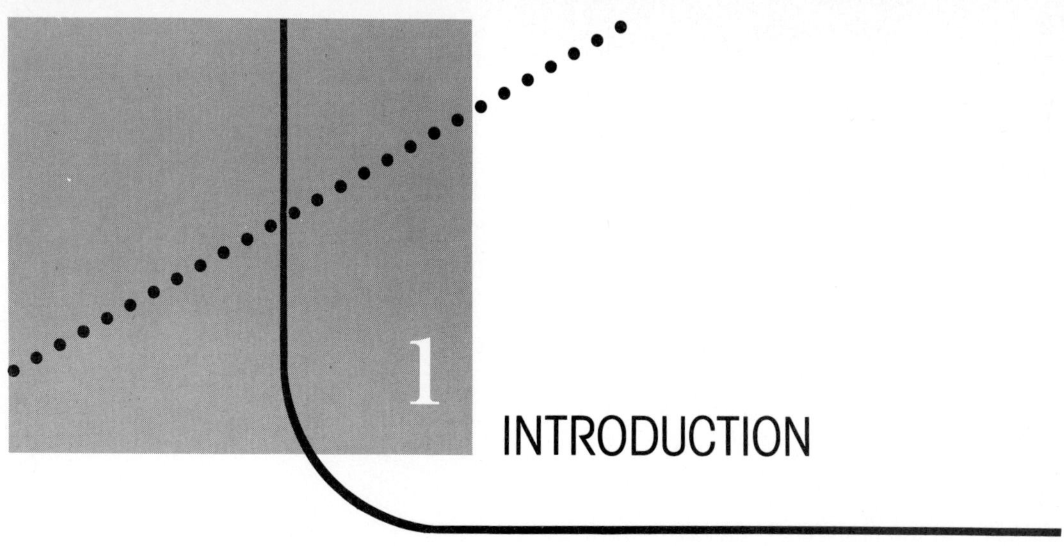

1 INTRODUCTION

The study of international trade and money has always been an especially lively and controversial part of economics. Many of the key insights of modern economic analysis first emerged in eighteenth and nineteenth century debates over international trade and monetary policy. Yet there was never a time when the study of international economics was as important as it is today. Through international trade in goods and services, and international flows of money, the economies of different countries are more closely linked to one another now than ever before. At the same time, the world economy is more turbulent than it has been in many decades. Keeping up with the shifting international environment has become a central concern of both business strategy and national economic policy.

A look at some basic trade statistics gives a first view of the increasing importance of international economics to the United States. Figure 1-1 shows the levels of U.S. exports and imports as shares of gross national product from 1965 to 1985. Two points are apparent from the figure. First, the United States exports much more of what it produces and imports much

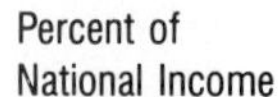

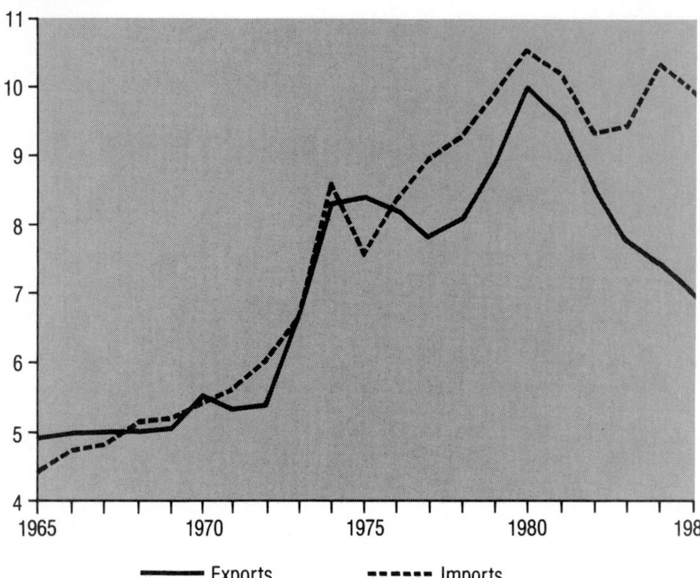

FIGURE 1-1 Exports and imports as a percent of U.S. national income. From the 1960s to 1980, both exports and imports rose steadily as shares of U.S. income. Since 1980, exports have plunged but imports have not.

more of what it consumes than it used to: from 1965 to 1980 the share of both exports and imports in GNP more than doubled. Second, something drastic has happened to U.S. trade since about 1980: exports have plunged relative to GNP, while imports have not. Both the long-term trend toward increasing trade and the recent sharp decline in U.S. exports relative to imports have been crucial developments for the U.S. economy. By 1980, hardly any discussion of domestic economic policy, be it antitrust, regulation, taxation, or labor issues, could ignore the role of international trade. Since 1980, rising imports and falling exports have been one of the most heated issues of U.S. economic controversy.

If international economics has become crucial to the United States, it is even more crucial to other nations. Figure 1-2 shows the 1984 shares of imports and exports in GNP for a sample of countries. The United States, by virtue of its size and the diversity of its resources, actually relies less on international trade than almost any other country. This means that for the rest of the world, international economics is even more important than it is for the United States.

This book introduces the main concepts and methods of international economics and illustrates them with applications drawn from the real world. It is in large part devoted to the grand tradition of international economics; the nineteenth century trade theory of David Ricardo and the even earlier international monetary analysis of David Hume remain quite relevant to the modern world. At the same time, we have made a special effort to bring the

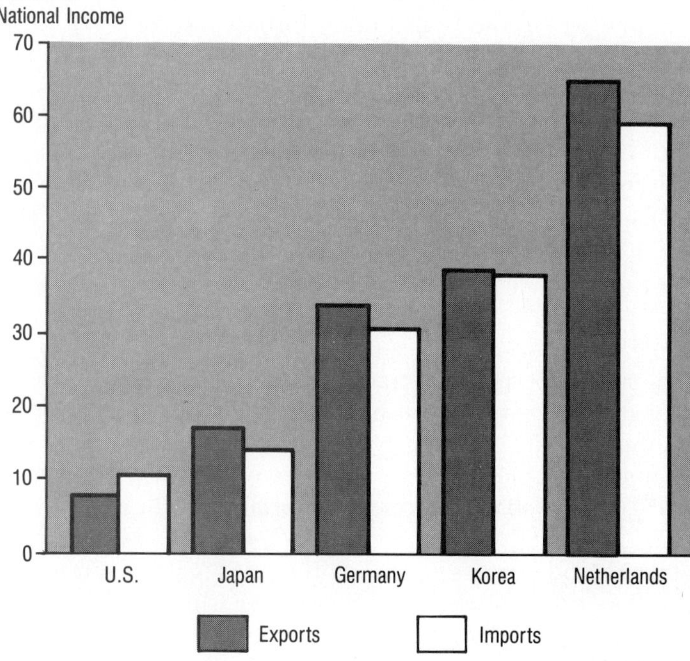

FIGURE 1-2 Exports and imports as percentages of national income in 1984. International trade is even more important to most other countries than it is to the United States.

analysis up to date. The field of international economics has been in a creative ferment in recent years, with new views emerging on such issues as the political economy of trade policy, strategic trade policy, exchange-rate determination, and the international coordination of macroeconomic policies. We have attempted to convey the key ideas of these new approaches while stressing the continuing usefulness of older ideas.

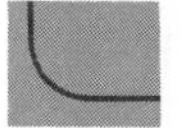

WHAT IS INTERNATIONAL ECONOMICS ABOUT?

International economics uses the same fundamental methods of analysis as other branches of economics, because the motives and behavior of individuals and firms are the same in international trade as they are in domestic transactions. When a bottle of Spanish wine appears on a London table, the sequence of events that brought it there is not very different from the sequence that brings a California bottle to a table in New York—and the distance traveled is much less! Yet international economics involves new and different concerns, because international trade and investment occur between independent nations. Spain and the United Kingdom are sovereign states; California and New York are not. Spain's wine shipments to the United Kingdom can be therefore be disrupted if the British government sets a quota that limits imports; Spanish wine may become suddenly cheaper to British wine drinkers if the foreign-exchange value of Spain's peseta falls against that of Britain's pound sterling. Neither of these events can happen within the United States, where the Constitution forbids restraints on interstate trade and there is only one currency.

The subject matter of international economics, then, consists of issues raised by the special problems of economic interaction between sovereign states. Seven themes in particular recur throughout the subject: the gains from trade, the pattern of trade, protectionism, the balance of payments, exchange-rate determination, international policy coordination, and the international capital market.

THE GAINS FROM TRADE

Everyone knows that some international trade is beneficial—nobody would suggest that Norway should grow its own oranges. Many people, however, are skeptical about the benefits of trading for goods that a country could produce for itself. Shouldn't Americans buy American goods whenever possible to help save U.S. jobs? Probably the most important insight in all of international economics is the idea that there are *gains from trade* —that is, that when countries sell goods and services to one another, this is almost always to their mutual benefit. The range of circumstances under which international trade is beneficial is much wider than most people appreciate. For example, many U.S. businessmen fear that if Japanese productivity overtakes that of the United States, trade with Japan will damage the U.S. economy because none of our industries will be able to compete. U.S. labor leaders charge that the United States is hurt by trade with less advanced countries, whose industries are less efficient than ours but who can sometimes undersell U.S. producers because they pay much lower wages. Yet the first model of trade in this book (Chapter 2) demonstrates that two countries can trade to their mutual advantage even when one of them is more efficient than the other at producing everything and producers in the less efficient economy can compete only by paying lower wages. Trade provides benefits by allowing countries to export goods whose production makes relatively heavy use of resources that are locally abundant while importing goods whose production makes heavy use of resources that are locally scarce (Chapter 4). International trade also allows countries to specialize in producing narrower ranges of goods, allowing them to gain greater efficiencies of large-scale production (Chapter 6). Nor are the benefits limited to trade in tangible goods: international migration and international borrowing and lending are also forms of mutually beneficial trade, the first a trade of labor for goods and services, the second a trade of current goods for the promise of future goods (Chapter 7). Finally, international exchanges of risky assets such as stocks and bonds can benefit all countries by allowing each country to diversify its wealth and reduce the variability of its income (Chapter 21). These invisible forms of trade yield gains as real as the trade that puts fresh fruit from Latin America in Toronto markets in February.

THE PATTERN OF TRADE

Economists cannot discuss the effects of international trade or recommend changes in government policies toward trade with any confidence unless they know that their theory is good enough to explain the international trade that is actually observed. Thus attempts to explain the pattern of international trade—who sells what to whom—have been a major preoccupation of international economists.

Some aspects of the pattern of trade are easy to understand. Climate and resources clearly explain why Brazil exports coffee and Saudi Arabia exports oil. Much of the pattern of trade is more subtle, however. Why does Japan export automobiles, while the United States exports aircraft? In the early nineteenth century English economist David Ricardo offered an explanation of trade in terms of international differences in labor productivity, an explanation that remains a powerful insight (Chapter 2). In the twentieth century, however, alternative explanations have also been proposed. One of the most influential, but still controversial, views links trade patterns to an interaction between the relative supplies of national resources such as capital, labor, and land on one side and the relative use of these factors in the production of different goods on the other. We present this theory in Chapter 4. Even as this book was being written, however, researchers presented new evidence that appears to show that this theory is less valid than many had previously thought. More recently still, some international economists have proposed theories that suggest a substantial random component in the pattern of international trade, theories that are developed in Chapter 6.

PROTECTIONISM

If the idea of gains from trade is the most important theoretical concept in international economics, the seemingly eternal battle between Free Trade and Protection is its most important policy theme. Since the emergence of modern nation-states in the sixteenth century, governments have worried about the effect of international competition on the prosperity of domestic industries and have tried either to shield industries from foreign competition by placing limits on imports or to help them in world competition by subsidizing exports. The single most consistent mission of international economics has been to analyze the effects of these so-called protectionist policies—and usually, though not always, to criticize protectionism and show the advantages of freer international trade.

The protectionist issue is especially intense in the United States because of the trends illustrated by Figure 1-1. Since World War II the United States has advocated free trade in the world economy, viewing international trade as a force not only for prosperity but also for world peace. With the growing role of trade in the U.S. economy from 1965 to 1980, however, many industries found that for the first time they were facing foreign competition in their home markets. Some of them found the foreign competition too much to handle and appealed for protection. During the 1970s these demands were opposed by other U.S. industries that were benefiting from increased export sales. In the 1980s, however, as exports plunged, the mood of Congress shifted toward protectionism. The Reagan administration resisted this political pressure but made a series of concessions, limiting imports of Japanese automobiles, European steel, Canadian lumber, and many other goods. Although the opposition of most international economists to protection remains as strong as ever, there seems to be a real possibility that over the next few years the United States will move sharply away from its four-decade-long commitment to the principle of free trade.

As befits both the historical importance and the current relevance of the protectionist issue, roughly a quarter of this book is devoted to this subject. Over the years, international economists have developed a simple yet powerful analytical framework for determining the effects of government policies that affect international trade. This framework not only predicts the effects of trade policies, it allows cost-benefit analysis and defines criteria for determining when government intervention is good for the economy. We present this framework in Chapters 8 and 9, and use it to discuss a number of policy issues in those chapters and in the following two.

In the real world, however, governments do not necessarily do what the cost-benefit analysis of economists tells them they should. This does not mean that analysis is useless. Economic analysis can help make sense of the politics of international trade policy, by showing who benefits and who loses from such government actions as quotas on imports and subsidies to exports. The key insight of this analysis is that conflicts of interest *within* nations are usually more important in determining trade policy than conflicts of interest *between* nations. Chapters 3 and 4 show that trade usually has very strong effects on income distribution within countries, while Chapters 9, 10, and 11 reveal that the relative power of different interest groups within countries, rather than some measure of overall national interest, is often the main determining factor in government policies toward international trade.

THE BALANCE OF PAYMENTS

In 1985, both Japan and Brazil ran large trade surpluses—that is, each of them sold more goods to the rest of the world than it bought in return. Japan's surplus of $56 billion brought complaints from many other countries that Japan was gaining at their expense; Brazil's surplus of $13 billion (which represented a much larger fraction of the country's national income) brought complaints from the Brazilians that *they* were being unfairly treated. What does it mean when a country runs a trade surplus or a trade deficit? To make sense of numbers like the trade deficit, it is essential to place them in the broader context of the whole of a nation's international transactions.

The record of a country's transactions with the rest of the world is called the balance of payments. Explaining the balance of payments, and diagnosing its significance, is a main theme of international economics. It emerges in a variety of specific contexts: in discussing international capital movements (Chapter 7), in relating international transactions to national income accounting (Chapter 12), and in discussing virtually every aspect of international monetary policy (Chapters 16 through 21). Like the problem of protectionism, the balance of payments has become a central issue for the United States because plunging exports and soaring imports have led to record trade deficits in every year since 1982.

EXCHANGE-RATE DETERMINATION

In February 1985, one U.S. dollar traded on international markets for 260 Japanese yen; in February 1987, a dollar was worth only 153 yen. This change had effects that reached far beyond financial markets. In February 1985, the average Japanese worker in manufacturing was paid a wage in yen that, converted into dollars at the prevailing rate of exchange, was only about half that of his U.S. counterpart. Two years later Japanese wages were about 80 percent of U.S. wages. With much of their labor cost advantage vis-à-vis the United States gone, and in the face of competition from low-wage competitors like Korea and Taiwan, Japanese manufacturers were forced into layoffs that drove the Japanese unemployment rate to its highest level since the 1950s.

One of the key differences between international economics and other parts of the field of economics is that different countries have different currencies. It is usually possible to convert one currency into another (though even this is illegal in some countries), but as the example of the dollar-yen exchange rate indicates, relative prices of currencies may change over time, sometimes drastically.

The study of exchange-rate determination is a relatively new part of international economics, for historical reasons. For most of the past century, exchange rates have been fixed by government action rather than determined in the marketplace. Before World War I the values of the world's major currencies were fixed in terms of gold, while for a generation after World War II the values of most currencies were fixed in terms of the U.S. dollar. The analysis of international monetary systems that fix exchange rates remains an important subject, especially since a return to fixed rates in the future remains a real possibility. Chapters 17 and 18 are devoted to the working of fixed-rate systems, and Chapter 19 to the debate over which system is better. For the time being, however, some of the world's most important exchange rates fluctuate minute by minute and the role of changing exchange rates remains at the center of the international economics story. Chapters 13 through 16 focus on the modern theory of floating exchange rates.

INTERNATIONAL POLICY COORDINATION

The international economy comprises sovereign nations, each free to choose its own economic policies. Unfortunately, in an integrated world economy one country's economic policies usually affect other countries as well. When West Germany raised taxes and interest rates in 1981, all of Europe went into a recession; when the United States imposed a tariff on imports of lumber during 1986, the Canadian lumber industry was placed into crisis. Differences in goals between countries often lead to conflicts of interest. Even when countries have similar goals, they may suffer losses if they fail to coordinate their policies. A fundamental problem in international economics is how to produce an acceptable degree of harmony among the international trade and monetary policies of different countries without a world government that can tell countries what to do.

For the last 40 years international trade policies have been governed by an international treaty known as the General Agreement on Tariffs and Trade, and massive international negotiations involving dozens of countries at a time have been held. We discuss the rationale for this system in Chapter 9 and look at whether the current rules of the game for international trade in the world economy can or should survive.

While cooperation on international trade policies is a well-established tradition, coordination of international macroeconomic policies is a newer and more uncertain topic. Only in the last few years have economists formulated at all precisely the case for macroeconomic policy coordination. Nonetheless, attempts at international macroeconomic coordination are occurring with growing frequency in the real world. Both the theory of international macroeconomic coordination and the developing experience are reviewed in Chapters 18 and 19.

THE INTERNATIONAL CAPITAL MARKET

During the 1970s banks in advanced countries lent hundreds of billions of dollars to firms and governments in poorer nations, especially in Latin America. In 1982, Mexico announced that it could no longer pay the money it owed without special arrangements that allowed it to postpone payments and borrow back part of its interest; soon afterward Brazil, Argentina, and a number of smaller countries found themselves in the same situation. While combined efforts of banks, governments, and countries avoided a world financial crisis in 1982, the debt difficulties of less-developed countries remained in a state of periodic crisis through 1987. The debt problem brought to the public's attention the growing importance of the international capital market.

In any sophisticated economy there is an extensive capital market: a set of arrangements by which individuals and firms exchange money now for promises to pay in the future. The growing importance of international trade since the 1960s has been accompanied by a growth in the *international* capital market, which links the capital markets of individual countries. Thus in the 1970s oil-rich Middle Eastern nations placed their oil revenues in banks in London or New York, and these banks in turn lent money to governments and corporations in Asia and Latin America. In the first half of the 1980s Japan converted much of the money it earned from its booming exports into investments in the United States, including the establishment of a growing number of U.S. subsidiaries of Japanese corporations.

International capital markets differ in important ways from national capital markets. They must cope with special regulations that many countries impose on foreign investment; they also sometimes offer opportunities to evade regulations placed on domestic markets. Since the 1960s, huge international capital markets have arisen, most notably the remarkable London Eurodollar market, in which billions of dollars are exchanged each day without ever touching the United States.

Some special risks are also associated with international capital markets. One risk is that of currency fluctuations: if the dollar falls suddenly against the Japanese yen, Japanese investors who bought U.S. bonds suffer a capital loss—as many discovered in 1985–1987. Another risk is that of national default: a nation may simply refuse to pay its debts (perhaps because it cannot), and there may be no effective way for its creditor to bring it to court. This remains a real possibility for the nations of Latin America; if all of them were to refuse payment, some major U.S. banks would themselves be at risk of going bankrupt.

The growing importance of international capital markets, and their new problems, demand greater attention than ever before. This book devotes two chapters to issues arising from international capital markets: one on the international debt problem (Chapter 20) and one on the functioning of global asset markets (Chapter 21).

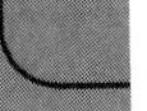

INTERNATIONAL ECONOMICS: TRADE AND MONEY

The economics of the international economy can be divided into two broad subfields: the study of *international trade* and the study of *international money.* International trade analysis focuses primarily on the *real* transactions in the international economy, that is, on those transactions that involve a physical movement of goods or a tangible commitment of economic resources. International monetary analysis focuses on the *monetary* side of the international economy, that is, on financial transactions such as foreign purchases of U.S. dollars. An example of an international trade issue is the conflict between the United States and Europe over Europe's subsidized exports of agricultural products; an example of an international monetary issue is the dispute over whether the foreign-exchange value of the dollar should be allowed to fall freely or be supported by government action.

In the real world there is no simple dividing line between trade and monetary issues. Most international trade involves monetary transactions, while, as the examples in this chapter already suggest, many monetary events have important consequences for trade. Nonetheless, the distinction between international trade and international money is useful. The first half of this book covers international trade issues. Part I (Chapters 2 through 7) develops the analytical theory of international trade, and Part II (Chapters 8 through 11) applies trade theory to the analysis of government policies toward trade. The second half of the book is devoted to international monetary issues. Part III (Chapters 12 through 17) develops international monetary theory, and Part IV (Chapters 18 through 21) applies this analysis to international monetary policy.

PART ONE

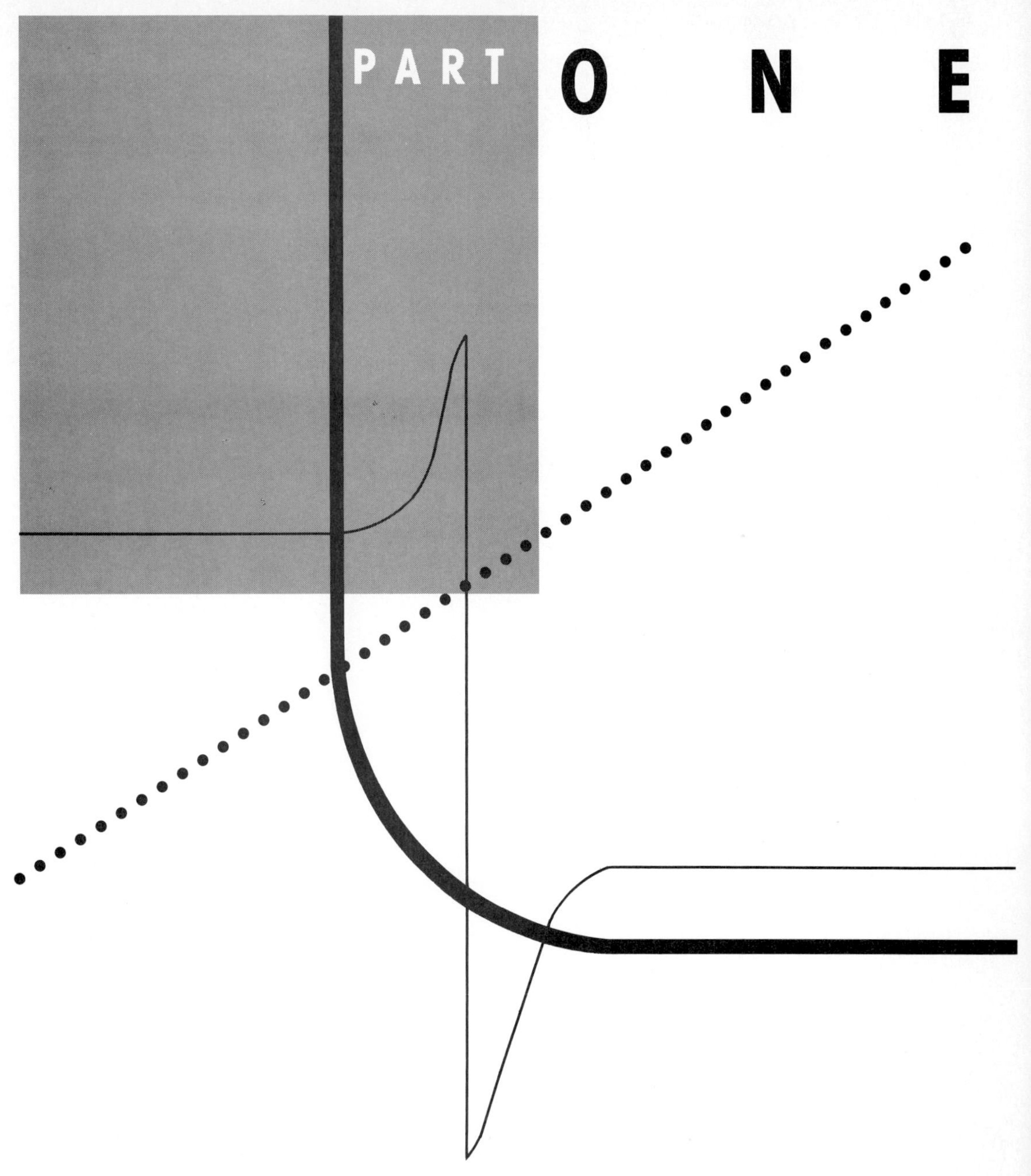

INTERNATIONAL TRADE THEORY

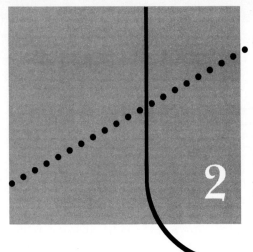

2 LABOR PRODUCTIVITY AND COMPARATIVE ADVANTAGE: THE RICARDIAN MODEL

Countries engage in international trade for two basic reasons, each of which can also be seen as a reason why countries gain from trade. First, countries trade because they are different from each other. Nations, like individuals, can benefit from their differences by reaching an arrangement in which each does the things it does relatively well. Second, countries trade in order to achieve economies of scale in production. That is, if each country produces only a limited range of goods, it can produce each of these goods at a larger scale and hence more efficiently than if it tried to produce everything. In the real world, patterns of international trade reflect the interaction of both these motives. As a first step toward understanding the causes and effects of trade, however, it is useful to look at simplified models in which only one of these motives is present.

The next four chapters develop a set of tools to help us to understand how differences between countries give rise to trade between them, and why this trade is mutually beneficial. The essential concept in this analysis is that of **comparative advantage.**

Although the idea of comparative advantage is a simple one, it can be somewhat confusing if stated in the abstract. The best way to grasp the concept properly is to examine a series of examples and models that demonstrate it. This chapter provides examples in which comparative advantage is solely the result of international differences in the productivity of labor. A model of comparative advantage resting on differences in labor productivity was first introduced in the early nineteenth century by the economist David Ricardo,[1] and is therefore referred to as the **Ricardian model.**

This chapter begins by examining a simple model of a Ricardian economy that does not trade with the rest of the world. Then we see what happens when two such economies are allowed to trade. A third section applies the results of this analysis to some often misunderstood policy issues. Finally, we consider some extensions of the basic model.

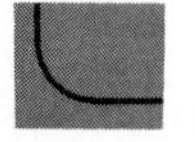

A ONE-FACTOR ECONOMY

To introduce the role of comparative advantage in determining the pattern of international trade, we begin by imagining that we are dealing with an economy—which we call Home—that has only one factor of production. (We extend the analysis to models in which there are several factors in later chapters.) Also we imagine that only two goods, wine and cheese, are produced. The technology of Home's economy can be summarized by the productivity of labor in each industry. It will turn out to be convenient to express productivity in terms of the **unit labor requirement,** the number of hours of labor required to produce a pound of cheese or a gallon of wine. For future reference, let us define a_{LW} and a_{LC} as the unit labor requirements in wine and cheese production, respectively. Also, the economy's total resources may be defined as L, the total labor supply.

PRODUCTION POSSIBILITIES

Because any economy has limited resources, there are limits on what it can produce, and there are always trade-offs; to produce more of one good the economy must sacrifice some production of another good. These trade-offs are illustrated graphically by a **production possibility frontier** (line PF in Figure 2-1), which shows the maximum amount of wine that can be produced once the decision has been made to produce any given amount of cheese, and vice versa.

When there is only one factor of production the production possibility frontier of an economy is simply a straight line. We can derive this line as follows: Let Q_W be the economy's production of wine and Q_C its production of cheese. Then the labor used in producing wine will be $a_{LW}Q_W$, the labor

[1]The classic reference is David Ricardo, *The Principles of Political Economy and Taxation*, first published in 1817.

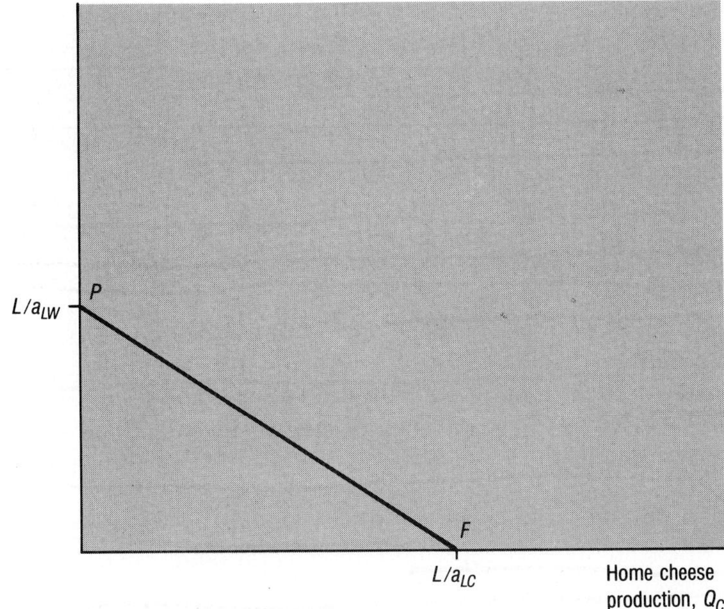

FIGURE 2-1 Home's production possibility frontier. The line *PF* shows the maximum amount of cheese that can be produced given any production of wine, and vice versa.

used in producing cheese $a_{LC}Q_C$. The production possibility frontier is determined by the limits on the economy's resources—in this case, labor. The economy's total labor supply is L. So the limits on production are defined by the inequality

$$a_{LC}Q_C + a_{LW}Q_W \leq L. \tag{2-1}$$

When the production possibility frontier is a straight line, the **opportunity cost** of cheese in terms of wine is constant. The opportunity cost is the number of gallons of wine the economy would have to give up in order to produce an extra pound of cheese. In this case, to produce another pound would require a_{LC} man-hours. Each of these man-hours could in turn have been used to produce $1/a_{LW}$ gallons of wine. Thus the opportunity cost of cheese in terms of wine is a_{LC}/a_{LW}. This is equal to minus the slope of the production possibility frontier, which itself is equal to the unit labor requirement in cheese (a_{LC} hours per pound) relative to that in wine (a_{LW} hours per gallon).

RELATIVE PRICES AND SUPPLY

The production possibility frontier illustrates the different mixes of goods the economy *can* produce. In order to determine what the economy will actually produce, however, we need to look at prices. Specifically, we need to know the relative price of the economy's two goods, that is, the price of one good in terms of the other.

In a competitive economy, supply is determined by the attempts of individuals to maximize their earnings. In our simplified economy, since labor is the only factor of production, the supply of cheese and wine will be determined by the movement of labor to whichever sector pays the higher wage.

Let P_C and P_W be the prices of cheese and wine, respectively. It takes a_{LC} man-hours to produce a pound of cheese; since there are no profits in our one-factor model, the hourly wage rate in the cheese sector will be equal to the value of what a worker can produce in an hour, P_C/a_{LC}. Since it takes a_{LW} man-hours to produce a gallon of wine, the hourly wage rate in the wine sector will correspondingly be equal to P_W/a_{LW}. Wages in the cheese sector will be higher if $P_C/P_W > a_{LC}/a_{LW}$; wages in the wine sector will be higher if $P_C/P_W < a_{LC}/a_{LW}$. But everyone will want to work in whichever industry offers the higher wage. The economy will therefore specialize in the production of cheese if $P_C/P_W > a_{LC}/a_{LW}$; it will specialize in the production of wine if $P_C/P_W < a_{LC}/a_{LW}$. Only when P_C/P_W is equal to a_{LC}/a_{LW} will both goods be produced.

What is the significance of the number a_{LC}/a_{LW}? We just saw that it is the opportunity cost of cheese in terms of wine. The general point, then, is the following: *The economy will specialize in the production of cheese if the relative price of cheese exceeds its opportunity cost; it will specialize in the production of wine if the relative price of cheese is less than its opportunity cost.*

In the absence of international trade, Home would have to produce both goods for itself. But it will produce both goods only if the relative price of cheese is just equal to its opportunity cost. Since opportunity cost equals the ratio of unit labor requirements in cheese and wine, we can summarize with a simple labor theory of value: *In the absence of international trade, the relative prices of goods are equal to their relative unit labor requirements.*

TRADE IN A ONE-FACTOR WORLD

To describe the pattern and effects of trade between two countries when each country has only one factor of production is simple. Yet the implications of this analysis can be surprising, and indeed often seem to those who have not thought about international trade to conflict with common sense. Even this simplest of trade models can offer some important guidance on real-world issues, such as what constitutes fair international competition and fair international exchange.

Before we get to these issues, however, let us get the model stated. Suppose that there are two countries. One of them we again call Home, and the other we call Foreign. Each of these countries has one factor of production (labor) and can produce two goods, wine and cheese. As before, we denote Home's labor force by L and Home's unit labor requirements in wine and cheese production by a_{LW} and a_{LC}, respectively. For Foreign we adopt a trick of notation that will turn out to be convenient throughout this book: when we want to refer to some aspect of Foreign, we will use the same symbol that we use for Home, but with an asterisk. Thus Foreign's labor force will be denoted by L^*; Foreign's unit labor requirements in wine and cheese will be denoted by a^*_{LW} and a^*_{LC}, respectively, and so on.

In general the unit labor requirements can follow any pattern. For example, Home could be less productive than Foreign in wine but more productive in cheese, or vice versa. For the moment, we make only one arbitrary assumption: that

$$a_{LC}/a_{LW} < a^*_{LC}/a^*_{LW} \tag{2-2}$$

or, equivalently, that

$$a_{LC}/a^*_{LC} < a_{LW}/a^*_{LW}. \tag{2-3}$$

In words, we are assuming that the ratio of the unit labor requirement in cheese to that in wine is lower in Home than it is in Foreign. More briefly still, we can say that Home's relative productivity in cheese is higher than it is in wine. In this case we will say that *Home has a comparative advantage in cheese production*. The significance of this will become apparent shortly.

One point should be noted immediately, however: the definition of comparative advantage involves all four unit labor requirements, not just two. You might think that to determine who will produce cheese, all you need to do is compare the two countries' unit labor requirements in cheese production, a_{LC} and a^*_{LC}. If $a_{LC} < a^*_{LC}$, Home labor is more efficient than Foreign in producing cheese. This is a situation where Home has an **absolute advantage** in cheese production. What we will see in a moment, however, is that we cannot determine the pattern of trade from absolute advantage alone. One of the most important sources of error in discussions of international trade is to confuse comparative advantage with absolute advantage.

Given the labor forces and the unit labor requirements in the two countries, we can draw the production possibility frontier for each country. We have already done this for Home, by drawing PF in Figure 2-1. The production possibility frontier for Foreign is shown as F^*P^* in Figure 2-2. Given our assumption about relative unit labor requirements, the Foreign production possibility frontier is steeper than Home's.

In the absence of trade the relative prices of cheese and wine in each country would be determined by the relative unit labor requirements. Thus in Home the relative price of cheese would be a_{LC}/a_{LW}; in Foreign it would be a^*_{LC}/a^*_{LW}.

Once we allow for the possibility of international trade, however, prices will no longer be determined purely by domestic considerations. If the relative price of cheese is higher in Foreign than in Home, it will be profitable to ship cheese from Home to Foreign and to ship wine from Foreign to Home. This cannot go on indefinitely; what will happen is that Home exports enough cheese, and Foreign enough wine, so as to equalize the relative price.

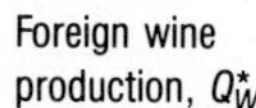

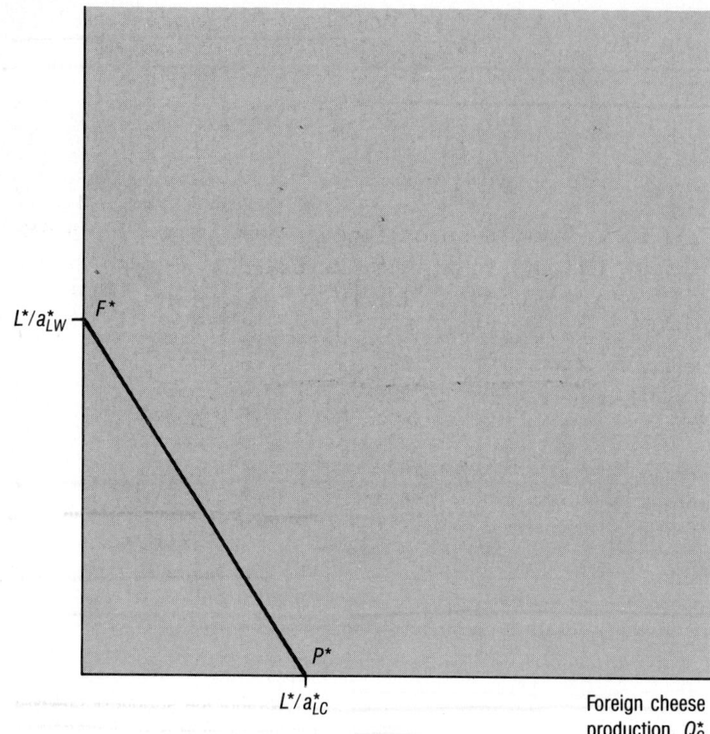

FIGURE 2-2 Foreign's production possibility frontier. Because Foreign's relative unit labor requirement in cheese is higher than Home's, its production possibility frontier is steeper.

So what we need to determine is the world relative price of cheese after trade.

DETERMINING THE RELATIVE PRICE AFTER TRADE

Prices of internationally traded goods, like other prices, are determined by supply and demand. In discussing comparative advantage, however, we must apply supply-and-demand analysis carefully. In some contexts, such as some of the trade policy analysis in Chapters 8 through 11, it is acceptable to focus only on supply and demand in a single market. In assessing the effects of U.S. import quotas on sugar, for example, it is reasonable to use **partial equilibrium analysis,** that is, to study a single market, the sugar market. When we study comparative advantage, however, it is crucial to keep track of the relationships between markets (in our example the markets for wine and cheese). Since Home exports cheese only in return for imports of wine, and Foreign exports wine in return for cheese, it can be misleading to look at the cheese and wine markets in isolation. What is needed is **general equilibrium analysis** that takes account of the linkages between the two markets.

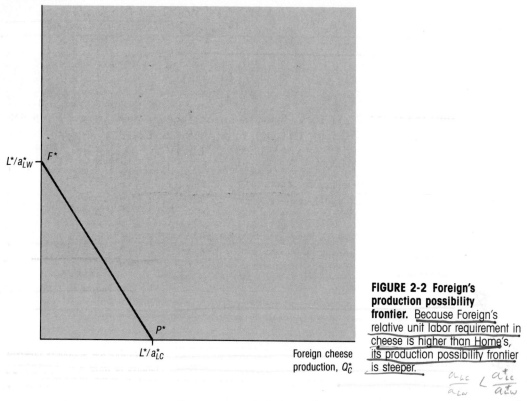

One useful way to keep track of two markets at once is to focus not just on the quantities of cheese and wine supplied and demanded but also on the *relative* supply and demand, that is, on the number of pounds of cheese supplied or demanded divided by the number of gallons of wine supplied or demanded.

Figure 2-3 shows world supply and demand for cheese relative to wine as functions of the price of cheese relative to that of wine. The **relative demand curve** is indicated by *RD*; the **relative supply curve** is indicated by *RS*. World general equilibrium requires that relative supply equal relative demand, and thus the world relative price is determined by the intersection of *RD* and *RS*.

The striking feature of Figure 2-3 is the funny shape of the relative supply curve *RS*: a "step" with flat sections linked by a vertical section. Once we understand the derivation of the *RS* curve, we will be almost home free in understanding the whole model.

First, as drawn, the *RS* curve shows that there is no supply of cheese if the world price drops below a_{LC}/a_{LW}. To see why, recall that we showed that

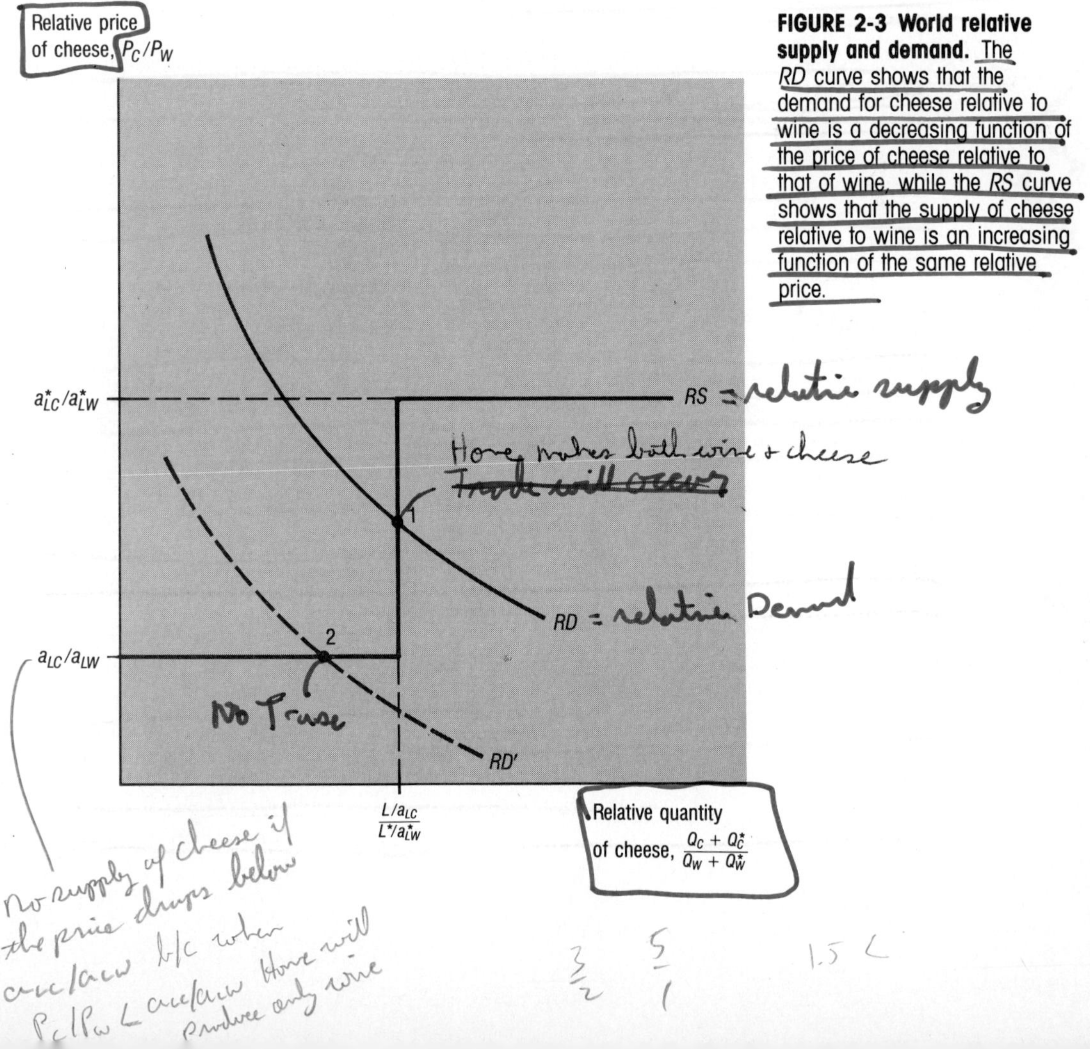

FIGURE 2-3 World relative supply and demand. The *RD* curve shows that the demand for cheese relative to wine is a decreasing function of the price of cheese relative to that of wine, while the *RS* curve shows that the supply of cheese relative to wine is an increasing function of the same relative price.

Home will specialize in the production of wine whenever $P_C/P_W < a_{LC}/a_{LW}$. Similarly, Foreign will specialize in wine production whenever $P_C/P_W < a^*_{LC}/a^*_{LW}$, which is by assumption greater than a_{LC}/a_{LW}. So at relative prices of cheese below a_{LC}/a_{LW}, there will be no world cheese production.

Next, when the relative price of cheese is exactly a_{LC}/a_{LW}, we know that workers in Home can earn exactly the same amount making either cheese or wine. So Home will be willing to supply any relative amount of the two goods, producing a flat section to the supply curve.

If P_C/P_W is above a_{LC}/a_{LW}, we have already seen that Home will specialize in the production of cheese. As long as $P_C/P_W < a^*_{LC}/a^*_{LW}$, however, Foreign will continue to specialize in producing wine. When Home specializes in cheese production, it produces L/a_{LC} pounds. Similarly, when Foreign specializes in wine it produces L^*/a^*_{LW} gallons. So for any relative price of cheese between a_{LC}/a_{LW} and a^*_{LC}/a^*_{LW} the relative supply of cheese is

$$(L/a_{LC})/(L^*/a^*_{LW}). \qquad \textbf{(2-4)}$$

At $P_C/P_W = a^*_{LC}/a^*_{LW}$, we know that Foreign workers are indifferent between producing cheese and wine. Thus here we again have a flat section of the supply curve.

Finally, for $P_C/P_W > a^*_{LC}/a^*_{LW}$, both Home and Foreign will specialize in cheese production. There will be no wine production, so that the relative supply of cheese will become infinite.

The relative demand curve *RD* does not require such exhaustive analysis. The downward slope of *RD* reflects substitution effects. As the relative price of cheese rises, consumers will tend to purchase less cheese and more wine, and so the relative demand for cheese falls.

The equilibrium relative price of cheese is determined by the intersection of the relative supply and relative demand curves. Figure 2-3 shows a relative demand curve *RD* that intersects the *RS* curve at point 1, where the relative price of cheese is between the two countries' pretrade prices. In this case each country specializes in the production of the good in which it has a comparative advantage: Home produces only cheese, Foreign only wine.

This is not, however, the only possible outcome. If the relevant *RD* curve were *RD′*, for example, relative supply and relative demand would intersect on one of the horizontal sections of *RS*. At point 2 the world relative price of cheese after trade is a_{LC}/a_{LW}, the same as the opportunity cost of cheese in terms of wine in Home.

What is the significance of this outcome? If the relative price of cheese is equal to its opportunity cost in Home, the Home economy need not specialize in producing either cheese or wine. And in fact at point 2 Home must be producing both some wine and some cheese; we can infer this from the fact that the relative supply of cheese is less than it would be if Home were in fact completely specialized. Since P_C/P_W is below the opportunity cost of cheese in terms of wine in Foreign, however, Foreign does specialize completely in producing wine. It therefore remains true that if a country does specialize, it will do so in the good in which it has a comparative advantage.

Let us for the moment leave aside the possibility that one of the two countries does not completely specialize. Except in this case, the normal result of trade is that the price of a traded good (e.g., cheese) relative to that of another good (wine) ends up somewhere in between its pretrade levels in the two countries.

The effect of this convergence in relative prices is that each country specializes in the production of that good in which it has the relatively lower unit labor requirement. The rise in the relative price of cheese in Home will lead Home to specialize in the production of cheese, producing at point F in Figure 2-1. The fall in the relative price of cheese in Foreign will lead Foreign to specialize in the production of wine, producing at point F^* in Figure 2-2.

THE GAINS FROM TRADE

We have now seen that countries whose relative labor productivities differ across industries will specialize in the production of different goods. We next show that both countries derive **gains from trade** from this specialization. This mutual gain can be demonstrated in two alternative ways.

The first way to show that specialization and trade are beneficial is to think of trade as an indirect method of production. Home could produce wine directly, but trade with Foreign allows it to "produce" wine by producing cheese and then trading the cheese for wine. This indirect method of "producing" a gallon of wine is a more efficient method than direct production. Consider two alternative ways of using an hour of labor. On one side Home could use the hour directly to produce $1/a_{LW}$ gallons of wine. Alternatively, Home could use the hour to produce $1/a_{LC}$ pounds of cheese. This cheese could then be traded for wine, with each pound trading for P_C/P_W gallons; so our original hour of labor yields $(1/a_{LC})(P_C/P_W)$ gallons of wine. This will be more wine than the hour could have produced directly as long as

$$(1/a_{LC})(P_C/P_W) > 1/a_{LW}, \qquad \text{(2-5)}$$

or

$$P_C/P_W > a_{LC}/a_{LW}.$$

But we just saw that in international equilibrium, if neither country produces both goods, we must have $P_C/P_W > a_{LC}/a_{LW}$. This shows that Home can "produce" wine more efficiently by making cheese and trading it than by producing for itself. Similarly, Foreign can "produce" cheese more efficiently by making wine and trading it. This is one way of seeing that both countries gain.

Another way to see the mutual gains from trade is to examine how trade affects each country's possibilities for consumption. In the absence of trade, consumption possibilities are the same as production possibilities (the solid lines *PF* and *F*P** in Figure 2-4). Once trade is allowed, however, each economy can consume a different mix of cheese and wine from the mix it produces. Home's consumption possibilities are indicated by the broken line *TF* in Figure 2-4a, while Foreign's consumption possibilities are indicated by *F*T** in Figure 2-4b. In each case trade has enlarged the range of choice, and therefore it must make residents of each country better off.

A NUMERICAL EXAMPLE

To solidify understanding of the points we have just made, it is useful to consider a numerical example. Suppose, then, that Home and Foreign have the unit labor requirements illustrated in Table 2-1.

A striking feature of this table is that Home has lower unit labor requirements, that is, has higher labor productivity, in *both* industries. Let us leave this observation on one side for a moment, however, and focus on the pattern of trade.

The first thing we need to do is determine the relative price of cheese P_C/P_W. This depends on demand; however, we know that it must lie between

FIGURE 2-4 Trade expands consumption possibilities. International trade allows Home and Foreign to consume anywhere within the broken lines, which lie outside the countries' production possibility frontiers.

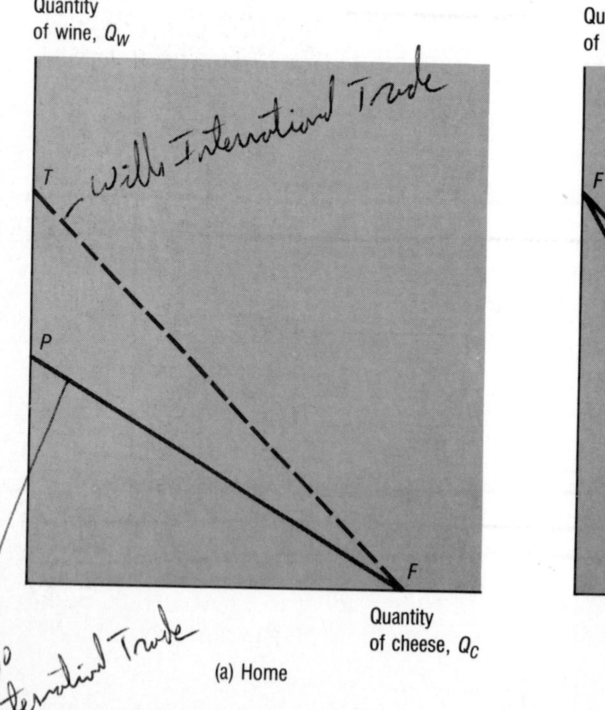

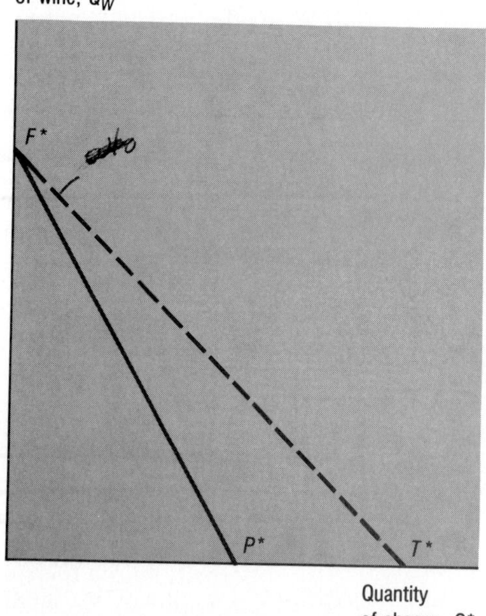

TABLE 2-1 Unit labor requirements

	Cheese	Wine
Home	$a_{LC} = 1$	$a_{LW} = 2$
Foreign	$a^*_{LC} = 6$	$a^*_{LW} = 3$

the opportunity cost of cheese in the two countries. In Home, we have $a_{LC} = 1$, $a_{LW} = 2$; so the opportunity cost of cheese in terms of wine is $a_{LC}/a_{LW} = 1/2$. In Foreign, $a^*_{LC} = 6$, $a^*_{LW} = 3$; so the opportunity cost of cheese is 2. In world equilibrium, the relative price of cheese must lie between these values. For the sake of the example, let us assume that in world equilibrium $P_C/P_W = 1$: a pound of cheese trades for a gallon of wine on world markets.

At this relative price of cheese, we can immediately see that each country will specialize, Home in cheese, Foreign in wine. To check this, notice that a worker in Home would earn only half as much producing wine as she does producing cheese, while the reverse is true for a worker in Foreign.

We can now check for gains from trade. First, we want to show that Home can "produce" wine more efficiently by making cheese and trading it for wine than by direct production. This is easy: in direct production, an hour of Home labor produces only 1/2 gallon of wine. The same hour could be used to produce 1 pound of cheese, which can then be traded for 1 gallon of wine. This shows that Home does indeed gain from trade. Similarly, Foreign could use 1 hour of labor to produce 1/6 pound of cheese; but it can instead use the hour to produce 1/3 gallon of wine, and trade the wine for 1/3 pound of cheese. In this particular example, each country can use labor twice as efficiently to trade for what it needs instead of producing its imports for itself.

Although it is not essential for analyzing the effect of trade on the welfare of either country, it is interesting to notice the implications of trade for the ratio of wage rates in the two countries. To determine the ratio of wage rates, first note what the wage rate of each country must be in terms of the good it produces. After trade, Home produces cheese; since it takes 1 hour of labor to produce 1 pound of cheese, the wage rate in Home is 1 pound of cheese per man-hour. Similarly, Foreign produces wine, needing 3 hours of labor per gallon; thus the foreign wage rate is 1/3 gallon of wine per man-hour.

To make these wage rates in terms of wine and cheese comparable, we must make use of the relative prices of the two goods. If 1 gallon of wine costs the same as 1 pound of cheese, then the wage rate in Foreign must be one-third the wage rate in Home. The ratio of the wage rates lies between the ratios of the two countries' productivities in the two industries. Home is six times as productive as Foreign in cheese, but only one-and-a-half times as productive in wine, and it ends up with a wage rate three times as high as Foreign's. It is precisely because the relative wage is intermediate between the relative productivities that each country ends up with a *cost* advantage in one good. Because of its lower wage rate, Foreign has a cost advantage in wine, even though it has lower labor productivity. Home has a cost advantage in cheese despite its higher wage rate, because the higher wage is more than offset by its higher productivity.

We have now developed the simplest of all models of international trade. Obviously the Ricardian one-factor model is far too simple to be a complete analysis of either the causes or the effects of international trade. Yet a focus on relative labor productivities can be a very useful tool for thinking about international trade. In particular, the simple one-factor model is a good way to deal with several common misconceptions about the meaning of comparative advantage and the nature of the gains from free trade. These misconceptions appear so frequently in public debate about international economic policy, and even in statements by those who regard themselves as experts, that in the next section we take time out to discuss some of the most common misunderstandings about comparative advantage in the light of our model.

MISCONCEPTIONS ABOUT COMPARATIVE ADVANTAGE

There is no shortage of muddled ideas in economics. Politicians, business leaders, and even economists frequently make statements that do not stand up to careful economic analysis. For some reason this seems to be especially true in international economics. Open the business section of any Sunday newspaper or weekly news magazine and you will probably find at least one article that makes foolish statements about international trade. Three misconceptions in particular have proved highly persistent, and our simple model of comparative advantage can be used to see why they are incorrect.

PRODUCTIVITY AND COMPETITIVENESS

Myth 1: Free trade is only beneficial if your country is productive enough to stand up to international competition. This argument, most often used with regard to less-developed countries, implies that poor countries should isolate themselves from the international economy until they are strong enough to compete. In 1983, for example, a columnist in the *Wall Street Journal* asserted that "Many small countries have no comparative advantage in anything."[2] This fallacy has been given a new lease on life by Japan's technological challenge to the United States. This challenge has produced fears that a failure of the United States to keep its technological lead will mean that trade will become a source of harm instead of gain.

[2]B. Bruce-Biggs, "The Coming Overthrow of Free Trade," *Wall Street Journal,* Feb. 28, 1983.

To see the fallacy in this reasoning, we need look no further than our simple numerical example of trade. In that example, Home has lower unit labor requirements and thus higher productivity in both the cheese and wine sectors. Yet, as we saw, both countries gain from trade. It is always tempting to suppose that the ability to export a good depends on an *absolute* advantage in productivity: what the *Wall Street Journal* columnist must have meant is that "many small countries have no absolute productivity advantage over other countries in anything." What he failed to understand is that an absolute productivity advantage over other countries in producing a good is neither a necessary nor a sufficient condition for having a *comparative* advantage in that good. In our one-factor model the reason why absolute productivity in an industry is neither necessary nor sufficient to yield competitive advantage is clear: *The competitive advantage of an industry depends not only on its productivity relative to the foreign industry, but also on the domestic wage rate relative to the foreign wage rate.* A country's wage rate, in turn, depends on relative productivity in its other industries. In our numerical example, Foreign is less efficient than Home in the manufacture of wine, but at even a greater relative productivity disadvantage in cheese. Because of its overall lower productivity, Foreign must pay lower wages than Home, sufficiently lower that it ends up with lower costs in wine production. Similarly, in the real world Portugal has low productivity in producing, say, clothing as compared with the U.S. clothing industry; but because Portugal's productivity disadvantage is even greater in other industries it pays low enough wages to have a comparative advantage in clothing all the same.

But isn't a competitive advantage based on low wages somehow unfair? Many people think so; their beliefs are summarized by our second misconception.

THE SWEATSHOP LABOR ARGUMENT

Myth 2: Foreign competition is unfair and hurts other countries when it is based on low wages. This argument, sometimes referred to as the **sweatshop labor argument,** is a particular favorite of labor unions seeking protection from foreign competition. People who adhere to this belief argue that industries should not have to cope with foreign industries that are less efficient but pay lower wages. This view is widespread and taken seriously by respectable opinion: during 1986 the *New York Times* printed three articles by Professor John Culbertson of the University of Wisconsin, arguing that foreign competition based on low wages is destructive to the United States.

Again, our simple example reveals the fallacy of this argument. In the example, Home is more productive than Foreign in both industries, and Foreign's lower cost of wine production is entirely due to its much lower wage rate. Foreign's lower wage rate is, however, irrelevant to the question of whether Home gains from trade. Whether the lower cost of wine produced in Foreign is due to high productivity or low wages does not matter. All that matters to Home is that it is cheaper in terms of its own labor for Home to produce cheese and trade it for wine than to produce wine for itself.

This is fine for Home; but what about Foreign? Isn't there something wrong with basing one's exports upon low wages? Certainly it is not an attractive position to be in, but the idea that trade is only good if you receive high wages is our final fallacy.

UNEQUAL EXCHANGE

Myth 3: Trade exploits a country and makes it worse off if the country uses more labor to produce the goods it exports than other countries use to produce the goods it receives in return. This argument, sometimes called the doctrine of **unequal exchange,** has its roots in the Marxist idea that value is created only by labor, and tends to be favored by third-world advocates of a redistribution of income from rich countries to poor.[3]

While there is a certain plausibility to the idea that a country is being exploited if its exports embody more labor than its imports, unequal exchange does not mean that the low-wage country loses from trade. In the numerical example Foreign exchanges 1 gallon of wine for each pound of cheese it receives, exchanging something it took 3 hours of labor to produce for something that Home produced with only 1 hour of labor. This inequality of labor input is, however, irrelevant to the conclusion that Foreign gains from trade. In asking whether trade is beneficial, you should not compare the domestic labor used to produce your exports with the foreign labor used to produce your imports. Rather, you should compare the labor used to produce your exports with the amount of labor it would have taken to produce your imports yourself. Through trade, Foreign is able to get 1 pound of cheese from 3 hours of labor, when it would have taken 6 hours to produce that pound domestically. If another country is able to produce your imports with much less labor than would have been required in your country, good for them; this fact does not reduce your own benefit from trade.

COMPARATIVE ADVANTAGE WITH MANY GOODS

In our discussion so far we have relied on a model in which only two goods are produced and consumed. This simplified analysis allows us to capture many essential points about comparative advantage and trade, and as we saw in the last section, it gives us a surprising amount of mileage as a tool for discussing policy issues. To move in the direction of realism, however, it is necessary to understand how comparative advantage functions in a model with a larger number of goods.

[3]As an example, see Arghiri Emmanuel, *Unequal Exchange* (NY: Monthly Review Press, 1972).

SETTING UP THE MODEL

Again, imagine a world of two countries, Home and Foreign. As before, each country has only one factor of production, labor. Each of these countries will now, however, be assumed to consume and to be able to produce a large number of goods—say, N different goods altogether. We assign each of the goods a number from 1 to N.

The technology of each country can be described by its unit labor requirement for each good, that is, the number of hours of labor it takes to produce one unit of each. We label Home's unit labor requirement for a particular good as a_{Li}, where i is the number we have assigned to that good. If cheese is now good number 7, a_{L7} will mean the unit labor requirement in cheese production. Following our usual rule, we label the corresponding Foreign unit labor requirements a^*_{Li}.

In order to analyze trade, we next pull one more trick. For any good we can calculate a_{Li}/a^*_{Li}, the ratio of Home's unit labor requirement to Foreign's. The trick is to relabel the goods so that the lower the number, the lower this ratio. That is, we reshuffle the order in which we number goods in such a way that

$$a_{L1}/a^*_{L1} < a_{2_{L2}}/a^*_{L2} < a_{L3}/a^*_{L3} < \cdots < a_{LN}/a^*_{LN}. \qquad \textbf{(2-6)}$$

RELATIVE WAGES AND SPECIALIZATION

We are now prepared to look at the pattern of trade. This depends on only one thing: the ratio of Home to Foreign wages. Once we know this ratio, we can determine who produces what.

Let w be the wage rate per hour in Home and w^* be the wage rate in Foreign. The ratio of wage rates, which is all that will concern us, is then w/w^*. The rule for allocating world production, then, is simply this: any good for which $a^*_{Li}/a_{Li} > w/w^*$ will be produced in Home, while any good for which $a^*_{Li}/a_{Li} < w/w^*$ will be produced in Foreign.

The reason for this result is that goods will always be produced where it is cheapest to make them. The cost of making some good, say good i, is the unit labor requirement times the wage rate. To produce good i in Home will cost wa_{Li}. To produce the same good in Foreign will cost $w^*a^*_{Li}$. It will be cheaper to produce the good in Home if

$$wa_{Li} < w^*a^*_{Li},$$

which can be rearranged to yield

$$a^*_{Li}/a_{Li} > w/w^*.$$

On the other hand, it will be cheaper to produce the good in Foreign if

$$wa_{Li} > w^*a^*_{Li},$$

which can be rearranged to yield

$$a^*_{Li}/a_{Li} < w/w^*.$$

We have already lined up the goods in increasing order of a_{Li}/a^*_{Li}. This criterion for specialization tells us that what happens is a "cut" in that lineup, determined by the ratio of the two countries' wage rates. All the goods to the left of the cut end up being produced in Home; all the goods to the right end up being produced in Foreign. (It is possible, as we will see in a moment, that the ratio of wage rates is exactly equal to the ratio of unit labor requirements for one good. In that case this borderline good may be produced in both countries.)

Table 2-2 offers a numerical example, in which Home and Foreign both consume and are able to produce *five* goods, apples, bananas, caviar, dates, and enchiladas.

The first two columns of this table are self-explanatory. The third column is the ratio of the Foreign unit labor requirement to the Home unit labor requirement for each good—or, what amounts to the same thing, the relative Home productivity advantage in each good. We have labeled the goods so that they are in the order of Home productivity advantage, with the Home advantage greatest for apples and least for enchiladas.

The determination of which country produces which goods depends on the ratio of Home and Foreign wage rates. Home will have a cost advantage in any good for which its relative productivity is higher than its relative wage, and Foreign will have the advantage in the others. If, for example, the Home wage rate is 5 times that of Foreign, apples and bananas will be produced in Home and caviar, dates, and enchiladas in Foreign. If the Home wage rate is only 3 times that of Foreign, Home will produce apples, bananas, and caviar, while Foreign will produce only dates and enchiladas.

Is such a pattern of specialization beneficial to both countries? We can see that it is by using the same method we used earlier: comparing the labor cost of producing a good directly in a country with that of indirectly "producing" it by producing another good and trading for the desired good.

TABLE 2-2 Home and foreign unit labor requirements

Good	Home unit labor requirement (a_{Li})	Foreign unit labor requirement (a^*_{Li})	Relative home productivity advantage (a^*_{Li}/a_{Li})
Apples	1	10	10
Bananas	5	40	8
Caviar	3	12	4
Dates	6	12	2
Enchiladas	12	9	0.75

If the Home wage rate is 3 times the Foreign wage, Home will import dates and enchiladas. A unit of dates requires 12 units of Foreign labor to produce, but its cost in Home labor, given the difference in wages, is only 4 man-hours—less than the 6 man-hours it would take to produce it at Home. For enchiladas, Foreign actually has higher productivity along with lower wages; it will cost Home only 3 man-hours to acquire a unit of enchiladas through trade, compared with the 12 man-hours it would take to produce it domestically. A similar calculation will show that Foreign also gains; for each of the goods Foreign imports it turns out to be cheaper in terms of domestic labor to trade for the good rather than produce the good domestically.

One piece is missing from this account, however: we have not yet explained how to determine the relative wage rate. This is the task to which we now turn.

DETERMINING THE RELATIVE WAGE IN THE MULTIGOOD MODEL

In the two-good model we determined relative wages by first calculating Home wages in terms of cheese and Foreign wages in terms of wine, then using the price of cheese relative to that of wine to deduce the ratio of the two countries' wage rates. We could do this because we knew that Home would produce cheese and Foreign wine. In the many-good case, who produces what depends on the relative wage rate; so this procedure is unworkable. Instead, to determine relative wages in a multigood economy we must look behind the relative demand for goods to the implied relative demand for labor. This is not a direct demand on the part of consumers; rather, it is a **derived demand** that results from the demand for goods produced with each country's labor.

The relative derived demand for Home labor will fall when the ratio of Home to Foreign wages rises, for two reasons. First, as Home labor becomes more expensive relative to Foreign, goods produced in Home also become relatively more expensive, and world demand for these goods falls. Second, as Home wages rise, fewer goods will be produced in Home and more in Foreign, further reducing the demand for Home labor.

We can illustrate these two effects using our numerical example. Suppose we start with the following situation: the Home wage is initially 3.5 times the Foreign wage. At that level, Home would produce apples, bananas, and caviar while Foreign would produce dates and enchiladas. If the relative Home wage were to increase from 3.5 to just under 4, say 3.99, the pattern of specialization would not change, but as the goods produced in Home became relatively more expensive, the relative demand for these goods would decline and the relative demand for Home labor would decline with it.

Suppose now that the relative wage were to increase slightly from 3.99 to 4.01. This small further increase in the relative Home wage would bring about a shift in the pattern of specialization. Because it is now cheaper to produce caviar in Foreign than in Home, the production of caviar shifts from Home to Foreign. What does this imply for the relative demand for Home labor? Clearly it implies that as the relative wage rises from a little less than 4 to a little more than 4 there is an abrupt drop-off in the relative demand, as Home production of caviar falls to zero and Foreign acquires a new industry. If the relative wage continues to rise, relative demand for Home labor will gradually decline, then drop off abruptly at a relative wage of 8, at which wage production of bananas shifts to Foreign.

We can illustrate the determination of relative wages with a diagram like Figure 2-5. Unlike Figure 2-3, this diagram does not have relative quantities of goods or relative prices of goods on its axes. Instead it shows the relative quantity of labor and the relative wage rate. The world demand for Home labor relative to its demand for Foreign labor is shown by the curve *RD*. The world supply of Home labor relative to Foreign labor is shown by the line *RS*.

The relative supply of labor is determined simply by the relative size of Home and Foreign labor forces. Assuming that the number of man-hours available does not vary with the wage, the relative wage has no effect on relative labor supply and thus *RS* is simply a vertical line.

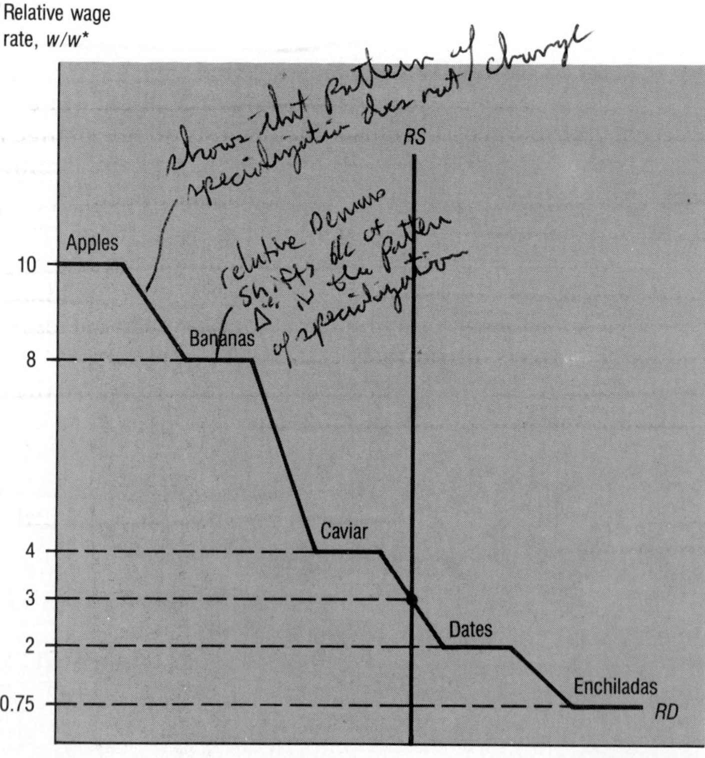

FIGURE 2-5 Determination of relative wages. In a many-good Ricardian model, relative wages are determined by the intersection of the derived relative demand curve for labor *RD* with the relative supply *RS*.

Our discussion of the relative demand for labor explains the "stepped" shape of *RD*. Whenever we increase the wage rate of Home workers relative to Foreign workers, the relative demand for goods produced in Home will decline, and the demand for Home labor will decline with it. In addition, the relative demand for Home labor will drop off abruptly whenever an increase in the relative Home wage makes a good cheaper to produce in Foreign. So the curve alternates between smoothly downward-sloping sections where the pattern of specialization does not change, and "flats" where the relative demand shifts abruptly because of shifts in the pattern of specialization. As shown in the figure, these "flats" correspond to relative wages that equal the ratio of Home to Foreign productivity for each of the five goods.

The equilibrium relative wage is determined by the intersection of *RD* and *RS*. As drawn, the equilibrium relative wage is 3. At this wage, Home produces apples, bananas, and caviar while Foreign produces dates and enchiladas. The outcome depends on the relative size of the countries (which determines the position of *RS*) and on the relative demand for the goods (which determines the shape and position of *RD*).

If the intersection of *RD* and *RS* happens to lie on one of the flats, both countries produce the good to which the flat applies.

ADDING TRANSPORT COSTS AND NONTRADED GOODS

To close this chapter, we extend our model another step closer to realism by considering the effects of transport costs. Transportation costs do not change the fundamental principles of comparative advantage or the gains from trade. Because transport costs pose obstacles to the movement of goods and services, however, they have important implications for the way that a trading world economy is affected by a variety of factors such as foreign aid, international investment, and balance of payments problems. While we will not deal with the effects of these factors yet, the multigood one-factor model is a good place to introduce the effects of transport costs.

The first thing to notice is that the world economy described by the model of the last section is marked by very extreme international specialization. At most there is one good that both countries produce; all other goods are produced either in Home or in Foreign, not in both.

There are three main reasons why specialization in the real international economy is not this extreme.

1. The existence of more than one factor of production reduces the tendency toward specialization (see the next two chapters).
2. Countries sometimes protect industries from foreign competition (a fact discussed at length in Chapters 8 through 11).
3. It is costly to transport goods and services, and in some cases the cost of transportation is enough to lead countries into self-sufficiency in certain sectors.

In the multigood example of the last section we found that at a relative Home wage of 3, Home could produce apples, bananas, and caviar more cheaply than Foreign, while Foreign could produce dates and enchiladas more cheaply than Home. *In the absence of transport costs,* then, Home will export the first three goods and import the last two.

Now suppose that there is a cost to transporting goods, and that this transport cost is a uniform fraction of production cost, say 100 percent. This transportation cost will discourage trade. Consider, for example, dates. One unit of this good requires 6 hours of Home labor or 12 hours of Foreign labor to produce. At a relative wage of 3, 12 hours of Foreign labor cost only as much as 4 hours of Home labor; so in the absence of transport costs Home imports dates. With a 100 percent transport cost, however, importing dates would cost the equivalent of 8 hours of Home labor; so Home will produce the good for itself instead.

A similar cost comparison shows that Foreign will find it cheaper to produce its own caviar than import it. A unit of caviar requires 3 hours of Home labor to produce. Even at a relative Home wage of 3, which makes this the equivalent of 9 hours of Foreign labor, this is cheaper than the 12 hours which Foreign would need to produce caviar for itself. In the absence of transport costs, then, Foreign would find it cheaper to import caviar than to make it domestically. With a 100 percent cost of transportation, however, imported caviar would cost the equivalent of 18 hours of Foreign labor, and would therefore be produced locally instead.

The result of introducing transport costs in this example, then, is that while Home still exports apples and bananas and imports enchiladas, caviar and dates become **nontraded goods** which each country produces for itself.

In this example we have assumed that transport costs are the same fraction of production cost in all sectors. In practice there is a wide range of transportation costs. In some cases transportation is virtually impossible: services such as haircuts and auto repair cannot be traded internationally (except where there is a metropolitan area that straddles a border, like Detroit-Windsor). There is also little international trade in goods with high weight-to-value ratios, like cement. (It is simply not worth the transport cost of importing cement, even if it can be produced much more cheaply abroad.) Many goods end up being nontraded either because of the absence of strong national cost advantages or because of high transportation costs.

The important point is that nations spend a large share of their income on nontraded goods. This observation is of surprising importance in our later discussion of international transfers of income (Chapter 5) and in international monetary economics.

SUMMARY

1. In this chapter we examined the *Ricardian model,* the simplest model that shows how differences between countries give rise to trade and *gains from*

trade. In this model labor is the only factor of production and countries differ only in the productivity of labor in different industries.

2. In the Ricardian model, countries will export goods that their labor produces relatively efficiently, and import goods that their labor produces relatively inefficiently. In other words, a country's production pattern is determined by *comparative advantage*.

3. That trade benefits a country can be shown in either of two ways. First, we can think of trade as an indirect method of production. Instead of producing a good for itself, a country can produce another good and trade it for the desired good. The simple model shows that whenever a good is imported it must be true that this indirect "production" requires less labor than direct production. Second, we can show that trade enlarges a country's consumption possibilities, implying gains from trade.

4. The distribution of the gains from trade depends on the relative prices of the goods countries produce. To determine these relative prices it is necessary to look at the *relative world supply and demand* for goods. The relative price implies a relative wage rate as well.

5. The proposition that trade is beneficial is unqualified. That is, there is no requirement that a country be "competitive" or that the trade be "fair." In particular, we can show that three commonly held beliefs about trade are wrong. First, a country gains from trade even if it has lower productivity than its trading partner in all industries. Second, trade is beneficial even if foreign industries are competitive only because of low wages. Third, trade is beneficial even if a country's exports embody more labor than its imports.

6. Extending the one-factor, two-good model to a world of many commodities does not alter these conclusions. The only difference is that it becomes necessary to focus directly on the relative demand for labor to determine relative wages rather than to work via relative demand for goods. Also, a many-commodity model can be used to illustrate the important point that transportation costs can give rise to a situation in which some *nontraded goods* exist.

KEY TERMS

comparative advantage
Ricardian model
unit labor requirement
production possibility frontier
opportunity cost
absolute advantage
partial equilibrium analysis
general equilibrium analysis
relative demand curve
relative supply curve
gains from trade
sweatshop labor argument
unequal exchange
derived demand
nontraded goods

PROBLEMS

1. Home has 1200 units of labor available. It can produce two goods, apples and bananas. The unit labor requirement in apple production is 3, while in banana production it is 2.

a) Graph Home's production possibility frontier.

b) What is the opportunity cost of apples in terms of bananas?

c) In the absence of trade, what would the price of apples in terms of bananas be? Why?

2. Home is as described in problem 1. There is now also another country, Foreign, with a labor force of 800. Foreign's unit labor requirement in apple production is 5, while in banana production it is 1.

a) Graph Foreign's production possibility frontier.

b) Construct the world relative supply curve.

3. Now suppose that world relative demand takes the following form:

Demand for apples/demand for bananas = price of bananas/price of apples

a) Graph the relative demand curve along with the relative supply curve.

b) What is the equilibrium relative price of apples?

c) Describe the pattern of trade.

d) Show that both Home and Foreign gain from trade.

4. Suppose that instead of 1200 workers, Home had 2400. Find the equilibrium relative price. What can you say about the division of the gains from trade between Home and Foreign in this case?

5. Suppose that Home has 2400 workers, but they are only half as productive in both industries as we have been assuming. Construct the world relative supply curve, and determine the equilibrium relative price. How do the gains from trade compare with those in the case described in problem 3?

6. "Korean workers earn less than $2 an hour; if we allow Korea to export as much as it likes to the United States, our workers will be forced down to the same level. You can't import a $3 shirt without importing the $2 wage that goes with it." Discuss.

7. Although Japanese labor productivity is generally somewhat lower than that of the United States, it is higher in some important sectors, such as steel and autos. In those sectors U.S. industries have been forced to contract because of Japanese competition. Does this mean that if Japan overtakes the United States in *overall* productivity, the whole U.S. economy will be forced into the same kind of decline as the steel and auto industries?

8. How does the fact that many goods are nontraded affect the extent of possible gains from trade?

9. We have focused on the case of trade involving only two countries. Suppose that there are many countries capable of producing two goods, and that each country has only one factor of production, labor. What could we say about the pattern of production and trade in this case? (Hint: Try constructing the world relative supply curve.)

FURTHER READING

Rudiger Dornbusch, Stanley Fischer, and Paul Samuelson, "Comparative Advantage, Trade and Payments in a Ricardian Model with a Continuum of Goods." *American Economic Review* 67 (December 1977), pp. 823–839. More recent theoretical modeling in the Ricardian mode, developing the idea of simplifying the many-good Ricardian model by assuming that the number of goods is so large as to form a smooth continuum.

G. D. A. MacDougall, "British and American Exports: A Study Suggested by the Theory of Comparative Costs." *Economic Journal* 61 (December, 1951), pp. 697–724; 62 (September 1952), pp. 487–521. In this famous study, MacDougall used comparative data on U.S. and U.K. productivity to test the predictions of the Ricardian model.

John Stuart Mill. *Principles of Political Economy.* London: Longmans, Green, 1917. Mill's 1848 treatise extended Ricardo's work into a full-fledged model of international trade.

David Ricardo. *The Principles of Political Economy and Taxation.* Homewood, IL: Irwin, 1963. The basic source for the Ricardian model is Ricardo himself in this book, first published in 1817.

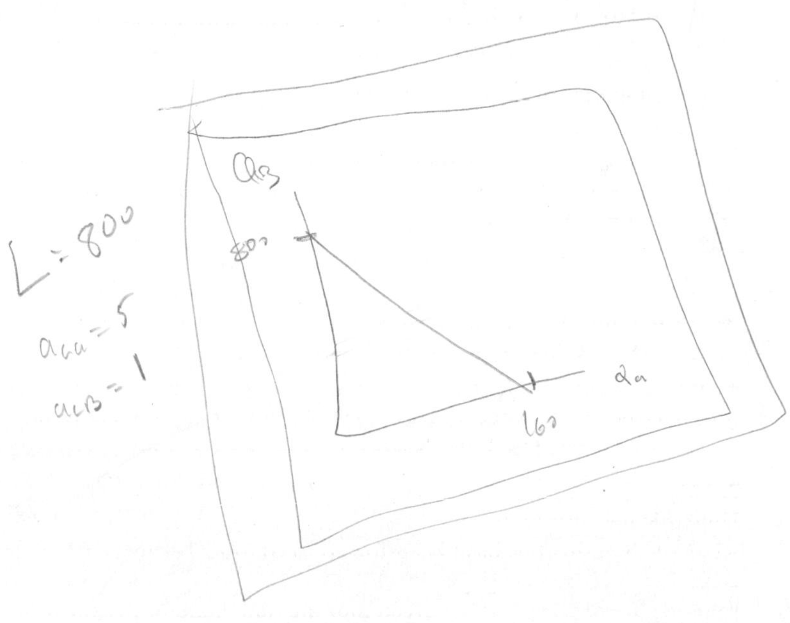

APPENDIX TO CHAPTER 2
A Ricardian Model with Very Many Goods

In this chapter our analysis became somewhat more complicated when we went from a model with only two goods to a model with a number of goods. Recently, however, trade theorists have noticed something surprising: if the number of goods becomes *very* large, so that one can think of them as virtually uncountable, the model actually becomes simpler again. A well-known 1977 article by Rudiger Dornbusch, Stanley Fischer, and Paul Samuelson of the Massachusetts Institute of Technology (see Further Reading) develops a Ricardian model with a very large number of goods that illustrates the points made in this chapter in a particularly clear way.

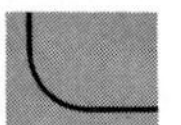

TECHNOLOGY AND SPECIALIZATION

Suppose that Home and Foreign still have only one factor of production, labor, available in quantities L and L^* in each country. Each country, however, consumes and is able to produce an extremely large number of goods. We label each of these goods with a number. These numbers will be assigned in a particular way that we will explain in a moment.

For each good both Home and Foreign will have a unit labor requirement in production. For good number z, let $a(z)$ be the unit labor requirement in Home and $a^*(z)$ be the unit labor requirement in Foreign. Then $a^*(z)/a(z)$ is the ratio of Home's productivity in that good to Foreign's. We define $A(z) = a^*(z)/a(z)$.

In labeling the goods we use the following rule: number the good with the highest A as good 1, the good with the next highest A as 2, etc., so that

$$A(1) > A(2) > A(3) \ldots.$$

That is, we order the goods in decreasing order of Home comparative advantage.

Now we graph $A(z)$ against z (Figure 2A-1). Here is where we use the assumption that there is a very large number of goods. In reality, z can take on only whole-number values, so that the curve $A(z)$ should be a series of discrete points at $z = 1, z = 2$, and so on. If there are thousands or millions of goods, however, any graph that compresses the z axis onto a single page will show an $A(z)$ that is indistinguishable from a solid curve. What we do is ignore the tiny holes that we know are there and treat $A(z)$ as if it were in fact a smooth, continuous mathematical relationship. It is of course downward-sloping, because we numbered the goods that way.

Which goods will be produced in Home, and which in Foreign? This depends on the ratio of the Home and Foreign wage rates. The cost of producing good z in Home is $wa(z)$, where w is the wage rate of Home workers. The cost of producing the same good in Foreign is $w^*a^*(z)$. The good will therefore be cheaper to produce in Home if

$$wa(z) < w^*a^*(z)$$

or, equivalently,

$$w/w^* < a^*(z)/a(z)$$

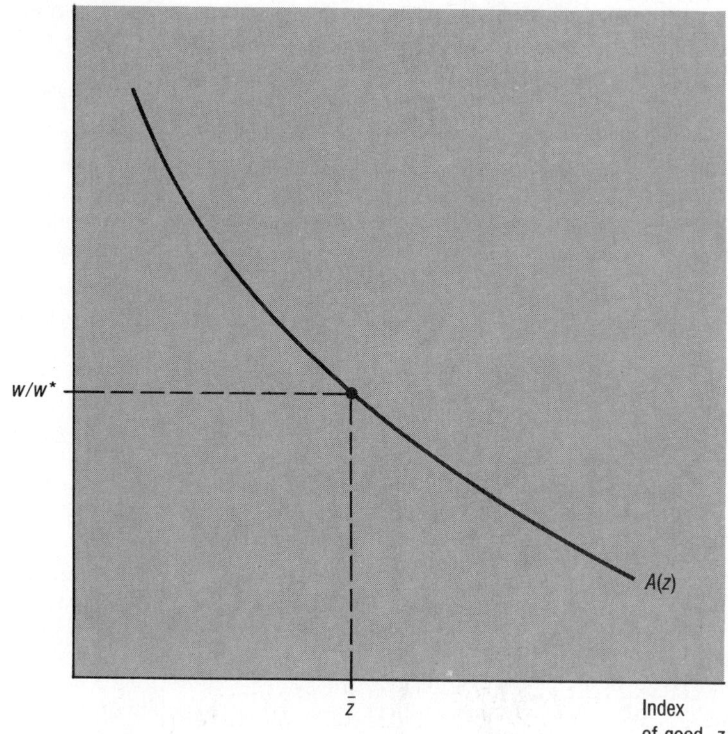

FIGURE 2A-1 Relative Home productivity. Goods are numbered in order of the ratio of Foreign to Home unit labor requirement, so that the curve $A(z)$ is downward-sloping.

or, finally,

$$A(z) > w/w^*.$$

Given the ratio of Home to Foreign wages w/w^*, then, we can establish the pattern of international specialization. There is a marginal good $\bar{z}$ for which $w/w^* = A(\bar{z})$ (see Figure 2A-1). All goods with lower numbers than $\bar{z}$ will be produced in Home, all goods with higher numbers in Foreign.

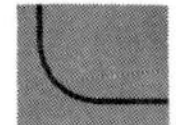

DEMAND AND EQUILIBRIUM

Next we turn to the determination of the relative wage. To do this we need to specify demand. A simple assumption about demand that is popular in international economics is that everyone in the world spends a constant share of his or her income on each good. For example, it might be the case that everyone spends 20 percent of income on food, 25 percent on housing, 15 percent on transportation, and so on. In our case, we assume that a fraction of income $b(z)$ of world income is spent on each good z.

What we need to know next is the fraction of world income spent on all goods manufactured in Home. This depends on which goods are made there—but we know that this will consist of all goods with numbers less than $\bar{z}$. Let $G(\bar{z})$ be the fraction of income spent on Home-made goods; it is equal to

$$G(\bar{z}) = b(1) + b(2) + \cdots + b(\bar{z}). \tag{2A-1}$$

Clearly $G(\bar{z})$ will be larger, the larger $\bar{z}$ is. Like $A(z)$, $G(z)$ describes a set of discrete points rather than a continuous curve, but with a very large number of goods we can ignore the holes.

Now we turn to the derived demand for Home labor. The total value of spending on Home goods will be $G(\bar{z})$ times world income. All this spending will accrue to Home workers as wages: thus we have

$$wL = G(\bar{z}) \times \text{world income}. \tag{2A-2}$$

World income, however, is the sum of the total wages earned in Home and Foreign, $wL + w^*L^*$. Thus we have

$$wL = G(\bar{z})(wL + w^*L^*), \tag{2A-3}$$

which can be rearranged as

$$\begin{aligned} w/w^* &= \frac{G(\bar{z})}{1 - G(\bar{z})} \times \frac{L^*}{L} \\ &= B(\bar{z})L^*/L. \end{aligned} \tag{2A-4}$$

The numerator of $B(z)$ is higher, the higher z is, while the denominator is less; therefore, $B(z)$ must rise when z rises. The intuition is that the more goods Home produces (and therefore the fewer Foreign produces), the higher the relative demand for Home labor and thus the higher Home's relative wage.

We have now established a relationship between the relative wage and the pattern of specialization, on one hand, and between the pattern of specialization and the relative wage, on the other. We can put these together on a single diagram (Figure 2A-2) to see how specialization and relative wages are simultaneously determined.

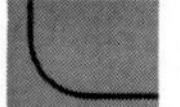

THE GAINS FROM TRADE

We can use this model to establish in a particularly neat way that trade is mutually beneficial to Home and Foreign. First, we ask what the prices of goods in international trade are. In a Ricardian one-factor economy, the price of a good will simply be the labor cost of production. Let $p(z)$ be the price of good z; then

$$\begin{aligned} p(z) &= wa(z) && \text{if the good is produced in Home} \\ &= w^*a^*(z) && \text{if the good is produced in Foreign.} \end{aligned}$$

Now we ask: is it more efficient for Home to trade for its imports rather than to produce them directly?

For Home to produce one unit of good z directly requires $a(z)$ man-hours. These man-hours earn an income $wa(z)$. If the good is imported, the income from the labor that would have been used to produce one unit of good z at Home can purchase $wa(z)/p(z)$ units of imports of z, where $p(z) = w^*a^*(z)$. It is cheaper for Home to im-

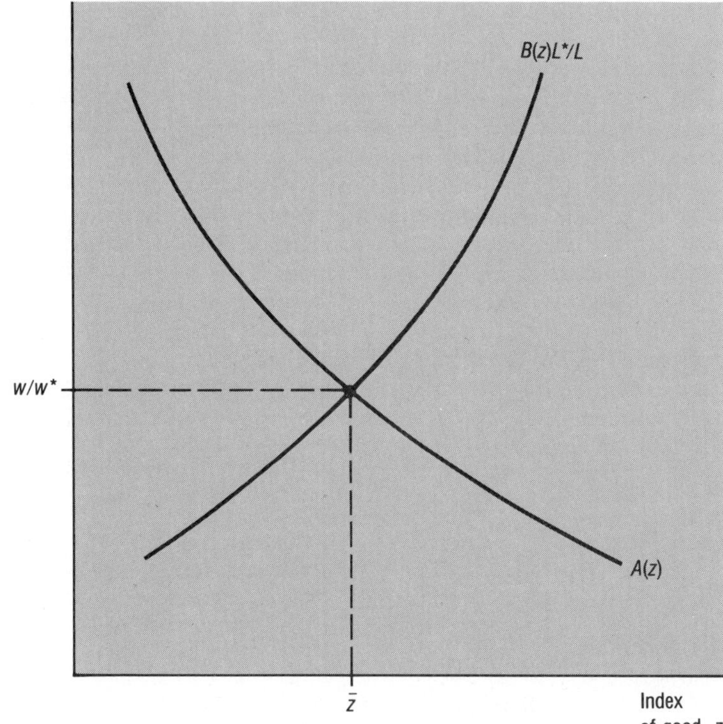

FIGURE 2A-2 Determining relative wages and the pattern of specialization. The ratio of Home to Foreign wage rates, and which country produces which goods, are determined simultaneously by the intersection of the relative productivity curve and the relative labor demand curve.

port good z if the labor that could produce a unit of z directly can indirectly generate more than one unit by producing instead exports to be traded, that is, if

$$wa(z)/p(z) = wa(z)/w^*a^*(z) > 1\,.$$

This is equivalent to

$$a^*(z)/a(z) = A(z) < w/w^*.$$

But we saw that the pattern of specialization is determined precisely by the requirement that Home produce all goods with $A(z) > w/w^*$, while Foreign produces all goods with $A(z) < w/w^*$. Gains from trade are therefore assured.

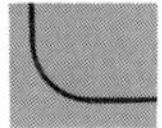

AN APPLICATION: PRODUCTIVITY GROWTH

An interesting application of this very-many-good model, one that is relevant to our discussion of misconceptions about international trade, is to ask what happens when one country's productivity increases. Is this good or bad for the other country?

Suppose that Foreign's productivity increases by 10 percent. We assume that this productivity increase takes place across the board, so that Foreign's unit labor requirement falls by 10 percent in every industry (if we didn't assume this, we would have to renumber the goods—can you see why?). Since $a^*(z)$ has fallen by 10 percent in all industries, $A(z)$ shifts down by 10 percent (Figure 2A-3). As the figure shows, Home's relative wage w/w^* falls. So does $\bar{z}$: the range of goods that Home produces also becomes narrower.

You might be tempted, looking at these results, to conclude that Home is worse off as a result of competition with Foreign. But this conclusion is exactly wrong. In fact, Home is unambiguously better off.

To see why, we look at Home's real wage, the wage rate divided by the price, in terms of each of the goods. If all real wages either stay the same or rise, Home is better off, and that is what happens. The reason is that while Home's relative wage falls, it falls by *less* than the 10 percent decline in Foreign unit labor requirements. This means that Foreign goods get cheaper in terms of Home labor.

Figure 2A-3 divides the goods into three groups: consistent Home exports, consistent imports, and transitional goods that shift from exports to imports. Let's examine what happens to Home's real wages in terms of each group.

The prices of goods that Home exports both before and after the change are proportional to the Home wage rate: $p(z) = wa(z)$; so the real wage rate $w/p(z)$ in terms of these goods does not change.

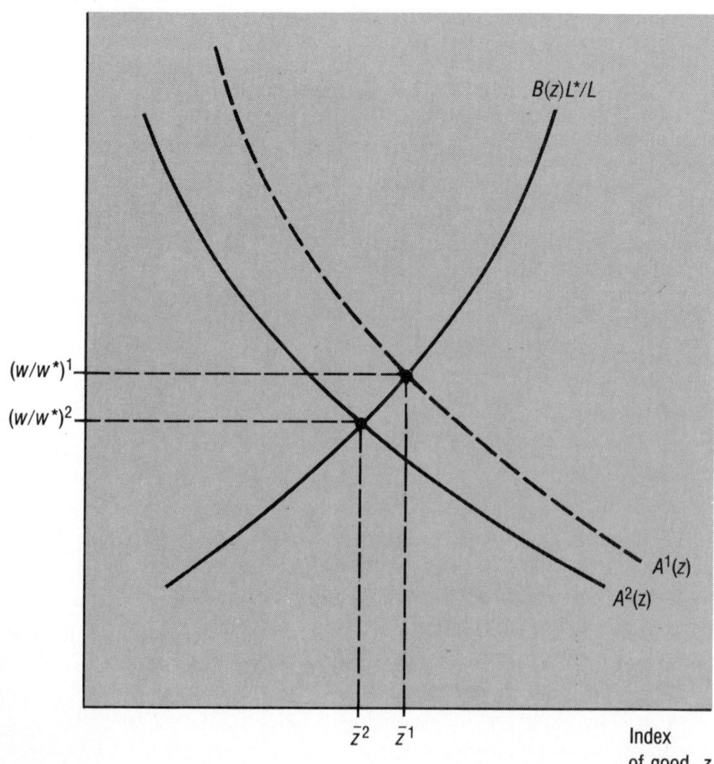

FIGURE 2A-3 Effects of an increase in Foreign productivity. An increase in Foreign's productivity shifts the relative productivity curve down from $A^1(z)$ to $A^2(z)$. The range of goods Home produces falls, and so does its relative wage. Nonetheless, the *real* wage earned by Home's workers increases.

The prices of goods that Home consistently imports depend on both Foreign wages and Foreign unit labor requirements:

$$p(z) = w^*a^*(z),$$

implying

$$w/p(z) = (w/w^*) \times [1/a^*(z)].$$

We know that w/w^* falls—but we also know that it falls proportionally less than $a^*(z)$, implying that for these consistent imports the Home real wage *rises*.

Finally, the transitional goods were produced in Home but are now produced in Foreign. Before the change Home's real wage in terms of each such good was $1/a(z)$, the inverse of the unit labor requirement. Home will only abandon production of a good if its price falls below production cost:

$$p(z) < wa(z),$$

or

$$w/p(z) > 1/a(z).$$

This says, however, that on transitional goods Home's real wage must also have risen.

On two out of three kinds of good, then, Home's real wage rises, while on the third there is no change. Home is unambiguously better off.

This example shows that the common belief that it is always bad when someone gains on you technologically is wrong.

3 IMMOBILE FACTORS AND INCOME DISTRIBUTION

International trade is potentially of mutual benefit to the nations that engage in it. Yet throughout history, governments have protected sectors of the economy from import competition. The government of the United States, for example, despite its commitment in principle to free trade, limits imports of steel, autos, textiles, sugar, and other commodities. Why is there opposition to the effects of international trade, when trade is such a good thing for the economy? To understand even the basics of the political economy of trade, it is necessary to look at the effects of trade, not just on a country as a whole, but on the distribution of income within that country.

The Ricardian model of international trade developed in Chapter 2 illustrates the potential benefits from trade. In that model trade leads to international specialization, with each country shifting its labor force from industries in which that labor is relatively inefficient to industries in which it is relatively more efficient. Because in the model there is only one factor of production, and this factor of production can move freely from one industry to another, there is no possibility that individuals will be hurt by trade. The Ricardian model thus suggests not only that all countries gain from trade, but that every *individual* is made better off as a result of international trade, because trade does not affect the distribution of income.

In the real world, unfortunately, trade has substantial effects on the income distribution within each trading nation, so that in practice the benefits of trade may be distributed very unevenly.

In this chapter we develop models that bring to center stage the income-distribution effects of trade that were assumed away in the Ricardian model. The key difference is in our assumption about the ability of factors of production to move between sectors. In the Ricardian model we assumed that labor could move immediately and costlessly from one sector to another. In this chapter, by contrast, we assume that at least some factors of production are completely immobile between sectors. Given this change in assumption, we see that trade that potentially makes a country better off can leave some individuals within that country worse off.

As in the last chapter, we begin by analyzing a simple economy in isolation, then ask what happens when two such economies trade. We then turn to a more elaborate model. The chapter concludes with a discussion of the implications of income-distribution effects for the politics of trade policy.

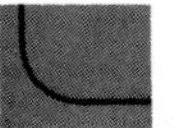

AN IMMOBILE FACTORS MODEL

To see the effects of trade on income distribution as simply as possible, imagine an economy similar to that described in Chapter 2. This economy—still named Home—produces and consumes only two goods, wine and cheese, and each good is produced with only one factor of production, labor. In this **immobile factors model,** however, wine is produced by winemakers, who cannot produce cheese, and cheese is produced by cheesemakers, who cannot produce wine. This immobility of labor changes the production possibilities of the economy, changes the shape of the relative supply curve, and requires that we ask what happens to the relative wages of winemakers and cheesemakers.

As in the last chapter, we define L as the labor supply of Home, a_{LW} and a_{LC} as the unit labor requirements in wine and cheese, respectively. P_C and Q_C will be the price and output of cheese, P_W and Q_W the price and output of wine. In addition some new notation becomes necessary. First, since winemakers and cheesemakers cannot move to the other sector, a distinction must be made between the two kinds of workers. Thus we let

L_C = Home's supply of cheesemaker-hours,

L_W = Home's supply of winemaker-hours.

Also, since winemakers cannot become cheesemakers or vice versa, their wage rate need not be the same. We define

w_C = wage rate of cheesemakers,

w_W = wage rate of winemakers.

PRODUCTION POSSIBILITIES

In the Ricardian model the production possibility curve is traced out by shifting labor from cheesemaking to winemaking. In an economy with immobile labor no such trade-off is possible. The maximum production of cheese is whatever all the cheesemakers can produce, regardless of how much wine the economy produces. The output of cheese cannot exceed the number of cheesemaker-hours available divided by the number of hours required to produce a pound of cheese:

$$Q_C \leq L_C/a_{LC}. \tag{3-1}$$

Similarly, the maximum production of wine is whatever the winemakers can produce:

$$Q_W \leq L_W/a_{LW}. \tag{3-2}$$

Because the production possibilities of the economy are defined by these two constraints, the production possibility frontier is right-angled (Figure 3-1).

RELATIVE DEMAND AND RELATIVE SUPPLY

With labor immobile between sectors and fully employed, relative supply is simple to describe. Because winemakers cannot produce cheese, they will

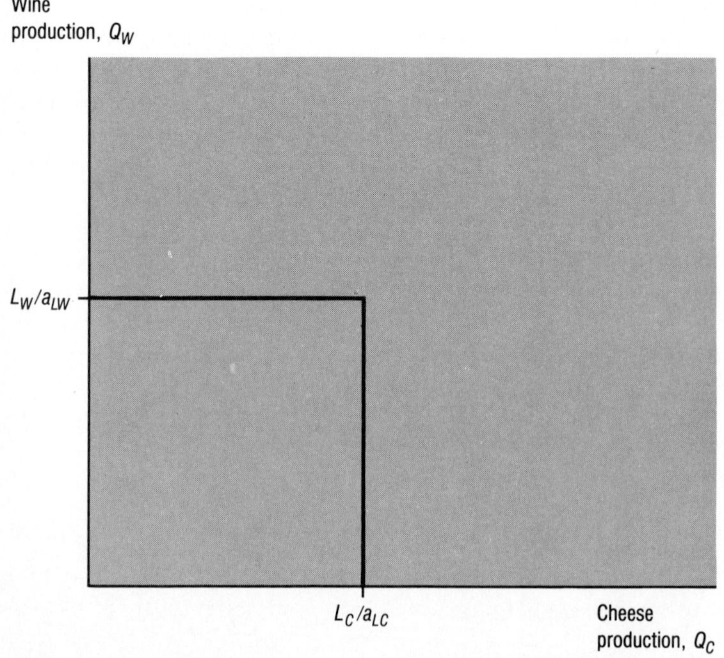

FIGURE 3-1 The production possibility frontier with immobile labor. The fixed supplies of cheesemakers and winemakers define constraints that give rise to a right-angled production possibility frontier.

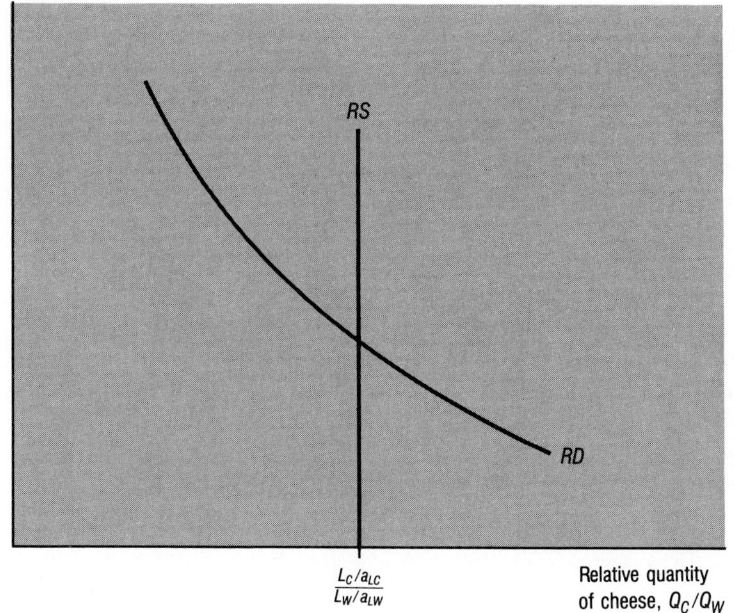

FIGURE 3-2 Relative supply with immobile labor. Because labor cannot move between sectors, relative supply is independent of the relative price of cheese.

always produce as much wine as they can (L_W/a_{LW} gallons), whatever the relative price of cheese. Similarly, cheesemakers will always produce L_C/a_{LC} pounds of cheese. The relative supply curve, *RS* in Figure 3-2, is therefore a vertical line.

Relative demand, illustrated by *RD*, continues to be a downward-sloping line. The equilibrium relative price P_C/P_W is determined by the intersection of *RS* and *RD*.

WAGES AND INCOME DISTRIBUTION

The wages of winemakers and cheesemakers need not be equal. Each type of worker receives a wage equal to the value of what she produces in an hour. It takes a_{LW} man-hours of labor to produce a gallon of wine that sells for P_W. Since a winemaker produces $1/a_{LW}$ gallons each hour, her wage rate is

$$w_W = P_W/a_{LW}. \tag{3-3}$$

Similarly, the wage rate of cheesemakers is

$$w_C = P_C/a_{LC}. \tag{3-4}$$

These expressions reveal some important information about the relationship between the prices of *goods* (wine and cheese) and the prices of *factors* (winemakers and cheesemakers). Dividing our expression for the cheesemaker wage by our expression for the winemaker wage shows that the ratio of cheesemakers' wages to those of winemakers is proportional to the price of cheese relative to that of wine:

$$w_C/w_W = (P_C/P_W) \times (a_{LW}/a_{LC}). \tag{3-5}$$

Equation (3-5) has a simple but important implication: if the relative price of cheese rises for some reason (such as an opening of the economy to international trade) the share of cheesemakers in the economy's income will rise and that of winemakers will fall.

While a rise in the relative price of cheese will raise the income of cheesemakers relative to that of winemakers, we have not yet established whether it will leave cheesemakers absolutely better off and winemakers absolutely worse off. To answer this question we look at the **real wages** of the two kinds of workers in terms of the two goods. The real wage of a worker in terms of a good is defined as her wage rate divided by the price of that good. By dividing the wage rate of winemakers by the price of wine, we find that the real wage of winemakers in terms of wine is simply the inverse of the unit labor requirement:

$$w_W/P_W = 1/a_{LW}. \tag{3-6}$$

When we divide the wage rate of winemakers instead by the price of cheese, we find that

$$\begin{aligned} w_W/P_C &= P_W/(P_C \times a_{LW}) \\ &= (1/a_{LW})/(P_C/P_W). \end{aligned} \tag{3-7}$$

These expressions indicate that an increase in the relative price of cheese will have no effect on the real wage of winemakers in terms of wine, while it reduces their real wage in terms of cheese. In other words, a rise in the relative price of cheese unambiguously reduces the purchasing power of winemakers' wages, leaving them worse off.

Similarly, for cheesemakers we can show that

$$w_C/P_C = 1/a_{LC}, \tag{3-8}$$

$$w_C/P_W = (1/a_{LC}) \times (P_C/P_W). \tag{3-9}$$

These equations say that a rise in the relative price of cheese leaves cheesemakers' real wage in terms of cheese unaffected, but raises their real wage in terms of wine. So an increase in P_C/P_W unambiguously raises the purchasing power of cheesemakers' income.

A rise in the relative price of cheese, then, not only raises the wage of cheesemakers relative to that of winemakers, it unambiguously makes cheesemakers better off and winemakers worse off.

INTERNATIONAL TRADE WITH IMMOBILE FACTORS

To analyze the effects of international trade in the immobile factors model, let's now suppose that there are two countries, Home and Foreign, both producing wine and cheese. In our analysis, we make two assumptions:

1. At any given P_C/P_W, relative demand is the same in the two countries; that is, if both countries face the same relative price of cheese, they will consume wine and cheese in the same proportions. This means that the two countries have the same relative demand curve.
2. The productivity of each type of labor is the same in the two countries.

The only difference between the countries is in their relative supplies of the two kinds of labor. Home has a higher ratio of cheesemakers to winemakers than Foreign and thus a larger relative supply of cheese. Given that relative demand is the same, Home's larger relative cheese supply implies that in the absence of trade the relative price of cheese P_C/P_W would be lower in Home than in Foreign. It is this difference in relative prices that gives rise to international trade.

TRADE AND RELATIVE PRICES

In this model, as always, international trade leads to a convergence of relative prices. This convergence is illustrated in Figure 3-3. Since relative demand is the same in Home and Foreign, *RD* is both each country's relative demand curve and the world relative demand curve when the two countries trade. The vertical lines RS_H, RS_F represent the relative supply curves of Home and Foreign, respectively. Because the ratio of cheesemakers to winemakers is higher in Home than in Foreign, RS_H lies to the right of RS_F. The pretrade relative price of cheese in Home, $(P_C/P_W)_H$, is lower than the pretrade relative price in Foreign, $(P_C/P_W)_F$.

When the two countries open trade, they create an integrated world economy whose production of wine and cheese is the sum of the national outputs of the two goods. The *world* relative supply of cheese (*RS*) thus lies in between the relative supplies in the two countries. The world relative price of cheese, $(P_C/P_W)_T$, therefore lies between the national pretrade prices. Trade has increased the relative price of cheese in Home and has lowered it in Foreign.

THE PATTERN OF TRADE

If trade occurs initially because of differences in relative prices of cheese, how does the convergence of P_C/P_W translate into a pattern of international trade? To answer this question, we need to state some basic relationships among prices, production, and consumption. In a country that cannot trade, the output of a good (Q_C, Q_W) must equal its consumption (D_C, D_W). Interna-

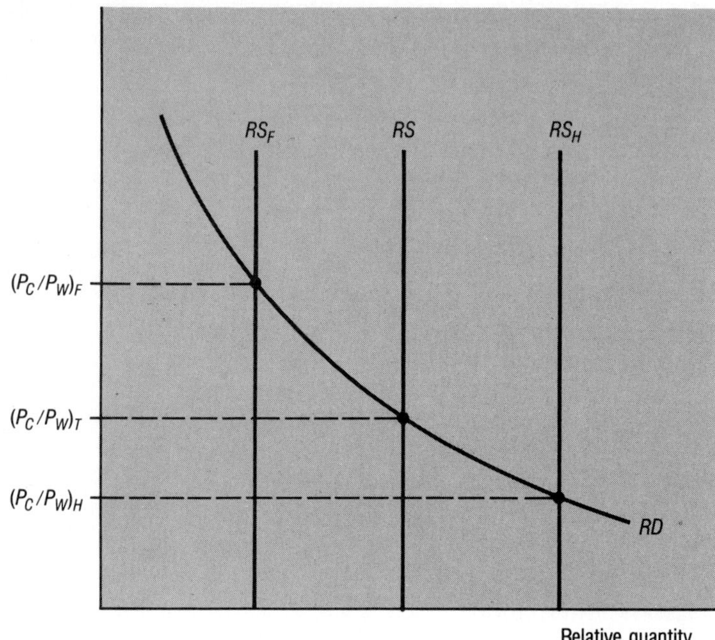

FIGURE 3-3 International trade leads to a convergence of relative prices. The posttrade relative price $(P_C/P_W)_T$ lies between the pretrade relative prices $(P_C/P_W)_H$ in Home and $(P_C/P_W)_F$ in Foreign.

tional trade makes it possible for the mix of cheese and wine consumed to differ from the mix produced. While the amounts of each good that a country consumes and produces may differ, however, a country cannot spend more than it earns: the *value* of consumption must be equal to the value of production. That is,

$$P_C D_C + P_W D_W = P_C Q_C + P_W Q_W . \qquad \textbf{(3-10)}$$

Equation (3-10) can be rearranged to yield the following:

$$D_W - Q_W = (P_C/P_W) \times (Q_C - D_C) . \qquad \textbf{(3-11)}$$

$D_W - Q_W$ is the economy's wine *imports,* the amount by which its consumption of wine exceeds its production. The right-hand side is the product of the relative price of cheese and the amount by which production of cheese exceeds consumption, that is, the economy's *exports* of cheese. The equation, then, states that imports of wine equal exports of cheese times the relative price of cheese. While it does not tell us how much the economy will import or export, the equation does show that the amount the economy can afford to import is constrained by the amount it exports. Equation (3-11) is therefore known as a **budget constraint.**[1]

Figure 3-4 illustrates two important features of the budget constraint for a trading economy. The first is that the budget constraint passes through the point representing production: if $Q_C = D_C$, then $D_W = Q_W$ (if the economy consumes all the cheese that it produces, it has no cheese left to export, so it cannot pay for any imports of wine). The second is that the slope of the budget constraint is minus P_C/P_W, the relative price of cheese.

We can now use the budget constraints of Home and Foreign to construct a picture of the trading equilibrium. In Figure 3-5, the outputs, budget constraints, and consumption choices of Home and Foreign are illustrated side by side. In Home, the rise in the relative price of cheese leads to a rise in the consumption of wine relative to cheese. Home produces Q_W of wine, but consumes D_W; it therefore becomes a cheese exporter and a wine importer. In Foreign, the posttrade fall in the relative price of cheese leads to the

[1]The constraint that the value of consumption equals that of production (or, equivalently, that imports equal exports in value) may not hold when countries can borrow from other countries or lend to them. For now we assume that these possibilities are not available and that the budget constraint [equation (3-11)] therefore holds. International borrowing and lending are examined in Chapter 7, which shows that an economy's consumption *over time* is still constrained by the necessity of paying its debts to foreign lenders.

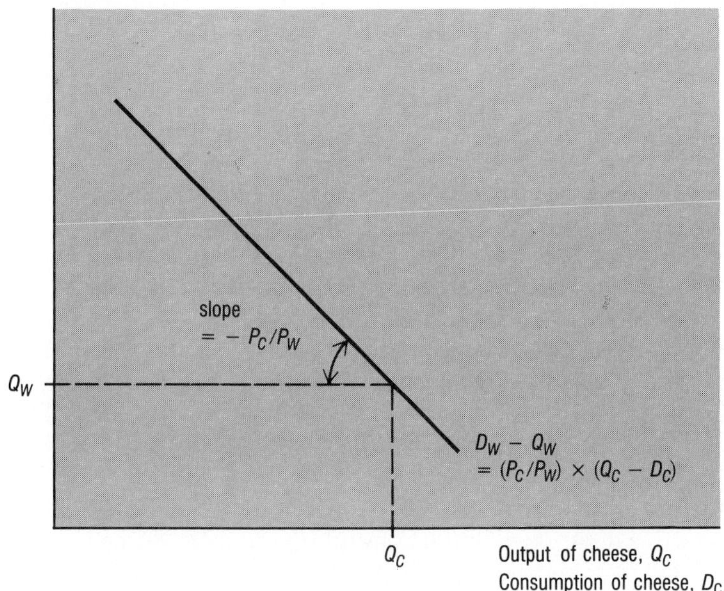

FIGURE 3-4 The budget constraint for a trading economy. The budget constraint is a line with a slope equal to $-P_C/P_W$ that passes through the production point Q_C, Q_W.

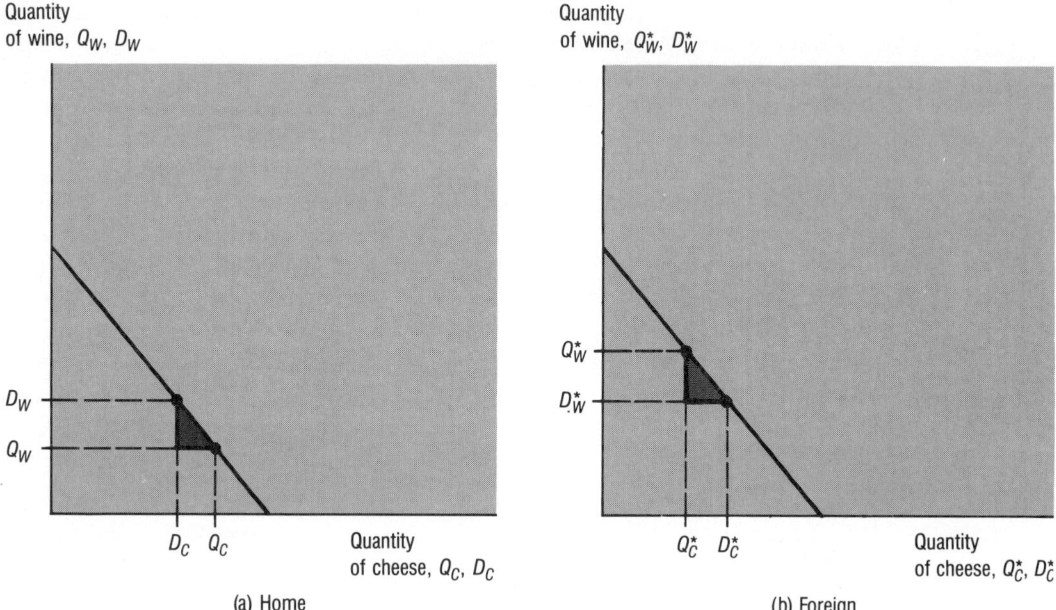

FIGURE 3-5 Trading equilibrium. Home's exports of cheese are exactly equal to Foreign's imports, and Home's imports of wine are exactly equal to Foreign's exports.

reverse result. In equilibrium Home's exports of cheese must exactly equal Foreign's imports, and Home's imports of wine exactly equal Foreign's exports. This equality is shown by the equality of the two shaded triangles in Figure 3-5.

INCOME DISTRIBUTION AND THE GAINS FROM TRADE

We are now in a position to ask the crucial question: who gains and who loses from international trade?

Consider first what happens in Home. Trade raises the price of cheese relative to that of wine. We saw, however, that a rise in P_C/P_W, while it makes cheesemakers better off, leaves winemakers worse off.

In Foreign, the effect of trade on relative prices is just the reverse: the relative price of cheese falls. So in Foreign winemakers are better off and cheesemakers worse off.

The general outcome, then, is simple: *Trade benefits workers in the export sector of each country but hurts workers in the import-competing sectors.*

Do the gains from trade outweigh the losses? One way you might think of trying to answer this question would be to sum up the gains of the winners and the losses of the losers and compare them. The problem with this procedure is that we are comparing welfare, which is an inherently subjective thing. Suppose that cheesemakers are dull people who get hardly any satisfaction out of increased consumption, while winemakers are bons vivants who get immense pleasure out of their incomes. Then one might well imagine that trade reduces the total amount of pleasure in Home. But the reverse could equally be true. More to the point, it is outside the province of what we normally think of as economic analysis to try to figure out how much enjoyment individuals get out of their lives.

A better way to approach the problem is to ask a different question: could those who gain from trade compensate those who lose, and still be better off themselves? If so, we can at least say that trade is *potentially* a source of gain to everyone.

To see that trade is, in fact, a source of potential gain for everyone, look at Figure 3-6. In the absence of trade, a country would have to consume a mix of goods it is able to produce. With trade, however, a country is able to choose any point on or inside its budget constraint. As we see from the figure, however, *all* of the area inside a country's production possibility frontier is also inside its budget constraint. Trade thus unambiguously *expands the*

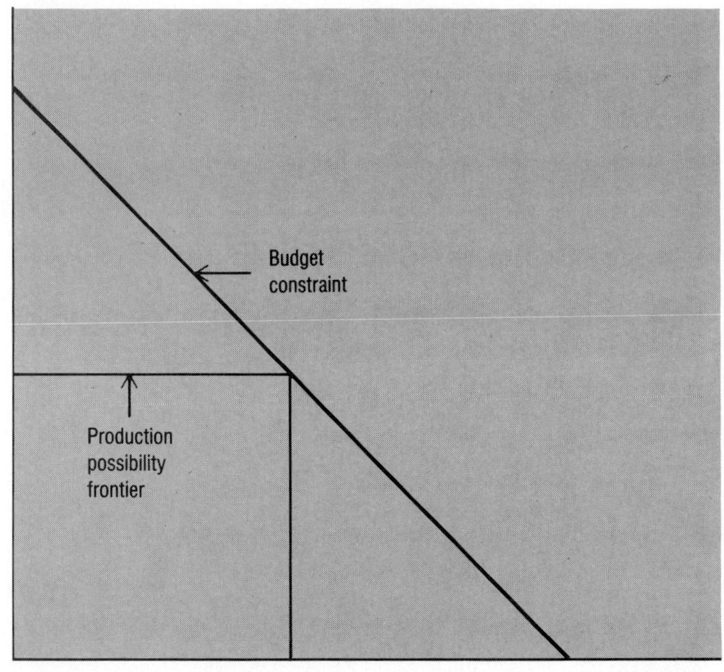

FIGURE 3-6 Trade expands an economy's choices. After trade, a country can choose any point inside its budget constraint, which includes all points inside the production possibility frontier and other points as well.

economy's choices. This expansion of choice means that it is always possible to redistribute income in such a way that everyone gains from trade.[2]

That everyone *could* gain from trade unfortunately does not mean that everyone actually does. In the real world, the presence of losers as well as winners from trade is one of the most important reasons why trade is not free.

MOBILE VS. SPECIFIC FACTORS

We learn some important lessons from a model where labor is completely unable to move between sectors. In the real world, however, matters are not quite this simple. Some factors of production—labor among them—are able to move from one employment to another, albeit at some cost. Other factors are more nearly immobile, because their usefulness is closely tied to certain kinds of production. For example, mechanical engineers are important to many industries, and are therefore a general-purpose factor that can shift from one sector to another. On the other hand, specialized equipment, like the presses used to stamp out auto bodies, cannot be converted to other uses. Economists refer to the distinction between factors of production that can move freely and those that cannot as the distinction between **mobile** and **specific** factors.

One particular model in which there are both mobile and specific factors has come into wide use among international economists as a convenient tool for analyzing a variety of issues. This model was developed by Paul Samuelson and Ronald Jones,[3] and is usually referred to as the **specific-factors model.**

ASSUMPTIONS OF THE MODEL

Imagine an economy—again called Home—that can produce two goods. This time, we call the goods manufactures and food. Instead of one factor, Home now has *three* factors of production: labor (L), capital (K), and land (T for "terrain"). Manufactures are produced using capital and labor (but not land). Food is produced using land and labor (but not capital). Labor is therefore a *mobile* factor that can be used in either sector, while land and capital are both *specific* factors that can be used only in the production of one good.

How much of each good does the economy produce? The economy's output of manufactures depends on how much capital and labor are used in

[2]The argument that trade is beneficial because it enlarges an economy's choices is much more general than this picture. For a thorough discussion see Paul Samuelson, "The Gains from International Trade Once Again," *Economic Journal* 72 (1962), pp. 820–829.

[3]Paul Samuelson, "Ohlin Was Right," *Swedish Journal of Economics* 73 (1971), pp. 365–384; and Ronald W. Jones, "A Three-Factor Model in Theory, Trade, and History," in Jagdish Bhagwati et al., eds., *Trade, Balance of Payments, and Growth* (Amsterdam: North-Holland, 1971), pp. 3–21.

that sector; we can summarize this by a **production function** that expresses the dependence of manufactures' output on inputs:

$$Q_M = Q_M(K, L_M) \tag{3-12}$$

where K is the economy's capital stock and L_M is that part of the country's labor force that is employed in manufactures. Similarly, for food we can write the production function

$$Q_F = Q_F(T, L_F) \tag{3-13}$$

where T is the economy's supply of land and L_F is the part of the labor force devoted to food production. For the economy as a whole, the labor employed must equal the total labor supply:

$$L_M + L_F = L\,. \tag{3-14}$$

PRODUCTION POSSIBILITIES

Given the supplies of capital, labor, and land, the more labor that is allocated to manufactures, the larger will be the output of manufactures and the less the output of food.

Figure 3-7 illustrates the relationship between labor input and output of manufactures. The larger the input of labor, for a given capital supply, the

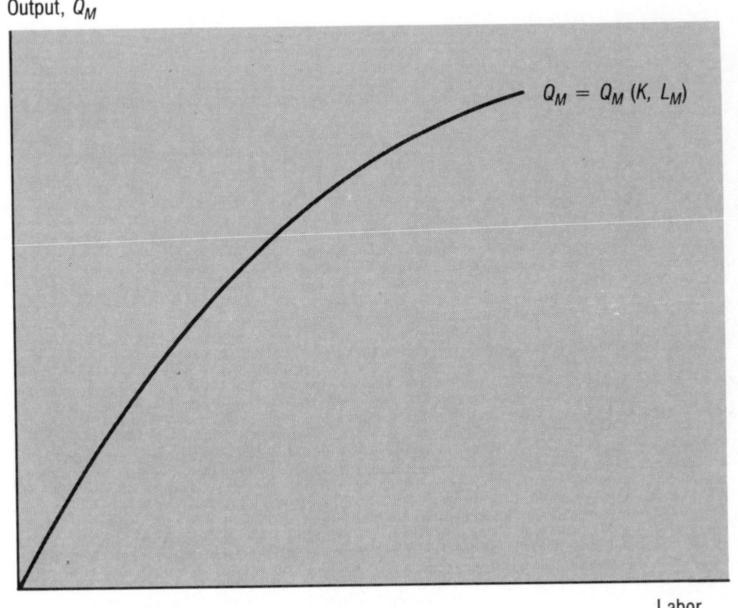

FIGURE 3-7 The production function for manufactures. The more labor that is employed in manufactures, the larger the output.

larger will be output. However, if labor input is increased without increasing capital as well, there will be diminishing returns: each successive increment of labor will add less to production than the last. In Figure 3-7, the slope of $Q_M(K, L_M)$ represents the **marginal product of labor,** that is, the addition to output generated by adding one more man-hour. **Diminishing returns** are shown by the fact that $Q_M(K, L_M)$ gets flatter as we move to the right, so that the marginal product of labor declines as more labor is used.

Figure 3-8 shows the same information a different way: in this figure we directly plot the marginal product of labor as a function of the labor employed. In the appendix to this chapter we show that the area under the marginal product curve, shaded in the figure, represents the total output of manufactures.

We can trace out Home's production possibilities (Figure 3-9) by varying the allocation of labor between manufactures and food. The more labor that is devoted to one sector, the less is available to the other. Thus the production possibility curve is downward-sloping. However, as we use more labor to produce manufactures, the marginal product of labor in manufacturing will decline, while at the same time the marginal product in food will rise. This means that the opportunity cost of manufactures in terms of food will be higher the more manufactures Home produces. This is reflected in the curvature of the production possibility frontier in Figure 3-9.

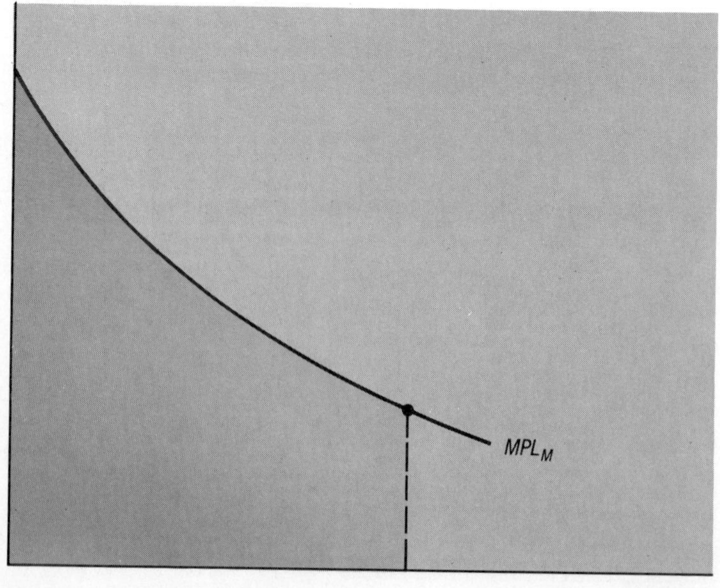

FIGURE 3-8 The marginal product of labor. The marginal product of labor in manufactures is lower, the more labor the sector employs. Total output of manufactures is measured by the area under the curve up to the level of employment.

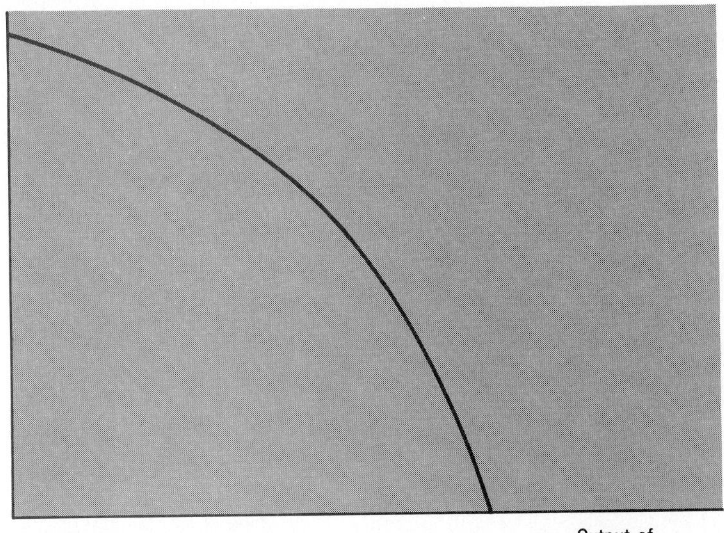

FIGURE 3-9 Production possibilities in the specific factors model. The more manufactures the economy produces, the less food it can produce, and vice versa. Diminishing returns make the frontier a curve instead of a straight line.

PRICES, WAGES, AND LABOR ALLOCATION

How much labor will be employed in each sector? The demand for labor in each sector depends on the price of output and the wage rate; the wage rate in turn depends on the combined demand for labor by food and manufactures.

In each sector, profit-maximizing employers will want to hire labor up to the point where the value produced by an additional man-hour equals the cost of employing that hour. The value of an additional man-hour in manufacturing is the marginal product of labor in manufacturing multiplied by the price of one unit of manufactures: $MPL_M \times P_M$. Similarly, the value of an additional man-hour in food is $MPL_F \times P_F$. Since labor is a mobile factor, it must be paid the same wage rate in both sectors; otherwise labor will move from the low-wage sector to the high-wage sector until wages are equalized. Let w be the wage rate of labor. Then in manufacturing we must have

$$MPL_M \times P_M = w\,. \tag{3-15}$$

Similarly, in food we must have

$$MPL_F \times P_F = w\,. \tag{3-16}$$

At the same time, total employment must equal total labor supply:

$$L_M + L_F = L\,. \tag{3-17}$$

By representing these three equations in a diagram (Figure 3-10), we can see how the wage rate and employment in each sector are determined given

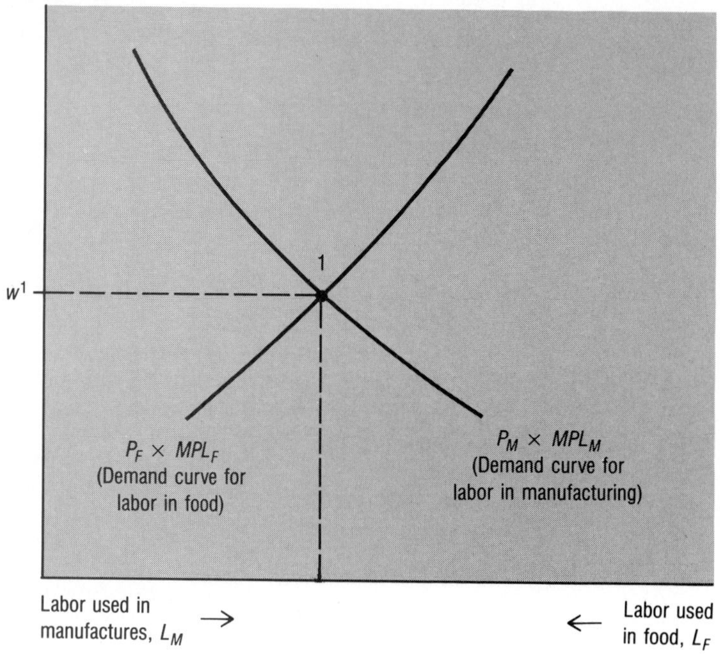

FIGURE 3-10 The allocation of labor. Labor is allocated so that the value of its marginal product is the same in manufactures and food. In equilibrium, the wage rate is equal to the value of labor's marginal product.

the prices of food and manufactures. Along the bottom of Figure 3-10 we show the total labor supply L. Measuring from the left of the diagram, we show the value of the marginal product of labor in manufactures, which is simply the MPL_M curve from Figure 3-8 multiplied by P_M. This is the demand curve for labor in the manufacturing sector. Measuring from the right, we show the value of the marginal product of labor in food, which is the demand for labor in food. The equilibrium is represented by point 1, which satisfies our three equations. At the wage rate corresponding to point 1, w^1, the sum of labor demanded by manufactures and food just equals the total labor supply. As the figure shows, this wage rate and the allocation of labor between manufactures and food are jointly determined.

PRICES AND THE DISTRIBUTION OF INCOME

We next ask what happens when the prices of food and manufactures change. This question can be simplified by noticing that any price change can be decomposed into two parts: an equal proportional change in both P_M and P_F, and a change in only one price. For example, suppose that the price of manufactures rises 17 percent and the price of food rises 10 percent. We can analyze the effects of this by first asking what happens if manufactures and food prices both rise by 10 percent, then finding what happens if manufactures prices rise by 7 percent. This allows us to separate the effect of changes in the overall price level from the effect of changes in relative prices.

Figure 3-11 shows the effect of an equal proportional increase in P_M and P_F. P_M rises from P_M^1 to P_M^2; P_F rises from P_F^1 to P_F^2. If both goods prices increase by 10 percent, the labor demand curves will both shift up by 10 percent as well. As you can see from the diagram, this will lead to a 10 percent increase in the wage rate from w^1 (point 1) to w^2 (point 2), while the allocation of labor between the sectors will not change.

What impact does this have on welfare? None at all. Workers receive a 10 percent wage increase, but the prices of both goods have also risen by 10 percent, leaving them in exactly the same real position as before. Owners of capital receive a 10 percent higher price, but their labor costs have also gone up in the same proportion; so their income will only rise in line with the increase in overall prices. The same is true of landowners. Thus we confirm for this model the basic economic principle that a pure increase in the overall level of prices, without changes in relative prices, has no real effects.

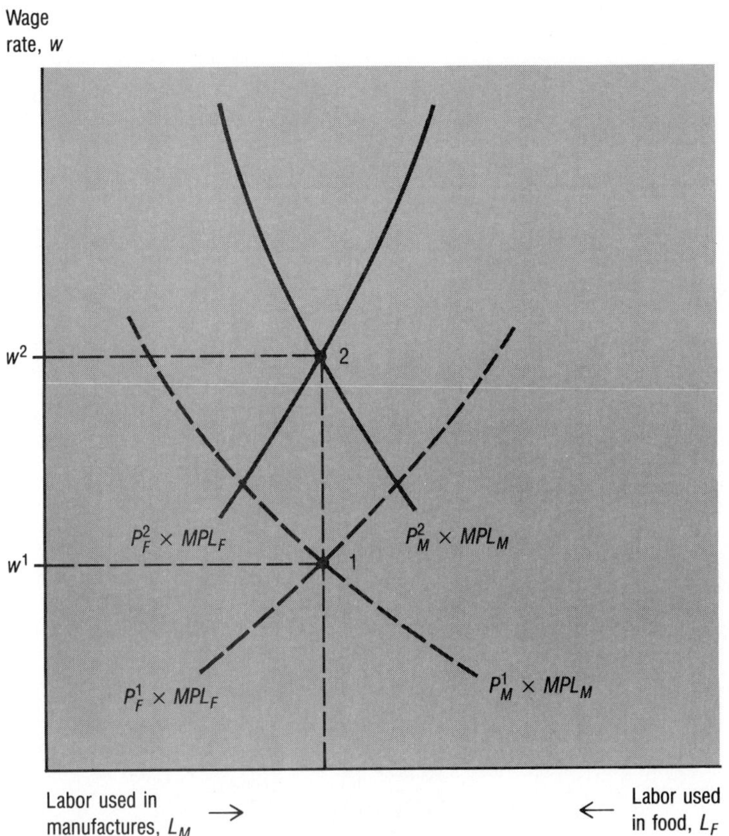

FIGURE 3-11 An equal proportional increase in the prices of manufactures and food. The labor demand curves in manufactures and food both shift up in proportion to the rise in P_M from P_M^1 to P_M^2 and the rise in P_F from P_F^1 to P_F^2. The wage rate rises in the same proportion, from w^1 to w^2; the allocation of labor does not change.

Figure 3-12 shows the effect of a change in the price of only one good, in this case a rise in P_M from P_M^1 to P_M^2. The initial effect of the increase in P_M is to shift up the manufacturing labor demand curve in the same proportion as the price increase. This shifts the equilibrium from point 1 to point 2. The important fact to notice is that in contrast to the case of a simultaneous rise in P_M and P_F, in this case w rises by *less* than P_M. Thus if manufacturing prices rise by 10 percent, we would expect the wage rate to rise by only, say, 5 percent.

Let's look at what this outcome implies for the real incomes of three groups: workers, owners of capital, and owners of land. Workers find that their wage rate has risen, but less than in proportion to P_M. Thus their real wage in terms of manufactures, w/P_M, falls, while their real wage in terms of food, w/P_F, rises. We cannot say in general whether workers are better or worse off.

Owners of capital are definitely better off. The real wage rate in terms of manufactures has fallen, so that the profits of capital owners in terms of what they produce rises. That is, the income of capital owners will rise more than proportionately with the rise in P_M. Since P_M in turn has risen relative to P_F, the gain for capitalists is unambiguous.

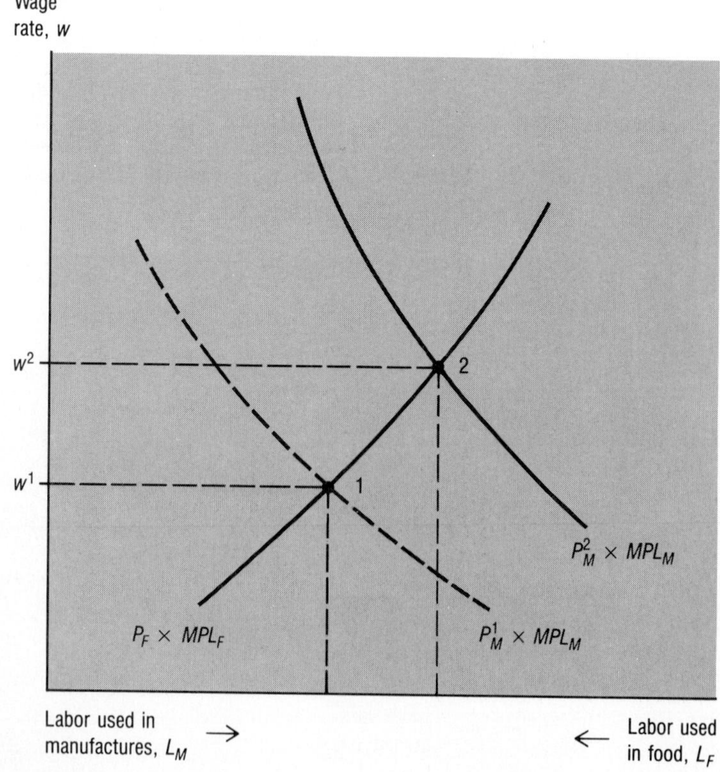

FIGURE 3-12 A rise in the price of manufactures. The manufacturing labor demand curve rises in proportion to the increase in P_M, but the wage rate rises less than proportionately. Output of manufactures rises; output of food falls.

SPECIFIC FACTORS AND THE BEGINNINGS OF TRADE THEORY

The modern theory of international trade began with the demonstration by David Ricardo, writing in 1817, that trade is mutually beneficial to countries. We studied Ricardo's model in Chapter 2. Ricardo used his model to argue for free trade, in particular for an end to the tariffs that at the time restricted England's imports of food. Yet almost surely the British economy of 1817 was better described by a specific factors model than by the one-factor model Ricardo presented.

To understand the situation, we need to recall our history. From the beginning of the French Revolution in 1789 until the defeat of Napoleon at Waterloo in 1815, Britain was almost continuously at war with France. This war interfered with Britain's trade: privateers (pirates licensed by foreign governments) raided shipping, and the French attempted to impose a blockade on British goods. Since Britain was an exporter of manufactures and an importer of agricultural products, this limitation of trade raised the relative price of food in Britain. The profits of manufacturers suffered, but landowners actually prospered during the long war.

After the end of the war, food prices in Britain fell. To avoid the consequences, the politically influential landowners were able to get legislation, the so-called Corn Laws, that imposed fees to discourage importation of grain. It was against these Corn Laws that Ricardo was arguing.

Now Ricardo knew that repeal of the Corn Laws would make capitalists better off but landowners worse off. From his point of view this was all to the good; as a London businessman himself, he preferred hard-working capitalists to idle landed aristocrats. But he chose to present his argument in the form of a model that assumed away issues of internal income distribution.

Why did he do this? Almost surely the answer is political: while Ricardo was in reality to some extent representing the interest of a single group, he emphasized the gains to the nation as a whole. This was a clever and thoroughly modern strategy. Ricardo thus pioneered the use of economic theory as a political instrument. Then as now, politics and intellectual progress are not incompatible: the Corn Laws were repealed well over a century ago, yet Ricardo's model of trade remains one of the great insights in economics.

Conversely, landowners are definitely worse off. They lose for two reasons: the real wage in terms of food rises, squeezing their income, and the rise in manufactures prices reduces the purchasing power of any given income.

INCOME DISTRIBUTION EFFECTS OF TRADE

All that we need to do now is point out that international trade will shift the relative prices of manufactures and food. Suppose that in the absence of trade Home would have had a lower relative price of manufactures than the rest of the world. Then trade, which leads to a convergence of relative prices, will mean a rise in P_M/P_F. As a result, owners of capital will be better off, workers will experience an ambiguous shift in their position, and landowners will be worse off.

The specific factors model thus confirms the insight from our simpler model: although trade may potentially be beneficial for the country as a whole, it can easily leave some groups worse off. We can also suggest a generalization: *Owners of factors specific to export sectors gain from trade; owners of factors specific to import-competing sectors lose from trade.* This was also true in our earlier model; the difference here is that there may also be mobile factors on which the effect of trade is ambiguous.

THE POLITICAL ECONOMY OF TRADE: A PRELIMINARY VIEW

Trade will often produce losers as well as winners. This insight is crucial if we are to understand the considerations that actually determine trade policy in the modern world economy. A detailed examination of trade policy will be given in Chapters 8 through 11; it is possible, however, to take a preliminary view at this point.

There are two ways to look at trade policy (or any government policy): (1) Given its objectives, what *should* the government do? What is its *optimal* trade policy? (2) What are governments likely to do in practice? The income-distribution effects of trade are important for the first way of looking at the issue, and are crucial for the second.

OPTIMAL TRADE POLICY

Suppose a government wants to maximize the welfare of its population. If everyone were exactly alike in tastes and in income there would be a straightforward solution: choose policies that make the representative individual as well off as possible. In this homogeneous economy, free international trade would clearly serve the government's objectives.

When people are not exactly alike, however, the government's problem is less well defined. The government must somehow weigh one person's gain against another person's loss. If, for example, the Home government is relatively more concerned about hurting winemakers than about helping cheesemakers, then international trade, which in our analysis benefited cheesemakers and hurt winemakers in Home, might turn out to be a bad thing from the government's point of view.

There are many reasons why one group might matter more than another, but the most compelling argument in practice is that some groups need special treatment because they are already relatively poor. There is widespread sympathy in the United States electorate for restrictions on imports of garments and shoes, even though the restrictions raise consumer prices, because workers in these industries are already poorly paid. The public feels that the gains that affluent consumers would realize if more imports were allowed do not matter as much to them as the losses that would be suffered by low-paid shoe and garment workers.

Does this mean that trade should be allowed only if it doesn't hurt lower-income people? Few international economists would agree. In spite of the real importance of income distribution, most economists remain strongly in favor of more or less free trade. There are three main reasons why economists do *not* generally put too much stress on the income-distribution effects of trade.

1. Income-distribution effects are not special to international trade. Every change in a nation's economy, including technological progress, shifting consumer preferences, exhaustion of old resources and discovery of new ones, and so on, has effects on income distribution. If every change in the economy were to be allowed only after it had been examined for its distributional effects, economic progress could easily end up snarled in red tape.
2. It is always better to allow trade and compensate those who are hurt by it than to prohibit the trade. (This applies to other forms of economic change as well.) All modern industrial countries provide some sort of "safety net" of income support programs that can somewhat cushion the losses of groups hurt by trade. Economists would argue that if this cushion is felt to be inadequate, more support rather than less trade is the right answer.
3. The politics of trade are such that those who stand to lose from increased trade are typically better organized than those who stand to gain. This imbalance creates a bias in the political process that requires a counterweight. It is the traditional role of economists to take a strong stand in favor of free trade, pointing to the overall gains from trade; those who are hurt usually have little trouble making their complaints heard.

Most economists, then, while acknowledging the effects of international trade on income distribution, believe that it is more important to stress the potential gains from trade than the possible losses to some groups within a country. Economists do not, however, often have the deciding voice in economic policy, especially when conflicting interests are at stake. Any realistic understanding of how trade policy is determined must look at the actual motivations of policy.

INCOME DISTRIBUTION AND TRADE POLITICS

It is easy to see why groups that lose from trade will lobby their governments to restrict trade and protect their incomes. You might expect that those who gain from trade would lobby equally strongly on the other side, but this is rarely the case. In the United States and in most countries, those who want trade limited seem to be much more effective politically than those who want it extended. Typically, those who gain from trade in any particular product are a much less concentrated, informed, and organized group than those who lose.

A good example of this contrast between the two sides is the U.S. sugar industry. The United States has limited imports of sugar for many years; at the time of writing the price of sugar in the U.S. market was about four times its price in the world market. One estimate puts the cost to U.S. consumers of this import limitation during the early 1970s at over a billion dollars a year—that is, about $5 for every man, woman, and child. The gains to producers were much smaller, less than half as large.

If producers and consumers were equally able to get their interests represented, this policy would never have been enacted. In absolute terms, however, each consumer suffered very little. Five dollars a year is not much; furthermore, most of the cost was hidden, because most sugar is consumed as an ingredient in other foods rather than purchased directly. Thus most consumers were unaware that the import quota even existed, let alone that it was reducing their standard of living. Even if they had been aware, $5 is not a large enough sum to provoke people into organizing protests and writing letters to their congressmen.

The sugar producers' situation was quite different. The average sugar producer gained thousands of dollars from the import quota. Furthermore, sugar producers are organized into trade associations and cooperatives that actively pursue their members' political interests. So the complaints of sugar producers about the effects of imports were loudly and effectively expressed.

As we will see in Chapters 8 through 11, the politics of import restriction in the sugar industry are an extreme example of a kind of political process that is quite common in international trade. That world trade in general became steadily freer from 1945 to 1980 depended, as we will see in Chapter 9, on a special set of circumstances that controlled what is probably an inherent political bias against international trade.

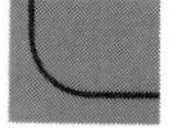

SUMMARY

1. When some factors of production cannot move freely between sectors, international trade produces losers as well as winners. In a model where labor is the only factor of production, we can show that workers employed in *exporting* sectors gain from trade, but those employed in *import-competing* sectors are made worse off, not only relative to other workers but in absolute terms as well.

2. Trade nonetheless produces overall gains in the limited sense that those who gain could in principle compensate those who lose while still remaining better off than before.

3. A more general and realistic model of income-distribution effects is the *specific-factors model,* which allows for a distinction between general-purpose factors that can move between sectors, and factors that are specific to partic-

ular uses. In this model factors specific to export sectors gain from trade, while factors specific to import-competing sectors lose. Mobile factors that can work in either sector may either gain or lose.

4. Most economists do not regard the effects of international trade on income distribution as a good reason to limit this trade. In its distributional effects, trade is no different from many other forms of economic change, which are not normally regulated. Furthermore, economists would prefer to address the problem of income distribution directly, rather than by interfering with trade flows.

5. Nonetheless, in the actual politics of trade policy income distribution is of crucial importance. This is true in particular because those who lose from trade are usually a much more informed, cohesive, and organized group than those who gain.

KEY TERMS

immobile factors model
real wages
budget constraint
mobile factors
specific factors
specific-factors model
production function
marginal product of labor
diminishing returns

PROBLEMS

1. In 1986, the price of oil on world markets dropped sharply. Since the United States is an oil-importing country, this was widely regarded as good for the U.S. economy. Yet in Texas and Louisiana 1986 was a year of economic decline. Why?

2. There are two kinds of workers, chicken farmers and duck farmers. Each kind of farmer can produce 15 birds per day, but neither can produce the other kind of bird. Home has a labor force of 500 chicken farmers and 800 duck farmers.

a) Graph Home's relative supply curve.

b) Suppose that the relative demand is:

Demand for chickens/demand for ducks = price of ducks/price of chickens

Find the relative price of chickens in the absence of trade, and the real wages of each kind of farmer in terms of each kind of good.

3. To the country described in problem 2, add a second country with 300 chicken farmers and 1000 duck farmers.

a) Find this second country's relative supply curve, and derive the relative price of chickens in the absence of trade.

b) If the countries can trade with each other, find the *world* relative supply curve.

c) Derive the world relative price after trade.

d) Find the real wages of each kind of farmer in each country in terms of each good, both before and after trade. Who gained from trade? Who lost?

e) [Optional] Derive the exports and imports of each country.

4. Consider a farmer who lives in Home but who unlike other Home farmers can produce both chickens and ducks—specifically, she can produce 5 chickens and 8 ducks. That is, she can produce birds in the same ratio as total Home production.

a) Assuming that this farmer has the same relative demand as everyone else, show that she is made better off by the relative price change that occurs with trade.

b) What does this result have to do with the proposition that everyone can *potentially* be made better off as a result of trade?

5. An economy can produce good 1 using labor and capital, and good 2 using labor and land. The total supply of labor is 100 units. Given the supply of capital, the output of good 1 depends on labor input as follows:

Labor input to good 1	*Output of good 1*
0	0.0
25	43.3
50	66.0
75	84.1
100	100.0

The output of good 2 depends on labor input as follows:

Labor input to good 2	*Output of good 2*
0	0.0
25	57.4
50	75.8
75	89.1
100	100.0

a) Graph the production functions for good 1 and good 2.

b) Graph the production possibility frontier. Why is it curved?

6. We developed a specific-factors model of a country that exports manufactures and imports food. We then considered the effects of a rise in the price of manufactures. What difference would it make if, instead of the price of manufactures rising, the price of food were to fall?

7. What would happen in the specific-factors model if the economy's supply of land were to increase (say because of a new irrigation scheme)? Analyze in particular the effects on the income of workers, capitalists, and the owners of the original land.

FURTHER READING

Avinash Dixit and Victor Norman. *Theory of International Trade.* Cambridge: Cambridge University Press, 1980. The problem of establishing gains from trade when some people may be made worse off has been the subject of a long debate. Dixit and Norman show that it is always possible in principle for a country's government to use taxes and subsidies to redistribute income in such a way that everyone is better off with free trade than with no trade.

Michael Mussa. "Tariffs and the Distribution of Income: The Importance of Factor Specificity, Substitutability, and Intensity in the Short and Long Run." *Journal of Political Economy* 82 (1974), pp. 1191–1204. An extension of the specific-factors model that relates it to the factor-proportions model of Chapter 4.

J. Peter Neary. "Short-Run Capital Specificity and the Pure Theory of International Trade." *Economic Journal* 88 (1978), pp. 488–510. A further treatment of the specific-factors model that stresses how differing assumptions about mobility of factors between sectors affect the model's conclusions.

Mancur Olson. *The Logic of Collective Action.* Cambridge: Harvard University Press, 1965. A highly influential book that argues the proposition that in practice government policies favor small, concentrated groups over large ones.

David Ricardo. *The Principles of Political Economy and Taxation.* Homewood, IL: Irwin, 1963. While Ricardo's *Principles* emphasizes the national gains from trade at one point, elsewhere in his book the conflict of interest between landowners and capitalists is a central issue.

APPENDIX TO CHAPTER 3

Further Details on Specific Factors

The specific-factors model developed in this chapter is such a convenient tool of analysis that we take the time here to spell out some of its details a little more fully than we did in the main body of the text. We give a fuller treatment of two related issues: (1) the relationship between marginal and total product within each sector; (2) the income-distribution effects of relative price changes.

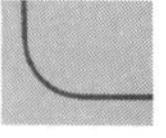

MARGINAL AND TOTAL PRODUCT

In the text we illustrated the production function in manufacturing two different ways. In Figure 3-7 we showed total output as a function of labor input, holding capital constant. We then observed that the slope of that curve is the marginal product of labor, and illustrated that marginal product in Figure 3-8. We now want to demonstrate that the total output is measured by the area under the marginal product curve.

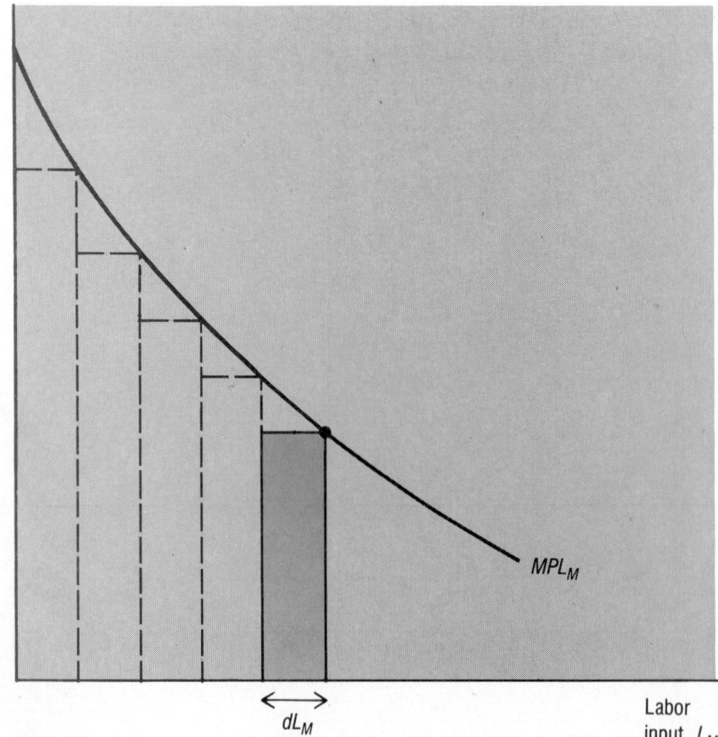

FIGURE 3A-1 Showing that output is equal to the area under the marginal product curve. By approximating the marginal product curve with a series of thin rectangles, one can show that the total output of manufactures is equal to the area under the curve.

(Students who are familiar with calculus will find this obvious: marginal product is the derivative of total, so total is the integral of marginal. Even for these students, however, an intuitive approach can be helpful.)

In Figure 3A-1 we show once again the marginal product curve in manufacturing. Suppose that we employ L_M man-hours. How can we show the total output of manufactures? Let's approximate this using the marginal product curve. First, let's ask what would happen if we used slightly fewer man-hours, say dL_M fewer. Then output would be less. The fall in output would be approximately

$$dL_M \times MPL_M,$$

i.e., the reduction in the work force times the marginal product of labor at the initial level of employment. This reduction in output is represented by the area of the shaded rectangle in Figure 3A-1. Now subtract another few man-hours; the output loss will be another rectangle. This time the rectangle will be taller, because the marginal product of labor rises as the quantity of labor falls. If we continue this process until all the labor is gone, our approximation of the total output loss will be the sum of all the rectangles shown in the figure. When no labor is employed, however, output will fall to zero. So we can approximate the total output of the manufacturing sector by the sum of the areas of all the rectangles under the marginal product curve.

This is, however, only an approximation, because we used the marginal product only of the first man-hour in each batch of labor removed. We can get a better ap-

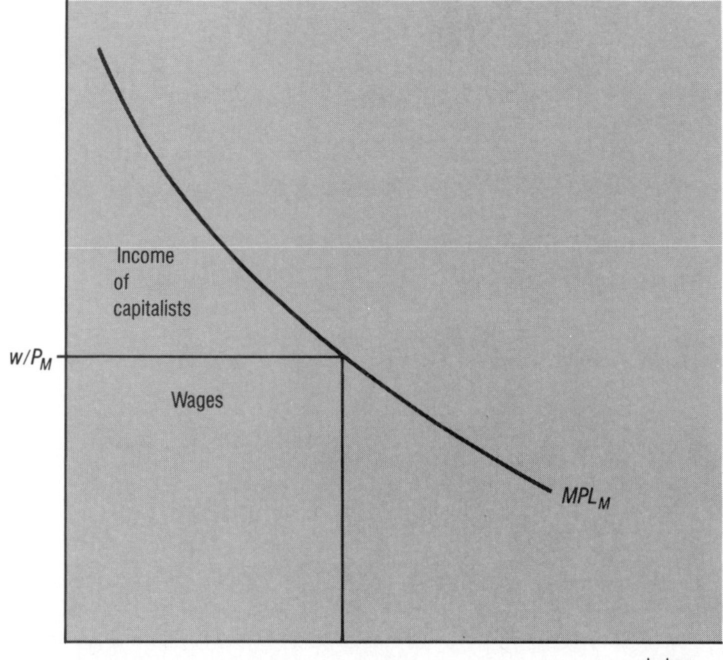

FIGURE 3A-2 The distribution of income within the manufacturing sector. Labor income is equal to the real wage times employment. The rest of output accrues as income to the owners of capital.

proximation if we take smaller groups—the smaller the better. As the groups of labor removed get infinitesimally small, however, the rectangles get thinner and thinner, and we approximate ever more closely the total area under the marginal product curve. In the end, then, we find that the total output of manufactures produced with labor L_M is equal to the area under the marginal product of labor curve MPL_M up to L_M.

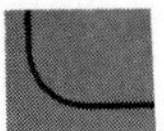

RELATIVE PRICES AND THE DISTRIBUTION OF INCOME

Figure 3A-2 uses the result we just found to show the distribution of income within the manufacturing sector for a given real wage. We know that employers will hire labor up to the point where the real wage in terms of manufactures, w/P_M, equals the marginal product. We can immediately read off the graph the total output of manufactures as the area under the marginal product curve. We can also read off the graph the part of manufacturing output that is paid out as wages, which is equal to the real wage times employment, and thus to the area of the rectangle shown. The part of the output that is kept by owners of capital, then, is the remainder. We can determine the distribution of food production between labor and landowners in the same way.

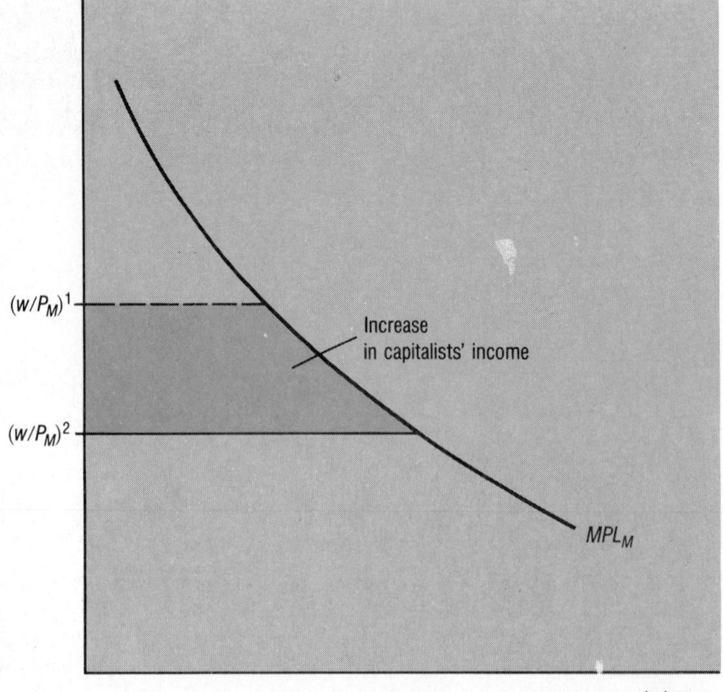

FIGURE 3A-3 A rise in P_M benefits the owners of capital. The real wage in terms of manufactures falls, leading to a rise in the income of capital owners.

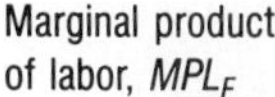

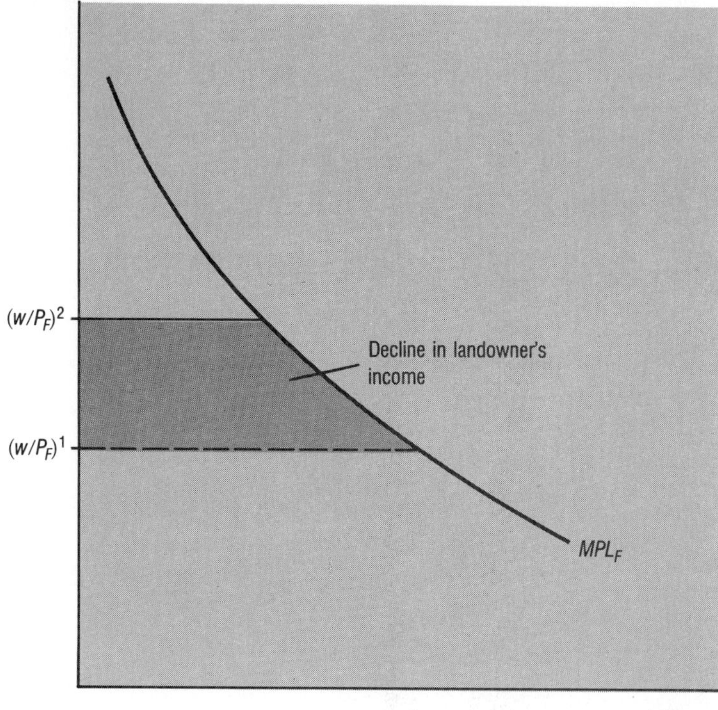

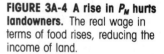

FIGURE 3A-4 A rise in P_M hurts landowners. The real wage in terms of food rises, reducing the income of land.

Suppose that the relative price of manufactures now rises. We saw in Figure 3-12 that a rise in P_M/P_F lowers the real wage in terms of manufactures while raising it in terms of food. The effects of this on the income of capitalists and landlords can be seen in Figures 3A-3 and 3A-4. In the manufactures sector, the real wage is shown as falling from $(w/P_M)^1$ to $(w/P_M)^2$; as a result capitalists receive increased income. In the food sector, the real wage rises from $(w/P_F)^1$ to $(w/P_F)^2$, and landlords receive less income.

This effect on incomes is reinforced by the change in P_M/P_F itself. Owners of capital receive more income *in terms of manufactures;* their purchasing power is further increased by the rise in the price of manufactures relative to food. Owners of land receive less income *in terms of food;* they are made still worse off because of the rise in the relative price of manufactures.

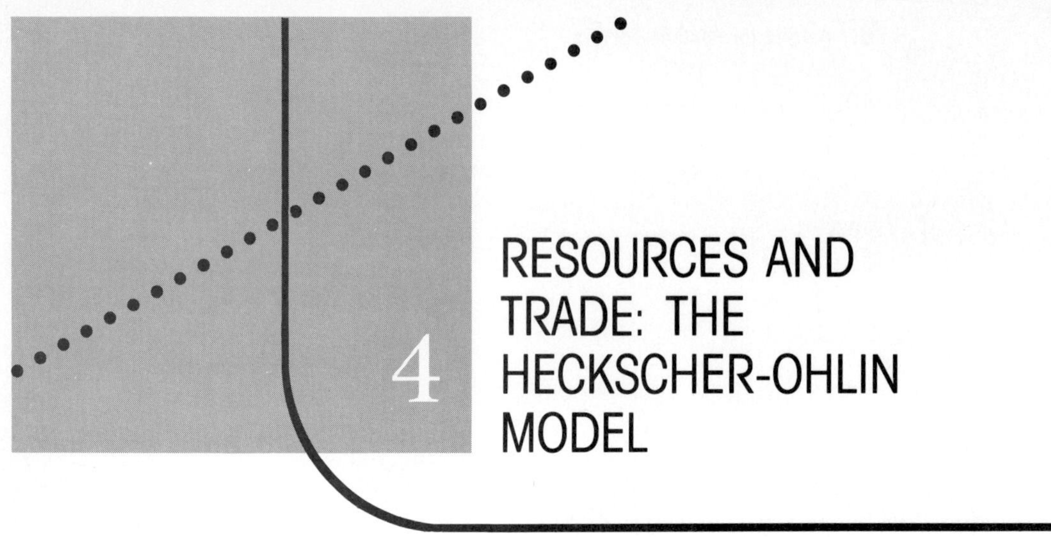

4 RESOURCES AND TRADE: THE HECKSCHER-OHLIN MODEL

If labor were the only factor of production, as the Ricardian model assumes, comparative advantage could arise only because of international differences in labor productivity. In the real world, however, while trade is partly explained by differences in labor productivity, it also reflects differences in countries' *resources.* Canada exports forest products to the United States, not because its lumbermen are more productive relative to their U.S. counterparts than other Canadians but because sparsely populated Canada has more forested land per capita than the United States. A realistic view of trade must allow for the importance, not just of labor, but of other factors of production such as land, capital, and mineral resources.

To explain the role of resource differences in trade, this chapter examines a model in which resource differences are the *only* source of trade. This model shows that comparative advantage is influenced by the interaction between the resources of nations (the relative **abundance** of factors of production) and the technology of production (which influences the relative **intensity** with which different factors of production are used in the production of different goods).

That international trade is largely driven by differences in countries' resources is one of the most influential theories in international economics. Developed by two Swedish economists, Eli Heckscher and Bertil Ohlin (Ohlin received the Nobel Prize in economics in 1977), the theory is often referred to as the **Heckscher-Ohlin theory.** Because the theory emphasizes the interplay between the proportions in which different factors of production are available in different countries, and the proportions in which they are used in producing different goods, it is also referred to as the **factor proportions theory.**

To develop the factor-proportions theory we begin by describing an economy that does not trade, then ask what happens when two such economies trade with each other. Since the factor-proportions theory is both an important theory and a controversial one, the chapter concludes with a discussion of the empirical evidence for and against the theory.

A MODEL OF A TWO-FACTOR ECONOMY

ASSUMPTIONS OF THE MODEL

The economy we are analyzing can produce two goods: cloth (measured in yards) and food (measured in calories). Production of these goods requires two inputs that are in limited supply: labor, which we measure in hours, and land, which we measure in acres. Initially we assume that the technology of production is one of **fixed coefficients**; that is, there is only one way to produce each good. A yard of cloth can only be produced using a certain fixed number of hours of labor and acres of land; we cannot use less land and more labor, or vice versa. The same is true for producing a calorie of food.

In general we would not expect the production of food and of cloth to require land and labor in the same proportions. Let's assume that cloth production is *labor-intensive,* that is, it requires a higher ratio of labor to land than food production. Food production is correspondingly more *land-intensive* than cloth production. Notice that the definition of labor or land intensity depends on the ratio of land to labor used in production, not the ratio of land or labor to output. Thus a good cannot be both land- and labor-intensive.

Let's define the following expressions:

a_{TC} = acres of land required per yard of cloth,

a_{LC} = hours of labor required per yard of cloth,

a_{TF} = acres of land required per calorie of food,

a_{LF} = hours of labor required per calorie of food,

L = economy's supply of labor,

T = economy's supply of land.

The assumption that cloth production is labor-intensive and food production land-intensive can be stated in two equivalent ways:

$$a_{LC}/a_{TC} > a_{LF}/a_{TF}$$

or

$$a_{LC}/a_{LF} > a_{TC}/a_{TF}.$$

PRODUCTION POSSIBILITIES

The principle that underlies the derivation of a production possibility frontier in this model is the same as in earlier ones: the economy cannot use more of either input than it has available. If the country produces Q_C yards of cloth and Q_F calories of food, it must use $a_{LC}Q_C + a_{LF}Q_F$ hours of labor to produce these goods, and this amount must not exceed the total labor force L. The economy will also use $a_{TC}Q_C + a_{TF}Q_F$ acres of land, and this must not exceed the total supply of land. Together, these two constraints define the economy's production possibilities. First, total use of labor cannot exceed the available supply:

$$a_{LC}Q_C + a_{LF}Q_F \leq L. \quad \textbf{(4-1)}$$

Second, total use of land must not exceed the available supply:

$$a_{TC}Q_C + a_{TF}Q_F \leq T. \quad \textbf{(4-2)}$$

The limited supplies of labor and land limit what the economy can produce.

By rearranging the labor constraint, we can write the expression

$$Q_F \leq L/a_{LF} - (a_{LC}/a_{LF})Q_C. \quad \textbf{(4-3)}$$

The logic behind this expression should be clear. If all labor (L) were used to produce food, there would be enough to produce at most L/a_{LF} calories, that is, the total labor force divided by the number of hours it takes to produce each calorie. If some cloth is also produced, each unit of cloth requires that a_{LC} units of labor be diverted from food production and thus reduces the maximum food output by a_{LC}/a_{LF} calories.

Similarly, by rearranging the land constraint we get

$$Q_F \leq T/a_{TF} - (a_{TC}/a_{TF})Q_C. \quad \textbf{(4-4)}$$

The labor and land constraints are illustrated in Figure 4-1. Because cloth is more labor-intensive than food—$a_{LC}/a_{LF} > a_{TC}/a_{TF}$—the labor constraint is a steeper line than the land constraint.

The heavy lines in Figure 4-1 show how the two constraints together determine the economy's production possibilities. If the economy is producing a high ratio of food to cloth, as at point 1, the *binding* constraint, that is, the constraint that actually limits production, is the land constraint. If, on the other hand, the economy is producing a low ratio of food to cloth, as at point 2, the labor constraint is the one that binds. The fact that which constraint is

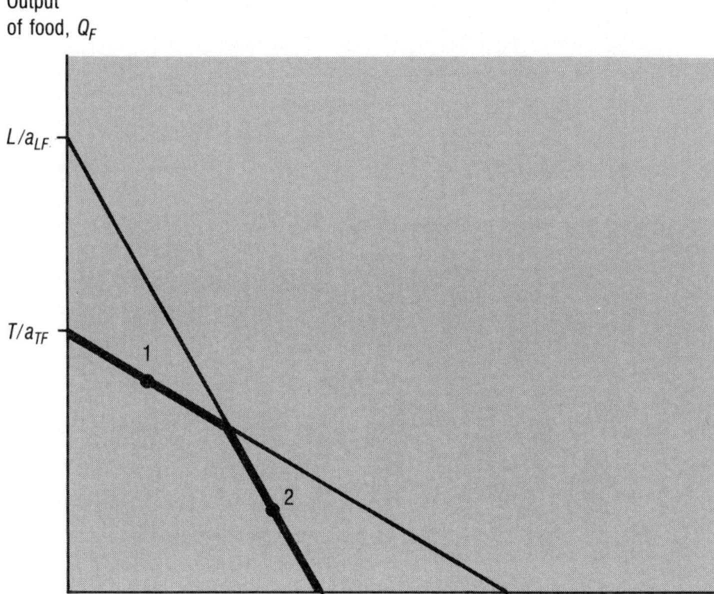

FIGURE 4-1 The production possibility frontier in the factor proportions model. The limited supplies of labor and land constrain the economy's production. Because cloth is more labor-intensive than food, the labor constraint is steeper than the land constraint.

binding depends on the mix of goods the economy produces suggests that changes in the economy's resources will have uneven effects on its ability to produce different goods. Specifically, an increase in the economy's supply of land will expand production possibilities more in the direction of food than in that of cloth, while an increase in the supply of labor will expand production possibilities more in the direction of cloth than in that of food.

Figure 4-2 shows explicitly how an increase in the supply of land changes production possibilities. When the supply of land is increased from T^1 to T^2, the land constraint on the economy's production possibilities is relaxed, so that the production possibility frontier is shifted outward. What is immediately clear from the diagram, however, is that this is a **biased expansion of production possibilities**—that is, the expansion is greater, the higher the ratio of food to cloth in production. In fact, if the economy tries to produce a high ratio of cloth to food, the expansion of land supply does not permit any increase in production at all.

The biased effect of increases in resources on production possibilities is the key to understanding how differences in resources give rise to international trade.[1] An increase in the supply of land expands production possibilities disproportionately in the direction of food production, while an increase

[1]The biased effect of resource changes on production was pointed out in a paper by the Polish economist T. M. Rybczynski, "Factor Endowments and Relative Commodity Prices," *Economica* 22 (1955), pp. 336–341. It is therefore known as the Rybczynski effect.

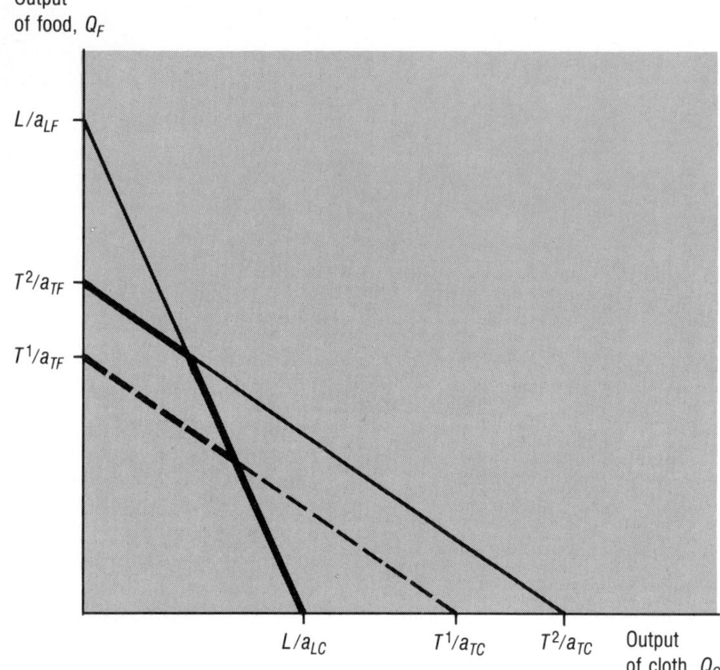

FIGURE 4-2 Increasing the supply of land. When land supply is increased from T^1 to T^2, the land constraint is relaxed. This expands production possibilities in a direction biased toward food production.

in the supply of labor expands them disproportionately in the direction of cloth production. Thus an economy with a high ratio of land to labor will be relatively better at producing food than an economy with a low ratio of land to labor. *More generally, an economy will tend to be relatively good at producing goods that are intensive in the factors with which the country is relatively well endowed.*

GOODS PRICES AND FACTOR PRICES

In Chapter 3 the immobility of labor when the price of a sector's output changed resulted in a change in the wage received by workers in that sector. The resulting effects on income distribution were significant enough to sharply qualify the conclusion that trade produces gains for everyone. In the Heckscher-Ohlin model factors of production can move between sectors, but because there are two factors income distribution may still be an issue. An analysis of the effects of changes in the prices of cloth and food on the earnings of land and labor involves the following:

P_C = price of 1 yard of cloth,

P_F = price of 1 calorie of food,

w = wage rate for 1 hour of labor,

r = rent that must be paid for the use of 1 acre of land.

To analyze the relationship between prices and earnings, we assume that there is perfect competition in the production of cloth and food. This perfect competition means that any monopoly profits are competed away, so that the price of each good is exactly equal to the cost of producing it. This cost, in turn, is the sum of the cost of land and labor used in production:

$$P_C = a_{LC}w + a_{TC}r, \quad \textbf{(4-5)}$$

$$P_F = a_{LF}w + a_{TF}r. \quad \textbf{(4-6)}$$

Equations (4-5) and (4-6) define combinations of w and r for which the cost of production equals the price for cloth and food respectively. These two relationships are shown in Figure 4-3. Remember that we have assumed that cloth production is more labor-intensive than food production—that is,

$$a_{LC}/a_{TC} > a_{LF}/a_{TF}.$$

This implies that the cloth line must be steeper than the food line, as drawn.

The economy will only produce both goods if price equals cost in both sectors. This equality holds for both goods at the point in the diagram where the two lines cross, point 1, where $w = w^1$ and $r = r^1$. The diagram thus shows that we can determine factor prices given goods prices. Notice that we did *not* need to ask about the relative supplies of land and labor to do this: as long as both goods are produced, there is a one-to-one relationship between goods prices and factor prices.

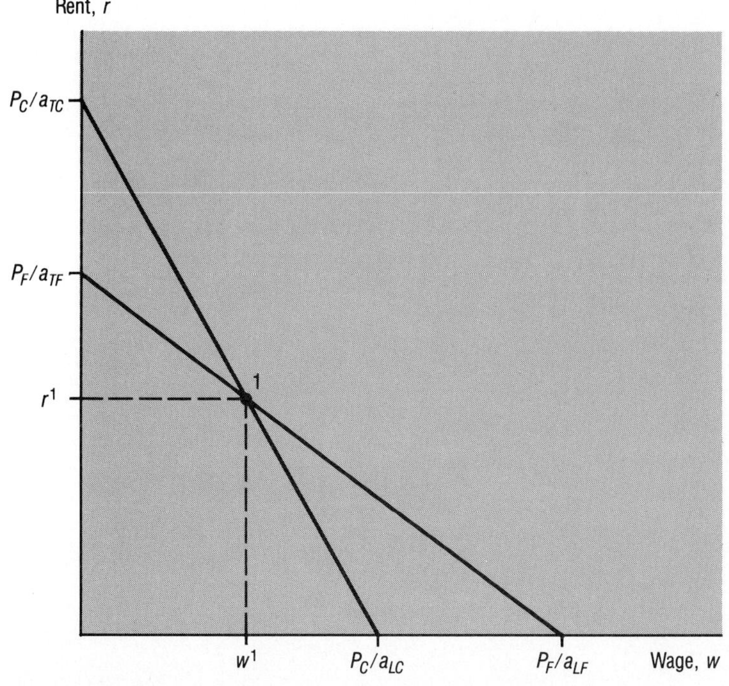

FIGURE 4-3 Determination of factor prices. The wage rate and the rental rate on land are determined by the requirement that price equal cost of production in both cloth and food.

When goods prices change, factor prices will also change. You might not be surprised to find that when the price of cloth is increased, the price of labor rises more than that of land. In fact, however, the effect on the relative price of land and labor is so strong that the price of land actually *falls*.

In Figure 4-4, we show what happens when the price of cloth is increased from P_C^1 to P_C^2. The increase in the price of cloth shifts the cloth line out. The equilibrium factor price point therefore shifts from point 1 to point 2. This movement involves a rise in the wage rate, from w^1 to w^2, and a fall in the rental rate on land, from r^1 to r^2. Similarly, a rise in the price of food would raise the rental rate on land and lower the wage rate.

When the price of cloth increases, the wage rate rises more than proportionately—that is, if the price of cloth increases by 10 percent, the wage rate will rise by more than 10 percent. This must be so because the rental on land actually falls. Consider the following numerical example. Initially, a yard of cloth takes 1 hour of labor and 1 acre of land to produce. The labor and the land each cost $5, and the price of cloth is $10. Now suppose that the price of cloth rises by 10 percent, to $11. When the price of cloth rises, we know that the rental on land actually falls, say to $4.50. Correspondingly, the wage rate must therefore have risen to $6.50—a 30 percent rise, three times as large as the increase in the price of cloth. This is an even stronger effect on

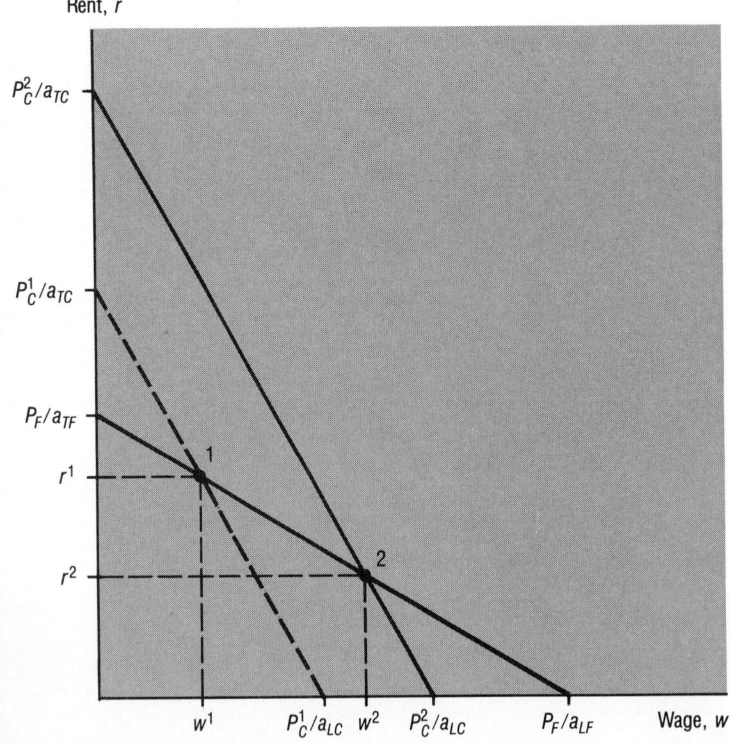

FIGURE 4-4 An increase in the price of cloth. When the price of cloth rises from P_C^1 to P_C^2, the wage rate rises from w^1 to w^2, while the rental rate on land actually declines from r^1 to r^2.

relative incomes than the effects on immobile labor that we studied in Chapter 3.

In a two-factor economy, then, changes in relative goods prices have very strong effects on income distribution, and these effects are even stronger than in the case of factor immobility. There is a **magnified effect of goods prices on factor prices.**[2] Because an increase in the price of cloth leads to a fall in the rent on land, someone who derives all his income from land rent will find his purchasing power reduced in terms of *both* goods. At the same time, the wage rate rises more than proportionately to the increase in the price of cloth; so someone who derives his income entirely from wages will find that his purchasing power has *increased* in terms of both goods.

ALLOWING SUBSTITUTION BETWEEN INPUTS

Up to now, we have examined an economy with fixed coefficients, where it takes a certain number of hours of labor and acres of land to make a yard of cloth and there is no way to trade off more land for less labor. The results must be modified slightly for an economy in which the ratio of land to labor in production can vary. (A more detailed discussion of the two-factor model with **variable coefficients** is given in the appendix to this chapter.)

One difference is that there is no longer a simple, physical definition of which goods are land-intensive and which are labor-intensive: the ratio of land to labor used in production depends on the relative price of land and labor. In the United States, where land is abundant, cattle raising is land-intensive compared with wheat growing. Yet in Japan, where land is very scarce, cows may be raised with a lower land-labor ratio than the United States uses in growing wheat. When comparing factor intensities, we must therefore be careful always to compare the land-labor ratio that would have been used given the same incentives. Specifically, we describe cloth production as more labor-intensive than food production as long as the cloth sector will use a higher labor-land ratio than the food sector *when the two sectors face the same factor prices.*

Another difference that arises when factor substitution is allowed is that we can no longer say that only one resource constrains production at each point in time. In the fixed-coefficients model, production possibilities are defined by two constraints. If the economy tries to produce a high ratio of food to cloth, only the land constraint matters; if it tries to produce a high ratio of cloth to food, only the labor constraint matters. Once we allow trade-offs between use of the two factors, however, this sharp-edged result gets a little fuzzy. Even if the economy is producing mostly food and very little cloth, an increase in the labor supply will allow it to produce more of *either* good by substituting labor for land.

[2]The effect of changes in relative goods prices on factor prices was first analyzed by Wolfgang Stolper and Paul Samuelson, "Protection and Real Wages," *Review of Economic Studies* 9 (1941), pp. 58–73, and is thus known as the **Stolper-Samuelson effect.**

Because of the additional flexibility allowed by land-labor substitution, the production possibility frontier loses the "kinked" shape that it has in the case of fixed coefficients. Instead, it becomes more of a smooth curve, as illustrated by *TT* in Figure 4-5.

Although the shape of the production possibility frontier is softened by allowing land-labor substitution, the basic result of our fixed-coefficient analysis remains valid: increases in factor supplies shift production possibilities in a biased way (Figure 4-6). An increase in the labor supply shifts the production possibility curve outward from T^1T^1 to T^2T^2, but it shifts production possibilities out more in the direction of the labor-intensive product (cloth) than in the direction of the land-intensive product (food). Similarly, an increase in the supply of land would shift production possibilities out more in the direction of food than in the direction of cloth.

One conclusion that is *not* softened by allowing factor substitution is the relationship between goods prices and factor prices: a rise in the price of cloth leads to a more than proportional increase in the wage rate, and to an actual fall in the price of land.

EFFECTS OF INTERNATIONAL TRADE BETWEEN TWO-FACTOR ECONOMIES

Having outlined the production structure of a two-factor economy, we can now look at what happens when two such economies, Home and Foreign, trade. As always, Home and Foreign are similar along many dimensions. They have the same tastes and therefore have identical relative demands for

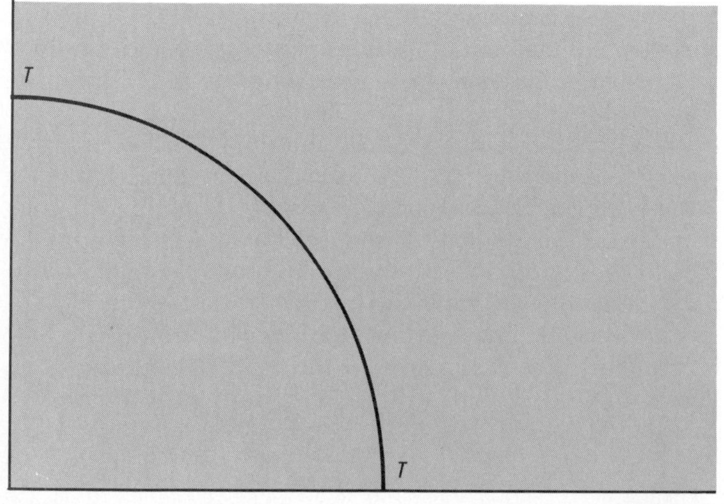

FIGURE 4-5 Production possibilities with land-labor substitution. The possibility of substitution removes the "kink" in the production possibility frontier, causing it instead to be a smooth curve.

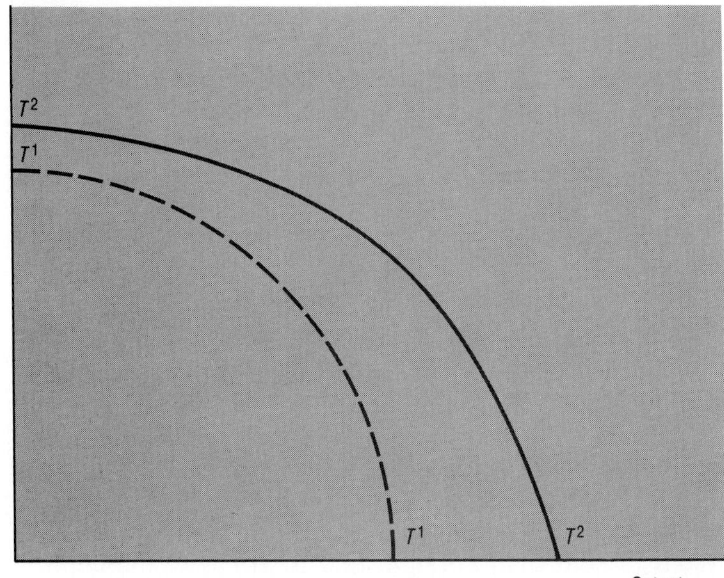

FIGURE 4-6 Biased expansion in production possibilities. An increase in the labor supply, which shifts the production possibility frontier out from T^1T^1 to T^2T^2, shifts it out more in the direction of cloth than of food.

food and cloth when faced with the same relative price of the two goods. They also have the same technology: a given amount of land and labor yields the same output of either cloth or food in the two countries. The only difference between the countries is in their resources: Home has a higher ratio of labor to land than Foreign does.

RELATIVE PRICES AND THE PATTERN OF TRADE

Since Home has a higher ratio of labor to land than Foreign, Home is *labor-abundant* and Foreign is *land-abundant.* Note that abundance is defined in terms of a ratio and not in absolute quantities. If America has 80 million workers and 200 million acres, while Britain has 20 million workers and 20 million acres, we consider Britain to be labor-abundant even though it has less total labor than America. "Abundance" is always defined in relative terms, by comparing the ratio of labor to land in the two countries, so that no country is abundant in everything.

Since cloth is the labor-intensive good, Home's production possibility frontier relative to Foreign's is shifted out more in the direction of cloth than in the direction of food. Thus, other things equal, Home tends to produce a higher ratio of cloth to food.

Because trade leads to a convergence of relative prices, one of the other things that will be equal is the price of cloth relative to food. Because the countries differ in their factor abundances, however, for any given ratio of the price of cloth to that of food Home will produce a higher ratio of cloth to food than Foreign will: Home will have a larger *relative supply* of cloth. Home's relative supply curve, then, lies to the right of Foreign's.

The relative supply schedules of Home (*RS*) and Foreign (*RS**) are illustrated in Figure 4-7. The relative demand curve, which we have assumed to be the same for both countries, is shown as *RD*. If there were no international trade, the equilibrium for Home would be at point 1, the equilibrium for Foreign at point 3. That is, in the absence of trade the relative price of cloth would be lower in Home than in Foreign.

When Home and Foreign trade with each other, their relative prices converge. The relative price of cloth rises in Home, declines in Foreign, and a new world relative price of cloth is established at a point somewhere between the pretrade relative prices, say at point 2. In Home, the rise in the relative price of cloth leads to a rise in the production of cloth and a decline in relative consumption; so Home becomes an exporter of cloth and an importer of food. Conversely, the decline in the relative price of cloth leads Foreign to become an importer of cloth and an exporter of food.

To sum up what we have learned about the pattern of trade: Home has a higher ratio of labor to land than Foreign; that is, Home is abundant in labor, and Foreign is abundant in land. Cloth production uses a higher ratio

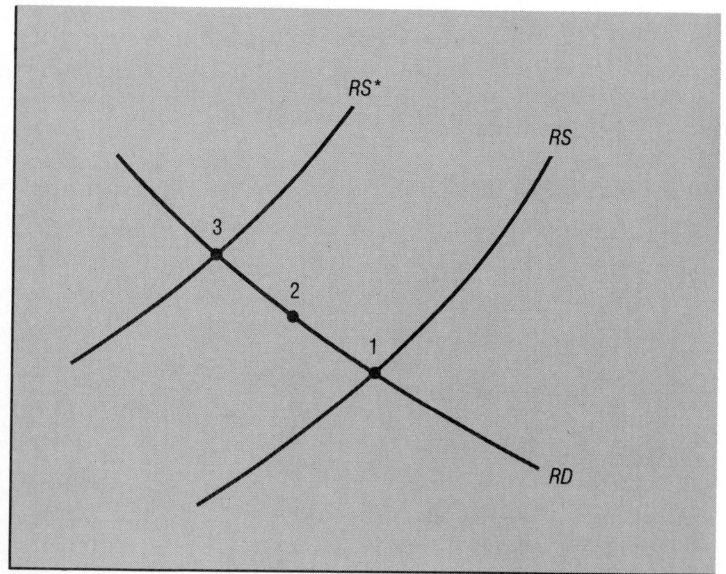

FIGURE 4-7 Trade leads to a convergence of relative prices. In the absence of trade, Home's equilibrium would be at point 1, where domestic relative supply *RS* intersects the relative demand curve *RD*. Similarly, Foreign's equilibrium would be at point 3. Trade leads to a world relative price that lies between the pretrade prices, e.g., at point 2.

of labor to land in its production than food; that is, cloth is labor-intensive and food is land-intensive. Home, the labor-abundant country, exports cloth, the labor-intensive good; Foreign, the land-abundant country, exports food, the land-intensive good. The general statement of the result is: *Countries tend to export goods whose production is intensive in factors with which they are abundantly endowed.*

TRADE AND THE DISTRIBUTION OF INCOME

Trade produces a convergence of relative prices. Changes in relative prices, in turn, have strong effects on the relative earnings of labor and land. A rise in the price of cloth raises the purchasing power of labor in terms of both goods while lowering the purchasing power of land in terms of both goods. A rise in the price of food has the reverse effect. Thus international trade has a powerful effect on income distribution. In Home, where the relative price of cloth rises, people who get their income from labor gain from trade but those who derive their income from land are made worse off. In Foreign, where the relative price of cloth falls, the opposite happens: laborers are made worse off and landowners are made better off.

The resource of which a country has a relatively large supply (labor in Home, land in Foreign) is the **abundant factor** in that country, and the resource of which it has a relatively small supply (land in Home, labor in Foreign) is the **scarce factor.** The general conclusion about the income distribution effects of international trade is: *Owners of a country's abundant factors gain from trade, but owners of a country's scarce factors lose.*

This conclusion is similar to the conclusion we reached in our analysis of the case of immobile factors. There we found that factors of production that are "stuck" in an import-competing industry lose from the opening of trade. Here we find that factors of production that are used intensively by the import-competing industry are hurt by the opening of trade. As a practical matter, however, there is an important difference between these two views. Immobility is presumably a temporary problem: garment makers cannot become computer manufacturers overnight, but given time the U.S. economy can shift its manufacturing employment from declining sectors to expanding ones. Thus income-distribution effects that arise because labor and other factors of production are immobile represent a temporary, transitional problem (which is not to say that such effects are not painful to those who lose). In contrast, effects of trade on the distribution of income among land, labor, and capital are more or less permanent.

We will see shortly that the trade pattern of the United States suggests that compared with the rest of the world the United States is abundantly endowed with highly skilled labor, and that low-skilled labor is correspondingly scarce. This means that international trade tends to make low-skilled workers in the United States worse off—not just temporarily, but on a sustained basis. The negative effect of trade on low-skill workers poses a persistent political problem. Industries that use low-skill labor intensively, such as apparel and shoes, consistently demand protection from foreign competition, and their demands attract considerable sympathy because low-skilled workers are relatively badly off to begin with.

The distinction between income-distribution effects due to immobility and those due to differences in factor intensity also reveals that there is frequently a conflict between short-term and long-term interests in trade. Consider a highly skilled U.S. worker who is employed in an industry that is intensive in low-skill labor. Her short-term interest is to restrict international trade, because she cannot instantly shift jobs. Over the longer term, however, she would be better off with free trade, which will raise the income of skilled workers generally.

FACTOR PRICE EQUALIZATION

In the absence of trade labor would earn less in Home than in Foreign, and land would earn more. Without trade, labor-abundant Home would have a lower relative price of cloth than land-abundant Foreign, and the difference in relative prices of *goods* implies an even larger difference in the relative prices of *factors*.

When Home and Foreign trade, the relative prices of goods converge. This convergence, in turn, causes convergence of the relative prices of land and labor. Thus there is clearly a tendency toward **equalization of factor prices.** How far does this tendency go?

The surprising answer is that in the model the tendency goes all the way. International trade leads to complete equalization of factor prices. Although Home has a higher ratio of labor to land than Foreign, once they trade with each other the wage rate and the rent on land are the same in both countries. To see this, refer back to Figure 4-3, which shows that given the prices of cloth and food we can determine the wage rate and the rental rate without reference to the supplies of land and labor. If Home and Foreign face the same relative prices of cloth and food, they will also have the same factor prices.

To understand how this equalization occurs, we have to realize that when Home and Foreign trade with each other more is happening than a simple exchange of goods. In an indirect way the two countries are in effect trading factors of production. Home lets Foreign have the use of some of its abundant labor, not by selling the labor directly but by trading goods produced with a high ratio of labor to land for goods produced with a low labor-land ratio. The goods that Home sells require more labor to produce than the goods it receives in return; that is, more labor is *embodied* in Home's exports than in its imports. Thus Home exports its labor, embodied in its labor-intensive exports. Conversely, Foreign's exports embody more land than its imports, and thus Foreign is indirectly exporting its land. When viewed this way, it is not surprising that trade leads to equalization of the two countries' factor prices.

Although this view of trade is clearly a very simple and appealing one, there is a major problem: in the real world factor prices are not equalized. For example, there is an extremely wide range of wage rates across countries (Table 4-1). While some of these differences may reflect differences in the quality of labor, they are too wide to be explained away on this basis alone.

To understand why the model doesn't give us an accurate prediction, we need to look at its assumptions. Three assumptions crucial to the prediction of factor price equalization are in reality certainly untrue. These are the assumptions that (1) both countries produce both goods; (2) technologies are the same; and (3) trade actually equalizes the prices of goods in the two countries.

1. To derive the wage and rental rates from the prices of cloth and food in Figure 4-3, we assumed that the country produced both goods. This need not, however, be the case. A country with a very high ratio of labor to land might produce only cloth, while a country with a very high ratio of land to labor produced only food. This implies that factor price equalization occurs only if the countries involved are sufficiently similar in their relative factor endowments. (A more thorough discussion of this point is given in the appendix to this chapter.) Thus, factor prices need not be equalized between countries with radically different ratios of capital to labor or of skilled to unskilled labor.

2. The proposition that trade equalizes factor prices will not hold if countries have different technologies of production. For example, a country with superior technology might have both a higher wage rate and a higher rental rate than a country with an inferior technology.

3. Finally, the proposition of complete factor price equalization depends on complete convergence of the prices of goods. In the real world, prices of goods are not fully equalized by international trade. This lack of convergence is due to both natural barriers (such as transportation costs) and man-made barriers to trade—tariffs, import quotas, and other restrictions.

TABLE 4-1 Comparative international wage rates

Country	Hourly wage rate in 1985 (dollars)
United States	12.97
Germany	9.82
Japan	6.45
Spain	4.85
Greece	3.53
Hong Kong	1.78
Taiwan	1.45
Korea	1.41

Source: OECD Economic Survey of Japan, 1986.

EMPIRICAL EVIDENCE ON THE HECKSCHER-OHLIN MODEL

Since the factor proportions theory of trade is one of the most influential ideas in international economics, it has been the subject of extensive empirical testing. The results of this testing have not been favorable: countries do not in fact export the goods the theory predicts. The question then is what to make of this—does the factor-proportions theory still have any relevance for thinking about international trade?

TESTING THE HECKSCHER-OHLIN MODEL

Tests on U.S. Data. Until recently, and to some extent even now, the United States has been a special case among countries. The United States was until a few years ago much wealthier than other countries, and U.S. workers visibly worked with more capital per person than their counterparts in other countries. Even now, although some Western European countries and Japan have largely caught up, the United States continues to be high on the scale of countries as ranked by capital-labor ratios.

One would expect, then, that the United States would be an exporter of capital-intensive goods and an importer of labor-intensive goods. Surprisingly, however, this is not the case. In a famous study published in 1953, the economist Wassily Leontief (winner of the Nobel Prize in 1973) found that U.S. exports were less capital-intensive than U.S. imports.[3] This result, confirmed over the years, is known as the *Leontief paradox*. It is the single biggest piece of evidence against the factor-proportions theory.

Table 4-2 illustrates the Leontief paradox as well as some other information about U.S. trade patterns. We compare the factors of production used to produce one million dollars' worth of U.S. exports with those used to pro-

TABLE 4-2 Factor content of U.S. exports and imports

	Imports	Exports
Capital	\$2,132,000	\$1,876,000
Labor (person-years)	119	131
Average years of education	9.9	10.1
Proportion of engineers and scientists	.0189	.0255

Source: Robert Baldwin, "Determinants of the Commodity Structure of U.S. Trade," *American Economic Review* 61 (March 1971), pp. 126–145.

[3]See Leontief, "Domestic Production and Foreign Trade: The American Capital Position Re-examined," *Proceedings of the American Philosophical Society* 97 (1953), pp. 331–349.

duce the same value of U.S. imports. As the first two lines in the table show, Leontief's paradox is still present: U.S. exports are produced with a lower ratio of capital to labor than U.S. imports. As the rest of the table shows, however, other comparisons of imports and exports are more in line with what one might expect. The U.S. exports products that are more skilled-labor-intensive than its imports. We also tend to export products that are "technology-intensive," requiring more scientists and engineers per unit of sales. These observations are consistent with the position of the United States as a high-skill country, with a comparative advantage in sophisticated products.

Why, then, do we observe the Leontief paradox? No one is quite sure. A plausible explanation, however, might be the following: The United States has a special advantage in producing new products or goods made with innovative technologies. Such products may well be *less* capital-intensive than products whose technology has had time to mature and become suitable for mass-production techniques. Thus the United States may be exporting goods that heavily use skilled labor and innovative entrepreneurship, while importing heavy manufactures that use large amounts of capital.

Tests on Global Data. More recently, economists have attempted to test the Heckscher-Ohlin model using data for a large number of countries. An important recent study by Harry P. Bowen, Edward E. Leamer, and Leo Sveikauskas[4] is based on the idea, described earlier, that trade in goods is actually an indirect way of trading factors of production. Thus if we were to calculate the factors of production embodied in a country's exports and imports, we should find that a country is a net exporter of the factors of production with which it is relatively abundantly endowed, a net importer of those with which it is relatively poorly endowed.

Table 4-3 shows one of Bowen et al.'s key tests. For a sample of 23 countries and 12 factors of production, the authors calculated the ratio of each country's endowment of each factor to the world supply. They then compared these ratios with each country's share of world income. If the factor-proportions theory were right, a country would always export factors for which the factor share exceeded the income share, import factors for which it was less. In fact, for nearly half of the factors of production trade ran in the predicted direction less than half the time. This result confirms the Leontief paradox on a broader level: trade just does not run in the direction that Heckscher-Ohlin theory predicts.

IMPLICATIONS OF THE TESTS

The negative results of tests of the factor-proportions theory place international economists in a difficult position. The Heckscher-Ohlin model has

[4]See Bowen, Leamer, and Sveikauskas, "Multicountry, Multifactor Tests of the Factor Abundance Theory," forthcoming in *American Economic Review.*

TABLE 4-3 Testing the Heckscher-Ohlin model

Factor of production	Predictive success*
Capital	.55
Labor	.51
Professional workers	.22
Managerial workers	.60
Clerical workers	.37
Sales workers	.44
Service workers	.44
Agricultural workers	.67
Production workers	.40
Arable land	.71
Pasture land	.78
Forest	.67

*Fraction of countries for which net exports of factor runs in predicted direction.
Source: Harry P. Bowen, Edward E. Leamer, and Leo Sveikauskas. "Multicountry, Multifactor Tests of the Factor Abundance Theory." *American Economic Review*, forthcoming.

long occupied a central place in trade theory, because it allows a simultaneous treatment of issues of income distribution and the pattern of trade. What model should we use, given what is by now strong evidence against Heckscher-Ohlin?

The best answer at this point seems to be to return to the Ricardian idea that trade is largely driven by international differences in technology rather than resources. For example, the United States exports computers and aircraft, not because its resources are specially suited to these activities but because it is simply relatively more efficient at producing these goods than it is at automobile or steel production. This still leaves the reasons for technology differences unexplained. Understanding the sources of technological differences between countries is now a key topic of research.

While we return to the Ricardian explanation of trade, however, we do not return to the view that trade has no effects on the distribution of income. As long as more than one factor is used in production, trade will have important effects on income distribution. Thus it is still important to ask what factors are embodied in a country's exports and imports. The United States exports skill-intensive goods and imports unskilled-labor-intensive products. Therefore, trade tends to benefit skilled U.S. workers at the expense of unskilled, even though U.S. factor endowments do not help us very much in predicting the pattern of trade. The Heckscher-Ohlin model thus retains a more limited use, as a way of predicting the income-distribution effects of trade and trade policy.

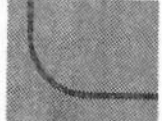

SUMMARY

1. To understand the role of resources in trade we begin by examining the effect of resources on a country's production possibilities. Increases in an

economy's supply of a factor of production such as land shift the production possibility frontier out in a *biased* way: an increase in the land supply shifts the frontier out more in the direction of land-intensive goods than in the direction of labor-intensive goods. As a result, countries are relatively good at producing goods whose production is *intensive* in resources of which they have a relatively abundant supply.

2. Changes in relative prices of goods have very strong effects on the relative incomes earned by different resources. An increase in the price of the land-intensive good will raise the rent earned on land more than in proportion, while actually reducing the wage rate.

3. A country that has a large supply of one resource relative to its supply of other resources is *abundant* in that resource. A country will tend to produce relatively more of goods that use its abundant resources intensively. The result is the basic *Heckscher-Ohlin theory* of trade: *Countries tend to export goods that are intensive in the factors with which the countries are abundantly supplied.*

4. Because changes in relative prices of goods have very strong effects on the relative earnings of resources, and because trade changes relative prices, international trade has strong income-distribution effects. The owners of a country's abundant factors gain from trade, but the owners of scarce factors lose.

5. In an idealized model international trade would actually lead to equalization of the prices of factors such as labor and capital between countries. In reality, complete *factor price equalization* is not observed because of wide differences in resources, barriers to trade, and international differences in technology.

6. Empirical evidence is generally negative on the idea that differences in resources are the main determinant of trade patterns. Instead, differences in technology probably play the key role, as we suggested in the Ricardian model. Nonetheless, the Heckscher-Ohlin model remains useful as a way to predict the income-distribution effects of trade.

KEY TERMS

factor abundance

factor intensity

Heckscher-Ohlin theory (or factor-proportions theory)

fixed coefficients

biased expansion of production possibilities

magnified effect of goods prices on factor prices (or Stolper-Samuelson effect)

variable coefficients

abundant factor

scarce factor

equalization of factor prices

PROBLEMS

1. To produce a ton of steel requires 10 units of labor and 5 units of land. To produce a ton of wheat requires 2 units of labor and 4 units of land. The economy has a supply of 100 units of labor and 100 units of land.

a) Graph the labor and land constraints on the economy's production.

b) Find the production possibility frontier.

c) Suppose that the labor supply were increased to 110. Show how this would affect production possibilities.

2. Maintaining the assumptions of problem 1, suppose that the price of steel is 3 and the price of wheat is 1.

a) Graph the lines along which the price and production cost are equal for steel and wheat.

b) Determine the equilibrium wage rate and rental rate on land.

c) Suppose that the price of steel were to rise to 3.5. Graph the effect of this change, and find the effects on the wage and rental rates.

3. "The world's poorest countries cannot find anything to export. There is no resource that is abundant—certainly not capital or land, and in small poor nations not even labor is abundant." Discuss.

4. The U.S. labor movement—which mostly represents blue-collar workers rather than professionals and highly educated workers—has traditionally favored limits on imports from less affluent countries. Is this a shortsighted policy or a rational one in view of the interests of union members? How does the answer depend on the model of trade?

5. There is substantial inequality of wage levels between regions within the United States. For example, wages of manufacturing workers in equivalent jobs are about 20 percent lower in the southeast than they are in the far west. Which of the explanations of failure of factor price equalization might account for this? How is this case different from the divergence of wages between the United States and Mexico (which is geographically closer to both the southeast and the far west than either is to the other)?

6. Explain why the "Leontief paradox" and the more recent Bowen, Leamer, and Sveikauskas results reported in the text contradict the factor-proportions theory.

7. Using the box diagram in the appendix, examine the impact of a reduction in the supply of labor (for example, due to emigration). Show that the production of cloth falls but that production of food actually rises.

FURTHER READING

Alan Deardorff. "Testing Trade Theories and Predicting Trade Flows," in Ronald W. Jones and Peter B. Kenen, eds. *Handbook of International Economics.* Vol. 1. Amsterdam: North-Holland, 1984. A survey of empirical evidence on trade theories, especially the factor-proportions theory.

Ronald W. Jones. "Factor Proportions and the Heckscher-Ohlin Theorem." *Review of Economic Studies* 24 (1956), pp. 1–10. This paper extends Samuelson's 1948–1949 analysis (cited below), which focuses primarily on the relationship between trade and income distribution, into an overall model of international trade.

Ronald W. Jones. "The Structure of Simple General Equilibrium Models." *Journal of Political Economy* 73 (1965), pp. 557–572. A restatement of the Heckscher-Ohlin-Samuelson model in terms of elegant algebra.

Ronald W. Jones and J. Peter Neary. "The Positive Theory of International Trade." in Ronald W. Jones and Peter B. Kenen, eds.. *Handbook of International Economics.* Vol. 1. Amsterdam: North-Holland, 1984. An up-to-date survey of many trade theories, including the factor-proportions theory.

Bertil Ohlin. *Interregional and International Trade.* Cambridge: Harvard University Press, 1933. The original Ohlin book presenting the factor-proportions view of trade remains interesting—its complex and rich view of trade contrasts with the more rigorous and simplified mathematical models that followed.

Paul Samuelson. "International Trade and the Equalisation of Factor Prices." *Economic Journal* 58 (1948), pp. 163–184, and "International Factor Price Equalisation Once Again." *Economic Journal* 59 (1949), pp. 181–196. The most influential formalizer of Ohlin's ideas is Paul Samuelson (again!), whose two *Economic Journal* papers on the subject are classics.

APPENDIX TO CHAPTER 4

The Heckscher-Ohlin Model with Variable Coefficients

In the main body of this chapter we examined a two-factor model with *fixed coefficients*. That is, the ratio of land to labor used in the production of each good was assumed to be wholly determined by technology. This is a useful simplification, but in the real world the possibility of substitution between factors is important. For example, firms in a country with cheap labor may choose to use less capital-intensive and more labor-intensive techniques of production than they would in a country with expensive labor. We want to be sure that the basic insights of our chapter are not lost when we allow for such substitution. This appendix briefly shows how a two-factor model of an economy works when coefficients are flexible.

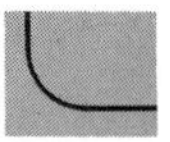

CHOICE OF TECHNIQUE

The key new element we need to introduce is that firms have a choice about the land or labor intensity of production of each good. They can choose to use less land per unit of output if they are willing to use more labor. Figure 4A-1 illustrates this trade-

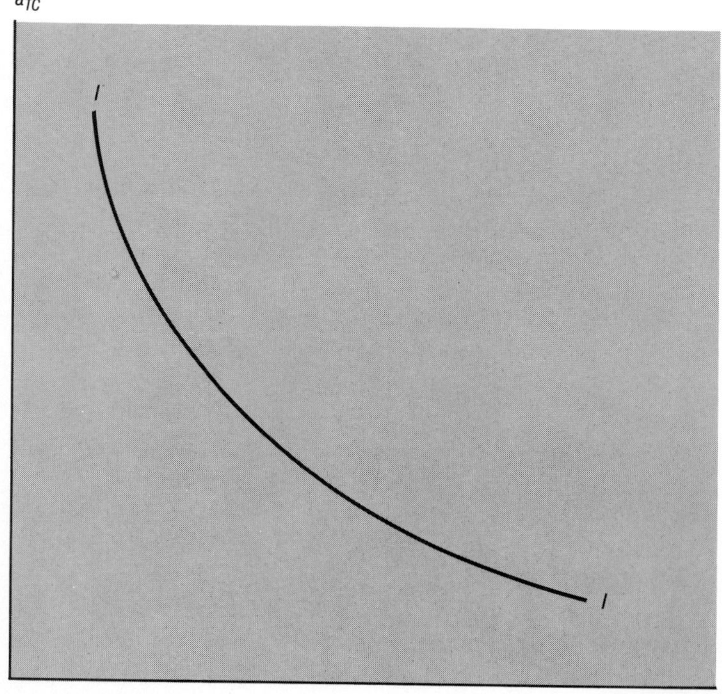

FIGURE 4A-1 The unit isoquant for cloth. The more labor that is used in producing a unit of cloth, the less land is needed.

off for cloth. Curve *II*, which shows different bundles of labor and land that can produce one unit of cloth, is referred to as the *unit isoquant* for cloth.

Firms will choose the ratio of land to labor that minimizes the cost of producing cloth. The details of this choice are discussed in microeconomics texts. The basic result is not surprising: the cost-minimizing land-labor ratio a_{TC}/a_{LC} is inversely related to the ratio of the price of land to that of labor, r/w.

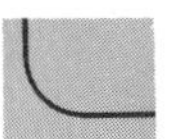

GOODS PRICES AND FACTOR PRICES

The price of each good must equal its cost of production. For any given price of a good, this requirement defines a set of possible factor prices. For example, given the price of cloth, the higher the wage rate w the lower must be the rental rate r (Figure 4A-2). The economy's factor prices must be such that the cost of production equals the price in both cloth and food (Figure 4A-3). Curve *CC* represents all combinations of w and r for which price equals cost in cloth, while *FF* represents all combinations for which price and cost are equal in food. Since cloth is more labor-intensive and less land-intensive than food, the wage rate has relatively more effect on the cost of cloth production, and the rental on land less effect. As a result, in order to offset the effect of higher w on cloth production cost, r must fall more than is true for food; thus *CC* is steeper than *FF*.

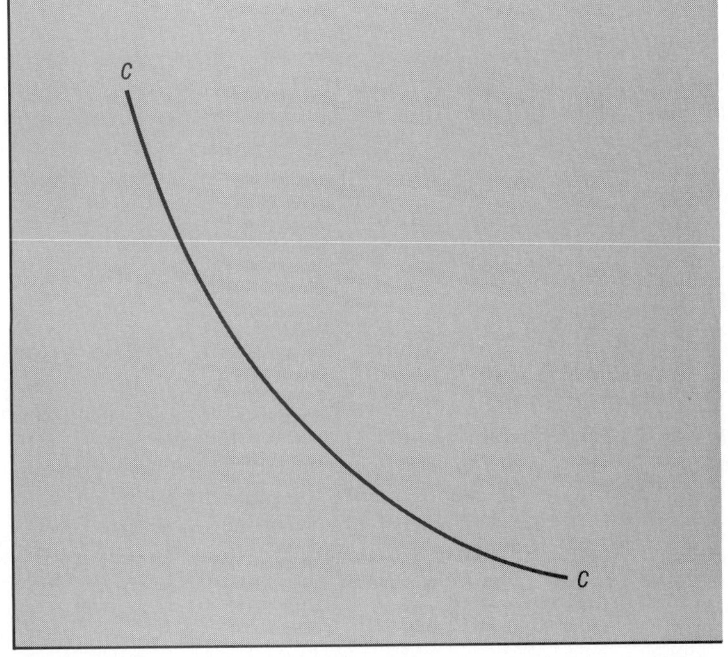

FIGURE 4A-2 Factor prices such that price equals cost. The curve *CC* shows all combinations of w and r such that the cost of producing a unit of cloth equals its price. The higher w is, the lower r must be to leave the production cost the same.

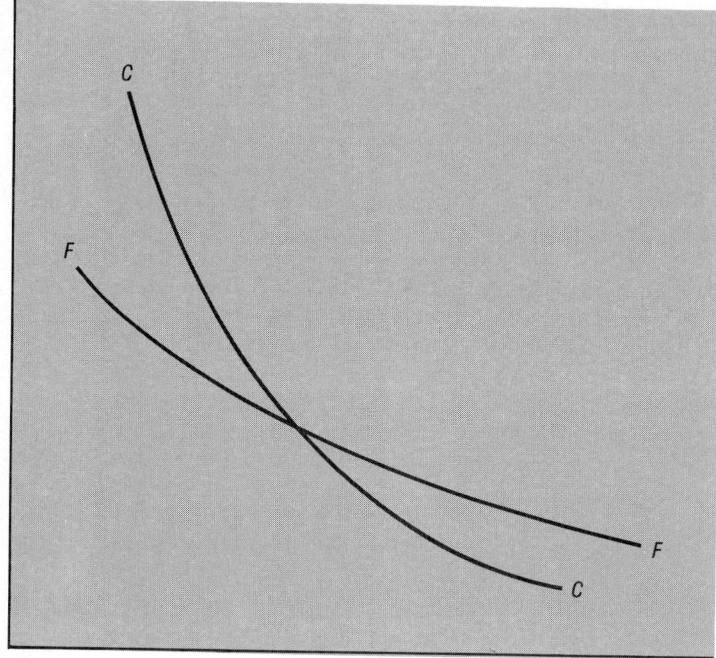

FIGURE 4A-3 Determination of *w* and *r*. In equilibrium, the cost of producing a unit of cloth must equal its price, and so must the cost of producing a unit of food. Thus *w* and *r* are determined by the intersection of *CC* and *FF*.

If the price of cloth rises, the cloth industry is able to pay a higher wage, a higher rent on land, or both: *CC* shifts out from C^1C^1 to C^2C^2 (Figure 4A-4). This raises the wage rate from w^1 to w^2, while lowering r from r^1 to r^2. The rise in w must be more than proportional to the increase in P_C. Thus in the flexible-coefficients model, as in the fixed-coefficients model, changes in relative prices have strong effects on the distribution of income.

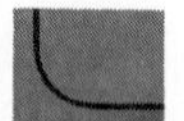

ALLOCATION OF RESOURCES

To determine how the economy allocates resources between cloth and food production, we follow three steps: (1) Use goods prices to determine factor prices. (2) Use factor prices to determine the land-labor ratio in each sector. (3) Use the assumption that land and labor are both fully employed to determine resource allocation.

Figure 4A-5 shows how step 3 works. The economy's resources are represented by the sides of a box. The width of the box represents the economy's supply of labor, while its height represents the supply of land. We measure resources used to produce cloth from the lower left corner of the box (O_C) and resources used to produce food from the upper right corner (O_F). The ratio of land to labor in cloth production is shown by the slope of the line O_CC, while the land-labor ratio in food is the slope of O_FF.

The allocation of land and labor that allows both to be fully employed is at point 1, where O_CC and O_FF cross. The economy allocates O_CL_C units of labor

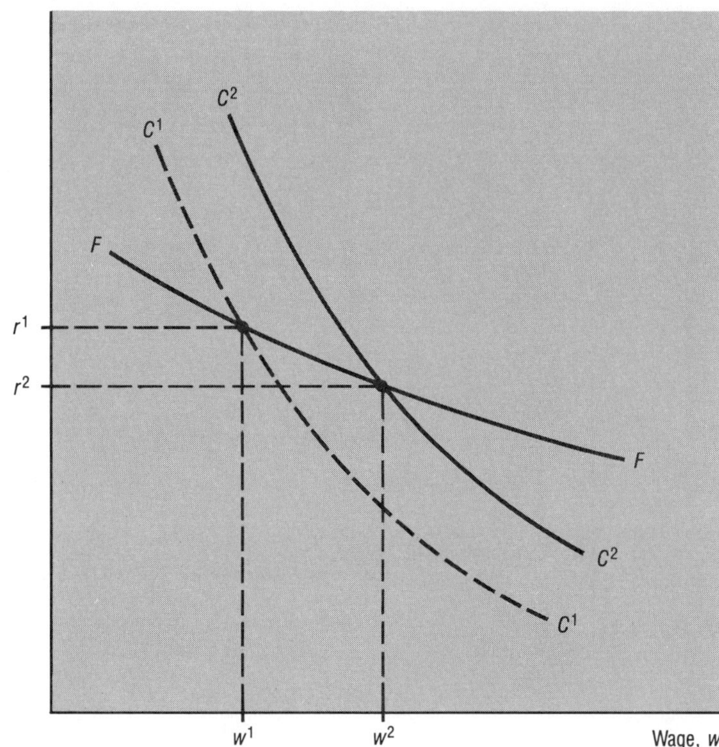

FIGURE 4A-4 A rise in the price of cloth. An increase in the price of cloth shifts *CC* out from C^1C^1 to C^2C^2. This raises the wage rate from w^1 to w^2, while lowering the rental rate from r^1 to r^2.

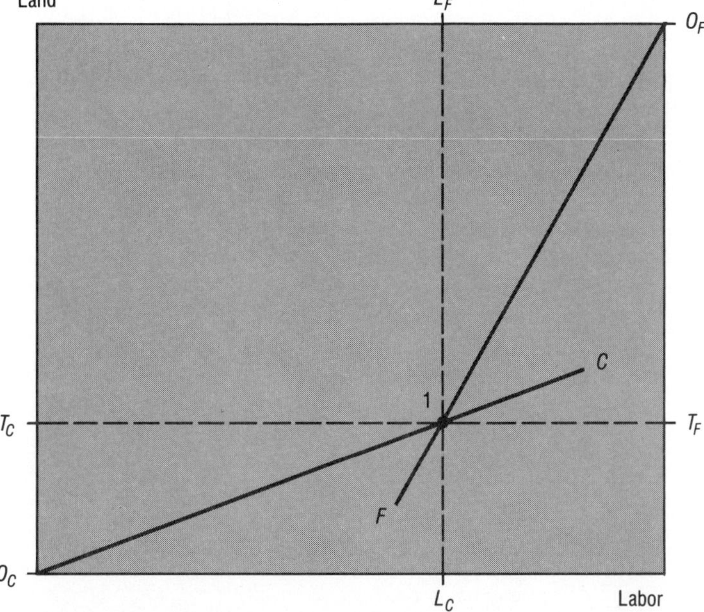

FIGURE 4A-5 Allocation of resources in the flexible coefficients case. Inputs to cloth production are measured from the lower left corner of the box, inputs to food production from the upper right corner. Given the land-labor ratios in the two industries, point 1 is the only allocation that fully employs both resources.

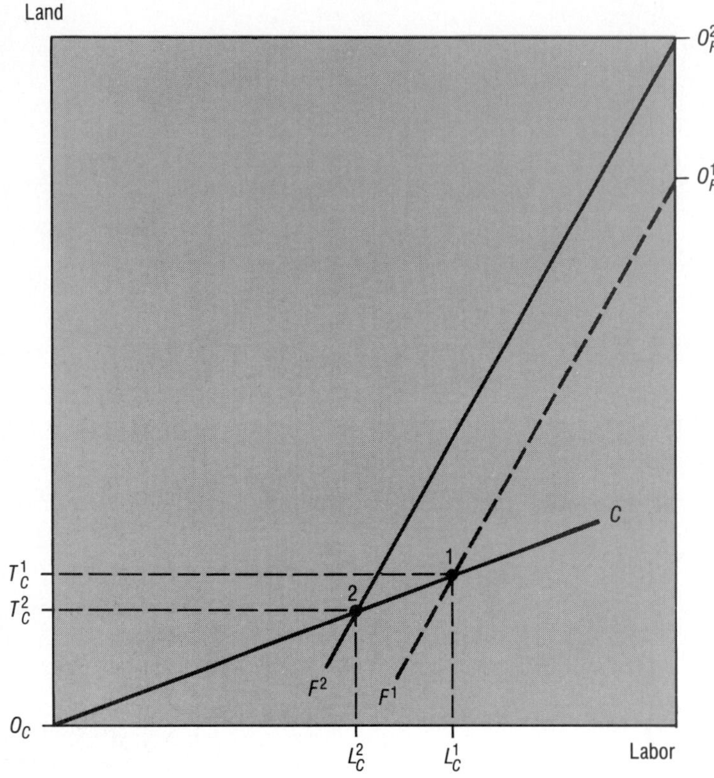

FIGURE 4A-6 An increase in the supply of land. An increase in the supply of land expands the box and shifts the allocation of resources from point 1 to point 2. Production of food rises, but production of cloth actually falls.

and $O_C T_C$ units of land to cloth production, $O_F L_F$ labor and $O_F T_F$ land to food production.

Now we ask what happens if the economy's supply of land increases (Figure 4A-6). The box expands, so that after the land-supply increase the resources used in food are measured from O_F^2 instead of O_F^1. The key point is to look at resources used in cloth production. As the equilibrium allocation shifts from point 1 to point 2, both land and labor used in cloth production *fall*, from $O_C T_C^1$ to $O_C T_C^2$ and from $O_C L_C^1$ to $O_C L_C^2$, respectively. As a result cloth production declines. Correspondingly, land and labor employed to produce food, and thus food production, must rise.

The result that an increase in land supply actually leads to a fall in the production of the labor-intensive good confirms our result from the fixed-coefficients model: increases in factor supplies have strongly *biased* effects on production.

Finally, it is clear from Figure 4A-6 that if we were to keep on increasing the economy's land supply, still holding goods prices fixed, eventually no resources at all would be used to produce cloth: the economy would specialize in food production. The general point is that a trading economy whose land-labor ratio is either very high or very low will specialize in producing only one good.

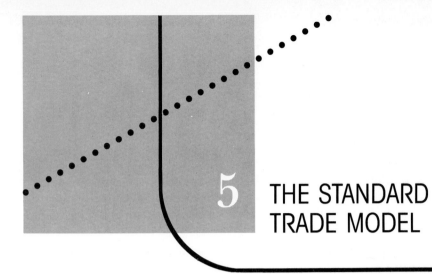

5 THE STANDARD TRADE MODEL

In previous chapters we have developed a number of different models, each of which illuminates a particular aspect of the supply side in international trade. In order to bring out important points as clearly as possible, each model leaves out aspects of reality that the others stress. When we analyze real problems, therefore, we often want to base our insights on a mixture of the models. For example, in the mid-1980s one of the central changes in world trade has been the rapid growth in exports from Japan, Korea, and Taiwan. These countries have experienced rapid productivity growth, with Japan overtaking the United States in many areas; to discuss the implications of this productivity growth we might want to apply the Ricardian model of Chapter 2. The changing pattern of trade has differential effects on different groups within the United States; to understand the effects of increased Pacific trade for U.S. income distribution, we may want to apply the specific-factors model of Chapter 3. Finally, over time the resources of the East Asian nations have changed, as they accumulate capital and their labor grows more educated, while unskilled labor becomes scarcer. To understand the implications of this shift, we may wish to turn to the Heckscher-Ohlin model of Chapter 4.

In spite of the differences in their details, moreover, all our models share a number of features.

1. The productive capacity of an economy can be summarized by its production possibility frontier, and differences in these frontiers give rise to trade.
2. Production possibilities determine a country's relative supply schedule.
3. World equilibrium is determined by world relative demand and a *world* relative supply schedule that lies between the national relative supply schedules.

Because of these common features, the models we have studied so far may be viewed as special cases of a more general model of a trading world economy. There are many important issues in international economics whose analysis can be conducted in terms of this general model, with only the details depending on which special model you choose. These include the effects of shifts in world supply resulting from economic growth; shifts in world demand resulting from foreign aid, war reparations, and other international transfers of income; and simultaneous shifts in supply and demand resulting from tariffs and export subsidies.

This chapter stresses those insights from international trade theory that are not strongly dependent on the details of the economy's supply side. We develop a standard model of a trading world economy of which the models of Chapters 2, 3, and 4 can be regarded as special cases, and use this model to ask how a variety of changes in underlying parameters affect the world economy.

A STANDARD MODEL OF A TRADING ECONOMY

The **standard trade model** is built upon four key relationships: (1) the relationship between the production possibility frontier and the relative supply curve; (2) the relationship between relative prices and demand; (3) the determination of world equilibrium by world relative supply and world relative demand; and (4) the effect of the **terms of trade**—the price of a country's exports divided by the price of its imports—on a nation's welfare.

PRODUCTION POSSIBILITIES AND RELATIVE SUPPLY

For the purposes of our standard model we assume that each country produces two goods, food (F) and cloth (C), and that each country's production possibility frontier is a smooth curve like that illustrated by TT in Figure 5-1.[1]

[1]We have seen that when there is only one factor of production, as in Chapter 2, the production possibility frontier is a straight line, while when factors are completely immobile between sectors, as in Chapter 3, it makes a right angle. For most models, however, it will be a smooth curve, and the Ricardian and immobile-factors results can be viewed as extreme cases.

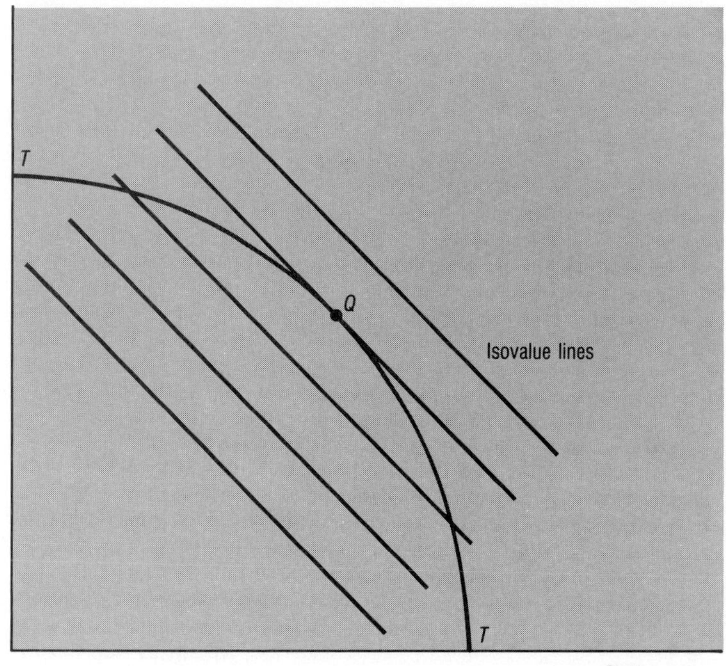

FIGURE 5-1 Relative prices determine the economy's output. An economy whose production possibility frontier is TT will produce at Q, which is on the highest possible isovalue line.

The point on its production possibility frontier at which an economy actually produces depends on the price of cloth relative to food, P_C/P_F. It is a basic proposition of microeconomics that a market economy that is not distorted by monopoly or other market failures is efficient in production—that is, it maximizes the value of output at given market prices, $P_C Q_C + P_F Q_F$.

We can indicate the market value of output by drawing a number of **isovalue lines**—that is, lines along which the value of output is constant. Each of these lines is defined by an equation of the form $P_C Q_C + P_F Q_F = V$, or by rearranging, $Q_F = V/P_F - (P_C/P_F)Q_C$, where V is the value of output. The higher V is, the farther out an isovalue line lies; thus isovalue lines farther from the origin correspond to higher values of output. The slope of an isovalue line is simply minus the relative price of cloth. The economy will produce the highest value of output it can, which can be achieved by producing at point Q, where TT is just tangent to an isovalue line.

Now suppose that P_C/P_F were to rise. Then the isovalue lines would be steeper than before. In Figure 5-2 the highest isovalue line the economy could reach before the change in P_C/P_F is shown as V^1V^1; the highest line after the price change is V^2V^2, the point at which the economy produces shifts from Q^1 to Q^2. Thus, as we might expect, a rise in the relative price of cloth

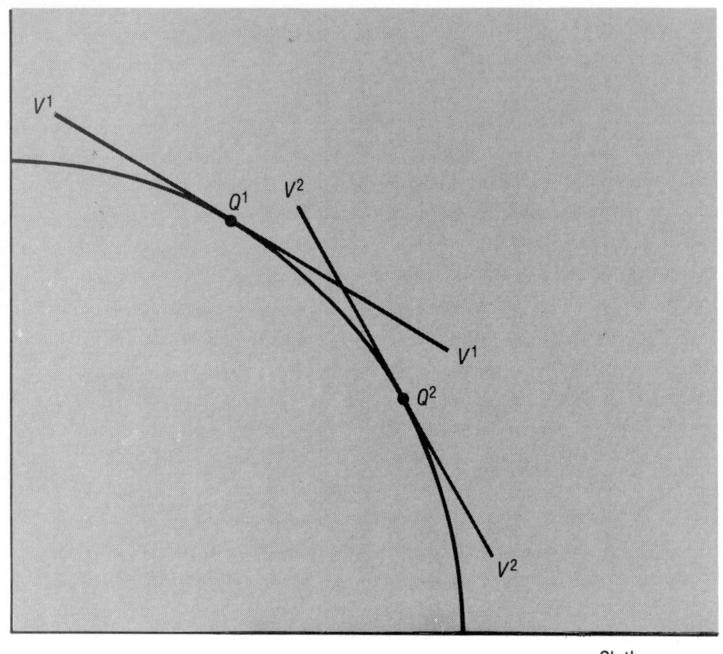

FIGURE 5-2 How an increase in the relative price of cloth affects relative supply. The isovalue lines become steeper, as shown by the shift from V^1V^1 to V^2V^2. As a result, equilibrium output shifts from Q^1 to Q^2.

leads the economy to produce more cloth and less food. The *relative* supply of cloth will therefore rise when the relative price of cloth rises.

RELATIVE PRICES AND DEMAND

Figure 5-3 shows the relationship among production, consumption, and trade in the standard model. As we pointed out in Chapter 3, the value of an economy's consumption equals the value of its production. Letting D_C and D_F be consumption of cloth and food, respectively, we must have

$$P_C D_C + P_F D_F = P_C Q_C + P_F Q_F = V.$$

The equation above says that production and consumption must lie on the same isovalue line.

The economy's choice of a point on the isovalue line depends on tastes. For our standard model, we make a useful simplifying assumption, namely, that the economy's consumption decisions may be represented as if they were based on the tastes of a single representative individual.[2]

[2]There are several sets of circumstances that can justify this assumption. One is that all individuals have the same tastes and the same share of all resources. Another is that the government redistributes income so as to maximize its view of overall social welfare. Essentially the assumption requires that effects of changing income distribution on demand not be too important.

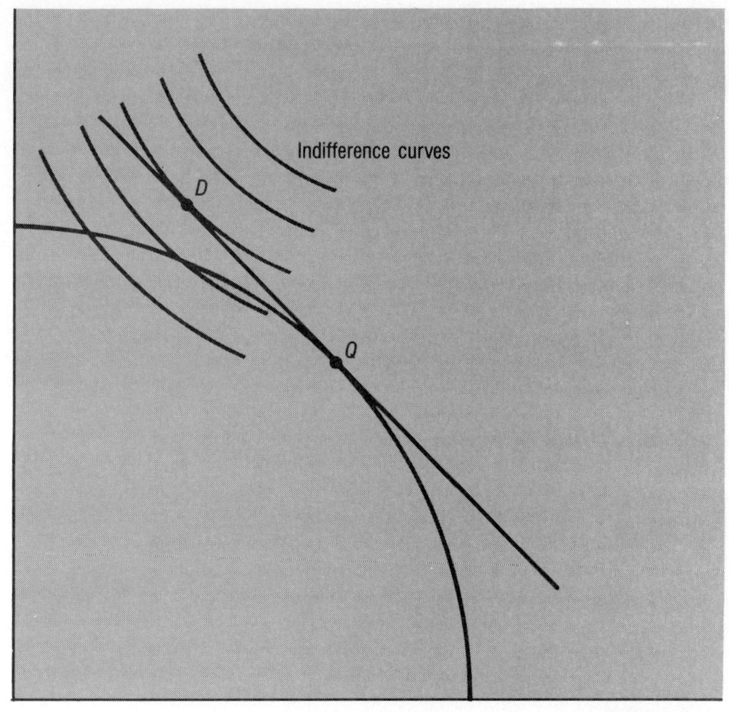

FIGURE 5-3 Production, consumption, and trade in the standard model. The economy produces at point Q and consumes at point D, which is the point where the isovalue line is tangent to the highest possible indifference curve.

The tastes of an individual can be represented graphically by a series of **indifference curves.** An indifference curve traces out a set of combinations of C and F that leave the individual equally well off. Indifference curves have three properties:

1. They are downward-sloping: if an individual is offered less F, then to be made equally well off she must be given more C.
2. The farther up and to the right an indifference curve lies, the higher the level of welfare to which it corresponds: an individual will prefer more of both goods to less.
3. Each indifference curve gets flatter as we move to the right: the more C and the less F an individual consumes, the more valuable a unit of F is at the margin compared with a unit of C; so more C will have to be provided to compensate for any further reduction in F.

In Figure 5-3 we show a set of indifference curves for the economy that have these three properties. The economy will choose the point on the isovalue line that yields the highest possible welfare. This point is where the isovalue line is tangent to the highest reachable indifference curve, at D. Notice that at this point the economy is an exporter of C and an importer of F. (If this is not obvious, refer back to our discussion of the pattern of trade in Chapter 3.)

Now consider what happens when P_C/P_F is increased. In Figure 5-4 we show the effects. First, the economy produces more C and less F, shifting production from Q^1 to Q^2. This shifts the isovalue line on which consumption must lie, from V^1V^1 to V^2V^2. The economy's consumption choice therefore also shifts, from D^1 to D^2.

The move from D^1 to D^2 reflects two effects of the rise in P_C/P_F. First, the economy has moved to a *higher* indifference curve: it is better off. The reason is that this economy is an exporter of cloth. When the relative price of cloth rises, the economy can afford to import more food for any given volume of exports. Thus the higher relative price of its export good represents an advantage. Second, the change in relative prices leads to a shift along the indifference curve, toward food and away from cloth.

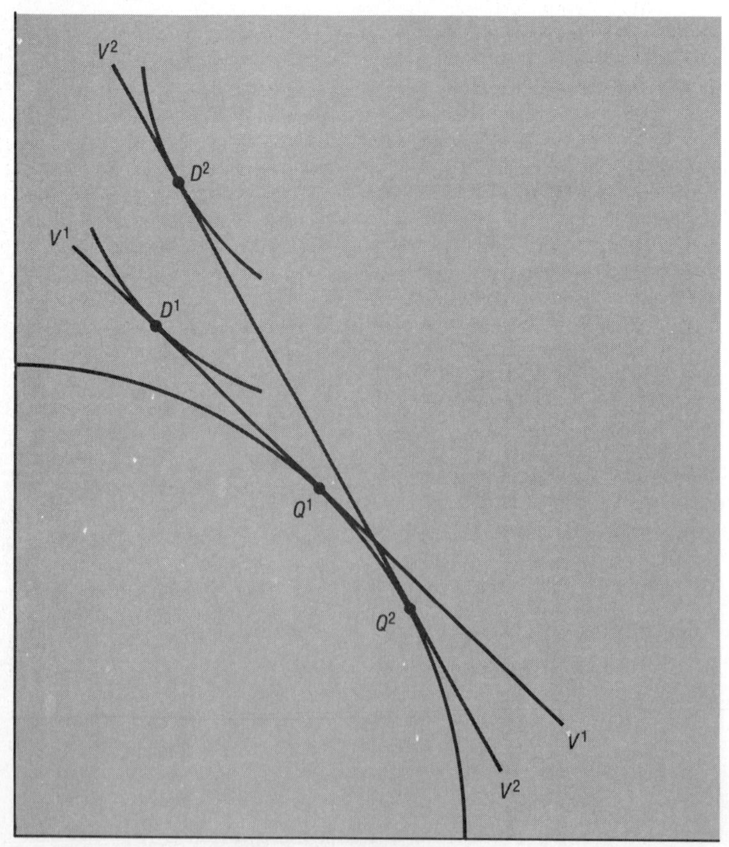

FIGURE 5-4 Effects of a rise in the relative price of cloth. The isovalue line rotates from V^1V^1 to V^2V^2. Production shifts from Q^1 to Q^2, while consumption shifts from D^1 to D^2.

These two effects are familiar from basic economic theory. The rise in welfare is an income effect; the shift in consumption at any given level of welfare is a substitution effect. The income effect tends to increase consumption of both goods, while the substitution effect acts to make the economy consume less C and more F.

It is possible in principle that the income effect will be so strong that when P_C/P_F rises, consumption of both goods actually rises. Normally, however, the ratio of C consumption to F consumption will fall, that is, *relative* demand for C will decline. This is the case shown in the figure.

THE WELFARE EFFECT OF CHANGES IN THE TERMS OF TRADE

When P_C/P_F increases, a country that initially exports C is made better off, as illustrated by the movement from D^1 to D^2 in Figure 5-4. Conversely, if P_C/P_F were to decline, the country would be made worse off—for example, consumption might move back from D^2 to D^1.

If the country were initially an exporter of food instead of cloth, the direction of this effect would of course be reversed. An increase in P_C/P_F would mean a fall in P_F/P_C, and the country would be worse off; a fall in P_C/P_F would make it better off.

We can cover all cases by defining the terms of trade as the price of the good a country initially exports divided by the price of the good it initially imports. The general statement, then, is that *a rise in the terms of trade increases a country's welfare, while a decline in the terms of trade reduces its welfare.*

DETERMINING RELATIVE PRICES

Let's now suppose that the world economy consists of two countries, once again named Home (which exports cloth) and Foreign (which exports food). Home's terms of trade are measured by P_C/P_F, while Foreign's are measured by P_F/P_C.

To determine P_C/P_F we find the intersection of world relative supply and world relative demand. The world relative supply curve (*RS* in Figure 5-5) is upward-sloping because an increase in P_C/P_F leads both countries to produce more cloth and less food. The world relative demand curve (*RD*) is downward-sloping because an increase in P_C/P_F leads both countries to shift their consumption away from cloth toward food. The intersection of the curves (point 1) determines the equilibrium relative price $(P_C/P_F)^1$.

Now that we know how relative supply, relative demand, the terms of trade, and welfare are determined in the standard model, we can use it to understand a number of important issues in international economics.

ECONOMIC GROWTH: A SHIFT OF THE *RS* CURVE

The effects of economic growth in a trading world economy are a perennial source of concern and controversy. The debate revolves around two ques-

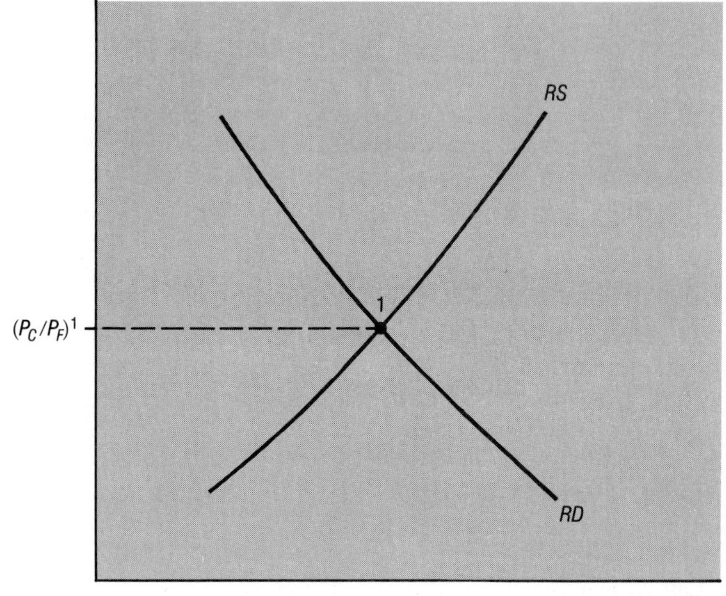

FIGURE 5-5 World relative supply and demand. The higher P_C/P_F is, the larger the world supply of cloth relative to food (*RS*) and the lower the world demand for cloth relative to food (*RD*).

tions. First, is economic growth in other countries good or bad for our nation? Second, is growth in a country more or less valuable when that nation is part of a closely integrated world economy?

In assessing the effects of growth in other countries, commonsense arguments can be made on either side. On one side, economic growth in the rest of the world may be good for our economy because it means larger markets for our exports. On the other side, growth in other countries may mean increased competition for our exporters.

Similar ambiguities seem present when we look at the effects of growth at home. On one hand, growth in an economy's production capacity should be more valuable when that country can sell some of its increased production to the world market. On the other hand, the benefits of growth may be passed on to foreigners in the form of lower prices for the country's exports rather than retained at home.

The standard model of trade developed in the last section provides a framework that can cut through these seeming contradictions and clarify the effects of economic growth in a trading world.

GROWTH AND THE PRODUCTION POSSIBILITY FRONTIER

Economic growth means an outward shift of a country's production possibility frontier. This growth can result either from increases in a country's resources or from improvements in the efficiency with which these resources are used.

The international trade effects of growth result from the fact that such growth typically has a bias. Biased growth takes place when the production possibility frontier shifts out more in one direction than in the other. Figure 5-6a illustrates growth biased toward cloth, and Figure 5-6b shows growth biased toward food. In each case the production possibility frontier shifts from T^1T^1 to T^2T^2.

As you may recall, growth may be biased for two main reasons:

1. The Ricardian model of Chapter 2 showed that technological progress in one sector of the economy will expand the economy's production possibilities more in the direction of that sector's output than in the direction of the other sector's output.
2. The factor-proportions model of Chapter 4 showed that an increase in a country's supply of a factor of production—say, an increase in the capital stock resulting from saving and investment—will produce an expansion biased in the direction of the good whose production is

FIGURE 5-6 Biased growth. Growth is biased if it shifts production possibilities out more toward one good than toward another. In both cases shown the production possibility frontier shifts out from T^1T^1 to T^2T^2. In case (a) this shift is biased toward cloth, in case (b) toward food.

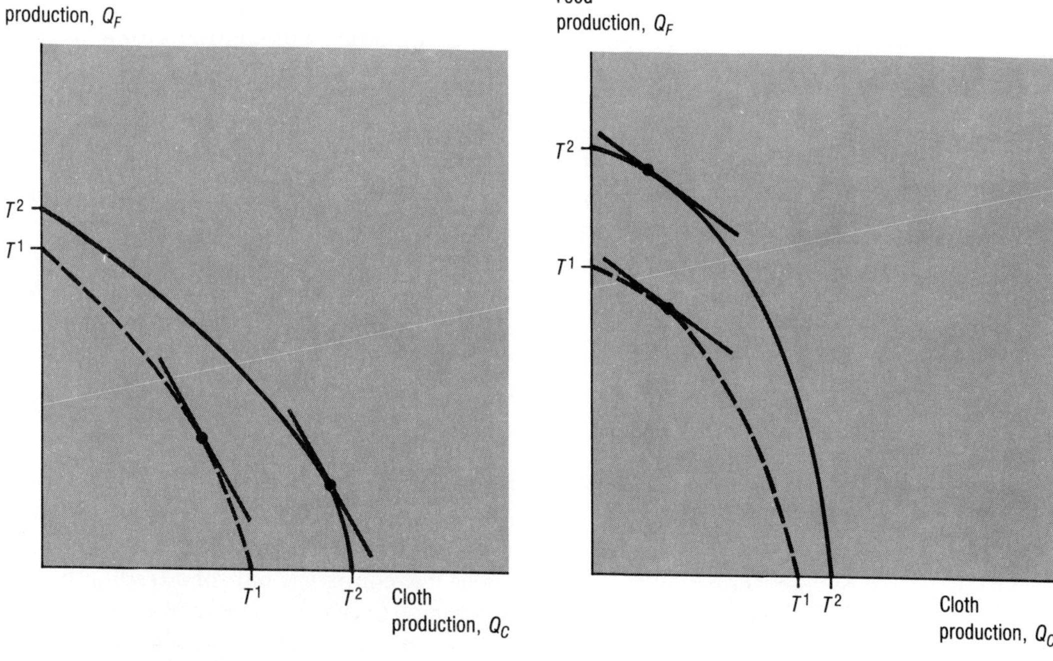

intensive in the factor whose supply has increased. Thus the same considerations that give rise to international trade will also lead to biased growth in a trading economy.

The biases of growth in Figure 5-6a and b are strong. In each case the economy is able to produce more of both goods, but at an unchanged relative price of cloth the output of food actually falls in Figure 5-6a, while the output of cloth actually falls in Figure 5-6b. Although growth is not always as strongly biased as it is in these examples, even growth that is more mildly biased toward cloth will lead, for any given relative price of cloth, to a rise in the output of cloth *relative* to that of food. The converse is true for growth biased toward food.

RELATIVE SUPPLY AND THE TERMS OF TRADE

Suppose now that Home experiences growth strongly biased toward cloth, so that its output of cloth rises at any given relative price of cloth, while its output of food declines. Then for the world as a whole the output of cloth relative to food will rise at any given price and the world relative supply curve will shift to the right from RS^1 to RS^2 (Figure 5-7a). This shift results in a decrease in the relative price of cloth from $(P_C/P_F)^1$ to $(P_C/P_F)^2$, which represents a worsening of Home's terms of trade and an improvement in Foreign's terms of trade.

Notice that the important consideration here is not which economy grows but the bias of the growth. If Foreign had experienced growth biased toward cloth, the effects on the relative supply curve and thus on the terms of trade would have been the same. On the other hand, either Home or Foreign growth biased toward food (Figure 5-7b) leads to a *leftward* shift of the RS curve (RS^1 to RS^2) and thus to a rise in the relative price of cloth from $(P_C/P_F)^1$ to $(P_C/P_F)^2$. This increase is an improvement in Home's terms of trade, a worsening of Foreign's.

Growth that disproportionately expands a country's production possibilities in the direction of the good it exports (cloth in Home, food in Foreign) is **export-biased growth.** Similarly, growth biased toward the good a country imports is **import-biased growth.** Our analysis leads to the following general principle: *Export-biased growth tends to worsen a growing country's terms of trade, to the benefit of the rest of the world; import-biased growth tends to improve a growing country's terms of trade at the rest of the world's expense.*

INTERNATIONAL EFFECTS OF GROWTH

Using this principle, we are now in a position to resolve our questions about the international effects of growth. Is growth in the rest of the world good or bad for our country? Does the fact that our country is part of a trading world economy increase or reduce the benefits of growth? In each case the answer depends on the *bias* of the growth. Export-biased growth in the rest of the

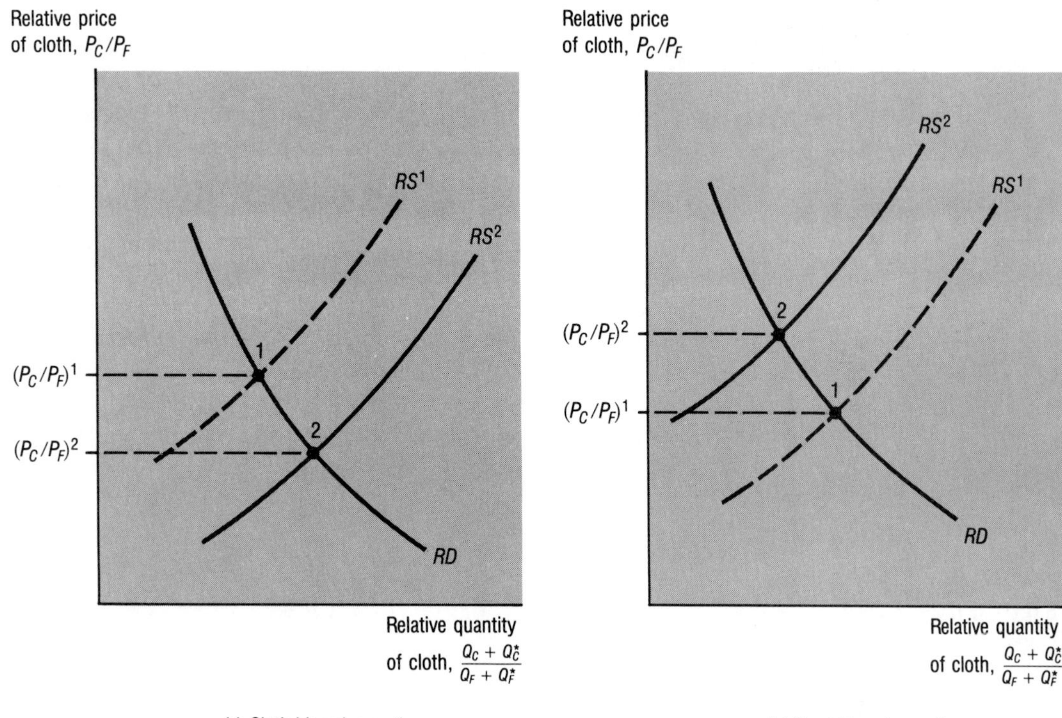

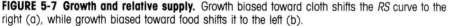

FIGURE 5-7 Growth and relative supply. Growth biased toward cloth shifts the *RS* curve to the right (a), while growth biased toward food shifts it to the left (b).

world is good for us, improving our terms of trade, while import-biased growth abroad worsens our terms of trade. Export-biased growth in our own country worsens our terms of trade, reducing the direct benefits of growth, while import-biased growth leads to an improvement of our terms of trade, a secondary benefit.

During the 1950s, many economists from poorer countries believed that their nations, which primarily exported raw materials, were likely to experience steadily declining terms of trade over time. They believed that growth in the industrial world would be marked by an increasing development of synthetic substitutes for raw materials, while growth in the poorer nations would take the form of a further extension of their capacity to produce what they were already exporting rather than a move toward industrialization. That is, the growth in the industrial world would be import-biased, while that in the less-developed world would be export-biased.

Some analysts suggested that growth in the poorer nations would actually be self-defeating. They argued that export-biased growth by poor nations would worsen their terms of trade so much that they would be worse off than if they had not grown at all. This situation is known to economists as the case of **immiserizing growth.**

In a famous paper published in 1958, the economist Jagdish Bhagwati of Columbia University showed that such perverse effects of growth can in fact arise within a rigorously specified economic model.[3] The conditions under which immiserizing growth can occur are, however, extreme: strongly export-biased growth must be combined with very steep *RS* and *RD* curves, so that the change in the terms of trade is large enough to offset the initial favorable effects of an increase in a country's productive capacity. Most economists now regard the concept of immiserizing growth as more a theoretical point than a real-world issue.

While growth at home normally raises our own welfare even in a trading world, however, this is by no means true of growth abroad. Import-biased growth is not an unlikely possibility, and whenever the rest of the world experiences such growth, it worsens our terms of trade. Indeed, as we point out below, it is possible that the United States has suffered some loss of real income because of foreign growth over the postwar period.

Case Study FOREIGN GROWTH AND THE U.S. TERMS OF TRADE

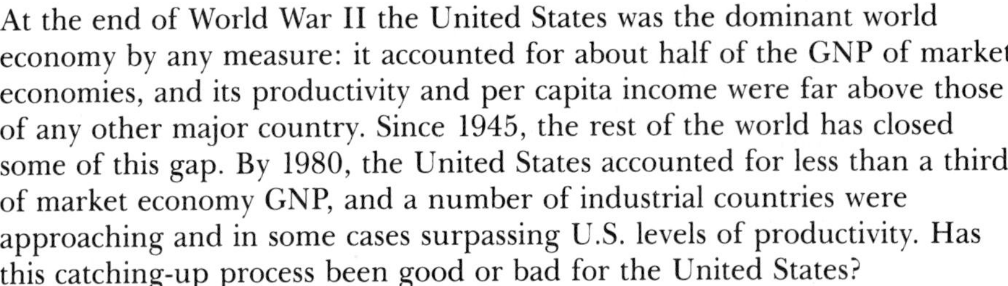

At the end of World War II the United States was the dominant world economy by any measure: it accounted for about half of the GNP of market economies, and its productivity and per capita income were far above those of any other major country. Since 1945, the rest of the world has closed some of this gap. By 1980, the United States accounted for less than a third of market economy GNP, and a number of industrial countries were approaching and in some cases surpassing U.S. levels of productivity. Has this catching-up process been good or bad for the United States?

In strictly economic terms, a good case can be made that the United States has been hurt by foreign growth. Consider Figure 5-8, which shows an index of the U.S. terms of trade, excluding oil and agricultural products, since the late 1960s. Until 1980, there was a consistent downward trend in the terms of trade, shown by the broken line in the figure. Most analysts would agree that the rise after 1980 is a temporary phenomenon associated with large inflows of foreign loans (see p. 563). Thus, as the broken line suggests, the evidence seems to indicate a persistent loss of U.S. terms of trade at about 1.5 percent per year.

Our standard model of trade suggests an explanation of this steady decline. Twenty years ago, the United States was ahead of the rest of the world in technology, skill of its labor force, and capital per worker. As the rest of the world began to catch up, other countries became *more like the United States.* This meant that their growth was naturally biased toward those sectors in which the U.S. advantage was initially greatest. For

[3]"Immiserizing Growth: A Geometrical Note," *Review of Economic Studies* 25 (June 1958), pp. 201–205.

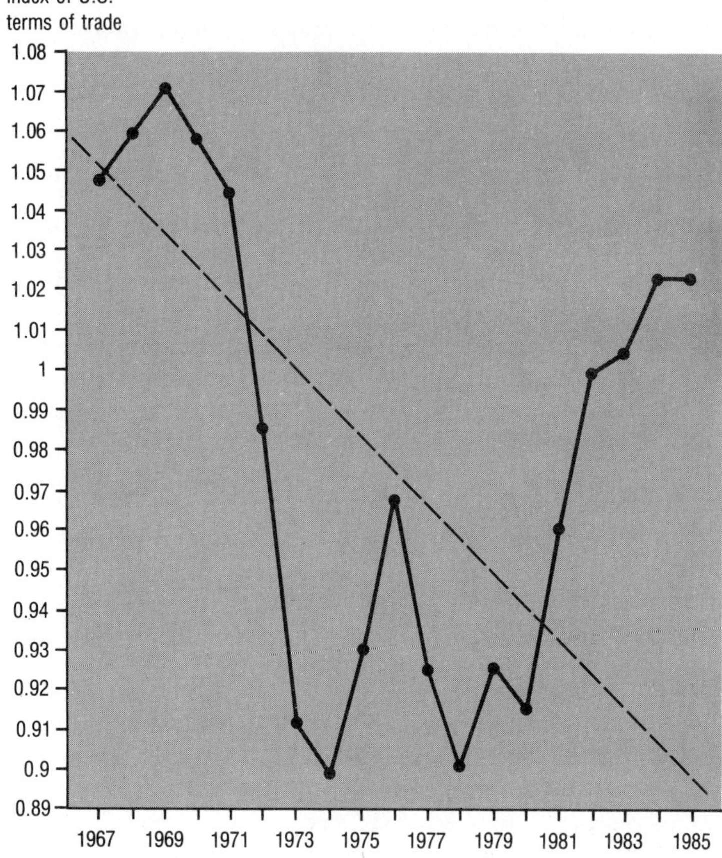

FIGURE 5-8 The U.S. terms of trade. Until the 1980s the U.S. terms of trade (excluding oil and agricultural goods) showed a persistent downward trend. Source: *Survey of Current Business.*

example, in the early 1950s Japan's comparative advantage lay in labor-intensive industries like textiles; over the decades that followed, it came to challenge the United States in capital-intensive industries like autos and steel. Growth in the rest of the world was import-biased, worsening the U.S. terms of trade.

One should not, however, jump to the conclusion that the United States made a mistake in helping Western Europe and Japan to recover from World War II! First, there were other considerations in aiding these countries besides the terms of trade—the United States had humanitarian and political reasons for seeking to restore prosperity to its allies. Second, the costs of the terms of trade loss, while not negligible, are not overwhelming. We show in the mathematical postscript to this book that the real income cost of a terms of trade loss is approximately equal to the percentage loss multiplied by the share of imports in GNP. Since imports were less than 10 percent of GNP through this period, a 1.5 percent per year terms of trade loss reduced the rate of growth of U.S. real income by at most 0.15 percent per year (over the period 1960–1985, U.S. growth averaged 3.1 percent annually). Finally, when the gains from economies of scale are taken into account (Chapter 6), growth in foreign markets may benefit a country even if its terms of trade worsen.

INTERNATIONAL TRANSFERS OF INCOME: SHIFTING THE *RD* CURVE

We now turn from terms of trade changes originating on the supply side of the world economy to changes that originate on the demand side.

Relative world demand for goods may shift for many reasons. For example, tastes may change: with the rise in concern over cholesterol, demand for fish has risen relative to the demand for red meat. Technology may also change demand: whale oil was a preferred fuel for lamps at one time but was supplanted first by kerosene, later by gas, and finally by electricity. In international economics, however, perhaps the most important and controversial issue is the shift in world relative demand that can result from international **transfers of income.**

In the past, transfers of income between nations have often occurred in the aftermath of wars. Germany demanded a payment from France after the latter's defeat in the Franco-Prussian war of 1871; after World War I the victorious Allies demanded large reparations payments from Germany (mostly never paid). More recently, international transfers have been more benign. After World War II, the United States provided aid to defeated Japan and Germany as well as to its wartime allies to help them rebuild. Since the 1950s, advanced countries have provided aid to poorer nations, although the sums have made a major contribution to the income of only a few of the very poorest countries.

International loans are not strictly speaking transfers of income, since the current transfer of spending power that a loan implies comes with an obligation to repay later. In the short run, however, the economic effects of a sum of money given outright to a nation and the same sum lent to that nation are similar. Thus an analysis of international income transfers is also useful in understanding the effects of international loans.

THE TRANSFER PROBLEM

The issue of how international transfers affect the terms of trade was raised in a famous debate between two great economists: Bertil Ohlin (one of the originators of the factor-proportions theory of trade) and John Maynard Keynes. The subject of the debate was the reparations payments demanded of Germany after World War I, and the question was how much of a burden these payments represented to the German economy.[4]

[4]See Keynes, "The German Transfer Problem" and Ohlin, "The German Transfer Problem: A Discussion," both in *Economic Journal* 39 (1929), pp. 1–7 and pp. 172–182, respectively.

Keynes, who made a forceful case that the vengeful terms of the Allies (the "Carthaginian peace") were too harsh, argued that the monetary sums being demanded were an understatement of the true burden on Germany. He pointed out that in order to pay money to other countries Germany would have to export more and import less. In order to do this, he argued, Germany would have to make its exports cheaper relative to its imports. The resulting worsening of Germany's terms of trade would add an excess burden to the direct burden of the payment.

Ohlin questioned whether Keynes was right in assuming that Germany's terms of trade would worsen. His counterargument was that when Germany raised taxes to finance its reparations, its demand for foreign goods would automatically decrease. At the same time, the reparation payment would be distributed in other countries in the form of reduced taxes or increased government spending, and some of the resulting increased foreign demand would be for German exports. Thus Germany might be able to reduce imports and increase exports without having its terms of trade worsen.

In the particular case in dispute the debate turned out to be beside the point: in the end, Germany paid very little of its reparations. The issue of the terms of trade effects of a transfer, however, arises in a surprisingly wide variety of contexts in international economics.

EFFECTS OF A TRANSFER ON THE TERMS OF TRADE

If Home makes a transfer of some of its income to Foreign, Home's income is reduced, and it must reduce its expenditure. Correspondingly, Foreign increases its expenditure. This shift in the national division of world spending may lead to a shift in world relative demand, thus affecting the terms of trade.

The shift in the *RD* curve (if it occurs) is the only effect of a transfer of income. The *RS* curve does not shift. As long as only income is being transferred, and not physical resources like capital equipment, the production of cloth and food for any given relative price will not change in either country. Thus the transfer problem is a purely demand-side issue.

The *RD* curve does not necessarily shift when world income is redistributed (this was Ohlin's point). If Foreign allocates its extra income between cloth and food in the same proportions that Home reduces its spending, then *world* spending on cloth and food will not change. The *RD* curve does not shift, and there is no terms of trade effect.

If the two countries do not allocate their change in spending in the same proportions, however, there will be a terms of trade effect, whose direction will depend on the difference in Home and Foreign spending patterns. Suppose that Home allocates a higher proportion of a marginal shift in expenditure to cloth than Foreign does. That is, Home has a higher **marginal propensity to spend** on cloth than Foreign. (Correspondingly, Home in this case must have a lower marginal propensity to spend on food.) Then at any given relative price Home's transfer payment to Foreign reduces demand for cloth and increases demand for food. The *RD* curve shifts to the left, from RD^1 to RD^2 (Figure 5-9) and equilibrium shifts from point 1 to point 2. This shift lowers the relative price of cloth from $(P_C/P_F)^1$ to $(P_C/P_F)^2$, worsening Home's terms of trade (because it exports cloth) while improving Foreign's. This is the case that Keynes described: the indirect effect of an international transfer on terms of trade reinforces its original effect on the incomes of the two countries.

There is, however, another possibility. If Home has a *lower* marginal propensity to spend on cloth, a transfer by Home to Foreign will shift the *RD* curve right, and improves Home's terms of trade at Foreign's expense. This effect offsets both the negative effect on Home's income and the positive effect on Foreign's income.

In general, then, *a transfer worsens the donor's terms of trade if the donor has a higher marginal propensity to spend on its export good than the recipient.* If the donor has a *lower* marginal propensity to spend on its export, its terms of trade will actually improve.

A paradoxical possibility is implied by this analysis. A transfer payment—say foreign aid—could conceivably improve the donor's terms of trade so

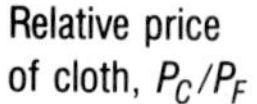

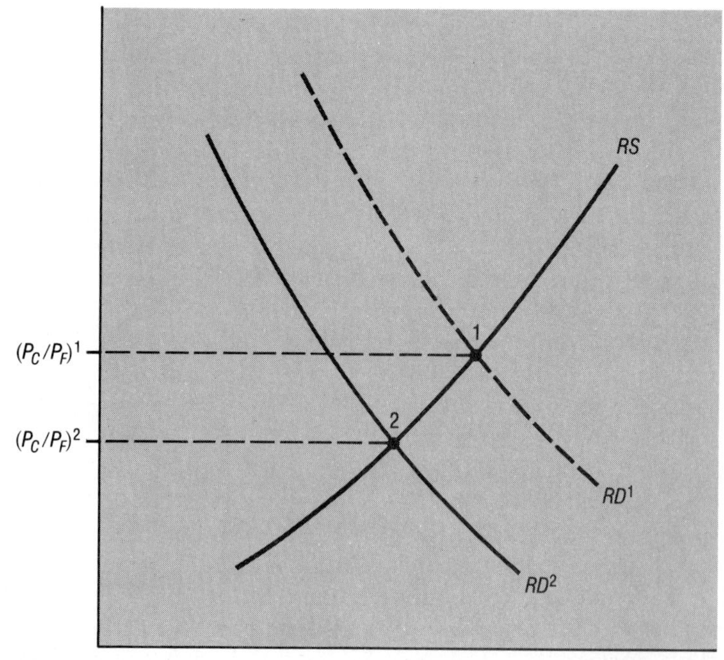

FIGURE 5-9 Effects of a transfer on the terms of trade. If Home has a higher marginal propensity to spend on cloth than Foreign, a transfer of income by Home to Foreign shifts the *RD* curve left from RD^1 to RD^2, reducing the equilibrium relative price of cloth.

much that it leaves the donor better off and the recipient worse off. In this case it is definitely better to give than to receive! Recent theoretical work has shown that this paradox, like the case of immiserizing growth, is possible in a rigorously specified model. The conditions are, however, even more stringent than those for immiserizing growth, and this possibility is almost surely purely theoretical.[5]

This analysis shows that the terms of trade effects of reparations and foreign aid can go either way. Thus Ohlin was right about the general principle. Many would still argue, however, that Keynes was right in suggesting that there is a presumption that transfers cause terms of trade effects that reinforce their effects on the incomes of donors and recipients.

PRESUMPTIONS ABOUT THE TERMS OF TRADE EFFECTS OF TRANSFERS

A transfer will worsen the donor's terms of trade if the donor has a higher marginal propensity to spend on its export good than the recipient. If differences in marginal propensities to spend were simply a matter of differences in taste, there would be no presumption either way: which good a country exports depends on differences in technology or resources, which need have nothing to do with tastes. When we look at actual spending patterns, however, each country seems to have a relative preference for its own goods. The United States, for example, produces only about one-third of the value of output of the world's market economies, so that total sales of U.S. goods are one-third of world sales. If spending patterns were the same everywhere, the United States would spend only one-third of its income on U.S. products. In fact, imports are only 10 percent of national income—that is, the United States spends 90 percent of its income domestically. On the other hand, the rest of the world spends only 4 percent of its income on U.S. products. This certainly suggests that if the United States were to transfer some of its income to foreigners, the relative demand for U.S. goods would fall and the U.S. terms of trade would decline, just as Keynes argued.

The United States spends so much of its income at home because of barriers to trade, both natural and artificial. Transportation costs, tariffs, and import quotas cause residents of each country to buy a variety of goods and services at home rather than abroad. As we noted in Chapter 2, the effect of such barriers to trade is to create a set of nontraded goods. Even if every country divides its income among different goods in the same proportions, local purchase of nontraded goods will ensure that spending has a national bias.

[5]For examples of how an immiserizing transfer might occur, see Graciela Chichilnisky, "Basic Goods, the Effects of Commodity Transfers and the International Economic Order," *Journal of Development Economics* 7 (1980), pp. 505–519; and Jagdish Bhagwati, Richard Brecher, and Tatsuo Hatta, "The Generalized Theory of Transfers and Welfare," *American Economic Review* 83 (1983), pp. 606–618.

Consider the following example. Suppose that there are not two but *three* goods: cloth, food, and haircuts. Only Home produces cloth, only Foreign produces food. Haircuts, however, are a nontraded good that each country produces for itself. Each country spends one-third of its income on each good. Even though these countries have the same tastes, each of them spends two-thirds of its income domestically and only one-third on imports.

Nontraded goods can give rise to what looks like a national preference for all goods produced domestically. But to analyze the effects of a transfer we need to know what happens to the supply and demand for *exports*. Here the crucial point is that nontraded goods compete with exports for resources. A transfer of income from the United States to the rest of the world lowers the demand for nontraded goods in the United States, releasing resources that can be used to produce U.S. exports. As a result, the supply of U.S. exports rises. At the same time, the rest of the world increases its demand for nontraded goods, drawing resources away from exports and reducing the supply of foreign exports (which are U.S. imports). The result is that a transfer by the United States to other countries may lower the price of U.S. exports relative to foreign, worsening our terms of trade.

Demand shifts also cause resources to move between the nontraded and import-competing sectors. As a practical matter, however, most international economists believe that the effect of barriers to trade *is* to validate the presumption that an international transfer of income worsens the donor's terms of trade. Thus, Keynes was right in practice.

Case Study THE TRANSFER PROBLEM FOR THE UNITED STATES

The magnitude of the terms of trade impacts from a transfer can be seen by looking at estimates for the United States. Based on estimates from past history, it appears that U.S. residents spend about 80 cents of a dollar of additional income on U.S. goods, while foreign residents will spend only 10 cents of that same dollar on goods made here. Thus a transfer to the United States will raise the relative demand for U.S. goods and hence improve U.S. terms of trade.

According to econometric estimates of supply and demand elasticities, a transfer to the United States of 1 percent of national income will lead to an improvement in the U.S. terms of trade of about 7 percent. This improvement in turn raises U.S. real income by about 0.7 percent. So in addition to the direct benefit of a transfer the United States would receive indirect benefits of only slightly smaller magnitude.

This calculation is relevant because at the time of writing the United States was receiving large inflows of loans from abroad. These are not true transfer payments, because they must eventually be repaid. For the time being, however, they not only allow the United States to spend more than its current income, they also raise the purchasing power of that income substantially. The transfer effect has been a major contributor to the large improvement in the U.S. terms of trade after 1980 (see Figure 5-8).

TARIFFS AND EXPORT SUBSIDIES: SIMULTANEOUS SHIFTS IN *RS* AND *RD*

Import tariffs and **export subsidies** are not usually put in place to affect a country's terms of trade. Government intervention in trade usually takes place for income-distribution reasons, to promote industries thought to be crucial to the economy or for balance-of-payments reasons (these motivations are examined in Chapters 9, 10, and 11). Whatever the motive for tariffs and subsidies, however, they do have terms of trade effects that can be understood using the standard trade model.

The distinctive feature of tariffs and export subsidies is that they create a difference between the prices at which goods are traded on the world market and their prices inside a country. The direct effect of a tariff (a tax levied on imports) is to make imported goods more expensive inside a country than they are outside. An export subsidy is a payment given to domestic producers who sell a good abroad; by giving an incentive to export, such subsidies raise the price of exported goods inside a country.

The price changes caused by tariffs and subsidies change both relative supply and relative demand. The result is a shift in the terms of trade of the country imposing the policy change and in the terms of trade of the rest of the world.

RELATIVE DEMAND AND SUPPLY EFFECTS OF A TARIFF

Tariffs and subsidies drive a wedge between the prices at which goods are traded internationally (**external prices**) and the prices at which they are traded within a country (**internal prices**). This means that we have to be careful in defining the terms of trade. The terms of trade are intended to measure the ratio at which countries exchange goods—for example, how many units of food can Home import for each unit of cloth that it exports? The terms of trade therefore correspond to external, not internal, prices. Thus we want to know how a tariff or export subsidy affects relative supply and demand *as a function of external prices.*

If Home imposes a 20 percent tariff on the value of food imports, the price of food relative to cloth faced by Home producers and consumers will be 20 percent higher than the relative price of food on the world market. Equivalently, the relative price of cloth on which Home residents base their decisions will be lower than that on the external market.

At any given world relative price of cloth, then, Home producers will face a lower relative cloth price and therefore will produce less cloth and more food. At the same time, Home consumers will shift their consumption toward cloth and away from food. From the point of view of the world as a whole, the relative supply of cloth will fall (from RS^1 to RS^2 in Figure 5-10) while the relative demand for cloth will rise (from RD^1 to RD^2). Clearly, the world relative price of cloth rises from $(P_C/P_F)^1$ to $(P_C/P_F)^2$, and thus Home's terms of trade improve at Foreign's expense.

The extent of this terms of trade effect depends on how large the country imposing the tariff is relative to the rest of the world—if the country is only a small part of the world, it cannot have much effect on world relative supply and demand and therefore cannot have much effect on relative prices. If the United States, a very large country, were to impose a 20 percent tariff, some estimates suggest that the U.S. terms of trade might rise by 15 percent. That is, the price of U.S. imports relative to exports might fall by 15 percent on the world market, while the relative price of imports rose only 5 percent inside the United States. On the other hand, if Luxembourg or

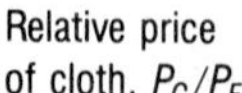

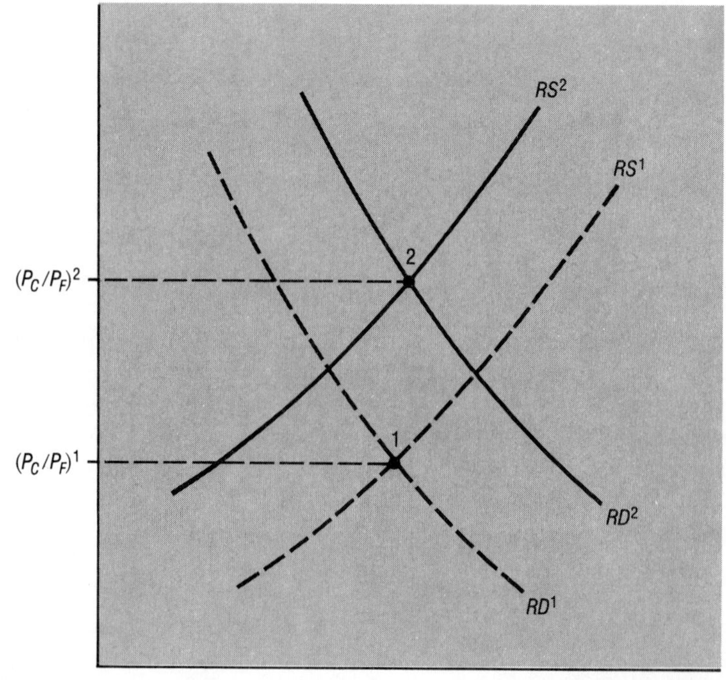

FIGURE 5-10 Effects of a tariff. An import tariff imposed by Home both reduces the relative supply of cloth (from RS^1 to RS^2) and increases the relative demand (from RD^1 to RD^2). As a result, the relative price of cloth must rise.

Paraguay were to impose a 20 percent tariff, the terms of trade effect would probably be too small to measure.

EFFECTS OF AN EXPORT SUBSIDY

Tariffs and export subsidies are often treated as similar policies, since they both seem to support domestic producers, but they have opposite effects on the terms of trade. Suppose that Home offers a 20 percent subsidy on the value of any cloth exported. For any given world prices this subsidy will raise Home's internal price of cloth relative to food by 20 percent. The rise in the relative price of cloth will lead Home producers to produce more cloth and less food, while leading Home consumers to substitute food for cloth. As illustrated in Figure 5-11, the subsidy will increase the world relative supply of cloth (from RS^1 to RS^2) and decrease the world relative demand for cloth (from RD^1 to RD^2), shifting equilibrium from point 1 to point 2. A Home export subsidy worsens Home's terms of trade and improves Foreign's.

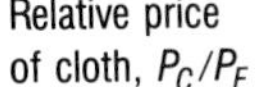

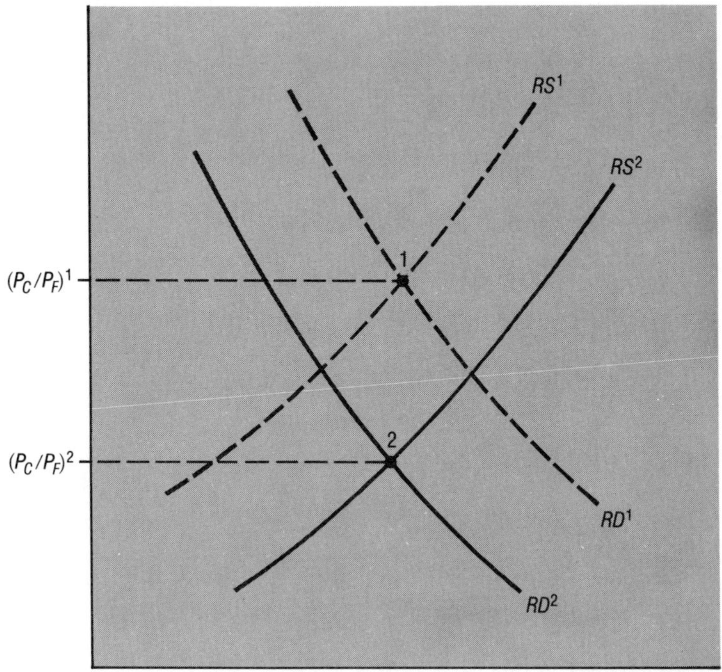

Relative quantity of cloth, $\frac{Q_C + Q_C^*}{Q_F + Q_F^*}$

FIGURE 5-11 Effects of a subsidy. An export subsidy's effects are the reverse of those of a tariff. Relative supply of cloth rises, while relative demand falls. Home's terms of trade decline.

IMPLICATIONS OF TERMS OF TRADE EFFECTS: WHO GAINS AND WHO LOSES?

The question of who gains and who loses from tariffs and export subsidies has two dimensions. First is the issue of the *international* distribution of income; second is the issue of the distribution of income *within* each of the countries.

The International Distribution of Income. If Home imposes a tariff, it improves its terms of trade at Foreign's expense. Thus tariffs hurt the rest of the world.

The effect on Home's welfare is not quite as clear-cut. The terms of trade improvement benefits Home; however, a tariff also imposes costs by distorting production and consumption incentives within Home's economy (see Chapter 8). The terms of trade gains will outweigh the losses from distortion only as long as the tariff is not too large: we will see later how to define an optimum tariff that maximizes net benefit. (For small countries that cannot have much impact on their terms of trade, the optimum tariff is near zero.)

The effects of an export subsidy are quite clear. Foreign's terms of trade improve at Home's expense, leaving it clearly better off. At the same time, Home loses from terms of trade deterioration *and* from the distorting effects of its policy.

This analysis seems to show that export subsidies never make sense. In fact, it is difficult to come up with any situation in which export subsidies would serve the national interest. The use of export subsidies as a policy tool usually has more to do with the peculiarities of trade politics than with economic logic.

The analysis seems to suggest that foreign tariffs are always bad for a country, while foreign export subsidies are always beneficial. Here we need to be a little careful. Our model is of a two-country world, where the other country exports the good we import and vice versa. In the real world of many countries, a foreign government may subsidize the export of a good that competes with U.S. exports; this foreign subsidy will obviously hurt the U.S. terms of trade. A good example of this effect is European subsidies to agricultural exports (see Chapter 8). Alternatively, a country may impose a tariff on something the United States also imports, lowering its price and benefiting the United States. We thus need to qualify our conclusions from a two-country analysis: subsidies to exports of things *the United States imports* help us, while tariffs *against U.S. exports* hurt us.

The view that subsidized foreign sales to the United States are good for us is not a popular one. When foreign governments are charged with subsidizing sales in the United States, the popular and political reaction is that this is unfair competition. Thus when a Commerce Department study determined that European governments were subsidizing exports of steel to the United States, our government demanded that they raise their prices. What the standard model tells us is that when we catch foreign governments subsidizing their exports to the United States, the appropriate response from a national point of view should be not to protest but to send them a note of thanks!

Of course this never happens, largely because of the effects of foreign subsidies on income distribution within the United States. If Europe subsidizes exports of steel to the United States, most U.S. residents gain from cheaper steel, but steelworkers, the owners of steel company stock, and industrial workers in general may not be so cheerful.

The Distribution of Income Within Countries. Foreign tariffs or subsidies change the relative prices of goods. Such changes have strong effects on income distribution because of factor immobility and differences in the factor intensity of different industries.

At first sight, the direction of the effect of tariffs and export subsidies on relative prices, and therefore on income distribution, may seem obvious. A tariff has the direct effect of raising the internal relative price of the imported good, while an export subsidy has the direct effect of raising the internal relative price of the exported good. We have just seen, however, that tariffs and export subsidies have an indirect effect on a country's terms of trade. The terms of trade effect suggests a paradoxical possibility. A tariff might improve a country's terms of trade so much—that is, raise the relative price of its export good so much on world markets—that even after the tariff rate is added, the internal relative price of the import good *falls.* Similarly, an export subsidy might worsen the terms of trade so much that the internal relative price of the export good falls in spite of the subsidy. If these paradoxical results occur, the income-distribution effects of trade policies will be just the opposite of what is expected.

The possibility that tariffs and export subsidies might have perverse effects on internal prices in a country was pointed out and demonstrated by the University of Chicago economist Lloyd Metzler and is known as the **Metzler paradox.**[6] This paradox has roughly the same status as immiserizing growth and a transfer that makes the recipient worse off: that is, it is something that is possible in theory but will happen only under extreme conditions and is not likely in practice.

Leaving aside the possibility of a Metzler paradox, then, a tariff will help the import-competing sector at home while hurting the exporting sector; an export subsidy will do the reverse. These shifts in the distribution of income *within* countries are often more obvious and more important to the formation of policy than the shifts in the distribution of income *between* countries that result from changes in the terms of trade.

[6]See Metzler, "Tariffs, the Terms of Trade, and the Distribution of National Income," *Journal of Political Economy* 57 (February 1949), pp. 1–29.

SUMMARY

1. The *standard trade model* derives a world relative supply curve from production possibilities and a world relative demand curve from preferences. The price of exports relative to imports, a country's *terms of trade*, is determined by the intersection of the world relative supply and demand curves. Other things equal, a rise in a country's terms of trade increases its welfare. Conversely, a decline in a country's terms of trade will leave the country worse off.

2. Economic growth means an outward shift in a country's production possibility frontier. Such growth is usually *biased* —that is, the production possibility frontier shifts out more in the direction of some goods than in the direction of others. The immediate effect of biased growth is to lead, other things equal, to an increase in the world relative supply of the goods toward which the growth is biased. This shift in the world relative supply curve in turn leads to a change in the growing country's terms of trade, which can go in either direction. If the growing country's terms of trade improve, this improvement reinforces the initial growth at home but hurts the rest of the world. If the growing country's terms of trade worsen, this decline offsets some of the favorable effects of growth at home but benefits the rest of the world.

3. The direction of the terms of trade effects depends on the nature of the growth. Growth that is *export-biased* (growth that expands the ability of an economy to produce the goods it was initially exporting more than it expands the ability to produce goods that compete with imports) worsens the terms of trade. Conversely, growth that is *import-biased,* disproportionately increasing the ability to produce import-competing goods, improves a country's terms of trade. It is possible for import-biased growth abroad to hurt a country, a situation that may actually have happened to a mild degree to the United States in the postwar period.

4. International *transfers of income* such as war reparations and foreign aid may affect a country's terms of trade by shifting the world relative demand curve. If the country receiving a transfer spends a higher proportion of an increase in income on its export good than the giver, a transfer raises world relative demand for the recipient's export good and thus improves its terms of trade. This improvement reinforces the initial transfer and provides an indirect benefit in addition to the direct income transfer. On the other hand, if the recipient has a lower *propensity to spend* on its export at the margin than the donor, a transfer worsens the recipient's terms of trade, offsetting at least part of the transfer's effect.

5. In practice, most countries spend a much higher share of their income on domestically produced goods than foreigners do. This is not necessarily due to differences in taste but rather to barriers to trade, natural and artificial, which cause many goods to be nontraded. If nontraded goods compete with

exports for resources, transfers will usually raise the recipient's terms of trade. The evidence suggests that this is, in fact, the case.

6. *Import tariffs* and *export subsidies* affect both relative supply and demand. A tariff raises relative supply of a country's import good while lowering relative demand. A tariff unambiguously improves the country's terms of trade at the rest of the world's expense. An export subsidy has the reverse effect, increasing the relative supply and reducing the relative demand for the country's *export* good, and thus worsening the terms of trade.

7. The terms of trade effects of an export subsidy hurt the subsidizing country and benefit the rest of the world, while those of a tariff do the reverse. This suggests that export subsidies do not make sense from a national point of view and that foreign export subsidies should be welcomed rather than countered. Both tariffs and subsidies, however, have strong effects on the distribution of income *within* countries, and these effects often weigh more heavily on policy than the terms of trade concerns.

KEY TERMS

standard trade model	transfers of income
terms of trade	marginal propensity to spend
isovalue lines	import tariff
indifference curves	export subsidy
export-biased growth	external price
import-biased growth	internal price
immiserizing growth	Metzler paradox

PROBLEMS

1. In some economies relative supply may be unresponsive to changes in prices. For example, in the immobile-factors model of Chapter 3 the production possibility frontier is right-angled, and output of the two goods does not depend on their relative prices. Is it still true in this case that a rise in the terms of trade increases welfare? Analyze graphically.

2. The counterpart to immobile factors on the supply side would be lack of substitution on the demand side. Imagine an economy where consumers always buy goods in rigid proportions—e.g., one yard of cloth for every pound of food, regardless of the prices of the two goods. Show that an improvement in the terms of trade benefits this economy, as well.

3. Japan primarily exports manufactured goods, while importing raw materials such as food and oil. Analyze the impact on Japan's terms of trade of the following events:

a) A war in the Middle East disrupts oil supply.

b) Korea develops the ability to produce automobiles that it can sell in Canada and the United States.

c) U.S. engineers develop a fusion reactor that replaces fossil-fuel electricity plants.

d) A harvest failure in the Soviet Union.

e) A reduction in Japan's tariffs on imported beef and citrus fruit.

4. Countries *A* and *B* have two factors of production, capital and labor, with which they produce two goods, *X* and *Y*. Technology is the same in the two countries. *X* is capital-intensive; *A* is capital-abundant.

Analyze the effects on the terms of trade and the welfare of the two countries of the following:

a) An increase in *A*'s capital stock.

b) An increase in *A*'s labor supply.

c) An increase in *B*'s capital stock.

d) An increase in *B*'s labor supply.

5. It is just as likely that economic growth will worsen a country's terms of trade as that it will improve them. Why, then, do most economists regard immiserizing growth, where growth actually hurts the growing country, as unlikely in practice?

6. In practice much foreign aid is "tied"; that is, it comes with restrictions that require that the recipient spend the aid on goods from the donor country. For example, France might provide money for an irrigation project in Africa, on the condition that the pumps, pipelines, and construction equipment be purchased from France rather than from Japan. How does such tying of aid affect the transfer problem analysis? Does tying of aid make sense from the donor's point of view? Can you think of a scenario in which tied aid actually makes the recipient worse off?

7. Suppose that one country subsidizes its exports and that the other country imposes a "countervailing" tariff that offsets its effect, so that in the end relative prices in the second country are unchanged. What happens to the terms of trade? What about welfare in the two countries?

Suppose, on the other hand, that the second country retaliates with an export subsidy of its own. Contrast the result.

FURTHER READING

Rudiger Dornbusch, Stanley Fischer, and Paul Samuelson. "Comparative Advantage, Trade, and Payments in a Ricardian Model with a Continuum of Goods." *American Economic Review,* 1977. This paper, which we cited in Chapter 2, also gives a clear exposition of the role of nontraded goods in establishing the presumption that a transfer improves the recipient's terms of trade.

J. R. Hicks. "The Long Run Dollar Problem." *Oxford Economic Papers* 2 (1953), pp. 117–135. The modern analysis of growth and trade has its origins in the fears of Europeans, in the early years after World War II, that the United States had established an economic lead that could not be overtaken (this sounds dated today, but many of the same arguments have now resurfaced about Japan). The paper by Hicks is the most famous exposition.

Harry G. Johnson. "Economic Expansion and International Trade." *Manchester School of Social and Economic Studies* 23 (1955), pp. 95–112. The paper that laid out the crucial distinction between export- and import-biased growth.

Paul Samuelson. "The Transfer Problem and Transport Costs." *Economic Journal* 62 (1952), pp. 278–304 (Part I) and 64 (1954), pp. 264–289 (Part II). The transfer problem, like so many issues in international economics, was given its basic formal analysis by Paul Samuelson.

John Whalley. *Trade Liberalization among Major World Trading Areas.* Cambridge: MIT Press, 1985. The impact of tariffs on the international economy has been the subject of extensive study. Most impressive are the huge "computable general equilibrium" models, numerical models based on actual data that allow computation of the effects of changes in tariffs and other trade policies. Whalley's book presents one of the most carefully constructed of these.

APPENDIX TO CHAPTER 5

Representing International Equilibrium with Offer Curves

For most purposes, analyzing international equilibrium in terms of relative supply and demand is the simplest and most useful technique. In some circumstances, however, it is useful to analyze trade in a diagram that shows directly what each country ships to the other. A diagram that does this is the *offer curve* diagram.

DERIVING A COUNTRY'S OFFER CURVE

In Figure 5-3 we showed how to determine a country's production and consumption given the relative price P_C/P_F. Trade is the difference between production and consumption. In an offer curve diagram we show directly the trade flows that correspond to any given relative price. On one axis of Figure 5A-1 we show the country's exports $(Q_C - D_C)$, on the other its imports $(D_F - Q_F)$. Point T in Figure 5A-1 corresponds to the situation shown in Figure 5-3 (production at Q, consumption at D). Since

$$(D_F - Q_F) = (Q_C - D_C) \times (P_C/P_F), \qquad \textbf{(5A-1)}$$

the slope of the line from the origin of Figure 5A-1 to T is equal to P_C/P_F. T is Home's *offer* at the assumed relative price: at that price, Home residents are willing to trade $(Q_C - D_C)$ units of cloth for $(D_F - Q_F)$ units of food.

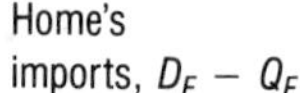

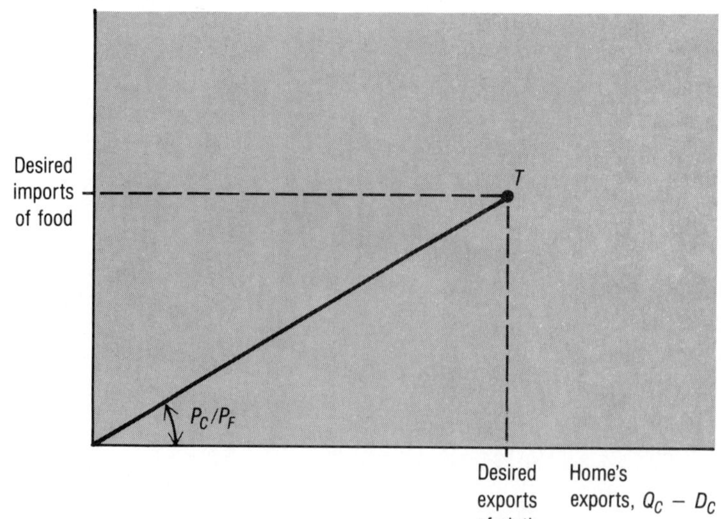

FIGURE 5A-1 Home's desired trade at a given relative price. At the relative price corresponding to the slope of the line from the origin, Home makes the offer to trade $Q_C - D_C$ units of cloth for $D_F - Q_F$ units of food.

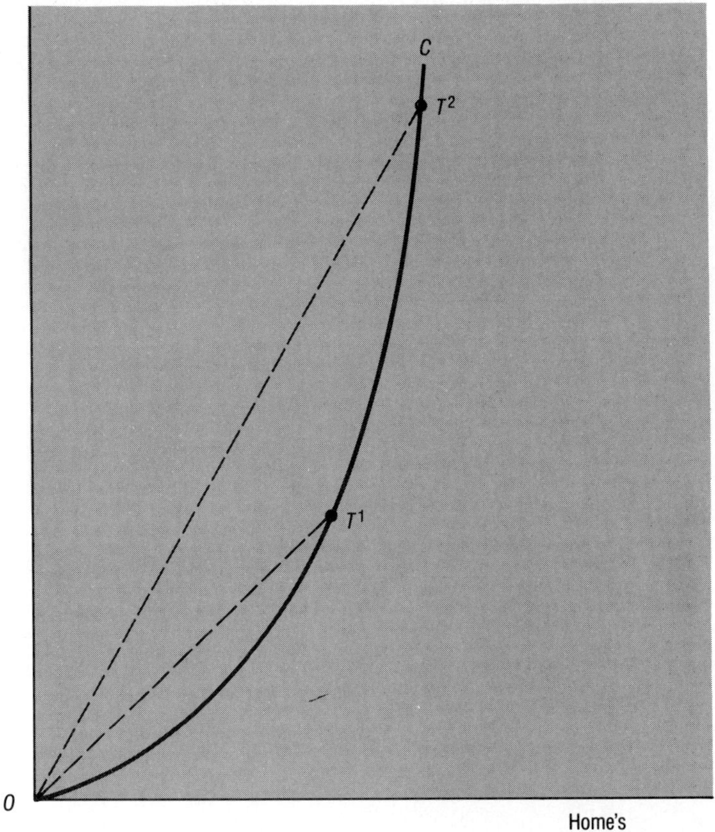

FIGURE 5A-2 Home's offer curve. The offer curve is generated by tracing out how Home's offer varies as the relative price of cloth is changed.

By calculating Home's offer at different relative prices, we trace out Home's *offer curve* (Figure 5A-2). We saw in Figure 5-4 that as P_C/P_F rises, Q_C rises, Q_F falls, D_F rises, and D_C may rise or fall. Desired $(Q_C - D_C)$ and $(D_F - Q_F)$, however, *both* normally rise if income effects are not too strong. In Figure 5A-2, T^1 is the offer corresponding to Q^1, D^1 in Figure 5-4; T^2 the offer corresponding to Q^2, D^2. By finding Home's offer at many prices, we trace out the Home offer curve OC.

Foreign's offer curve OF may be traced out in the same way (Figure 5A-3). On the vertical axis we plot $(Q_F^* - D_F^*)$, Foreign's desired exports of food, while on the horizontal axis we plot $(D_C^* - Q_C^*)$, desired imports of cloth. The lower P_C/P_F is, the more food Foreign will want to export and the more cloth it will want to import.

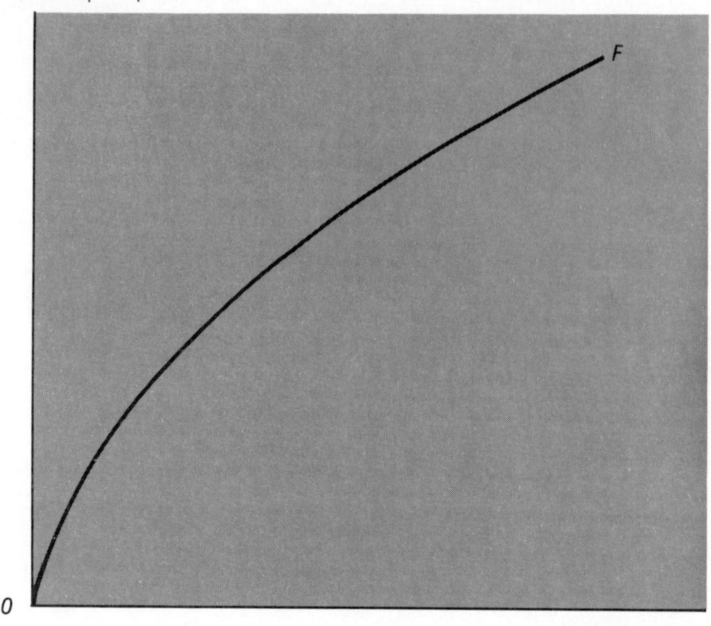

FIGURE 5A-3 Foreign's offer curve. Foreign's offer curve shows how that country's desired imports of cloth and exports of food vary with the relative price.

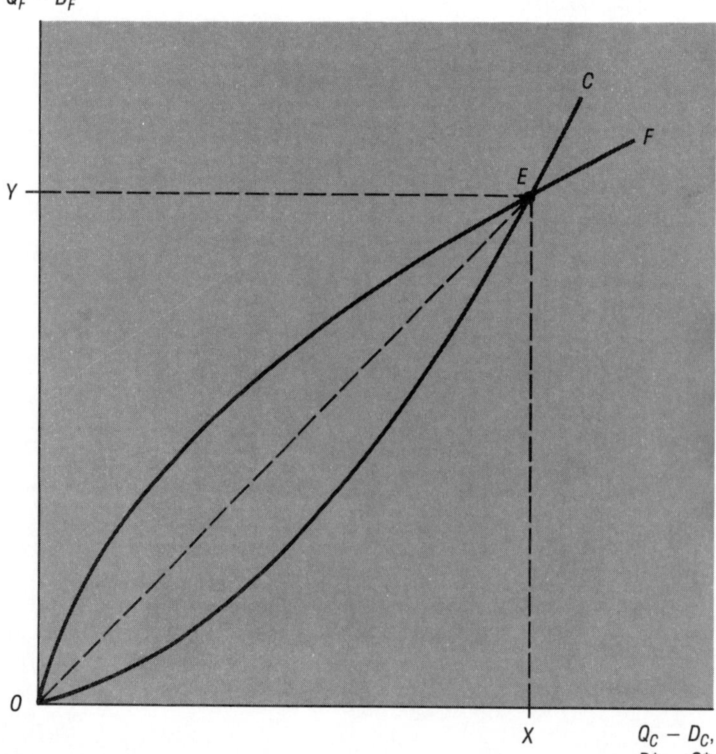

FIGURE 5A-4 Offer curve equilibrium. World equilibrium is where the Home and Foreign offer curves intersect.

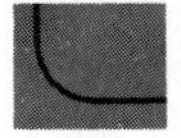

INTERNATIONAL EQUILIBRIUM

In equilibrium it must be true that $(Q_C - D_C) = (D_C^* - Q_C^*)$, and also that $(D_F - Q_F) = (Q_F^* - D_F^*)$. That is, world supply and demand must be equal for both cloth and food. Given these equivalences, we can plot the Home and Foreign offer curves on the same diagram (Figure 5A-4). Equilibrium is at the point where the Home and Foreign offer curves cross. At the equilibrium point E the relative price of cloth is equal to the slope of OE. Home's exports of cloth, which equal Foreign's imports, are OX. Foreign's exports of food, which equal Home's imports, are OY.

This representation of international equilibrium helps us see that equilibrium is in fact *general* equilibrium, in which supply and demand are equalized in both markets at the same time.

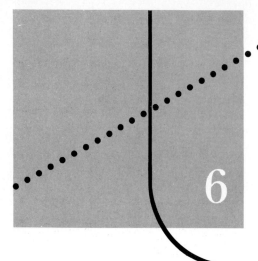

6 ECONOMIES OF SCALE AND INTERNATIONAL TRADE

In Chapter 2 we pointed out that there are two quite different reasons why countries specialize and trade. One is the fact that countries differ either in their resources or in technology, and specialize in doing the things they do relatively well; the other is that there are **economies of scale,** or **increasing returns,** that make it advantageous for each country to specialize in the production of only a limited range of goods and services. For the past four chapters we have considered models in which all trade is based on comparative advantage—that is, models in which differences between countries are the only reason for trade. The time has now come to bring in the role of economies of scale.

The analysis of trade based on economies of scale presents certain problems that we have so far avoided. Up to this point we have assumed that markets are perfectly competitive, so that all monopoly profits are always competed away. When there are increasing returns, however, large firms will usually have an advantage over small, so that markets will tend to end up being dominated by only one firm—a situation of monopoly—or more usually by a few firms—a situation of oligopoly. Unfortunately the analysis of oligopolistic markets, where there are some monopoly profits but also some competition, is one of the most problematic areas in economics. The essential aspects of the role of economies of scale in international trade can be understood, however, by focusing on two special cases where scale economies do *not* give rise to monopoly profits. The first of these is the case where the economies of scale take the form of **external economies:** that is, costs are decreasing in the size of the industry, but large firms do not have any advantage over small ones. The second is the case of **monopolistic competition,** in which the entry of a large number of firms into an industry, each producing a somewhat differentiated product, squeezes out any monopoly profits.

We begin with an analysis of trade based on scale economies that are external to firms. This analysis lets us see in as simple as possible a form why economies of scale give rise to international trade, and why trade based on scale economies can be mutually beneficial. We then proceed to the case of monopolistic competition. This case is useful because it allows us to see how scale economies and comparative advantage interact in international trade.

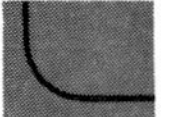

EXTERNAL ECONOMIES AND TRADE

We say that economies of scale are *external* to firms when the productivity of a firm depends on how large an industry it is part of rather than on the size of the firm itself. For example, garment makers in New York have traditionally been quite small firms, but for much of the past century they had an advantage over garment makers elsewhere in the United States because of the size of the New York industry. This advantage derived from a number of factors. New York firms were able to respond faster to changes in fashion because of the flow of news and ideas between firms, they had greater flexibility because of New York's large specialized labor market, they had better access to suppliers of intermediate goods, and so on. The nature of the garment industry was such that productivity of firms was relatively high if they were close to other similar firms, even though large firms were no more efficient than smaller firms.

External scale economies are difficult to measure but have probably been important since the beginnings of industrialization. We need only notice the tendency of many industries to clump together geographically. We have already mentioned the New York garment industry, which emerged in the late nineteenth century, but the phenomenon can be found as early as the eighteenth century, when cotton spinning was concentrated in the county of Lancashire in England, and it remains important today, when semiconductor manufacture is concentrated in California's Silicon Valley.

A MODEL WITH EXTERNAL ECONOMIES

Imagine a world consisting of two countries—Home and Foreign, of course. To concentrate on the effects of increasing returns, we return to the one-factor analysis of Chapter 2, assuming that each country has only one factor of production, labor. Each country can produce two goods: a good that is subject to external economies, such as a high-technology good where firms learn from each others' discoveries, and a good where there are no economies of scale. Let us call the first industry chips and the second fish. In keeping with our usual strategy of isolating particular causes of trade, let us also assume that these countries have identical technologies. That is, the unit labor requirement for fish production is the same in both, and so is the unit labor requirement in chips production, *other things being equal.*

Other things will not necessarily be equal, however. Chips is subject to external scale economies, so that productivity in each country depends on the size of that country's industry. That is, the unit labor requirement in chips is a function of output:

$$a_{LC} = A(Q_C), \tag{6-1}$$

$$a^*_{LC} = A(Q^*_C). \tag{6-2}$$

The function $A(.)$, assumed to be the same in both countries, is illustrated in Figure 6-1. Because the function is the same, Home and Foreign would have the same productivity in chips if they had the same output. Otherwise, however, their productivity will differ. The figure shows a case where $Q_C > Q^*_C$. In this case we see that Home has a lower unit labor requirement in chips than Foreign, not because it is inherently more efficient but because of the economies of scale associated with a larger industry.

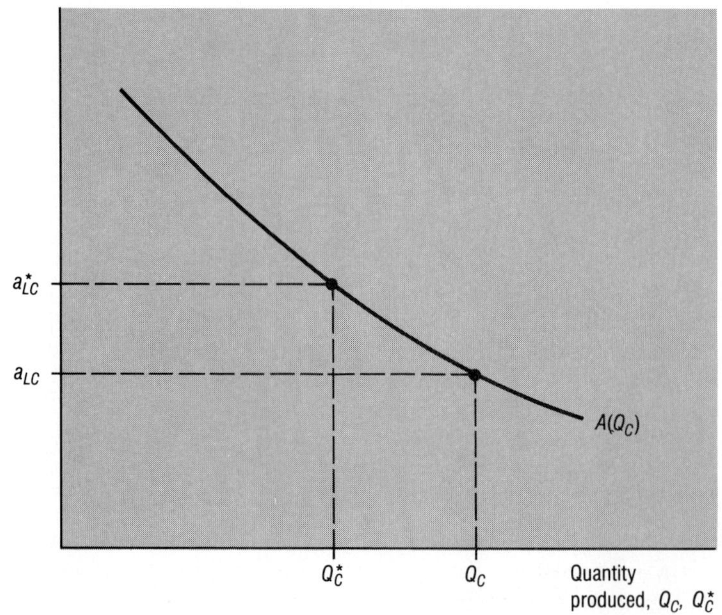

FIGURE 6-1 Unit labor requirements as a function of output. The higher a country's output of chips, the less labor is required to produce each unit.

Now suppose that Home and Foreign are able to trade with each other, with zero transportation cost. Then even though the countries have the same technology, they will end up specializing in the production of different goods. To see this, suppose that one country's chips industry starts out larger than the other's—maybe only slightly so. Then that country will have a lower unit labor requirement in chips. If both countries are producing fish, they will pay the same wage rates; so chips will be cheaper to produce in the country with the larger industry. The result will be that the chips industry will steadily expand in the country where it was initially larger and contract in the country where it was initially smaller. This process will continue until one of two things happens. Either the contracting chips industry will disappear, meaning that the country in which it is located specializes completely in the production of fish, or the expanding chips industry will run out of labor when its home country ceases to produce any more fish.

The only way that both countries could continue to produce both goods would be if they started out with exactly the same size chips industry. Such a position would, however, be *unstable.* If anything were to make one chips industry even slightly larger than the other, the larger industry would have a cost advantage that would lead it to expand relative to the other, reinforcing its advantage and setting in motion a snowballing process of specialization. The only outcomes that will not be displaced by slight shocks will be those where the countries do not both produce both goods.

A stable pattern of production must have at least one country specializing in the production of one good. Six such outcomes are possible; they are shown in Table 6-1. These six outcomes are of three types, with two outcomes corresponding to each type.

1. The chips industry is entirely concentrated in one country, which also produces some fish, while the other country produces only fish.
2. Both countries specialize, one producing only fish while the other produces only chips.
3. One country produces both chips and fish while the other produces only chips.

TABLE 6-1 Possible patterns of specialization with external economies

I. *Both countries produce fish*
   A. Chips production concentrated in Home
   B. Chips production concentated in Foreign
II. *Both countries specialize*
   A. Chips produced in Home
   B. Chips produced in Foreign
III. *Both countries produce chips*
   A. Home specializes in chips
   B. Foreign specializes in chips

The type of outcome depends on the relative demand for fish and chips. If the demand for chips is not too large, the first outcome, where only one country produces the scale economy good and that country still has some labor left over to produce the other good, is the likely one. As the relative demand for chips grows, the second and third possibilities become more likely.

All these outcomes have in common, however, the fact that a world economy in which we have ruled out any form of comparative advantage ends up with countries specialized in producing different goods. One country either ends up with the whole of world chips production or ends up specialized in the production of chips, while the other ends up either specialized in fish or as the only fish producer.

THE PATTERN OF TRADE WITH EXTERNAL ECONOMIES

External economies of scale lead to international specialization. This international specialization necessarily leads to international trade. In each of the cases we considered, at least one of the two goods is produced in only one of the two countries. As long as both countries demand both goods, the country that has the larger chips industry therefore exports chips and imports fish. So even though neither country started out with any advantage in terms of technology or resources that would give it a reason to specialize in one good or the other, we end up with international trade.

But which country will export which good? The surprising answer in this simple model is that either country may end up as the chips exporter. That is, we cannot predict the pattern of trade. To see this, let's focus on the case (outcome type 1) where the demand for chips is not too large, so that whichever country produces chips also ends up producing some fish as well. Then there are two possible patterns of specialization, shown in the upper part of Table 6-1. In one pattern the chips industry ends up concentrated in Home; in the other it ends up concentrated in Foreign. In either outcome the fact that the industry is concentrated gives the country where it is located a productivity advantage that ensures that the industry stays there.

The result that the international pattern of specialization and trade is impossible to predict may seem disturbing. In interpreting the real-world implications of the result, however, the right way to think of it is to say that initial advantages can cumulate over time, so that history and accidental factors—which we do not capture with our simple model—can have a persistent effect on the pattern of international trade. Consider, for example, the Swiss watch industry. In the eighteenth century, the particular skills of Swiss workers and the fact that clockmaking did not require a strong natural resource base led to a Swiss lead in that nascent industry. By the mid-twentieth century the technology of watchmaking, the character of the Swiss labor force, the nature of the world market, and virtually everything else one might consider had changed beyond recognition. Yet the Swiss advantage in watches has only recently been challenged by Japan. The enduring Swiss advantage in watch manufacture, like the dominant position of New York's garment industry, is based on the fact that such an advantage is self-reinforcing, because a large industry supports a good flow of information, a flexible labor market, specialized suppliers and services, and so on.

The unpredictability of the pattern of specialization in our model, then, does not reflect an actual indeterminacy. We should instead interpret it as meaning that when external economies are important, the pattern of specialization and trade is likely to be determined to an important extent by accident and by historical factors rather than by broad national characteristics.

THE GAINS FROM TRADE

We have just seen that the pattern of trade may be arbitrary and impossible to predict from the model. This might suggest that the benefits of trade are also uncertain. In particular, the fact that the chips industry is more productive the larger it is may seem to suggest that the country that ends up exporting chips gains from trade while the other country loses. This is a misinterpretation. The strong presumption is that trade that is based on economies of scale benefits everyone.

Let's continue to consider the case where chips production ends up concentrated in one country, while both countries produce some fish. We can assess the benefits of trade in the same way that we did in Chapter 2. That is, we ask whether the real wage in terms of each of the goods rises or falls. If the real wage in terms of both goods is higher or no lower as a result of trade, we can say that a country gains from trade.

First, look at real wages before trade. The price of each good will be the unit labor requirement times the wage rate. Thus in Home we have

$$\tilde{P}_F = \tilde{w} a_{LF}, \qquad \textbf{(6-3)}$$

$$\tilde{P}_C = \tilde{w} a_{LC} = \tilde{w} A(\tilde{Q}_C), \qquad \textbf{(6-4)}$$

where a tilde ("~") over a variable means "pretrade." The real wages will then be

$$(\tilde{w}/\tilde{P}_F) = 1/a_{LF}, \qquad \textbf{(6-5)}$$

$$(\tilde{w}/\tilde{P}_C) = 1/A(\tilde{Q}_C). \qquad \textbf{(6-6)}$$

Similarly, in Foreign the pretrade real wages will be

$$(\tilde{w}/\tilde{P}_F)^* = 1/a_{LF}, \qquad \textbf{(6-7)}$$

$$(\tilde{w}/\tilde{P}_C)^* = 1/A(\tilde{Q}_C^*). \qquad \textbf{(6-8)}$$

When Home and Foreign open trade, we assume that they both continue to produce fish. Since unit labor requirements for fish are the same, this means that they must pay the same wage rate—otherwise fish would be cheaper to produce in one country than in the other. We represent this common wage rate as w. The price of fish must therefore equal wa_{LF}, implying a real posttrade wage in terms of fish common to both countries,

$$w/P_F = 1/a_{LF}\,, \tag{6-9}$$

which is the same as the pretrade wage.

Only one country will produce chips; as we saw, we cannot predict which one. However, this uncertainty does not matter. Let $\overline{Q}_C$ be the posttrade output of chips in whichever country does produce them. This is also the world output. Then the unit labor requirement in that country is $A(\overline{Q}_C)$. The price of chips is the wage rate times the unit labor requirement,

$$P_C = wA(\overline{Q}_C)\,, \tag{6-10}$$

which in turn implies that both countries will have a posttrade real wage in terms of chips

$$w/P_C = 1/A(\overline{Q}_C)\,.$$

Now compare this posttrade real wage with the pretrade real wages in the two countries. It is immediately apparent that trade will give Home a higher real wage as long as $\overline{Q}_C > \tilde{Q}_C$, and Foreign a higher real wage as long as $\overline{Q}_C > \tilde{Q}_C^*$. It does not matter whether $\overline{Q}_C$ is produced in Home or Foreign, since the country that does not produce chips can buy them at the same price as the country that does.

The important point is that the criterion for gains from trade for *both* countries is that the chips industry of the trading world economy be larger than their national industry before trade. That is, the criterion does not depend on whether the country actually produces chips or not. We can state the criterion for gains from trade more generally: *In a world characterized by external scale economies, countries will gain from trade provided that the world scale of increasing returns industries is larger as a result of trade than the national scale of those industries would have been in the absence of trade.*

It should be apparent that this criterion is almost surely going to be satisfied. The world market is bigger than any one country's market; so there is a strong presumption that the scale of production will be larger in a trading world economy than any one country could achieve.

SIGNIFICANCE OF THE RESULTS

We have now examined the simplest possible model of the role of economies of scale in international trade. This simple model yields three basic insights about trade. First, economies of scale lead to international specialization and trade even when countries are similar in resources and technology—or more generally, scale economies are an additional source of trade over and above the sources of comparative advantage we studied in Chapters 2 to 5. Second, the pattern of specialization and trade generated by economies of scale typically contains an element of unpredictability. Who produces what may be determined in part by historical circumstance rather than by the fundamental characteristics of countries. Third, despite this unpredictability, trade based on increasing returns produces gains by allowing production at a larger scale, which raises productivity.

The external economies model is incomplete in two major respects, however. On one side, all economies of scale are not in fact external to firms. We would like to be able to discuss the case of increasing returns at the level of the firm as well. On the other side, the model we have developed allows no role for comparative advantage. We would like to be able to discuss the combined roles of scale economies and comparative advantage in a single model.

Recent work in the theory of international trade has led to an alternative model that meets both these complaints. This is the monopolistic competition model of trade, to which we now turn.

MONOPOLISTIC COMPETITION AND TRADE

Up to this point we have assumed, as economists often do, that markets are perfectly competitive. By this we mean that each firm is small enough relative to its market to view itself as unable to affect the price it receives for its output. If there are important economies of scale at the level of the firm, however, perfect competition breaks down. Large firms have an advantage over small, and industries end up dominated by only one or a few firms. Thus economies of scale normally lead to some form of **imperfect competition.**

Imperfect competition can take several forms. The simplest is pure monopoly: only one firm produces each product. The most complex is oligopoly: several firms produce each product and engage in a mixture of rivalry and cooperation. We consider each of these forms of competition later in the book—monopoly is an important issue for the analysis of protection in Chapter 8, and oligopoly is key to the analysis of industrial policy in Chapter 11. To understand the role of economies of scale in trade, however, economists have found it useful to focus on the intermediate case of monopolistic competition, a concept first proposed by the Harvard economist Edward Chamberlin.[1] The basic idea of monopolistic competition is that each firm in an industry produces a good that consumers view as different from the products of its competitors. Thus each firm is in effect a monopolist producing a unique good, and firms make their decisions about prices as if they were simple monopolists. If firms in the industry are seen to be making above-normal profits, however, additional firms will enter. By offering alternative products, these new entrants will draw off demand from the existing firms, reducing their profits. In the end, the field becomes crowded enough that profits are reduced to normal levels. We end up with an industry con-

[1]Chamberlin, *The Theory of Monopolistic Competition: A Re-orientation of the Theory of Value* (Cambridge: Harvard University Press, 1933).

sisting of a number of little monopolists, none of whom is earning any monopoly profits.

To understand monopolistic competition, we first need to review the basic theory of monopoly. Then we can describe monopolistic competition at the level of a single industry. Finally, we can turn to the interaction between monopolistic competition and international trade.

THE THEORY OF MONOPOLY

Figure 6-2 shows the position of a single, monopolistic firm. The firm faces a downward-sloping demand curve, shown in the figure as *D*. This shows how the price of the firm's output falls as it tries to sell more units. As we know from basic microeconomics, corresponding to the demand curve is another curve that represents the **marginal revenue** that the firm gains from selling an additional unit. Marginal revenue for a monopolist is always less than the price, because to sell an additional unit the firm must lower the price of the units it would have sold otherwise. Thus the marginal revenue curve, *MR*, lies below the demand curve.

AC represents the firm's average cost of production. It is downward-sloping; this reflects our assumption that there are economies of scale, so

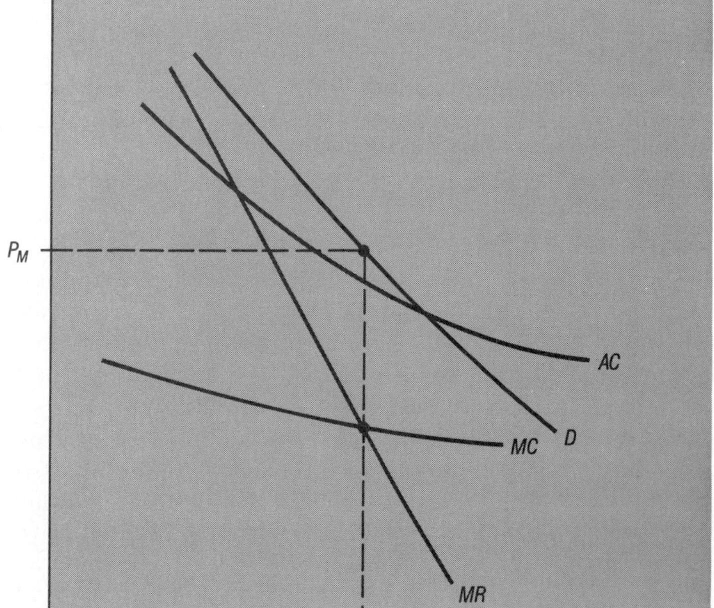

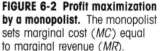

FIGURE 6-2 Profit maximization by a monopolist. The monopolist sets marginal cost (*MC*) equal to marginal revenue (*MR*).

that the larger the firm, the lower its costs. *MC* represents the firm's **marginal cost.** We know from basic economics that when average costs are a decreasing function of output, marginal cost is always less than average. Thus *MC* lies below *AC*.

The profit-maximizing output is where marginal revenue equals marginal cost, i.e., where *MC* and *MR* cross. In the figure we can see that at this output Q_M the price P_M exceeds average cost. This means that the monopolist is in fact earning some monopoly profits.

THE THEORY OF MONOPOLISTIC COMPETITION

We now imagine an industry consisting of many firms producing products that consumers view as good but not perfect substitutes for one another. These are referred to as **differentiated products.** In such an industry the demand curve facing each firm depends on how many other firms are producing competing products.

The firm shown in Figure 6-2 has a price above its average cost; i.e., it is earning monopoly profits. Suppose that this firm is now only one of a number of firms producing differentiated products and that additional firms are free to enter the industry. If the typical firm is earning monopoly profits, new firms will enter. This will reduce the demand facing firms already in the market: *D* will shift left, making each firm less profitable. In the end, we will have the zero-profit equilibrium illustrated in Figure 6-3. Each firm is a monopolist and charges a price above marginal cost. However, because of the crowding of the field by other firms, the firm is unable to earn monopoly profits. At the profit-maximizing output, price is, therefore, just equal to average cost. At any other output price would be below average cost; so the equilibrium is one where average cost is tangent to the demand curve.

EFFECTS OF MARKET SIZE ON MONOPOLISTIC COMPETITION

One of the effects of international trade is to create a world market that is larger than any one country's market would be by itself. We will turn to international trade in a moment. First, however, let us consider the general effects of an increase in market size in a monopolistically competitive industry.

Suppose that the size of the market expands, say because of an increase in population or a rise in per capita income. The initial effect will be to increase the demand facing each individual firm. This will raise profits. This in turn will lead to entry by new firms, pushing the demand curve facing each firm back until the monopoly profits have been eliminated. Thus an increase in market size will lead to an increase in the number of firms (and thus an expansion in the number of products from which consumers can choose).

There is usually more to the story than this, however. As the number of products increases, each consumer faces a choice among increasingly good substitutes. This will usually make the demand for each individual good

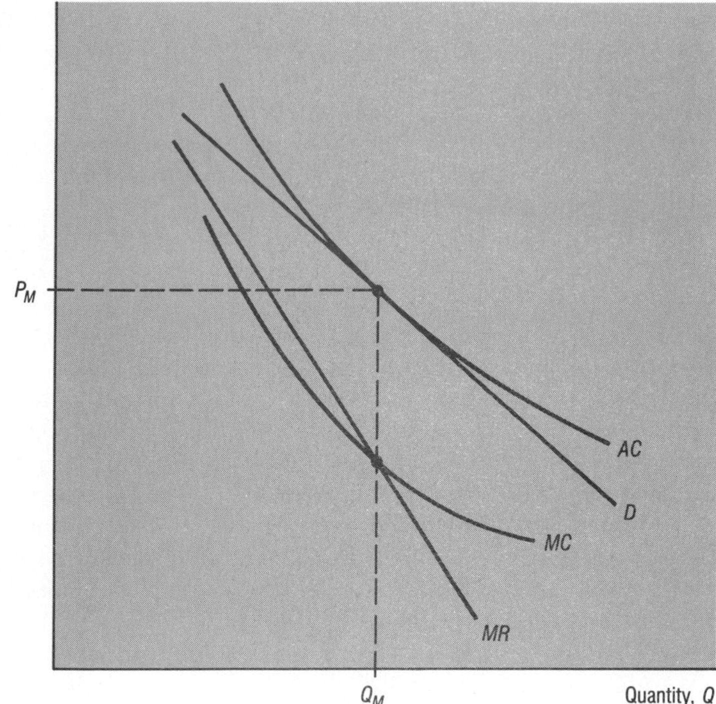

FIGURE 6-3 Zero-profit equilibrium. Entry has crowded the market, so that each monopolistic firm can at most charge a price that just covers average cost.

more sensitive to price: the more alternatives are available, the more readily consumers will switch when the price of one of them changes. So the demand curve will not only shift left, it will get *flatter.*

The implication of this shift is shown in Figure 6-4, which compares zero-profit equilibrium before and after an expansion in the market. Before the expansion the demand curve facing a representative firm is D^1; after the expansion it is D^2. The tangency between AC and the demand curve after a market expansion therefore involves a fall in the price, from P^1 to P^2, and a rise in the output of the typical firm, from Q^1 to Q^2.

Notice that consumers gain from a larger market in two ways. They have a wider range of choice, because more products are available, and they pay lower prices, because firms produce larger output and thus have lower average costs. These two gains from a larger market represent new sources of gains from international trade over and above those arising from comparative advantage.

A MONOPOLISTIC COMPETITION MODEL OF TRADE

Let us now imagine a world economy consisting as usual of our two countries Home and Foreign. Each of these countries has two factors of production,

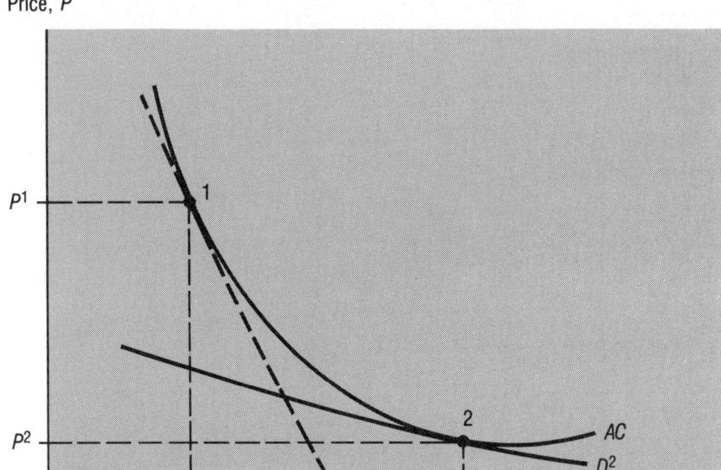

FIGURE 6-4 A larger market increases the scale of production. In a larger market, each firm faces a flatter demand curve (D^1 instead of D^2). The zero-profit equilibrium output rises from Q^1 to Q^2, while the price falls from P^1 to P^2.

capital and labor. We assume that Home has a higher overall capital-labor ratio than Foreign, i.e., that Home is the capital-abundant country. Let's also imagine that there are two industries, manufactures and food, with manufactures the more capital-intensive industry.

The difference between this model and the model of Chapter 4 is that we now suppose that manufactures is not a perfectly competitive industry producing a homogeneous product. Instead, it is a monopolistically competitive industry in which a number of firms all produce differentiated products. *Because of economies of scale, neither country is able to produce the full range of products by itself; thus although both countries may produce some manufactures, they will be producing different things.* This makes an important difference to the trade pattern. This difference can best be seen by first asking what would happen if manufactures were not a monopolistically competitive sector.

If manufactures were *not* a differentiated product sector, we already know from Chapter 4 what the trade pattern would look like. Because Home is capital-abundant and manufactures is capital-intensive, Home would have a larger relative supply of manufactures and would therefore export manufactures and import food. Schematically, we can represent the trade pattern with a diagram like Figure 6-5. The length of the arrows indicates the value of trade in each direction; what the figure shows is that Home would export manufactures equal in value to the food it imports.

But we are assuming that manufactures is a monopolistically competitive sector. That is, each firm produces a product that is differentiated from what

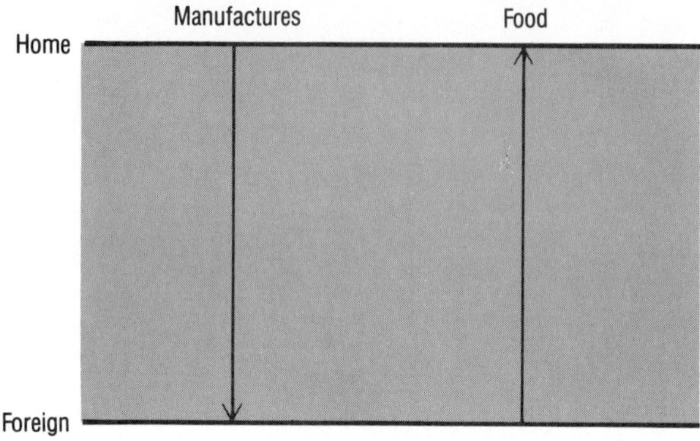

FIGURE 6-5 The trade pattern in the absence of product differentiation. Home exports but does not import manufactures, imports but does not export food.

other firms are producing. Now it will continue to be true that Home will be a *net* exporter of manufactures and an importer of food. However, Foreign firms in the manufactures sector will now be producing products different from those that Home firms are producing. Some Home consumers will prefer Foreign varieties; thus Home, although running a trade surplus in manufactures, will import as well as export within the industry. The pattern of trade will thus look like Figure 6-6. There will be two-way trade *within* the manufacturing sector. We can think of world trade as consisting of two parts. Some trade is in effect an exchange of manufactures for manufactures; this is referred to as **intraindustry trade.** The rest is in effect an exchange of manufactures for food; this is referred to as **interindustry trade.**

Four points should be noticed about this pattern of trade:

1. *Interindustry* trade reflects comparative advantage. The pattern of interindustry trade is that Home, the capital-abundant country, is a net exporter of capital-intensive manufactures and a net importer of labor-intensive food. So comparative advantage continues to be a major part of the story about trade.

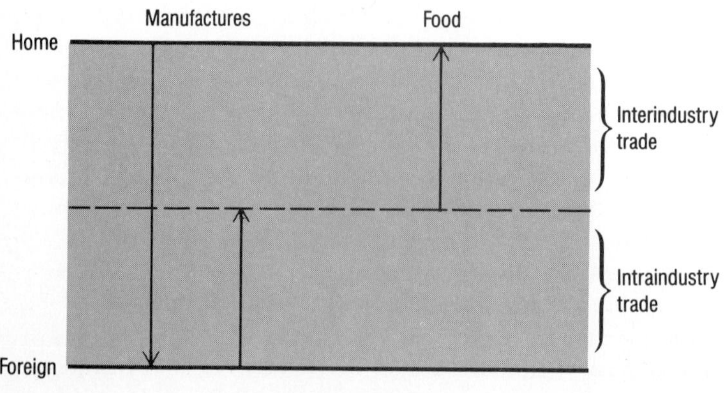

FIGURE 6-6 The trade pattern with differentiated products. Home both exports and imports manufactures; the two-way trade in manufactures is referred to as intraindustry trade. The remaining trade, which is an exchange of manufactures for food, is interindustry trade.

2. On the other hand, *intraindustry* trade does *not* reflect comparative advantage. Even if the countries had the same overall capital-labor ratio, their firms would continue to produce differentiated products, and the demand of consumers for products made abroad would continue to generate intraindustry trade. It is economies of scale that keep each country from producing the full range of products for itself; so what we are seeing here, as in the external economies model above, is that economies of scale can be an independent source of international trade. This time, however, there are both scale economies and comparative advantage operating at the same time.

3. The pattern of intraindustry trade itself is unpredictable. We have not said anything about which country produces which goods within the manufactures sector, because there is nothing in the model to tell us. All that we know is that the countries will produce different products. This indeterminacy is of course similar to the indeterminacy we saw in the last section and again should be interpreted to mean that history and accident determine the details of the trade pattern. An unpredictable component of the trade pattern is an inevitable feature of a world where economies of scale are important. Notice, however, that the unpredictability is not total. While the precise pattern of intraindustry trade within the manufactures sector is arbitrary, the pattern of interindustry trade between manufactures and food is determined by underlying differences between countries.

4. The character of international trade depends on how similar countries are. Suppose that Home and Foreign were very similar in their capital-labor ratios; then there would be very little interindustry trade, and intraindustry trade, based ultimately on economies of scale, would be dominant. On the other hand, suppose that the capital-labor ratios were very different, so that, for example, Foreign were to specialize completely in food production. Then there would be no intraindustry trade, and all trade would in fact be based on comparative advantage.

THE SIGNIFICANCE OF INTRAINDUSTRY TRADE

The monopolistic competition model shows us how comparative advantage and economies of scale interact to produce international trade. Comparative advantage determines the pattern of *interindustry* trade, in just the way that we examined in Chapters 2 through 5. Because of economies of scale, however, countries specialize within industries, giving rise to *intraindustry* trade that is additional to the trade that our earlier models would have predicted. The next question is what difference this extra trade makes.

The first point to make is that intraindustry trade will produce extra gains from international trade. This is because intraindustry trade creates a larger market. By engaging in intraindustry trade a country can simultaneously reduce the number of products it produces and increase the variety of goods available to domestic consumers. Suppose, for example, that two countries each produce 15 different models of automobile. If they trade automobiles with each other, each could reduce the number of models it produces to, say, 10, yet consumers would actually have a wider range of choice (20 models).

Each of these changes is an advantage. By producing fewer varieties, a country can produce each at larger scale and thus with higher productivity. At the same time, consumers benefit from the increased range of choice. As we will see from the example of the North American auto industry, the advantages of creating an integrated industry in two countries can be substantial.

In our earlier analysis of the distribution of gains from trade, in Chapters 3 and 4, we were pessimistic about the prospects that everyone will benefit from trade, even though potentially international trade could raise everyone's income. The reason was that in the models discussed there, trade had all its effects through a change in relative prices, and changes in relative prices have very strong effects on the distribution of income.

Suppose, however, that intraindustry trade is the dominant source of gains from trade. This will happen when countries are similar in their relative factor supplies, so that there is not much interindustry trade, and when scale economies and product differentiation are important, so that the gains from increased choice and larger scale are large. Then the income-distribution effects of trade will be small and there will be substantial extra gains from intraindustry trade. The result may well be that despite the effects of trade on income distribution, everyone gains from trade.

When will this be most likely to happen? Intraindustry trade will tend to be prevalent between countries that are similar in their capital-labor ratios, skill levels, and so on; this means that intraindustry trade will be important between countries at a similar level of economic development. The gains from this trade will be large when there are important economies of scale and products are highly differentiated, a situation more characteristic of sophisticated manufactured goods than of raw materials or more traditional sectors. The implication is that trade without serious income-distribution effects is most likely to happen in manufactures trade between advanced industrial countries.

This conclusion is borne out by postwar experience, particularly in Western Europe. In 1957 the major countries of continental Europe established a free trade area in manufactured goods, the Common Market, or European Economic Community (EEC). (The United Kingdom entered the EEC later, in 1973.) The result was a rapid growth of trade: trade within the EEC grew twice as fast as world trade as a whole during the 1960s. One might have expected this rapid growth in trade to produce substantial dislocations and political problems. As it turned out, however, the growth in trade was almost entirely a growth in intraindustry rather than interindustry trade. This meant that not much drastic economic change was called for. Instead of, say, workers in France's electrical machinery industry being hurt while those in Germany gained, workers in both sectors gained from the increased efficiency of the integrated European industry. The result was that the growth in trade within Europe presented far fewer social and political problems than anyone had anticipated.

There is both a good and a bad side to this favorable view of intraindustry trade. The good side is that under some circumstances trade is relatively easy to live with and therefore relatively easy to support politically. The bad side is that not all trade is like this. Trade between very different countries or where scale economies and product differentiation are not important remains politically problematic. In fact, the progressive liberalization of trade that, as we will see in Chapter 9, characterized the 30-year period from 1950 to 1980 was primarily concentrated on trade in manufactures among the advanced nations. If progress on other kinds of trade is important, the past record does not give us much encouragement.

Case Study INTRAINDUSTRY TRADE IN ACTION: THE NORTH AMERICAN AUTO PACT

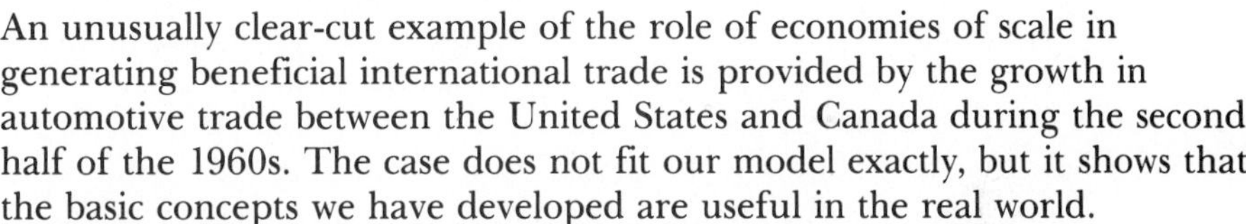

An unusually clear-cut example of the role of economies of scale in generating beneficial international trade is provided by the growth in automotive trade between the United States and Canada during the second half of the 1960s. The case does not fit our model exactly, but it shows that the basic concepts we have developed are useful in the real world.

Before 1965, tariff protection by Canada and the United States produced a Canadian auto industry that was largely self-sufficient, neither importing nor exporting much. The Canadian industry was controlled by the same firms as the U.S. industry—a departure from our model, since we have not yet examined the role of multinational firms—but these firms found it cheaper to have largely separate production systems than to pay the tariffs. Thus the Canadian industry was in effect a miniature version of the U.S. industry, at about one-tenth the scale.

The Canadian subsidiaries of U.S. firms found that small scale was a substantial disadvantage. Partly this was because Canadian plants had to be smaller than their U.S. counterparts. Perhaps more important, U.S. plants could often be "dedicated"—that is, devoted to producing a single model or component—while Canadian plants had to produce several different things, requiring the plants to shut down periodically to change over from one item to another, to hold larger inventories, to use less specialized machinery, and so on. The Canadian auto industry had a labor productivity about 30 percent lower than that of the United States.

In an effort to remove these problems, the United States and Canada agreed in 1964 to establish a free trade area in automobiles (subject to certain restrictions with which we need not concern ourselves). This allowed the auto companies to reorganize their production. Canadian subsidiaries of the auto firms sharply cut the number of products made in Canada. For example, General Motors cut the number of models assembled in Canada in half. The overall level of production and employment in Canada was, however, maintained. This was achieved by importing the products no longer made in Canada from the United States, and exporting the remaining products. In 1962, Canada exported 16 million dollars' worth of automotive products to the United States while importing 519 million dollars' worth. By 1968 the numbers were 2.4 and 2.9 billion dollars, respectively. In other words, both exports and imports increased sharply: intraindustry trade in action.

The gains seem to have been substantial. By the early 1970s the Canadian industry was comparable to the U.S. industry in productivity.

SUMMARY

1. Although our analysis in Chapters 2 through 5 was based on the assumption that international trade is based on comparative advantage, *economies of scale* can serve as an independent motivation for trade. This chapter derived some key insights about the role of scale economies in the international economy by examining two particular models of trade with *increasing returns.* First is the case of *external economies,* scale economies that apply at the level of the industry but not at the level of the firm. Second is the case of *monopolistic competition,* where entry of many firms into an industry eliminates monopoly profits. These two models together give us a number of suggestive conclusions about international trade.

2. Even when countries have the same technology and resources, economies of scale give rise to international trade. If one country starts with even slightly larger production in an industry subject to scale economies, this advantage will tend to snowball until at least one of the countries becomes specialized.

3. The pattern of trade generated by economies of scale is generally somewhat unpredictable. That is, more than one pattern of trade may be consistent with countries' underlying resources and technology. This unpredictability should be interpreted as giving a substantial role to history and accident in the detailed pattern of international trade.

4. Even though the pattern of trade is somewhat unpredictable, international trade based on scale economies is generally beneficial to all countries. The reason is that the concentration of production that results from trade raises productivity, increasing the purchasing power of countries' resources. These gains occur even for countries that lose increasing returns sectors as a result of trade.

5. The monopolistic competition model shows that trade based on scale economies can coexist with trade based on comparative advantage. We may distinguish between two kinds of trade. The first is *interindustry trade,* which is

based on comparative advantage. The second is *intraindustry trade,* which is based on economies of scale. Intraindustry trade happens because, with economies of scale, each country produces only a limited range of products within an industry. Thus countries produce different goods within industries and import some even as they are exporting others.

6. The relative importance of intraindustry trade and interindustry trade depends on the similarity of countries. If countries are similar in their resources and their technology, their trade will typically be intraindustry in character. Intraindustry trade will persist even between countries that are identical in their resources.

7. Intraindustry trade produces extra gains over and above those from interindustry trade. These gains take the form of increased scale of production, which raises productivity, and an increased range of choice for consumers.

8. When there are large gains from intraindustry trade and not too much interindustry trade, the gains from a larger market can outweigh the income-distribution effects we analyzed in Chapters 3 and 4. This is most likely to happen in trade in manufactured goods between the advanced countries, and this is in fact where most of the successful trade liberalization of the past 40 years has been concentrated.

KEY TERMS

economies of scale
increasing returns
external economies
monopolistic competition
imperfect competition
marginal revenue
marginal cost
differentiated products
intraindustry trade
interindustry trade

PROBLEMS

1. Suppose that there are three countries, America, Britain, and Canada, and three goods, xylophones, yttrium, and zebras. Each country has only one factor of production, labor. Xylophones and yttrium are produced with external economies, while zebras are not.

Assume that because of the external economies the production of xylophones will always end up concentrated in only one country, and the same is true of yttrium. What are the possible patterns of specialization and trade?

2. How would you evaluate the relative importance of economies of scale and comparative advantage in causing the following?

a) Most of the world's aluminum smelting takes place in Norway and Canada.

b) Half of the world's large jet aircraft are assembled in Seattle.

c) Most semiconductors are manufactured either in the United States or in Japan.

d) Most Scotch whiskey comes from Scotland.

e) Much of the world's best wine comes from France.

3. Home and Foreign both produce fish and chips with labor the only factor of production. Each country has a labor force of 100. The unit labor requirement in fish production is 1 in both countries. The unit labor requirement in chips production takes the following form:

$$a_{LC} = 1 + 20/Q_C.$$

In the absence of trade each country produces 20 units of chips. After trade one of the countries produces 60 units of chips, while the other country produces none.

a) Calculate the output of fish in each country in the absence of trade, and the real wage of labor in terms of both goods.

b) Calculate the output of fish in each country after trade, and the real wage of labor in terms of each good.

c) Have both countries gained from trade? Relate the result to the criterion for gain given in the text.

4. In a monopolistically competitive industry, the average cost curve of a typical firm is $AC = 1 + 20/Q$. Before trade is opened, the demand curve facing each firm is $Q = 60 - 20P$. After trade, the demand curve is $Q = 105 - 45P$.

a) Graph the average cost curve and the pre- and posttrade demand curves. Show that each demand curve corresponds to a zero-profit equilibrium.

b) Find the price and output per firm before and after trade.

5. Normally an increase in the variety of products available to consumers will make their demand curve for each product flatter, but this is not always the case. Analyze the effects of increasing the size of the market on consumers when the slope of the demand curve for each product does *not* change. Does this eliminate any scale economy gains from trade?

6. There is serious discussion of the possibility of free trade between the United States and Canada; on the other hand, despite large potential gains, free trade between the United States and Mexico is not politically realistic. Explain why in terms of the theory of intraindustry trade.

FURTHER READING

Bela Balassa. *Trade Liberalization among Industrial Countries.* New York: McGraw-Hill, 1967. A clear discussion of different sources of gains from trade, and an informal exposition of the role of economies of scale.

Herbert Grubel and Peter Lloyd. *Intra-Industry Trade.* New York: John Wiley and Sons, 1975. A discussion of the role of intraindustry trade backed by extensive data.

Elhanan Helpman and Paul Krugman. *Market Structure and Foreign Trade: Increasing Returns, Imperfect Competition, and the International Economy.* Cambridge: MIT Press, 1985. A technical presentation of new models of international trade.

Henryk Kierzkowski, ed. *Monopolistic Competition in International Trade.* Oxford: Clarendon Press, 1984. The monopolistic competition model of trade and other formal treatments of increasing returns have been the subject of extensive research since the late 1970s. Many of the leading researchers have papers in this volume.

Staffan Burenstam Linder. *An Essay on Trade and Transformation.* New York: John Wiley and Sons, 1961. An early and influential statement of the view that trade in manufactures among advanced countries reflects forces other than comparative advantage.

APPENDIX TO CHAPTER 6

Price Discrimination and Dumping in International Markets

Most of the time, firms charge all their customers the same price, regardless of whether they are domestic or foreign. In imperfectly competitive markets, however, firms will sometimes charge a different price for a good when that good is exported than they charge for the same good when it is sold domestically. In general, when a firm charges different customers different prices, we describe this as price discrimination. The most common form of price discrimination in international trade is where a firm sells at a lower price on export markets than it does at home; charging a lower price for exports than on domestic sales is known as *dumping*.

Dumping can occur only if two conditions are met. First, the industry must be imperfectly competitive, so that firms set prices rather than taking market prices as given. Second, markets must be *segmented:* it must not be easy for domestic residents to purchase goods intended for export.

Given these conditions, a monopolistic firm may find that it is profitable to engage in dumping. Figure 6A-1 shows an industry in which there is a single monopolistic domestic firm. The firm sells on two markets: a domestic market, where it faces the demand curve *D*, and an export market. In the export market the firm can sell as much as it wants at the price P_X. We assume that the firm can charge a higher price on domestic sales than on exports without consumers diverting export sales to domestic use.

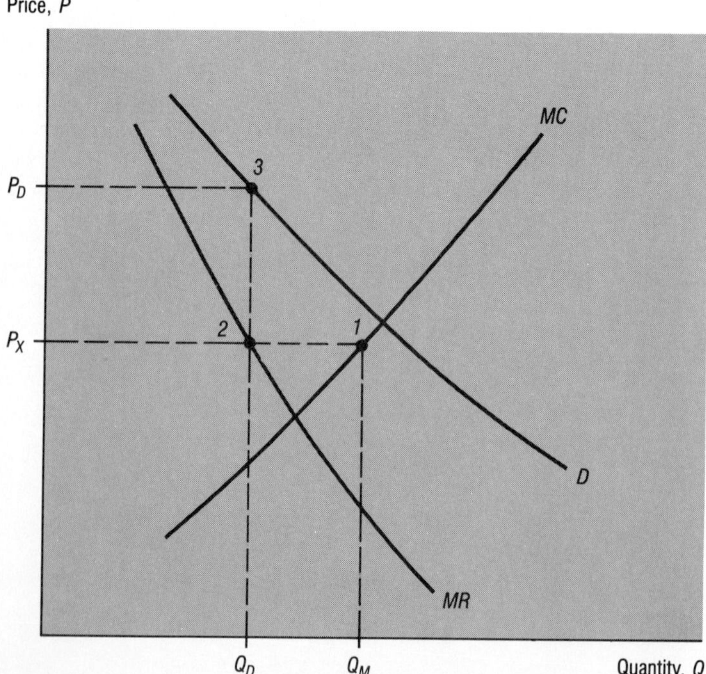

FIGURE 6A-1 Dumping by a monopolistic firm. The firm sets marginal cost equal to the export price P_X (point 1), while setting it equal to marginal revenue at home (point 2). The result is that the domestic price P_D exceeds the export price (point 3).

To maximize profits, the firm must set marginal revenue equal to marginal cost in *each* market. Marginal revenue on domestic sales is defined by the curve MR, which lies below D. Export sales take place at a constant price P_X; so the marginal revenue from an additional unit exported is just P_X. The solution that sets marginal cost equal to marginal revenue in both markets is to produce the quantity Q_M (point 1), to sell Q_D on the domestic market (point 2), and to export $Q_M - Q_D$. The cost of producing an additional unit in this case is equal to P_X, the marginal revenue from exports, which in turn is equal to marginal revenue from domestic sales.

The domestic price is P_D, above the export price (point 3). Thus the firm is indeed dumping, selling more cheaply abroad than at home.

The basic reason why dumping is profitable in this case is the difference in the market conditions that the firm faces for exports and domestic sales. Increased exports, we have assumed, do not depress the price; so marginal revenue and price coincide on the export market. Domestically, by contrast, increased sales do lower the price. This is an extreme example of the general condition for price discrimination presented in microeconomics courses: firms will price-discriminate when they face a more elastic demand in one market than in another. (In this case we have assumed that export demand is infinitely elastic.)

Dumping is widely regarded as an unfair practice in international competition. There is no good economic justification for regarding dumping as particularly harmful, but U.S. trade law prohibits foreign firms from dumping in our market and automatically imposes tariffs when such dumping is discovered.[1]

Reverse dumping is the situation where a firm charges more for export sales than for domestic sales. A notable example of reverse dumping occurred for European luxury automobiles in 1984 and 1985. When the dollar rose sharply against European currencies, European manufacturers such as Volvo and Mercedes chose not to cut their U.S. prices, even though the equivalent dollar price of their cars in Europe had dropped a great deal. Thus a Mercedes could be bought in Germany for as much as 40 percent less than it cost in the United States. The gap was so large that many buyers started purchasing cars in Europe and shipping them to the United States themselves. The situation probably could not have gone on forever, but it was eventually resolved through a decline in the dollar rather than a change in pricing policy.

[1]Actually, U.S. law offers some alternative definitions of dumping, such as selling below cost. The economic justification for these alternative definitions is unclear, however, and not much can be said about them analytically.

7 INTERNATIONAL FACTOR MOVEMENTS

Up to this point we have concerned ourselves entirely with international *trade.* That is, we have focused on the causes and effects of international exchanges of goods and services. Movement of goods and services is not, however, the only form of international integration. This chapter is concerned with another form of integration, international movements of factors of production, or **factor movements.** Factor movements include labor migration, the transfer of capital via international borrowing and lending, and the subtle international linkages involved in the formation of multinational corporations.

The principles of international factor movement do not differ in their essentials from those underlying international trade in goods. Both international borrowing and lending and international labor migration can be thought of as analogous in their causes and effects to the movement of goods we analyzed in Chapters 2 through 5. The role of the multinational corporation may be understood by extending some of the concepts we developed in Chapter 6. So when we turn from trade in goods and services to factor movements we do not make a radical shift in emphasis.

Although there is a fundamental economic similarity between trade and factor movements, however, there are major differences in the political context. A labor-abundant country may under some circumstances import capital-intensive goods, under other circumstances acquire capital by borrowing abroad. A capital-abundant country may import labor-intensive goods or begin employing migrant workers. A country that is too small to support firms of efficient size may import goods where large firms have an advantage or allow those goods to be produced locally by subsidiaries of foreign firms. In each case the alternative strategies may be similar in their purely economic consequences but radically different in their political acceptability.

On the whole, international factor movement tends to raise even more political difficulties than international trade. Thus factor movements are subject to more restriction than trade in goods. Immigration restrictions are universal. Controls on capital movements are often present between pairs of countries, such as France and Germany, that have virtually free trade in goods with each other. Investment by foreign-based multinational corporations is regarded with suspicion and tightly regulated through much of the world. The result is that factor movements are probably less important in practice than trade in goods, which is why we took an analysis of trade in the absence of factor movements as our starting point. Nonetheless, factor movements are very important, and it is valuable to spend a chapter on their analysis.

This chapter is in three parts. We begin with a simple model of international labor mobility. We then proceed to an analysis of international borrowing and lending, in which we show that this lending can be interpreted as trade *over time:* the lending country gives up resources now in order to receive repayment in the future, while the borrower does the reverse. Finally, the last section of the chapter analyzes multinational corporations.

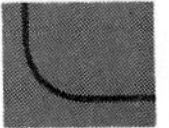

INTERNATIONAL LABOR MOBILITY

A ONE-GOOD MODEL WITHOUT FACTOR MOBILITY

As in the analysis of trade, the best way to understand factor mobility is to begin with a world that is not economically integrated, then examine what happens when international transactions are allowed. Let's assume that we have, as usual, a two-country world consisting of Home and Foreign, each with two factors of production, land and labor. We assume for the moment, however, that this world is even simpler than the one we examined in Chapter 4, in that the two countries produce only *one* good, which we will simply refer to as "output." Thus there is no scope for ordinary trade, the exchange of different goods, in this world. The only way for these economies to become integrated with each other is via a movement of either land or labor. Land almost by definition cannot move; so this is a model of integration via international labor mobility.

Before we introduce factor movements, however, let us analyze the determinants of the level of output in each country. Land and labor are the only scarce resources. Thus the output of each country will depend, other things equal, on the quantity of these factors available. The relationship between the supplies of factors on one side and the output of the economy on the other is referred to as the economy's production function.

We have already encountered the idea of a production function in Chapter 3. As we noted there, a useful way to look at the production function is to ask how output depends on the supply of one factor of production, holding the quantity of the other factor fixed. This is done in Figure 7-1, which shows how a country's output varies as its employment of labor is varied, holding fixed the supply of land; the figure is the same as Figure 3-7. The slope of the production function measures the increase in output that would be gained by using a little more labor and is thus referred to as the *marginal product of labor.* As the curve is drawn in Figure 7-1, the marginal product of labor is assumed to fall as the ratio of labor to land rises. This is the normal case: as a country seeks to employ more labor on a given amount of land, it must move to increasingly labor-intensive techniques of production, and this will normally become increasingly difficult the farther the substitution of labor for land goes.

Figure 7-2, corresponding to Figure 3-8, contains the same information as Figure 7-1 but plots it in a different way. We now show directly how the marginal product of labor depends on the quantity of labor employed. We also indicate on the diagram that the real wage earned by each unit of labor is equal to labor's marginal product. This will be true as long as the economy is perfectly competitive, which we assume to be the case.

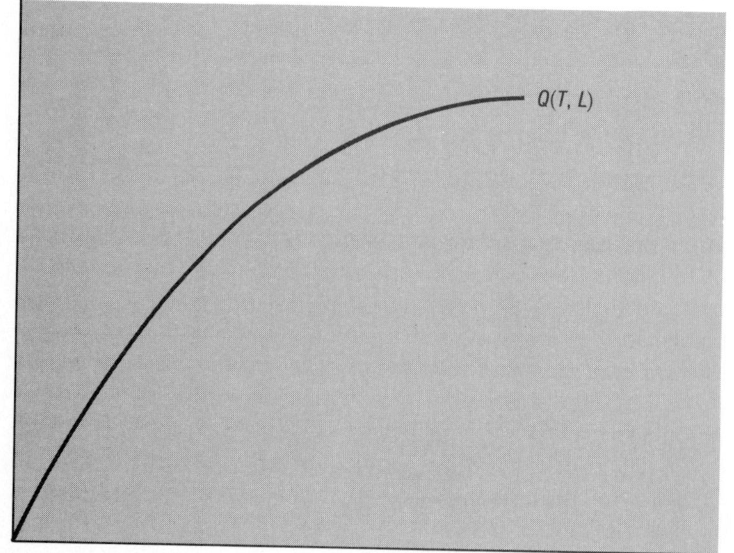

FIGURE 7-1 An economy's production function. The larger the supply of labor, the larger is output; however, the marginal product of labor declines as more workers are employed.

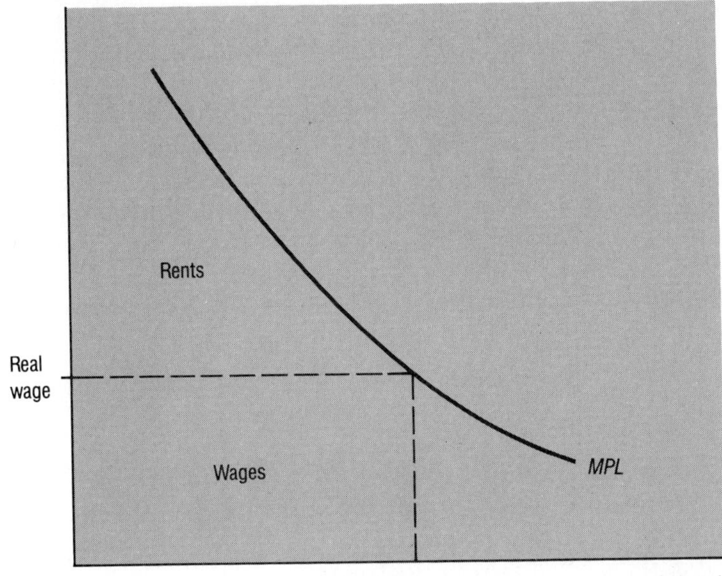

FIGURE 7-2 The marginal product of labor. The marginal product of labor declines with employment. The area under the marginal product curve equals total output.

What about the income earned by land? As we showed in the appendix to Chapter 3, the total output of the economy can be measured by the area under the marginal product curve. Of that total output, wages equal the real wage rate times the employment of labor, and hence equal the indicated area on the figure. The remainder, also shown, equals rents earned by landowners.

Assume that Home and Foreign have the same technology but different overall land-labor ratios. If Home is the labor-abundant country, workers in Home will earn less than those in Foreign, while land in Home earns more than in Foreign. This obviously creates an incentive for factors of production to move. Home workers would like to move to Foreign; Foreign landowners would also like to move their land to Home, but we are supposing that this is impossible. Our next step is to allow workers to move and see what happens.

INTERNATIONAL LABOR MOVEMENT

Now suppose that workers are able to move between our two countries. Workers will move from Home to Foreign. This movement will reduce the Home labor force and thus raise the real wage in Home, while increasing the labor force and reducing the real wage in Foreign. If there are no obstacles to labor movement, this process will continue until the marginal product of labor is the same in the two countries.

Figure 7-3 illustrates the causes and effects of international labor mobility. The horizontal axis represents the total world labor force. The workers employed in Home are measured from the left, the workers employed in Foreign from the right. On the vertical axis is shown the marginal product of labor in each country. Initially we assume that there are OL^1 workers in Home, L^1O* workers in Foreign. Given this allocation, the real wage rate would be lower in Home than in Foreign. If workers can move freely to whichever country offers the higher real wage, they will move from Home to Foreign until the real wage rates are equalized. The eventual distribution of the world's labor force will be one with OL^2 workers in Home, L^2O* workers in Foreign.

Three points should be noted about this redistribution of the world's labor force.

1. It leads to a convergence of real wage rates. Real wages rise in Home, fall in Foreign.
2. It increases the world's output as a whole. Foreign's output rises by the area under its marginal product curve from L^1 to L^2, while Home's falls by the corresponding area under its marginal product curve. We see from the figure that Foreign's gain is larger than Home's loss, by an amount equal to the shaded area in the figure.

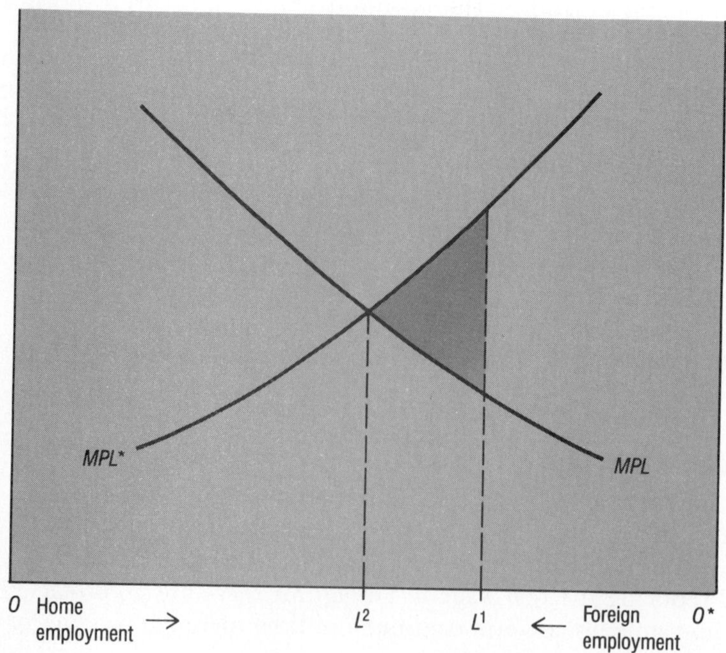

FIGURE 7-3 Causes and effects of international labor mobility. Initially OL^1 workers are employed in Home, while L^1O* workers are employed in Foreign. Labor migrates from Home to Foreign until OL^2 workers are employed in Home, L^2O* in Foreign, and wages are equalized.

3. Despite this gain, some people are hurt by the change. Those who would originally have worked in Home receive higher real wages, but those who would originally have worked in Foreign receive lower real wages. Landowners in Foreign benefit from the larger labor supply, but landowners in Home are made worse off. As in the case of the gains from international trade, then, international labor mobility, while allowing everyone to be made better off in principle, leaves some groups worse off in practice.

EXTENDING THE ANALYSIS

We have just seen that a very simple model tells us quite a lot about both why international factor movements occur and what effects they have. Labor mobility in our simple model, like trade in the model of Chapter 4, is driven by international differences in resources; also like trade, it is beneficial in the sense that it increases world production yet is associated with strong income-distribution effects that make those gains problematic.

To conclude this basic analysis, we consider briefly how the analysis is modified when we add some of the complications we have assumed away.

The most important extension is to remove the assumption that the two countries produce only one good. Suppose, then, that the countries produce two goods, one more labor-intensive than the other. What we already know from our discussion of the factor-proportions model in Chapter 4 is that in this case trade offers an alternative to factor mobility. Home can in a sense export labor and import land by exporting the labor-intensive good and importing the land-intensive good. It is possible in principle for such trade to lead to a complete equalization of factor prices without any need for factor mobility. If this happened, it would of course remove any incentive for labor to move from Home to Foreign.

In practice, while trade is indeed a substitute for international factor movement, it is not a perfect substitute. The reasons are those we have already summarized in Chapter 4 as reasons why complete factor price equalization is not observed in the real world. Countries are sometimes too different in their resources to remain unspecialized; there are barriers to trade, both natural and artificial, and there are differences in technology as well as resources between countries.

We might wonder on the other side whether factor movements do not remove the incentive for international trade. Again the answer is that while in a simple model movement of factors of production can make international trade in goods unnecessary, in practice there are substantial barriers to free movement of labor, capital, and other potentially mobile resources. And some resources cannot be brought together—Canadian forests and Caribbean sunshine cannot migrate.

Extending the simple model of factor mobility, then, does not change its fundamental message. The main point is that trade in factors is in purely

INTERNATIONAL LABOR MOBILITY IN PRACTICE: "GUEST WORKERS" IN EUROPE

The great age of international labor mobility was the late nineteenth and early twentieth centuries, when tens of millions of workers moved from Europe to North and South America, and millions of Indians and Chinese emigrated to Africa, the West Indies, and Southeast Asia. Since 1920, great movements of population have been limited by immigration restrictions, and most large population shifts have been political consequences of war and civil strife. A major example of economically based migration, however, has been the mobility of labor within Europe. From the 1950s to the mid-1970s the affluent countries of Western Europe attracted about 30 million workers from the less prosperous areas to the south and southeast: Portugal, Spain, southern Italy, Yugoslavia, Greece, Turkey, North Africa. These so-called guest workers often stayed only temporarily and left their families behind in their home countries.

The guest worker phenomenon illustrates both the potential benefits and the problems raised by international labor mobility. By migrating, workers were able to earn much more—sometimes ten times more—than they could have earned at home. During the 1960s and early 1970s, with the Western European economies at near-full employment, the availability of migrant workers helped to keep growth in Europe from being constrained by labor supply. Although a simple model suggests that West European workers would have been better off without competition from immigrants, by and large immigrants ended up in low-skill jobs that domestic workers were not anxious to take.

Even during the period of rapid growth, however, migration raised serious social and political issues. Guest workers inevitably came to constitute a sort of second-class citizenry in their host countries, especially in Switzerland, where by the early 1970s they were one-third of the labor force. Inevitably, the position of migrants as hewers of wood and drawers of water for wealthier societies produces feelings of bitterness and inferiority, well dramatized in the movie *Bread and Chocolate.* The Swiss author Max Frisch wrote, "We asked for workers, but human beings came." With the slowdown in European growth after 1973, many foreign workers left Western Europe.

economic terms very much like trade in goods, occurring for much the same reasons and producing similar results.

INTERNATIONAL BORROWING AND LENDING

International movements of capital are a prominent feature of the international economic landscape. It is tempting to analyze these movements in a way parallel to our analysis of labor mobility, and this is sometimes a useful exercise. There are some important differences, however. When we speak of international labor mobility, it is clear that workers are physically moving from one country to another. International capital movements are not so simple. When we speak of capital flows from the United States to Mexico, we do not mean that U.S. machines are literally being unbolted and shipped south. We are instead talking of a *financial* transaction. A U.S. bank lends to a Mexican firm, or U.S. residents buy stock in Mexico, or a U.S. firm invests through its Mexican subsidiary. We focus for now on the first type of transaction, in which U.S. residents make loans to Mexicans—that is, the U.S. residents grant Mexicans the right to spend more than they earn today in return for a promise to repay in the future.

The full analysis of financial aspects of the international economy is the subject of the second half of this book. It is important to realize, however, that financial transactions do not exist simply on paper. They have real consequences. International borrowing and lending, in particular, can be interpreted as a kind of international trade. The trade is not of one good for another at a point in time but of goods today for goods in the future. This kind of trade is known as **intertemporal trade;** we will have much more to say about it in the second half of this book, but for present purposes a simple model will be sufficient to make our point.[1]

INTERTEMPORAL PRODUCTION POSSIBILITIES AND TRADE

Even in the absence of international capital movements, any economy faces a trade-off between consumption now and consumption in the future. Economies usually do not consume all of their current output; some of their output takes the form not of current consumption but of investment in machines, buildings, and other forms of productive capital. The more investment an economy undertakes now, the more it will be able to produce and consume in the future. In order to invest more, however, an economy must release resources by consuming less (unless there are unemployed resources, a possibility we temporarily disregard). Thus there is a trade-off between current and future consumption.

Let's imagine an economy that consumes only one good and will exist for only two periods, which we will call present and future. Then there will be a trade-off between present and future production of the consumption good, which we can summarize by drawing an **intertemporal production possibility frontier.** Such a frontier is illustrated in Figure 7-4. It looks just like the production possibility frontiers we have been drawing between two goods at a point in time.

The shape of the intertemporal production possibility frontier will differ among countries. Some countries will have production possibilities that are biased toward present output, while others are biased toward future output.

[1]The appendix to this chapter contains a more detailed examination of the model developed in this section.

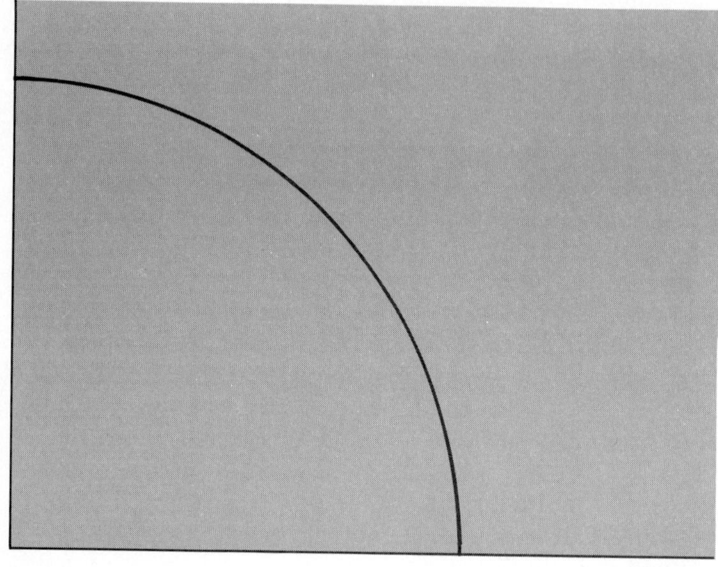

FIGURE 7-4 The intertemporal production possibility frontier. A country can trade off current for future consumption in the same way that it can produce more of one good by producing less of another.

We will try to ask what real differences these biases correspond to in a moment, but first let's simply suppose that there are two countries, Home and Foreign, with different intertemporal production possibilities. Home's possibilities are biased toward current consumption, while Foreign's are biased toward future consumption.

Reasoning by analogy, we already know what to expect. In the absence of international borrowing and lending, we would expect the relative price of future consumption to be higher in Home than in Foreign, and thus if we open the possibility of trade over time, we would expect Home to export present consumption and import future consumption.

This may, however, seem a little puzzling. What is the relative price of future consumption, and how does one trade over time?

The answer to the second question is that a country, like an individual, can trade over time by borrowing or lending. Consider what happens when an individual borrows: she is initially able to spend more than her income, or in other words to consume more than her production. Later, however, she must repay the loan with interest, and therefore in the future she consumes *less* than she produces. By borrowing, then, she has in effect traded future consumption for current consumption. The same is true of a borrowing country.

Clearly the price of future consumption in terms of present has something to do with the interest rate. As we will see in the second half of this book, in the real world the interpretation of interest rates is complicated by the possibility of changes in the overall price level. Let's bypass that problem for now by supposing that loan contracts are specified in "real" terms: when a country borrows, it gets the right to purchase some quantity of consumption in present in return for repayment of some larger quantity in future. Specifically, the quantity of repayment in future will be $(1 + r)$ times the quantity borrowed in present. Then r is the **real interest rate** on borrowing. And it is clear also that, since the trade-off is one unit of consumption in present for $(1 + r)$ units in future, the relative price of future consumption is $1/(1 + r)$.

The parallel with our standard trade model is now complete. If borrowing and lending are allowed, the relative price of future consumption, and thus the world real interest rate, will be determined by the world relative supply and demand for future consumption. Home, whose intertemporal production possibilities are biased toward present consumption, will export present consumption and import future consumption. That is, Home will lend to Foreign in the first period and receive repayment in the second.

We have assumed that Home's intertemporal production possibilities are biased toward present production. But what does this mean? The sources of intertemporal comparative advantage are somewhat different from those which give rise to ordinary trade.

A country that has a comparative advantage in future production of consumption goods is one that in the absence of international borrowing and lending would have a high real interest rate. This high real interest rate corresponds to a high return on investment—that is, a high return to diverting resources from current production of consumption goods to production of capital goods, construction, and other activities that enhance the economy's future ability to produce. So countries that borrow in the international market will be those where highly productive investment opportunities are available relative to current productive capacity, while countries that lend will be those where such opportunities are not available domestically.

The pattern of international borrowing and lending in the 1970s illustrates the point. Table 20-2 (p. 597) compares the international lending of three groups of countries: industrial countries, non-oil developing countries, and major oil exporters. From 1973 to 1981, the oil exporters lent \$384 billion, the less-developed countries borrowed \$409 billion, and the industrial countries borrowed a much smaller amount, \$64 billion. In the light of our model, this is not surprising. During the 1970s, as a result of a spectacular increase in oil prices, oil exporters like Saudi Arabia found themselves with very high current income. They did not, however, find any comparable increase in their domestic investment opportunities. With small populations, limited resources other than oil, and little expertise in industrial or other production, their natural reaction was to invest much of their increased earnings abroad. By contrast, rapidly developing countries such as Brazil and Korea expected to have much higher incomes in the future and saw highly productive investment opportunities in their growing industrial sectors.

DIRECT FOREIGN INVESTMENT AND MULTINATIONAL FIRMS

In the last section we focused on international borrowing and lending. This is a relatively simple transaction, in that the borrower makes no demands on the lender other than that of repayment. An important part of international capital movement, however, takes a different form, that of **direct foreign investment.** By direct foreign investment we mean international capital flows in which a firm in one country creates or expands a subsidiary in another. The distinctive feature of direct foreign investment is that it involves not only a transfer of resources but also the acquisition of *control.* That is, the subsidiary does not simply have a financial obligation to the parent company; it is part of the same organizational structure.

Multinational firms are often a vehicle for international borrowing and lending. Parent companies often provide their foreign subsidiaries with capital, in the expectation of eventual repayment. To the extent that multinational firms provide financing to their foreign subsidiaries, direct foreign investment is an alternative way of accomplishing the same things as international lending. This still leaves open the question, however, of why direct investment rather than some other way of transferring funds is chosen. In any case, the existence of multinational firms does not necessarily reflect a net capital flow from one country to another. Multinationals sometimes raise money for the expansion of their subsidiaries in the country where the subsidiary operates rather than in their home country. Furthermore, there is a good deal of two-way foreign direct investment among industrial countries: U.S. firms expanding their European subsidiaries at the same time that European firms expand their U.S. subsidiaries, for example.

The point is that while multinational firms sometimes act as a vehicle for international capital flows, it is probably a mistake to view direct foreign investment as primarily an alternative way for countries to borrow and lend. Instead, the main point of direct foreign investment is to allow the formation of multinational organizations. That is, it is the extension of control that is the essential purpose.

But why do firms seek to extend control? We should admit at the outset that economists do not have as fully worked out a theory of multinational enterprise as they do of many other issues in international economics. There is some theory on the subject, however, which we now review.

THE THEORY OF MULTINATIONAL ENTERPRISE

The basic necessary elements of a theory of multinational firms can be seen most clearly if we look at an example. Consider the Mexican auto industry. In terms of production Mexico is largely self-sufficient in automobiles, assembling nearly all the cars sold there and producing most of the components for those cars as well. The firms that produce the autos, however, are subsidiaries of major U.S. automakers. This arrangement is familiar, but we should realize that there are two obvious alternatives. On one side, instead of producing in Mexico the U.S. firms could produce in the United States and export to Mexico. On the other side, firms owned and controlled by residents of Mexico could produce automobiles. Why, then, do we have this particular arrangement, in which the *same* firms produce in *different* countries?

The modern theory of multinational enterprise starts by making a distinction between the two questions of which this larger question is composed. First, why is a good produced in two (or more) different countries rather than one? This is know as the question of **location**. Second, why is production in different locations done by the same firm rather than by separate firms? This is known, for reasons that will become apparent in a moment, as the question of **internalization**. We need a theory of location to explain why Mexico does not import its automobiles from the United States; we need a theory of internalization to explain why Mexico's auto industry is not independently controlled.

Now the theory of location is not a difficult one in principle. It is, in fact, just the theory of trade that we developed in Chapters 2 through 6. The location of production is often determined by resources. Aluminum mining must be located where the bauxite is, aluminum smelting near cheap electricity. Minicomputer manufacturers locate their skill-intensive design facilities in Massachusetts or northern California, their labor-intensive assembly plants in Ireland or Singapore. Alternatively, transport costs and other barriers to trade may determine location. The Mexican auto industry exists in large part because of import quotas and other protective measures that limit imports. The point is that the factors that determine a multinational corporation's decisions about where to produce are probably not much different from those which determine the pattern of trade in general.

The theory of internalization is another matter. Why not have independent auto companies in Mexico? We may note first that there are always important transactions between a multinational's operations in different countries. The output of one subsidiary is often an input into the production of another. Or technology developed in one country may be used in others. Or management may usefully coordinate the activities of plants in several countries. These transactions are what tie the multinational firm together, and the firm presumably exists so as to facilitate these transactions. But international transactions need not be carried out inside a firm. Components can be sold in an open market, and technology can be licensed to other firms. Multinationals exist because it turns out to be more profitable to carry out these transactions within a firm rather than between firms. This is why the motive for multinationals is referred to as "internalization."

We have defined a concept, but we have not yet explained what gives rise to internalization. Why are some transactions more profitably conducted within a firm rather than between firms? Here there are a variety of theories, none as well grounded either in theory or in evidence as our theories of location. We may note two influential views, however, about why activities in different countries may usefully be integrated in a single firm.

The first view stresses the advantages of internalization for **technology transfer.** Technology, broadly defined as any kind of economically useful knowledge, can sometimes be sold or licensed. There are important difficulties in doing this, however. Often the technology involved in, say, running a factory has never been written down; it is embodied in the knowledge of a group of individuals and cannot be packaged and sold. Also, it is difficult for a prospective buyer to know how much knowledge is worth—if the buyer knew as much as the seller, there would be no need to buy! Finally, property rights in knowledge are often hard to establish. If a European firm licenses technology to a U.S. firm, other U.S. firms may legally imitate that technology. All these problems may be reduced if a firm, instead of selling technology, sets about capturing the returns in other countries by setting up foreign subsidiaries.

The second view stresses the advantages of internalization for **vertical integration.** If one firm (the "upstream" firm) produces a good that is used as an input for another firm (the "downstream" firm), a number of problems can result. For one thing, if each has a monopoly position, they may get into a conflict as the downstream firm tries to hold the price down while the upstream firm tries to raise it. There may be problems of coordination if demand or supply is uncertain. Finally, a fluctuating price may impose excessive risk on one or the other party. Again, if the upstream and downstream firms are combined into a single "vertically integrated" firm, these problems may be avoided or at least reduced.

It should be clear that these views are by no means as rigorously worked out as the analysis of trade that we have carried out elsewhere in this book. The unfortunate fact is that the economic theory of organizations—which is really what we are talking about when we try to develop a theory of multinational corporations—is still in its infancy. What makes this particularly unfortunate is that multinationals are a subject of heated controversy in practice.

MULTINATIONAL FIRMS IN PRACTICE

Multinational firms play an important part in world trade and investment. For example, about half of U.S. imports are transactions between "related parties." By this we mean that the buyer and the seller are to a significant extent owned and presumably controlled by the same firm. Thus half of U.S. imports can be regarded as transactions between branches of multinational firms. At the same time, 24 percent of U.S. assets abroad consists of the value of foreign subsidiaries of U.S. firms. So U.S. trade and investment, while not dominated by multinational firms, are to an important extent conducted by such firms. Presumably the same is true of other countries as well.

The important question, however, is what difference multinationals make. Since we have only a limited understanding of why multinationals ex-

FOREIGN DIRECT INVESTMENT IN THE UNITED STATES

Until recently, the United States was almost always thought of as a "home" country for multinational enterprises rather than a "host" country for foreign-based multinationals. To a large extent the political battle lines on multinationals continue to be drawn as if this were still the case. The U.S. government defends the role of multinational enterprise against foreign countries who fear economic domination by U.S. firms; U.S. labor groups condemn multinational firms for exporting U.S. jobs.

In reality, however, the United States has started to become as much a target as a source of direct foreign investment. Since 1981, investments by foreign firms in the United States have consistently exceeded investments by U.S. firms abroad. Examples of foreign control of U.S. firms have become increasingly common—for example, the Japanese firm Honda manufactures automobiles in Ohio. In some cases consumers have gotten used to the idea of buying foreign goods but are now, without knowing it, often buying goods made here. Japanese exports of color televisions to the United States actually peaked in 1976, and since 1978 more Japanese TV sets have been made in the United States than were imported (more than twice as many in 1985).

Why are foreign firms coming to the United States? As we have stressed, we need to understand both why goods are produced in the United States and why foreign firms rather than U.S. firms produce them. The explanations of the location decision seem complicated. One explanation is a shift in relative costs; U.S. wages, which used to be the highest in the world, are not so high any longer—at the exchange rates of early 1987 they were lower than German wages and not much higher than Japanese wages. Another explanation is fear of protectionism: foreign firms, especially Japanese firms, were setting up production in the United States either in anticipation of import quotas or in order to buy off protectionist sentiment by providing jobs in the United States. As for why foreign rather than U.S. firms were doing the producing, it seems that foreign firms now often believe that they have superior technology or management technique that allows them to produce more efficiently than local U.S. competitors.

The interesting question is how the United States will react to a growing foreign role in our economy. Will we start to worry about losing our national sovereignty to foreigners? Will the same U.S. officials who ridiculed Third World complaints about multinationals dust off those arguments and use them against the Japanese?*

*While this book was in production, political pressure led the Japanese multinational Fujitsu to abandon its plans to acquire Fairchild Semiconductor, suggesting that the U.S. backlash against foreign-owned firms has already begun.

ist, this is a hard question to answer. Nonetheless, the existing theory suggests some preliminary answers.

The first point to notice is that much of what multinationals do could be done without multinationals, although perhaps not as easily. Two examples are the shift of labor-intensive production from industrial countries to labor-abundant nations, and capital flows from capital-abundant countries to capital-scarce countries. Multinational firms are sometimes the agents of these changes and are therefore either praised or condemned for their actions (depending on the commentator's point of view). But these shifts reflect the "location" aspect of our theory of multinationals, which is really no different from ordinary trade theory. If multinationals were not there, the same things would still happen, though perhaps not to the same extent. This observation leads international economists as a group to attribute less significance to multinational enterprise than most lay observers.

The second point to notice is that in a broad sense what multinational corporations do, by creating organizations that extend across national boundaries, is similar to the effects of trade and simple factor mobility; that is, it is a form of international economic integration. By analogy with the other forms of international integration we have studied, we would expect multinational enterprise to produce overall gains but to produce income-distribution effects that are strong enough that some people are made worse off. These income-distribution effects are probably mostly effects *within* rather than *between* countries.

The upshot of this discussion is that multinational corporations probably are not as important a factor in the world economy as their visibility would suggest, and that their role is neither more nor less likely to be beneficial than other international linkages. This does not, however, prevent them from being cast in the role of villains or (more rarely) heroes, as we will see in our discussion of trade and development in Chapter 10.

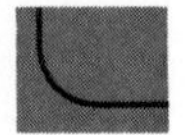

SUMMARY

1. International *factor movements* can sometimes substitute for trade. So it is not surprising that international migration of labor is similar in its causes and effects to international trade based on differences in resources. Labor moves from countries where it is abundant to countries where it is scarce. This movement raises total world output, but it also generates strong income-distribution effects, so that some groups are hurt.

2. International borrowing and lending can be viewed as a kind of international trade, but one that involves trade of present consumption for future consumption rather than trade of one good for another. The relative price at which this *intertemporal trade* takes place is one plus the *real rate of interest.*

3. Multinational firms, while they often serve as vehicles for international borrowing and lending, primarily exist as ways of extending control over ac-

tivities taking place in two or more different countries. The theory of multinational firms is not as well developed as other parts of international economics. A basic framework can be set out, however, that stresses two crucial elements in explaining the existence of a multinational: a *location* motive that leads the activities of the firm to be in different countries, and an *internalization* motive that leads these activities to be integrated in a single firm.

4. The location motives of multinationals are the same as those behind all international trade. The internalization motives are less well understood; current theory points to two main motives, the need for a way to *transfer technology* and the advantages in some cases of *vertical integration.*

KEY TERMS

factor movement

intertemporal trade

intertemporal production possibility frontier

real interest rate

direct foreign investment

location and internalization motives of multinationals

technology transfer

vertical integration

PROBLEMS

1. In Home and Foreign there are two factors of production, land and labor, used to produce only one good. The land supply in each country, and the technology of production, are exactly the same. The marginal product of labor in each country depends on employment as follows:

Number of workers employed	Marginal product of last worker
1	20
2	19
3	18
4	17
5	16
6	15
7	14
8	13
9	12
10	11
11	10

Initially, there are 11 workers employed in Home, but only 3 workers in Foreign.

Find the effect of free movement of labor from Home to Foreign on employment, production, real wages, and the income of landowners in each country.

2. Suppose that a labor-abundant country and a land-abundant country both produce labor- and land-intensive goods with the same technology. Drawing on the analysis in Chapter 4, first analyze the conditions under which trade between the two countries eliminates the incentive for labor to migrate. Then show, using the analysis in Chapter 5, that a tariff by one country will create an incentive for labor migration.

3. Explain the analogy between international borrowing and lending and ordinary international trade.

4. Which of the following countries would you expect to have intertemporal production possibilities biased toward current consumption goods, and which biased toward future consumption goods?

a) A country, like Argentina or Canada in the last century, that has only recently been opened for large-scale settlement and is receiving large inflows of immigrants.

b) A country, like the United Kingdom in the late nineteenth century or the United States today, that leads the world technologically but is seeing that lead eroded as other countries catch up.

c) A country that has discovered large oil reserves that can be exploited with little new investment (like Saudi Arabia).

d) A country that has discovered large oil reserves that can be exploited only with massive investment (like Norway, whose oil lies under the North Sea).

e) A country like South Korea that has somehow discovered the knack of producing industrial goods and is rapidly catching up to advanced countries.

5. Which of the following is a direct foreign investment, and which is not?

a) A Saudi businessman buys $10 million of IBM stock.

b) The same businessman buys a New York apartment building.

c) A French company merges with an American company; stockholders in the U.S. company exchange their stock for shares in the French firm.

d) An Italian firm builds a plant in the Soviet Union and manages the plant as a contractor to the Soviet government.

6. The Karma Computer Company has decided to open a Brazilian subsidiary. Brazilian import restrictions have prevented the firm from selling into that market, while the firm has been unwilling to sell or lease its patents to Brazilian firms because it fears that this will eventually hurt its technological advantage in the U.S. market. Analyze Karma's decision in terms of the theory of multinational enterprise.

FURTHER READING

Richard A. Brecher and Robert C. Feenstra. "International Trade and Capital Mobility between Diversified Economies." *Journal of International Economics* 14 (May 1983), pp. 321–339. A recent synthesis of the theories of trade and international factor movements.

Richard E. Caves. *Multinational Enterprises and Economic Analysis.* Cambridge: Harvard University Press, 1982. A recent view of multinational firms' activities.

Wilfred J. Ethier. "The Multinational Firm." *Quarterly Journal of Economics* 101 (November 1986), pp. 805–833. Models the internalization motive of multinationals.

Irving Fisher. *The Theory of Interest.* New York: Macmillan, 1930. The "intertemporal" approach described in this chapter owes its origin to Fisher.

Charles P. Kindleberger. *American Business Abroad.* New Haven: Yale University Press, 1969. A good discussion of the nature and effects of multinational firms, written at a time when such firms were primarily United States-based.

Charles P. Kindleberger. *Europe's Postwar Growth: The Role of Labor Supply.* Cambridge: Harvard University Press, 1967. A good account of the role of labor migration in Europe during its height.

G. D. A. MacDougall. "The Benefits and Costs of Private Investment from Abroad: A Theoretical Approach." *Economic Record* 36 (1960), pp. 13–35. A clear analysis of the costs and benefits of factor movement.

Robert A. Mundell. "International Trade and Factor Mobility." *American Economic Review* 47 (1957), pp. 321–335. The paper that first laid out the argument that trade and factor movement can substitute for each other.

Jeffrey Sachs. "The Current Account and Macroeconomic Adjustment in the 1970s." *Brookings Papers on Economic Activity,* 1981. A study of international capital flows that takes the approach of viewing such flows as intertemporal trade.

APPENDIX TO CHAPTER 7
More on Intertemporal Trade

This appendix contains a more detailed examination of the two-period intertemporal trade model described in the chapter. The concepts used are the same as those used in Chapter 5 to analyze international exchanges of different consumption goods at a *single* point in time. In the present setting, however, the trade model explains international patterns of investment and borrowing and the determination of the *intertemporal* terms of trade (that is, the real interest rate).

First consider Home, whose intertemporal production possibility frontier is shown in Figure 7A-1. Recall that the quantities of present and future consumption goods produced at Home depend on the amount of present consumption goods invested to produce future goods. As currently available resources are diverted from present consumption to investment, production of present consumption, Q_P, falls and production of future consumption, Q_F, rises. Increased investment therefore shifts the economy up and to the left along the intertemporal production possibility frontier.

The chapter showed that the price of future consumption in terms of present consumption is $1/(1 + r)$, where r is the real interest rate. Measured in terms of

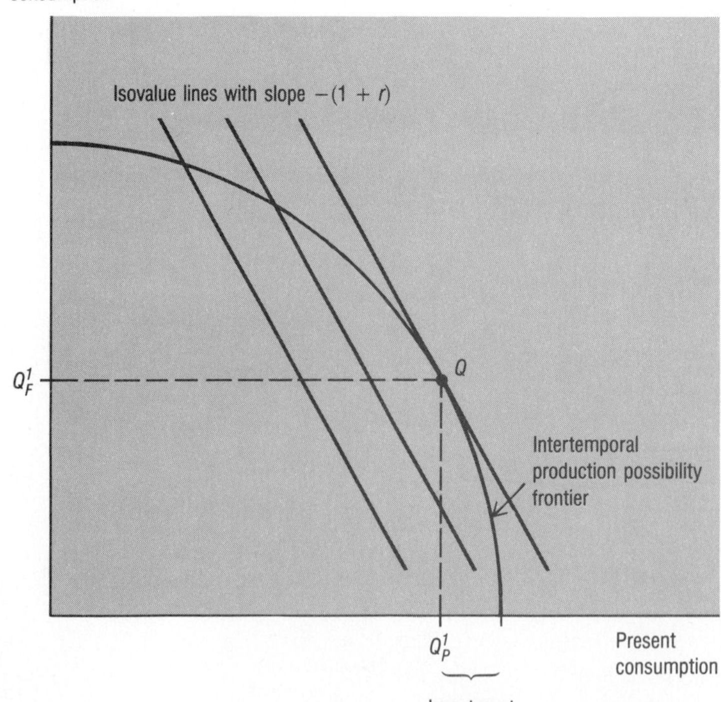

FIGURE 7A-1 Determining Home's intertemporal production pattern. At a world real interest rate of r, Home's investment level maximizes the value of production over the two periods that the economy exists.

present consumption, the value of the economy's total production over the two periods of its existence is therefore

$$V = Q_P + Q_F/(1 + r).$$

Figure 7A-1 shows the isovalue lines corresponding to the relative price $1/(1 + r)$ for different values of V. These are straight lines with slope $-(1 + r)$ (because future consumption is on the vertical axis). As in the standard trade model, firms' decisions lead to a production pattern that maximizes the value of production at market prices, $Q_P + Q_F/(1 + r)$. Production therefore occurs at point Q. The economy invests the amount shown, leaving Q_P^1 available for present consumption and producing an amount Q_F^1 of future consumption when the first-period investment pays off.

Notice that at point Q, the extra future consumption that would result from investing an additional unit of present consumption just equals $(1 + r)$. It would be inefficient to push investment beyond point Q because the economy could do better by lending additional present consumption to foreigners instead. Figure 7A-1 implies that a rise in the world real interest rate r, which steepens the isovalue lines, causes investment to fall.

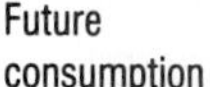

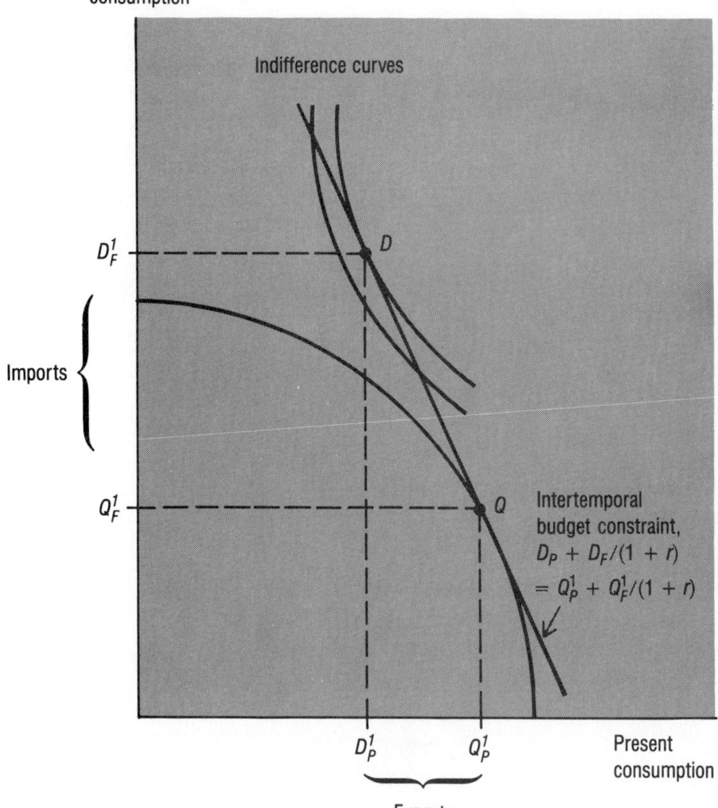

FIGURE 7A-2 Determining Home's intertemporal consumption pattern. Home's consumption places it on the highest indifference curve touching its intertemporal budget constraint. The economy exports $Q_P^1 - D_P^1$ units of present consumption and imports $D_F^1 - Q_F^1 = (1 + r) \times (Q_P^1 - D_P^1)$ units of future consumption.

Figure 7A-2 shows how Home's consumption pattern is determined for a given world interest rate. Let D_P and D_F represent the demands for present and future consumption goods, respectively. Since production is at point Q, the economy's consumption possibilities over the two periods are limited by the *intertemporal budget constraint:*

$$D_P + D_F/(1 + r) = Q_P^1 + Q_F^1/(1 + r).$$

This constraint states that the value of Home's consumption over the two periods (measured in terms of present consumption) equals the value of consumption goods produced in the two periods (also measured in present consumption units). Put another way, production and consumption must lie on the same isovalue line.

Point D, where Home's budget constraint touches the highest attainable indifference curve, shows the present and future consumption levels chosen by the economy. Home's demand for present consumption, D_P^1, is smaller than its production of present consumption, Q_P^1; so it exports (that is, lends) $Q_P^1 - D_P^1$ units of present consumption to Foreigners. Correspondingly, Home imports $D_F^1 - Q_F^1$ units of future consumption from abroad when its first-period loans are repaid to it with interest. The intertemporal budget constraint implies that $D_F^1 - Q_F^1 = (1 + r) \times (Q_P^1 - D_P^1)$, so that trade is *intertemporally* balanced.

Figure 7A-3 shows how investment and consumption are determined in Foreign. Foreign is assumed to have a comparative advantage in producing *future* consumption

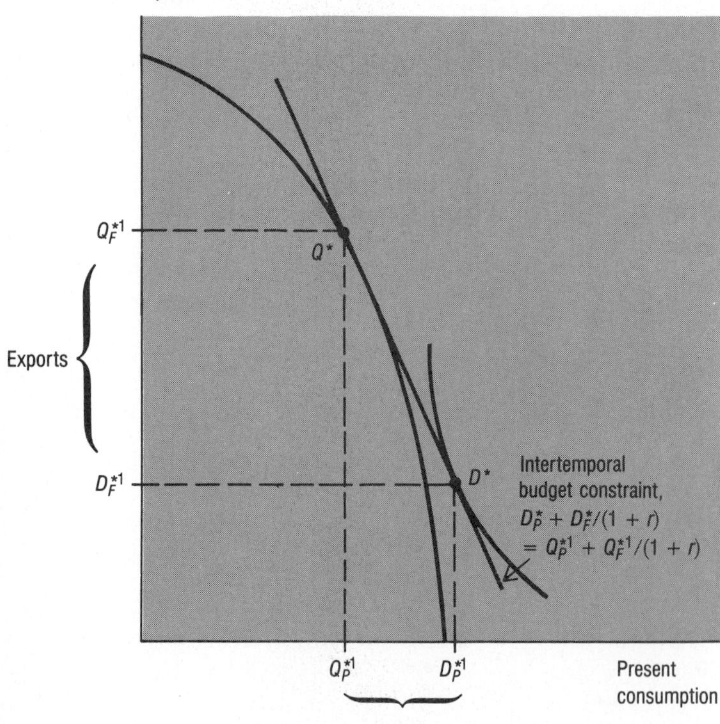

FIGURE 7A-3 Determining Foreign's intertemporal production and consumption patterns. Foreign produces at point Q^* and consumes at point D^*, importing $D_P^{*1} - Q_P^{*1}$ units of present consumption and exporting $Q_F^{*1} - D_F^{*1} = (1 + r) \times (D_P^{*1} - Q_P^{*1})$ units of future consumption.

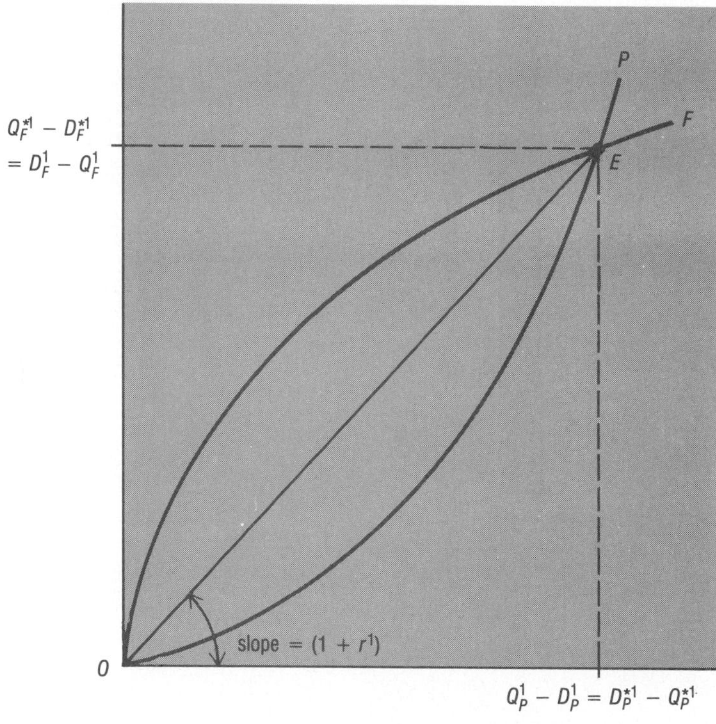

FIGURE 7A-4 International intertemporal equilibrium in terms of offer curves. Equilibrium is at point E (with interest rate r^1) because desired Home exports of present consumption equal desired Foreign imports and desired Foreign exports of future consumption equal desired Home imports.

goods. The diagram shows that at a real interest rate of r, foreign borrows consumption goods in the first period and repays this loan using consumption goods produced in the second period. Because of its relatively rich domestic investment opportunities and its relative preference for present consumption, Foreign is an importer of present consumption and an exporter of future consumption.

As in Chapter 5 (appendix), international equilibrium can be portrayed by an offer-curve diagram. Recall that a country's offer curve is the result of plotting its desired exports against its desired imports. Now, however, the exchanges plotted involve present and future consumption. Figure 7A-4 shows that the equilibrium real interest rate is determined by the intersection of the Home and Foreign offer curves OP and OF at point E. The ray OE has slope $(1 + r^1)$, where r^1 is the equilibrium world interest rate. At point E, Home's desired export of present consumption equals Foreign's desired import of present consumption. Put another way, at point E, Home's desired first-period lending equals Foreign's desired first-period borrowing. Supply and demand are therefore equal in both periods.

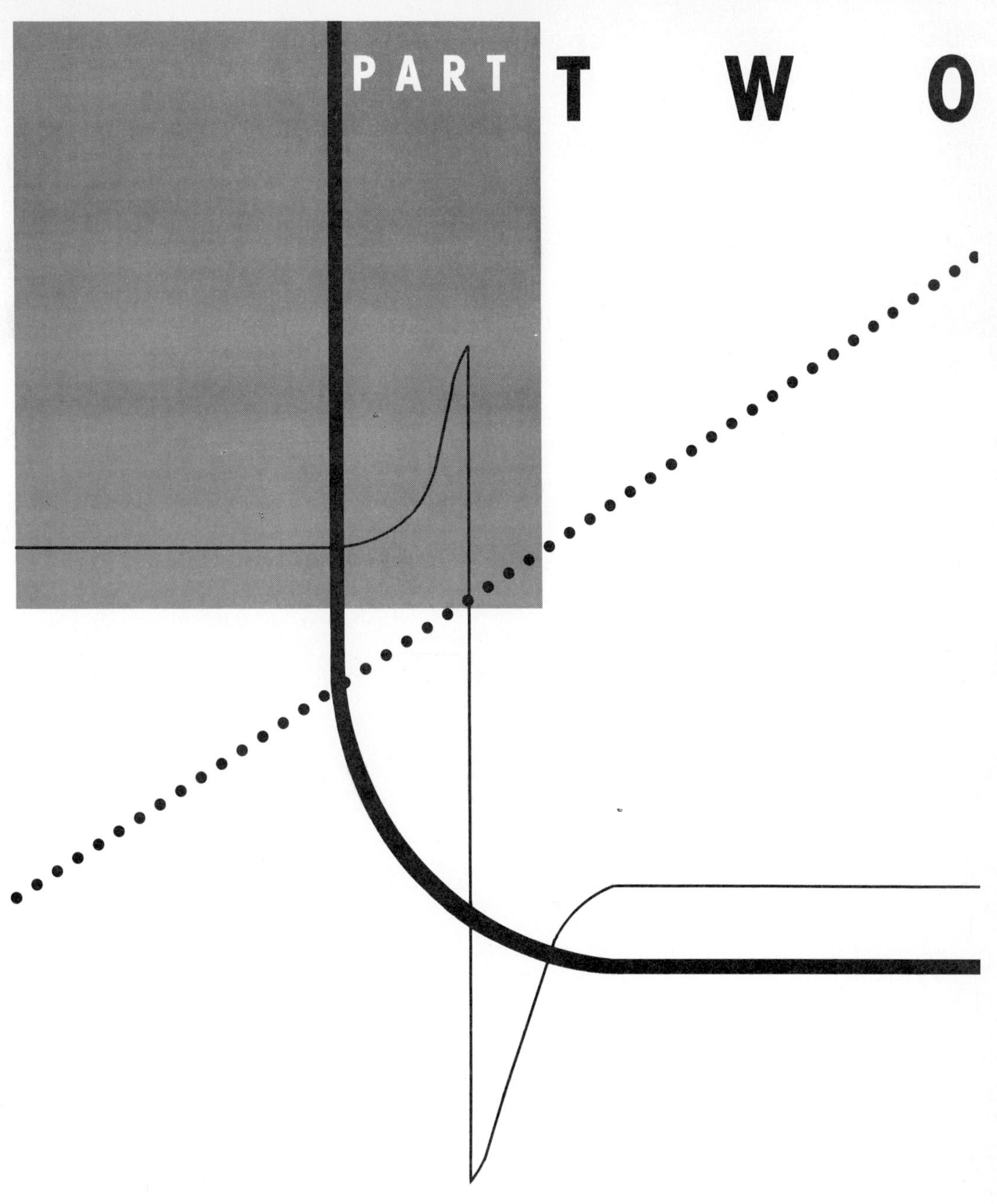

PART TWO

INTERNATIONAL TRADE POLICY

8 THE INSTRUMENTS OF TRADE POLICY

Previous chapters have answered the question, "Why do nations trade?" by *describing* the causes and effects of international trade and the functioning of a trading world economy. While this question is interesting in itself, its answer is much more interesting if it helps answer the question, "What should a nation's trade policy be?" Should the United States use a tariff or an import quota to protect its automobile industry against competition from Japan and Korea? Who will benefit and who will lose from an import quota? Will the benefits outweigh the costs?

In this chapter, the focus shifts to an examination of the policies that governments adopt toward international trade, policies that involve a number of different actions, including taxes on some international transactions, subsidies for other transactions, legal limits on the value or volume of particular imports, and many other measures. This chapter provides a framework for understanding the effects of the most important instruments of trade policy.

BASIC TARIFF ANALYSIS

A tariff, the simplest of trade policies, is a tax levied when a good is imported. **Specific tariffs** are levied as a fixed charge for each unit of goods imported (for example, $3 per barrel of oil). **Ad valorem tariffs** are taxes that are levied as a fraction of the value of the imported goods (for example, the 25 percent U.S. tariff on imported trucks). In either case the effect of the tariff is to raise the cost of shipping goods to a country.

Tariffs are the oldest form of trade policy and have traditionally been used as a source of government income. Until the introduction of the income tax, for instance, the U.S. government raised most of its revenue from tariffs. Their true purpose, however, has usually been not only to provide revenue but to protect particular domestic sectors. In the early nineteenth century the United Kingdom used tariffs (the famous Corn Laws) to protect its agriculture from import competition. In the late nineteenth century both Germany and the United States protected their new industrial sectors by imposing tariffs on imports of manufactured goods. The importance of tariffs has declined in modern times, because modern governments usually prefer to protect domestic industries through a variety of **nontariff barriers**. Nonetheless, an understanding of the effects of a tariff remains a vital basis for understanding other trade policies.

In developing the theory of trade in Chapters 2 through 7 we adopted a *general equilibrium* perspective. That is, we took considerable care to keep in mind the point that events in one part of the economy have repercussions elsewhere. However, in many (though not all) cases trade policies toward one sector can be reasonably well understood without going into detail about the repercussions of that policy in the rest of the economy. For the most part, then, trade policy can be examined in a *partial equilibrium* framework. The rest of the economy is always there in the background, however. When the effects on the economy as a whole become crucial, we will refer back to general equilibrium analysis.

SUPPLY, DEMAND, AND TRADE IN A SINGLE INDUSTRY

Let's suppose that there are two countries, Home and Foreign, both of which consume and produce wheat, which can be costlessly transported between the countries. In each country wheat is a simple competitive industry in which the supply and demand curves are functions of the market price. Normally Home supply and demand will depend on the price in terms of Home currency, and Foreign supply and demand will depend on the price in terms of Foreign currency, but we assume that the exchange rate between the currencies is not affected by whatever trade policy is undertaken in this market. Thus, we quote prices in both markets in terms of Home currency.

Trade will arise in such a market if prices are different in the absence of trade. Suppose that in the absence of trade the price of wheat is higher in Home than it is in Foreign. Now allow foreign trade. Since the price of wheat in Home exceeds the price in Foreign, shippers begin to move wheat from Foreign to Home. The export of wheat raises its price in Foreign and lowers its price in Home until the difference in prices has been eliminated.

To determine the world price and the quantity traded, it is helpful to define two new curves: the Home **import demand curve** and the Foreign **export supply curve,** which are derived from the underlying domestic supply and demand curves. Home import demand is the excess of what Home consumers demand over what Home producers supply; Foreign export supply is the excess of what Foreign producers supply over what Foreign consumers demand.

Figure 8-1 shows how the Home import demand curve is derived. At the price P^1 Home consumers demand D^1, while Home producers supply only S^1, so Home import demand is $D^1 - S^1$. If we raise the price to P^2, Home consumers demand only D^2, while Home producers raise their supply to S^2, so import demand falls to $D^2 - S^2$. Thus the import demand curve *MD* is downward-sloping. At P_A, Home supply and demand are equal in the absence of trade; so at that price the Home import demand curve crosses zero.

FIGURE 8-1 Deriving Home's import demand curve. As the price of the good increases, Home consumers demand less, while Home producers supply more, so that the demand for imports declines.

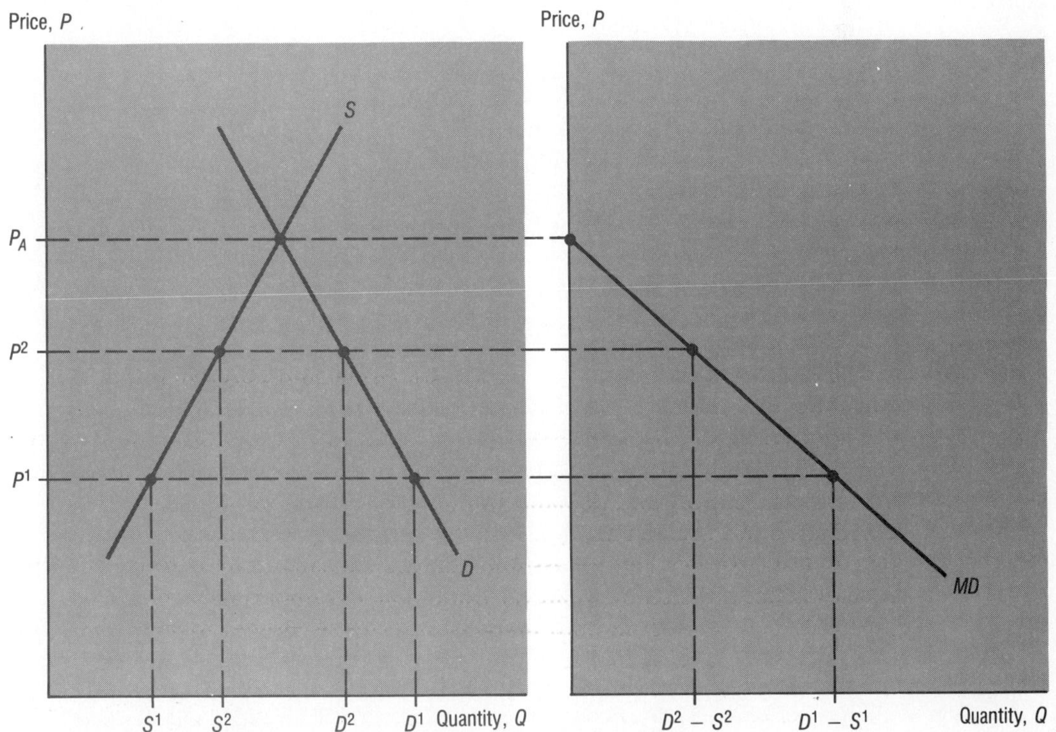

Figure 8-2 shows how the Foreign export supply curve XS is derived. At P^1 Foreign producers supply S^{*1}, while Foreign consumers demand only D^{*1}, so the supply available for export is $S^{*1} - D^{*1}$. At P^2 Foreign producers raise their supply to S^{*2}, Foreign consumers lower their demand to D^{*2}, so export supply rises to $S^{*2} - D^{*2}$. Thus the Foreign export supply curve is upward-sloping. If the price were as low as P^*_A, supply and demand would be equal in the absence of trade; so the Foreign export supply curve crosses zero at P^*_A.

World equilibrium occurs when Home import demand equals Foreign export supply (Figure 8-3). At the price P_W, where the two curves cross, world supply equals world demand. At the equilibrium point 1 in Figure 8-3,

$$\text{Home demand} - \text{Home supply} = \text{Foreign supply} - \text{Foreign demand}.$$

By adding and subtracting from both sides, this can be rearranged to say that

$$\text{Home demand} + \text{Foreign demand} = \text{Home supply} + \text{Foreign supply}$$

or, in other words,

$$\text{world demand} = \text{world supply}.$$

FIGURE 8-2 Deriving Foreign's export supply curve. As the price of the good rises, Foreign producers supply more while Foreign consumers demand less, so that the supply available for export rises.

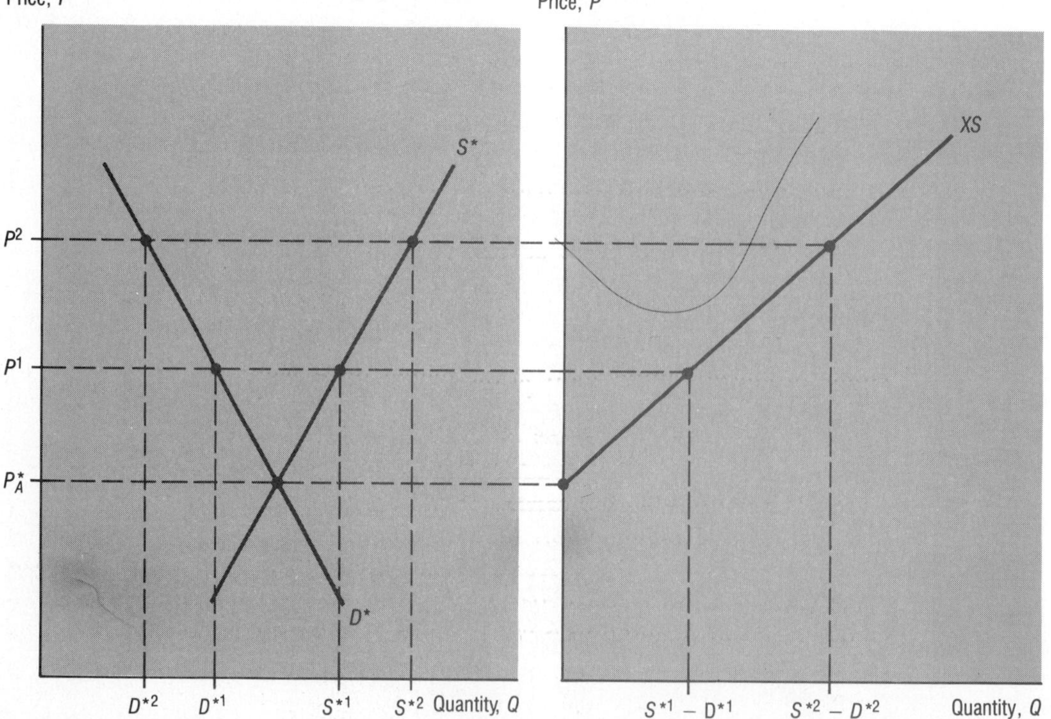

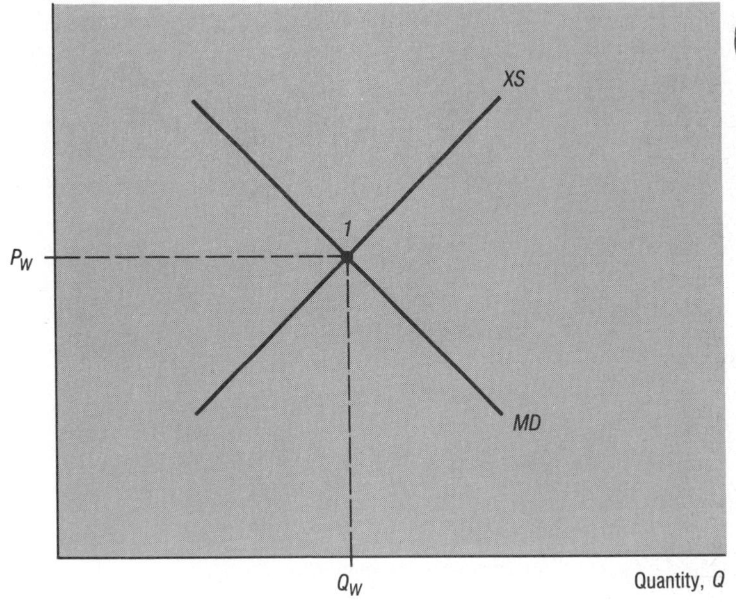

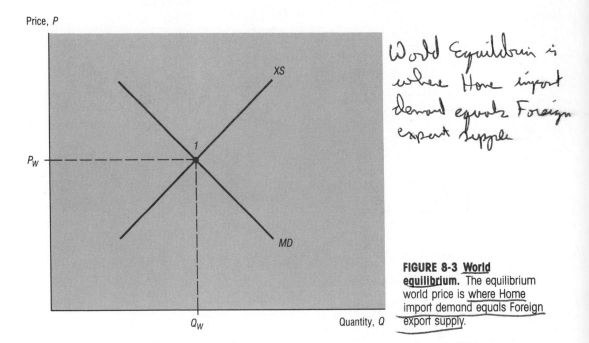

FIGURE 8-3 World equilibrium. The equilibrium world price is where Home import demand equals Foreign export supply.

EFFECTS OF A TARIFF

From the point of view of someone shipping goods, a tariff is just like a cost of transportation. If Home imposes a tax of $2 on every bushel of wheat imported, shippers will be unwilling to move the wheat unless the price difference between the two markets is at least $2.

Figure 8-4 illustrates the effects of a specific tariff of $\$t$ per unit of wheat. In the absence of a tariff, the price of wheat would be equalized at P_W in both Home and Foreign. With the tariff in place, however, shippers are not willing to move wheat from Foreign to Home unless the Home price exceeds the Foreign price by at least $\$t$. Thus the price in Home rises, and the price in Foreign falls, until the price difference is $\$t$. Introducing a tariff drives a wedge between the prices in the two markets. The tariff raises the price in Home to P_T and lowers the price in Foreign to $P_T^* = P_T - t$. In Home producers supply more at the higher price, while consumers demand less, so that fewer imports are demanded. In Foreign the lower price leads to reduced supply and increased demand, and thus a smaller export supply. Thus the volume of wheat traded declines from Q_W, the free-trade volume, to Q_T, the volume with a tariff. At the trade volume Q_T, Home import demand equals Foreign export supply when $P_T - P_T^* = t$.

The increase in the price in Home, from P_W to P_T, is less than the amount of the tariff, because part of the tariff is reflected in a decline in Foreign's export price and thus is not passed on to Home consumers. This is the normal result of a tariff and of any trade policy that limits imports. The size of this effect, however, is often in practice very small. When a small country

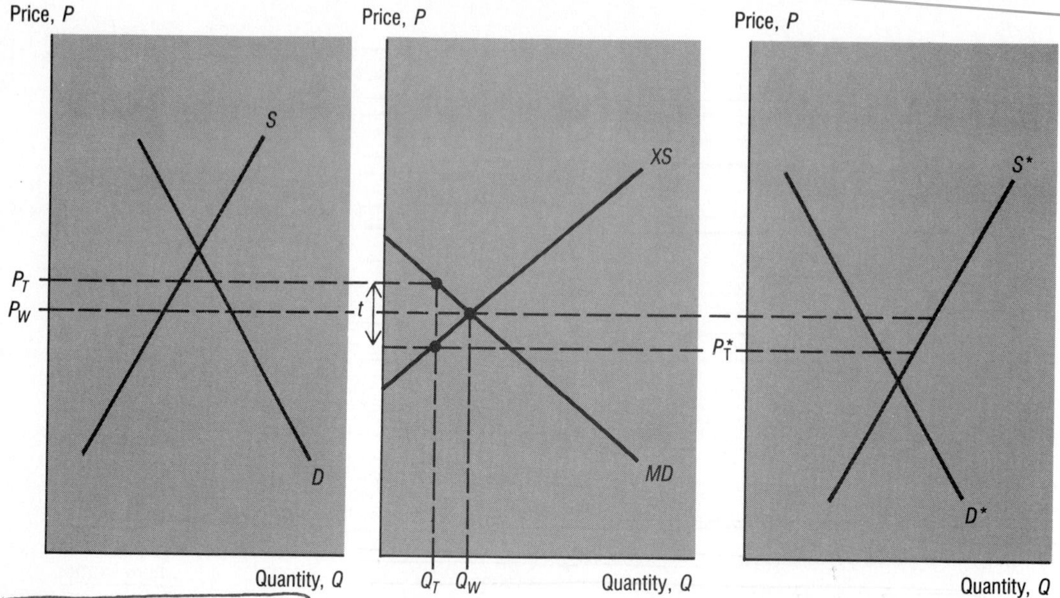

FIGURE 8-4 Effects of a tariff. A tariff raises the price in Home while lowering the price in Foreign. The volume traded declines.

imposes a tariff, its share of the world market for the goods it imports is usually minor to begin with, so that its import reduction has very little effect on the world price. For all practical purposes, the foreign export price of imported goods can be taken as given in many cases.

The effects of a tariff in the "small country" case where a country cannot affect foreign export prices are illustrated in Figure 8-5. In this case a tariff raises the price of the imported good by the full amount of the tariff, from P_W to $P_W + t$. Production rises from S^1 to S^2, while consumption falls from D^1 to D^2.

MEASURING THE AMOUNT OF PROTECTION

A tariff on an imported good raises the price received by domestic producers of that good. This effect is often the tariff's principal objective—to *protect* domestic producers from the low prices that would result from import competition. In analyzing trade policy in practice, it is important to ask how much protection a tariff or other trade policy actually provides. The answer to this question is usually expressed as a percentage of the price that would prevail under free trade. An import quota on sugar could, for example, raise the price received by U.S. sugar producers by 45 percent.

It might seem at first that measuring protection would be straightforward in the case of a tariff: if the tariff is an ad valorem tax that is pro-

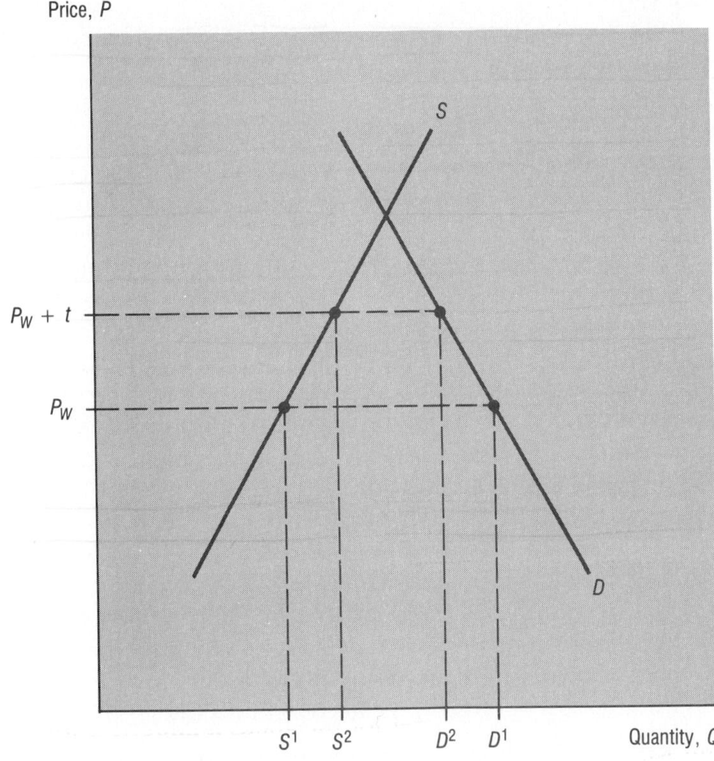

FIGURE 8-5 A tariff in a small country. When a country is small, a tariff cannot lower the foreign price of the good it imports.

portional to the value of the imports, the tariff rate itself should measure the amount of protection; if the tariff is specific, dividing the tariff by the price net of the tariff gives us the ad valorem equivalent.

There are two problems in trying to calculate the rate of protection this simply. First, if the small-country assumption is not a good approximation, part of the effect of a tariff will be to lower foreign export prices rather than to raise domestic prices, and the effect of trade policies on foreign export prices is sometimes significant. In theory (though rarely in practice) it is actually possible that a tariff will lower the price received by domestic producers (the Metzler paradox discussed in Chapter 5).

The second problem is that tariffs may have very different effects on different stages of production of a good. A simple example illustrates this point.

Suppose that an automobile sells on the world market for \$8000 and that the parts out of which that automobile is made sell for \$6000. Let's compare two countries: one that wants to encourage the development of an auto assembly industry and one that already has an assembly industry and wants to develop a parts industry.

To encourage a domestic auto industry, the first country places a 25 percent tariff on imported autos, allowing domestic assemblers to charge

\$10,000 instead of \$8000. In this case it would be wrong to say that the assemblers receive only 25 percent protection. Before the tariff, domestic assembly would take place only if it could be done for \$2000 (the difference between the \$8000 price of a completed automobile and the \$6000 cost of parts) or less; now it will take place even if it costs as much as \$4000 (the difference between the \$10,000 price and the cost of parts). That is, the 25 percent tariff rate provides assemblers with an **effective rate of protection** of 100 percent.

Now suppose that the second country, in order to encourage domestic production of parts, imposes a 10 percent tariff on imported parts, raising the cost of parts to domestic assemblers from \$6000 to \$6600. Even though there is no change in the tariff on assembled automobiles, this policy makes it less advantageous to assemble domestically. Before the tariff it would have been worth assembling a car locally if it could be done for \$2000 (\$8000 − \$6000); after the tariff local assembly takes place only if it can be done for \$1400 (\$8000 − \$6600). The tariff on parts, then, while providing positive protection to parts manufacturers, provides negative effective protection to assembly at the rate of −30 percent (−600/2000).

Reasoning similar to that seen in this example has led economists to make elaborate calculations to measure the degree of effective protection actually provided to particular industries by tariffs and other trade policies. Trade policies aimed at promoting economic development, for example (Chapter 10), often lead to rates of effective protection much higher than the tariff rates themselves.

COSTS AND BENEFITS OF A TARIFF

A tariff raises the price of a good in the importing country and lowers it in the exporting country. As a result of these price changes, consumers lose in the importing country and gain in the exporting country. Producers gain in the importing country and lose in the exporting country. In addition, the government imposing the tariff gains revenue. To compare these costs and benefits, it is necessary to quantify them. The method for measuring costs and benefits of a tariff depends on two concepts common to much microeconomic analysis: consumer and producer surplus.

CONSUMER AND PRODUCER SURPLUS

Consumer surplus measures the amount a consumer gains from a purchase by the difference between the price he actually pays and the price he would have been willing to pay. If, for example, a consumer would have been willing to pay \$8 for a bushel of wheat but the price is only \$3, the consumer surplus gained by the purchase is \$5.

Consumer surplus can be derived from the market demand curve (Figure 8-6). For example, suppose that the maximum price at which consumers

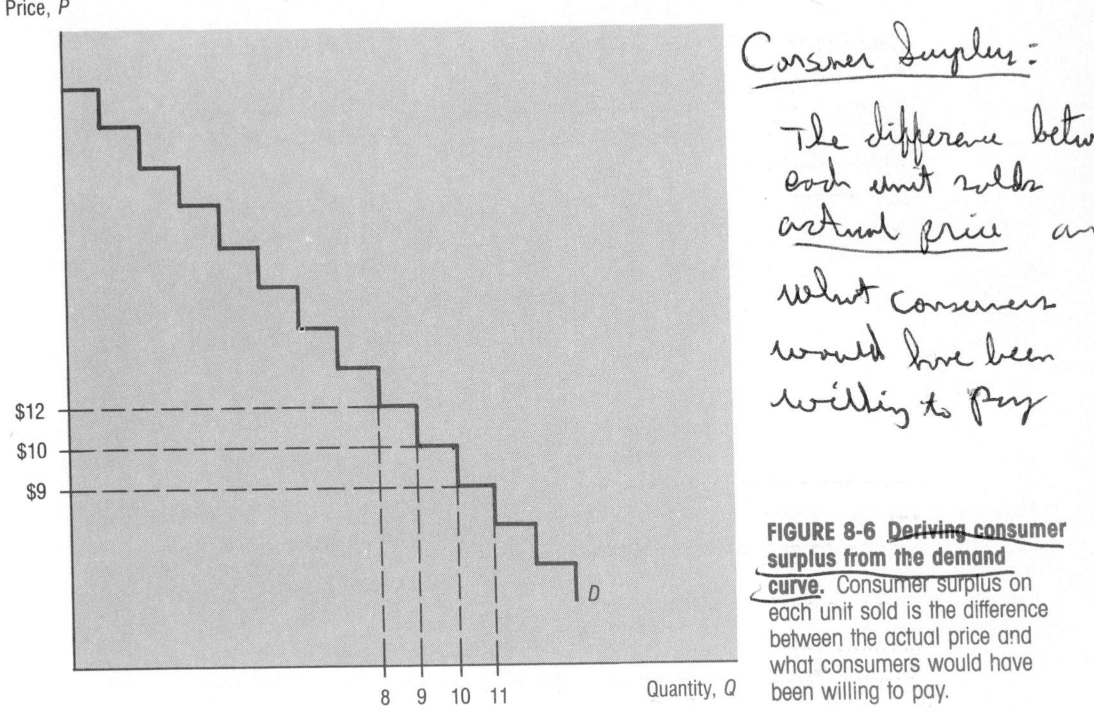

FIGURE 8-6 Deriving consumer surplus from the demand curve. Consumer surplus on each unit sold is the difference between the actual price and what consumers would have been willing to pay.

will buy 10 units of a good is \$10. Then the tenth unit of the good purchased must be worth \$10 to consumers. If it were worth less, they would not purchase it; if it were worth more, they would have been willing to purchase it even if the price were higher. Now suppose that in order to get consumers to buy 11 units the price must be cut to \$9. Then the eleventh unit must be worth only \$9 to consumers.

Suppose that the price is \$9. Then consumers are just willing to purchase the eleventh unit of the good, and thus receive no consumer surplus from their purchase of that unit. They would have been willing to pay \$10 for the tenth unit, however, and thus receive \$1 in consumer surplus from that unit. They might have been willing to pay \$12 for the ninth unit; if so, they receive \$3 of consumer surplus on that unit, and so on.

Generalizing from this example, if P is the price of a good and Q the quantity demanded at that price, then consumer surplus is calculated by subtracting P times Q from the area under the demand curve up to Q (Figure 8-7). If the price is P^1, the quantity demanded is Q^1, and the consumer surplus is measured by the area labeled a. If the price falls to P^2, the quantity demanded rises to Q^2, and consumer surplus rises to equal a plus the additional area b.

Producer surplus is an analogous concept. If a producer would have been willing to sell a good for \$2 but receives a price of \$5, she gains a pro-

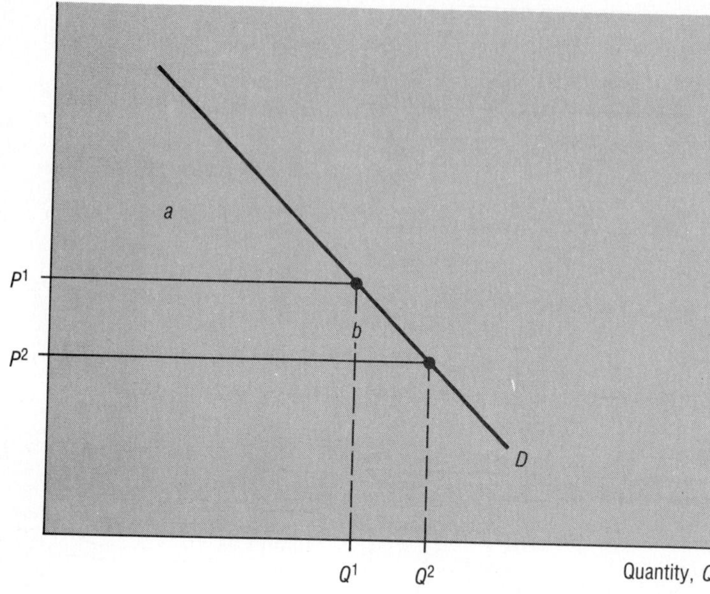

FIGURE 8-7 Geometry of consumer surplus. Consumer surplus is equal to the area under the demand curve.

ducer surplus of $3 from the sale. By the same procedure used to derive consumer surplus from the demand curve, producer surplus can be derived from the supply curve. If P is the price and Q the quantity supplied at that price, then producer surplus is P times Q minus the area under the supply curve up to Q (Figure 8-8). If the price is P^1, the quantity supplied will be Q^1, and producer surplus is measured by the area c. If the price rises to P^2, the quantity supplied rises to Q^2, and producer surplus rises to equal c plus the additional area d.

The concepts of consumer and producer surplus are subject to some difficulties. Some of the difficulties are technical issues of calculation that can safely be neglected for most practical purposes. More important is the question of whether the direct gains to producers and consumers in a given market accurately measure the *social* gains. Arguments that suggest additional benefits and costs not captured by consumer and producer surplus are at the core of the case for trade policy activism discussed in Chapter 9. For now, however, we reserve these issues and focus on costs and benefits as measured by consumer and producer surplus.

MEASURING THE COSTS AND BENEFITS

Figure 8-9 illustrates the costs and benefits of a tariff for the importing country.

The tariff raises the domestic price from P_W to P_T but lowers the foreign export price from P_W to P_T^* (refer back to Figure 8-4). Domestic production

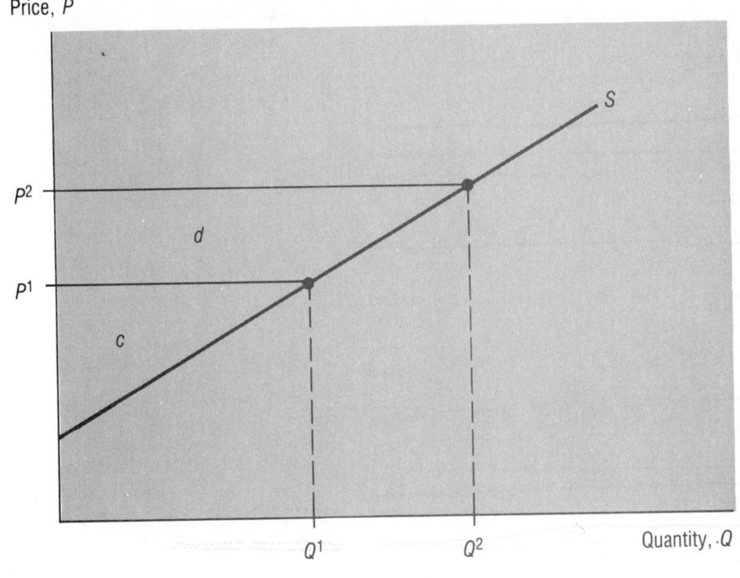

Producer Surplus is equal to the area above the Supply curve

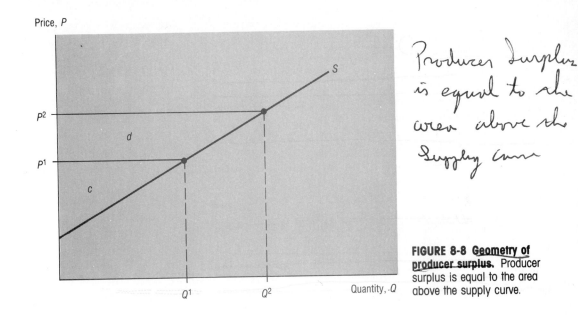

FIGURE 8-8 Geometry of producer surplus. Producer surplus is equal to the area above the supply curve.

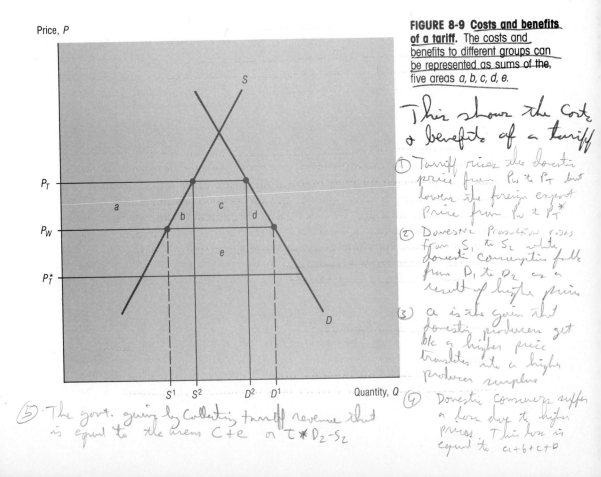

FIGURE 8-9 Costs and benefits of a tariff. The costs and benefits to different groups can be represented as sums of the five areas *a*, *b*, *c*, *d*, *e*.

This shows the Costs & benefits of a tariff

(1) Tariff rises the domestic price from P_W to P_T but lowers the foreign export price from P_W to P_T^*

(2) Domestic Production rises from S_1 to S_2 while domestic consumption falls from D_1 to D_2 as a result of higher price

(3) a is the gain that domestic producers get b/c a higher price translates into a higher producer surplus

(4) Domestic Consumers suffer a loss due to higher prices. This loss is equal to a+b+c+d

(5) The govt. gains by Collecting tariff revenue that is equal to the areas C+e or T * D2-S2

rises from S^1 to S^2, while domestic consumption falls from D^1 to D^2. The costs and benefits to different groups can be expressed as sums of the areas of five regions, labeled a, b, c, d, e.

Consider first the gain to domestic producers. They receive a higher price and therefore have higher producer surplus. Referring back to Figure 8-8, their gain may be measured by a, the increase in the difference between $P \times Q$ and the area under the supply curve.

Domestic consumers also face a higher price and are therefore worse off. Referring to Figure 8-7, the loss to domestic consumers is equal to the sum $a + b + c + d$, the reduction in the difference between the area under the demand curve and $P \times Q$.

There is a third player here as well: the government. The government gains by collecting tariff revenue. This is equal to the tariff rate t times the volume of imports $Q_T = D^2 - S^2$. Since $t = P_T - P_T^*$, the government's revenue is equal to the sum of the two areas c and e.

Since these gains and losses accrue to different people, the overall cost-benefit evaluation of a tariff depends on how much we value a dollar's worth of benefit to each group. If, for example, the producer gain accrues mostly to wealthy owners of resources, while the consumers are poorer than average, the tariff will be viewed differently than if the good is a luxury bought by the affluent but produced by low-wage workers. Further ambiguity is introduced by the role of the government: will it use its revenue to finance vitally needed public services or waste it on cost overruns? Despite these problems, it is common for analysts of trade policy to attempt to compute the net effect of a tariff on national welfare by assuming that at the margin a dollar's worth of gain or loss to each group is of the same social worth.

Let's look, then, at the net effect of a tariff on welfare. The net cost of a tariff is

$$\text{consumer loss} - \text{producer gain} - \text{government revenue} \qquad \textbf{(8–1)}$$

or, replacing these concepts by the areas in Figure 8-9,

$$(a + b + c + d) - a - (c + e) = b + d - e. \qquad \textbf{(8–2)}$$

That is, there are two "triangles" whose area measures loss, and a "rectangle" whose area measures an offsetting gain. A useful way to interpret these gains and losses is the following: the loss triangles represent the **efficiency loss** that arises because a tariff distorts incentives, while the rectangle represents the **terms of trade gain** that arises because a tariff lowers foreign export prices.

The gain depends on the ability of the tariff-imposing country to drive down foreign export prices. If the country cannot affect world prices (the "small country" case illustrated in Figure 8-5), region e, which represents the terms of trade gain, disappears, and it is clear that the tariff reduces welfare. It distorts the incentives of both producers and consumers by inducing them to act as if imports were more expensive than they actually are. The cost of an additional unit of consumption to the economy is the price of an additional unit of imports, yet because the tariff raises the domestic price above the world price, consumers reduce their consumption to the point where that marginal unit yields them welfare equal to the tariff-inclusive domestic price. The value of an additional unit of production to the economy is the price of the unit of imports it saves, yet domestic producers expand production up to the point where the marginal cost is equal to the tariff-inclusive price. Thus the economy produces at home additional units of the good that it could purchase more cheaply abroad.

The net welfare effects of a tariff, then, are summarized in Figure 8-10. The negative effects consist of the two triangles *b* and *d*. The first triangle is a **production distortion loss,** resulting from the fact that the tariff leads domestic producers to produce too much of this good. The second triangle is a domestic **consumption distortion loss,** resulting from the fact that a tariff leads consumers to consume too little of the good. Against these losses must be set the terms of trade gain measured by the rectangle *e*, which results from the decline in the foreign export price that results from a tariff. In the important case of a small country that cannot significantly affect foreign

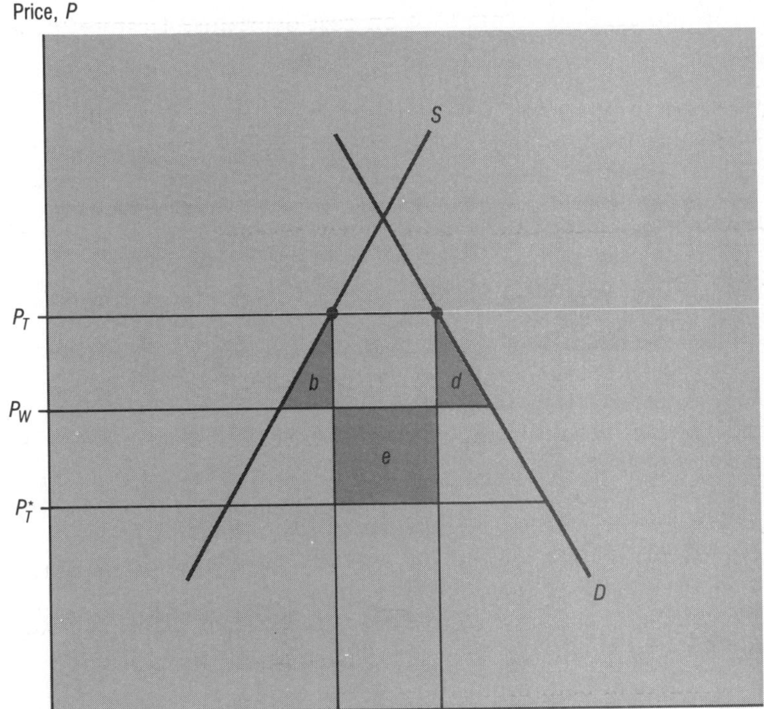

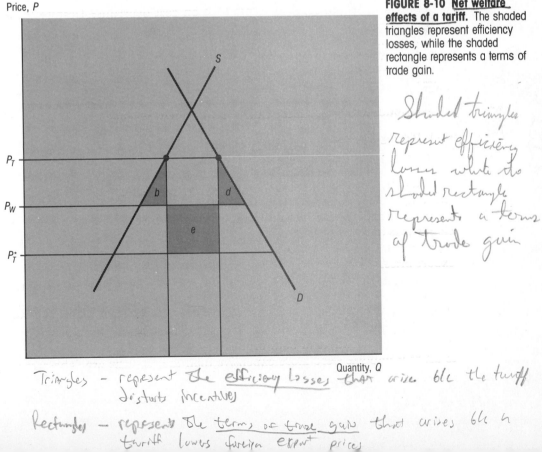

FIGURE 8-10 Net welfare effects of a tariff. The shaded triangles represent efficiency losses, while the shaded rectangle represents a terms of trade gain.

prices, this last effect drops out, so that the costs of a tariff unambiguously exceed its benefits.

OTHER INSTRUMENTS OF TRADE POLICY

Tariffs are the simplest trade policies, but in the modern world most government intervention in international trade takes other forms. The most prominent of these other forms are export subsidies, import quotas, voluntary export restraints, and local content requirements. Fortunately, once we understand tariffs it is not too difficult to understand these other trade instruments as well.

EXPORT SUBSIDIES: THEORY

An export subsidy is a payment given to a firm or individual that ships a good abroad. Like a tariff, an export subsidy can be either specific (a fixed sum per unit) or ad valorem (a proportion of the value exported). When the government offers an export subsidy, shippers will export the good up to the point where the domestic price exceeds the foreign price by the amount of the subsidy.

The effects of an export subsidy on prices are exactly the reverse of those of a tariff (Figure 8-11). The price in the exporting country rises from

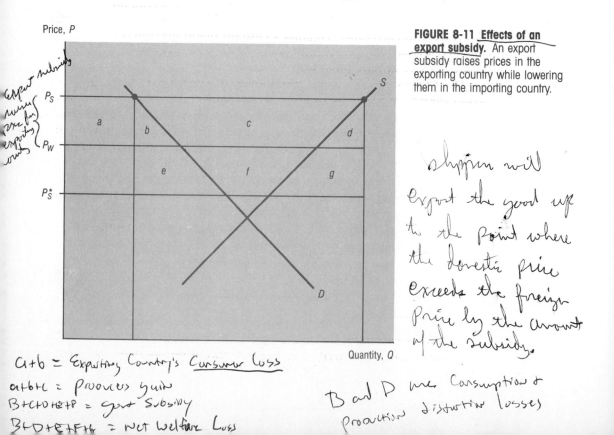

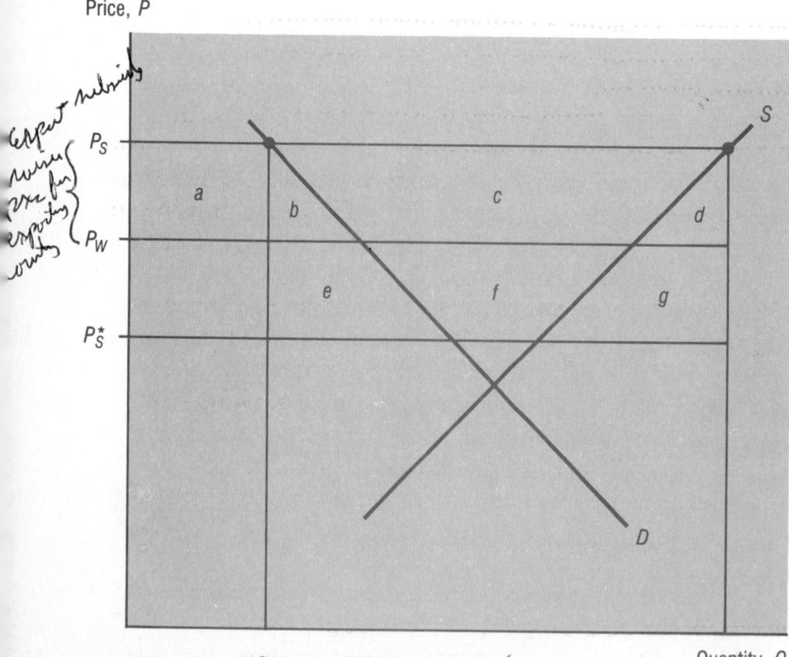

FIGURE 8-11 Effects of an export subsidy. An export subsidy raises prices in the exporting country while lowering them in the importing country.

P_W to P_S, but because the price in the importing country falls from P_W to P_S^*, the price rise is less than the subsidy. In the exporting country, consumers are hurt, producers gain, and the government loses because it must expend money on the subsidy. The consumer loss is the area $a + b$; the producer gain is the area $a + b + c$; the government subsidy is the area $b + c + d + e + f + g$. The net welfare loss is therefore the sum of the areas $b + d + e + f + g$. Of these, b and d represent consumption and production distortion losses of the same kind that a tariff produces. In addition, and in contrast to a tariff, the export subsidy *worsens* the terms of trade by lowering the price of the export in the foreign market from P_W to P_S^*. This leads to the additional terms of trade loss $e + f + g$, equal to $P_W - P_S^*$ times the quantity exported with the subsidy. So an export subsidy unambiguously leads to costs that exceed its benefits.

Case Study EUROPE'S COMMON AGRICULTURAL POLICY

Since 1957, six Western European nations—Germany, France, Italy, Belgium, the Netherlands, and Luxembourg—have been members of the European Economic Community (EEC); they were later joined by the United Kingdom, Ireland, Denmark, Greece, and most recently Spain and Portugal. The EEC fulfills a number of functions, but its two biggest effects are on trade policy. First, the members of the EEC have removed all tariffs with respect to each other, creating a customs union (discussed in the next chapter). Second, the agricultural policy of the EEC has developed into a massive export subsidy program.

The EEC's Common Agricultural Policy (CAP) did not start as an export subsidy. It began as an effort to guarantee high prices to European farmers by having the EEC buy agricultural products whenever the prices fell below specified support levels. To prevent this policy from drawing in large quantities of imports, it was initially backed by tariffs that offset the difference between European and world agricultural prices.

Since the 1970s, however, the support prices set by the EEC have turned out to be so high that Europe, which would under free trade be an importer of most agricultural products, was producing more than consumers were willing to buy. The result was that the EEC found itself obliged to buy and store huge quantities of food. At the end of 1985, European nations had stored 780,000 tons of beef, 1.2 million tons of butter, and 12 million tons of wheat. To avoid unlimited growth in these stockpiles, the EEC turned to a policy of subsidizing exports to dispose of surplus production.

Figure 8-12 shows how the CAP works. It is of course exactly like the export subsidy shown in Figure 8-11, except that Europe would actually be an importer under free trade. The support price is set not only above the

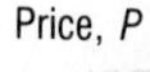

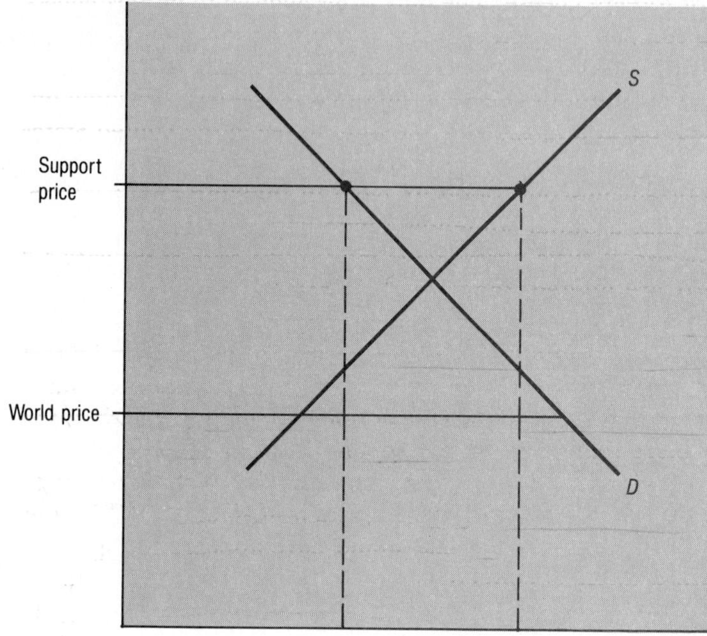

FIGURE 8-12 Europe's common agricultural program. Agricultural prices are fixed above world market levels, and an export subsidy is used to dispose of the resulting surplus.

world price that would prevail in its absence but also above the price that would equate demand and supply even without imports. To export the resulting surplus, an export subsidy is paid that offsets the difference between European and world prices. The subsidized exports themselves tend to depress the world price, increasing the required subsidy. Cost-benefit analysis would clearly show that the combined costs to European consumers and taxpayers exceed the benefits to producers.

At the time of writing the Common Agricultural Policy was under substantial political pressure. This concern did not primarily reflect cost-benefit analysis, however. Instead, the problems were the budgetary strain from the subsidies—12 billion dollars in 1985—and conflict with the United States. The United States is also an exporter of agricultural products and also has a farm surplus problem, so that European subsidies that depress prices have been a major U.S. sore point.

IMPORT QUOTAS: THEORY

An **import quota** is a direct restriction on the quantity of some good that may be imported. The restriction is usually enforced by issuing licenses to some group of individuals or firms. For example, the United States has a quota on imports of foreign cheese. The only firms allowed to import cheese are certain trading companies, each of which is allocated the right to import a maximum number of pounds of cheese each year; the size of each firm's quota is based on the amount of cheese it imported in the past. In some important cases, notably sugar and apparel, the right to sell in the United States is given directly to the governments of exporting countries.

The most important misconception to avoid in thinking about import quotas is the idea that a quota somehow limits imports without raising domestic prices. *An import quota always raises the domestic price of the imported good.* When imports are limited, the immediate result is that at the initial price the demand for the good exceeds domestic supply plus imports. This causes the price to be bid up until the market clears. In the end, an import quota will raise domestic prices by the same amount as a tariff that limits imports to the same level (except in the case of domestic monopoly, when the quota raises prices more than this; see the appendix to this chapter).

The difference in effect between a quota and a tariff is that with a quota the government receives no revenue. When a quota instead of a tariff is used to restrict imports, the sum of money that would have appeared as government revenue with a tariff is collected by whoever receives the import licenses. License holders are able to buy imports and resell them at a higher price in the domestic market. The profits received by the holders of import licenses are known as the **quota rents.** In assessing the costs and benefits of an import quota, a crucial issue is to determine who gets the rents. When the rights to sell in the domestic market are assigned to governments of exporting countries, as is often the case, the transfer of rents abroad makes the costs of a quota substantially higher than the equivalent tariff.

Case Study AN IMPORT QUOTA IN PRACTICE: U.S. SUGAR

The U.S. sugar problem is similar in its origins to the European agricultural problem: a domestic price guarantee by the Federal government has led to U.S. prices above world market levels. Unlike the EEC, however, the United States has not gotten to the point where the domestic supply exceeds domestic demand. Thus the United States has been able to keep domestic prices at the target level with an import quota on sugar.

As it happens, a quantification of the likely costs and benefits of the sugar quota has been performed by the Federal Trade Commission (FTC), allowing us to place numbers into our framework.[1] Before we proceed to

[1]David G. Tarr and Morris E. Morkre, *Aggregate Costs to the United States of Tariffs and Quotas on Imports* (Washington, D.C.: Federal Trade Commission, 1984).

these numbers, however, it is important to note two special features of U.S. sugar policy that affect the results.

The first special feature is that the import quota is combined with a tariff. The effect of this is to make the rents associated with the quota smaller than they would otherwise have been or, to put it another way, to allow the U.S. government to capture part of those rents. The second special feature is that the rights to sell in the United States—the import licenses—are allocated to 24 foreign governments, who then allocate these to their own residents. Thus whatever rents are not captured by the tariff accrue to foreigners.

Figure 8-13 shows the effects of the sugar quota, as estimated by the Federal Trade Commission. Notice that the United States is assumed to be a "small" country in terms of the world sugar market; this reflects a judgment that, given time, world sugar supply is highly elastic. The FTC estimates the normal world sugar price at 15 cents a pound, requiring a quota to raise the U.S. price to its support level of 21.8 cents. The difference between U.S. and world prices is thus 6.8 cents. Since the tariff rate is only 2.8 cents, the right to sell in the United States is worth $6.8 - 2.8 = 4.0$ cents per pound. Under free trade, imports would be 13.04 billion pounds, but under the quota they are restricted to 5.96 billion pounds.

The welfare effects of the sugar quota are indicated by the five areas f, g, h, i, j. Because the quota raises the price, U.S. consumers lose the consumer surplus $f + g + h + i + j$. The value of this lost surplus is

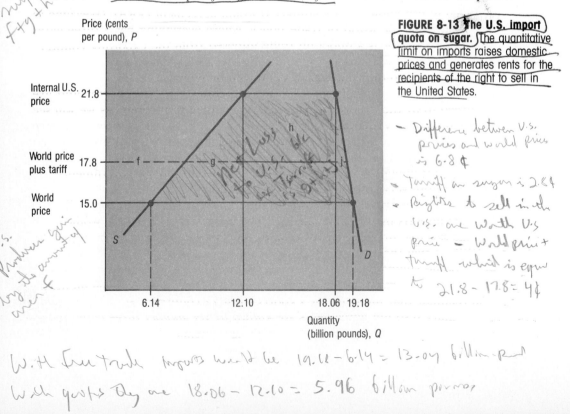

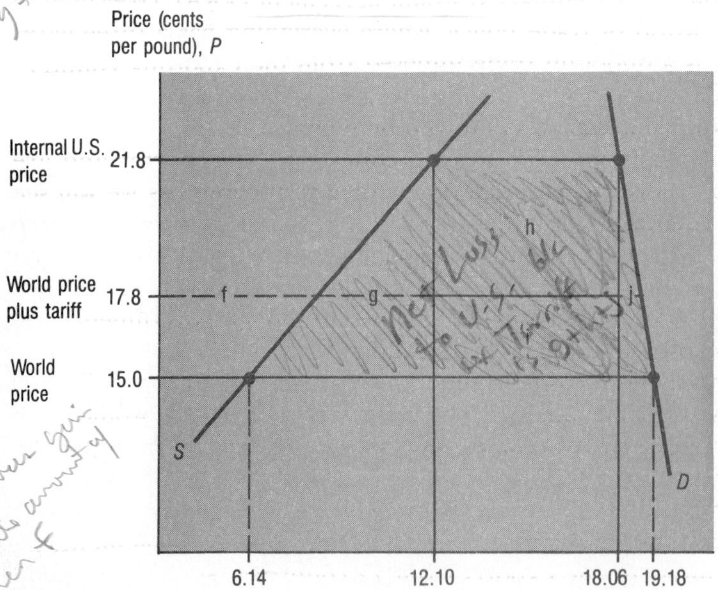

FIGURE 8-13 The U.S. import quota on sugar. The quantitative limit on imports raises domestic prices and generates rents for the recipients of the right to sell in the United States.

$1.266 billion. U.S. producers gain from the higher price, with the area f measuring their gain; the value of this gain is $616 million. The U.S. government also collects tariff revenue, in the amount measured by the area i; this is simply the volume of imports times the tariff rate equaling $167 million.

The net effect to the United States is a loss: $f + g + h + i + j - f - i = g + j + h$ = $483 million. Of this net loss, the areas g and j represent the production distortion and consumption distortion losses. Area h consists of rents collected by foreigners; it equals $238 million. This sum, which represents a pure transfer to foreigners, is thus just as important a part of the U.S. loss as efficiency costs.

A final postscript: during 1985 there was a sharp fall in the world price of sugar, to levels well below the FTC's estimates. The difference between U.S. and world sugar prices became so large as to make extreme efforts to evade the quota profitable. For example, some firms began importing Canadian pancake mix, which contains a high proportion of sugar but is not subject to the quota, and processing it to extract the sugar.

VOLUNTARY EXPORT RESTRAINTS

A variant on the import quota is the **voluntary export restraint (VER),** which is also known as a voluntary restraint agreement (VRA). (Welcome to the bureaucratic world of trade policy, where everything has a three-letter symbol.) A VER is a quota on trade imposed from the exporting country's side instead of the importer's. The most famous example is the limitation on auto exports to the United States enforced by Japan since 1981.

VERs are generally imposed at the request of the importer and are agreed to by the exporter to forestall other trade restrictions. As we will see in Chapter 9, VERs have certain political and legal advantages that have made them preferred instruments of trade policy in recent years. From an economic point of view, however, a voluntary export restraint is exactly like an import quota where the licenses are assigned to foreign governments and is therefore very costly to the importing country.

A VER is always more costly to the importing country than a tariff that limits imports by the same amount. The difference is that what would have been revenue under a tariff becomes rents earned by foreigners under the VER, so that the VER clearly produces a loss.

Some voluntary export agreements cover more than one country. The most famous multilateral agreement is the Multifiber Arrangement, an agreement that limits textile exports from 22 countries. Such multilateral voluntary restraint agreements are known by yet another three-letter abbreviation as OMAs, for orderly marketing agreements.

THE CASE OF THE FORBIDDEN PHONE BOOTHS

Anyone who has visited Britain remembers the distinctive red steel telephone booths found throughout the country. Although the British phone booth has long been popular, in 1985 the British phone service began dismantling them to replace them with more open, accessible, and vandalproof models. Peculiarly, this led to a trade dispute with the United States.

The problem began when the British, rather than simply melting down the old phone booths, decided to try to sell them. They soon discovered that they had a market in the United States. Many Americans, it turned out, were interested in buying a traditional British phone booth, whether to decorate shopping malls, to place in the gardens of Beverly Hills homes, or for other purposes. There seemed to be a perfect match between America's idea of the old Britain and Britain's march toward the future.

When the phone booths began to arrive in the United States, however, they were impounded by U.S. Customs because of an orderly marketing agreement in iron and steel products between the United States and Europe, including Britain. This agreement sets a limit on the quantity of iron and steel products that Britain may export to the United States. Since old phone booths are mostly iron and steel, the United States refused to allow them in unless Britain reduced its exports of some other product. (Specifically, the United States contended that the phone booths fell under a category defined in the OMA as "other other.") The British, of course, denounced this action, claiming that phone booths should be classified, not as iron and steel, but as antiques—a category for which there is so far no U.S. import restriction. At the time of writing the phone booths were the subject of high-level negotiations.

Case Study A VOLUNTARY EXPORT RESTRAINT IN PRACTICE: JAPANESE AUTOS

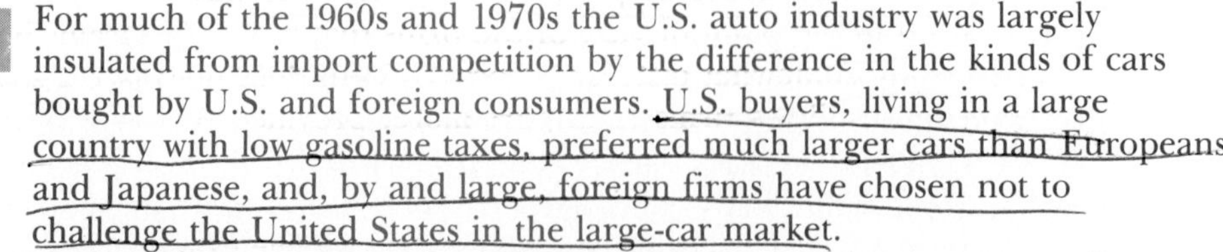

For much of the 1960s and 1970s the U.S. auto industry was largely insulated from import competition by the difference in the kinds of cars bought by U.S. and foreign consumers. U.S. buyers, living in a large country with low gasoline taxes, preferred much larger cars than Europeans and Japanese, and, by and large, foreign firms have chosen not to challenge the United States in the large-car market.

In 1979, however, sharp oil price increases and temporary gasoline shortages caused the U.S. market to shift abruptly toward smaller cars. Japanese producers, whose costs had been falling relative to their U.S.

competitors in any case, moved in to fill the new demand. As the Japanese market share soared and U.S. output fell, strong political forces in the United States demanded protection for the U.S. industry. Rather than act unilaterally and risk creating a trade war, the U.S. government asked the Japanese government to limit its exports. The Japanese, fearing unilateral U.S. protectionist measures if they did not do so, agreed to limit their sales. The first agreement, in 1981, limited Japanese exports to the United States to 1.68 million automobiles. A revision raised that total to 1.85 million in 1984–1985. In 1985, the agreement was allowed to lapse, but the Japanese government indicated its intention to continue to restrict its exports.

The effects of this voluntary export restraint are complicated by several factors. First, Japanese and U.S. cars are clearly not perfect substitutes. Second, the Japanese industry to some extent responded to the quota by upgrading its quality, selling larger autos with more extra features. Third, the auto industry is clearly not perfectly competitive. Nonetheless, the basic results were what the discussion of voluntary export restraints earlier would have predicted: the price of Japanese cars in the United States rose, with the rent captured by Japanese firms. The FTC estimates the total costs to the United States at nearly one billion dollars per year, primarily transfers to Japan rather than efficiency losses.

LOCAL CONTENT REQUIREMENTS

A **local content requirement** is a regulation that requires that some specified fraction of a final good be produced domestically. In some cases this fraction is specified in physical units, like the U.S. oil import quota in the 1960s (see below). In other cases the requirement is stated in value terms, by requiring that some minimum share of the price of a good represent domestic value added. Local content laws have been widely used by developing countries trying to shift their manufacturing base from assembly back into intermediate goods. In the United States, a local content bill for automobiles was proposed in 1982 but was never acted upon.

From the point of view of the domestic producers of parts, a local content regulation provides protection in the same way that an import quota does. From the point of view of the firms that must buy locally, however, the effects are somewhat different. Local content does not place a strict limit on imports. It allows firms to import more, provided that they also buy more domestically. This means that the effective price of inputs to the firm is an average of the price of imported and domestically produced inputs.

Consider, for example, the earlier automobile example in which the cost of imported parts is $6000. Suppose that to purchase the same parts domestically would cost $10,000 but that assembly firms are required to use 50 percent domestic parts. Then they will face an average cost of parts of

\$8000 (0.5 × \$6000 + 0.5 × \$10,000), which will be reflected in the final price of the car.

The important point is that a local content requirement does not produce either government revenue or quota rents. Instead, the difference between the prices of imports and domestic goods in effect gets averaged in the final price and is passed on to consumers.

An interesting innovation in local content regulations has been to allow firms to satisfy their local content requirement by exporting instead of using parts domestically. This has become important in several cases: for example, U.S. auto firms operating in Mexico have chosen to export some components from Mexico to the United States, even though those components could be produced in the United States more cheaply, because this allows them to use less Mexican content in producing cars in Mexico for Mexico's market.

Case Study A LOCAL CONTENT SCHEME: THE OIL IMPORT QUOTA IN THE 1960s

Local content regulations are widely used as part of the industrialization strategies of less-developed countries. In most cases, however, the details of the schemes are too complex to be easily summarized. To illustrate a fairly simple local content scheme in practice, we reach back into history to describe the working of the U.S. oil import quota in the 1960s and early 1970s.

As its name suggests, the oil import quota was intended to set a quantitative limit on U.S. oil imports. Unlike many import limitations, however, this legislation did not allocate rights to import on a fixed basis to foreign governments or domestic firms. Instead, it allowed domestic firms to compete for quota rights in a way that turned it effectively into a local content requirement.

Imported oil is not sold directly to final consumers. It must first be processed into refined products such as gasoline and heating oil. The oil import quota based the amount of imported oil that a refiner was allowed to purchase on the total amount of oil it refined. That is, by refining, say, eight barrels of domestic crude oil the refiner would be allowed to purchase one barrel of cheaper imported oil. (In fact the proportions depended on the size of the refiner; small refiners were allowed to purchase a higher proportion of imported oil than large.)

What was particularly interesting about the scheme was that refiners were not required to use or even actually take delivery of the imported oil. They could instead sell their import rights (known as "tickets") to other refiners. In general, inland refiners sold their rights to coastal ones, generating a substantial market in which the right to import sold at a well-defined price.

The results were straightforward. Domestic oil sold at a higher price than imported: about $3.25 per barrel versus $2.00. Correspondingly, the price of an import "ticket" was about $1.25. Consumer prices of refined products appeared to reflect the average price of oil, which lay between the import and domestic prices.

Estimates of the effects of the oil import quota suggest that it cost consumers about $5 billion per year. Most of this, however, was a redistribution to oil producers rather than a net cost to the economy as a whole; the net cost may have been on the order of $1 to $2 billion.

OTHER TRADE POLICY INSTRUMENTS

There are many other ways in which governments influence trade. We list some of them briefly.

Export credit subsidies. This is like an export subsidy except that it takes the form of a subsidized loan to the buyer. The United States, like most countries, has a government institution, the Export-Import Bank, that is devoted to providing at least slightly subsidized loans to aid exports.

National procurement. Purchases by the government or by strongly regulated firms can be directed toward domestically produced goods even when these goods are more expensive than imports. The classic example is the European telecommunications industry. The nations of the European Economic Community in principle have free trade with each other. The main purchasers of telecommunications equipment, however, are phone companies—and in Europe these companies have until recently all been government-owned. These government-owned telephone companies buy from domestic suppliers even when these suppliers charge higher prices than suppliers in other countries. The result is that there is very little trade in telecommunications equipment within Europe.

Red-tape barriers. Sometimes a government wants to restrict imports without doing so formally. Fortunately or unfortunately, it is easy to twist normal health, safety, and customs procedures so as to place substantial obstacles in the way of trade. The classic example here is the French decree in 1982 that all Japanese videocassette recorders must pass through the tiny customs house at Poitiers—effectively limiting the actual imports to a handful.

SUMMARY

1. In contrast to our earlier analysis, which stressed the general equilibrium interaction of markets, for analysis of trade policy it is usually sufficient to use a *partial equilibrium* approach.

2. A tariff drives a wedge between foreign and domestic prices, raising the domestic price, but by less than the tariff rate. An important and relevant special case, however, is that of a "small" country that cannot have any substantial influence on foreign prices. In the small country case a tariff is fully reflected in domestic prices.

3. The costs and benefits of a tariff or other trade policy may be measured using the concepts of *consumer surplus* and *producer surplus*. Using these concepts, we can show that the domestic producers of a good gain, because a tariff raises the price they receive; the domestic consumers lose, for the same reason. There is also a gain in government revenue.

4. If we add together the gains and losses from a tariff, we find that the net effect on national welfare can be separated into two parts. There is an *efficiency loss,* which results from the distortion in the incentives facing domestic producers and consumers. On the other hand, there is a *terms of trade gain,* reflecting the tendency of a tariff to drive down foreign export prices. In the case of a small country that cannot affect foreign prices, the second effect is zero, so that there is an unambiguous loss.

5. The analysis of a tariff can be readily adapted to other trade policy measures, such as *export subsidies, import quotas,* and *voluntary export restraints*. An export quota causes efficiency losses similar to a tariff but compounds these losses by causing a deterioration of the terms of trade. Import quotas and voluntary export restraints differ from tariffs in that the government gets no revenue. Instead, what would have been government revenue accrues as *rents* to the recipients of import licenses in the case of a quota, to foreigners in the case of a voluntary export restraint.

KEY TERMS

specific tariff
ad valorem tariff
nontariff barriers
import demand curve
export supply curve
effective rate of protection
consumer surplus
producer surplus
efficiency loss
terms of trade gain
production distortion loss
consumption distortion loss
import quota
quota rent
voluntary export restraint (VER)
local content requirement

PROBLEMS

1. Home's demand curve for wheat is

$$D = 100 - 20P.$$

Its supply curve is

$$S = 20 + 20P.$$

Derive and graph Home's *import* demand schedule. What would the price of wheat be in the absence of trade?

2. Now add Foreign, which has a demand curve

$$D^* = 80 - 20P$$

and a supply curve

$$S^* = 40 + 20P.$$

a) Derive and graph Foreign's *export* supply curve, and find the price of wheat that would prevail in Foreign in the absence of trade.

b) Now allow Foreign and Home to trade with each other, at zero transportation cost. Find and graph the equilibrium under free trade. What is the world price? What is the volume of trade?

3. Home imposes a specific tariff of 0.5 on wheat imports.

a) Determine and show graphically the effects of the tariff on the following: (1) The price of wheat in each country; (2) the quantity of wheat supplied and demanded in each country; (3) the volume of trade.

b) Determine the effect of the tariff on the welfare of each of the following groups: (1) Home import-competing producers; (2) Home consumers; (3) the Home government.

c) Show graphically and calculate the terms of trade gain, the efficiency loss, and the total effect on welfare of the tariff.

4. Suppose that Foreign had been a much larger country, with domestic demand

$$D^* = 800 - 200P,$$

$$S^* = 400 + 200P.$$

(Notice that this implies that the Foreign price of wheat in the absence of trade would have been the same as in problem 2.)

Recalculate the free trade equilibrium and the effects of a 0.5 tariff by Home. Relate the difference in results to the discussion of the "small country" case in the text.

5. The aircraft industry in Europe receives aid from several governments, according to some estimates equal to 20 percent of the purchase price of each aircraft. For example, an airplane that sells for $50 million may have cost $60 million to produce, with the difference made up by European governments. At the same time, approximately half the purchase price of a "European" aircraft represents the cost of components purchased from other countries (incuding the United States). If these estimates are correct, what is the *effective* rate of protection received by European aircraft producers?

6. Return to the example of problem 2. Starting from free trade, assume that Foreign offers exporters a subsidy of 0.5 per unit. Calculate the effects on the price in each country and on welfare, both of individual groups and of the economy as a whole, in both countries.

7. The nation of Acirema is "small," unable to affect world prices. It imports peanuts at the price of $10 per bag. The demand curve is

$$D = 400 - 10P.$$

The supply curve is

$$S = 50 + 5P.$$

Determine the free trade equilibrium. Then calculate and graph the following effects of an import quota that limits imports to 50 bags.

a) The increase in the domestic price
b) The quota rents
c) The consumption distortion loss
d) The production distortion loss

FURTHER READING

Jagdish Bhagwati. "On the Equivalence of Tariffs and Quotas," in Robert E. Baldwin et al., eds. *Trade, Growth, and the Balance of Payments.* Chicago: Rand McNally, 1965. The classic comparison of tariffs and quotas under monopoly.

W. M. Corden. *The Theory of Protection.* Oxford: Clarendon Press, 1971. A general survey of the effects of tariffs, quotas, and other trade policies.

Robert W. Crandall. *Regulating the Automobile.* Washington, D.C.: Brookings Institution, 1986. Contains an analysis of the most famous of all voluntary export restraints.

Ilse Mintz. *U.S. Import Quotas: Costs and Consequences.* Washington, D.C.: American Enterprise Institute, 1973. Description and analysis of some actual U.S. trade policies.

D. Rousslang and A. Suomela. "Calculating the Consumer and Net Welfare Costs of Import Relief." U.S. International Trade Commission Staff Research Study 15. Washington, D.C.: International Trade Commission, 1985. An exposition of the framework used in this chapter, with a description of how the framework is applied in practice to real industries.

APPENDIX TO CHAPTER 8

Tariffs and Import Quotas in the Presence of Monopoly

The trade policy analysis in this chapter assumed that markets are perfectly competitive, so that all firms take prices as given. As we argued in Chapter 6, however, many markets for internationally traded goods are imperfectly competitive. The effects of international trade policies can be affected by the nature of the competition in a market.

When we analyze the effects of trade policy in imperfectly competitive markets, a new consideration appears: international trade limits monopoly power, and policies that limit trade may therefore increase monopoly power. Even if a firm is the only producer of a good in a country, it will have little ability to raise prices if there are many foreign suppliers and free trade. If imports are limited by a quota, however, the same firm will now be free to raise prices without fear of competition.

The link between trade policy and monopoly power may be understood by examining a model in which a country imports a good and its import-competing production is controlled by only *one* firm. The country is small on world markets, so that the price of the import is unaffected by its trade policy. For this model, we examine and compare the effects of free trade, a tariff, and an import quota.

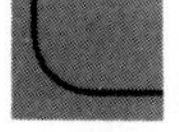

THE MODEL WITH FREE TRADE

Figure 8A-1 shows free trade in a market where a domestic monopolist faces competition from imports. D is the domestic demand curve: demand for the product by domestic residents. P_W is the world price of the good; imports are available in unlimited quantities at that price. The domestic industry is assumed to consist of only a single firm, whose marginal cost curve is MC.

If there were no trade in this market, the domestic firm would behave as an ordinary profit-maximizing monopolist. Corresponding to D is a marginal revenue curve MR, and the firm would choose the monopoly profit-maximizing level of output Q_M and price P_M.

With free trade, however, this monopoly behavior is not possible. If the firm tried to charge P_M, or indeed any price above P_W, nobody would buy its product, because cheaper imports would be available. Thus international trade puts a lid on the monopolist's price at P_W.

Given this limit on its price, the best the monopolist can do is produce up to the point where marginal cost is equal to the world price, at Q_f. At the price P_W, domestic consumers will demand D_f units of the good, so imports will be $D_f - Q_f$. This outcome, however, is exactly what would have happened if the domestic industry had been perfectly competitive. With free trade, then, the fact that the domestic industry is a monopoly does not make any difference to the outcome.

THE MODEL WITH A TARIFF

The effect of a tariff is to raise the maximum price the domestic industry can charge. If a specific tariff t is charged on imports, the domestic industry can now charge

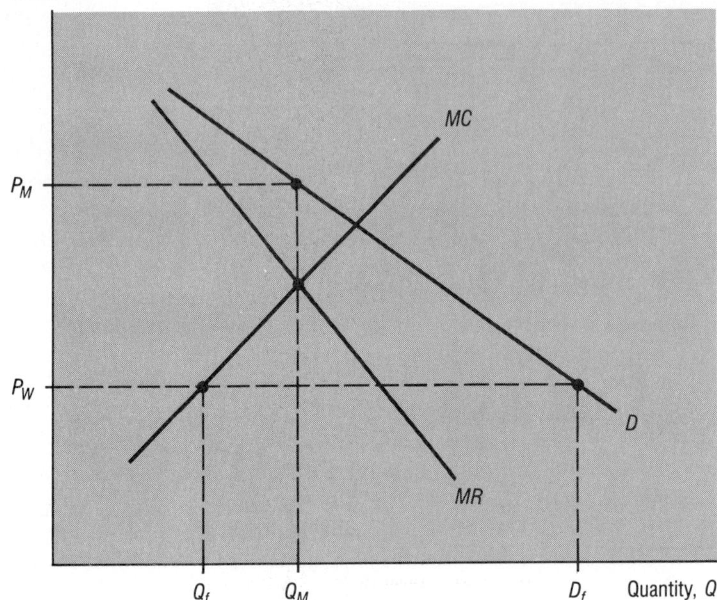

FIGURE 8A-1 A monopolist under free trade. The threat of import competition forces the monopolist to behave like a perfectly competitive industry.

$P_W + t$ (Figure 8A-2). The industry is still not free to raise its price all the way to the monopoly price, however, because consumers will still turn to imports if the price rises above the world price plus the tariff. Thus the best the monopolist can do is to set price equal to marginal cost, at Q_t. The tariff raises the domestic price as well as the output of the domestic industry, while demand falls to D_t and thus imports fall. However, the domestic industry still produces the same quantity as if it were perfectly competitive.[1]

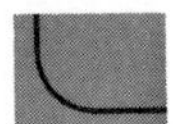

THE MODEL WITH AN IMPORT QUOTA

Suppose the government imposes a limit on imports, restricting their quantity to a fixed level $\overline{Q}$. Then the monopolist knows that when it charges a price above P_W, it will not lose all its sales. Instead, it will sell whatever domestic demand is at that price, minus the allowed imports $\overline{Q}$. Thus the demand facing the monopolist will be domestic demand less allowed imports. We define the postquota demand curve as D_q; it is parallel to the domestic demand curve D but shifted $\overline{Q}$ units to the left (Figure 8A-3).

Corresponding to D_q is a new marginal revenue curve MR_q. The firm protected by an import quota maximizes profit by setting marginal cost equal to this new

[1]There is one case in which a tariff will have different effects on a monopolistic industry than on a perfectly competitive one. This is the case where a tariff is so high that imports are completely eliminated (a prohibitive tariff). For a competitive industry, once imports have been eliminated, any further increase in the tariff has no effect. A monopolist, however, will be forced to limit its price by the *threat* of imports even if actual imports are zero. Thus an increase in a prohibitive tariff will allow a monopolist to raise its price closer to the profit-maximizing price P_M.

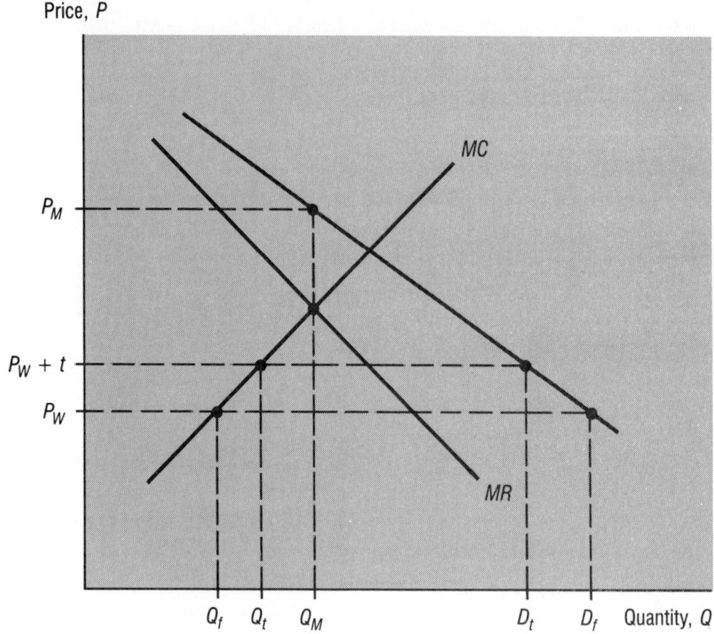

FIGURE 8A-2 A monopolist protected by a tariff. The tariff allows the monopolist to raise its price, but the price is still limited by the threat of imports.

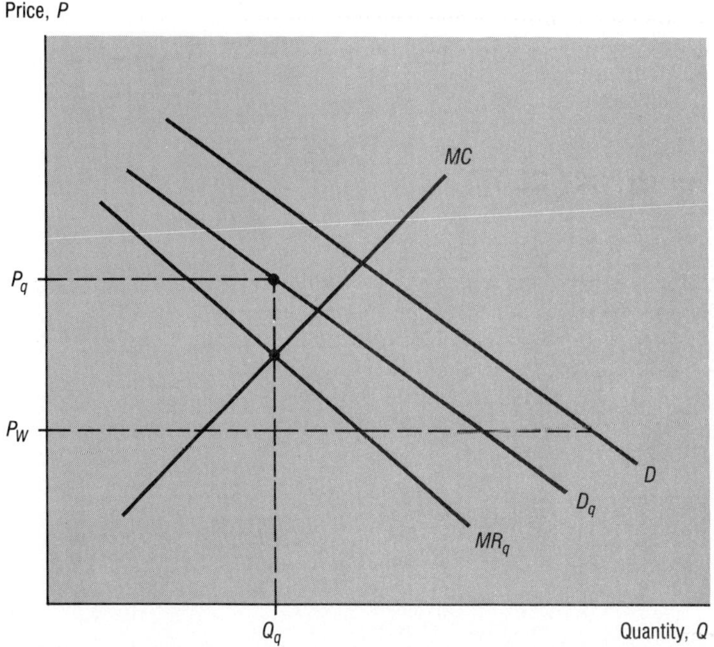

FIGURE 8A-3 A monopolist protected by an import quota. The monopolist is now free to raise prices, knowing that the domestic price of imports will rise too.

marginal revenue, producing Q_q and charging the price P_q. (The license to import one unit of the good will therefore yield a rent of $P_q - P_W$.)

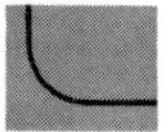

COMPARING A TARIFF AND A QUOTA

We now ask how the effects of a tariff and a quota compare. To do this, we compare a tariff and a quota that lead to *the same level of imports* (Figure 8A-4). The tariff level t leads to a level of imports $\overline{Q}$; we therefore ask what would happen if instead of a tariff the government simply limited imports to $\overline{Q}$.

We see from the figure that the results are not the same. The tariff leads to domestic production of Q_t and a domestic price of $P_W + t$. The quota leads to a lower level of domestic production, Q_q, and a higher price, P_q. When protected by a tariff the monopolistic domestic industry behaves as if it were perfectly competitive; when protected by a quota it clearly does not.

The reason for this difference is that an import quota creates more monopoly power than a tariff. When a monopolistic industry is protected by a tariff, domestic firms know that if they raise their prices too high they will still be undercut by imports. An import quota, on the other hand, provides absolute protection: no matter how high the domestic price, imports cannot exceed the quota level.

This comparison seems to say that if governments are concerned about domestic monopoly power, they should prefer tariffs to quotas as instruments of trade policy. In fact, however, protection has increasingly drifted away from tariffs toward nontariff barriers, including import quotas. To explain this, we need to look at considerations other than economic efficiency that motivate governments.

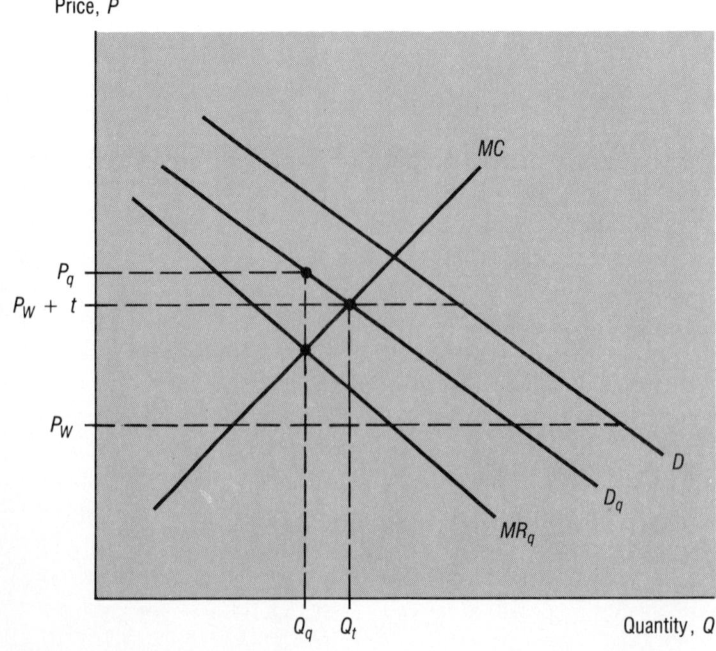

FIGURE 8A-4 Comparing a tariff and a quota. A quota leads to lower domestic output and a higher price than a tariff that yields the same level of imports.

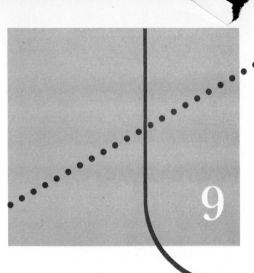

9 THE POLITICAL ECONOMY OF TRADE POLICY

In 1981, the United States asked Japan to limit its exports of autos to the United States. This raised the prices of imported cars and forced U.S. consumers to buy domestic autos they clearly did not like as much. While Japan was willing to accommodate the U.S. government on this point, however, it was unwilling to meet another U.S. request, that it eliminate import quotas on beef and citrus products—quotas that forced Japanese consumers to buy incredibly expensive domestic products instead of cheap imports from the United States. The governments of both countries were thus determined to pursue policies that, according to the cost-benefit analysis we developed in Chapter 8, produced more costs than benefits. Clearly, government policies must reflect objectives that go beyond simple measures of cost and benefit.

In this chapter we examine some of the reasons why governments either should not or at any rate do not base their policy on economists' cost-benefit calculations. The examination of the forces motivating trade policy in practice continues in Chapters 10 and 11, which discuss the characteristic trade policy issues facing developing and advanced countries, respectively.

The first step toward understanding actual trade policies is to ask what reasons there are for governments *not* to interfere with trade—that is, what is the case for free trade? With this question answered, arguments for intervention can be examined as challenges to the assumptions underlying the case for free trade.

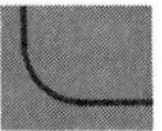

THE CASE FOR FREE TRADE

Few countries have anything approaching completely free trade. The city-state of Hong Kong may be the only modern nation with no tariffs or import quotas. Nonetheless, since the time of Adam Smith economists have advocated free trade as an ideal toward which trade policy should strive. The reasons for this advocacy are not quite as simple as the idea itself. At one level, theoretical models of trade suggest that free trade will avoid the efficiency losses associated with protection. Many economists believe that free trade produces additional gains that go beyond the elimination of production and consumption distortions. Finally, even among economists who believe that free trade is a less than perfect policy, many believe that free trade is usually better than any other policy that a government is likely to follow.

FREE TRADE AND EFFICIENCY

The **efficiency case for free trade** is simply the reverse of the cost-benefit analysis of a tariff. Figure 9-1 shows the basic point once again for the case of a small country that cannot influence foreign export prices. A tariff causes a net loss to the economy measured by the area of the two triangles; it does so by distorting the economic incentives of both producers and consumers. Conversely, a move to free trade eliminates these distortions and increases national welfare.

A number of efforts have been made to add up the total costs of distortions due to tariffs and import quotas in particular economies. Table 9-1 presents some representative estimates. It is noteworthy that the costs of protection to the United States are measured as quite small relative to national income. This situation reflects two facts: (1) the United States is rela-

TABLE 9-1 Estimated cost of protection, as a percentage of national income

Brazil (1966)	9.5
Pakistan (1963)	6.2
Mexico (1960)	2.5
United States (1983)	0.26

Source: Bela Balassa. *The Structure of Protection in Developing Countries.* Baltimore: The Johns Hopkins Press, 1971; and David G. Tarr and Morris E. Morkre. *Aggregate Costs to the United States of Tariffs and Quotas on Imports.* Washington, D.C.: Federal Trade Commission, 1984.

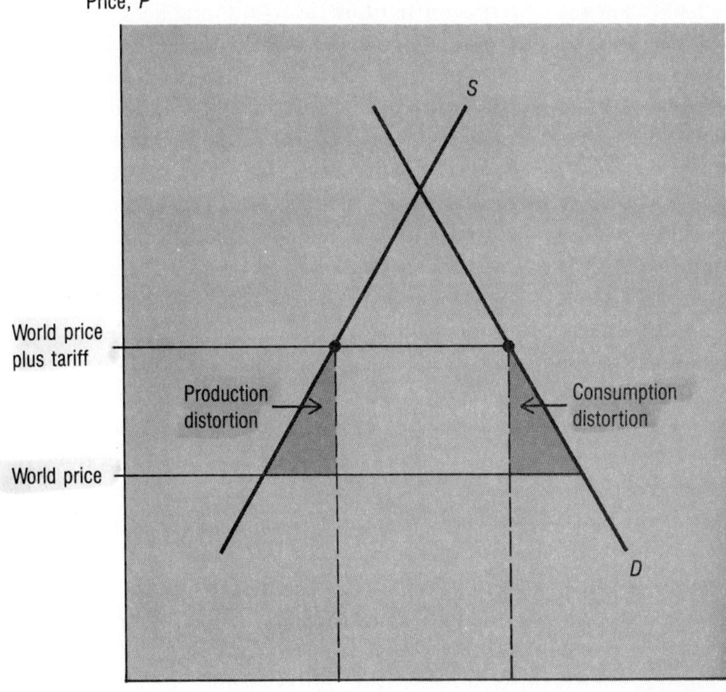

FIGURE 9-1 The efficiency case for free trade. A trade restriction, such as a tariff, leads to production and consumption distortions.

tively less dependent on trade than other countries, and (2) with some major exceptions, U.S. trade is fairly free. By contrast, some smaller countries that impose very restrictive tariffs and quotas are estimated to lose as much as 10 percent of their potential national income to distortions caused by their trade policies.

ADDITIONAL GAINS FROM FREE TRADE[1]

There is a widespread belief among economists that calculations of the kind reported in Table 9-1, even though they report substantial gains from free trade in some cases, do not represent the whole story. In small countries in general and developing countries in particular, many economists would argue that there are important gains from free trade that are not accounted for in conventional cost-benefit analysis.

One kind of additional gain involves economies of scale. Protected markets not only fragment production internationally, but by reducing competition and raising profits, they also lead too many firms to enter the protected

[1]The additional gains from free trade that are discussed here are sometimes referred to as "dynamic" gains, because increased competition and innovation may take more time to take effect than the elimination of production and consumption distortions.

industry. With a proliferation of firms in narrow domestic markets, the scale of production of each firm becomes inefficient. A good example of how protection leads to inefficient scale is the case of the Argentine automobile industry, which emerged because of import restrictions. An efficient scale assembly plant should make from 80 thousand to 200 thousand automobiles per year; yet in 1964 the Argentine industry, which produced only 166 thousand cars, contained no less than 13 firms! Some economists argue that the need to deter excessive entry and the resulting inefficient scale of production is a reason for free trade that goes beyond the standard cost-benefit calculations.

Another argument for free trade is that by providing entrepreneurs with an incentive to seek out new ways to export or compete with imports, free trade offers more opportunities for learning and innovation than are provided by a system of "managed" trade where the government largely dictates the pattern of imports and exports. Chapter 10 discusses the experiences of less-developed countries that discovered unexpected export opportunities when they shifted from systems of import quotas and tariffs to more open trade policies.

These additional arguments for free trade are for the most part not quantified. Recently, however, the Canadian economists Richard Harris and David Cox have attempted to quantify the gains for Canada of free trade with the United States, taking into account the gains from a more efficient scale of production within Canada. They estimate that Canada's real income would rise by 8.6 percent—an increase about three times as large as the one typically estimated by economists who do not take the gains from economies of scale into account.

If the additional gains from free trade are as large as some economists believe, the costs of distorting trade with tariffs, quotas, export subsidies, etc., are correspondingly larger than the conventional cost-benefit analysis measures.

POLITICAL ARGUMENT FOR FREE TRADE

A **political argument for free trade** reflects the fact that a political commitment to free trade may be a good idea in practice even though there may be better policies in principle. In discussing U.S. trade policies in particular, economists often argue that trade policies in practice are dominated by special-interest politics rather than consideration of national costs and benefits. Economists can sometimes show that in theory a selective set of tariffs and export subsidies could increase national welfare, but in reality any government agency attempting to pursue a sophisticated program of intervention in trade would probably be captured by interest groups and converted into a device for redistributing income to politically influential sectors. If this argument is correct, it may be better to advocate free trade without exceptions, even though on purely economic grounds free trade may not always be the best conceivable policy.

The three arguments outlined in the previous section probably represent the standard view of most international economists, at least in the United States.

1. The conventionally measured costs of deviating from free trade are large.
2. There are other benefits from free trade that add to the costs of protectionist policies.
3. Any attempt to pursue sophisticated deviations from free trade will be subverted by the political process.

Nonetheless, there are intellectually respectable arguments for deviating from free trade, and these arguments deserve a fair hearing.

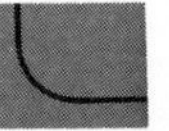

NATIONAL WELFARE ARGUMENTS AGAINST FREE TRADE

Most tariffs, import quotas, and other trade policy measures are undertaken primarily to protect the income of particular interest groups. Politicians often claim, however, that the policies are being undertaken in the interest of the nation as a whole, and sometimes they are even telling the truth. Although economists often argue that deviations from free trade reduce national welfare, there are, in fact, some theoretical grounds for believing that activist trade policies can sometimes increase the welfare of the nation as a whole.

THE TERMS OF TRADE ARGUMENT FOR A TARIFF

One argument for deviating from free trade comes directly out of cost-benefit analysis: for a large country that is able to affect the prices of foreign exporters, a tariff lowers the price of imports and thus generates a terms of trade benefit. This benefit must be set against the costs of the tariff, which arise because the tariff distorts production and consumption incentives. It is possible, however, that in some cases the terms of trade benefits of a tariff outweigh its costs so there is a **terms of trade argument for a tariff.**

The appendix to this chapter shows that for a sufficiently small tariff the terms of trade benefits must outweigh the costs. Thus at small tariff rates a country's welfare is higher than with free trade (Figure 9-2). As the tariff rate is increased, however, the costs eventually begin to grow more rapidly than the benefits, and the curve relating national welfare to the tariff rate turns down. A tariff rate that completely prohibits trade (t_P in Figure 9-2) leaves the country worse off than with free trade; further increases in the tariff rate beyond t_P have no effect, so the curve flattens out.

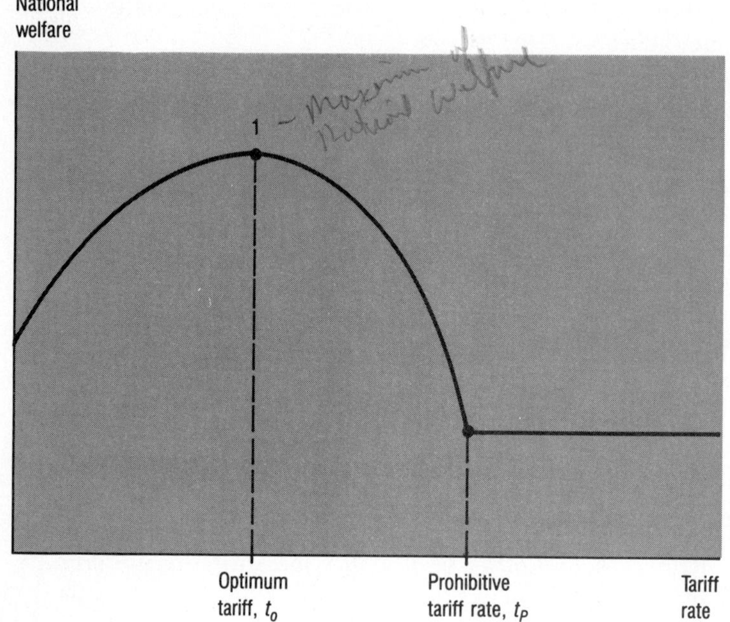

FIGURE 9-2 The optimum tariff. For a large country, there is an optimum tariff t_O at which the marginal gain from improved terms of trade just equals the marginal efficiency loss from production and consumption distortion.

At point 1 on the curve in Figure 9-2, corresponding to the tariff rate t_O, national welfare is maximized. The tariff rate t_O that maximizes national welfare is the **optimum tariff.** (By convention the phrase "optimum tariff" is usually used to refer to the tariff justified by a terms of trade argument rather than to the best tariff given all possible considerations.) The optimum tariff rate is always positive, but less than the prohibitive rate (t_P) that would eliminate all imports.

What policy would the terms of trade argument dictate for *export* sectors? Since an export subsidy *worsens* the terms of trade, and therefore unambiguously reduces national welfare, the optimal policy in export sectors must be a negative subsidy—that is, a *tax* on exports that raises the price of exports to foreigners. Like the optimum tariff, the optimum export tax is always positive, but less than the prohibitive tax that would eliminate exports completely.

The policy of Saudi Arabia and other oil exporters has been to tax their exports of oil, raising the price to the rest of the world. Although oil prices fell in the mid-1980s, it is hard to argue that Saudi Arabia would have been better off under free trade.

The terms of trade argument against free trade has some important limitations, however. Most small countries have very little ability to affect the world prices of either their imports or other exports, so that the terms of trade argument is of little practical importance. For big countries like the United States, the problem is that the terms of trade argument amounts to an argument for using national monopoly power to extract gains at other countries' expense. The United States could surely do this to some extent, but such a predatory policy would probably bring retaliation from other large countries. A cycle of retaliatory trade moves would, in turn, undermine the attempts at international trade policy coordination described later in this chapter.

The terms of trade argument against free trade, then, is intellectually impeccable but of doubtful usefulness. In practice, it is emphasized more by economists as a theoretical proposition than it is used by governments as a justification for trade policy.

THE DOMESTIC MARKET FAILURE ARGUMENT AGAINST FREE TRADE

Leaving aside the issue of the terms of trade, the basic theoretical case for free trade rested on cost-benefit analysis using the concepts of consumer and producer surplus. Many economists have made a case against free trade based on the counterargument that these concepts, producer surplus in particular, do not properly measure costs and benefits.

Why might producer surplus not properly measure the benefits of producing a good? We consider a variety of reasons in the next two chapters: these include the possibility that the labor used in a sector would otherwise be unemployed or underemployed, the existence of defects in the capital or labor markets that prevent resources from being transferred as rapidly as they should be to sectors that yield high returns, and the possibility of technological spillovers from industries that are new or particularly innovative. These can all be classified under the general heading of **domestic market failures.** That is, each of these examples is one in which some market within the country is not doing its job right—the labor market is not clearing, the capital market is not allocating resources efficiently, and so on.

Suppose, for example, that the production of some good yields experience that will improve the technology of the economy as a whole but that the firms in the sector cannot appropriate this benefit and therefore do not take it into account in deciding how much to produce. Then there is a **marginal social benefit** to additional production that is not captured by the producer surplus measure. This marginal social benefit can serve as a justification for tariffs or other trade policies.

Figure 9-3 illustrates the domestic market failure argument against free trade. Figure 9-3a shows the conventional cost-benefit analysis of a tariff for a small country (which rules out terms of trade effects). Figure 9-3b shows the marginal benefit from production that is not taken account of by the producer surplus measure. The figure shows the effects of a tariff that raises the domestic price from P_W to $P_W + t$. Production rises from S^1 to S^2, with a resulting production distortion indicated by the area labeled a. Consumption falls from D^1 to D^2, with a resulting consumption distortion indicated by the area b. If we considered only consumer and producer surplus, we would find

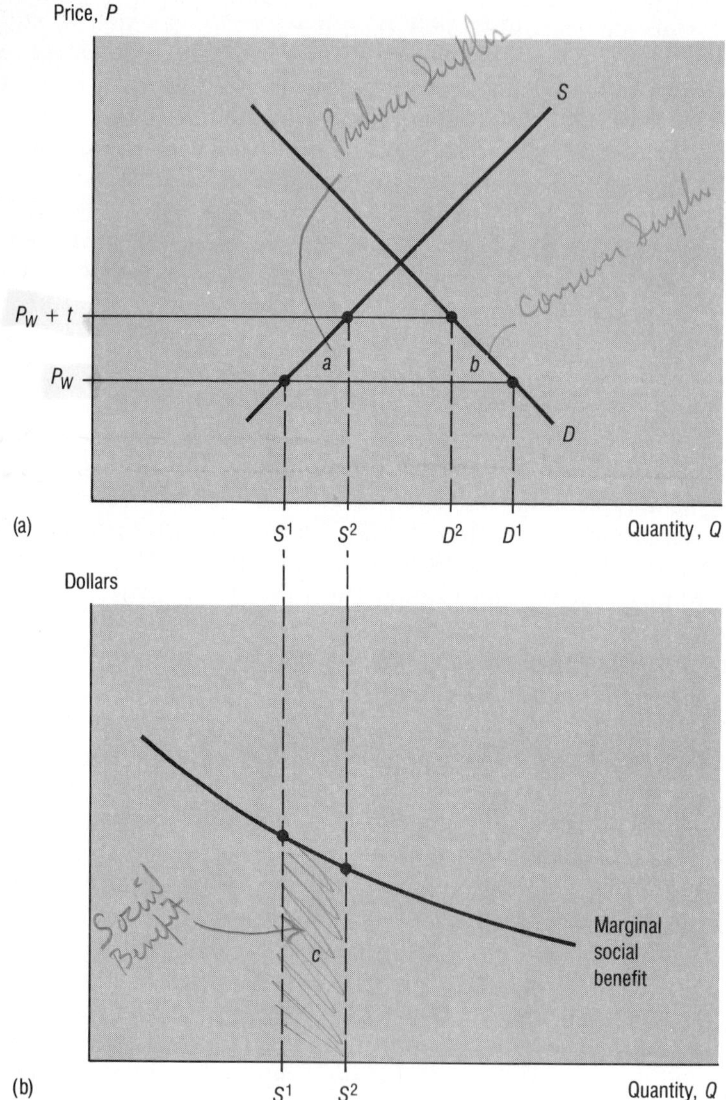

FIGURE 9-3 The domestic market failure argument for a tariff. If production of a good yields extra social benefits not captured as producer surplus, a tariff can increase welfare.

that the costs of the tariff exceed its benefits. Figure 9-3b shows, however, that this calculation overlooks an additional benefit that may make the tariff preferable to free trade. The increase in production yields a social benefit that may be measured by the area under the marginal social benefit curve from S^1 to S^2, indicated by *c*. In fact, by an argument similar to that in the terms of trade case, we can show that if the tariff is small enough the area *c* must always exceed the area $a + b$, and that there is some welfare-maximizing tariff that yields a level of social welfare higher than that of free trade.

The domestic market failure argument against free trade is a particular case of a more general concept known in economics as the **theory of the second best.** This theory states that a hands-off policy is desirable in any one market only if all other markets are working properly. If they are not, a government intervention that appears to distort incentives in one market may actually increase welfare by offsetting the consequences of market failures elsewhere. For example, if the labor market is malfunctioning and fails to deliver full employment, a policy of subsidizing labor-intensive industries, which would be undesirable in a full-employment economy, might turn out to be a good idea. It would be better to fix the labor market, for example, by making wages more flexible; but if for some reason this cannot be done, intervening in other markets may be a "second-best" way of alleviating the problem.

When economists apply the theory of the second best to trade policy, they argue that imperfections in the *internal* functioning of an economy may justify interfering in its *external* economic relations. This argument accepts that international trade is not the source of the problem but suggests nonetheless that trade policy can provide at least a partial solution.

HOW CONVINCING IS THE MARKET FAILURE ARGUMENT?

When they were first proposed, market failure arguments for protection seemed to undermine much of the case for free trade. After all, who would want to argue that the real economies we live in are free from market failures? In poorer nations, in particular, market imperfections seem to be legion. For example, unemployment and massive differences between rural and urban wage rates are present in many less-developed countries (Chapter 10). The evidence that markets work badly is less glaring in advanced countries, but it is easy to develop hypotheses suggesting major market failures there as well—for example, the inability of innovative firms to reap the full rewards of their innovations. How can we defend free trade given the likelihood that there are interventions that could raise national welfare?

There are two lines of defense for free trade. The first is the argument that domestic market failures should be corrected by domestic policies aimed at their source. The second is the argument that economists cannot diagnose market failure well enough to prescribe policy in any case.

The point that domestic market failure calls for domestic policy changes, not international trade policies, can be made by cost-benefit analysis, modified to account for any unmeasured marginal social benefits. The situation illustrated in Figure 9-3 again showed that a tariff might raise welfare, despite the production and consumption distortion it causes, because it leads to additional production that yields social benefits. If the same production increase were achieved via a production subsidy rather than a tariff, however, the price to consumers would not increase, and the consumption loss b would be avoided. In other words, by targeting directly the particular activity we want to encourage, a production subsidy would avoid some of the side costs associated with a tariff.

This example illustrates a general principle when dealing with market failures: it is always preferable to deal with market failures as directly as possible, because indirect policy responses lead to unintended distortions of incentives elsewhere in the economy. Thus, trade policies justified by domestic market failure are never the most efficient response; they are always "second-best" rather than "first-best" policies.

This insight has important implications for trade policymakers: any proposed trade policy should always be compared with a purely domestic policy aimed at correcting the same problem. If the domestic policy appears too costly or has undesirable side effects, the trade policy is almost surely even less desirable—even though the costs are less apparent.

In the United States, for example, an import quota on automobiles has been supported on the grounds that it is necessary to save the jobs of autoworkers. The advocates of an import quota argue that U.S. labor markets are too inflexible for autoworkers to remain employed either by cutting their wages or by finding jobs in other sectors. Now consider a purely domestic policy aimed at the same problem: a subsidy to firms that employ autoworkers. Such a policy would encounter massive political opposition. For one thing, to preserve current levels of employment without protection would require large subsidy payments, which would either increase the federal government budget deficit or require a tax increase. Furthermore, autoworkers are among the highest-paid workers in the manufacturing sector; the general public would surely object to subsidizing them. It is hard to believe that an employment subsidy for autoworkers could pass Congress. Yet an import quota *would be even more expensive,* because while bringing about the same increase in employment, it would also distort consumer choice. The only difference is that the costs would be less visible, taking the form of higher pices rather than direct government outlays.

Critics of the domestic market failure justification for protection argue that this case is typical: most deviations from free trade are adopted not because their benefits exceed their costs but because the public fails to understand their true costs. Comparing the costs of trade policy with alternative domestic policies is a useful way to focus attention on how large these costs are.

The second defense of free trade is that because market failures are typically hard to identify precisely, it is difficult to be sure about the appropriate policy response. For example, suppose that there is urban unemployment in a less-developed country; what is the appropriate policy? One hypothesis (examined more closely in Chapter 10) says that a tariff to protect urban industrial sectors will draw the unemployed into productive work and thus generate social benefits that more than compensate for its costs. Another hypothesis says, however, that this policy will encourage so much migration to urban areas that unemployment will, in fact, increase. It is difficult to say which of these hypotheses is right. While economic theory has a good deal to say about the working of markets that function properly, it gives much less guidance on those that don't; there are many ways in which markets can malfunction, and the choice of a second-best policy depends on the details of the market failure.

The difficulty of ascertaining the right second-best trade policy to follow reinforces the political argument for free trade mentioned earlier. If trade policy experts are highly uncertain about how policy should deviate from free trade, and disagree among themselves, it is all too easy for trade policy to ignore national welfare altogether and become dominated by special-interest politics. If the market failures are not too bad to start with, a commitment to free trade might in the end be a better policy than opening the Pandora's box of a more flexible approach.

This is, however, a judgment about politics rather than economics. We need to realize that economic theory does *not* provide a dogmatic defense of free trade, something that it is often accused of doing.

INCOME DISTRIBUTION AND TRADE POLICY

The discussion so far has focused on national welfare arguments for and against tariff policy. It is appropriate to start there, both because a distinction between national welfare and the welfare of particular groups helps to clarify the issues and because the advocates of trade policies usually claim that they will benefit the nation as a whole. When looking at the actual politics of trade policy, however, it becomes necessary to deal with the reality that there is no such thing as national welfare; there are only the desires of individuals, which get more or less imperfectly reflected in the objectives of government.

The previous discussion showed that a tariff or other trade policy usually has opposite effects on the welfare of domestic producers and consumers. While no single theory explains how governments decide on their trade policy, several influential hypotheses have been offered.

WEIGHTED SOCIAL WELFARE

According to one view of trade policy, the government (at least implicitly) goes through calculations like the cost-benefit analysis in Chapter 8, but with a difference: A dollar of gain to different groups is not weighted equally. Instead, some groups are counted more heavily than others, with the result that deviations from free trade serve the purpose of redistributing income to the favored groups. This is referred to as **weighted social welfare.**

In the United States, government policy often seems to favor low-wage workers. In many less-developed countries, and in resource-rich industrial countries such as Australia, the government seems to consistently favor urban workers over agricultural interests.

This view is appealing because it incorporates the politics of trade policy into our basic analysis with only a small modification (weighted dollars of gain). In itself, however, it is not enough to explain many features of actual trade policy.

CONSERVATIVE SOCIAL WELFARE

An idea that often seems useful for looking at fairly short-run changes in trade policy is the **conservative social welfare** view that governments are reluctant to allow large changes in income distribution regardless of who gains and who loses. If import competition threatens to make producers in an industry much worse off, they are liable to get protection regardless of whether they are a group normally favored by public policy. Thus the U.S. government was unwilling to let its auto industry suffer at foreign hands after 1979, even though the Reagan administration was in principle strongly committed to free trade.

An intriguing aspect of the conservative social welfare view is that it helps explain how temporary trade policies can become permanent. Consider the case of Latin American industrialization. During the 1930s, many Latin American countries imposed import quotas and tariffs as an emergency response to the balance-of-payments problems brought on by the worldwide depression. These barriers led to the emergence of domestic industries, which produced substitutes for imports. Because of World War II, imports continued to be restricted through the mid-1940s. By the time a return to freer trade was possible, so much capital was invested and so many workers were employed in the import-substituting industries that removal of import restrictions had become politically unthinkable. Such restrictions remain in much of Latin America to this day.

The irreversibility of protection that results from conservative social welfare is often used as another argument for free trade. Even where a temporary tariff could be desirable, it may be better to avoid risking the creation of a vested interest in permanent protection.

COLLECTIVE ACTION

Many trade policies seem to involve heavy costs to the general public compared with the benefits they provide. How can such apparently irrational policies come into existence? A frequently offered answer draws on the famous insight by the economist Mancur Olson that political action, or **collective action,** while it may be in the interest of a *group,* is not usually in the interest of any individual member of that group.[2] Only if interest groups are small and/or well organized will they make themselves felt politically.

[2]See Olson, *The Logic of Collective Action* (Cambridge: Harvard University Press, 1965).

The sugar quota discussed in Chapter 8, for example, cost consumers \$1.266 billion, while benefiting sugar producers and the government by only \$783 million—not a very good bargain. The consumer loss, however, comes to less than \$5 per capita: something few people would notice, especially since most sugar is purchased as an ingredient in other foods rather than directly. In fact, only a tiny fraction of the American voting public is aware that there is a sugar quota or that it raises their cost of living. And, since an individual's protest will not by itself change the policy, it is not in the interests of individual consumers to be any better informed.

The sugar producers, by contrast, are well aware of their stake in the quota. The quota can easily be worth tens or even hundreds of thousands of dollars to an individual sugar producer. Furthermore, sugar producers are an organized group, with the ability to act collectively to lobby Congressmen and make political contributions. It is therefore not too surprising to find that a policy that by any estimate produces far more costs than benefits is also almost unchallengeable politically.

The upshot of theories that emphasize the problem of collective political action is that trade policy generally favors groups that are small or well organized, even when cost-benefit calculations suggest that the protection is a bad idea or when the beneficiaries are not the groups one expects the political system to favor in general.

WHO GETS PROTECTED?

We have now discussed three possible views of how concerns over income distribution affect trade policy. To conclude this section, we consider briefly who actually gets protected in the world economy.

At a broad level, two generalizations stand out. In countries with strong comparative advantage in manufacturing, farmers get protected, while in countries with a comparative advantage in agricultural or natural resource production, the industrial sector gets protected. Thus Europe and Japan, densely populated areas with highly productive industry, provide price supports, import restrictions, and (in the case of Europe) export subsidies that provide their farmers with prices as much as ten times as high as world levels. At the same time, resource-rich countries like Australia and less-developed economies like India offer their industrial sectors rates of effective protection that sometimes run to hundreds of percent.

In the case of the United States, we can describe specifically who gets protected. Although a number of small industries—ranging from color TVs to motorcycles to pasta—receive trade protection, most U.S. protection is concentrated on just four industries: autos, steel, sugar, and textiles and clothing.

What is noticeable is how disparate these industries are. Autos and steel are capital-intensive industries whose workers receive wages much higher than the U.S. average. Textiles and especially clothing is a labor-intensive industry whose workers are among the most poorly paid in the manufacturing sector. Sugar is an agricultural sector, unique primarily in that sugar is one of the few agricultural products in which the United States has both domestic production (unlike, say, coffee) and a comparative disadvantage (unlike wheat). What this means is that we should take generalizations about the politics of trade policy cautiously. In the United States, at least, there is no "typical" protected industry.

INTERNATIONAL NEGOTIATIONS AND TRADE POLICY

Our discussion of the politics of trade policy up to this point has not been very encouraging. We have argued that it is very difficult to devise trade policies that actually raise national welfare, and that in practice trade policy is often dominated by interest group politics. It is not hard in looking at the experience of the United States and other countries to come up with "horror stories" of trade policies that produce costs that greatly exceed any conceivable benefits. On the whole, it is easy to become highly cynical about the practical side of trade theory.

Yet, in fact, from the mid-1930s until about 1980 the United States and other advanced countries gradually removed tariffs and some other barriers to trade, and by so doing aided a rapid increase in international integration. Most economists believe that this progressive trade liberalization was highly beneficial. Given what we have said about the politics of trade policy, however, how was this removal of tariffs politically possible?

At least part of the answer is that the great postwar liberalization of trade was achieved through **international negotiation.** That is, governments made agreements to engage in mutual tariff reduction. These agreements had the effect of linking reduced protection for each country's import-competing industries to reduced protection by other countries against that country's export industries. Such a linkage, as we will now argue, helps to offset some of the political difficulties that would otherwise prevent countries from adopting good trade policies.

THE ADVANTAGES OF NEGOTIATION

There are at least two reasons why it is easier to lower tariffs as part of a mutual agreement to do so than as a unilateral policy. First, a mutual agreement helps mobilize support for freer trade. Second, negotiated agreements on trade can help governments avoid getting caught in destructive "trade wars."

The effect of international negotiations on support for freer trade is straightforward. We have noted that import-competing producers are usually better informed and organized than consumers. What international negotiations can do is bring in domestic exporters as a counterweight. The United States and Japan, for example, could reach an agreement in which the United States refrains from imposing import quotas to protect some of its manufacturers from Japanese competition in return for removal of Japanese barriers to U.S. exports of agricultural or high-technology products to Japan. U.S. consumers might not be effective politically in opposing such import quotas on foreign goods, even though these quotas may be costly to them; but exporters who want access to foreign markets may, through their lobbying for mutual elimination of import quotas, protect consumer interests.

Beyond this effect of international negotiation on the constituency for freer trade is the usefulness of coordination as a way of avoiding a **trade war.** The concept of a trade war can best be illustrated with a stylized example.

Let's imagine that there are only two countries in the world, the United States and Japan, and that these countries have only two policy choices, free trade or protection. Finally, let's suppose that these are unusually clear-headed governments that can assign definite numerical values to their satisfaction with any particular policy outcome (Table 9-2).

The particular values of the payoffs given in the table have been chosen to represent two assumptions. The first is that each country's government would choose protection if it could take the other country's policy as given. That is, whichever policy Japan chooses, the U.S. government is better off with protection. This assumption is by no means necessarily true; many economists would argue that free trade is the best policy for the nation, regardless of what other governments do. Governments, however, must act not only in the public interest but in their own political interest. For the reasons discussed in the previous section, governments often find that it is politically difficult to avoid giving protection to some industries.

The second assumption built into Table 9-2 is that even though each government acting individually would be better off with protection, they would both be better off if both chose free trade. That is, the U.S. government has more to gain from an opening of Japanese markets than it has to lose from opening its own markets, and the same is true for Japan. We can justify this assumption simply by appealing to the gains from trade.

To those who have studied game theory, this situation is known as a **Prisoner's Dilemma.** Each government, making the best decision for itself, will

TABLE 9-2 The problem of trade warfare

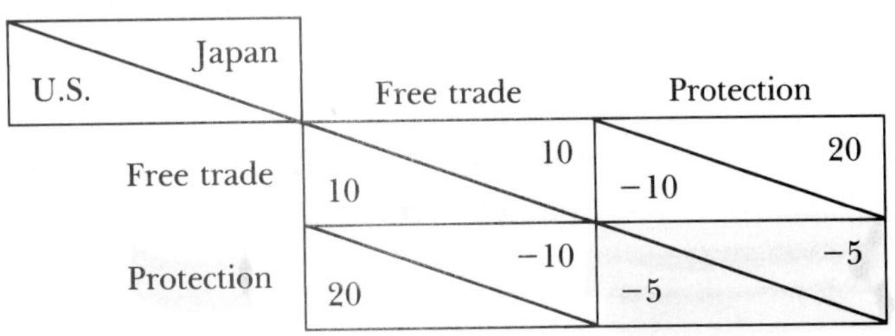

U.S. \ Japan	Free trade	Protection
Free trade	10 10	20 −10
Protection	−10 20	−5 −5

choose to protect. These choices lead to the outcome in the lower right box of the table. Yet both governments are better off if neither protects: the upper left box of the table yields a payoff which is higher for both countries. By acting unilaterally in what appear to be their best interests, the governments fail to achieve the best outcome possible. If the countries act unilaterally to protect, there is a trade war that leaves both worse off. Trade wars are not as serious as shooting wars, but the problem of avoiding them is similar to the problem of avoiding armed conflict or arms races.

Obviously, Japan and the United States need to establish an agreement (such as a treaty) to refrain from protection. Each government will be better off if it limits its own freedom of action, provided that the other country limits its freedom of action as well. A treaty can make everyone better off.

This is a highly simplified example. In the real world of trade policy there are both many countries and many gradations of trade policy between free trade and complete protection against imports. Nonetheless, the example suggests both that there is a need to coordinate trade policies through international agreements and that such agreements can actually make a difference. Indeed, the current system of international trade is built around a series of international agreements.

INTERNATIONAL TRADE AGREEMENTS: A BRIEF HISTORY

The origins of internationally coordinated tariff reduction as a trade policy date back to the 1930s. In 1930, the United States passed a remarkably irresponsible tariff law, the Smoot-Hawley act. Under this act, tariff rates rose steeply and U.S. trade fell sharply; some economists argue that the Smoot-Hawley act helped deepen the Great Depression. Within a few years after the act's passage, the U.S. administration concluded that tariffs needed to be reduced, but this posed serious problems of political coalition building. Any tariff reduction would be opposed by Congressmen whose districts contained firms producing competing goods, while the benefits would be so widely diffused that few Congressmen could be mobilized on the other side. To get the tariff rates down, it was necessary to link each tariff reduction to some concrete benefits for exporters. The initial solution to this political problem was bilateral tariff negotiations. These took the following form: the United States would approach some country that was a major exporter of some good—say, a sugar exporter—and offer to lower tariffs on sugar if that country would lower its tariffs on some goods that the United States exported. In the United States, the attractiveness of the deal to U.S. exporters would help counter the political weight of the sugar interest. In the foreign country, the attractiveness of the deal to sugar exporters would balance the political influence of import-competing interests. Such bilateral negotiations helped reduce the average duty on U.S. imports from 59 percent in 1932 to 25 percent shortly after World War II.

Bilateral negotiations, however, do not take full advantage of the scope for international coordination. For one thing, benefits from a bilateral negotiation may "spill over" to countries that have not made any concessions. For example, if the United States reduces tariffs on coffee as a result of a deal with Brazil, Colombia will also gain from a higher world coffee price. Furthermore, some advantageous deals may inherently involve more than two countries: the United States sells more to Europe, Europe sells more to Saudi Arabia, Saudi Arabia sells more to Japan, and Japan sells more to the United States. Thus the next step in international trade liberalization was to proceed to multilateral negotiations involving a number of countries.

Since 1945, there have been seven major multilateral trade agreements. The first five of these took the form of "parallel" bilateral negotiations. In these negotiations, each country would be negotiating pairwise with a number of countries at once. This meant that if Germany, say, was thinking of offering a tariff reduction that would benefit both France and Italy, it could ask both of them for reciprocal concessions. The ability to make more extensive deals, together with the worldwide economic recovery from the war, helped to permit substantial tariff reductions.

The sixth multilateral trade agreement, known as the Kennedy round, was completed in 1967. This agreement involved an across-the-board 50 percent reduction in tariffs by the major industrial countries, except for specified industries whose tariffs were left unchanged. The negotiations were over which industries to exempt rather than over the size of the cut for industries not given special treatment. Overall, the Kennedy round reduced average tariffs by about 35 percent.

Finally, the so-called Tokyo round of trade negotiations (completed in 1979) reduced tariffs by a formula more complex than that of the Kennedy round. In addition, new codes were established in an effort to control the proliferation of nontariff barriers, such as voluntary export restraints and orderly marketing agreements. At the time of writing, an eighth round of multilateral trade negotiations was in its preliminary stages.

The multilateral tariff reductions since World War II have taken place under the umbrella framework of the **General Agreement on Tariffs and Trade (GATT),** established in 1947. The GATT embodies a set of rules of conduct for international trade policy that are monitored by a bureaucracy headquartered in Geneva. Like any law, the provisions of the GATT are complex in detail, but the main constraints it places on trade policy are:

1. Export subsidies: Signatories to the GATT may not use export subsidies, except for agricultural products (an exception originally insisted on by the United States but now primarily exploited by the EEC).
2. Import quotas: Signatories to the GATT may not impose unilateral quotas on imports, except when imports threaten "market disruption"

(an undefined phrase usually interpreted to mean surges of imports that threaten to put a domestic sector suddenly out of business).

3. Tariffs: Any new tariff or increase in a tariff must be offset by reductions in other tariffs in order to compensate the affected exporting countries.

Not all countries are members of the GATT. In particular, developing countries are by and large outside these rules. Nearly all advanced countries are members, however, and the trade policies they adopt are to some extent conditioned by the need to remain "GATT-legal."

PREFERENTIAL TRADING AGREEMENTS

The international trade agreements that we have described so far all involved a "nondiscriminatory" reduction in tariff rates. For example, when the United States agrees with Germany to lower its tariff on imported machinery, the new tariff rate applies to machinery from any nation rather than just imports from Germany. Such nondiscrimination is normal in most tariffs. Indeed, the United States grants many countries a status known formally as that of "most favored nation" (MFN), a guarantee that their exporters will pay tariffs no higher than that of the nation that pays the lowest. All countries granted MFN status pay the same rates.

There are some important cases, however, in which nations establish **preferential trading agreements** under which the tariffs they apply to each others' products are lower than the rates on the same goods coming from other countries. The simplest case is one in which two or more countries eliminate all tariffs on trade with each other while continuing to maintain tariff barriers against the rest of the world. Such agreements are known variously as **customs unions, common markets,** and **free-trade areas.** The most important customs union in the modern world is the European Economic Community, which unites 12 European nations in a zone without any tariffs or explicit quotas (although a variety of administrative obstacles to trade still persist). Since more than a third of world trade takes place within this European free-trade area, preferential trading arrangements are an important real-world issue. Furthermore, a number of other customs unions exist, albeit on a smaller scale, and the formation of a Canadian-U.S. free-trade area is currently a subject of widespread discussion.

Subject to the qualifications mentioned earlier in this chapter, tariff reduction is a good thing that raises economic efficiency. At first sight it might seem that preferential tariff reductions are also a good thing, if not as good as reducing tariffs all round. After all, isn't half a loaf better than none?

Perhaps surprisingly, this conclusion is too optimistic. It is possible for a country to make itself worse off by joining a customs union. The reason may be illustrated by a hypothetical example, using Britain, France, and the United States. The United States is a low-cost producer of wheat ($4 per bushel), France a medium-cost producer ($6 per bushel), and Britain a high-cost producer ($8 per bushel). Both Britain and France maintain tariffs against all wheat imports. If Britain forms a customs union with France, the tariff against French, but not U.S., wheat will be abolished. Is this good or bad for Britain? To answer this, let's consider two cases.

First, suppose that Britain's initial tariff was high enough to exclude wheat imports from either France or the United States. For example, with a tariff of $5 per bushel it would cost $9 to import U.S. wheat and $11 to import French wheat; so British consumers would buy $8 British wheat instead. When the tariff on French wheat is eliminated, imports from France will replace British production. From Britain's point of view this is a gain, because it costs $8 to produce a bushel of wheat domestically, while Britain needs to produce only $6 worth of export goods to pay for a bushel of French wheat.

On the other hand, suppose that the tariff was lower, for example, $3 per bushel, so that before joining the customs union Britain bought its wheat from the United States (at a cost to consumers of $7 per bushel) rather than producing its own wheat. When the customs union is formed, consumers will buy French wheat at $6 rather than U.S. wheat at $7. So imports of wheat from the United States will cease. However, U.S. wheat is really cheaper than French wheat; the $3 tax that British consumers must pay on U.S. wheat returns to Britain in the form of government revenue and is therefore not a net cost to the British economy. Britain will have to devote more resources to exports in order to pay for its wheat imports and will be worse rather than better off.

This possibility of a loss is another example of the theory of the second best. Think of Britain as initially having two policies that distort incentives: a tariff against U.S. wheat and a tariff against French wheat. Although the tariff against French wheat may seem to distort incentives, it may help to offset the distortion of incentives resulting from the tariff against the United States, by encouraging consumption of the cheaper U.S. wheat. Thus, removing the tariff on French wheat can actually reduce welfare.

Returning to our two cases, notice that Britain gains if the formation of a customs union leads to new trade—French wheat replacing domestic production—while it loses if the trade within the customs union simply replaces trade with countries outside the union. In the analysis of preferential trading arrangements, the first case is referred to as that of **trade creation,** while the second is **trade diversion.** Whether a customs union is desirable or undesirable depends on whether it largely leads to trade creation or trade diversion.

SUMMARY

1. Although few countries practice free trade, most economists continue to hold up free trade as a desirable policy. This advocacy rests on three lines of argument. First, there is a formal case for the efficiency gains from free

trade that is simply the cost-benefit analysis of trade policy read in reverse. Second, many economists believe that free trade produces additional gains that go beyond this formal analysis. Finally, given the difficulty of translating complex economic analysis into real policies, even those who do not see free trade as the best imaginable policy see it as a useful rule of thumb.

2. There is an intellectually respectable case for deviating from free trade. One argument that is clearly valid in principle is that countries can improve their *terms of trade* through optimal tariffs and export taxes. This argument is not too important in practice, however. Small countries cannot have much influence on their import or export prices; so they cannot use tariffs or other policies to raise their terms of trade. Large countries, on the other hand, *can* influence their terms of trade, but in imposing tariffs they run the risk of disrupting trade agreements and provoking retaliation.

3. The other argument for deviating from free trade rests on *domestic market failures.* If some domestic market, such as the labor market, fails to function properly, deviating from free trade can sometimes help reduce the consequences of this malfunctioning. The *theory of the second best* states that if one market fails to work properly it is no longer optimal for the government to abstain from intervention in other markets. A tariff may raise welfare if there is a marginal social benefit to production of a good that is not captured by producer surplus measures.

4. Although market failures are probably common, the domestic market failure argument should not be applied too freely. First of all, it is an argument for domestic policies rather than trade policies; tariffs are always an inferior, "second-best" way to offset domestic market failure, which is always best treated at its source. Furthermore, market failure is difficult to analyze well enough to be sure of the appropriate policy recommendation.

5. In practice, trade policy is dominated by considerations of income distribution. No single way of modeling the politics of trade policy exists, but several useful ideas have been proposed. First is the concept of *weighted social welfare.* In this view, governments weight an additional dollar of gain or loss differently depending on who is affected, so that trade policy attempts to benefit favored groups. Second is the idea of *conservative social welfare;* in this view, governments are reluctant to allow any group to suffer large losses. Third is the problem of *collective action;* in this view, trade policy is determined by the differential ability of groups to organize to act politically in their collective interest, even though it may be in the interest of individuals to abstain.

6. If trade policy were made on a purely domestic basis, progress toward freer trade would be very difficult to achieve. In fact, however, industrial countries have achieved substantial reductions in tariffs through a process of *international negotiation.* International negotiation helps the cause of tariff reduction in two ways: it helps broaden the constituency for freer trade by giv-

ing exporters a direct stake, and it helps governments avoid the m… disadvantageous *trade wars* that internationally uncoordinated policies … bring.

7. Although some progress was made in the 1930s toward trade liberalization via bilateral agreements, since World War II international coordination has taken place primarily via multilateral agreements under the auspices of the *General Agreement on Tariffs and Trade*. The GATT, which comprises both a bureaucracy and a set of rules of conduct, is the central institution of the international trading system.

8. Finally, in addition to the overall reductions in tariffs that have taken place through multilateral negotiation, some groups of countries have negotiated *preferential trading agreements* under which they lower tariffs with respect to each other but not with respect to the rest of the world. The simplest examples are those of *customs unions*. The economic value of joining a customs union is ambiguous. If joining leads to replacement of high-cost domestic production by imports from within the customs union—the case of *trade creation*—the country gains. If, on the other hand, joining leads to replacement of cheap imports from outside the union by more expensive imports from inside—the case of *trade diversion*—the country loses.

KEY TERMS

efficiency case for free trade
political argument for free trade
terms of trade argument for a tariff
optimum tariff
domestic market failure
marginal social benefit
theory of the second best
weighted social welfare
conservative social welfare
collective action
international negotiation
trade war
Prisoner's Dilemma
General Agreement on Tariffs and Trade (GATT)
preferential trading agreements
customs union
common market
free-trade area
trade creation
trade diversion

PROBLEMS

1. "For a small country like the Philippines, a move to freer trade would have huge advantages. It would let consumers and producers make their choices based on the real costs of goods, not artificial prices determined by government policy; it would allow escape from the confines of a narrow domestic market; it would open new horizons for entrepreneurship; and most important, it would help to clean up domestic politics." Separate out and identify the arguments for free trade in this statement.

2. Which of the following are potentially valid arguments for tariffs or export subsidies, and which are not (explain your answers)?

a) "The more oil the United States imports, the higher the price of oil will go in the next world shortage."

b) "The growing exports of off-season fruit from Chile, which now accounts for 80 percent of the U.S. supply of such produce as winter grapes, are contributing to sharply falling prices of these former luxury goods."

c) "U.S. farm exports don't just mean higher incomes for farmers—they mean higher income for everyone who sells goods and service to the U.S. farm sector."

d) "Semiconductors are the crude oil to technology; if we don't produce our own chips, the flow of information that is crucial to every industry that uses microelectronics will be impaired."

e) "The real price of timber has fallen forty percent, and thousands of timber workers have been forced to look for other jobs."

3. A small country can import a good at a world price of 10 per unit. The domestic supply curve of the good is

$$S = 50 + 5P\ .$$

The demand curve is

$$D = 400 - 10P\ .$$

In addition, each unit of production yields a marginal social benefit of 10.

a) Calculate the total effect on welfare of a tariff of 5 per unit levied on imports.

b) Calculate the total effect of a production subsidy of 5 per unit.

c) Why does the production subsidy produce a greater gain in welfare than the tariff?

d) What would the *optimal* production subsidy be?

4. Suppose that demand and supply are exactly as described in problem 3 but that there is no marginal social benefit to production. However, for political reasons the government counts a dollar's worth of gain to producers as being worth two dollars of either consumer gain or government revenue. Calculate the effects *on the government's objective* of a tariff of 5 per unit.

5. "There is no point in the United States complaining about trade policies in Japan and Europe. Each country has a right to do whatever is in its own best interest. Instead of complaining about foreign trade policies, the United States should let other countries go their own way, and give up our own prejudices about free trade and follow suit." Discuss both the economics and the political economy of this viewpoint.

6. Which of the following actions would be legal under GATT, and which would not?

a) A U.S. tariff of 20 percent against any country that exports more than twice as much to the U.S. as it imports in return.

b) A subsidy to U.S. wheat exports, aimed at recapturing some of the markets lost to the EEC.

c) A U.S. tariff on Canadian lumber exports, not matched by equivalent reductions on other tariffs.

d) A Canadian tax on lumber *exports,* agreed to at the demand of the United States in order to placate U.S. lumber producers.

e) A program of subsidized research and development in areas related to high-technology goods such as electronics and semiconductors.

f) Special government assistance for workers who lose their jobs because of import competition.

FURTHER READING

Robert E. Baldwin. *The Political Economy of U.S. Import Policy.* Cambridge: MIT Press, 1985. A basic reference on how and why trade policies are made in the United States.

Robert E. Baldwin, ed. *Recent Issues and Initiatives in U.S. Trade Policy.* Cambridge: National Bureau of Economic Research, 1984. Essays on some of the issues that are relevant to current policy debate.

Robert E. Baldwin. "Trade Policies in Developed Counties," in Ronald W. Jones and Peter B. Kenen, eds. *Handbook of International Economics.* Vol. 1. Amsterdam: North-Holland, 1984. A comprehensive survey of theory and evidence on a broad range of trade-related policies.

Jagdish Bhagwati, ed. *Import Competition and Response.* Chicago: University of Chicago Press, 1982. Analytical papers on the economic and political issues raised when imports compete with domestic production.

W. Max Corden. *Trade Policy and Economic Welfare.* Oxford: Clarendon Press, 1974. A careful survey of economic arguments for and against protection.

Dominick Salvatore, ed. *The New Protectionist Threat to World Welfare.* Amsterdam: North-Holland, 1987. A collection of essays on the causes and consequences of increasing protectionist pressure in the 1980s.

Robert M. Stern. *U.S. Trade Policies in a Changing World Economy.* Cambridge: MIT Press, 1987. More essays on current trade policy issues.

APPENDIX TO CHAPTER 9
Proving that the Optimum Tariff Is Positive

A tariff always improves the terms of trade of a large country but at the same time distorts production and consumption. This appendix shows that for a sufficiently small tariff the terms of trade gain is always larger than the distortion loss. Thus there is always an optimal tariff that is positive.

To make the point, we focus on the case where all demand and supply curves are *linear,* that is, are straight lines.

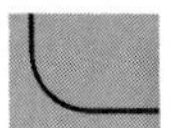

DEMAND AND SUPPLY

We assume that Home, the importing country, has a demand curve whose equation is

$$D = a - b\tilde{P}, \qquad \text{(9A-1)}$$

where $\tilde{P}$ is the internal price of the good, and a supply curve whose equation is

$$Q = e + f\tilde{P}. \qquad \text{(9A-2)}$$

Home's import demand is equal to the difference between domestic demand and supply,

$$D - Q = (a - e) - (b + f)\tilde{P}. \qquad \text{(9A-3)}$$

Foreign's export supply is also a straight line,

$$(Q^* - D^*) = g + hP_W, \qquad \text{(9A-4)}$$

where P_W is the world price. The internal price in Home will exceed the world price by the tariff,

$$\tilde{P} = P_W + t. \qquad \text{(9A-5)}$$

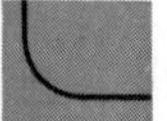

THE TARIFF AND PRICES

A tariff drives a wedge between internal and world prices, driving the internal Home price up and the world price down (Figure 9A-1).

In world equilibrium, Home import demand equals Foreign export supply:

$$(a - e) - (b + f) \times (P_W + t) = g + hP_W. \qquad \text{(9A-6)}$$

Let P_F be the world price that would prevail if there were no tariff. Then a tariff t will raise the internal price to

$$\tilde{P} = P_F + th/(b + f + h), \qquad \text{(9A-7)}$$

while lowering the world price to

$$P_W = P_F - t(b + f)/(b + f + h). \qquad \text{(9A-8)}$$

(For a small country, foreign supply is highly elastic, i.e., h is very large. So for a small country a tariff will have little effect on the world price while raising the domestic price almost one-for-one.)

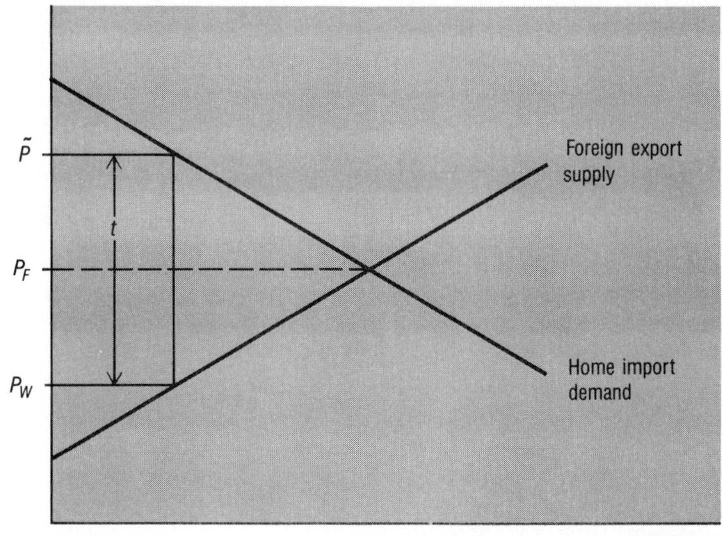

FIGURE 9A-1 Effects of a tariff on prices. In a linear model we can calculate the exact effect of a tariff on prices.

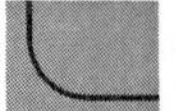

THE TARIFF AND DOMESTIC WELFARE

We now use what we have learned to derive the effects of a tariff on Home's welfare (Figure 9A-2). Q^1 and D^1 represent the free-trade levels of consumption and production. With a tariff the internal price rises, with the result that Q rises to Q^2 and D falls to D^2, where

$$Q^2 = Q^1 + tfh/(b + f + h) \tag{9A-9}$$

and

$$D^2 = D^1 - tbh/(b + f + h). \tag{9A-10}$$

The gain from a lower world price is the area of the rectangle in Figure 9A-2, the fall in the price multiplied by the level of imports after the tariff:

$$\begin{aligned} \text{gain} &= (D^2 - Q^2) \times t(b + f)/(b + f + h) \\ &= t \times (D^1 - Q^1) \times (b + f)/(b + f + h) \\ &\quad - (t)^2 \times h(b + f)^2/(b + f + h)^2. \end{aligned} \tag{9A-11}$$

The loss from distorted consumption is the sum of the areas of the two triangles in Figure 9A-2,

$$\begin{aligned} \text{loss} &= (1/2) \times (Q^2 - Q^1) \times (\tilde{P} - P_F) \\ &\quad + (1/2) \times (D^1 - D^2) \times (\tilde{P} - P_F) \\ &= (t)^2 \times (b + f) \times (h)^2/2(b + f + h)^2. \end{aligned} \tag{9A-12}$$

The net effect on welfare, therefore, is

$$\text{gain} - \text{loss} = t \times U - (t)^2 \times V, \tag{9A-13}$$

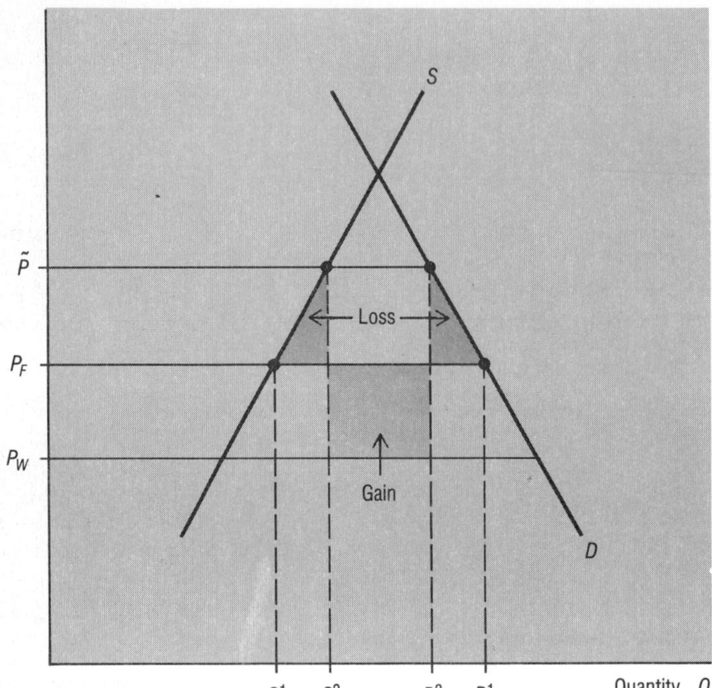

FIGURE 9A-2 Welfare effects of a tariff. The net benefit of a tariff is equal to the area of the shaded rectangle minus the area of the two shaded triangles.

where U and V are complicated expressions that are, however, independent of the level of the tariff. That is, the net effect is the sum of a positive number times the tariff rate and a negative number times the *square* of the tariff rate.

We can now see that when the tariff is small enough, the net effect must be positive. The reason is that when we make a number smaller the square of that number gets smaller faster than the number itself. Suppose that a tariff of 20 percent turns out to produce a net loss. Then let's try a tariff of 10 percent. The positive term in that tariff's effect will be only half as large as with a 20 percent tariff, but the negative part will be only one-quarter as large. If the net effect is still negative, try a 5 percent tariff; this will again reduce the negative effect twice as much as the positive effect. At some sufficiently low tariff, the negative effect will have to be outweighed by the positive effect.

10 TRADE POLICY IN DEVELOPING COUNTRIES

So far we have analyzed the instruments of trade policy and its objectives without specifying the context—that is, without saying much about the country undertaking these policies. Each country has its own distinctive history and issues, but in discussing economic policy, one broad distinction is between two groups of countries. On one side are the developed or advanced countries: North America, Western Europe, Japan, and a few others. These countries, whatever their economic problems, are by the standards of the rest of the world highly successful economies. With only about 15 percent of the world's population, the advanced countries account for about 60 percent of the world's production and international trade. Given how well these economies perform, it is reasonable to suppose that their economic systems are fairly efficient, so neither the demands on trade policy nor the expectations placed on it are usually very large.

Most of the world's population, however, lives in **developing countries** that lag far behind these advanced nations.[1] Developing countries span the

[1]Developing country is a term used by international organizations that has now become standard, even though some "developing" countries have had declining living standards for a decade or more. A more descriptive but less polite term is less-developed countries (LDCs).

range from rapidly growing nations such as South Korea (which may soon be "graduated" into the category of advanced countries) to nations like Ethiopia that live on the edge of subsistence. Despite the huge differences among developing countries, however, their shared relative backwardness creates some common themes in their trade policies. First, many developing nations have tried to use trade policy to favor manufacturing as opposed to traditional sectors such as agriculture and mining in the hope that this would help them catch up with wealthier countries. Second, many poorer countries have tried to use trade policy to cure the problem of uneven development or dualism *within* the country. Finally, developing countries sometimes argue that their relative poverty is not their own fault but is instead due to an unfair international economic system, and they have at times tried to use international negotiation to bring about changes in that system.

In this chapter we examine the special issues of trade policy raised by each of these considerations. In the next chapter we turn to the different concerns of the advanced countries.

TRADE POLICY TO PROMOTE MANUFACTURING

Perhaps the most distinctive difference between trade policy in advanced countries and in poor countries is that in developing countries policy is more consistently preoccupied with the encouragement of manufacturing as opposed to other sectors of the economy. This preoccupation is, to some extent, a result of the symbolic importance of manufacturing as a sign of national development. Most advanced nations are mainly exporters of manufactured goods, while poor nations are usually exporters of "primary" products such as agricultural produce and minerals. Thus, countries seeking to demonstrate their strength and independence often want to have conspicuous domestic industries such as steel or petrochemicals. Beyond the symbolism of manufacturing development, however, governments in many nations have been strongly influenced by theoretical arguments for trade policy to promote manufacturing. The most important of these arguments is the **infant industry argument** for temporary protection of the manufacturing sector against import competition.

WHY MANUFACTURING IS FAVORED: THE INFANT INDUSTRY ARGUMENT

According to the infant industry argument, developing countries have a *potential* comparative advantage in manufacturing, but new manufacturing industries in developing countries cannot initially compete with well-established manufacturing in developed countries. In order to allow manufacturing to get a toehold, governments should temporarily support new industries, until they have grown strong enough to meet international competition. Thus it makes sense, according to this argument, to use tariffs or import quotas as temporary measures to get industrialization started. It is a historical fact that the world's three largest market economies all began their industrialization behind trade barriers: the United States and Germany had high tariff rates on manufacturing in the nineteenth century, while Japan had extensive import controls until the 1970s.

Problems with the Infant Industry Argument. The infant industry argument seems highly plausible, and in fact it has been persuasive to many governments. Yet economists have pointed out many pitfalls in the argument, suggesting that it must be used cautiously.

First, it is not always a good idea to try to move today into the industries that will have a comparative advantage in the future. Suppose that a country that is currently labor-abundant is in the process of accumulating capital: when it accumulates enough capital, it will have a comparative advantage in capital-intensive industries. That does not mean that it should try to develop these industries immediately. In the 1980s, for example, Korea has become an exporter of automobiles; it would probably not have been a good idea for Korea to have tried to develop its auto industry in the 1960s, when capital and skilled labor were still very scarce.

Second, protecting manufacturing does no good unless the protection itself helps make industry competitive. Pakistan and India have protected their manufacturing sectors for decades and have recently begun to develop significant exports of manufactured goods. The goods they are exporting, however, are light manufactures like textiles, not the heavy manufactures that they protected; a good case can be made that they would have developed their manufactured exports even if they had never protected manufacturing. Some economists have warned of the case of the "pseudo infant industry," where industry is initially protected, then becomes competitive for reasons that have nothing to do with the protection. In this case infant industry protection ends up looking like a success but may actually have been a net cost to the economy.

More generally, the fact that it is costly and time-consuming to build up an industry is not an argument for government intervention unless there is some domestic market failure. If an industry is supposed to be able to earn high enough returns to capital, labor, and other factors of production to be worth developing, then why don't private investors develop the industry without government help? Sometimes it is argued that private investors take into account only the current returns in an industry and fail to take account of the future prospects, but this is not consistent with market behavior. In advanced countries at least, investors often back projects whose returns are uncertain and lie far in the future. (Consider, for example, the U.S. biotechnology industry, which attracted hundreds of millions of dollars of capital years before it made even a single commercial sale.)

Market Failure Justifications for Infant Industry Protection. To justify the infant industry argument, it is necessary to go beyond the plausible but questionable view that industries always need to be sheltered when they are new. Whether infant industry protection is justified depends on an analysis of the kind we discussed in Chapter 9. That is, the argument for protecting an industry in its early growth must be related to some particular set of market failures that prevent private markets from developing the industry as rapidly as they should. Sophisticated proponents of the infant industry argument have identified two market failures as reasons why infant industry protection may be a good idea: **imperfect capital markets** and the problem of **appropriability**.

The *imperfect capital markets justification* for infant industry protection is as follows: If a developing country does not have a set of financial institutions (such as efficient stock markets and banks) that would allow savings from traditional sectors (such as agriculture) to be used to finance investment in new sectors (such as manufacturing), then growth of new industries will be restricted by the ability of firms in these industries to earn current profits. Thus low initial profits will be an obstacle to investment even if the long-term returns on this investment are high. The first-best policy is to create a better capital market; but protection of new industries, which would raise profits and thus allow more rapid growth, can be justified as a second-best policy option.

The *appropriability argument* for infant industry protection can take many forms, but all have in common the idea that firms in a new industry generate social benefits for which they are not compensated. For example, the firms that first enter an industry may have to incur "start-up" costs of adapting technology to local circumstances or of opening new markets. If other firms are able to follow their lead without incurring these start-up costs, the pioneers will be prevented from reaping any returns from these outlays. Thus, pioneering firms may, in addition to producing physical output, create intangible benefits (such as knowledge or new markets) in which they are unable to establish property rights. In some cases the social benefits from creation of a new industry will exceed its costs, yet because of the problem of appropriability, no private entrepreneurs will be willing to enter. The first-best answer is to compensate firms for their intangible contributions. When this is not possible, however, there is a second-best case for encouraging entry into a new industry by using tariffs or other trade policies.

Both the imperfect capital markets argument and the appropriability case for infant industry protection are clearly special cases of the *market failures* justification for interfering with free trade (Chapter 9). The difference is that in this case the arguments apply specifically to new industries rather than to any industry. The general problems with the market failure approach remain, however. In practice it is difficult to evaluate which industries really warrant special treatment, and there are risks that a policy intended to promote development will end up being captured by special interests. There are many stories of infant industries that have never grown up and remain dependent upon protection.

HOW MANUFACTURING IS FAVORED: IMPORT-SUBSTITUTING INDUSTRIALIZATION

Although there are doubts about the infant industry argument, many developing countries have seen this argument as a compelling reason to provide special support for the development of manufacturing industries. In principle such support could be provided in a variety of ways. For example, countries could provide subsidies to manufacturing production in general, or they could focus their efforts on subsidies for the export of some manufactured goods in which they believe they can develop a comparative advantage. In most developing countries, however, the basic strategy for industrialization has been to develop industries oriented toward the domestic market by using trade restrictions such as tariffs and quotas to encourage the replacement of imported manufactures by domestic products. The strategy of encouraging domestic industry by limiting imports of manufactured goods is known as the strategy of **import-substituting industrialization.**

One might ask why a choice needs to be made. Why not encourage both import substitution and exports? The answer goes back to the general equilibrium analysis of tariffs in Chapter 5: a tariff that reduces imports also necessarily reduces exports. By protecting import-substituting industries, countries draw resources away from actual or potential export sectors. So a country's choice to seek to substitute for imports is also a choice to discourage export growth.

The reasons why import substitution rather than export growth has usually been chosen as an industrialization strategy are a mixture of economics and politics. First, until the 1970s many developing countries were skeptical about the possibility of exporting manufactured goods (although this skepticism also calls into question the infant industry agrument for manufacturing protection). They believed that industrialization was necessarily based on a substitution of domestic industry for imports rather than on a growth of manufactured exports. Second, in many cases import-substituting industrialization policies dovetailed naturally with existing political biases. We have already noted the case of Latin American nations that were compelled to develop substitutes for imports during the 1930s because of the Great Depression and during the first half of the 1940s because of the wartime disruption of trade (Chapter 9). In these countries import substitution directly benefited powerful, established interest groups, while export promotion had no natural constituency.

The 1950s and 1960s saw the high tide of import-substituting industrialization. Developing countries typically began by protecting final stages of industry, such as food processing and automobile assembly. In the larger developing countries, domestic products almost completely replaced imported consumer goods (although the manufacturing was often carried out by foreign multinational firms). Once the possibilities for replacing consumer goods imports had been exhausted, these countries turned to protection of intermediate goods, such as automobile bodies, steel, and petrochemicals.

In most developing economies, the import-substitution drive stopped short of its logical limit: sophisticated manufactured goods such as computers, precision machine tools, and so on continued to be imported. Nonetheless, the larger countries pursuing import-substituting industrialization reduced their imports to remarkably low levels. Usually, the smaller a country's economic size (as measured, for example, by the value of its total output) the larger will be the share of imports and exports in national income. Yet as Table 10-1 shows, Brazil, with a domestic market less than 10 percent as large as that of the United States, exported the same fraction of its output as the United States. India is the most extreme case: in 1983, exports were only 6 percent of output, a share less than that of the United States and far less than that of large industrial countries such as Japan and Germany.

As a strategy for encouraging growth of manufacturing, import-substituting industrialization has clearly worked. Latin American economies now generate almost as large a share of their output from manufacturing as advanced nations. (India generates less, but only because its poorer population continues to spend a high proportion of its income on food.) For these countries, however, the encouragement of manufacturing was not a goal in itself; it was a means to the end goal of economic development. Has import-substituting industrialization promoted economic development? Here many doubts have appeared. Although many economists approved of import-substitution measures in the 1950s and early 1960s, since the 1960s import-substituting industrialization has come under increasingly harsh criticism. Indeed, much of the focus of economic analysts and of policymakers has shifted from trying to encourage import substitution to trying to correct the damage done by bad import-substitution policies.

RESULTS OF FAVORING MANUFACTURING: PROBLEMS OF IMPORT-SUBSTITUTING INDUSTRIALIZATION

The attack on import-substituting industrialization starts from the fact that many countries that have pursued import substitution have not shown any

TABLE 10-1 Exports as a percentage of national income, 1983

India	6
Brazil	8
United States	8
Japan	14
West Germany	30
South Korea	37
Hong Kong	95
Singapore	176

Source: World Bank. *World Development Report.* Washington, D.C.: World Bank, 1985.

signs of catching up with the advanced countries. In some cases, the development of a domestic manufacturing base seems to have led to a stagnation of per capita income instead of an economic takeoff. This is true of India, which, after 20 years of ambitious economic plans between the early 1950s and the early 1970s, found itself with per capita income only a few percent higher than before. It is also true of Argentina, once considered a wealthy country, whose economy has grown at a snail's pace for decades. Other countries, such as Mexico, have achieved economic growth but have not narrowed the gap between themselves and advanced countries. Only a few developing countries really seem to have moved dramatically upward on the income scale—and these countries either have never pursued import substitution or have moved sharply away from it.

Why didn't import-substituting industrialization work the way it was supposed to? The most important reason seems to be that the infant industry argument was not as universally valid as many people assumed. A period of protection will not create a competitive manufacturing sector if there are fundamental reasons why a country lacks a comparative advantage in manufacturing. Experience has shown that the reasons for failure to develop often run deeper than a simple lack of experience with manufacturing. Poor countries lack skilled labor, they lack entrepreneurs, they lack managerial competence, and they have problems of social organization that make it difficult to maintain reliable supplies of everything from spare parts to electricity. These problems may not be beyond the reach of economic policy, but they cannot be solved by *trade* policy: an import quota can allow an inefficient manufacturing sector to survive, but it cannot directly make that sector more efficient. The infant industry argument is that, given the temporary shelter of tariffs or quotas, the manufacturing industries of less-developed nations will learn to be efficient. In practice, this is not always, or even usually, true.

With import substitution failing to deliver the promised benefits, attention has turned to the costs of the policies used to promote industry. On this issue, a growing body of evidence shows that the protectionist policies of many less-developed countries have badly distorted incentives. Part of the problem has been that many countries have used excessively complex methods to promote their infant industries. That is, they have used elaborate and often overlapping import quotas, exchange controls, and domestic content rules instead of simple tariffs. It is often difficult to determine how much protection an administrative regulation is actually providing, and studies show that the degree of protection is often both higher and more variable across industries than the government intended. As Table 10-2 shows, some industries in Latin America and South Asia have been protected by regulations that are the equivalent of tariff rates of 200 percent or more. These high rates of effective protection have allowed industries to exist even when their cost of production is three or four times the price of the imports they replace. Even the most enthusiastic advocates of market failure arguments for protection find rates of effective protection that high difficult to defend.

TABLE 10-2 Effective protection of manufacturing in some developing countries (percent)

Mexico (1960)	26
Philippines (1965)	61
Brazil (1966)	113
Chile (1961)	182
Pakistan (1963)	271

Source: Bela Balassa. *The Structure of Protection in Developing Countries.* Baltimore: The Johns Hopkins Press, 1971.

A further cost that has received considerable attention is the tendency of import restrictions to promote production at inefficiently small scale. Even the largest developing countries have domestic markets that are only a small fraction the size of that of the United States or the European Economic Community. Often, the whole domestic market is not large enough to allow an efficient-scale production facility. Yet when this small market is protected, say, by an import quota, if only a single firm were to enter the market it could earn monopoly profits. The competition for these profits typically leads several firms to enter a market that does not really even have room enough for one, and production is carried out at highly inefficient scale. The answer for small countries to the problem of scale is, as noted in Chapter 6, to specialize in the production and export of a limited range of products and to import other goods. Import-substituting industrialization eliminates this option by focusing industrial production on the domestic market.

Those who criticize import-substituting industrialization also argue that it has aggravated other problems, such as income inequality and unemployment (problems discussed later in this chapter under the heading of the dual economy).

Despite the criticism of import-substituting industrialization by economists, few countries that followed policies of import substitution have dismantled their trade barriers. The reason for this reluctance to change policy is only partly that they continue to believe in import substitution as a development strategy. An equally important factor is that at this point a lot of capital has been invested in industries that could not survive without protection, and many workers in protected industries would be hurt if that protection were removed. Thus there is now a vested interest in the continuation of import-substitution policies.

ANOTHER WAY TO FAVOR MANUFACTURING: INDUSTRIALIZATION THROUGH EXPORTS

Although the attempt to promote industrialization through import substitution has now fallen into disfavor among economists, not all industrialization among less-developed countries has been a failure. Since the mid-1960s, a small group of initially poor countries has combined rapid growth of output and living standards with industrialization oriented primarily toward export rather than domestic markets. These countries are often referred to as **newly industrializing countries,** or **NICs**. The most spectacular performers among the NICs have been the four Asian countries of South Korea, Hong Kong, Taiwan, and Singapore, sometimes referred to facetiously as the "Gang of Four" (after the allegedly villainous clique ousted by the current Chinese government).

Aside from their rapid growth, the most remarkable thing about the Gang of Four is their openness to international trade. Table 10-1 shows some

THE KOREAN SUCCESS STORY

The largest of the Asian NICs, both in population and in national income, is South Korea. In 1986, South Korea achieved a major symbolic economic success when it began selling an automobile, the Hyundai Excel, in the United States. However, the rise of Korea's auto industry is only a recent stage in an extraordinary economic takeoff.

In 1960, few expected great things from South Korea. The Korean War of 1950–1953 had devastated and permanently divided the country. Before World War II Korea, then controlled by Japan, had experienced some industrial development, but that development was concentrated in areas that became part of Communist North Korea. In 1960, predominantly rural South Korea had an annual per capita income of only $157. Furthermore, the economy showed few signs of dynamism; from 1955 to 1960 the economy's real output per capita grew only 2.1 percent.

In the early 1960s, South Korea instituted a series of economic reforms that liberalized trade and freed up domestic markets. To everyone's surprise, including its own, Korea began to export manufactured goods. Initially, the principal exports were unglamorous items such as plywood and wigs. Had the development strategy been dependent on government selection of industries to protect, one wonders whether these industries would have been considered. Yet these exports laid the base for an extraordinary economic expansion. From 1960 to 1970, per capita output grew by 89 percent; from 1970 to 1980, it grew by another 86 percent. South Korea is still poor compared with Japan, Western Europe, or the United States, but it is now officially classed by the World Bank as an "upper-middle income" nation.

The lessons of Korea's experience are a subject of intense debate. Whatever one's explanation, however, the Korean accomplishment is encouraging: it shows that it is possible for poor nations to move up in the world.

comparative figures for the shares of exports in national income. The contrast between the NICs and the import-substituting industrializers is clear.[2]

For the most part, the NICs have not followed policies of strict free trade (except for Hong Kong, which is the least regulated economy in the world). Compared with the import-substituting nations, however, all of the highly successful countries seem to have rates of protection that are both lower and less variable across sectors.

The big question about the NICs is whether their success can be emulated by other developing countries. Does Korea do so well because of its relatively low rate of protection or because of other factors? If (say) Mexico were to abandon its strategy of import substitution, would its growth rate sharply accelerate? Obviously countries differ, and it might be that the successful NICs do well because of social factors such as a national commitment to education or work ethic. On the other hand, 25 years ago, few people would have said that Korea had a society well suited to economic growth. It was only after trade policy changed that Korea began to look like a winner. Was this success just a coincidence?

Whatever the final verdict on the causes of success in the NICs, the remarkable achievements of export-oriented development have shattered the old belief that industrialization must be aimed at the domestic market.

PROBLEMS OF THE DUAL ECONOMY

While the trade policy of less-developed countries is partly a response to their relative backwardness as compared with advanced nations, it is also a response to uneven development *within* the country. Often a relatively modern, capital-intensive, high-wage industrial sector exists in the same country as a very poor traditional agricultural sector. The division of a single economy into two sectors that appear to be at very different levels of development is referred to as **economic dualism,** and an economy that looks like this is referred to as a **dual economy.**

Why does dualism have anything to do with trade policy? One answer is that dualism is probably a sign of markets working poorly: in an efficient economy, for example, workers would not earn hugely different wages in different sectors. Whenever markets are working badly, there may be a market failure case for deviating from free trade. The presence of economic dualism is often used to justify tariffs that protect the apparently more efficient manufacturing sector.

[2]It may seem puzzling that Singapore's export share exceeds 100 percent. However, no paradox is involved. National income, as explained in Chapter 12, measures the value *added* by the economy, not the total value of the goods it produces. Singapore often buys partly finished manufactures from abroad, processes them further, then exports them. For example, fabric woven in the United States may be sewn by Singapore workers into garments, which are then exported. The value added—the difference between what the imported fabric cost and the price of the finished clothing—can easily be less than the cost of the fabric. When this is the typical pattern, imports and exports will end up larger than national income.

A second reason for linking dualism to trade policy is that trade policy may itself have a great deal to do with dualism. As import-substituting industrialization has come under attack, some economists have argued that import-substitution policies have actually helped to create the dual economy or at least to aggravate some of its symptoms.

THE SYMPTOMS OF DUALISM

There is no precise definition of a dual economy, but in general, a dual economy is one in which there is a "modern" sector (typically producing manufactured goods that are protected from import competition) that contrasts sharply with the rest of the economy in a number of ways:

1. The value of output per worker is much higher in the modern sector than in the rest of the economy. In most developing countries, the goods produced by a worker in the manufacturing sector carry a price several times that of the goods produced by an agricultural worker. Sometimes this difference runs as high as fifteen to one.
2. Accompanying the high value of output per worker is a higher wage rate. Industrial workers may earn ten times what agricultural laborers make (although their wages still seem low in comparison with North America or Western Europe).
3. Although wages are high in the manufacturing sector, however, returns on capital are not necessarily higher. In fact, it often seems to be the case that capital earns *lower* returns in the industrial sector.
4. The high value of output per worker in the modern sector is at least partly due to a higher capital intensity of production. Manufacturing in less-developed countries typically has much higher capital intensity than agriculture (this is *not* true of advanced countries, where agriculture is quite capital-intensive). In the developing world, agricultural workers often work with primitive tools, while industrial facilities are not much different from those in advanced nations.
5. Finally, many less-developed countries have a persistent unemployment problem. Especially in urban areas, there are large numbers of people either without jobs or with only occasional, extremely low-wage employment. These urban unemployed coexist with the relatively well-paid urban industrial workers.

Case Study ECONOMIC DUALISM IN INDIA

The economy of India presents a classic case of economic dualism. In a country of over 700 million people, only 6 million are employed in the manufacturing sector. These manufacturing workers, however, produce

15 percent of the gross national product and receive wages more than six times as high as agricultural wages. Manufacturing is far more capital-intensive than agriculture; indeed, for the past 30 years investment on capital equipment for the tiny manufacturing labor force has consistently been larger than total investment in agriculture.

This sharp distinction between manufacturing and agriculture has actually grown over time. Since 1960, for example, the real wages of manufacturing workers have risen by about 80 percent, while those of farm workers have risen only about 5 percent.

Why is the gap between sectors so large? It seems likely that government policies play a key role. In India, government subsidies and protectionist policies have encouraged investment in manufacturing, and investment in the most capital-intensive sectors in particular. At the same time, labor laws designed to protect workers' interests have probably helped the bargaining position of unions, enabling organized workers to win large wage increases even though there are millions of workers who would be willing to take their jobs at lower wages.

Will India's manufacturing sector grow and absorb the traditional economy? Unfortunately, there is little reason to think so. From 1960 to 1980, manufacturing employment grew at an annual rate of only 3 percent, not much faster than India's population.

DUAL LABOR MARKETS AND TRADE POLICY

The symptoms of dualism are present in many countries and are clear signs of an economy that is not working well, especially in its labor markets. The trade policy implications of these symptoms have been a subject of great dispute among students of economic development.

In the 1950s, many economists argued that wage differences between manufacturing and agriculture provided another justification, beyond the infant industry argument, for encouraging manufacturing at agriculture's expense. This argument, known as the **wage differentials argument,** can be stated in market failure terms. Suppose that, for some reason, an equivalent worker would receive a higher wage in manufacturing than he would in agriculture. Whenever a manufacturing firm decides to hire an additional worker, then, it generates a marginal social benefit for which it receives no reward, because a worker gains an increase in his wage when he moves from agriculture to manufacturing. This is in contrast to what would happen without a wage difference, where the marginal worker would be indifferent between manufacturing and agricultural employment and there would be no marginal social benefit of hiring a worker other than the profits earned by the hiring firm.

The effects of a wage differential on the economy's allocation of labor can be illustrated using the *specific-factors model* presented in Chapter 3. Assume that an economy produces only two goods, manufactures and food. Manufactures are produced using labor and capital; food is produced using labor and land. Then the allocation of resources can be represented with a diagram like Figure 10-1. The vertical axis represents wage rates and marginal products; the horizontal axis represents employment. Employment in manufactures is measured from the left origin O_M, while employment in food is measured from the right origin O_F. MPL_M is the marginal product of labor in manufactures, MPL_F the marginal product in food; P_M is the price of manufactures, P_F the price of food. Thus the two curves in the figure represent the *value* of the marginal product of an additional worker in each sector.

When there is a wage differential, workers in manufactures must be paid a higher wage than workers in food; in the figure the manufactures wage is assumed to be w_M, the food wage w_F. Employers in each sector will hire workers up to the point where the value of a worker's marginal product equals his wage; thus employment in manufactures is $O_M L^1$, employment in food is $L^1 O_F$.

Suppose that the economy were now able to shift one worker from food to manufactures. Manufactures output would rise; food output would fall. The value of the additional manufactures output, however, would be the

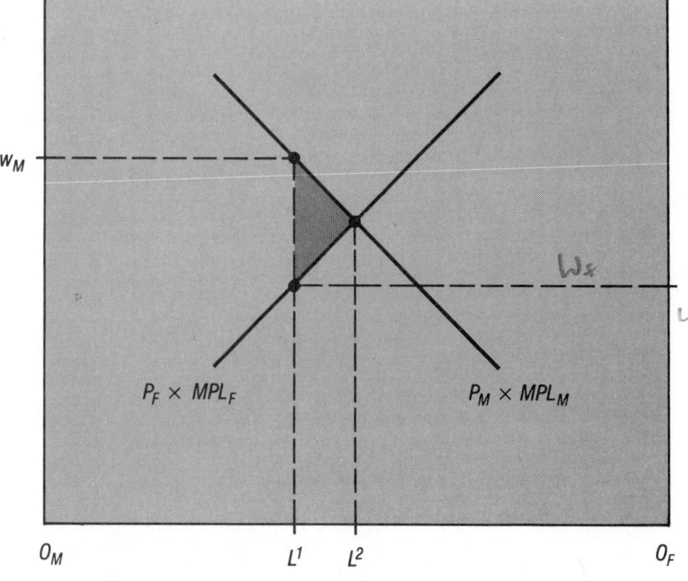

FIGURE 10-1 The effects of a wage differential. If manufactures must pay a higher wage than food, the economy will employ too few workers in manufactures and too many in food.

wage rate in manufactures, w_M, while the value of the reduction in food output would be the lower wage rate in food, w_F. The total value of the economy's output, then, would rise by $w_M - w_F$. The fact that the value of output can be increased by shifting labor from food to manufactures shows that the economy is allocating too little labor to manufactures. An efficient economy would set the marginal product of labor equal in both sectors, which would be achieved if $O_M L^2$ workers were employed in manufactures, $L^2 O_F$ in food. (The increase in output achieved by moving to this efficient allocation of labor would be equal to the shaded area in the figure.)

If there is a wage differential, then, markets will misallocate labor; firms in the industrial sector will hire too few workers. A government policy that induces them to hire more can raise national welfare.

As usual, trade policy is not the first-best policy to expand manufacturing employment. Ideally, government policy should target employment directly, either by eliminating the wage differential or by subsidizing firms to hire more workers. A subsidy to manufacturing production is not as good, because it encourages capital as well as labor to move into manufacturing[3]—and capital does not receive an especially high return in manufacturing. A tariff or import quota is still worse, because it also distorts demand. Nonetheless, as a second-best alternative (or more strictly third-best), a tariff on manufactures could be justified by the wage differentials argument.

In the 1950s and 1960s this seemed to be a fairly convincing argument. In a famous paper published in 1970, however, the economists Harris and Todaro offered a devastating reinterpretation of the labor markets of less-developed countries.[4] They pointed out a link between rural-urban migration and unemployment that undermines the case for favoring manufacturing employment, even though manufacturing does offer higher wages.

Harris and Todaro began from the observation that countries with highly dualistic economies also seem to have a great deal of urban unemployment. Although one might suppose that this unemployment strengthens the case for creating more urban jobs in manufacturing, Harris and Todaro pointed out that despite this unemployment, migration from rural to urban areas continues. They concluded that rural workers were willing to come to the cities and take the risk of being unemployed in return for the chance of getting high-paying industrial jobs. The chance of getting a job depends, of course, on how many jobs are available.

According to the Harris-Todaro model, an increase in the number of manufacturing jobs will lead to a rural-urban migration so large that urban

[3]This cannot be seen in the specific-factors model, because that model assumes that capital cannot be used in the agricultural sector. In the factor-proportions model, however, the superiority of a wage subsidy to a production subsidy can be demonstrated. See Harry G. Johnson, "Optimal Trade Intervention in the Presence of Domestic Distortions," in Robert E. Baldwin et al., *Trade, Growth, and the Balance of Payments* (Chicago: Rand McNally, 1965), pp. 3–34.

[4]John R. Harris and Michael P. Todaro, "Migration, Unemployment, and Development: A Two-Sector Analysis," *American Economic Review* 60 (1970), pp. 126–142.

unemployment actually rises. When an additional worker is hired by the manufacturing sector, two or three more workers may leave agriculture to swell the ranks of the urban unemployed. Although the lucky worker gains, his wage gain will be largely (maybe even completely) offset by the wage losses of the newly unemployed. The supposed social benefit of additional manufacturing employment is therefore lost.

Like the infant industry argument, the wage differentials argument for protection is now in disfavor with economists. This is partly because of arguments like that of Harris and Todaro and partly because of the general backlash against import-substitution policies. In fact, trade policies adopted as a response to economic dualism are now often accused of actually making that dualism worse.

TRADE POLICY AS A CAUSE OF ECONOMIC DUALISM

Trade policy has been accused both of widening the wage differential between manufacturing and agriculture and of fostering excessive capital intensity.

The reasons for huge wage differentials between agriculture and industry are not well understood. Some economists believe that these differentials are a natural market response. Firms, so the argument goes, offer high wages as a way to ensure low turnover and high work effort in countries where the discipline of industrial work does not come naturally. Other economists argue, however, that the wage differentials also reflect the monopoly power of unions whose industries are sheltered by import quotas from foreign competition. With freer trade, they argue, industrial wages would be lower and agricultural wages higher. If so, dualism—and unemployment—may be worsened by import restrictions, especially those undertaken in the name of import substitution.

The capital intensity of manufacturing is partly due to relatively high wages, which give firms an incentive to substitute capital for labor. To the extent that trade restrictions are responsible for these high wages, they are to blame. Also, in some countries a controlled banking system in effect provides subsidized credit to industrial firms, making capital-labor substitution cheap. The most direct channel, however, has been through selective import control. In many cases, imports of capital goods enter without tariff or other restriction, and sometimes with de facto import subsidies. This policy further encourages the use of capital-intensive techniques.

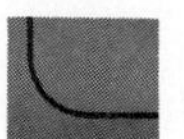

NEGOTIATIONS BETWEEN DEVELOPING AND ADVANCED COUNTRIES: THE NORTH-SOUTH DEBATE

So far we have focused on how individual developing countries have tried to use their own trade policies to help themselves grow. Since World War II, however, developing countries have also tried to get the advanced countries to change their policies. The result has been a set of running arguments that are often called the **North-South debate** because (with the exception of Australia and New Zealand) all the advanced countries are in the temperate zones of the Northern Hemisphere, while most developing countries lie in the tropics.

Three questions have been at the heart of the North-South debate:

1. Have poor nations been exploited? Is the affluence of the advanced nations achieved to some degree at the expense of developing countries?
2. What is the role of foreign capital in development? Is investment by advanced nations in developing countries good or bad for them?
3. Should the prices of developing-country exports be higher? Should cartels be organized to raise the prices of raw materials?

ARE POOR NATIONS EXPLOITED?

Poor nations, and their advocates in the advanced countries, have often claimed that the wealth of the rich nations is based on exploitation. This position was easier to argue when much of the less-developed world was under direct political domination from Europe. (Actually, at the height of imperialism, few colonies paid enough tribute to repay the cost of administering them. But there were some examples of brutal exploitation, especially in Africa.) In the modern world, the case for exploitation must rest on something about the transactions between North and South that works to the South's disadvantage.

It is clear that trade between advanced countries and developing countries is marked by "unequal exchange." Developing nations use much more labor to produce the goods they export to advanced nations than these nations use to produce the goods they supply in return. The Ricardian model presented in Chapter 2 showed, however, that this is not a useful way to look at international exchange. Given the low productivity of developing countries in both manufacturing and agriculture, unequal exchange is inevitable: it is not an indication that the poor countries are losing from their trade.

A more sophisticated view of exploitation comes from the same line of thought as the infant industry argument. Suppose that developing countries could potentially develop efficient manufacturing industries but that they cannot get started in the face of competition from established industries in the advanced nations. Then it might be that the division of the world into rich manufacturing nations and poor agricultural countries is a historical accident—the rich countries just got there first, and their industrial development precluded development by the rest of the world. This view is sometimes called the doctrine of **uneven development.** Unlike the concept of unequal exchange, which the model in Chapter 2 showed to be misconceived, but like the infant industry argument, uneven development is an idea that makes sense. The question is whether it is true.

The answer is that uneven development is hard to justify given the experience of the last few decades. On one side, the doctrine depends on the correctness of the infant industry argument. Yet the history of import-substitution policies shows that even with decades of protection from foreign competition, many developing countries have not been able to develop efficient manufacturing sectors. On the other hand, some developing countries have done very well at selling manufactures in world markets without infant industry protection. Both the failure of protected industries to achieve efficiency and the success of unprotected industries indicate that competition from established industries in advanced countries is not the main factor inhibiting growth in developing countries.

Many people — not all of them from developing countries — would like to believe that the poverty of most of the world is caused by the wealth of the lucky advanced nations. The sheer awfulness of world poverty makes us want to find villains. In fact, however, it is hard to find evidence that the wealth of the advanced countries has been achieved at the expense of developing nations.

THE ROLE OF FOREIGN CAPITAL AND MULTINATIONAL FIRMS IN DEVELOPMENT

The doctrine of uneven development concerns the effects of foreign *trade* on development. Many LDCs have been equally concerned about the effects of foreign *investment,* especially when it comes as direct investment by multinational firms. Does an important role by foreign multinationals hurt the economy of a less-developed country?

At one level the opposition to foreign multinationals is based on concern over national sovereignty. In the past, some countries have felt that foreign firms dominate their economies and have too much influence over their politics. The caricature of the "banana republic" that is virtually owned by the United Fruit Company has sometimes had a basis in reality. Even in a country as large as Mexico, foreign companies dominated the economy and had powerful political influence in the early years of this century; it was partly a nationalistic reaction to this foreign control that set off the Mexican revolution of 1910–1920. As is the case for international investment generally, foreign ownership declined during the period between the wars and has never regained the relative importance it had in the years before World War I. Despite some scare talk, national sovereignty has not been much threatened in the postwar period. A rise in multinational operations during the 1950s and 1960s did, however, raise some legitimate economic concerns.

Essentially, recent concern over multinationals has focused on technology: the kind that multinationals use (the issue of **appropriate technology**) and the way in which it is made available to others (the issue of **technology transfer**).

Appropriate Technology. Those who raise the appropriate technology issue argue that multinational firms bring with them a technology that is suited to the capital-abundant, labor-scarce economies in which they are based but not to the poor economies to which they come. The slogan "small is beautiful," coined by the development theorist F. W. Schumacher, has popularized the view that LDCs need small-scale, labor-intensive methods rather than the large-scale, capital-intensive methods that allegedly characterize the operations of multinationals.

Defenders of multinationals reply that multinationals are no more inclined to use inappropriate technology than domestically owned firms, and that when they do it is because they are given inappropriate incentives. When multinationals produce manufactures in dualistic economies, for example, they face relatively high wages and government policies that encourage them to import expensive machinery. Given these incentives the multinationals adopt capital-intensive techniques similar to the ones they use at home. Given different incentives, they would behave differently.

There is some evidence to support this view. Consider Mexico, which has traditionally pursued a policy of import-substituting industrialization and which has the characteristic problems of dualism: a capital-intensive manufacturing sector that offers too few jobs to employ the growing population of urban unemployed. Since 1965, U.S. firms have been allowed to establish plants in northern Mexico that export to the United States and receive special exemption from both U.S. and Mexican restrictions on trade: raw materials can be imported from the United States without tariff or import restrictions, and the United States has agreed to charge tariffs only on the value-added, not the total value of goods exported from Mexico. Because powerful unions are absent, wages in these export-oriented manufacturing plants are lower than wages in the older import-substituting industries. Also, no special incentives have been offered to these new plants to import expensive capital goods. The results are dramatic: the plants in northern Mexico are only about one-tenth as capital-intensive as the traditional manufacturing sector. Despite having only modest investment, the offshore manufacturing now employs some 25 percent of Mexican industrial workers. The Mexican experience suggests that when multinationals are given an incentive to use appropriate technology, they are as likely to use it as domestic firms.

Technology Transfer. The technology transfer issue is a cousin to the infant industry issue of appropriability. Recall that infant industries are supposed to yield extra benefits in the form of experience and knowledge that diffuse to the rest of the economy. Critics of multinationals argue that when an infant industry consists of foreign firms, the technology is developed elsewhere and is not *transferred* to the rest of the domestic economy. These critics would prefer to see domestically owned firms that either license technology from abroad or develop it themselves. They believe that even though these firms might initially have higher costs than a multinational, the indirect benefits would be larger.

While there is no hard evidence on how technology transfer by multinationals compares with that by domestic firms, it might be informative to ask whether the NICs, which seem to have been successful at adopting advanced technology, have relied on multinationals. The answer is that they vary enormously. On one side, Korea and Hong Kong have relied primarily on local entrepreneurs to develop their industry. On the other side, Taiwan and Singapore rely heavily on multinationals—so much so in the case of Singapore that some observers have characterized it as a "contract labor" economy that hires itself out to foreign firms. All four economies have done spectacularly well at improving their living standards.

RAISING THE EXPORT PRICES OF DEVELOPING COUNTRIES: COMMODITY EXPORT CARTELS

Despite their efforts at industrialization, most developing countries remain exporters of agricultural products and minerals—often called "commodities"—and importers of manufactures. Thus, the terms of trade of developing countries as a group are related to the prices of commodities relative to those of manufactured goods. Governments of poor nations have therefore always been interested in ways to raise commodity prices. The most promising route to increased commodity prices has often seemed to be the formation of **commodity export cartels,** in which a group of countries exporting the same commodity agree to restrict supply and drive up the price.

We saw in Chapter 9 that a country that is a large exporter of some good can raise its welfare at other countries' expense by imposing an export tax. If there are several exporting nations, however, each individual country will be restrained from imposing a large export tax, because some of the benefit of the higher prices that result will accrue to other exporters rather than the taxing country. The basic idea of an export cartel is that several exporters acting together will take into account the benefits that each gains from the export taxes of the others, and that they will therefore succeed in raising prices (and their welfare) more than if they acted independently.

For example, suppose that Brazil and Colombia were the world's only coffee exporters. If Brazil were to impose a tax on its coffee exports in order to raise world prices, some consumers would shift to Colombian coffee; this shift would limit how high an export tax Brazil could profitably impose. Colombia would feel similarly constrained. If Brazil and Colombia agreed to raise coffee prices together, however, they would both feel free to raise prices higher, to their mutual gain (and the rest of the world's loss).

The scope for gains from forming a cartel is greatest when the cartel controls much of world production, when there is little ability on the part of consumers to switch away from the product, and when alternative sources of supply are difficult to develop. Over the years there have been many attempts to form export cartels, in commodities ranging from coffee to oil to tin. For the most part, however, these cartels either broke apart or were less successful in raising prices than their founders hoped. The reasons have partly to do with the limits on cartel power: most cartels have controlled too little of world production and have faced both substitution by consumers and competition from alternative sources. Equally important, cartels have trouble imposing discipline on their own members. Each country has an incentive to cheat, undercutting the rest of the cartel so as to sell more. If too many members cheat, the "honest" members will find that it is not worth their while trying to support the price.

Case Study OPEC

Most commodity export cartels have been unimpressive in their results, but there has been one spectacular exception. The Organization of Petroleum Exporting Countries (OPEC), founded in 1961, was able during the 1970s to engineer a huge rise in the price of oil. For a time, it seemed as though OPEC could serve as a model for other commodity exporters. In fact, however, OPEC's success has remained unique, and OPEC itself fell on hard times in the mid-1980s.

What was special about OPEC? Part of the answer is that political disturbances helped disrupt the supply of oil and drive up the price: the Arab-Israeli war of 1973 led to an Arab embargo, while the fall of the Shah in Iran (1979) and the Iran-Iraq war (begun in 1980) reduced deliveries from the Persian Gulf. Also, OPEC accounted for more than half of world oil production outside the U.S.S.R. in the early 1970s, and both the supply and demand for oil are inelastic in the short run.

The problem of cheating by cartel members was less of a problem for OPEC than other cartels, at least at first, because of the dominant role of Saudi Arabia. In effect, the Saudis had a large enough market share that they were willing to support the price by reducing output even when other members of OPEC produced more than they were supposed to.

These special circumstances explain why oil could be more effectively cartelized than other commodities. And even OPEC eventually ran into problems: by 1986, long-run shifts in demand and increasing supply from non-OPEC sources had forced price reductions to levels that, in real terms, were the lowest since 1973.

Despite the failure of attempts to raise prices through export cartels, developing countries continue to argue that something should be done to improve their terms of trade, which fell during the mid-1980s to the lowest levels since the Depression. At times they have proposed that advanced countries fund price-support programs, in which international organizations would buy up commodities whenever their prices fell to some minimum level; such programs would be extremely expensive, however, and there is no sentiment in the industrial countries for providing the necessary resouces.

SUMMARY

1. Trade policy in less-developed countries can be analyzed using the same analytical tools used to discuss advanced countries. The particular issues characteristic of *developing countries* are, however, different. In particular, trade policy in developing countries is concerned with three objectives: promoting industrialization, coping with the uneven development of the domestic economy, and attempting to undo what is perceived as unfair or exploitative economic relations with advanced countries.

2. Government policy to promote industrialization has often been justified by the *infant industry* argument, which says that new industries need a temporary period of protection from competition from established competitors in other countries. The infant industry argument is valid only if it can be cast as a market failure argument for intervention. Two usual justifications are the existence of *imperfect capital markets* and the problem of *appropriability* of knowledge generated by pioneering firms.

3. Using the infant industry argument as justification, many LDCs have pursued policies of *import-substituting industrialization* in which domestic industries are created under the protection of tariffs or import quotas. Although these policies have succeeded in promoting manufacturing, by and large they have not delivered the expected gains in economic growth and living standards. Many economists are now harshly critical of the results of import substitution, arguing that it has fostered high-cost, inefficient production.

4. A small group of developing countries has managed to industrialize not through import substitution but through development of manufactured exports. These *newly industrializing countries* (NICs) have achieved rapid growth in output and living standards. A major question is whether other countries, by moving away from import-substitution policies, can achieve similar success.

5. Most developing countries are characterized by economic *dualism:* a high-wage, capital-intensive industrial sector coexists with a low-wage traditional sector. Dual economies also often have a serious problem of urban unemployment.

6. The difference in wages between the modern and traditional sectors has sometimes been used as a case for tariff protection of the industrial sector. This is the *wage differentials* case for protection. This view no longer receives much credence among economists, however. More recent analyses suggest

that protection will lead to more rural-urban migration, which worsens the urban unemployment problem and may worsen the symptoms of dualism.

7. Governments of developing countries and their supporters have argued that the current international economic system is unfair and that the poverty of the developing world is related to advanced countries' wealth. The most coherent view of this kind is the doctrine of *uneven development*, which is related to the infant industry argument. According to this doctrine, advanced countries were just lucky in getting established in the industrial sector first, forestalling industrial development by later competitors. A review of the evidence, however, finds little support for the view that advanced nations grew wealthy at the expense of others.

8. On a less global level, multinational enterprises have been accused of failing to provide benefits to their host countries, either because they use *inappropriate technology* or because they fail to make a *technology transfer* that improves the technological level of the rest of the economy. Defenders of multinationals argue that multinationals use inappropriate technology because they are faced with distorted incentives. On the technology transfer issue, some countries have done well with extensive foreign investment and others have done well without it, so that it is hard to reach any definite answer.

9. Finally, most developing countries export commodities, and they have always tried to find ways to raise commodity prices. In the 1970s the success of OPEC led to hopes that *commodity export cartels* could improve the terms of trade of many developing countries. It seems, however, that OPEC benefited from uniquely favorable conditions (and OPEC itself has come on hard times).

KEY TERMS

developing countries
infant industry argument
imperfect capital markets
appropriability
import-substituting industrialization
newly industrializing countries (NICs)
economic dualism
dual economy
wage differentials argument
North-South debate
uneven development
appropriate technology
technology transfer
commodity export cartels

PROBLEMS

1. "Japan's experience makes the infant industry case for protection better than any theory. In the early 1950s Japan was a poor nation that survived by exporting textiles and toys. The Japanese government protected what at first were inefficient, high-cost steel and automobile industries, and those industries came to dominate world markets." Discuss critically.

2. A country currently imports automobiles at $8000 each. Its government believes that domestic producers could manufacture autos for only $6000 given time but that there would be an initial shakedown period during which autos would cost $10,000 to produce domestically.

a) Suppose that each firm that tries to produce autos must go through the shakedown period of high costs on its own. Under what circumstances would the existence of the initial high costs justify infant industry protection?

b) Now suppose, on the contrary, that once one firm has borne the costs of learning to produce autos at $6000 each, other firms can imitate it and do the same. Explain how this can prevent development of a domestic industry, and how infant industry protection can help.

3. Why can't a country use export subsidies at the same time it imposes import tariffs, so that it achieves import substitution without reducing its exports?

4. Why might import substituting industrialization be more successful in large developing countries such as Brazil than in smaller nations such as Ghana?

5. The very small economy of Cantabrigia has a total labor force of 20 workers. These workers can produce two goods, manufactures and food. In production of manufactures, the *marginal* product of labor depends on employment as follows:

Number of workers	Marginal product of last worker
1	20
2	18
3	16
4	14
5	12
6	11
7	10
8	9
9	8
10	7

In the food sector the marginal product of labor is independent of employment, and is 9. The world price of a unit of manufactures is $10; so is the world price of a unit of food.

a) Suppose that there were no distortion in the labor market; find the wage rate, the allocation of labor between manufactures and food, and the output of each good.

b) Now suppose that for some reason the minimum wage in the manufactures sector is $150. Full employment, however, is maintained. Find the output of the economy in this case. How large is the cost of the distortion?

c) Finally, suppose that workers migrate from the country to the city until the wage of city workers multiplied by the probability of being employed equals the rural wage. Find the level of output and unemployment.

6. "Import quotas on capital-intensive industrial goods, and subsidies for the import of capital equipment, were meant to create manufacturing jobs in many developing countries. Unfortunately, they have probably helped create the urban unemployment problem." Explain this remark.

7. Explain the distinction between the doctrines of unequal exchange and uneven development. Why is there a natural relationship between the uneven development doctrine and the case for import-substituting industrialization?

8. Suppose two countries produce bauxite for the world market. In each country the cost of producing bauxite is \$10 per ton. The world demand curve for bauxite may be written

$$P = 40 - 0.1Q,$$

where Q is the total production by both countries combined. Note that this demand curve is written showing price as a function of quantity; it could equally well be written the other way, in which case the curve would be

$$Q = 400 - 10P.$$

It is possible to show that if the two countries choose independent profit-maximizing levels of bauxite output, each will produce 100 tons; if they agree to maximize their profits jointly, each will produce only 75 tons.

a) Compare the profits of each when they each produce 100 tons with profits when they organize a cartel and each produces 75 tons.

b) What happens if one of the countries honors its agreement to produce only 75 tons, but the other cheats and produces 100 tons after all?

FURTHER READING

Jagdish N. Bhagwati, ed. *The New International Economic Order.* Cambridge: MIT Press, 1977. The North-South debate reached its height in the late 1970s, with widespread demands for a "new international economic order" that would redistribute income from rich to poor nations. This volume gives a good overview of the debate.

Jagdish N. Bhagwati and T. N. Srinivasan, "Trade Policy and Development," in Rudiger Dornbusch and Jacob A. Frenkel, eds. *International Economic Policy: Theory and Evidence.* Baltimore: Johns Hopkins University Press, 1979, pp. 1–35. Reviews research findings on the links between trade policy and economic development.

W. Max Corden. *Trade Policy and Economic Welfare.* Oxford: Clarendon Press, 1974. A clear analytical discussion of the role of trade policy in economic development.

Anne O. Krueger. "Trade Policies in Developing Countries," in *Handbook of International Economics,* vol. 1, Ronald W. Jones and Peter B. Kenen, eds. Amsterdam: North-Holland, 1984. A recent analytical survey of developing-country trade issues.

W. Arthur Lewis. *The Theory of Economic Development.* Homewood, IL: Irwin, 1955. A good example of the upbeat view taken of trade policies for economic development during the import-substitution high tide of the 1950s and 1960s.

I. M. D. Little. *Economic Development.* New York: Basic Books, 1982. An entertaining discussion of the not always scientific process by which ideas about trade policy for developing countries have come into and out of vogue.

I. M. D. Little, Tibor Scitovsky, and Maurice Scott. *Industry and Trade in Some Developing Countries.* New York: Oxford University Press, 1970. A key work in the emergence of a more downbeat view of import substitution in the 1970s and 1980s.

11 INDUSTRIAL POLICY IN ADVANCED COUNTRIES

Most of the world's income is generated by a handful of advanced industrial countries: the nations of Western Europe and North America, plus Japan, Australia, and New Zealand. These are lucky countries, whose prosperity is the envy of the rest of the world. Even wealthy countries, however, want to add to their wealth through economic growth. Throughout the industrial world, economic growth has been much slower in the 1970s and 1980s than it was in the 1950s and 1960s. In Western Europe, this slower growth has been accompanied by rising unemployment. In the United States, employment has grown steadily but productivity growth has been sluggish, and important segments of the population are worse off economically than they were in 1970. In Japan, growth continues to outpace that in the rest of the industrial world, but there too its pace has slowed.

How can a country accelerate the pace of its economic growth? One possible answer is to adopt an **industrial policy,** in which the government attempts to channel resources into sectors that it views as important for future economic growth. This chapter reviews the debate over the usefulness and appropriate form of industrial policy for an advanced nation like the United States. The first part of the chapter considers some popular arguments for industrial policy that are *not* based on careful economic analysis, and criticizes their weaknesses. The second part reviews some sophisticated arguments that do make good economic sense, and asks how they might be applied in practice. The third part turns to a brief survey of experience with industrial policy, in Japan and elsewhere.

POPULAR ARGUMENTS FOR INDUSTRIAL POLICY

Industrial policy is an attempt by a government to encourage resources to move into particular sectors that the government views as important to future economic growth. Since this means moving resources out of other sectors, industrial policy always promotes some parts of the domestic economy at the expense of others. The case for such a policy therefore stands or falls on the issue of **criteria for selection:** how do we choose which sectors should be encouraged at the expense of the rest?

It is important not to confuse the question of which sectors the government should encourage with the question of which sectors should grow. In a market economy some sectors will be growing, others shrinking, as a result of natural market forces. To devise a useful industrial policy, a government must do more than decide which are the industries of the future; it must answer the much more difficult question: Which sectors should be growing or shrinking *more rapidly than they would if left to the market?* For example, we may be able to say that U.S. comparative advantage is shifting from traditional "smokestack" industries like steel and automobiles to new high-technology areas like computers and biotechnology. But this observation does not necessarily imply that the U.S. government should actively encourage workers and investment to move into the new sectors, since these resources are shifting to the new industries in any case as a result of market incentives. To justify an active government program that encourages the shift of resources, it would be necessary to show that for some reason the shift is taking place too slowly—that there is a market failure justification for government intervention.

Currently popular arguments for industrial policy are not usually cast in market failure form. Instead, they suggest plausible criteria for identifying desirable industries that the government should encourage. In particular, proponents of a U.S. industrial policy have argued that the U.S. government should encourage the growth of (1) industries with high value added per worker, (2) industries that have a "linkage" role with regard to other industries, (3) industries that have future growth potential, and (4) industries that have been targeted by foreign governments. While on the surface these criteria seem reasonable, a close analysis reveals that each is badly flawed.

ENCOURAGING INDUSTRIES WITH HIGH VALUE ADDED PER WORKER

The value added by an industry is the difference between the value of its output and the value of the inputs it buys from other industries. The sum of value added in all industries is a country's national income. Value added per worker varies considerably across industries. This has led many commentators to argue that a country can raise its national income by shifting its industrial mix toward those industries with **high value added per worker.**

The problem with this argument is that it fails to ask *why* some sectors have higher value added per worker than others. Commentators often presume that high-value-added sectors must pay higher wage rates or earn higher rates of profit than low-value-added sectors. But if that were the case, labor and capital would have a market incentive to move into high-value-added industries, without need for special government encouragement. In fact, however, high value added per worker usually reflects high inputs per worker. High-value-added sectors are often capital-intensive, like petrochemicals. In such industries the high value added per worker is compensated for by extremely high capital costs, so that neither wages nor profit rates are particularly out of line. In other cases, high value added reflects human capital: high levels of training or skill.

Suppose for a moment that high-value-added sectors are those that have large inputs of capital per worker. Could we then argue that a country can raise its national income by expanding these sectors? As we saw in Chapter 4, if a country accumulates capital, it will indeed both grow richer and shift its industrial mix toward capital-intensive sectors and away from labor-intensive sectors. This shift does not, however, need a special government policy, because it will happen as a natural consequence of market forces. The government might encourage saving and investment, which will lead to capital accumulation and will eventually automatically lead to a shift in industrial structure toward capital goods. Encouraging saving, however, is not industrial policy. An industrial policy would involve deliberately subsidizing or otherwise encouraging growth of the capital-intensive industries for a *given* supply of capital.

Will such an industrial policy raise national welfare? Not unless it helps correct some market failure. If there is no market failure, the initial allocation of resources will already be optimal, and the government-sponsored reallocation cannot improve upon it. If there *is* a market failure, there is still no reason to assume that the market failure leads to insufficient allocation of resources to capital-intensive sectors, rather than excessive allocation to these sectors.

What would happen if a country did subsidize its capital-intensive industries? Other things equal, a given amount of capital will employ fewer workers in capital- than in labor-intensive sectors. So a shift of capital toward the capital-intensive part of the economy will initially tend to reduce employment. Although the unemployment may eventually be eliminated by a fall in real wages that encourages all sectors to substitute labor for capital, the initial increase in unemployment is hardly the result that one looks for from an industrial policy.

ENCOURAGING LINKAGE INDUSTRIES

A recurrent view in discussions of industrial policy has been that governments should offer special encouragement to sectors that supply inputs to the rest of the economy. The idea is that expansion of industries producing intermediate goods has multiplied effects through the encouragement of industries that use what they produce. For example, some observers argue that Japanese subsidies to investment in steel, by leading to cheaper steel, encouraged growth of all those industries that use steel, like shipbuilding and autos.

The popularity of the **linkage argument** stems from the feeling that producing intermediate goods that can be used in a variety of sectors is a more fundamental economic activity than producing consumer goods that simply provide satisfaction to households. It is hard to escape the feeling that the makers of steel or semiconductors are doing something more serious than the makers of toys or toothpaste.

Again, however, if there is no market failure, there is no reason to expect markets to devote too few resources to the production of intermediate goods. A basic proposition of economics is that with competitive markets the earnings of any input are equal to the value of its marginal product. Thus at the margin a dollar's worth of capital services will add one dollar to the value of production of the sector in which it is employed, whether it be steel, autos, shipbuilding, or any other. It is also true that a dollar's worth of steel will similarly be worth one dollar in any alternative use.

The linkage argument is that the government should direct more investment into steel as opposed to autos or shipbuilding than the private market would have. Will this raise national income? In the absence of a market failure, it will not. A dollar of capital services reallocated from autos to steel lowers the value of auto output by one dollar and raises the value of steel output by one dollar. The extra steel output can now be used to raise auto output back to its original level, *but not higher;* this only confirms that the original allocation was optimal in that it could not be improved upon.

PROMOTING INDUSTRIES WITH FUTURE GROWTH POTENTIAL

Another common argument is that industrial policy should seek to channel resources into industries with high potential for future growth. There is no question that technological change, shifting patterns of demand, and shifting comparative advantage lead to very different growth rates of industries within an economy. Sometimes, though not always, it is possible to predict which industries will grow fastest. Should the government try to "pick winners" and encourage labor and capital to move into the industries with the highest growth prospects?

Again the answer is that properly functioning markets will make such a government role unnecessary. Firms making investment choices and workers choosing their careers are already trying to pick the winning industries. Only if the government can do a better job of picking the winners than these private market participants can it improve on the market outcome. To put the point another way, if everyone knows that an industry will grow rapidly, capital and labor will move into that industry even without special government encouragement. Unless there is some market failure, adding additional incentives to move into the sector will actually overdo it. It *is* possible to invest too much in a high-growth industry, as the later discussion of experience with steel and aircraft will make clear.

The argument that the government should always promote growth sectors amounts to saying that private markets systematically undervalue future growth prospects. This argument is close to the infant industry argument (Chapter 10). The infant industry argument has been strongly criticized on the grounds that there is no clear evidence for the kinds of market failures that would make it valid. The same criticism applies with even more force in the case of advanced industrial countries, where markets presumably work more efficiently. In the United States, private investors often support ventures, such as the Alaskan oil pipeline and the development of biotechnology, that involve large initial expenditures in return for profits that will occur only after a long delay and which may be highly uncertain. Looking at these examples, both of which have attracted huge amounts of private investment, it is hard to argue that private markets are systematically shortsighted.

COUNTERING THE EFFECTS OF OTHER COUNTRIES' INDUSTRIAL POLICIES

A final criterion for industrial policy that is particularly popular in U.S. discussion is the idea of industrial policy as a defensive measure. Suppose that other countries provide support to an industry, leading to a contraction of that industry in the United States. Shouldn't the United States respond by supporting the industry? If it does not, the argument runs, the United States will, in effect, be allowing its industrial structure to be determined by other countries' industrial policies.

To see what is wrong with this argument, let's first imagine a different scenario. Suppose that other countries get more efficient at producing some good, say textiles, and that as a result textile prices on world markets fall. What is the appropriate U.S. response? Because this is a shift in comparative advantage, the United States should accommodate it by moving resources out of textiles and into other sectors. Furthermore, markets will tend to make this adjustment automatically, because the reduced relative price of textiles will provide the incentive. Unless there is some market failure in the U.S. economy, there is no need for a special government policy either to stop or to accelerate the pace of adjustment.

Now return to the issue of industrial targeting, and suppose that the price of textiles falls, not because of a shift in comparative advantage but because other countries subsidize textile production. Should the United States respond differently? It should not. *From the point of view of the United States,* it makes no difference whether the price of textiles falls because of changes in foreign technology or because of foreign subsidies. In either case, the response that maximizes U.S. welfare is to shift resources out of textiles. A farmer deciding whether to grow wheat or corn needs to know their relative price, but the right decision does not depend on whether this price is the result of natural market forces or of government price supports. The same is true of a country setting its industrial mix. The French economist Frédéric Bastiat once wrote that the fact that other countries have rocks in their harbors is no reason to throw rocks in our own—that is, the fact that other countries distort their production with protection and subsidies is no reason for us to distort our own.

The usual counterargument is that if the United States does not respond to foreign industrial targeting, other countries will drive us out of key industries. This presumes, however, that the sectors other countries are targeting are especially important for economic growth. Certainly the fact that another country chooses to target a sector is not in and of itself evidence of a market failure requiring government intervention. The defensive argument for industrial policy in effect commits us to accepting other countries' judgments about which sectors should be encouraged—and as we will see, the record on judgment either by the United States or by other governments is not especially good.

What we have done so far is to examine a series of criteria for industrial policy that have been influential in popular discussion. These criteria all seem appealing but do not stand up well to thoughtful economic analysis. Should the government dismiss the case for activist industrial policy? If its advocates cannot come up with better arguments than these, why should thoughtful observers take industrial policy seriously? There are two answers to this. The first is a practical one: although these ideas may not convince economists, they remain influential in actual policy. Thus it is important to ask how industrial policy has worked out in practice (the evidence on this issue is covered later in this chapter).

The second answer to a dismissal of the idea of industrial policy is that to restrict the discussion to popular criteria is not to give the idea of industrial policy a fair hearing. Although popular criteria for industrial policy may not hold up too well, there are more carefully conceived arguments that we should examine carefully. These arguments do not carry the political appeal of the simplistic arguments above, but they do have more intellectual substance.

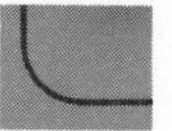

SOPHISTICATED ARGUMENTS FOR INDUSTRIAL POLICY

There is nothing in the analytical framework developed in Chapters 8 and 9 that rules out the desirability of industrial policy. What that framework *does* show is that activist government policy needs a specific kind of justification—namely, it must offset some preexisting domestic market failure. The problem with the popular arguments for industrial policy in the previous pages is precisely that they do not link the case for government intervention to any particular failure of the assumptions on which the case for laissez-faire rests.

The problem with market failure arguments for intervention is how to know a market failure when you see one. In recent years economists studying industrial countries have identified two kinds of market failure that seem to be present and relevant to the industrial policies of advanced countries. One of these is the inability of firms in high-technology industries to capture the benefits of that part of their contribution to knowledge that spills over to other firms. The other is the presence of monopoly profits in highly concentrated oligopolistic industries.

TECHNOLOGY AND EXTERNALITIES

The discussion of the infant industry argument in Chapter 10 noted that there is a potential market failure arising from difficulties of appropriating knowledge. If firms in an industry generate knowledge that other firms can also use without paying for it, the industry is in effect producing some extra output—the marginal social benefit of the knowledge—that is not reflected in the incentives of firms. Where such **externalities** (benefits that accrue to parties external to the firms) can be shown to be important, there is a good case for subsidizing the industry.

At an abstract level this argument is the same for the infant industries of less-developed countries as it is for the established industries of the advanced countries. In advanced countries, however, the argument has a special edge because in those countries there are some industries in which the generation of knowledge is in many ways the central aspect of the enterprise. These industries, called **high-technology industries,** include computers, electronics, and aerospace. In high-technology industries, firms devote a great deal of their resources to improving technology, either by explicit spending on research and development or by being willing to take initial losses on new products and processes in order to gain experience. Such activities take place in nearly all industries, of course, so that there is no sharp line between high-tech and the rest of the economy. There are clear differences in degree, however, and it makes sense to talk of a high-technology sector in which investment in knowledge is the key part of the business.

The point for industrial policy is that while firms can appropriate some of the benefits of their own investment in knowledge (otherwise they would not be investing!), they usually cannot appropriate them fully. Some of the benefits accrue to other firms that can imitate the ideas and techniques of the leaders. In electronics, for example, it is not uncommon for firms to "reverse engineer" their rivals' designs, taking their products apart to figure out how they work and how they were made. Because patent laws provide only weak protection for innovators, there is a reasonable presumption that under laissez-faire high-technology firms do not receive as strong an incentive to innovate as they should.

The Case for Government Support of High-Technology Industries. Should the government of the United States subsidize high-technology industries? While there is a pretty good case for such subsidy, we need to exercise some caution. Two questions in particular arise, regarding the ability of government policy to target the right thing and the quantitative importance of the argument.

Although high-technology industries probably produce extra social benefits because of the knowledge they generate, much of what goes on even in a high-technology industry has nothing to do with generating knowledge. There is no reason to subsidize the employment of capital or nontechnical workers in high-technology industries; on the other hand, innovation and technological spillovers happen to some extent even in industries that are mostly not at all high-tech. A general principle is that trade and industrial policy should be targeted specifically on the activity in which the market failure occurs. Thus policy should seek to subsidize the generation of knowledge that firms cannot appropriate. A general subsidy for a set of industries in which this kind of knowledge generation is believed to go on is a pretty blunt instrument for the purpose.

Perhaps, instead, government should subsidize research and development wherever it occurs. The problem here is one of definition. How do we know when a firm is engaged in creating knowledge? A loose definition could lend itself to abuse: who is to say whether paper clips and company cars were really supporting the development of knowledge or were placed in the research department's budget to inflate the subsidy? A strict definition, on the other hand, would risk favoring large, bureaucratic forms of research where the allocation of funds can be strictly documented over the smaller, informal organizations that are widely believed to be the key to the most original thinking.

The United States *does* in effect subsidize research and development, at least as compared with other kinds of investment. R&D can be claimed by firms as a current expense and thus counts as an immediate deduction against the corporate profit tax. By contrast, investment in plant and equipment cannot be claimed as an immediate expense and can be written off only through gradual depreciation. This effective favorable treatment for knowledge is an accident of tax history rather than an explicit policy, but we should note it before concluding that the United States spends too little on R&D or that the high-technology sector needs further encouragement. To reach such a conclusion we would need to know how much subsidy is justified.

How Important are Externalities? The question of the appropriate level of subsidy for high technology depends on the answer to a difficult empirical problem: How important, quantitatively, is the technological spillover argument for targeting high-technology industries? Is the optimal subsidy 10, 20, or 100 percent? The honest answer is that no one has a good idea. It is in the nature of externalities, benefits that do not carry a market price, that they are hard to measure.

Further, even if the externalities generated by high-technology industries could be shown to be large, there may be only a limited incentive for any one country to support these industries. The reason is that many of the benefits of knowledge created in one country may in fact accrue to firms in other countries. Thus if, say, a Belgian firm develops a new technique for steelmaking, most of the firms that can imitate this technique will be in other European countries, the United States, and Japan rather than in Belgium. A world government might find it worthwhile to subsidize this innovation; the Belgian government might not. Such problems of appropriability at the level of the *nation* (as opposed to the firm) are less severe but still important even for a nation as large as the United States.

Despite the criticism, the technological spillover argument is probably the best case one can make intellectually for an active industrial policy. In contrast to the simplistic criteria for choosing industries, which can be strongly rejected, the case for or against targeting "knowledge-intensive" industries is a judgment call.

IMPERFECT COMPETITION AND STRATEGIC TRADE POLICY

Very recently a new argument for industrial targeting has received substantial theoretical attention. Originally proposed by the economists Barbara Spencer and James Brander of the University of British Columbia, this argument locates the market failure that justifies government intervention in the lack of perfect competition. In some industries, they point out, there are only a few firms in effective competition. Because of the small number of firms, the assumptions of perfect competition do not apply. In particular, there will typically be **excess returns;** that is, firms will make profits above what equally risky investments elsewhere in the economy can earn. There will be an international competition over who gets these profits.

Spencer and Brander noticed that, in this case, it is possible in principle for a government to alter the rules of the game to shift these excess returns from foreign to domestic firms. In the simplest case, a subsidy to domestic firms, by deterring investment and production by foreign competitors, can raise the profits of domestic firms by more than the amount of the subsidy. Setting aside the effects on consumers—for example, when the firms are selling only in foreign markets—this capture of profits from foreign competitors would mean that the subsidy raises national income at other countries' expense.

The Brander-Spencer Analysis: An Example. The **Brander-Spencer analysis** can be illustrated with a simple example in which there are only two firms competing, each from a different country. Bearing in mind that any resemblance to actual events may be coincidental, let's call the firms Boeing and Airbus, and the countries the United States and Europe. Suppose that there is a new product, 150-seat aircraft, that both firms are capable of making. For simplicity, assume that each firm can make only a yes/no decision: either to produce 150-seat aircraft or not.

Table 11-1 illustrates how the profits earned by the two firms might depend on their decisions. (The setup is similar to the one we used to examine the interaction of different countries' trade policies in Chapter 9.) Each row corresponds to a particular decision by Boeing, each column to a decision by Airbus. In each box are two entries: the entry on the lower left represents the profits of Boeing, while that on the upper right represents the profits of Airbus.

As set up, the table reflects the following assumption: either firm alone could earn profits making 150-seat aircraft, but if both firms try to produce them, both will make losses. Which firm will actually get the profits? This depends on who gets there first. Suppose that Boeing is able to get a small head start and commits itself to produce 150-seat aircraft before Airbus can get going. Airbus will find that it has no incentive to enter. The outcome will be in the upper right of the table, with Boeing earning profits.

Now comes the Brander-Spencer point: the European government can reverse this situation. Suppose that the European government commits itself to pay its firm a subsidy of 25 if it enters. The result will be to change the table of payoffs to that represented in Table 11-2. It is now profitable for Airbus to produce 150-seat aircraft whatever Boeing does.

Let's work through the implications of this shift. Boeing now knows that whatever it does, it will have to compete with Airbus and will therefore lose money if it chooses to produce. So now it is Boeing that will be deterred from entering. In effect, the government subsidy has removed the advantage

TABLE 11-1 Two-firm competition

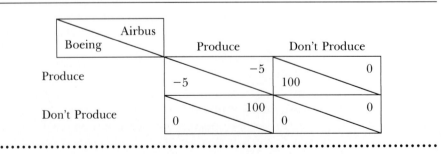

Boeing \ Airbus	Produce	Don't Produce
Produce	Boeing: −5; Airbus: −5	Boeing: 100; Airbus: 0
Don't Produce	Boeing: 0; Airbus: 100	Boeing: 0; Airbus: 0

TABLE 11-2 Effects of a subsidy to Airbus

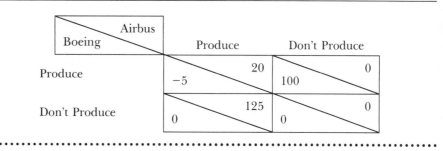

Boeing \ Airbus	Produce	Don't Produce
Produce	Boeing −5, Airbus 20	Boeing 100, Airbus 0
Don't Produce	Boeing 0, Airbus 125	Boeing 0, Airbus 0

of a head start that we assumed was Boeing's and has conferred it on Airbus instead.

The end result is that the equilibrium shifts from the upper right of Table 11-1 to the lower left of Table 11-2. Airbus ends up with profits of 125 instead of 0, profits that arise because of a government subsidy of only 25. That is, the subsidy raises profits by more than the amount of the subsidy itself, because of its deterrent effect on foreign competition. The subsidy has this effect because it creates an advantage for Airbus comparable with the *strategic* advantage it would have had if it, not Boeing, had had a head start in the industry. For this reason the argument for industrial policy based on imperfect competition is often referred to as the **strategic trade policy** argument.

Problems with the Brander-Spencer Analysis. This hypothetical example might seem to indicate that the strategic trade policy argument provides a compelling case for government activism. A subsidy by the European government sharply raises profits of a European firm at the expense of its foreign rivals. Leaving aside the interest of consumers, this seems to clearly raise European welfare (and reduce U.S. welfare). Shouldn't the U.S. government go ahead and put this argument into practice?

In fact, the strategic justification for trade policy, while it has attracted a great deal of interest, has also come in for a great deal of criticism. The critics argue that to make practical use of the theory would require more information than is likely to be available, that such policies would risk foreign retaliation, and that in any case the domestic politics of trade and industrial policy would prevent use of such subtle analytical tools.

The problem of insufficient information has two aspects. The first is that even when looking at an industry in isolation, it may be difficult to fill in the entries in a table like Table 11-1 with any confidence. And if the government gets it wrong, a subsidy policy may turn out to be a costly misjudgment. To see this, suppose that instead of Table 11-1, the reality is represented by the

TABLE 11-3 Two-firm competition: an alternative case

Boeing \ Airbus	Produce	Don't Produce
Produce	5 (Boeing) / −20 (Airbus)	125 (Boeing) / 0 (Airbus)
Don't Produce	0 (Boeing) / 100 (Airbus)	0 (Boeing) / 0 (Airbus)

seemingly similar payoffs in Table 11-3. The numbers are not much different, but the difference is crucial. In Table 11-3, Boeing is assumed to have some underlying advantage—maybe a better technology—so that even if Airbus enters, Boeing will still find it profitable to produce. Airbus, however, cannot produce profitably if Boeing enters.

In the absence of a subsidy, the outcome in Table 11-3 will be in the upper right corner; Boeing produces, and Airbus does not. Now suppose that, as in the previous case, the European government provides a subsidy of 25, which is sufficient to induce Airbus to produce. The new table of payoffs is illustrated as Table 11-4. The result is that both firms produce: the outcome is in the upper left. In this case Airbus, which receives a subsidy of 25, earns profits of only 5. That is, we have reversed the result above, in which a subsidy raised profits by more than the amount of the subsidy. The reason for the difference in outcome is that this time the subsidy has failed to act as a deterrent to Boeing.

Initially the two cases look very similar, yet in one case a subsidy looks like a very good idea, while in the other it looks like a terrible idea. It seems

TABLE 11-4 Effects of a subsidy to Airbus

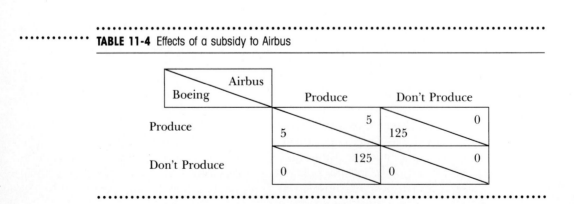

Boeing \ Airbus	Produce	Don't Produce
Produce	5 (Boeing) / 5 (Airbus)	125 (Boeing) / 0 (Airbus)
Don't Produce	0 (Boeing) / 125 (Airbus)	0 (Boeing) / 0 (Airbus)

to be a general property of strategic trade policies that their desirability depends on an exact reading of the situation. This leads some economists to ask whether we are ever likely to have enough information to use the theory effectively.

The information requirement is complicated by the fact that we cannot consider industries in isolation. If one industry is subsidized, it will draw resources from other industries and lead to increases in their costs. Thus, even a policy that succeeds in giving U.S. firms a strategic advantage in one industry will tend to cause strategic disadvantage elsewhere. To ask whether the policy is justified, the U.S. government needs to weigh these offsetting effects. Even if the government has a precise understanding of one industry, this is not enough; it needs an equally precise understanding of those industries with which that industry competes for resources.

If a proposed strategic trade policy can overcome these criticisms, it still faces the problem of foreign retaliation, essentially the same problem faced when considering the use of a tariff to improve the terms of trade (Chapter 9). Strategic policies are **beggar-thy-neighbor policies** that increase our welfare at other countries' expense. These policies therefore risk a trade war that leaves everyone worse off. Few economists would advocate that the United States be the initiator of such policies. Instead, the most that is usually argued for is that the United States itself be prepared to retaliate when other countries appear to be using strategic policies aggressively.

Finally, can theories like this ever be used in a political context? We discussed this issue in Chapter 9, where the reasons for skepticism were placed in the context of a political skeptic's case for free trade.

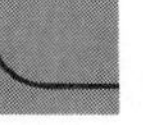

INDUSTRIAL POLICY IN PRACTICE

The theory of industrial policy is a special case of the domestic market failure analysis laid out in Chapter 9. The principles are therefore fairly simple, even though the details may be complex. No such underlying simplicity ties together the *practice* of industrial policy, however. There is a great deal of controversy even over what the industrial policies of major countries have tried to accomplish, let alone how successful they were. What follows is a brief review of some salient facts about industrial policy, followed by a discussion of some famous cases.

THE INDUSTRIAL POLICY OF JAPAN

Japan is the spectacular success story of the advanced industrial world, having emerged from postwar devastation and economic weakness into decades of spectacular growth. Japan also has had the most visible industrial policy of the industrial countries. But what was the content of that policy?

Experts on Japan point out that it is necessary to distinguish two phases in Japan's industrial policy.[1] From 1950 until the early 1970s, the Japanese economy was run in such a way that government agencies had a great deal of direct control over the allocation of resources. Since the mid-1970s, the government's role has been more subtle and ambiguous. It is a mistake to discuss the current role of the Japanese government in electronics and computers in the same context as its earlier role in steel, shipbuilding, and other heavy industries.

Early Japanese Industrial Policy. From the end of World War II until the 1970s, Japan was run as a "shortage" economy. Both the price of foreign currency and the interest rate were kept below the levels at which supply would have equaled demand, so that foreign exchange and credit were rationed. The allocation of these scarce resources was essentially controlled by the government, especially by the Ministry of Finance and the famous Ministry of International Trade and Industry (MITI). Their control over vital resources gave these ministries great power over the direction of the economy's growth. This power was further reinforced by the use of tariffs and import restrictions to protect selected industries.

During the 1950s and 1960s, the ministries used this power to follow a growth strategy similar to what the advocates of the "popular" criteria we discussed earlier might have suggested. The government channeled funds into heavy industries with high value added per worker and away from traditional labor-intensive industries such as textiles. They tried to encourage those industries that they believed reflected Japan's future comparative advantage rather than its current trade pattern. Intermediate goods industries such as steel were special favorites.

The result is history: Japan's economy grew extremely rapidly. Indeed, it is Japan's success that helps lend plausibility to the popular arguments we discussed.

The crucial question is whether Japan's industrial policy was really the key to the rapid growth. Might the economy have grown just as rapidly without the policy? There are at least two reasons to be cautious about attributing success primarily to the industrial policy.

First, we are not sure whether the activities of Japan's government were actually pushing Japan into heavy industry faster than they would have gone under laissez-faire. Japan's industrial policy was not applied to an otherwise unregulated economy. Instead, the government first disconnected the normal channels of allocation, by rationing foreign exchange and credit, then made up for the lack of a market by allocating these resources directly. Some economists have argued that in the end Japan arrived at the same outcome

[1]For a clear summary of Japan's industrial policy, see Kozo Yamamura, "Caveat Emptor: The Industrial Policy of Japan," in Paul R. Krugman, ed., *Strategic Trade Policy and the New International Economics* (Cambridge: MIT Press, 1986).

as if the government had stayed out of the picture throughout. To put it another way, the government may have been making sensible investment decisions, but the market would have made similar decisions if left to itself. There is some evidence supporting this view in Japan's pattern of trade in the 1970s, which was not very different from what would have been predicted from its resources and level of economic development, even without its industrial policy.

Second, there is the possibility that the dynamism of Japanese industry had its roots in factors other than industrial policy and that Japan would have done well in any case. Reasons for Japan's success are many: Japan had the highest savings rate in the world, an effective educational system, good labor-management relations, and a business-oriented culture in which the most ambitious and talented channeled their energy into corporate management. It is possible that industrial policy may have been a minor positive factor or even a drag on economic growth. Some of Japan's most successful industries, notably automobiles and consumer electronics, were not among those that received high priority.

The Japanese industrial policy of the 1950s and 1960s remains the picture of Japan that many retain. The country is seen as "Japan, Inc.," a society in which the allocation of resources is under the central control of MITI. Such a picture has become increasingly out of date, however. Since 1970, the traditional levers of Japanese industrial policy have lost much of their force. Foreign exchange and credit are no longer scarce and rationed, while the use of trade restrictions has become constrained by the demand of other countries that Japan open its markets. Industrial policy since 1975 or so has taken a different and more subtle form.

Current Japanese Industrial Policy. Japan's industrial policy since the mid-1970s has aimed at encouraging a new set of industries, the "knowledge-intensive," or high-technology, industries. The tools of industrial policy have been a combination of modest subsidies for research and development and encouragement of joint government-industry research projects aimed at developing promising new technologies. The whole enterprise has been on a much smaller scale relative to the total economy than the old industrial policy.

The justification for targeting high technology is not especially clear. The Japanese themselves do not seem to be clear whether they are targeting high technology because it is the growth sector of the future or because it is a generator of technological spillovers. The new Japanese industrial policy is, however, easier to justify in terms of a market failure argument than the old one.

How much effect do the new policies have? The industries targeted since 1975 remain a small part of Japan's economy. Neither automobiles nor consumer electronics (TVs, stereos, VCRs, and so on) are part of the high-technology area that has been the focus of research joint ventures. So the

Japanese consumer products that have made Japan's export success so visible do not reflect the new industrial policy. Japan has, however, become a significant producer of some products in which recent industrial policy has played a key role. Most famous and most important of these is semiconductor chips, a case we will examine shortly.

This brief history gives some perspective on the reality of Japan's policy. Japan is often seen as an almost militarily organized society, centrally commanded against economic objectives. This view exaggerated the role of the Japanese government even during its period of greatest influence and exaggerates it still more today.

INDUSTRIAL POLICY IN OTHER COUNTRIES

Other countries have pursued industrial policies to some degree in the postwar period, though none with the degree of government control, or of success, that Japan did. France has pursued industrial policies with varying degrees of vigor. Also, the United States, though without an explicit industrial strategy, does have policies—notably its support of agriculture and its military procurement—that look to some observers like industrial policies.

French Industrial Policy. The aspect of French industrial policy that has attracted the most attention has been the efforts of the government to bolster French firms in technological competition with foreign firms. Since the 1960s, the French government has worried that world technology will become dominated by large U.S. or, more recently, Japanese companies. To prevent this domination, the government has attempted to make sure that there are French firms, called national champions, that can compete on world markets. To create national champions, the French government has encouraged mergers of smaller firms into large units. It has also made use of the government's influence over demand to provide privileged markets, for example, by requiring the state-run phone company to buy its telecommunications and computer equipment from French firms. And in a few cases, notably aircraft, extensive government subsidies have been used to promote industries that are regarded as key ones.

How has France's industrial policy worked? The French economy performed quite well until the late 1970s, achieving rates of growth slightly higher than Germany's and much higher than Britain's. Since then France has had a severe unemployment problem, but this is a problem shared by almost all of Europe. Notable about France, however, is that while the economy as a whole has done well, the sectors most coveted by the government have not done as well. France's computer industry remains dependent on protected markets, and her efforts to develop an aircraft industry have achieved technological success only at the cost of heavy monetary losses. For this reason few would regard France's industrial policy as the key to her economic growth.

U.S. Industrial Policy. The United States has a commitment to free-market ideology that would preclude any explicit government direction of the economy such as that of Japan during the early phase. There are some areas, however, in which the U.S. government has had a major role in promoting industries.

The most notable of these areas is agriculture. Here the U.S. government has come closest to the kind of industrial policy that we might recommend on the basis of the sophisticated criteria discussed earlier. Recall that the problem of appropriating knowledge can be a reason for intervening in an industry. In agriculture, which remains mostly a matter of family farms, this problem is especially acute: a farmer who makes a major innovation can be imitated by thousands of others, who derive the benefits without sharing in the risks. To alleviate this problem, the U.S. government has long engaged both in research into agricultural techniques and in the dissemination of improved techniques through the Agricultural Extension Service. Also, the government has taken a leading role in large-scale projects, such as irrigation facilities, that require collective action. These interventions fit nicely into a market failure framework and are commended even by economists who are skeptical about most industrial policy.

Another major role for the U.S. government is in defense. Both because it has a larger national income than other industrial countries and because it spends relatively more on defense, the U.S. government is far and away the world's largest market for military hardware. Not surprisingly, the United States dominates the production of military goods such as fighter aircraft that involve large economies of scale. In some cases it is likely that U.S. spending on military goods has helped give U.S. firms an advantage in civilian markets as well. For example, one of the most successful civilian aircraft produced by Boeing, the Boeing 707 (introduced in 1960), owed a great deal to a previously developed military plane (the B-52 bomber). The military market surely sometimes helps U.S. firms gain economies of scale that help them in civilian markets—the Boeing 707 continues to be manufactured, long after its civilian sales are over, as the AWACS reconnaissance plane. Military research and development sometimes gives U.S. firms knowledge that they can apply elsewhere. As usual in industrial policy issues, however, the quantitative importance of these effects is a matter of dispute. European commentators, who sometimes feel that they are losing a race with the United States and Japan, have suggested that in practice the United States has as effective an industrial policy as Japan.

CASE STUDIES OF INDUSTRIAL POLICY

How effective is industrial policy? Industrial policy has been applied in a wide variety of industries. To see the difficulties involved in evaluation, we examine three examples: Japan's targeting of steel in the 1960s and early

1970s, European support of aircraft production, and Japan's targeting of semiconductors in the late 1970s and early 1980s.

Case Study JAPANESE TARGETING OF STEEL (1960–EARLY 1970s)

Beginning in the 1950s the Japanese government designated steel as a sector that should receive priority in growth. Japanese steel production tripled from 1963 to 1970, not only meeting the rapidly growing demands of the domestic economy but also making Japan the world's largest exporter. This development was especially remarkable given that virtually all the raw materials for steelmaking have to be imported into resource-poor Japan from other countries. When a world steel glut developed after the energy crisis in 1973, Japan's industry had the most modern plants with the lowest operating costs and was thus able to continue to operate in an environment in which the steel industries of other industrial countries were either contracting sharply (as in the United States) or being supported by government subsidy (as in Europe).

This experience raises two major questions. Was government policy the cause of steel's rapid growth? Was this policy good for Japan's economy?

Given the previous description of Japan's industrial policy, we must ask whether the government's targeting of steel only moved the economy in the same direction market forces would have moved it anyway. Japan would probably have developed a comparative advantage in steel even with laissez-faire. On one side, Japan's high savings rate gave it a growing comparative advantage in capital-intensive industries like steel. On the other side, falling transport costs and the emergence of new sources of iron ore and coal made it less necessary for steel industries in general to locate near coalfields or iron deposits. Thus Japan might well have had a growing steel industry even without government intervention. Nonetheless, it is a good guess that the Japanese government encouraged steel to grow even faster than it would have in a free-market economy. This guess is supported by the observation that Japan's steel industry grew rapidly despite a profit rate substantially *below* the average for Japanese manufacturing.

The more important question, however, is whether the policy accelerated Japanese economic growth. In answering this question, it is important to be careful. The policy was successful in making the steel industry grow—but that is not the question. The question is whether it made the Japanese economy *as a whole* grow faster. This amounts to asking whether the resources used in steel yielded a higher payoff to society than they would have had elsewhere.

As noted above, the return directly earned by the resources used in steel was actually not as high as the same resources were earning elsewhere.

Capital invested in steel earned a rate of return only a little more than half the average rate of return in Japanese manufacturing even during the prosperous 1960s, and ended up earning an even lower return during the 1970s.[2] Japan's promotion of steel can be justified only if there were marginal social benefits not included in the market return.

Economists who have studied the issue have not identified important marginal social benefits. Steel is not a "high-technology" industry that could be expected to yield important technological externalities. Nor is it an industry where there are high returns to be snatched from foreign rivals by strategic trade policy. Creation of jobs did not represent an extra benefit in Japan, because the economy was already running at full employment. Unless a plausible source of marginal social benefits can be identified, we must conclude that the targeting of steel—despite the industry's growth—was a mistake. It diverted resources to areas where their return was lower than elsewhere and thus acted as a drag on Japan's growth.

The case of Japanese steel is an instructive one. It is a reminder that the economic success of an industrial policy cannot be measured simply by looking at the growth or market share of the targeted industry.

Case Study EUROPEAN SUPPORT OF AIRCRAFT IN THE 1970s AND 1980s

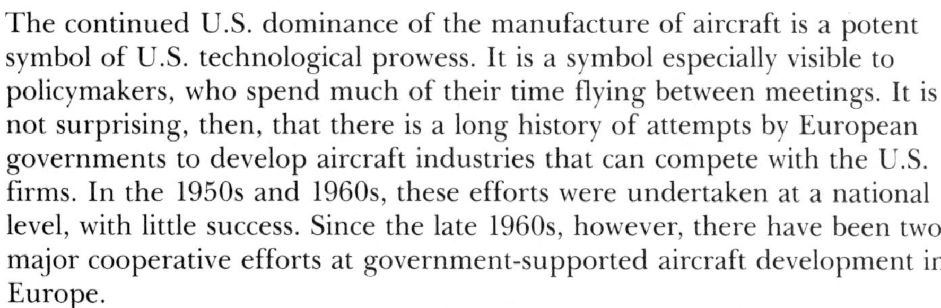

The continued U.S. dominance of the manufacture of aircraft is a potent symbol of U.S. technological prowess. It is a symbol especially visible to policymakers, who spend much of their time flying between meetings. It is not surprising, then, that there is a long history of attempts by European governments to develop aircraft industries that can compete with the U.S. firms. In the 1950s and 1960s, these efforts were undertaken at a national level, with little success. Since the late 1960s, however, there have been two major cooperative efforts at government-supported aircraft development in Europe.

One of these efforts was the joint development by Britain and France of a supersonic aircraft, the Concorde. Construction of a supersonic passenger plane became technologically feasible in the late 1960s, but private airplane manufacturers were unconvinced that it would be profitable to develop. A political campaign to have the U.S. government finance development of such a plane failed. In Europe, however, France and Britain agreed to foot the bill for development. The logic behind this agreement was complex. To some extent there was hope of large

[2]See Paul R. Krugman, "Targeted Industrial Policies: Theory and Evidence," in Dominick Salvatore, ed., *The New Protectionist Threat to World Welfare* (Amsterdam: North-Holland, 1987).

technological spillovers. More important, however, was the prestige appeal of the project and the usefulness of the Concorde as a symbol of European cooperation.

In commercial terms the results have been disastrous. Concordes are extremely expensive to run, and the saving of a few hours in travel time has not been enough to counteract this difference in expense. Only a few Concordes have been sold, and those were bought by the state-owned airlines of Britain and France. The best that can be said of the Concorde is that the experience of its development may have yielded technological spillovers to the next European attempt at aircraft production, the Airbus.

Airbus is a consortium of European governments that produces large passenger airplanes that compete directly with the main U.S. strength. The costs of capital and some of the other costs have been subsidized by the member governments. Unlike the Concorde project, Airbus has succeeded in producing planes that are commercially viable: the A300 family of wide-bodied, medium-range passenger jets is comparable in performance and operating costs with U.S. planes and has achieved significant sales. Unfortunately, after years of subsidy Airbus continues to have production costs substantially higher than Boeing, its chief U.S. competitor. Airbus has taken a sizable market share, but only at the cost of continuing subsidy.

What makes the Airbus experience particularly interesting is that it fits well into our discussion of strategic trade policy. The economies of scale in large passenger aircraft production are so huge that there is probably room for only one or two profitable producers in the whole world market. The European subsidy to Airbus could be viewed as an attempt to overcome Boeing's head start and snatch some of that profitable market for Europe. Unfortunately, the outcome looks more like Tables 11-3 and 11-4 than like Tables 11-1 and 11-2. Boeing has *not* been driven out, and Airbus is absorbing a lot of government money.

Case Study JAPANESE TARGETING OF SEMICONDUCTORS (MID-1970s TO DATE)

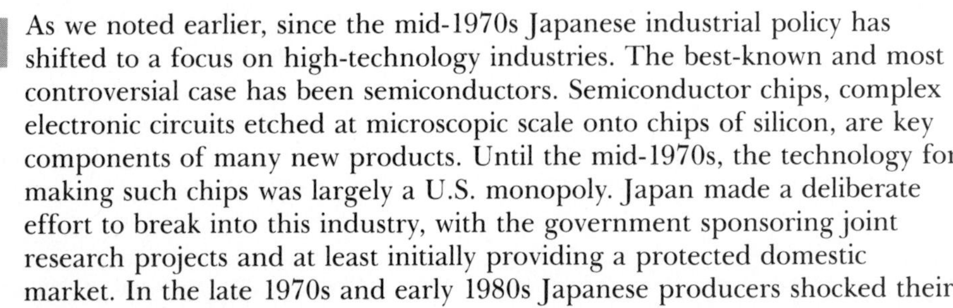

As we noted earlier, since the mid-1970s Japanese industrial policy has shifted to a focus on high-technology industries. The best-known and most controversial case has been semiconductors. Semiconductor chips, complex electronic circuits etched at microscopic scale onto chips of silicon, are key components of many new products. Until the mid-1970s, the technology for making such chips was largely a U.S. monopoly. Japan made a deliberate effort to break into this industry, with the government sponsoring joint research projects and at least initially providing a protected domestic market. In the late 1970s and early 1980s Japanese producers shocked their

U.S. competitors by taking a dominant share of the market for one kind of chip, random access memories.

That Japan targeted semiconductors, and that the industry achieved a large market share, is known. What is hotly disputed is how much support the Japanese industry actually received, how decisive that support was, and whether the policy helped Japan and/or hurt the United States.

We know that not much government money was provided; the subsidy component of the targeting was actually quite small. We also know that explicit home market protection, by tariffs and quotas, was mostly removed after the mid-1970s. Some would argue that, in fact, the Japanese semiconductor industry succeeded with little government help.

Others argue that more subtle government help was crucial. The proponents of this view argue that the joint research projects, which would have been blocked in the United States by antitrust laws, were a highly effective way of improving the technology. They also argue that the Japanese market was effectively closed through a tacit "buy-Japanese" policy discreetly encouraged by the government. As evidence they note that U.S. firms had a much smaller market share in Japan than in either the United States or Europe.

Economists do not know which of these views is correct. (It may be that the Japanese don't know either.) If we assume for the sake of argument that government policy was, in fact, crucial, was it a good idea?

As in the case of steel, the direct returns on Japan's investment in semiconductors have been quite low. Exact figures are not available, but it is generally believed that Japanese firms have earned a low rate of return on semiconductors since the late 1970s. So any gains from the encouragement of chips must be located in the technological externalities.

Now comes the great uncertainty. Unlike steel, semiconductor production—a highly dynamic industry where knowledge is the main source of competitive advantage—is exactly the kind of sector where the external economy argument should apply. But were the externalities large enough to justify the cost? Nobody knows.

This brief survey of three industrial policies in practice is not comprehensive. Each example does, however, illustrate an important point: an industrial policy cannot be judged by asking whether the targeted industries grew. All three cases are of industries that did eventually grow and achieve substantial market share, but this does not mean that they accelerated economic growth, because an industrial policy will not accelerate overall growth unless it corrects a market failure. In the case of steel, it is hard to identify a market failure, so that the Japanese government's promotion of steel probably retarded economic growth by channeling resources into an area of low return. In the case of aircraft, European subsidy could in principle have helped Airbus gain a strategic advantage, but it is doubtful whether any advantage was gained in fact. In the case of semiconductors, the justification for the Japanese targeting rests on presumed external economies that have not been measured.

Some extravagant claims have been made about the effectiveness of industrial policy. We cannot show that such policies never work, but we can show that they have not always worked and that assessing them requires a more careful analysis of data than most observers have carried out.

SUMMARY

1. *Industrial policy* is an attempt by a government to shift the allocation of resources to promote economic growth. Industrial policy has been extensively practiced in Japan, is important in France, and exists to some extent in many countries, including the United States.

2. Advocates of industrial policy often base their case for intervention on criteria that do not have their basis in economic theory. The most often cited criteria are the alleged need to target industries with *high value added per worker, linkage* industries, industries with high growth prospects, and industries that have been targeted by foreign governments. A careful examination of these criteria shows that they are badly flawed and likely to lead to undesirable results if used as the basis for government policy.

3. More sophisticated criteria for industrial policy are based on the existence of domestic market failures. Two arguments for industrial policy in particular have attracted the attention of international economists. One is the argument that governments should promote industries that yield *technological externalities.* The other is the *strategic trade policy* argument that says that governments can help domestic firms seize monopoly profits from foreign competitors. These criteria are valid in terms of economic theory. The worry of many economists is that they are too subtle and require too much information to be useful in practice.

4. Industrial policy in practice is much more varied and uncertain in effect than popular descriptions might indicate. Japan's industrial policy has shifted from an extensive government control over the economy in the 1950s and 1960s to a much lighter government hand today. Other countries have had less consistent policies; even the United States has, in effect, had a widely approved industrial policy in agriculture, and some foreigners allege that the U.S. defense budget acts like an industrial policy for the high-technology industries.

5. Assessing the effect of industrial policies is not easy. Looking at market shares or the growth of the industry is not enough. Instead, one must do a cost-benefit analysis. An examination of some major examples of industrial policy is not very encouraging about the track record of governments in their targeting.

KEY TERMS

industrial policy
criteria for selection
high value added per worker
linkage argument
externalities
high-technology industries
excess returns
Brander-Spencer analysis
strategic trade policy
beggar-thy-neighbor policies

PROBLEMS

1. Suppose that the U.S. government were able to determine which industries will grow most rapidly over the next 20 years. Why doesn't this automatically mean that the nation should have a policy of supporting these industries' growth?

2. The U.S. Commerce Department has urged that the United States provide special support for its high-technology industries. It argues that these industries have the prospect of rapid future growth, provide inputs to many other industries, and generate technology that benefits the whole economy. Furthermore, some U.S. high-technology industries such as aircraft and microelectronics face challenges by government-supported foreign competitors. Which of these arguments might be valid reasons for the United States to have an industrial policy targeting these industries?

3. If the United States had its way, it would demand that Japan spend more money on basic research in science and less on applied research into industrial applications. Explain why in terms of the analysis of appropriability.

4. In Tables 11-1 and 11-2 we presented a situation in which the European government was able to use a subsidy to achieve a strategic advantage, while in Tables 11-3 and 11-4 we presented a situation in which it could not. What is the crucial distinction between these two cases? That is, what is the general rule for determining when a subsidy can work?

5. "The new strategic trade policy argument demonstrates the wisdom of policies like that of Korea, which subsidizes its exports across the board. The subsidy gives each industry the strategic advantage it needs to establish itself in world competition." Discuss.

6. Explain the difference between pre-1970 and post-1975 Japanese industrial policy. How is it possible to reconcile Japan's spectacular growth rate before 1970 with the assertion that the industrial policy was of doubtful value?

7. It appears that Japan earned a low market rate of return on both its investment in steel in the late 1960s and early 1970s, and its investment in semiconductors in the late 1970s and 1980s. What possible justification for these investments can be given? Why is the text more sympathetic to the possibility that semiconductor targeting was a good policy than it is to the case for steel targeting?

FURTHER READING

James A. Brander and Barbara J. Spencer. "International R&D Rivalry and Industrial Strategy." *Review of Economic Studies* 50 (1983), pp. 707–722. The first exposition of the case for "strategic" industrial policy.

James A. Brander and Barbara J. Spencer. "Export Subsidies and International Market Share Rivalry." *Journal of International Economics* 16 (1985), pp. 83–100. A basic reference on the potential role of subsidies as a tool of strategic trade policy.

Avinash K. Dixit and A. S. Kyle. "The Use of Protection and Subsidies for Entry Promotion and Deterrence." *American Economic Review* 75 (1985), pp. 139–152. An extension of the Brander-Spencer analysis that looks at the broader game between governments as well as the competition between firms.

Paul R. Krugman. "The U.S. Response to Foreign Industrial Targeting." *Brookings Papers on Economic Activity,* 1: 1984, pp. 77–131. An examination of the evidence that other countries' industrial policies have contributed to the international competitiveness problem of the United States.

Paul R. Krugman, ed. *Strategic Trade Policy and the New International Economics.* Cambridge: MIT Press, 1986. A collection of papers by leading exponents and critics of the idea of strategic trade policy.

Ira Magaziner and Robert Reich. *Minding America's Business.* New York: Random House, 1982. An eloquent and clearly written tract in favor of a national industrial policy for the United States.

PART THREE

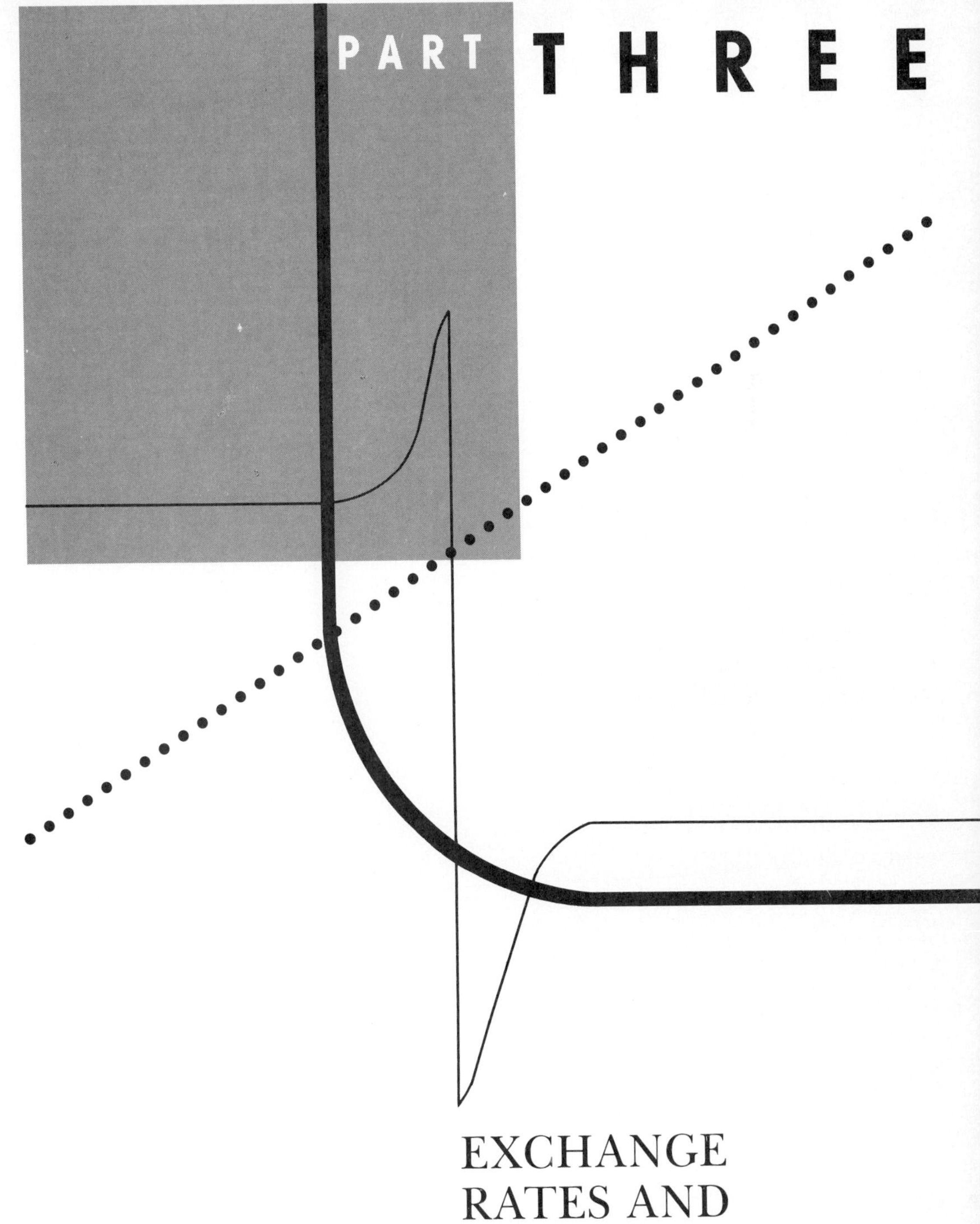

EXCHANGE RATES AND OPEN-ECONOMY MACROECONOMICS

12 NATIONAL INCOME ACCOUNTING AND THE BALANCE OF PAYMENTS

Between 1979 and 1983, the percentage of unemployed workers in the industrial countries' labor force rose from 5.1 to 8.7, and has remained high. Unemployment rates in the early 1980s were without precedent since the Great Depression of the 1930s, and they inflicted immense economic and personal hardships on many people throughout the world. Was this worldwide slump an inexplicable accident? Or can economic analysis throw light on its causes and suggest ways to avoid similar contractions in the future?

Previous chapters have been concerned primarily with the problem of making the best use of the world's scarce productive resources at a single point in time. The branch of economics called **microeconomics** studies this problem from the perspective of individual firms and consumers. Microeconomics works "from the bottom up" to show how individual economic actors, by pursuing their own interests, collectively determine how resources are used. In our study of international microeconomics we have learned how individual production and consumption decisions produce patterns of international trade and specialization. We have seen that while free trade in many instances leads to efficient resource use, government intervention or market failures can cause waste even when all factors of production are fully employed.

With this chapter we shift our focus and ask: How can we ensure that factors of production *are* always fully employed? And what determines how an economy's capacity to produce goods and services changes over time? To answer these questions we must understand **macroeconomics**, the branch of economics that studies how economies' overall levels of production and employment are determined. Like microeconomics, macroeconomics is concerned with the effective use of scarce resources. But while microeconomics focuses on the economic decisions of individuals, macroeconomics analyzes the behavior of the economy as a whole. In our study of international macroeconomics, we will learn how the interactions of national economies influence the worldwide patterns of employment and economic growth.

Macroeconomic analysis emphasizes four aspects of economic life that we have usually kept in the background up until now to simplify our discussion of international economics:

1. *Unemployment.* We know that in the real world workers may be unemployed and factories may be idle. Macroeconomics studies the factors that give rise to unemployment and the steps governments can take to prevent it. A main concern of international macroeconomics is the problem of ensuring full employment in economies open to international trade.

2. *Saving.* In earlier chapters of the book we often assumed that every country consumes an amount exactly equal to its income—no more and no less. In reality, though, households can put aside part of their income to provide for the future, or they can temporarily spend more than their income by borrowing. A country's saving or borrowing behavior affects domestic employment and future levels of national wealth. From the standpoint of the international economy as a whole, the world saving level determines how quickly the world stock of productive capital can grow.

3. *Trade imbalances.* As we saw in earlier chapters, the value of a country's imports equals the value of its exports when spending equals income. This state of balanced trade is seldom attained by actual economies, however. Trade imbalances play a large role in the following chapters because they redistribute wealth among countries and are a main channel through which one country's macroeconomic policies affect its trading partners. It should be no surprise, therefore, that trade imbalances, particularly when they are large and persistent, quickly become a cause of international concern.

4. *Money and the price level.* The trade theory you have studied so far is a barter theory, one in which goods are exchanged directly for other goods on the basis of their relative prices. In practice it is more convenient to use money, a widely acceptable medium of exchange, in transactions, and to quote prices in terms of money. Because money changes hands in virtually

every transaction that takes place in a modern economy, fluctuations in the supply of money or the demand for it can affect both output and employment. International macroeconomics takes into account that each country has its own individual money and that a monetary change in one country (for example, a change in money supply) can have effects that spill across its borders to other countries. Stability in money price levels is an important goal of international macroeconomic policy.

This chapter takes the first step in our study of international macroeconomics by explaining the accounting concepts economists use to describe a country's level of production and its international transactions. To get a complete picture of the macroeconomic linkages among economies that engage in international trade, we have to master two related and essential tools. The first of these tools, **national income accounting,** records all the expenditures that contribute to a country's income and output. The second tool, **balance of payments accounting,** helps us keep track of both changes in a country's indebtedness to foreigners and the fortunes of its export and import-competing industries. The balance of payments accounts also show the connection between foreign transactions and national money supplies.

THE NATIONAL INCOME ACCOUNTS

Of central concern to macroeconomic analysis is a country's **gross national product (GNP),** the value of all final goods and services produced by its factors of production and sold on the market in a given time period. GNP, which is the basic measure of a country's output studied by macroeconomists, is calculated by adding up the market value of all expenditures on final output. GNP therefore includes the value of goods like bread sold in a supermarket and textbooks sold in a bookstore, as well as the value of services provided by supermarket checkers and baggers and by university professors. Because output cannot be produced without the aid of factor inputs, the expenditures that make up GNP are closely linked to the employment of labor, capital, and other factors of production.

In order to distinguish among the different types of expenditure that make up a country's GNP, government economists and statisticians who compile national income accounts divide GNP among the four possible uses for which a country's output is purchased: *consumption* (the amount consumed by private domestic residents), *investment* (the amount put aside by firms to build new plant and equipment for future production), *government purchases* (the amount used by the government), and the *current account balance* (the amount of net exports of goods and services to foreigners). The term "national income accounts" is used to describe this fourfold classification, rather than "national output accounts," because a country's income in fact equals its output. Thus, the national income accounts can be thought of as classifying each transaction that contributes to national income according to the type of ex-

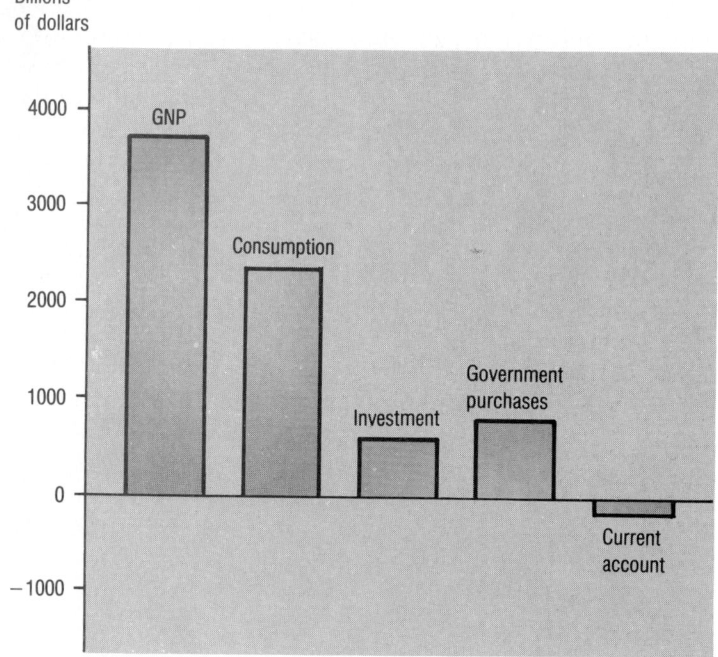

FIGURE 12-1 U.S. GNP and its components, 1984

penditure that gives rise to it. Figure 12-1 shows how U.S. GNP was divided among its four components in 1984.[1]

Why is it useful to divide GNP into consumption, investment, government purchases, and the current account? One major reason is that we cannot hope to understand the cause of a particular recession or boom without knowing how the main categories of spending have changed. And without such an understanding, we cannot recommend a sound policy response. In addition, the national income accounts provide information essential for studying why some countries are rich—that is, have a high level of GNP relative to population size—while some are poor.

NATIONAL PRODUCT AND NATIONAL INCOME

Our first task in understanding how economists analyze GNP is to explain in greater detail why the GNP a country generates over some time period must equal its **national income,** the income earned in that period by its factors of production.

[1]Neither our definition of the current account nor our identification of national income and output is strictly accurate when a country is a net donor or recipient of foreign gifts. We describe later in this chapter how the definitions of national income and the current account must be changed in such cases.

The reason for this equality is that every dollar used to purchase goods or services automatically ends up in somebody's pocket. A visit to the doctor provides the simplest example of how an increase in national output raises national income by the same amount. The $75 you pay the doctor represents the market value of the services she provides for you; so your visit raises GNP by $75. But the $75 you pay the doctor also raises her income. So national income rises by $75.

The principle that output and income are the same also applies to goods, even goods that are produced with the help of many factors of production. Consider the example of an economics textbook. When you purchase a new book from the publisher, the value of your purchase enters GNP. But your payment enters the income of the productive factors that have cooperated in producing the book because the publisher must pay for their services with the proceeds of his sales. First, there are the authors, editors, artists, and typesetters who provide the labor inputs necessary for the book's production. Second, there are the publishing company's shareholders, who receive dividends for having financed acquisition of the capital used in production. Finally, there are the suppliers of paper and ink, who provide the intermediate materials used in producing the book.

The paper and ink purchased by the publishing house to produce the book are *not* counted separately in GNP because their contribution to the value of national output is already included in the book's price. It is to avoid such double counting that we allow only the sale of *final* goods and services to enter into the definition of GNP: sales of intermediate goods, such as paper and ink purchased by a publisher, are not counted. Notice also that the sale of a used textbook does not enter GNP. Our definition counts only final goods and services that are *produced,* and a used textbook does not qualify: it was counted in GNP at the time it was first sold. Equivalently, the sale of a used textbook does not generate income for any factor of production.

CAPITAL DEPRECIATION AND INTERNATIONAL TRANSFERS

Because we have defined GNP and national income so that they are necessarily equal, their equality is really an identity. Two adjustments to GNP must be made, however, before this identification is entirely correct.

1. GNP does not take into account the economic loss due to the tendency of machinery and structures to wear out as they are used. This loss, called *depreciation,* reduces the income of capital owners. To calculate national income over a given period, we must therefore subtract from GNP the depreciation of capital over the period. GNP less depreciation is called *net national product* (NNP).

2. A country's income may include gifts from residents of foreign countries, called *unilateral transfers.* Examples of unilateral transfers are pension payments to retired citizens living abroad, reparation payments, and foreign

aid such as relief funds donated to drought-stricken nations. Unilateral transfers are part of a country's income but are not part of its product, and they must be added to NNP in calculations of national income.

National income equals GNP *less* depreciation *plus* unilateral transfers. The difference between GNP and national income, though not always an insignificant number, is of little importance in macroeconomics. Therefore, we usually use the terms "GNP" and "national income" interchangeably for the balance of the book.

NATIONAL INCOME ACCOUNTING IN A CLOSED ECONOMY

Before discussing the national income accounts for an open economy, that is, one that trades with other economies, we discuss the hypothetical case of a closed economy that does not trade with the outside world. Because a closed economy's residents cannot purchase foreign output or sell their own output to foreigners, there are only three types of expenditure that generate national income in an economy closed to international trade: consumption, investment, and government purchases. Put another way, the fourth component of spending on an *open* economy's output, the current account, makes no contribution to national income in a *closed* economy because exports and imports both must equal zero.

While no economy is truly closed to international trade, a hypothetical closed economy is a good starting point for our discussion of national income accounting because the relations among the components of expenditure on GNP are simpler there than in an open economy. In addition, a preliminary exploration of the closed-economy case will serve to highlight the central role of trade in the macroeconomics of open economies.

CONSUMPTION

The portion of GNP purchased by the private sector to fulfill current wants is called **consumption**. Purchases of movie tickets, food, dental work, and washing machines all fall in this category. Consumption expenditure is the largest component of GNP in most economies. In the United States, for example, the percentage of GNP devoted to consumption has been fairly stable since the Korean War, fluctuating in a range of about 62 to 65 percent.

INVESTMENT

The part of output used by firms to produce future output is called **investment**. Investment spending may be viewed as the portion of GNP used to increase the nation's stock of capital. Steel and bricks used to build a factory are part of investment spending, as are services provided by a technician who helps build business computers. Firms' purchases of inventories are also counted in investment spending because the carrying of inventories is just another way for firms to transfer output from current use to future use. Investment is usually more variable than consumption. In the U.S., it has fluctuated between 12 and 18 percent of GNP in recent years. While we often use the word "investment" to describe individual households' purchases of stocks, bonds, or real estate, you should be careful not to confuse this everyday meaning of the word with the economic definition of investment as a component of GNP. When you buy a share of IBM stock, you are buying neither a good nor a service; so your purchase does not show up in GNP.

The criteria used by national income accountants to distinguish investment from consumption may at times seem arbitrary. This is because they adopt the convention that investment activity can be carried out only by firms. An individual's purchase of a book from its publisher is considered consumption, but when a bookstore buys the same book the transaction is counted in inventory investment.

A related practice in national income accounting is the treatment as consumption of household spending on consumer durables, goods that are not consumed at once (as are milk and fresh fruit) but are used continuously over many years. The purchase of a washing machine, which yields services over a long period, seems like a form of investment, but according to the definitions used to construct GNP accounts it is not. Because of its importance to the economy, one type of consumer-durable spending, spending on newly built private homes, is counted in investment. For the sake of consistency, GNP accounts treat a homeowner as a firm selling housing services to herself. Correspondingly, estimated rental payments reflecting the value of these housing services are included in GNP as part of consumption.

GOVERNMENT PURCHASES

Any goods and services purchased by federal, state, or local governments are classified as **government purchases** in the national income accounts. Included in government purchases are federal military spending, government support of cancer research, and government funds spent on highway repair and education. Government transfer payments are certainly a part of the government's total expenditure, but transfer payments do not require the recipient to give the government any goods or services in return. Thus, transfer payments like social security, unemployment, and welfare benefits are not included in government purchases.

Government purchases currently take up about 20 percent of U.S. GNP, and this share has not risen much since the late 1950s. (The corresponding figure for 1959, for example, was also 20 percent.) In 1929, however, government purchases accounted for only 8.5 percent of U.S. GNP.

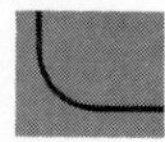

THE NATIONAL INCOME IDENTITY FOR A CLOSED ECONOMY

For a closed economy, the division of GNP into consumption, investment, and government purchases is exhaustive. Any good or service that is not purchased by households or the government must be used by firms to produce new plant, equipment, and inventories. What happens to consumption goods that cannot be sold immediately to consumers or the government? Firms (perhaps reluctantly) add such goods to their existing inventories, thus increasing investment.

Our reasoning leads to a fundamental identity for closed economies. Let Y stand for GNP, C for consumption, I for investment, and G for government purchases. Since all of a closed economy's output must be consumed, invested, or bought by the government, we can write

$$Y = C + I + G.$$

The relationship above is an identity because C, I, and G are defined to ensure that it always holds.[2] You should be careful not to confuse identities, which hold by definition, with equilibrium conditions, which describe the equality of market supply and demand. Equilibrium conditions hold true only when price and quantity are at their equilibrium levels.

AN IMAGINARY CLOSED ECONOMY

Table 12-1 shows the national income accounts for an imaginary closed economy, Agraria, whose only output is wheat. Each citizen of Agraria is a consumer of wheat, but each is also a farmer and therefore can be viewed as a firm. Farmers invest by putting aside a portion of each year's crop as seed for the following year's planting. There is also a government that appropriates part of the crop to feed the Agrarian army. Of Agraria's total annual crop of 100 bushels of wheat, 65 bushels are consumed by civilians in the current year, 25 are stored away to be used in the future as seed, and 10 go to feed the army in the current year.

TABLE 12-1 National income accounts for Agraria, a closed economy

	GNP (total output)	=	consumption	+	investment	+	government purchases
Bushels of wheat	100	=	65	+	25	+	10

[2]If Y is thought of as national income rather than GNP, the identity holds if investment is defined as *net* investment, that is, investment less depreciation.

IMPLICATIONS FOR NATIONAL SAVING

Simple as it is, the GNP identity has many illuminating implications. To explain the most important of these implications, we define the concept of **national saving,** that is, the portion of output, Y, that is not devoted to household consumption, C, or government purchases, G[3]. *In a closed economy, national saving always equals investment.* This fact tells us that the economy as a whole can increase its wealth only by accumulating new capital.

Let S stand for national saving. Our definition of S tells us that

$$S = Y - C - G.$$

Since the GNP identity, $Y = C + I + G$, may also be written as $I = Y - C - G$, then

$$S = I,$$

and national saving must equal investment in a closed economy.

If you return to Table 12-1, you will see that saving and investment are indeed equal in the imaginary economy of Agraria. Current use of wheat by the private sector and government is 65 + 10 = 75 bushels. The 25 bushels that are invested by farmers are the same 25 bushels that the economy saves.

The finding that saving equals investment may be surprising because households can save but, according to the rules of GNP accounting, they cannot invest (except in owner-occupied housing). The key to understanding why saving must equal investment is that S is the sum of *all* the saving decisions of every household, firm, and government agency in the economy. Suppose that a household lowers its consumption by \$100 to buy a bond from the U.S. government. The government then uses the \$100 to buy white paint to touch up the columns of the White House. In this case, neither investment nor *national* saving is affected: the \$100 increase in household saving is exactly offset by an additional \$100 government purchase (a \$100 decrease in *government* saving). Suppose, however, that the same household uses its savings to purchase a newly issued \$100 corporate bond from IBM, and that IBM in turn uses the money to buy bricks for a new office building. Then national saving and investment both rise by \$100. The \$100 in resources that the household makes available to IBM is used by the firm to increase the stock of plant and equipment that can be used to produce output in the future.

What happens to national saving, S, when a household saves by buying a piece of land in the country? Doesn't national saving rise without any corresponding increase in investment? The answer to this question is "not necessarily": when one household raises its saving to acquire land, the household

[3]The U.S. national income accounts assume that government purchases are not used to enlarge the nation's capital stock. We follow this convention here. However, most other countries' national accounts distinguish between government consumption and government investment. Often the latter category includes armament purchases.

that sells the land may be lowering its saving, by an equal amount, through the action of selling some of its wealth so that it can consume more. Overall saving, S, would not change in this case. In a closed economy, saving can take place *in the aggregate* only through enlarging the stock of capital.

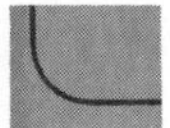

NATIONAL INCOME ACCOUNTING FOR AN OPEN ECONOMY

In this section we extend the national income accounting framework to open economies. In an open economy, the national income identity must be modified because some domestic output is exported to foreigners while some domestic income is spent on imported foreign goods.

The main lesson of this section concerns the relation between national saving, investment, and trade imbalances. We will see that in open economies, saving and investment are not necessarily equal as they are in a closed economy. This is because countries can save by exporting more than they import, and they can dissave—that is, reduce their wealth—by exporting less than they import.

THE NATIONAL INCOME IDENTITY FOR AN OPEN ECONOMY

We derived the national income identity for a closed economy by assuming that all output was consumed or invested by the country's citizens or purchased by the government. When foreign trade is possible, however, some output is purchased by foreigners while some domestic spending goes to purchase goods and services produced abroad. The GNP identity for open economies shows how the national income a country earns by selling its goods and services is divided between sales to domestic residents and sales to foreign residents.

Since residents of an open economy may spend some of their income on imports, that is, goods and services purchased from abroad, only the portion of their spending that is not devoted to imports is part of domestic GNP. The value of imports, denoted by IM, must be subtracted from total domestic spending, $C + I + G$, to find the portion of domestic spending that generates domestic national income. Imports from abroad add to foreign countries' GNPs but do not add directly to domestic GNP.

Similarly, the goods and services sold to foreigners make up a country's exports. Exports, denoted by EX, are the amount foreign residents' purchases add to the national income of the domestic economy.

The national income of an open economy is therefore the sum of domestic and foreign expenditure on the goods and services produced by domestic factors of production. Thus, the national income identity for an open economy is

$$Y = C + I + G + EX - IM. \qquad \textbf{(12-1)}$$

To make this identity concrete, let's suppose that the imaginary country Agraria can import milk from the rest of the world in exchange for exports of wheat. We cannot draw up the Agrarian national income accounts without knowing the price of milk in terms of wheat because all the components in the GNP identity (12-1) must be measured in the same units. If we assume that the price of milk is 0.5 bushel of wheat per gallon, and that at this price Agrarians want to consume 40 gallons of milk, then Agraria's imports are equal to 20 bushels of wheat.

In Table 12-2, we see that, as before, Agraria's total output is 100 bushels of wheat. Consumption is now divided between wheat and milk, however, with 55 bushels of wheat and 40 gallons of milk (equal in value to 20 bushels of wheat) consumed over the year. The value of consumption in terms of wheat is $55 + (0.5 \times 40) = 55 + 20 = 75$.

The 100 bushels of wheat produced by Agraria are used as follows: 55 are consumed by domestic residents, 25 are invested, 10 are purchased by the government, and 10 are exported abroad. National income ($Y = 100$) equals domestic spending ($C + I + G = 110$) plus exports ($EX = 10$) less imports ($IM = 20$).

THE CURRENT ACCOUNT AND FOREIGN INDEBTEDNESS

In reality a country's foreign trade is exactly balanced only rarely. The difference between exports of goods and services and imports of goods and services is known as the **current account balance.** (We usually call it the current account for short.) If we denote the current account by CA, we can express this definition in symbols as

$$CA = EX - IM.$$

When a country's imports exceed its exports, we say that the country has a *current account deficit.* A country has a *current account surplus* when its exports exceed its imports.[4]

TABLE 12-2 National income accounts for Agraria, an open economy

	GNP (total output)	= consumption	+ investment	+ government purchases	+ exports	− imports
Bushels of wheat	100	= 75[a]	+ 25	+ 10	+ 10	− 20[b]

[a]55 bushels of wheat plus (0.5 bushel per gallon) × (40 gallons of milk).
[b]0.5 bushel per gallon × 40 gallons of milk.

[4]In addition to net exports of goods and services, the current account balance includes net unilateral transfers, which we discussed briefly above. Following our earlier assumption, we continue to ignore transfers for now to simplify the discussion. We will see how transfers enter the current account later in this chapter when we analyze the U.S. balance of payments in detail.

The GNP identity, equation (12-1), shows one reason why the current account is important in international macroeconomics. Since the right-hand side of (12-1) is total expenditure on domestic output, changes in the current account can be associated with changes in output and, thus, employment.

The current account is also important because it measures the size and direction of international borrowing. When a country imports more than it exports, it is buying more from foreigners than it sells to them and must somehow finance this current account deficit. How does it pay for additional imports once it has spent its export earnings? Since the country as a whole can import more than it exports only if it can borrow the difference from foreigners, a country with a current account deficit must be increasing its net foreign debts by the amount of the deficit.[5]

Similarly, a country with a current account surplus is earning more from its exports than it spends on imports. This country finances the current account deficit of its trading partners by lending to them. The foreign wealth of a surplus country rises because foreigners pay for any imports not covered by their exports by issuing IOUs that they will eventually have to redeem. The preceding reasoning shows that: *A country's current account balance equals the change in its net foreign wealth.*

We have defined the current account as the difference between exports and imports. Equation (12-1) says that the current account is also equal to the difference between national income Y and domestic residents' spending $C + I + G$:

$$Y - (C + I + G) = CA.$$

It is only by borrowing abroad that a country can have a current account deficit and use up more output than it is currently producing. And if it uses up less than its output, it has a current account surplus and is lending the surplus to foreigners.[6] International borrowing and lending were identified with *intertemporal trade* in Chapter 7. A country with a current account deficit is importing present consumption, exporting future consumption. A country with a current account surplus is exporting present consumption, importing future consumption.

As an example, consider again the imaginary economy of Agraria described in Table 12-2. The total value of its consumption, investment, and government purchases, at 110 bushels of wheat, is greater than its output of 100 bushels. This inequality would be impossible in a closed economy; it *is* possible in this open economy because Agraria now imports 40 gallons of milk, worth 20 bushels of wheat, but exports only 10 bushels of wheat. The

[5]Alternatively, a country could finance a current account deficit by using previously accumulated foreign wealth to pay for imports. This country would be running down its net foreign wealth, which is the same as running up its net foreign debts.

[6]The sum $C + I + G$ is often called domestic *absorption* in the literature on international macroeconomics. Using this terminology, we can describe the current account surplus as the difference between income and absorption.

current account deficit of 10 bushels is the value of Agraria's borrowing from foreigners, which the country will have to repay in the future.

SAVING AND THE CURRENT ACCOUNT

In a closed economy, saving and investment must always be equal. In an open economy, however, saving and investment can differ. Remembering that national saving, S, equals $Y - C - G$ and that $CA = EX - IM$, we can rewrite the GNP identity (12-1) as

$$S = I + CA.$$

The equation highlights an important difference between open and closed economies: *An open economy can save either by building up its capital stock or by acquiring foreign wealth, but a closed economy can save only by building up its capital stock.*

Unlike a closed economy, an open economy with profitable investment opportunities does not have to increase its saving in order to exploit them. The preceding expression shows that it is possible to simultaneously raise investment and foreign borrowing without changing saving. For example, if Brazil decides to build a profitable hydroelectric plant, it can import the materials it needs from the United States and borrow American funds to pay for them. This transaction raises Brazil's domestic investment because the imported materials contribute to expanding Brazil's capital stock. The transaction also raises Brazil's current account deficit by an amount equal to the increase in investment. Brazil's saving does not have to change, even though investment rises. For this to be possible, however, U.S. residents must be willing to save more so that the resources needed to build the plant are freed for Brazil's use. The result is another example of intertemporal trade, in which Brazil imports present consumption (when it borrows from the United States) and exports future consumption (when it pays off the loan).

Because one country's savings can be borrowed by a second country to increase the second country's stock of capital, a country's current account surplus is often referred to as its *net foreign investment.* Of course, when one country lends to another to finance investment, part of the income generated by the investment in future years must be used to pay back the lender. Domestic investment and foreign investment are two different ways in which a country can use current output to increase its future income.

PRIVATE AND GOVERNMENT SAVING

So far, our discussion of saving has not stressed the distinction between saving decisions made by the private sector and saving decisions made by the government. Unlike private saving decisions, however, government saving decisions are often made with an eye toward their effect on output and employment. The national income identity can help us to analyze the channels through which government saving decisions influence macroeconomic conditions. To use the national income identity in this way, we first have to divide national saving into its private and government components.

Private saving is defined as the part of disposable income that is saved rather than consumed. Disposable income is national income, Y, less the net taxes collected from households and firms by the government, T.[7] Private saving, denoted S^p, can therefore be expressed as

$$S^p = Y - T - C.$$

Government saving is defined similarly to private saving. The government's "income" is its net tax revenue, T, while its "consumption" is government purchases, G. If we let S^g stand for government saving, then

$$S^g = T - G.$$

The two types of saving we have defined, private and government, do add up to national saving. To see why, recall the definition of national saving, S, as $Y - C - G$. Then

$$S = Y - C - G = Y - T - C + T - G = S^p + S^g.$$

We can use the definitions of private and government saving to rewrite the national income identity in a form that is useful for analyzing the effects of government saving decisions on open economies. Because $S = S^p + S^g = I + CA$,

$$S^p = I + CA - S^g = I + CA - (T - G) = I + CA + (G - T). \tag{12-2}$$

Equation (12-2) relates private saving to domestic investment, the current account surplus, and government saving. To interpret equation (12-2), we define the **government budget deficit** as $G - T$, that is, as government saving preceded by a minus sign. The government budget deficit measures the extent to which the government is borrowing to finance its expenditures. Equation (12-2) then states that a country's private saving must take one of three forms: investment in domestic capital (I), purchases of IOUs from foreigners (CA), and purchases of the domestic government's debt ($G - T$).[8]

The usefulness of equation (12-2) is illustrated by the following case study.

[7]Net taxes are taxes less government transfer payments. The term "government" refers to the federal, state, and local governments considered as a single unit.

[8]In a closed economy the current account is always zero; so equation (12-2) is simply $S^p = I + (G - T)$.

Case Study DO GOVERNMENT BUDGET DEFICITS WORSEN THE CURRENT ACCOUNT?

Unusually large imbalances in the current accounts of the United States and Japan developed in the 1980s, with America's current account moving to a record deficit and Japan's to a record surplus. The huge U.S. deficit led many Americans to favor protection for industries whose sales were hurt by the availability of cheaper foreign imports. Because much of Japan's export surplus went to the United States, Japan became the leading target for many of the proposed measures.

Some international policymakers blamed the current account imbalances on growing U.S. government budget deficits and shrinking government budget deficits in Japan. The administration of President Ronald Reagan, which had engineered the American government deficits, tried to deflect blame for the U.S. current account's deterioration by pointing to buoyant domestic investment as the cause.

Identity (12-2), which can be written as

$$CA = S^p - I - (G - T),$$

provides a framework for analyzing the current accounts of the United States and Japan in the 1980s. Because private saving, investment, the current account, and the government deficit are jointly determined variables, we cannot fully determine the cause of a current account change by using the identity above alone. Nonetheless, the identity can give us some useful clues.

The table below presents data on the four variables linked by identity (12-2) for the United States. (The variables are expressed as percentages of GNP so that their values in different years can be compared more easily; they may not add up exactly as required by (12-2) because of rounding errors.)

United States (percentage of GNP)

Year	CA	S^p	I	$G - T$
1981	0.3	18.0	16.9	1.0
1982	0.0	17.6	14.1	3.5
1983	−1.0	17.7	14.8	3.8
1984	−2.4	18.4	17.9	2.9
1985	−2.9	17.5	16.8	3.5

Source: *Economic Report of the President, 1986.*

Identity (12-2) tells us that, all else equal, a rise in private saving must increase the current account surplus; a rise in investment or the government budget deficit must lower the current account surplus. The U.S. data above show that from 1981 to 1983, the current account moved from a small surplus to a deficit of 1 percent of GNP as the government budget deficit rose sharply from 1 to 3.5 percent of GNP. A large fall in investment accompanied the U.S. economy's slide into a recession in 1981–1982.

The American economy grew quickly in 1984 and investment recovered sharply. Private saving rose slightly, and because government tax revenues increased automatically as the economy grew, the government deficit declined relative to GNP. But the investment surge of 1984 was so large that the current account deficit (measured as a fraction of GNP) widened to a level unprecedented since the middle of the nineteenth century.

The events of 1981–1984 do not, however, establish the Reagan administration's case that high investment caused the U.S. current account deficit to widen. If we compare 1985, when the recovery from recession leveled off, with 1981, we see that private savings and investment rates are comparable in the two years but that both the government and current account deficits are much higher in the latter year. Higher government budget deficits would have resulted in much higher current account deficits in 1982 and 1983 had investment not plummeted in the recession. This fall in investment temporarily masked the effect on the current account of the higher government deficits, but that effect was apparent in 1985 once investment had returned close to its 1981 level. The government and current account deficits both remained high in 1986 and 1987.

Let's look next at the same figures for Japan so that we can analyze its current account surplus:

Japan (percentage of GNP)

	CA	S^p	I	$G - T$
Year				
1981	0.5	34.9	30.6	3.8
1982	0.7	34.1	29.8	3.6
1983	1.8	33.5	28.0	3.7
1984	2.8	32.8	27.8	2.2
1985	3.7	32.8	27.7	1.4

Source: Organization for Economic Co-operation and Development, *Economic Outlook,* December 1986.

Japan's current account surplus swelled after 1981 despite a decline in its private saving rate. (Japan's private saving rate remained, however, nearly double that of the United States!) The growing current account surplus reflected both a declining investment rate and a shrinking government budget deficit. Unlike the U.S. national income accounts, the Japanese accounts classify investment spending by the government as part of I rather than of G. Part of the fall in investment after 1981 resulted from the Japanese government's attempt to reduce its borrowing by cutting its investment spending.

As in the U.S. case, we see that changes in the Japanese government budget deficit are an important factor behind that country's current account performance in the 1980s. With unchanged private saving, increases in the government budget deficit tend to lower the current account surplus while decreases in the government budget deficit tend to raise the current account surplus.

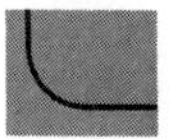

THE BALANCE OF PAYMENTS ACCOUNTS

In the previous section, we examined the components of the national income accounts: consumption, investment, government purchases, and the current account (the measure of a country's net foreign investment or, equivalently, of the difference between its exports and imports). In addition to national income accounts, government economists and statisticians also keep balance of payments accounts, a detailed record of the composition of the current account balance and of the many transactions that finance it. Balance of payments figures are of great interest to the general public, as indicated by the attention that various news media pay to them. But should we be alarmed or cheered by a *Wall Street Journal* headline proclaiming "U.S. Chalks Up Record Balance of Payments Deficit"? A thorough understanding of balance of payments accounting will help us evaluate the implications of a country's international transactions.

A country's balance of payments accounts keep track of both its payments to and its receipts from foreigners. Any transaction resulting in a payment to foreigners is entered in the balance of payments accounts as a *debit* and is given a negative (−) sign. Any transaction resulting in a receipt from foreigners is entered as a *credit* and is given a positive (+) sign.

Two types of international transaction are recorded in the balance of payments:

1. Transactions that involve the export or import of goods or services and therefore enter directly into the current account. When a Frenchman imports American blue jeans, for example, the transaction enters the U.S. balance of payments accounts as a credit on current account.

2. Transactions that involve the purchase or sale of assets. An **asset** is any one of the forms in which wealth can be held, such as money, stocks, factories, government debt, land, or rare postage stamps. The **capital account** of the balance of payments records all international purchases or sales of assets.

When an American buys a French chateau, the transaction enters the U.S. balance of payments as a debit on capital account. It may seem strange to give a negative sign to a purchase of assets and a positive sign to a sale of assets. It will seem less so if you think in terms of the U.S. "importing" (purchasing) assets and the U.S. "exporting" (selling) assets and give the transaction the same sign you would give to an import (−) or export (+) transaction recorded in the current account. The difference between a country's exports and imports of assets is called its capital account balance, but we usually call that balance the capital account for short.

You will find the complexities of the balance of payments accounts less confusing if you keep in mind the following simple rule of double-entry bookkeeping: *Every international transaction automatically enters the balance of payments twice, once as a credit and once as a debit.* This principle of balance of payments accounting holds true because every transaction has two sides: if you buy something from a foreigner you must pay him in some way, and the foreigner must then somehow spend or store your payment. An example will clarify how the principle operates in practice.

Imagine that you buy a typewriter from the Italian firm Olivetti and pay for your purchase with a $1000 check. Since your purchase represents a payment to a foreigner, it enters the current account of the U.S. balance of payments as a $1000 debit. On the other side of the transaction, Olivetti now has your check and must do something with it. It if deposits the check in an American bank, Olivetti has purchased a U.S. asset—a bank deposit worth $1000—and the transaction shows up as a $1000 credit in the U.S. balance of payments capital account. But suppose Olivetti deposits the check at its Italian bank. Now the Italian bank must do something with the check, and any action it takes will ultimately result in a credit item in the U.S. balance of payments. If, for example, the Italian bank lends the $1000 to an Italian firm that uses it to import personal computers from the United States, $1000 must be credited to the U.S. current account. We can never be sure where the flip side of a given transaction will show up, but we can be sure that it will show up somewhere.

Because any international transaction automatically gives rise to two offsetting entries in the balance of payments, the current account balance and the capital account balance automatically add up to zero:

$$\text{Current account} + \text{capital account} = 0. \quad \textbf{(12-3)}$$

This identity can also be understood by recalling the relation between the current account and international lending and borrowing. Because the current account is the change in a country's net foreign wealth, the current account necessarily equals the difference between a country's purchases of assets from foreigners and its sales of assets to them, that is, the capital account balance preceded by a minus sign.

We now turn to a more detailed description of the balance of payments accounts, using as an example the U.S. accounts for 1982. Table 12-3 reproduces the record of America's international transactions in that year.

TABLE 12-3 The U.S. balance of payments accounts for 1982 (billions of dollars)

	Credits	Debits
Current account		
(1) Exports	+348.3	
Of which:		
Merchandise	+211.2	
Investment income received	+84.1	
Other services	+53.0	
(2) Imports		−351.5
Of which:		
Merchandise		−247.6
Investment income paid		−56.8
Other services		−47.1
(3) Net unilateral transfers		−8.0
Balance on current account [(1) + (2) + (3)]		−11.2
Capital account		
(4) U.S. assets held abroad (increase −)		−118.0
Of which:		
Official reserve assets		−5.0
Other assets		−113.0
(5) Foreign assets held in U.S. (increase +)	+87.9	
Of which:		
Official reserve assets	+3.2	
Other assets	+84.7	
Balance on capital account [(4) + (5)]		−30.1
Statistical discrepancy	+41.4	

THE CURRENT ACCOUNT, ONCE AGAIN

As you have learned, the current account balance measures a country's net exports of goods and services. Table 12-3 shows that U.S. exports were $348.3 billion in 1982 while U.S. imports were $351.5 billion. Because imports give rise to payments to foreigners, these enter the accounts with a negative sign, as shown.

The balance of payments accounts divide exports and imports into three finer categories. The first category is *merchandise* trade, that is, exports or imports of goods. The second category, *investment income,* is made up of interest and dividend payments between countries. If you own a share of a German firm's stock and receive a dividend payment of $50, that payment shows up in the accounts as a U.S. investment income receipt of $50. The final category, *other services,* includes items such as tourists' expenditures and shipping fees.

We include income on foreign investments in the current account because interest and dividend payments are compensation for the *services* provided by foreign investments. When a U.S. corporation builds a Canadian plant, for instance, the productive services the plant generates are viewed as a service export from the United States to Canada equal in value to the profits the plant yields for its American owner. To be consistent, we must be sure to include these profits in American GNP and not in Canadian GNP. Remember, the definition of GNP refers to goods and services generated by a country's factors of production, but it does *not* specify that those factors must work within the country that owns them.

Before calculating the current account, we must include one additional type of international transaction that we have largely ignored up until now. In discussing the relation between GNP and national income, we defined unilateral transfers between countries as international gifts, that is, payments that do not correspond to the purchase of any good, service, or asset. Net unilateral transfers are considered part of the current account as well as part of national income, and the identity $Y = C + I + G + CA$ holds exactly if Y is interpreted as national income. In 1982, the U.S. balance of unilateral transfers was −$8.0 billion.[9]

The table shows a 1982 current account balance of $348.3 billion − $351.5 billion − $8.0 billion = −$11.2 billion, a deficit. The negative sign means that current payments exceeded current receipts and that U.S. residents used up more output than they produced. Since these current account transactions were paid for in some way, we know that this negative $11.2 billion entry must be offset by a positive $11.2 billion entry in the other part of the balance of payments, the capital account.

THE CAPITAL ACCOUNT

Just as the current account is the difference between our sales of goods and services to foreigners and our purchases of goods and services from them, the capital account measures the difference between our sales of assets to foreigners and our purchases of assets located abroad. When the United States borrows $1 from foreigners, it is selling them an asset—a promise that they will be repaid $1, with interest, in the future. Such a transaction enters the capital account with a positive sign because the loan is itself a payment to the United States, or a **capital inflow.** When the United States lends abroad, however, a payment is made to foreigners and the capital account is debited. This transaction involves the purchase of an asset from foreigners and is called a **capital outflow.**

[9]This item also includes workers' remittances—wages workers earn abroad and send home to their dependents. These remittances could be classified more appropriately as a payment made to the home country for the export of labor services, and therefore as part of GNP; in practice, however, they are not.

To cover its current account deficit in 1982, the United States required a net capital inflow of $11.2 billion. In other words, its net borrowing or sales of assets to foreigners should have amounted to $11.2 billion. We can look again at Table 12-3 to see exactly how this net capital inflow came about.

The table records separately increases in U.S. holdings of assets located abroad (which are capital outflows and enter with a negative sign) and increases in foreign holdings of assets located in the United States (which are capital inflows and enter with a positive sign).

According to Table 12-3, U.S. assets held abroad increased by $118.0 billion in 1982, contributing a −$118.0 billion entry to the U.S. balance of payments. Foreign assets held in the United States rose by $87.9 billion in the year, and these purchases are shown with a positive sign. We calculate the balance on capital account as $87.9 billion − $118.0 billion = −$30.1 billion, a deficit.

We come out with a capital account deficit of −$30.1 billion rather than the $11.2 billion capital account surplus we expected. Because it is difficult to measure many international transactions, the balance of payments accounts seldom balance in practice as they must in theory. Account keepers make the two sides balance by adding to the accounts a statistical discrepancy (here $41.4 billion) which is in part attributable to errors in measuring capital account transactions. If the statistical discrepancy is added to the measured capital account balance of −$30.1 billion, we get a surplus item of $11.3 billion, which is just equal (apart from rounding error) to the measured current account deficit.

Current accounts are, like capital accounts, measured with error. Accurate measurement of international interest and dividend payments is particularly difficult. (See the box on pages 300–301.) But while we cannot be absolutely certain about the size of the current account, our best guess would be that in 1982, the United States spent around $11.2 billion more than it earned. Foreigners financed this deficit by buying around $11.2 billion more assets from the United States than they sold to the United States.

OFFICIAL RESERVE TRANSACTIONS

Although there are many types of capital-account transaction, one type is important enough to merit separate discussion. This type of transaction involves the purchase or sale of official reserve assets by central banks.

An economy's **central bank** is the institution responsible for managing the supply of money. In the United States, the central bank is the Federal Reserve System. **Official international reserves** are foreign assets held by central banks as a cushion against national economic misfortune. At one time official reserves consisted largely of gold, but today central banks' reserves include substantial foreign financial assets, particularly U.S. dollar assets such as Treasury bills. The Federal Reserve itself holds only a small level of offi-

THE MYSTERY OF THE MISSING SURPLUS

Because the world as a whole is a closed economy, world saving must equal world investment and world spending must equal world output. Individual countries can run current account surpluses or deficits to invest or borrow abroad. Because one country's lending is another country's borrowing, however, the sum of all these individual current account imbalances necessarily equals zero.

Or does it? National current account data show that the world as a whole is running a substantial current account *deficit* that increased sharply in the early 1980s and has remained high. On the opposite page are figures for the sum total of all countries' current account balances since 1978.

The global discrepancies in the table are far greater in magnitude than most reported national current accounts. Since positive and negative errors cancel out in the summation leading to the global figures, discrepancies of this size raise the worrisome possibility that the national current account statistics on which policymakers base decisions are seriously inaccurate.

What explains the theoretically impossible deficit shown by total world current account numbers? Your first reaction may be to blame the problem on the statistical discrepancies that bedevil the national income and balance of payments accounts of individual countries. An additional complication is introduced by timing factors. Goods that leave one country's ports near the end of an accounting year, for example, may not reach their destination in time to be recorded in the recipient's import statistics for the same year.

A general appeal to accounting anomalies such as these does not explain, however, why the world as a whole should appear to be persistently in deficit (rather than in surplus) or why that deficit should

cial reserve assets other than gold; its own holdings of dollar assets are not considered to be international reserves.

Central banks often buy or sell international reserves in private asset markets to affect macroeconomic conditions in their economies. Official transactions of this type are called **official foreign exchange intervention.** One reason why foreign exchange intervention can alter macroeconomic conditions is that it is a way for the central bank to inject money into the economy or withdraw it from circulation. We will have much more to say later about the causes and consequences of foreign exchange intervention.

When a central bank purchases or sells a foreign asset, the transaction appears in its country's capital account just as if the same transaction had been carried out by a private citizen. A transaction in which the central bank of Germany (called the Bundesbank) acquires dollar assets might occur as have tripled in the 1980s. A more plausible hypothesis links the missing surplus to one specific cause of accounting discrepancies at the national level, the systematic misreporting of international interest income flows. Interest payments earned abroad are often not reported to government authorities in the recipient's home country. In many cases such interest payments are credited directly to a foreign bank account and do not even cross national borders. There is thus a consistent tendency to observe a negative global balance of international interest flows.

World interest rates rose sharply after 1980, and the size of the world interest-payment discrepancy increased with them. The interest-payment hypothesis therefore offers a potential explanation for the recent increase in the global deficit. Are interest-rate changes the whole story? The downturn in world interest rates after the mid-1980s provides a test. If the interest-payment theory is correct, the measured world current account deficit should drop dramatically.

Measured World Current Account Balance, 1978–1986 (billions of U.S. dollars)

1978	1979	1980	1981	1982	1983	1984	1985	1986
−29.5	−24.9	−38.5	−71.5	−113.5	−80.8	−96.9	−90.8	−64.3

Source: International Monetary Fund, *World Economic Outlook,* April 1986, table A30. The 1986 figure is a projection. Estimates for Soviet bloc countries are included in the totals above.

follows: A U.S. auto dealer imports a Volkswagen from Germany and pays the auto company with a check for $15,000. Volkswagen does not want to invest the money in dollar assets, but it so happens that the Bundesbank is willing to give Volkswagen German money in exchange for the $15,000 check. The Bundesbank's international reserves rise by $15,000 as a result of the deal. Because the Bundesbank's dollar reserves are part of total German assets held in the United States, the latter rise by $15,000. This transaction therefore results in a positive $15,000 entry in the U.S. capital account, the other side of the −$15,000 entry in the U.S. current account due to the purchase of the car.[10]

[10]To test your understanding, see if you can explain why the same sequence of actions causes a $15,000 improvement in Germany's current account but a $15,000 worsening of its capital account.

Table 12-3 shows the size and direction of official reserve transactions involving the United States. United States official reserve assets—that is, international reserves held by the Federal Reserve—rose by $5.0 billion (recall that a negative sign here means an increase in U.S. assets held abroad, that is, an "import" of assets from foreigners). Foreign central banks purchased $3.2 billion to add to their international reserves. The *net* increase in U.S. official reserves is the balance of official reserve transactions, also called the **official settlements balance** or (in less formal usage) the **balance of payments.** This balance was $5.0 billion − $3.2 billion = $1.8 billion. Non-central bank foreign lending to the United States in 1982 had to finance both the United States's current account deficit of $11.2 billion *and* its $1.8 billion net acquisition of international reserves (a net official capital outflow).

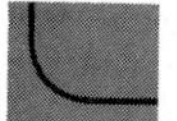

SUMMARY

1. International *macroeconomics* is concerned with the full employment of scarce economic resources and price-level stability throughout the world economy. Because they reflect national expenditure patterns and their international repercussions, the *national income accounts* and the *balance of payments accounts* are essential tools for studying the macroeconomics of open, interdependent economies.

2. A country's *gross national product* (GNP) is equal to the income received by its factors of production. The national income accounts divide national income up according to the types of spending that generate it: *consumption, investment, government purchases,* and the *current account balance.*

3. In an economy closed to international trade, GNP must be consumed, invested, or purchased by the government. By using current output to build plant, equipment, and inventories, investment transforms present output into future output. For a closed economy, investment is the only way to save in the aggregate; so the sum of the saving carried out by the private and public sectors, *national saving,* must equal investment.

4. In an open economy, GNP equals the sum of consumption, investment, government purchases, and net exports of goods and services. Trade does not have to be balanced if the economy can borrow from the rest of the world. The difference between the economy's exports and its imports, the current account balance, equals the difference between the economy's output and its total use of goods and services.

5. The current account also equals the country's net lending to foreigners. Unlike a closed economy, an open economy can save by investing domestically *and* by foreign investment. National saving therefore equals domestic investment plus the current account balance.

6. Balance of payments accounts provide a detailed picture of the composition and financing of the current account. All transactions between a country and the rest of the world are recorded in its balance of payments accounts.

The accounts are based on the convention that any transaction resulting in a payment to foreigners is entered with a minus sign while any transaction resulting in a receipt from foreigners is entered with a plus sign.

7. Transactions involving goods and services appear in the current account of the balance of payments while international sales or puchases of *assets* appear in the *capital account.* Any current account deficit must be matched by an equal capital account surplus, and any current account surplus by a capital account deficit. This feature of the accounts reflects the fact that discrepancies between export earnings and import expenditures must be matched by a promise to repay the difference, usually with interest, in the future.

8. International asset transactions carried out by *central banks* are included in the capital account. Any central bank transaction in private markets for foreign-currency assets is called *official foreign exchange intervention.* One reason intervention is important is that central banks use it as a way of altering the amount of money in circulation.

KEY TERMS

microeconomics
macroeconomics
national income accounting
balance of payments accounting
gross national product (GNP)
national income
consumption
investment
government purchases
national saving
current account balance
private saving
government budget deficit
asset
capital account
capital inflow
capital outflow
central bank
official international reserves
official foreign exchange intervention
official settlements balance (or balance of payments)

PROBLEMS

1. We stated above that GNP accounts avoid double counting by including only the value of *final* goods and services sold on the market. Should the measure of imports used in the GNP accounts therefore be defined to include only imports of final goods and services from abroad? What about exports?

2. Equation (12-2) tells us that to reduce a current account deficit, a country must increase its private saving, reduce domestic investment, or cut its government budget deficit. Yet, as we saw in the case study of the American and Japanese current accounts in the 1980s, many people recommended restrictions on imports from Japan and other countries to reduce the American current account deficit. How do you think higher U.S. barriers to imports would affect its private saving, domestic investment, and government deficit? Do you agree that import restrictions would necessarily reduce a U.S. current account deficit?

3. Explain how each of the following transactions generates two entries—a credit and a debit—in the American balance of payments accounts, and describe how each entry would be classified:

a) An American buys a share of German stock, paying by writing a check on his account with a Swiss bank.

b) An American buys a share of German stock, paying the seller with a check on an American bank.

c) The French government carries out an official foreign exchange intervention in which it uses dollars held in an American bank to buy French currency from its citizens.

d) A tourist from Detroit buys a meal at an expensive restaurant in Lyons, France, paying with a VISA credit card.

e) A California winegrower contributes a case of his best cabernet sauvignon for a London wine tasting.

4. A New Yorker travels to New Jersey to buy a $100 telephone answering machine. The New Jersey company that sells the machine then deposits the $100 check in its account at a New York bank. How would these transactions show up in the balance of payments accounts of New York and New Jersey? What if the New Yorker pays cash for the machine?

5. The nation of Pecunia had a current account deficit of $1 billion and a non-central bank capital account surplus of $500 million in 1987.

a) What was the balance of payments of Pecunia in that year? What happened to the country's net foreign assets?

b) Assume that foreign central banks neither buy nor sell Pecunian assets. How did the Pecunian central bank's international reserves change in 1987? How would this official intervention show up in the balance of payments accounts of Pecunia?

c) How would your answer to (b) change if you learned that foreign central banks had purchased $600 million of Pecunian assets in 1987? How would these official purchases enter foreign balance of payments accounts?

d) Draw up the Pecunian balance of payments accounts for 1987 under the assumption that the event described in (c) occurred in that year.

6. Can you think of reasons why a government might be concerned about a large current account deficit or surplus? Why might a government be concerned about its official settlements balance (that is, its balance of payments)?

FURTHER READING

William H. Branson. "Trends in United States International Trade and Investment Since World War II," in Martin S. Feldstein, ed. *The American Economy in Transition.* Chicago: University of Chicago Press, 1980, pp. 183–257. Surveys postwar changes in the structure of the U.S. current and capital accounts.

Robert J. Gordon. *Macroeconomics,* 4th edition, Chapter 2. Boston: Little, Brown and Company, 1987. A more detailed description of national income accounting.

International Monetary Fund. "Statistical Asymmetry in Global Current Account Balances." Supplementary note 11 in *World Economic Outlook,* May 1983. Washington, D.C.: International Monetary Fund, pp. 161–167. Discusses the statistical discrepancy in the world current account balance, along with its implications for policy analysis.

Rita M. Maldonado. "Recording and Classifying Transactions in the Balance of Payments." *International Journal of Accounting* 15 (Fall 1979), pp. 105–133. Provides detailed examples of how various international transactions enter the balance of payments accounts.

Oskar Morgenstern. *On the Accuracy of Economic Observations,* 2d edition. Princeton: Princeton University Press, 1965. Chapter 9 examines problems in measuring balance of payments flows.

Robert A. Mundell. *International Economics,* Chapter 10. New York: Macmillan, 1968. An analytical discussion of balance of payments concepts.

Robert M. Stern, Charles F. Schwartz, Robert Triffin, Edward M. Bernstein, and Walther Lederer. *The Presentation of the Balance of Payments: A Symposium,* Princeton Essays in International Finance 123. International Finance Section, Department of Economics, Princeton University, August 1977. A discussion of changes in the presentation of the U.S. balance of payments accounts.

U.S. Bureau of the Budget, Review Committee for Balance of Payments Statistics. *The Balance of Payments Statistics of the United States: A Review and Appraisal.* Washington, D.C.: Government Printing Office, 1965. A major official reappraisal of U.S. balance of payments accounting procedures. Chapter 9 focuses on conceptual difficulties in defining surpluses and deficits in the balance of payments.

13 EXCHANGE RATES AND THE FOREIGN-EXCHANGE MARKET: AN ASSET APPROACH

In Chapter 12 we learned that there are two important ways in which a country's current account measures its macroeconomic interactions with other countries. First, the current account equals the difference between exports and imports; so it is a component of the overall demand for the country's national product. Second, the current account equals the economy's net accumulation of assets located abroad—the change in its net foreign wealth.

In 1985, the United States registered one of the largest current account deficits in its history—$117.7 billion, equal to 2.9 percent of U.S. GNP. In the same year, the prices of foreign currencies in terms of dollars were on average around 40 percent lower than they had been 6 years earlier. The huge current account deficit and the change in the dollar's value were closely connected. Low dollar prices of foreign currencies encouraged Americans to import more goods and services from abroad than ever before. For the same reason, foreigners reduced their demand for American exports and instead spent more of their income on the less expensive goods produced in their home countries.

The price of one currency in terms of another currency is called an **exchange rate.** At 3 P.M. New York time on October 21, 1985, you would have needed 37.91 cents to buy one unit of the West German currency, the Deutschemark (DM); so the dollar's exchange rate against the DM was 0.3791 dollars per DM. Because of their strong influence on the current account and other macroeconomic variables, exchange rates are among the most important prices in an open economy.

Because an exchange rate, the price of one country's money in terms of another country's money, is also an asset price, the principles governing the behavior of other asset prices also govern the behavior of exchange rates. As you will recall from Chapter 12, the defining characteristic of an asset is that it is a form of wealth, a way of transferring purchasing power from the present into the future. The price that an asset commands today is therefore directly related to the goods and services buyers expect it to yield in the future. Similarly, *today's* dollar/DM exchange rate is closely tied to people's expectations about the *future* level of that rate. Just as the price of IBM stock rises immediately on favorable news about IBM's future prospects, so do exchange rates respond immediately to any news concerning future currency values.

Our general goals in this chapter are to understand the role of exchange rates in international trade and how exchange rates are determined. To begin, we first learn how exchange rates allow us to compare the prices of different countries' goods and services. Next we describe the international asset market in which currencies are traded and show how equilibrium exchange rates are determined in that market. A final section underlines our asset-market approach by showing how today's exchange rate responds to changes in the expected future values of exchange rates.

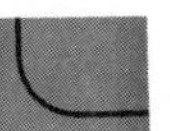

EXCHANGE RATES AND INTERNATIONAL TRANSACTIONS

Each country has a currency in which the prices of goods and services are quoted—the dollar in the United States, the DM in Germany, the pound sterling in Britain, the yen in Japan, and the austral in Argentina, to name just a few. Exchange rates play a central role in international trade because they allow us to compare the prices of goods and services produced in different countries. A consumer deciding which of two American cars to buy must compare their dollar prices, for example, \$25,000 (for a Lincoln Continental) or \$12,000 (for a Ford Taurus). But how is the same consumer to compare either of these prices with the 2,200,000 yen (¥2,200,000) it costs to import a Subaru from Japan? To make this comparison, she must know the relative price of dollars and yen.

The relative prices of currencies are reported daily in newspapers' financial sections. Table 13-1 shows the dollar exchange rates for currencies traded in New York at 3 P.M. on October 21, 1985, as reported in the *Wall Street Journal.* Notice that each exchange rate can be quoted in two ways,

TABLE 13-1 Exchange-rate quotations

FOREIGN EXCHANGE

Monday, October 21, 1985

The New York foreign exchange selling rates below apply to trading among banks in amounts of $1 million and more, as quoted at 3 P.M. Eastern time by Bankers Trust Co. Retail transactions provide fewer units of foreign currency per dollar.

	U.S. $ equiv.		*Currency per U.S. $*	
Country	*Mon.*	*Fri.*	*Mon.*	*Fri.*
Argentina (Austral)	1.2484	1.2484	.801	.801
Australia (Dollar)	.7030	.7055	1.4225	1.4174
Austria (Schilling)	.05420	.05397	18.45	18.53
Belgium (Franc)				
Commercial rate	.01874	.01871	53.35	53.46
Financial rate	.01838	.01859	54.405	53.80
Brazil (Cruzeiro)	.0001241	.0001281	8060.00	7805.00
Britain (Pound)	1.4335	1.4290	.6976	.6998
30-Day Forward	1.4288	1.4248	.6999	.7019
90-Day Forward	1.4215	1.4208	.7035	.7038
180-Day Forward	1.4120	1.4174	.7082	.7055
Canada (Dollar)	.7339	.7328	1.3625	1.3646
30-Day Forward	.7337	.7326	1.3629	1.3650
90-Day Forward	.7332	.7323	1.3638	1.3655
180-Day Forward	.7899	.7321	1.2660	1.3659
Chile (Official rate)	.005686	.005705	175.88	175.27
China (Yuan)	.3269	.3281	3.0582	3.0475
Colombia (Peso)	.006253	.006293	159.93	158.90
Denmark (Krone)	.1047	.1047	9.5500	9.5550
Ecuador (Sucre)				
Official rate	.01504	.01504	66.48	66.48
Floating rate	.008722	.008877	114.65	112.65
Finland (Markka)	.1749	.1761	5.7175	5.6775
France (Franc)	.1244	.1243	8.0400	8.0435
30-Day Forward	.1243	.1242	8.0460	8.0525
90-Day Forward	.1240	.1240	8.0645	8.0645
180-Day Forward	.1234	.1238	8.1190	8.0795
Greece (Drachma)	.006494	.006472	154.00	154.50
Hong Kong (Dollar)	.1283	.1283	7.7935	7.7920
India (Rupee)	.082713	.08403	12.08	11.90
Indonesia (Rupiah)	.0008905	.0008913	1123.00	1122.00
Ireland (Punt)	1.1760	1.1750	.8503	.8511
Israel (Shekel)	.0006803	.0006729	1470.00	1486.00
Italy (Lira)	.0005624	.0005624	1778.00	1778.00
Japan (Yen)	.004639	.004649	215.55	215.08
30-Day Forward	.004646	.004656	215.23	214.78
90-Day Forward	.004659	.004663	214.66	214.47
180-Day Forward	.004679	.004669	213.71	214.20

Country	U.S. $ equiv. Mon.	U.S. $ equiv. Fri.	Currency per U.S. $ Mon.	Currency per U.S. $ Fri.
Jordan (Dinar)	2.7353	2.7427	.3656	.3646
Kuwait (Dinar)	3.3772	3.3738	.2961	.2964
Lebanon (Pound)	.05427	.05391	18.425	18.55
Malaysia (Ringgit)	.4080	.4073	2.4510	2.4550
Malta (Lira)	2.2857	2.2857	.4375	.4375
Mexico (Peso)				
Floating rate	.002545	.002532	393.00	395.00
Netherlands (Guilder)	.3366	.3359	2.9705	2.9770
New Zealand (Dollar)	.5820	.5840	1.7182	1.7123
Norway (Krone)	.1267	.1263	7.8900	7.9150
Pakistan (Rupee)	.06227	.06410	16.06	15.60
Peru (Sol)	.00007173	.00007173	13942.00	13942.00
Philippines (Peso)	.05345	.05356	18.71	18.67
Portugal (Escudo)	.006079	.006192	164.50	161.50
Saudi Arabia (Riyal)	.2739	.2740	3.6500	3.6490
Singapore (Dollar)	.4688	.4675	2.1330	2.1390
South Africa (Rand)	.3860	.3810	2.5907	2.6247
South Korea (Won)	.001121	.001122	892.40	891.60
Spain (Peseta)	.006223	.006202	160.70	161.25
Sweden (Krona)	.1262	.1259	7.9250	7.9400
Switzerland (Franc)	.4620	.4615	2.1645	2.1670
30-Day Forward	.4637	.4630	2.1564	2.1596
90-Day Forward	.4662	.4646	2.1449	2.1523
180-Day Forward	.4705	.4657	2.1255	2.1473
Taiwan (Dollar)	.02494	.02489	40.10	40.17
Thailand (Baht)	.03759	.03759	26.60	26.60
United Arab (Dirham)	.2723	.2723	3.673	3.673
Uruguay (New Peso)				
Financial	.008667	.008763	115.38	114.12
Venezuela (Bolivar)				
Official rate	.1333	.1333	7.50	7.50
Floating rate	.06849	.06840	14.60	14.62
W. Germany (Mark)	.3791	.3794	2.6375	2.6358
30-Day Forward	.3804	.3805	2.6291	2.6279
90-Day Forward	.3824	.3817	2.6150	2.6202
180-Day Forward	.3857	.3827	2.5930	2.6132
SDR	1.06712	1.06566	0.937102	0.938384
ECU	0.840505	0.838531	...	...

Special Drawing Rights are based on exchange rates for the U.S., West German, British, French, and Japanese currencies. Source: International Monetary Fund.

ECU is based on a basket of community currencies. Source: European Community Commission.

z-Not quoted.

Source: Reprinted by permission of *The Wall Street Journal,* © Dow Jones & Company, Inc. 1985.

as the price of the foreign currency in terms of dollars (for example, $0.004639 per yen) or as the price of dollars in terms of the foreign currency (for example, ¥215.55 per dollar).

Households and firms use exchange rates to translate foreign prices into domestic-currency terms. Once the money prices of domestic goods and imports have been expressed in terms of the same currency, households and firms can compute the *relative* prices that affect international trade flows.

DOMESTIC AND FOREIGN PRICES

If we know the exchange rate between two countries' currencies, we can compute the price of one country's exports in terms of the other country's money. For example, how many dollars would it cost to buy an Edinburgh Woolen Mill sweater costing 50 British pounds (£50)? The answer is found by multiplying the price of the sweater in pounds, 50, by the price of a pound in terms of dollars—the dollar's exchange rate against the pound. At an exchange rate of $1.50 per pound, the dollar price of the sweater is (1.50 $/£) × (£50) = $75.

A change in the dollar/pound exchange rate would alter the sweater's dollar price. At an exchange rate of $1.25 per pound, the sweater would cost only (1.25 $/£) × (£50) = $62.50, assuming its price in terms of pounds remained the same. At an exchange rate of $1.75 per pound, the sweater's dollar price would be higher and equal to (1.75 $/£) × (£50) = $87.50.

Changes in exchange rates are described as depreciations or appreciations. A **depreciation** of the pound against the dollar is a fall in the dollar price of pounds, for example, a change in the exchange rate from $1.50 per pound to $1.25 per pound. The preceding example shows that *all else equal, a depreciation of a country's currency makes its goods cheaper for foreigners.* A rise in the pound's price in terms of dollars—for example, from $1.50 per pound to $1.75 per pound—is an **appreciation** of the pound against the dollar. *All else equal, an appreciation of a country's currency makes its goods more expensive for foreigners.*

The exchange rate changes discussed in the our example simultaneously alter the prices Britons must pay for American goods. At an exchange rate of $1.50 per pound, the pound price of a pair of American designer jeans costing $45 is ($45)/(1.50 $/£) = £30. A change in the exchange rate from $1.50 per pound to $1.25 per pound, while a depreciation of the pound against the dollar, is also a rise in the pound price of dollars, an *appreciation* of the dollar against the pound. This appreciation of the dollar makes the American jeans more expensive for Britons by raising their pound price to ($45)/(1.25 $/£) = £36. The change in the exchange rate from $1.50 per pound to $1.75 per pound—an appreciation of the pound against the dollar but a depreciation of the dollar against the pound—lowers the pound price of the jeans to ($45)/(1.75 $/£) = £25.71.

As you can see, descriptions of exchange-rate changes as depreciations or appreciations can be bewildering, because when one currency depreciates against a second, the second currency must simultaneously appreciate against the first. To avoid confusion in discussing exchange rates, we must always keep track of which of the two currencies we are examining has depreciated or appreciated against the other.

If we remember that a depreciation of the dollar against the pound is at the same time an appreciation of the pound against the dollar, we reach the following conclusion: *When a country's currency depreciates, foreigners find that its exports are cheaper and domestic residents find that imports from abroad are more expensive. An appreciation has opposite effects: foreigners pay more for the country's products and domestic consumers pay less for foreign products.*

EXCHANGE RATES AND RELATIVE PRICES

Import and export demands, like the demands for all goods and services, are influenced by *relative* prices, such as the price of sweaters in terms of designer jeans. We have just seen how exchange rates allow individuals to compare domestic and foreign money prices by expressing them in a common currency unit. Carrying this analysis one step further, we can see that exchange rates also allow individuals to compute the relative prices of goods and services whose prices are quoted in different currencies.

An American trying to decide how much to spend on American jeans and how much to spend on British sweaters must translate their prices into a common currency in order to compute the price of sweaters in terms of jeans. As we have seen, an exchange rate of $1.50 per pound means that an American pays $75 for a sweater priced at £50 in Britain. Because the price of a pair of American jeans is $45, the price of sweaters in terms of jeans is ($75 per sweater)/($45 per pair of jeans) = 1.67 pairs of jeans per sweater. Naturally, a Briton faces the same relative price of (£50 per sweater)/(£30 per pair of jeans) = 1.67 pairs of jeans per sweater.

Table 13-2 shows the relative prices implied by exchange rates of $1.25 per pound, $1.50 per pound, and $1.75 per pound, on the assumption that

TABLE 13-2 $/£ exchange rates and the relative price of American designer jeans and British sweaters

Exchange rate ($/£)	1.25	1.50	1.75
Relative price (pairs of jeans/sweater)	1.39	1.67	1.94

Note: The above calculations assume unchanged money prices of $45 per pair of jeans and £50 per sweater.

HAVE DOLLARS, WILL TRAVEL

From December 1983 to January 1985, the British pound depreciated sharply against the dollar to levels never seen before. In little more than a year, the dollar price of a pound plummeted from $1.4506 to $1.1275, a pound depreciation of about 22 percent. British raingear, cashmere sweaters, china, suits, jams, and autos all became cheaper for foreigners as a result of the pound's fall.

British goods became so much cheaper for foreigners that many flew to London for weekend shopping. Hoping to attract footloose and relatively wealthy Americans, posh British department stores advertised their post-Christmas sales in the United States. One of the stores, Harrods, even placed a joint ad with Pan Am airlines and American Express in the *New York Times*. Apparently the foreign advertising efforts were successful. In the first 2 days of its 1985 sale, Harrods took in $11 million, 20 percent more than it had taken in during the first 2 days of its 1984 sale.

A spokesman for Harrods reported that one American couple had flown to London on the Concorde for a single day of shopping. The couple felt that the money they saved by buying in London rather than in the United States was more than sufficient to cover their air fare!*

*See "Weak Pound: An Opportunity," *New York Times*, January 18, 1985.

the dollar price of jeans and the pound price of sweaters are unaffected by the exchange-rate changes. To test your understanding, try to calculate these relative prices for yourself and confirm that the outcome of the calculation is the same for a Briton and for an American.

The table shows that if money prices do not change, an appreciation of the dollar against the pound makes sweaters cheaper in terms of jeans (each pair of jeans buys more sweaters) while a depreciation of the dollar against the pound makes sweaters more expensive in terms of jeans (each pair of jeans buys fewer sweaters). The computations illustrate a general principle: *All else equal, an appreciation of a country's currency raises the relative price of its exports and lowers the relative price of its imports. Conversely, a depreciation lowers the relative price of a country's exports and raises the relative price of its imports.*

THE FOREIGN-EXCHANGE MARKET

Just as other prices in the economy are determined by the interaction of buyers and sellers, exchange rates are determined by the interaction of the households, firms, and financial institutions that buy and sell foreign currencies in order to make international payments. The market in which international currency trades take place is called the **foreign-exchange market.**

THE ACTORS

The major participants in the foreign-exchange market are commercial banks, corporations that engage in international trade, nonbank financial institutions such as brokerage firms and insurance companies, and central banks. Individuals also participate in the foreign-exchange market—for example, the tourist who buys foreign currency from his hotel—but such cash transactions are an insignificant fraction of total foreign-exchange trading.

We now describe the major actors in the market and their roles.

1. *Commercial banks.* Commercial banks are at the center of the foreign-exchange market because almost every sizable international transaction involves the debiting and crediting of accounts at commercial banks in various financial centers. Thus, the vast majority of foreign-exchange transactions involve the exchange of *bank deposits* denominated in different currencies.

Let's look at an example. Suppose Exxon Corporation wishes to pay DM160,000 to a German supplier. First, Exxon gets an exchange-rate quotation from its own commercial bank, the Third National Bank. Then, it instructs Third National to debit Exxon's dollar account and pay DM160,000 into the supplier's account at a German bank. If the exchange rate quoted to Exxon by Third National is \$0.35 per DM, \$56,000 (= \$0.35 per DM × DM160,000) is debited from Exxon's account. The final result of the transaction is the exchange of a \$56,000 deposit at Third National Bank (now owned by the German bank that supplied the DM) for the DM160,000 deposit used by Third National to pay Exxon's German supplier.

As the example shows, banks routinely enter the foreign-exchange market to meet the needs of their customers—primarily corporations. A bank may also transact in foreign currencies to alter the currency composition of its own assets and liabilities. In addition, it is normal practice in the foreign-exchange market for a bank to quote to other banks exchange rates at which it is willing to buy currencies from them and sell currencies to them.

Foreign-currency trading among banks—called **interbank trading**—accounts for most of the activity in the foreign exchange market. In fact, the exchange rates listed in Table 13-1 are interbank rates, the rates banks charge to each other. No amount less than \$1 million is traded at those rates. The rates available to corporate customers, called "retail" rates, are usually less favorable than the "wholesale" interbank rates. The differential between the retail and wholesale rates is the bank's compensation for doing the business.

Because their international operations are so extensive, large commercial banks are well suited to bring buyers and sellers of currencies together. A multinational corporation wishing to convert \$100,000 into Swedish kronor might find it difficult and costly to locate other corporations wishing to sell the right amount of kronor. By serving many customers simultaneously through a single large purchase of kronor, a bank can economize on these search costs.

2. *Corporations.* Corporations with operations in several countries frequently make or receive payments in currencies other than that of the country in which they are headquartered. To pay workers at a plant in Mexico, for example, IBM may need Mexican pesos. If IBM has only dollars earned by selling computers in the United States, it can acquire the pesos it needs by buying them with its dollars in the foreign-exchange market.

3. *Nonbank financial institutions.* In recent years, deregulation of financial markets in the United States, the United Kingdom, Japan, and other countries has encouraged nonbank financial institutions to offer their customers a broader range of services, many of them indistinguishable from those offered by banks. Among these have been services involving foreign-exchange transactions.

4. *Central banks.* In the previous chapter we learned that central banks sometimes intervene in foreign-exchange markets. While the volume of central bank transactions is typically not large, the impact of these transactions may be great. The reason for this impact is that participants in the foreign-exchange market watch central bank actions closely for clues about future macroeconomic policies that may affect exchange rates. Government agencies other than central banks may also trade in the foreign-exchange market, but central banks are the most regular official participants.

CHARACTERISTICS OF THE MARKET

Foreign-exchange trading takes place in many financial centers, with the largest volume of trade occurring in such major cities as London (the largest market), New York, Tokyo, Frankfurt, and Singapore. The worldwide volume of foreign-exchange trading is enormous, and it has ballooned in recent years. In April 1983, for example, the total value of foreign-exchange transactions carried out in the United States alone was $544 billion. In the same month, the volume of foreign-exchange trading in Tokyo was $249 billion; in Canada, $102 billion; and in Singapore, $123 billion. Three years later, in March 1986, the average volume of worldwide currency trading was well over $200 billion *per day,* of which $90 billion were traded daily in London, $50 billion in New York, and $48 billion in Tokyo.[1]

[1]For April 1983 figures, see Michael D. Andrews, "Recent Trends in the U.S. Foreign Exchange Market," *Federal Reserve Bank of New York Quarterly Review* (Summer 1984), pp. 38–47. March 1986 figures come from surveys carried out simultaneously by the Federal Reserve Bank of New York, the Bank of England, and the Bank of Japan. See, for example, "The Market for Foreign Exchange in London," *Bank of England Quarterly Bulletin* 26 (September 1986), pp. 379–382.

Direct telephone links among the major foreign-exchange trading centers make each a part of a single world market on which the sun never sets. Economic news released at any time of the day is immediately transmitted around the world and may set off a flurry of activity by market participants. Even after trading in New York has finished, New York-based banks and corporations with affiliates in other time zones can remain active in the market. Some banks allow their foreign-exchange traders to deal from their homes when a late-night phone call alerts them to important developments in a financial center on another continent.

The integration of financial centers implies that there can be no significant difference between the dollar/DM exchange rate quoted in New York at 9 A.M. and the dollar/DM exchange rate quoted in London at the same time (which corresponds to 3 P.M. London time). If the DM was selling for $0.30 in New York and $0.35 in London, profits could be made through **arbitrage**, the process of buying a currency cheap and selling it dear. At the prices listed above, a trader could, for instance, purchase DM1,000,000 in New York for $300,000 and immediately sell her DM in London for $350,000, making a pure profit of $50,000. As all traders tried to cash in on the opportunity, however, their demand for DM in New York would drive the dollar price of DM there up and their supply of DM in London would drive the dollar price of DM there down. Very quickly, the difference between the New York and London exchange rates would disappear. Since foreign-exchange traders carefully watch their computer screens for arbitrage opportunities, the few opportunities that arise are small and very short-lived.

While a foreign-exchange transaction can involve any two currencies, most transactions between banks involve exchanges of foreign currencies for U.S. dollars. This is true even when a bank's goal is to sell one nondollar currency and buy another! A bank wishing to sell Dutch guilders and buy Austrian schillings, for example, will usually sell its guilders for dollars and then use the dollars to buy schillings. While this procedure may appear roundabout, it is actually cheaper for the bank than the alternative of trying to find a holder of schillings who wishes to buy guilders. The advantage of trading through the dollar is a result of the United States's importance in the world economy. Because the volume of international transactions involving dollars is so great, it is not hard to find parties willing to trade large amounts of dollars against guilders or schillings. In contrast, relatively few transactions require direct exchanges of guilders for schillings.[2]

Because of its pivotal role in so many foreign-exchange deals, the dollar is sometimes called a **vehicle currency.** A vehicle currency is one that is

[2]The guilder/schilling exchange rate can be calculated from the dollar/guilder and dollar/schilling rates as the dollar/schilling rate divided by the dollar/guilder rate. If the dollar/guilder rate is $0.30 per guilder and the dollar/schilling rate is $0.06 per schilling, then the guilder/schilling exchange rate is (0.06 $/schilling)/(0.30 $/guilder) = 0.20 guilders/schilling. Exchange rates between nondollar currencies are called "cross rates" by foreign-exchange traders.

widely used to denominate international contracts made by parties who do not reside in the country that issues the vehicle currency.[3]

After the dollar, the DM and the yen play the most important roles in the foreign-exchange market. In March 1986, 34 percent of all foreign-exchange transactions in U.S. financial centers involved DM and 23 percent involved yen. The pound sterling, once second only to the dollar as a key international currency, has declined in importance. Its March 1986 share in U.S. foreign-exchange trading was only 19 percent.

SPOT RATES AND FORWARD RATES

The foreign-exchange transactions we have been discussing take place on the spot: two parties agree to an exchange of bank deposits and execute the deal immediately. Exchange rates governing such "on-the-spot" trading are called **spot exchange rates,** and the deal is called a spot transaction.

The term "spot" is a bit misleading because even spot exchanges become effective only 2 days after a deal is struck. The delay occurs because in most cases it takes 2 days for payment instructions (such as checks) to be cleared through the banking system.[4] Suppose Apple Computers has pounds in an account at the National Westminster bank in London but sells them to the Bank of America in San Francisco, which has offered Apple a more favorable spot exchange rate for pounds than the bank where it has its dollar account, Wells Fargo. On Monday, June 20, Apple pays the pounds to Bank of America with a pound check drawn on Nat West, while Bank of America, to pay Apple, writes a dollar check on itself that Apple deposits with Wells Fargo. Normally, Apple cannot use the dollars it has bought, nor can Bank of America use its pounds, until Wednesday, June 22, 2 business days later. In the jargon of the foreign-exchange market, the *value date* for a spot transaction—the date on which the parties actually receive the funds they have purchased—occurs 2 business days after the deal is made.

Foreign-exchange deals sometimes specify a value date farther away than 2 days—30 days, 90 days, 180 days, or even several years. The exchange rates quoted in such a transactions are called **forward exchange rates.** In a 30-day forward transaction, for example, two parties may agree on March 1 to exchange £100,000 for $136,000 on March 31. The 30-day forward exchange rate is therefore $1.36 per pound, and it is generally different from the spot rate and from the forward rates applied to different value dates. When you agree to sell pounds for dollars on a future date at a forward rate agreed on today, you have "sold pounds forward" and "bought dollars forward."

[3]For a more detailed discussion of vehicle currencies, see Stephen P. Magee and Ramesh K. S. Rao, "Vehicle and Nonvehicle Currencies in International Trade," *American Economic Review* 70 (May 1980), pp. 368–373.

[4]A major exception involves trades of U.S. dollars for Canadian dollars in New York. These are consummated with a 1-day lag.

Table 13-1 shows forward exchange rate quotations for the most heavily traded foreign currencies. Forward and spot exchange rates, while not necessarily equal, do tend to move closely together, as illustrated for dollar/pound rates in Figure 13-1. The appendix to this chapter, which discusses how forward exchange rates are determined, explains this close relationship between movements in spot and forward rates.

An example shows why parties may wish to engage in forward exchange transactions. Suppose an American who imports radios from Japan knows that in 30 days he must pay yen to a Japanese supplier for a shipment arriving then. The importer must pay his supplier ¥25,000 per radio and can sell each radio for $100 in the United States; so his profits depend on the dollar/yen exchange rate. At the current spot exchange rate of $0.0038 per yen, the importer would pay ($0.0038 per yen) × (¥25,000 per radio) = $95 per radio, and he would therefore make $5 on each radio imported. But the importer will not have the funds to pay his supplier until the radios arrive and are sold. If over the next 30 days the dollar unexpectedly depreciates to $0.0041 per yen, the importer will have to pay ($0.0041 per yen) × (¥25,000 per radio) = $102.50 per radio, and so will take a $2.50 *loss* on each.

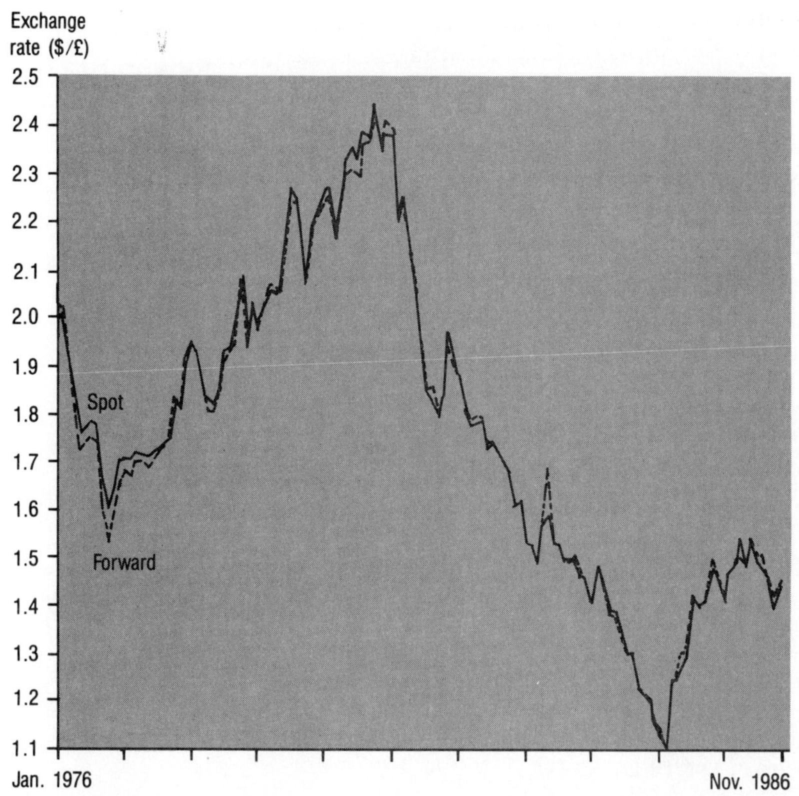

FIGURE 13-1 Dollar/pound spot and forward exchange rates, 1976–1986. Rates shown are 90-day forward exchange rates and spot exchange rates, at end of month.
Source: OECD, *Main Economic Indicators.*

To avoid this risk, the importer can make a 30-day forward exchange deal with his bank. If the bank agrees to sell yen to the importer in 30 days at a rate of \$0.0039, the importer is assured that he will pay no more than (\$0.0039 per yen) × (¥25,000 per radio) = \$97.50 per radio to his supplier. By buying yen and selling dollars forward, the importer guarantees himself a profit of \$2.50 per radio and insures himself against the possibility that a sudden exchange-rate change turns a profitable importing deal into a loss.

From now on, when we mention an exchange rate without specifying whether it is a spot rate or a forward rate, we will always be referring to the spot rate.

THE DEMAND FOR FOREIGN-CURRENCY ASSETS

We have now seen how banks, corporations, and other institutions trade foreign-currency bank deposits in a worldwide foreign-exchange market that operates 24 hours a day. To understand how exchange rates are determined by the foreign-exchange market, we first must ask how the major actors' demands for different types of foreign-currency deposits are determined.

The demand for a foreign-currency bank deposit is influenced by the same considerations that influence the demand for any other asset. Chief among these considerations is our view of what the deposit will be worth in the future. A foreign-currency deposit's future value depends in turn on two factors: the interest rate it offers and the expected change in the currency's exchange rate against other currencies.

ASSETS AND ASSET RETURNS

As you will recall, people can hold wealth in many forms—stocks, bonds, cash, real estate, rare wines, diamonds, and so on. The object of acquiring wealth—of saving—is to transfer purchasing power into the future. We may do this to provide for our retirement years or for our heirs, or simply because we earn more than we need to spend in a particular year and prefer to save the balance for a "rainy day."

Because the object of saving is to provide for future consumption, we judge the desirability of an asset largely on the basis of its **rate of return,** that is, the proportional increase in its value over some time period. For example, a diamond purchased for \$50,000 in 1985 and worth \$60,000 a year later has given its owner a rate of return of 20 percent over the year [(60,000 − 50,000)/50,000 = 0.20]. Because we often cannot know with certainty the price that an asset will command in the future, our decisions must be based on an *expected* rate of return. To calculate an expected rate of return over some time period, you make your best forecast of the asset's total value at the end of the period. The proportional difference between that expected future value and the price you pay for the asset today equals the asset's expected rate of return over the time period.

MATCHMAKING IN THE FOREIGN-EXCHANGE MARKET

Banks wishing to buy or sell foreign currencies don't always take the direct approach of phoning another bank. Often, they use the services of foreign-exchange brokers who specialize in bringing buyers and sellers together. The advantage of working through a broker comes from the additional information the broker can provide. At any moment, the broker may know the prices at which fifty or even a hundred banks are willing to buy and sell currencies. This knowledge puts the broker in an ideal position to get the best price for her customers.

Foreign-exchange brokers require vast communications networks to maintain up-to-the-second information on prospective matches. The *New York Times* reported in 1986 that one of the largest brokerage firms, Noonan, Astley & Pearce Inc., has around 1750 phone lines. These include lines dedicated to particular bank customers, sometimes up to 20 per bank. The multiplicity of dedicated lines serves to separate dealings in different currencies and in the spot and forward markets.*

The foreign-exchange brokerage business has been revolutionized in recent years through international mergers and acquisitions. The firm of Noonan, Astley & Pearce, for example, resulted from the 1978 merger of Noonan, based in New York, with Astley & Pearce, based in London. The internationalization of the brokerage industry makes it easier for brokers to arrange deals between customers located in different countries. As a reflection of its increasing market role, Noonan has more than tripled its brokerage force in the last decade.

Days are long and fees are lean. Trading begins at 5:30 A.M. and continues until midnight so that customers in both London and the Pacific basin can be served. Commissions are negotiated, but fierce competition among brokers assures a fee that is usually no more than $10 per million dollars traded.

*See "Money's Swift Matchmakers," *New York Times,* August 25, 1986.

When we measure an asset's rate of return, we compare its value on two dates. In the previous example, we compared the prices of a diamond in 1985 ($50,000) and in 1986 ($60,000) to conclude that the rate of return on the diamond was 20 percent per year. We call this a *dollar* rate of return because the two values we compare are expressed in terms of dollars. It is also possible, however, to compute different rates of return by expressing the two values in terms of a foreign currency or a commodity like gold.

The expected rate of return that savers consider in deciding which assets to hold is the expected **real rate of return,** the rate of return computed by measuring the asset's value in terms of a typical "basket" of goods consumed by a representative household in one week. It is the expected real return that matters because the ultimate goal of saving is future consumption, and only the *real* return measures the amount of consumption we can enjoy in the future in return for giving up some consumption (that is, saving) today.

To continue our example, suppose that the dollar price of diamonds increased by 20 percent between 1985 and 1986 but that the dollar prices of all consumption goods *also* increased by 20 percent. Then in terms of consumption goods—that is, in *real* terms—a diamond would be worth no more in 1986 than in 1985. With a real rate of return of zero, a diamond would not be a very desirable asset.

Although savers care about expected real rates of return, rates of return expressed in terms of a currency can still be used to *compare* the returns on *different* assets. Even if all dollar prices rise by 20 percent between 1985 and 1986, a share of stock that pays no dividends but whose dollar price rises by 25 percent is still a better deal than a diamond whose dollar price rises by only 20 percent. The real rate of return offered by the share is 5 percent (= 25 percent − 20 percent) while that offered by the diamond is 0 percent (= 20 percent − 20 percent). Notice that the difference between the dollar returns of the two assets (25 percent − 20 percent) must equal the difference between their real returns (5 percent − 0 percent). The reason for this equality is that, given the two assets' dollar returns, a change in the rate at which the dollar prices of goods are rising changes both assets' real returns by the same amount.

The distinction between real rates of return and dollar rates of return illustrates an important concept in studying how savers evaluate different assets: the returns on two assets cannot be compared unless they are measured in the *same* units. For example, it makes no sense to directly compare the real return on a diamond (0 percent in our example) with the dollar return on stocks (25 percent), or to compare the dollar return on old paintings with the DM return on gold. Only after the returns are expressed in terms of a common unit of measure—for example, all in terms of dollars—can we tell which asset offers the highest expected real rate of return.

RISK AND LIQUIDITY

All else equal, individuals prefer to hold those assets offering the highest expected real rate of return. Our later discussions of particular assets show, however, that "all else" is sometimes not equal. Some assets may be valued by savers for attributes other than the expected real rate of return they offer. Savers care about two main characteristics of an asset other than its return, its **risk**, that is, the variability it contributes to savers' wealth, and its **liquidity**, that is, the ease with which the asset can be sold or exchanged for goods.

1. *Risk.* An asset's real return is usually unpredictable and may turn out to be quite different from what savers expect when they purchase the asset. In our

earlier example, we saw that savers found the expected real rate of return on a share of stock (5 percent) by subtracting from the expected rate of increase in the share's dollar price (25 percent) the expected rate of increase in dollar prices (20 percent). But if expectations turn out to be wrong and dollar prices rise at a rate of 30 percent instead of 20 percent, for example, the rate of return actually realized by the saver is *minus* 5 percent (= 25 percent − 30 percent). Savers dislike uncertainty and are reluctant to hold assets that make their wealth highly variable. An asset with a high expected rate of return may appear undesirable to savers if its realized rate of return fluctuates widely.

2. *Liquidity.* Assets also differ according to the cost and speed at which savers can dispose of them. A house, for example, is not very liquid because its sale usually requires time and the services of brokers and lawyers. In contrast, cash is the most liquid of assets: it is always acceptable at face value as payment for goods or other assets. Savers prefer to hold some liquid assets as a precaution against unexpected expenses that might force them to sell less liquid assets at a loss. If a saver's wealth is held mostly in illiquid form, he will therefore consider an asset's liquidity as well as its expected return and risk in deciding whether to hold it.

INTEREST RATES

As in other asset markets, participants in the foreign-exchange market base their demands for deposits of different currencies on a comparison of these assets' expected real rates of return. To compare returns on different deposits, market participants need two pieces of information. First, they need to know how the money values of the deposits will change. Second, they need to know how exchange rates will change so that they can translate rates of return measured in different currencies into comparable terms.

The first piece of information needed to compute the rate of return on a deposit of a particular currency is the currency's **interest rate,** the amount of that currency an individual can earn by lending a unit of the currency for a year. At a dollar interest rate of 0.10 (quoted as 10 percent per year), the lender of $1 receives $1.10 at the end of the year, $1 of which is principal and 10 cents of which is interest. Looked at from the other side of the transaction, the interest rate on dollars is also the amount that must be paid to borrow $1 for a year. When you buy a U.S. government bond, you earn the interest rate on dollars because you are lending dollars to the U.S. government.

Interest rates play an important role in the foreign-exchange market because the large deposits traded there pay interest, each at a rate reflecting its currency of denomination. For example, when the interest rate on dollars is 10 percent per year, a $100,000 deposit is worth $110,000 after a year; when the interest rate on DM is 5 percent per year, a DM100,000 deposit is worth DM105,000 after a year. Deposits pay interest because they are really

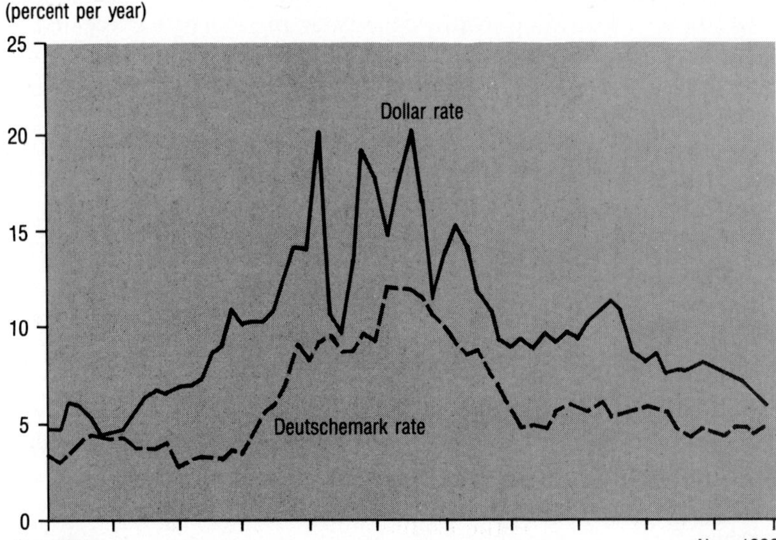

FIGURE 13-2 Interest rates on dollar and Deutschemark deposits, 1976–1986. Rates shown are one-month Euro-deposit rates, at end of month.
Source: Morgan Guaranty Trust Company of New York, *World Financial Markets.*

loans from the depositor to the bank. When a corporation or a financial institution deposits a currency in a bank, it is lending that currency to the bank rather than using it for some current expenditure. In other words, the depositor is acquiring an asset denominated in the currency it deposits.

The dollar interest rate is simply the dollar rate of return on dollar deposits. You "buy" the deposit by lending a bank $100,000, and when you are paid back with 10 percent interest at the end of the year, your asset is worth $110,000. This gives a rate of return of (110,000 − 100,000)/100,000 = 0.10, or 10 percent per year. Similarly, a foreign currency's interest rate measures the foreign-currency return on deposits of that currency. Figure 13-2 shows the behavior of the interest rates on dollars and DM since 1976.[5]

EXCHANGE RATES AND ASSET RETURNS

The interest rates offered by a dollar and a DM deposit tell us how their dollar and DM values will change over a year. The other piece of information we need to compare the real rates of return offered by dollar and DM deposits is the expected change in the dollar/DM exchange rate over the year.

[5]Chapter 7 discussed *real* interest rates, which are simply real rates of return on loans, that is, interest rates expressed in terms of a consumption basket. Interest rates expressed in terms of currencies are called *nominal* interest rates. The connection between real and nominal interest rates is discussed in detail in Chapter 14.

An example will show how exchange rates are used together with interest rates to calculate comparable rates of return. Suppose that the dollar interest rate is 10 percent per year while the DM interest rate is 5 percent per year. This means that a deposit of a dollar pays $1.10 after a year while a deposit of a Deutschemark pays DM1.05 after a year. To see which of these deposits offers a higher rate of return, you must ask the question: If I use dollars to buy a DM deposit, how many dollars will I get back after a year? When you answer this question, you are calculating the dollar rate of return on a DM deposit because you are comparing its dollar price today with its dollar value a year from today.

The answer can be found in three steps. First, use today's dollar/DM exchange rate to figure out the dollar price of a DM deposit of, say, DM1. Second, use the DM interest rate to find the amount of DM you will have a year from now if you purchase a DM1 deposit today. Third, use the exchange rate you expect to prevail a year from today to calculate the dollar value of those DM.

1. Step 1 is easy. If the exchange rate today is $0.350 per DM, the dollar price of a DM1 deposit is just $0.350.
2. Step 2 is also easy. You know that the interest rate on DM deposits is 5 percent per year. So at the end of a year your DM1 deposit is worth DM1.05.
3. Step 3 is a bit harder because you do not actually know what the exchange rate will be a year from now. If you expect the dollar to depreciate against the DM over the coming year so that the exchange rate 12 months from today is $0.380 per DM, then you'd expect the dollar value of your DM deposit to be ($0.380 per DM) × (DM1.05) = $0.399 after a year.

Now that you know the dollar price of a DM1 deposit today ($0.350) and can forecast its value in a year ($0.399), you can calculate the expected *dollar* rate of return on a DM deposit as (0.399 − 0.350)/0.350 = 0.14, or 14 percent per year. Since the dollar rate of return on dollar deposits is only 10 percent per year, you would expect to do better by holding your wealth in the form of DM deposits.

A SIMPLE RULE

There is a simple rule that shortens this calculation. First, define the **rate of depreciation** of the dollar against the DM as the percentage increase in the dollar/DM exchange rate over a year. In the example, the dollar's expected depreciation rate is (0.380 − 0.350)/0.350 = 0.086, or roughly 9 percent per year. Once you have calculated the rate of depreciation of the dollar against the DM, our rule is this: *The dollar rate of return on DM deposits is approximately the DM interest rate plus the rate of depreciation of the dollar against the DM.* In other words, to translate the DM return on DM deposits into dollar terms, you need to add the rate at which the DM's dollar price rises over a year to the DM interest rate.

In our example, the sum of the DM interest rate (5 percent) and the expected depreciation rate of the dollar (roughly 9 percent) is about 14 percent, which is what we found the expected dollar return on DM deposits to be in our first calculation.

We summarize our discussion by introducing some notation:

R_{DM} = today's interest rate on DM deposits,

$E_{\$/DM}$ = today's price of DM in terms of dollars (number of dollars per DM),

$E^e_{\$/DM}$ = dollar/DM exchange rate (number of dollars per DM) expected to prevail a year from today.

(The superscript e attached to this last exchange rate indicates that it is a forecast of the future exchange rate based on what people know today.)

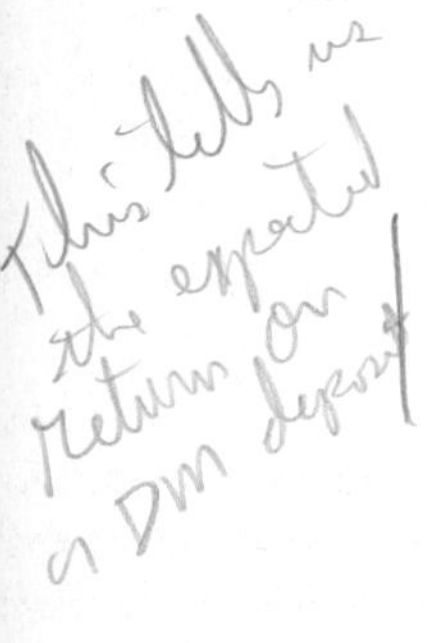

Using these symbols, we write the expected rate of return on a DM deposit, measured in terms of dollars, as the sum of (1) the DM interest rate and (2) the expected rate of dollar depreciation against the DM,

$$R_{DM} + (E^e_{\$/DM} - E_{\$/DM})/E_{\$/DM}.$$

This expected return is what must be compared with the dollar interest rate $R_\$$ in deciding whether dollar or DM deposits offer the higher expected *real* rate of return.[6] The expected real rate of return difference between dollar and DM deposits is therefore equal to $R_\$$ less the above expression,

$$R_\$ - [R_{DM} + (E^e_{\$/DM} - E_{\$/DM})/E_{\$/DM}] = R_\$ - R_{DM} - (E^e_{\$/DM} - E_{\$/DM})/E_{\$/DM}. \quad \textbf{(13-1)}$$

When the difference above is positive, dollar deposits yield the higher expected real rate of return, and when it is negative, DM deposits yield the higher expected real rate of return.

Table 13-3 carries out some illustrative comparisons. In case 1, the interest difference in favor of dollar deposits is 4 percent per year ($R_\$ - R_{DM} = 0.10 - 0.06 = 0.04$), and no change in the exchange rate is expected [$(E^e_{\$/DM} - E_{\$/DM})/E_{\$/DM} = 0.00$]. This means that the expected annual real rate of return on dollar deposits is 4 percent higher than that on DM, so that, all else equal, you would prefer to hold your wealth as dollar rather than DM

[6]If you compute the expected dollar return on DM deposits using the exact three-step method we described before introducing the simple rule, you'll find that it actually equals

$$(1 + R_{DM})(E^e_{\$/DM}/E_{\$/DM}) - 1.$$

This exact formula can be rewritten, however, as

$$R_{DM} + (E^e_{\$/DM} - E_{\$/DM})/E_{\$/DM} + R_{DM} \times (E^e_{\$/DM} - E_{\$/DM})/E_{\$/DM}.$$

This formula is very close to the formula derived from the simple rule when, as is usually the case, the product $R_{DM} \times (E^e_{\$/DM} - E_{\$/DM})/E_{\$/DM}$ is a small number.

TABLE 13-3 Comparing dollar rates of return on dollar and DM deposits

Case	Dollar interest rate $R_\$$	DM interest rate R_{DM}	Expected rate of dollar depreciation against DM $\frac{E^e_{\$/DM} - E_{\$/DM}}{E_{\$/DM}}$	Rate of return difference between dollar and DM deposits $R_\$ - R_{DM} - \frac{(E^e_{\$/DM} - E_{\$/DM})}{E_{\$/DM}}$
1	0.10	0.06	0.00	0.04
2	0.10	0.06	0.04	0.00
3	0.10	0.06	0.08	−0.04
4	0.10	0.12	−0.04	0.02

deposits. In case 2 the interest difference is the same (4 percent), but it is just offset by an expected depreciation rate of the dollar of 4 percent. The two assets therefore have the same expected rate of return.

Case 3 is similar to the one discussed earlier: a 4 percent interest difference in favor of dollar deposits is more than offset by an 8 percent expected depreciation of the dollar; so DM deposits are preferred by market participants. In case 4, there is a 2 percent interest difference in favor of DM deposits, but the dollar is expected to *appreciate* against the DM by 4 percent over the year. The expected real rate of return on dollar deposits is therefore 2 percent per year higher than that on DM.

So far we have been translating all returns into dollar terms. But the rate of return differentials we calculated would have been the same had we chosen to express returns in terms of DM or in terms of some third currency. Suppose, for example, we had wanted to measure the return on dollar deposits in terms of DM. Following our simple rule, we would add to the dollar interest rate $R_\$$ the expected rate of depreciation of the DM against the dollar. But the expected rate of depreciation of the DM against the dollar is approximately the expected **rate of appreciation** of the dollar against the DM, that is, the expected rate of depreciation of the dollar against the DM with a minus sign in front of it. This means that in terms of DM, the return on a dollar deposit is

$$R_\$ - (E^e_{\$/DM} - E_{\$/DM})/E_{\$/DM}.$$

The difference between the expression above and R_{DM} is identical to (13-1). Thus, it makes no difference to our comparison whether we measure returns in dollar terms or in DM terms, so long as we measure them in terms of a single currency.

RETURN, RISK, AND LIQUIDITY IN THE FOREIGN-EXCHANGE MARKET

We observed earlier that a saver deciding which assets to hold may care about assets' riskiness and liquidity in addition to their expected real rates of return. Similarly, the demand for foreign-currency assets depends not only on returns but on risk and liquidity. Even if the expected dollar return on DM deposits is higher than that on dollar deposits, for example, people may be reluctant to hold DM deposits if the payoff to holding them varies erratically.

There is no consensus among economists about the importance of risk in the foreign-exchange market. Even the definition of "foreign-exchange risk" is a topic of debate. For now we will avoid the complex questions involved by assuming that the real returns on all deposits have equal riskiness, regardless of the currency of denomination. In other words, we are assuming that risk differences do not influence the demand for foreign-currency assets. We discuss the role of foreign-exchange risk in greater detail, however, in Chapters 17 and 21.[7]

Some market participants may be influenced by liquidity factors in deciding which currencies to hold. Most of these participants are firms and individuals involved in international trade. An American importer of French goods, for example, may find it convenient to hold French francs for routine payments even if the expected rate of return on francs is lower than that on dollars. Because payments connected with international trade make up a very small fraction of total foreign-exchange transactions, we ignore the liquidity motive for holding foreign currencies.

We are therefore assuming for now that participants in the foreign-exchange market base their demands for foreign-currency assets exclusively on a comparison of those assets' expected rates of return. The main reason for making this assumption is that is simplifies our analysis of how exchange rates are determined in the foreign-exchange market. In addition, the risk and liquidity motives for holding foreign currencies appear to be of secondary importance for many of the international macroeconomic issues discussed in the next few chapters.

EQUILIBRIUM IN THE FOREIGN-EXCHANGE MARKET

We now use what we have learned about the demand for foreign-currency assets to describe how exchange rates are determined. We will show that the exchange rate at which the market settles is the one that makes market participants content to hold existing supplies of deposits of all currencies. When

[7]In discussing spot and forward foreign-exchange transactions, some textbooks make a distinction between foreign-exchange "speculators"—market participants who allegedly care only about expected returns—and "hedgers"—market participants whose concern is to avoid risk. We depart from this textbook tradition because it can mislead the unwary: while the speculative and hedging motives are both potentially important in exchange-rate determination, the same person can be both a speculator and a hedger if she cares about both return and risk. Our assumption that risk is unimportant in determining the demand for foreign-currency assets means, in terms of the traditional language, that the speculative motive for holding foreign currencies is far more important than the hedging motive.

market participants willingly hold the existing supplies of deposits of all currencies, we say that the foreign-exchange market is in equilibrium.

The description of exchange-rate determination given in this section is only a first step: a full explanation of the exchange rate's current level can be given only after we examine how participants in the foreign-exchange market form their expectations about exchange rates they expect to prevail in the future. The next two chapters explain how expectations of future exchange rates are determined. For now, however, we will be taking expected future exchange rates as given.

INTEREST PARITY: THE BASIC EQUILIBRIUM CONDITION

The foreign-exchange market is in equilibrium when the expected returns on deposits of all currencies are the same. The condition that the expected returns on deposits of any two currencies must be equal when expressed in the same currency is called the **interest parity condition.** It implies that potential holders of foreign-currency deposits view them all as equally desirable assets.

Let's see why the foreign-exchange market is in equilibrium only when the interest parity condition holds. Suppose that the dollar interest rate is 10 percent and the DM interest rate is 6 percent, but that the dollar is expected to depreciate against the DM at an 8 percent rate over a year. (This is case 3 in Table 13-3.) In the circumstances described, the rate of return on DM deposits would be 4 percent per year higher than that on dollar deposits. We assumed at the end of the last section that individuals always prefer to hold deposits of currencies offering the highest expected return. This means that if the expected return on DM deposits is 4 percent greater than that on dollar deposits, no one will be willing to continue holding dollar deposits, and holders of dollar deposits will be trying to sell them for DM deposits. There will therefore be an excess supply of dollar deposits and an excess demand for DM deposits in the foreign-exchange market.

As a contrasting example, suppose that dollar deposits again offer a 10 percent interest rate but that DM deposits offer a 12 percent rate and that the dollar is expected to *appreciate* against the DM by 4 percent over the coming year. (This is case 4 in Table 13-3.) Now the return on dollar deposits is 2 percent higher. In this case no one would demand DM deposits; so these would be in excess supply and dollar deposits would be in excess demand.

When, however, the dollar interest rate is 10 percent, the DM interest rate is 6 percent, and the dollar's expected depreciation rate against the DM is 4 percent, dollar and DM deposits offer the same rates of return and participants in the foreign-exchange market are willing to hold either. (This is case 2 in Table 13-3.)

Only when all expected rates of return are equal—that is, when the interest parity condition holds—is there no excess supply of some type of deposit and no excess demand for another. The foreign-exchange market is in equilibrium when no type of deposit is in excess demand or excess supply.

We can therefore say that the foreign-exchange market is in equilibrium when the interest parity condition holds.

To express interest parity between dollar and DM deposits symbolically, we can use expression (13-1), which shows the difference between these two assets' expected rates of return. The two expected rates of return are equal when

$$R_{\$} = R_{DM} + (E^{e}_{\$/DM} - E_{\$/DM})/E_{\$/DM}. \tag{13-2}$$

HOW CHANGES IN THE CURRENT EXCHANGE RATE AFFECT EXPECTED RETURNS

As a first step in understanding how the foreign-exchange market finds its equilibrium, we must see how changes in today's exchange rate affect the expected return on a foreign-currency deposit when interest rates and expectations about the future exchange rate do not change.

It is easiest to begin with an example, in which we ask how a change in today's dollar/DM exchange rate, all else held constant, changes the expected return on DM deposits measured in terms of dollars. Suppose that today's dollar/DM rate is \$0.365 per DM and that the exchange rate you expect for this day next year is \$0.383 per DM. Then the expected rate of dollar depreciation against the DM is $(0.383 - 0.365)/0.365 = 0.05$, or 5 percent per year. This means that when you buy a DM deposit, you not only earn the interest R_{DM} but also get a 5 percent "bonus" in terms of dollars. Now suppose that today's exchange rate suddenly jumps up to \$0.370 per DM (a depreciation of the dollar and an appreciation of the DM) but that the expected future rate is still \$0.383 per DM. What has happened to the "bonus" you expected to get from the DM's increase in value in terms of dollars? The expected rate of dollar depreciation is now only $(0.383 - 0.370)/0.370 = 0.035$, or 3.5 percent instead of 5 percent. Since R_{DM} has not changed, the dollar return on DM deposits, which is the sum of R_{DM} and the expected rate of dollar depreciation, has *fallen* by 1.5 percent per year (= 5 percent − 3.5 percent).

In Table 13-4 we work out the dollar return on DM deposits for various levels of today's dollar/DM exchange rate $E_{\$/DM}$, always assuming that the expected *future* exchange rate remains fixed at \$0.383 per DM and that the DM interest rate is 5 percent per year. As you can see, a rise in today's dollar/DM exchange rate (a depreciation of the dollar against the DM) always *lowers* the expected dollar return on DM deposits (as in our example), while a fall in today's dollar/DM rate (an appreciation of the dollar against the DM) always *raises* this return.

It may run counter to your intuition that a depreciation of the dollar against the DM makes DM deposits less attractive relative to dollar deposits (by lowering the expected dollar return on DM deposits) while an appreciation of the dollar makes DM deposits more attractive. This result will seem less surprising if you remember that we have assumed that the expected future dollar/DM rate and interest rates do not change. A dollar depreciation

TABLE 13-4 Today's dollar/DM exchange rate and the expected dollar return on DM deposits when $E^e_{\$/DM}$ = \$0.383 per DM

Today's dollar/DM exchange rate $E_{\$/DM}$	Interest rate on DM Deposits R_{DM}	Expected dollar depreciation rate against DM $\frac{0.383 - E_{\$/DM}}{E_{\$/DM}}$	Dollar return on DM deposits $R_{DM} + \frac{0.383 - E_{\$/DM}}{E_{\$/DM}}$
0.395	0.05	−0.03	0.02
0.383	0.05	0.00	0.05
0.375	0.05	0.02	0.07
0.370	0.05	0.035	0.085
0.365	0.05	0.05	0.10

today, for example, means that the dollar now needs to depreciate by a *smaller* amount to reach any expected future level. If the expected future dollar/DM exchange rate does not change when the dollar depreciates today, the dollar's expected future depreciation against the DM therefore falls, or, alternatively, the dollar's expected future appreciation rises. With interest rates also unchanged, today's dollar depreciation thus makes DM deposits less attractive compared with dollar deposits.

Put another way, a current dollar depreciation that affects neither exchange-rate expectations nor interest rates leaves the expected future dollar payoff of a DM deposit the same but raises the deposit's current dollar cost. This change naturally makes DM deposits less attractive relative to dollars.

Figure 13-3 shows the calculations in Table 13-4 in a graphical form that will be helpful in our analysis of exchange-rate determination. The vertical axis in the figure measures today's dollar/DM exchange rate and the horizontal axis measures the expected dollar return on DM deposits. For fixed values of the expected future dollar/DM exchange rate and the DM interest rate, the relation between today's dollar/DM exchange rate and the expected dollar return on DM deposits defines a downward-sloping schedule.

THE EQUILIBRIUM EXCHANGE RATE

Now that we understand why the interest parity condition must hold if the foreign-exchange market is in equilibrium and how today's exchange rate affects the expected return on foreign-currency deposits, we can see how equilibrium exchange rates are determined. Our main conclusion will be that exchange rates always adjust to maintain interest parity.

Figure 13-4 illustrates how the equilibrium dollar/DM exchange rate is determined for *given* values of the dollar interest rate $R_\$$, the DM interest

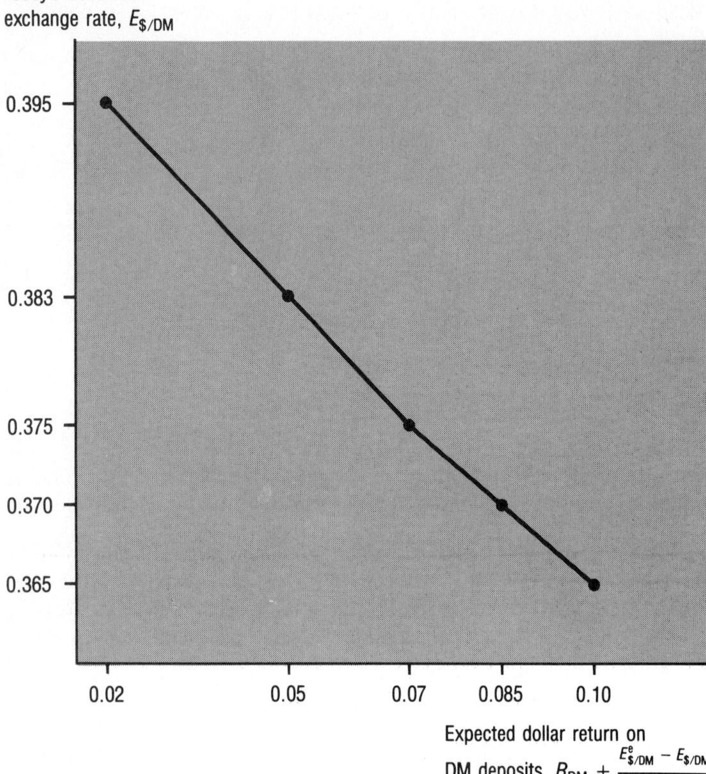

FIGURE 13-3 How changes in the dollar/DM exchange rate affect the dollar return on DM deposits, given $E^e_{\$/DM} = 0.383$ and $R_{DM} = .05$. An appreciation of the dollar against the DM raises the expected return on DM deposits, measured in terms of dollars.

rate R_{DM}, and the expected future dollar/DM exchange rate $E^e_{\$/DM}$. The vertical schedule in the graph indicates the given level of $R_\$$, the return on dollar deposits measured in terms of dollars. The downward-sloping schedule shows how the expected return on DM deposits measured in terms of dollars depends on the current dollar/DM exchange rate. This second schedule is derived in the same way as the one shown in Figure 13-3.

The equilibrium dollar/DM rate is the one indicated by the intersection of the two schedules at point 1, $E^1_{\$/DM}$. At this exchange rate, the returns on dollar and DM assets are equal, so that the interest parity condition (13-2),

$$R_\$ = R_{DM} + (E^e_{\$/DM} - E_{\$/DM})/E_{\$/DM},$$

is satisfied.

Let's see why the exchange rate will tend to settle at point 1 in Figure 13-4 if it is initially at a point like 2 or 3. Suppose first that we are at point 2, with the exchange rate equal to $E^2_{\$/DM}$. The downward-sloping schedule measuring the expected dollar return on DM deposits tells us that at the exchange rate $E^2_{\$/DM}$, the rate of return on DM deposits is less than the rate of

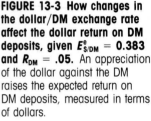

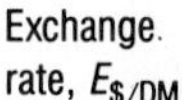
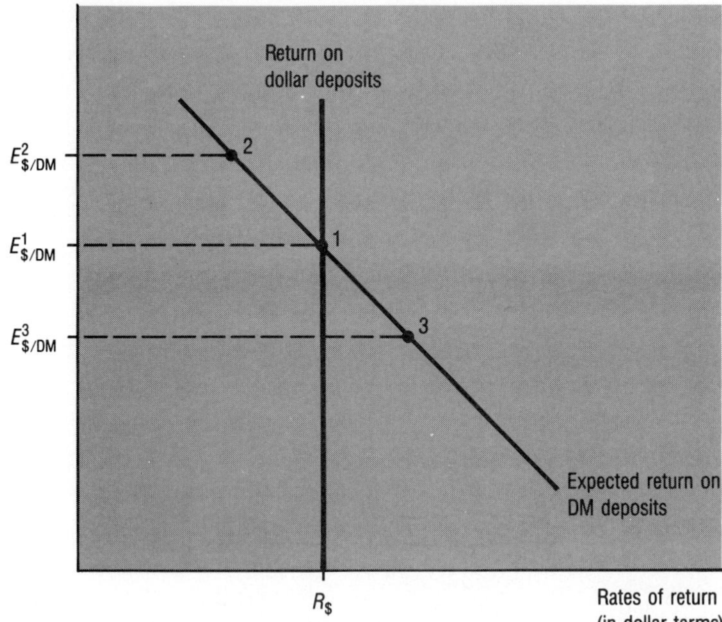

FIGURE 13-4 Determination of the equilibrium dollar/DM exchange rate. Equilibrium in the foreign exchange market is at point 1, where the expected dollar returns on dollar and DM deposits are equal.

return on dollar deposits, $R_\$$. In this situation anyone holding DM deposits wishes to sell them for the more lucrative dollar deposits: the foreign-exchange market is out of equilibrium because participants are *unwilling* to hold DM deposits.

How does the exchange rate adjust? The unhappy owners of DM deposits attempt to sell them for dollar deposits, but because the return on dollar deposits is higher than that on DM deposits at the exchange rate $E^2_{\$/DM}$, no holder of a dollar deposit is willing to sell it for DM at that rate. As DM holders try to entice dollar holders to trade by offering them a better price for dollars, the dollar/DM exchange rate falls toward $E^1_{\$/DM}$; that is, DM become cheaper in terms of dollars. Once the exchange rate reaches $E^1_{\$/DM}$, DM and dollar deposits offer equal returns and holders of DM deposits no longer have an incentive to try to sell them for dollars. The foreign-exchange market is therefore in equilibrium. In falling from $E^2_{\$/DM}$ to $E^1_{\$/DM}$, the exchange rate equalizes the expected returns on the two types of deposit by increasing the rate at which the dollar is expected to depreciate in the future, therefore making DM deposits more attractive.

The same process works in reverse if we are initially at point 3 with an exchange rate of $E^3_{\$/DM}$. At point 3, the return on DM deposits exceeds that on dollar deposits; so there is now an excess supply of the latter. As unwilling holders of dollar deposits bid for the more attractive DM deposits, the price of DM in terms of dollars tends to rise; that is, the dollar tends to depreciate against the DM. When the exchange rate has moved to $E^1_{\$/DM}$, rates of return are equalized across currencies and the market is in equilibrium. The depreciation of the dollar from $E^3_{\$/DM}$ to $E^1_{\$/DM}$ makes DM deposits less attractive relative to dollar deposits by reducing the rate at which the dollar is expected to depreciate in the future.[8]

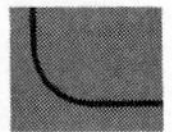

INTEREST RATES, EXPECTATIONS, AND EQUILIBRIUM

Having seen how exchange rates are determined, we now take a look at how current exchange rates are affected by changes in interest rates and in expectations about the future. In our discussion we will see that the exchange rate (which is the relative price of two assets) responds to factors that alter the expected rates of return on those two assets.

THE EFFECT OF CHANGING INTEREST RATES ON THE CURRENT EXCHANGE RATE

We often read in the newspaper that the dollar is strong because U.S. interest rates are high or that it is falling because U.S. interest rates are falling. Can these statements be explained using our analysis of the foreign-exchange market?

To answer this question we again turn to our diagram. Figure 13-5 shows a rise in the interest rate on dollars, from $R^1_\$$ to $R^2_\$$, as a rightward shift of the vertical schedule. At the initial exchange rate $E^1_{\$/DM}$, the expected return on dollar deposits is now higher than that on DM deposits by an amount equal to the distance between points 1 and 1′. As we have seen, this difference causes the dollar to appreciate to $E^2_{\$/DM}$ (point 2). Because there has been no change in the DM interest rate or in the expected future exchange rate, the dollar's appreciation today raises the expected dollar return on DM deposits by increasing the rate at which the dollar is expected to depreciate in the future.

Figure 13-6 shows the effect of a rise in the DM interest rate R_{DM}. This change causes the downward-sloping schedule (which measures the expected dollar return on DM deposits) to shift rightward. (To see why, ask yourself how a rise in the DM interest rate alters the dollar return on DM deposits, given the current exchange rate and the expected future rate.)

At the initial exchange rate $E^1_{\$/DM}$ the expected depreciation rate of the dollar is the same as before the rise in R_{DM}; so the expected return on DM deposits now exceeds that on dollar deposits. The dollar/DM exchange rate rises (from $E^1_{\$/DM}$ to $E^2_{\$/DM}$) in order to eliminate the excess supply of dollar as-

[8] We could have developed our diagram from the perspective of Germany, with the DM/dollar exchange rate $E_{DM/\$}$ ($= 1/E_{\$/DM}$) on the vertical axis, a schedule vertical at R_{DM} to indicate the DM return on DM deposits, and a downward-sloping schedule showing how the DM return on dollar deposits varies with $E_{DM/\$}$. An exercise at the end of the chapter asks you to show that this alternative way of looking at equilibrium in the foreign-exchange market gives the same answers as the method used in the text.

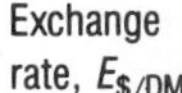

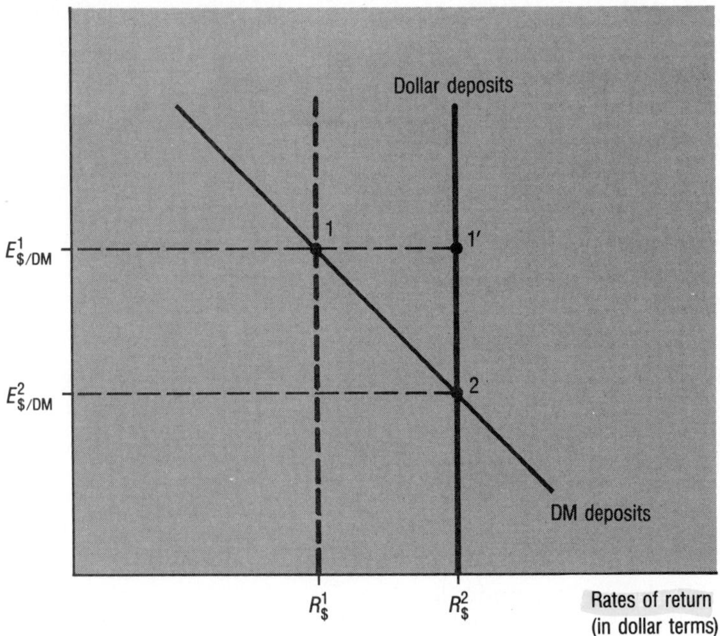

FIGURE 13-5 Effect of a rise in the dollar interest rate. A rise in the interest rate offered by dollar deposits causes the dollar to appreciate from $E^1_{\$/DM}$ (point 1) to $E^2_{\$/DM}$ (point 2).

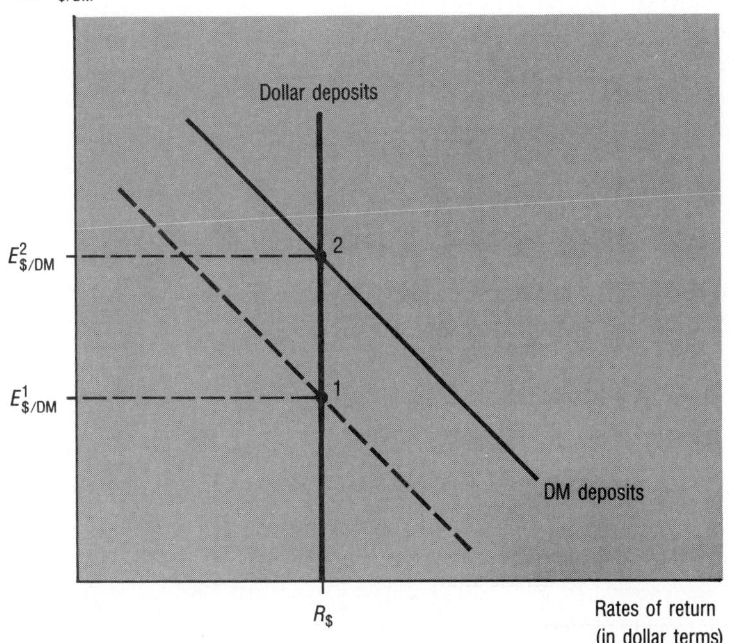

FIGURE 13-6 Effect of a rise in the DM interest rate. A rise in the interest rate paid by DM deposits causes the dollar to depreciate from $E^1_{\$/DM}$ (point 1) to $E^2_{\$/DM}$ (point 2). (This figure also describes the effect of a rise in the expected future \$/DM exchange rate.)

sets at point 1. As before, the dollar's depreciation against the DM eliminates the excess supply of dollar assets by lowering the expected dollar rate of return on DM deposits. A rise in German interest rates therefore leads to a depreciation of the dollar against the DM or, looked at from the German perspective, an appreciation of the DM against the dollar.

Our discussion shows that, all else equal, *an increase in the interest paid on deposits of a currency causes that currency to appreciate against foreign currencies.*

Before we conclude that the newspaper account of the effect of interest rates on exchange rates is correct, we must be aware that our assumption of a *constant* expected future exchange rate is very unrealistic. In most cases a change in interest rates will be accompanied by a change in the expected future exchange rate. This change in the expected future exchange rate will depend, in turn, on the economic causes of the interest-rate change. We discuss the connection between interest rates and expected future exchange rates in Chapter 14. Keep in mind for now that in the real world, we cannot predict how a given interest-rate change will alter exchange rates unless we know *why* the interest rate is changing.

THE EFFECT OF CHANGING EXPECTATIONS ON THE CURRENT EXCHANGE RATE

Figure 13-6 may also be used to study the effect on today's exchange rate of a rise in the expected future dollar/DM exchange rate, $E^e_{\$/DM}$.

Given today's exchange rate, a rise in the expected future price of DM in terms of dollars raises the dollar's expected depreciation rate. For example, if today's exchange rate is \$0.365 per DM and the rate expected to prevail in a year is \$0.383 per DM, the expected depreciation rate of the dollar against the DM is $(0.383 - 0.365)/0.365 = 0.05$; if the expected future exchange rate now rises to \$0.387 per DM, the expected depreciation rate rises too, to $(0.387 - 0.365)/0.365 = 0.06$.

Because a rise in the expected depreciation rate of the dollar raises the expected dollar return on DM deposits, the downward-sloping schedule shifts to the right, as in Figure 13-6. At the initial exchange rate $E^1_{\$/DM}$ there is now an excess supply of dollar deposits. The dollar therefore depreciates against the DM until equilibrium is reached at point 2.

We conclude that, all else equal, *a rise in the expected future exchange rate causes a rise in the current exchange rate. Similarly, a fall in the expected future exchange rate causes a fall in the current exchange rate.*

SUMMARY

1. An *exchange rate* is the price of one country's currency in terms of another country's currency. Exchange rates play a role in spending decisions because they enable us to translate different countries' prices into comparable terms. All else equal, a *depreciation* of a country's currency against foreign currencies makes its exports cheaper and its imports more expensive; and an *appreciation* of its currency makes its exports more expensive and its imports cheaper.

2. Exchange rates are determined in the *foreign-exchange market.* The major participants in that market are commercial banks, international corporations, nonbank financial institutions, and national central banks. Commercial banks play a pivotal role in the market because they facilitate the exchanges of interest-bearing bank deposits that make up the bulk of foreign-exchange trading. Even though foreign-exchange trading takes place in many financial centers around the world, modern telecommunication technology links those centers together into a single market that is open 24 hours a day. One important category of foreign-exchange trading is *forward* trading, in which parties agree to exchange currencies on some future date at a prenegotiated exchange rate.

3. Because the exchange rate is the relative price of two assets, it is most appropriately thought of as being an asset price itself. The basic principle of asset pricing is that an asset's current value depends on its expected future purchasing power. In evaluating different assets, savers look at the expected *rates of return* they offer, that is, the rates at which their values are expected to rise over time. It is possible to measure an asset's expected rate of return in different ways, each depending on the units in which the asset's value is measured. Savers care about an asset's expected *real rate of return,* the rate at which its value is expected to rise when expressed in terms of a representative basket of consumption goods.

4. When relative asset returns are relevant, as in the foreign-exchange market, it is appropriate to compare expected changes in assets' currency values provided those values are expressed in the same currency. If *risk* and *liquidity* factors do not strongly influence the demands for foreign-currency assets, participants in the foreign-exchange market always prefer to hold those assets yielding the highest expected rate of return.

5. The returns on deposits traded in the foreign-exchange market depend on *interest rates* and expected exchange-rate changes. To compare the expected rates of return offered by dollar and DM deposits, for example, the return on DM deposits must be expressed in dollar terms by adding to the DM interest rate the expected *rate of depreciation* of the dollar against the DM (or *rate of appreciation* of the DM against the dollar) over the deposit's holding period.

6. Equilibrium in the foreign-exchange market requires *interest parity;* that is, deposits of all currencies must offer the same expected rate of return when returns are measured in comparable terms.

7. For given interest rates and a given expectation of the future exchange rate, the interest parity condition tells us the current equilibrium exchange rate. When the expected return on DM deposits exceeds that on dollar deposits, for example, the dollar immediately depreciates against the DM. Other things equal, a dollar depreciation today reduces the expected return on DM deposits by reducing the depreciation rate of the dollar against the DM expected for the future. Similarly, when the expected return on DM deposits is below that on dollar deposits, the dollar must immediately appreci-

ate against the DM. Other things equal, a current appreciation of the dollar makes DM deposits more attractive by increasing the dollar's expected future depreciation against the German currency.

8. All else equal, a rise in dollar interest rates causes the dollar to appreciate against the DM while a rise in DM interest rates causes the dollar to depreciate against the DM. Today's exchange rate is also altered by changes in its expected future level. If there is a rise in the expected future level of the dollar/DM rate, for example, then at unchanged interest rates, today's dollar/DM rate will also rise.

KEY TERMS

exchange rate
depreciation
appreciation
foreign-exchange market
interbank trading
arbitrage
vehicle currency
spot exchange rate
forward exchange rate
rate of return
real rate of return
risk
liquidity
interest rate
rate of depreciation
rate of appreciation
interest parity condition

PROBLEMS

1. In Munich a bratwurst costs 2 DM; a hot dog costs $1 at Boston's Fenway Park. At an exchange rate of $0.5 per DM, what is the price of a bratwurst in terms of hot dogs? All else equal, how does this relative price change if the dollar appreciates to $0.4 per DM? Compared with the initial situation, has a hot dog become more or less expensive relative to a bratwurst?

2. A U.S. dollar costs 8 French francs, but the same dollar can be purchased for 2 Swiss francs. What is the French franc/Swiss franc exchange rate?

3. Calculate the dollar rates of return on the following assets:

a) A painting whose price rises from $200,000 to $250,000 in a year.

b) A bottle of a rare Burgundy wine, Domaine de la Romanée-Conti 1978, whose price rises from $180 to $216 between 1985 and 1986.

c) A £10,000 deposit in a London bank in a year when the interest rate on pounds is 10 percent and the $/£ exchange rate moves from $1.50 per pound to $1.38 per pound.

4. What would be the real rates of return on the assets in the preceding question if the price changes described were accompanied by a simultaneous 10 percent increase in all dollar prices?

5. Suppose that the dollar interest rate is 5 percent per year and that the pound sterling interest rate is the same, 5 percent per year. What is the relation between the current equilibrium \$/£ exchange rate and its expected future level? Suppose that the expected future \$/£ exchange rate, \$1.52 per pound, remains constant as Britain's interest rate rises to 10 percent per year. If the U.S. interest rate also remains constant, what is the new equilibrium \$/£ exchange rate?

6. Traders in asset markets suddenly learn that the interest rate on dollars will decline in the near future. Use the diagrammatic analysis of the chapter to determine the effect on the *current* dollar/DM exchange rate, assuming that current interest rates on dollar and DM deposits do not change.

7. We noted that we could have developed our diagrammatic analysis of foreign-exchange market equilibrium from the perspective of Germany, with the DM/dollar exchange rate $E_{DM/\$}$ ($= 1/E_{\$/DM}$) on the vertical axis, a schedule vertical at R_{DM} to indicate the DM return on DM deposits, and a downward-sloping schedule showing how the DM return on dollar deposits varies with $E_{DM/\$}$. Derive this alternative picture of equilibrium, and use it to examine the effect of changes in interest rates and the expected future exchange rate. Do your answers agree with those we found earlier?

8. Suppose that the dollar exchange rates of the DM and the pound are equally variable. The DM, however, tends to depreciate unexpectedly against the dollar when the return on the rest of your wealth is unexpectedly high, while the pound tends to appreciate unexpectedly in the same circumstances. Which currency, the DM or the pound, would you consider to be riskier?

9. In October 1979, the U.S. central bank (the Federal Reserve System) announced that it would play a less active role in limiting fluctuations in dollar interest rates. After this new policy was put into effect, the dollar's exchange rates against foreign currencies became more volatile. Does our analysis of the foreign-exchange market suggest any connection between these two events?

10. Imagine that everyone in the world pays a tax of τ percent on interest earnings and on any capital gains due to exchange-rate changes. How would such a tax alter the analysis of the interest parity condition? How does the answer change if the tax applies to interest earnings but *not* to capital gains, which are untaxed?

11. Suppose that the 1-year forward \$/DM exchange rate is \$0.38 per DM and that the spot exchange rate is \$0.362 per DM. What is the forward premium on DM (the forward discount on dollars)? What is the difference between the interest rate on 1-year dollar deposits and that on 1-year DM deposits (assuming no political risk)?

FURTHER READING

Peter B. Kenen. *The Role of the Dollar as an International Currency,* Occasional Paper 13. New York: Group of Thirty, 1983. Recent evidence on the U.S. dollar's use in international trade and financial transactions.

John Maynard Keynes. *A Tract on Monetary Reform,* Chapter 3. London: Macmillan, 1923. The classic early analysis of the forward-exchange market and covered interest parity.

Paul R. Krugman. "The International Role of the Dollar: Theory and Prospect," in John F. O. Bilson and Richard C. Marston, eds. *Exchange Rate Theory and Practice.* Chicago: University of Chicago Press, 1984, pp. 261–278. Theoretical and empirical analysis of the dollar's position as an "international money."

Roger M. Kubarych. *Foreign Exchange Markets in the United States,* revised edition. New York: Federal Reserve Bank of New York, 1983. A detailed description of the structure and functions of the foreign-exchange market.

Ronald I. McKinnon. *Money in International Exchange: The Convertible Currency System.* New York: Oxford University Press, 1979. Theoretical and institutional analysis of the place of the foreign-exchange market in international monetary relations.

Michael Mussa. "Empirical Regularities in the Behavior of Exchange Rates and Theories of the Foreign Exchange Market," in Karl Brunner and Allan H. Meltzer, eds. *Policies for Employment, Prices and Exchange Rates,* Carnegie-Rochester Conference Series on Public Policy 11. Amsterdam: North-Holland, 1979, pp. 9–57. Examines the empirical basis of the asset-price approach to exchange-rate determination.

APPENDIX TO CHAPTER 13

Forward Exchange Rates and Covered Interest Parity

This appendix explains how forward exchange rates are determined. Under the assumption that the interest parity condition always holds, a forward exchange rate equals the spot exchange rate expected to prevail on the forward contract's value date.

As the first step in the discussion, we point out the close connection among the forward exchange rate between two currencies, their spot exchange rate, and the interest rates on deposits denominated in those currencies. The connection is described by the *covered interest parity* condition, which is similar to the (noncovered) interest parity condition defining foreign-exchange market equilibrium but involves the forward exchange rate rather than the expected future spot exchange rate.

To be concrete, we again consider dollar and DM deposits. Suppose that you want to buy a DM deposit with dollars but would like to be *certain* about the number of dollars it will be worth at the end of a year. You can avoid exchange-rate risk by buying a DM deposit and, at the same time, selling the proceeds of your investment forward. When you buy a DM deposit with dollars and at the same time sell the principal and interest forward for dollars, we say that you have "covered" yourself, that is, avoided the possibility of an unexpected depreciation of the DM.

The covered interest parity condition states that the rates of return on dollar deposits and "covered" foreign deposits must be the same. An example will clarify the meaning of the condition and illustrate why it must always hold. Let $F_{\$/DM}$ stand for the 1-year forward price of DM in terms of dollars, and suppose $F_{\$/DM} = \$0.387$ per DM. Assume that at the same time, the spot exchange rate $E_{\$/DM} = \$0.365$ per DM, that $R_{\$} = 0.10$, and that $R_{DM} = 0.05$. The (dollar) rate of return on a dollar deposit is clearly 0.10, or 10 percent per year. What is the rate of return on a covered DM deposit?

We answer this question as in the text. A DM1 deposit costs \$0.365 today, and it is worth DM1.05 after a year. If you sell DM1.05 forward today at the forward exchange rate of \$0.387 per DM, the dollar value of your investment at the end of a year is (\$0.387 per DM) × DM1.05 = \$0.406. The rate of return on a covered purchase of a DM deposit is therefore (0.406 − 0.365)/0.365 = 0.11. This 11 percent per year rate of return exceeds the 10 percent offered by dollar deposits; so covered interest parity does not hold. In this situation, no one would be willing to hold dollar deposits; everyone would prefer covered DM deposits.

More formally, we can express the covered return on a DM deposit as

$$\frac{F_{\$/DM}(1 + R_{DM}) - E_{\$/DM}}{E_{\$/DM}},$$

which is approximately equal to

$$R_{DM} + \frac{F_{\$/DM} - E_{\$/DM}}{E_{\$/DM}},$$

when $F_{\$/DM}$ and $E_{\$/DM}$ do not differ greatly. The covered interest parity condition can therefore be written

$$R_{\$} = R_{DM} + \frac{F_{\$/DM} - E_{\$/DM}}{E_{\$/DM}}.$$

The quantity

$$\frac{F_{\$/DM} - E_{\$/DM}}{E_{\$/DM}}$$

is called the *forward premium* on DM against dollars. (It is also called the *forward discount* on dollars against DM.) Using this terminology, we can state the covered interest parity condition as follows: *The interest rate on dollar deposits equals the interest rate on DM deposits plus the forward premium on DM against dollars (the forward discount on dollars against DM).*

There is strong empirical evidence that the covered interest parity condition holds for different foreign-currency deposits issued within a single financial center. Indeed, currency traders often set the forward exchange rates they quote by looking at current interest rates and spot exchange rates and using the covered interest parity formula.[1] Deviations from covered interest parity can occur, however, when the deposits being compared are located in different countries. These deviations occur when asset holders fear that governments may unexpectedly impose regulations that prevent the free movement of foreign funds across national borders. Our derivation of the covered interest parity condition implicitly assumed that there was no "political risk" of this kind.[2]

By comparing the (noncovered) interest parity condition,

$$R_{\$} = R_{DM} + (E^{e}_{\$/DM} - E_{\$/DM})/E_{\$/DM},$$

with the *covered* interest parity condition, you will find that both conditions can be true at the same time only if the 1-year forward \$/DM rate quoted today equals the spot exchange rate people expect to materialize a year from today:

$$F_{\$/DM} = E^{e}_{\$/DM}.$$

This makes intuitive sense. When two parties agree to trade foreign exchange on a date in the future, the exchange rate they agree on is the spot rate they expect to prevail on that date. The important difference between covered and noncovered transactions should be kept in mind, however. Covered transactions do not involve exchange-rate risk, noncovered transactions do.[3]

[1]Empirical evidence supporting the covered interest parity condition is provided by Frank McCormick in "Covered Interest Arbitrage: Unexploited Profits? Comment," *Journal of Political Economy* 87 (April 1979), pp. 411–417.

[2]For a more detailed discussion of the role of political risk in the forward exchange market, see Robert Z. Aliber, "The Interest Parity Theorem: A Reinterpretation," *Journal of Political Economy* 81 (November/December 1973), pp. 1451–1459. Of course, actual restrictions on cross-border money movements can also cause covered interest parity deviations.

[3]We noted in the text that the (noncovered) interest parity condition, while a useful simplification, may not always hold exactly if the riskiness of currencies influences demands in the foreign-exchange market. Therefore, the forward rate may differ from the expected future spot rate by a risk factor even if *covered* interest parity holds true. As noted earlier, the role of risk in exchange-rate determination is discussed more fully in Chapters 17 and 21.

The theory of covered interest parity helps explain the close correlation between movements in spot and forward exchange rates shown in Figure 13-1, a correlation typical of all major currencies. The unexpected economic events that affect expected asset returns often have a relatively small effect on international interest-rate differences between deposits with short maturities (for example, 3 months). To maintain covered interest parity, therefore, spot and forward rates for the corresponding maturities must change roughly in proportion to each other.

We conclude this appendix with one further application of the covered interest parity condition. To illustrate the role of forward exchange rates, the chapter used the example of an American importer of Japanese radios anxious about the $/¥ exchange rate he would face in 30 days when the time came to pay his supplier. In the example, the importer solved his problem by selling forward for yen enough dollars to cover the cost of the radios. But he could have solved his problem in a different, more complicated way. He could have (1) borrowed dollars from his bank; (2) sold those dollars immediately for yen at the spot exchange rate and placed the yen in a 30-day yen bank deposit; (3) then, after 30 days, used the proceeds of his maturing yen deposit to pay his Japanese supplier; and (4) used the realized proceeds of his U.S. radio sales, less his profits, to repay his original dollar loan.

Which course of action—the forward purchase of yen or the sequence of four transactions described in the preceding paragraph—is more profitable for the importer? We leave it to you, as an exercise, to show that the two strategies yield the same profit when the covered interest parity condition holds.

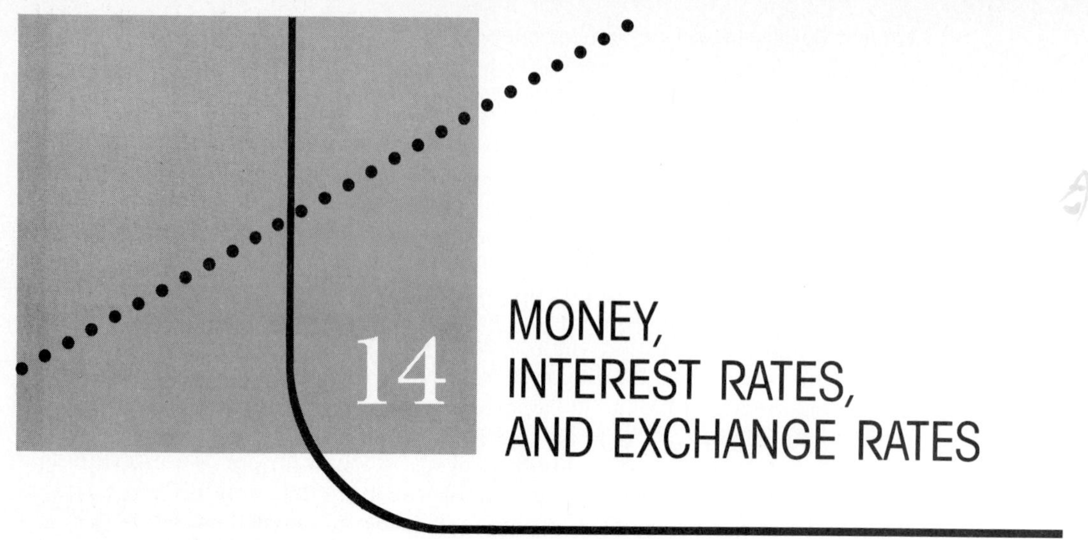

14 MONEY, INTEREST RATES, AND EXCHANGE RATES

Chapter 13 showed how the exchange rate between two currencies depends on two factors, the interest that can be earned on deposits of those currencies and the expected future exchange rate. To fully understand the determination of exchange rates, however, we have to learn how interest rates are determined and how expectations of future exchange rates are formed. In the next three chapters we examine these topics by building an economic model that links exchange rates, interest rates, and other important macroeconomic variables such as the inflation rate and output.

The first step in building the model is to explain the effects of a country's money supply and of the demand for its money on its interest rate and exchange rate. Because exchange rates are the relative prices of national monies, factors that affect a country's money supply or demand are among the most powerful determinants of its currency's exchange rate against foreign currencies. It is therefore natural to begin a deeper study of exchange-rate determination with a discussion of money supply and money demand.

Monetary developments influence the exchange rate *both* by changing interest rates *and* by changing people's expectations about future exchange rates. Expectations about future exchange rates are closely connected with expectations about the future money prices of countries' products; and these price movements, in turn, depend on changes in money supply and demand. In examining monetary influences on the exchange rate, we therefore look at how monetary factors influence output prices along with interest rates. Expectations of future exchange rates depend on many factors other than money, however, and these nonmonetary factors are taken up in the next chapter.

Once the theories and determinants of money supply and demand are laid out, we use them to examine how equilibrium interest rates are determined by the equality of money supply and money demand. Then we combine our model of interest-rate determination with the interest parity condition to study the effects of monetary shifts on the exchange rate, given the prices of goods and services and market expectations about the future. Finally, we look at the effect of monetary changes on output prices and expected future exchange rates.

MONEY DEFINED: A BRIEF REVIEW

We are so accustomed to using money that we seldom notice the roles it plays in almost all of our everyday transactions. As with many other modern conveniences, we take money for granted until something goes wrong with it! In fact, the easiest way to appreciate the importance of money is to imagine what economic life would be like without it.

In this section we do just that. Our purpose in carrying out this "thought experiment" is to distinguish money from other assets and to describe the characteristics of money that induce people to hold it. These characteristics are central to an analysis of the demand for money.

MONEY AS A MEDIUM OF EXCHANGE

The most important function of money is to serve as a *medium of exchange,* a generally accepted means of payment. To see why a medium of exchange is necessary, just imagine how time-consuming it would be for people to purchase goods and services in a world where the only type of trade possible was barter trade—the trade of goods or services for other goods or services.

Money eliminates the enormous search costs connected with a barter system because it is universally acceptable. It eliminates these search costs by enabling an individual to sell the goods and services she produces to people other than the producers of the goods and services she wishes to consume. A complex modern economy would cease functioning without some standardized and convenient means of payment.

MONEY AS A UNIT OF ACCOUNT

Money's second important role is as a *unit of account,* that is, as a widely recognized measure of value. It is in this role that we encountered money in Chapter 13: prices of goods, services, and assets are typically expressed in terms of money; exchange rates allow us to translate different countries' money prices into comparable terms.

The convention of quoting prices in money terms simplifies economic calculations by making it easy to compare the prices of different commodities. The international price comparisons in Chapter 13, which used exchange rates to compare the prices of different countries' outputs, are similar to the calculations you would have to do many times each day if different commodities' prices were not expressed in terms of a standardized unit of account. If the calculations in Chapter 13 gave you a headache, imagine what it would be like to have to calculate the relative prices of each good and service you consume in terms of several other goods and services. This thought experiment should give you a keener appreciation of using money as a unit of account.

MONEY AS A STORE OF VALUE

Because money can be used to transfer purchasing power from the present into the future, it is also an asset, or a *store of value.* This attribute is essential for any medium of exchange because no one would be willing to accept it in payment if its value in terms of goods and services evaporated immediately.

Money's usefulness as a medium of exchange, however, automatically makes it the most *liquid* of all assets. As you will recall from the last chapter, an asset is said to be liquid when it can be transformed into goods and services rapidly and without incurring high transaction costs, such as brokers' fees. Since money is readily acceptable as a means of payment, money sets the standard against which the liquidity of other assets is judged.

WHAT IS MONEY?

Currency and bank deposits on which checks may be written certainly qualify as money. These are widely accepted means of payment that can be transferred between owners at low cost. Households and firms hold currency and checking deposits as a convenient way of financing routine transactions as they arise. Assets such as real estate do not qualify as money because, unlike currency and checking deposits, they lack the essential property of liquidity.

When we speak of the **money supply** in this book, we are referring to the monetary aggregate that the Federal Reserve calls M1, that is, the total amount of currency and checking deposits held by households and firms. In the United States at the end of 1986, the total money supply amounted to \$746 billion.[1]

The large deposits traded by participants in the foreign-exchange market are not considered part of the money supply. These deposits are less liquid than money and are not used to finance routine transactions.

HOW THE MONEY SUPPLY IS DETERMINED

An economy's money supply is controlled by its central bank. The central bank directly regulates the amount of currency in existence and also has indirect control over the amount of checking deposits issued by private banks. The procedures through which the central bank controls the money supply are complex, and we assume for now that the central bank simply sets the size of the money supply at the level it desires. We go into the money supply process in more detail, however, in Chapters 17 and 21.

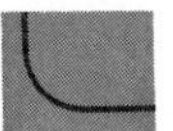

THE DEMAND FOR MONEY BY INDIVIDUALS

Having discussed the role of money and the definition of the money supply, we now examine the factors that determine the amount of money an individual desires to hold. The determinants of individual money demand can be derived from the theory of asset demands discussed in the last chapter.

We saw in the last chapter that individuals base their demand for an asset on three characteristics:

1. The expected return the asset offers compared with the returns offered by other assets.
2. The riskiness of the asset's expected return.
3. The asset's liquidity.

While liquidity plays no important role in determining the demands for the assets traded in the foreign-exchange market, households and firms hold money *only* because of its liquidity. To understand how the households and firms in the economy decide how much money to hold, we must look more closely at how the three considerations listed above influence the demand for money.

[1]A broader Federal Reserve measure of money supply, M2, includes time deposits, but these are less liquid than the assets included in M1 because the funds in them typically cannot be withdrawn early without penalty. An even broader measure, known as M3, is also tracked by the Fed. A decision on where to draw the line between money and near-money must be somewhat arbitrary and therefore controversial. For further discussion of this question, see Frederic S. Mishkin, *The Economics of Money, Banking and Financial Markets*. Boston: Little, Brown and Company, 1986, Chapter 2.

EXPECTED RETURN

Currency and checking deposits pay no interest. When you hold money, you therefore sacrifice the interest you could earn by holding your wealth in a government bond, a large time deposit, or some other relatively illiquid asset.[2] The difference between the rate of return offered by money and that offered by an interest-paying asset is simply the interest paid on money (that is, zero) less the interest rate. Thus, the difference in rates of return between money and less liquid alternative assets is measured by the interest rate: the higher the interest rate, the more you sacrifice by holding wealth in the form of money.

Suppose, for example, that the interest rate you could earn from a U.S. Treasury bill is 10 percent per year. If you use $10,000 of your wealth to buy a Treasury bill, you will be paid $11,000 by Uncle Sam at the end of a year, but if you choose instead to keep the $10,000 as cash in a safe-deposit box, you give up the $1000 interest you could have earned by buying the Treasury bill. You thus sacrifice a 10 percent rate of return by holding your $10,000 as money.

The theory of asset demand developed in the last chapter shows how changes in the rate of interest affect the demand for money. The theory states that, all else equal, people prefer assets offering higher expected returns. Because an increase in the interest rate is a rise in the rate of return on illiquid assets relative to the rate of return on money, individuals will want to hold more of their wealth in assets that pay interest and less of their wealth in the form of money if the interest rate rises. *We conclude that all else equal, a rise in the interest rate causes the demand for money to fall.*[3]

We can also describe the influence of the interest rate on money demand in terms of the economic concept of *opportunity cost*—the amount you sacrifice by taking one course of action rather than another. The interest rate measures the opportunity cost of holding money rather than interest-bearing bonds. A rise in the interest rate therefore raises the cost of holding money and causes money demand to fall.

RISK

Risk is not an important factor in money demand. It is risky to hold money because an unexpected increase in the prices of goods and services could re-

[2]As a result of financial deregulation in the United States, some checking deposits do pay interest. But because changes in the interest rates they offer do not always keep pace with changes in the higher interest rates offered by less liquid assets, our analysis remains applicable to most "checkable" deposits.

[3]Many of the illiquid assets that individuals can choose from do not pay their returns in the form of interest. Stocks, for example, pay returns in the form of dividends and capital gains. The family summer house on Cape Cod pays a return in the form of capital gains and the pleasure of vacations at the beach. The assumption behind our analysis of money demand is that, once allowance is made for risk, all assets other than money offer an expected rate of return (measured in terms of money) equal to the interest rate. This assumption allows us to use the interest rate to summarize the return an individual forgoes by holding money rather than an illiquid asset.

duce the value of your money in terms of the commodities you consume. Since interest-paying assets such as government bonds have face values fixed in terms of money, however, the same unexpected increase in prices would reduce the real value of those assets by the same percentage. Because any change in the riskiness of money causes an equal change in the riskiness of bonds, changes in the risk of holding money need not cause individuals to reduce their demand for money and increase their demand for interest-paying assets.

LIQUIDITY

The main benefit of holding money comes from its liquidity. Households and firms hold money because it is the easiest way of financing their everyday purchases. Some large purchases can be financed through the sale of a substantial illiquid asset. An art collector, for example, could sell one of her Picassos to buy a house. To finance a continuing stream of smaller expenditures at various times and for various amounts, however, households and firms have to hold some money.

An individual's need for liquidity rises when the average daily value of his transactions rises. A student who takes the bus every day, for example, does not need to hold as much cash as a business executive who takes taxis during rush hour. *We conclude that a rise in the average value of transactions carried out by a household or firm causes its demand for money to rise.*

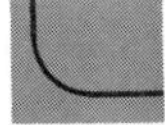

AGGREGATE MONEY DEMAND

Our discussion of how individual households and firms determine their demand for money can now be applied to derive the determinants of **aggregate money demand,** the total demand for money by all households and firms in the economy. Aggregate money demand is just the sum of all the economy's individual money demands.

Three main factors determine aggregate money demand:

1. *The interest rate.* A rise in the interest rate causes each individual in the economy to reduce her demand for money. All else equal, aggregate money demand therefore falls when the interest rate rises.

2. *The price level.* The economy's **price level** is the price of a typical weekly consumption basket in terms of currency. If the price level rises, each individual must spend more money than before to purchase her usual basket of goods and services. To maintain the same level of liquidity as before the price-level increase, she will therefore have to demand more money.

3. *Real national income.* When real national income (GNP) rises, more goods and services are being sold in the economy. This increase in the real value of transactions raises the demand for money, given the price level.

If P is the price level, R is the interest rate, and Y is real GNP, the aggregate demand for money, M^d, can be expressed as

$$M^d = P \times L(R, Y), \tag{14-1}$$

where the value of $L(R, Y)$ falls when R rises and rises when Y rises.[4] To see why we have specified that aggregate money demand is *proportional* to the price level, imagine that all prices doubled but that the interest rate and everyone's *real* incomes remained unchanged. The money value of each individual's average daily transactions would then simply double, as would the amount of money each wished to hold.

We usually write the aggregate money demand relation (14-1) in the equivalent form

$$M^d/P = L(R, Y), \tag{14-2}$$

and call $L(R, Y)$ aggregate *real* money demand. This way of expressing money demand shows that the aggregate demand for liquidity, $L(R, Y)$, is not a demand for a certain number of currency units but is instead a demand to hold a certain amount of purchasing power in liquid form. Real money holdings, M^d/P—that is, money holdings measured in terms of a typical consumption basket—equal the amount of purchasing power held in liquid form. For example, if people are holding \$1000 and the price level is \$100 per consumption basket, real money holdings are equivalent to \$1000/\$100 = 10 consumption baskets. If the price level doubles (to \$200 per consumption basket), real money holdings are halved, and can now purchase only 5 consumption baskets.

Figure 14-1 shows how aggregate real money demand is affected by the interest rate given a fixed level of real income, Y. The aggregate real money demand schedule $L(R, Y)$ slopes downward because a fall in the interest rate raises desired real money holdings of all the households and firms in the economy.

For a given level of real GNP, changes in interest rates cause movements *along* the $L(R, Y)$ schedule. Changes in real GNP, however, cause the schedule itself to shift. Figure 14-2 shows how a rise in real GNP from Y^1 to Y^2 affects aggregate real money demand. Because a rise in real GNP raises aggregate real money demand for a given interest rate, the schedule $L(R, Y^2)$ lies to the right of $L(R, Y^1)$ when Y^2 is greater than Y^1.

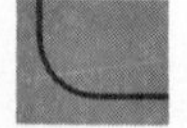

THE EQUILIBRIUM INTEREST RATE: THE INTERACTION OF MONEY SUPPLY AND DEMAND

As you might expect from other economics courses you've taken, the money market is in equilibrium when the money supply set by the central bank equals aggregate money demand. In this section we see how the interest

[4]Naturally, $L(R, Y)$ rises when R falls and falls when Y falls.

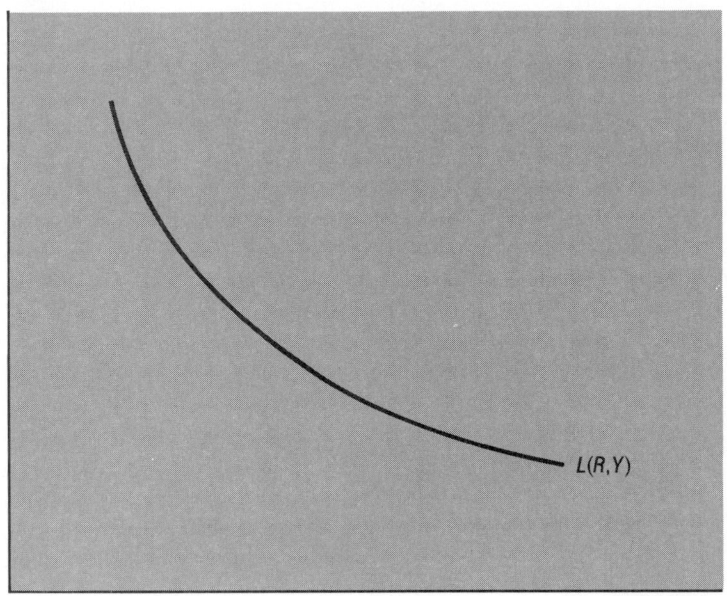

FIGURE 14-1 How aggregate real money demand depends on the interest rate for a given real income level, Y. The graph shows that for a given income level, real money demand rises as the interest rate falls.

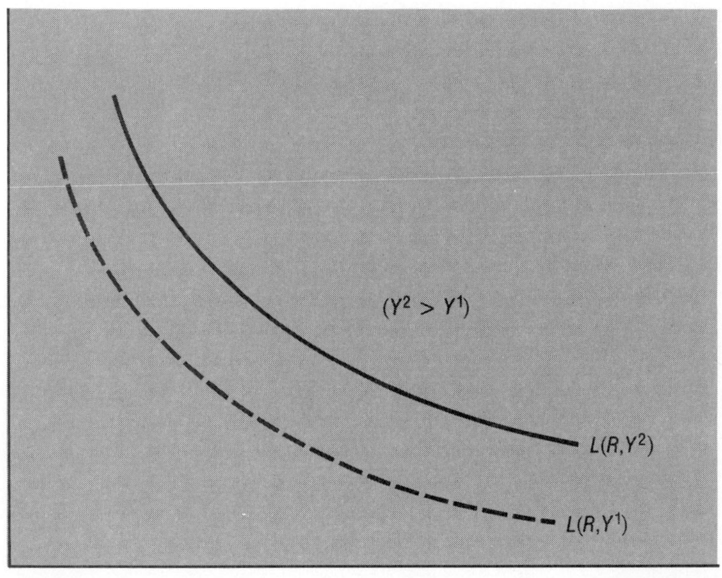

FIGURE 14-2 Effect on the aggregate real money demand schedule of a rise in real income from Y^1 to Y^2. An increase in real income causes the demand for real money balances to rise at every level of the interest rate.

rate is determined by money-market equilibrium, given the price level and output.

EQUILIBRIUM IN THE MONEY MARKET

If M^s is the money supply, the condition for equilibrium in the money market is

$$M^s = M^d. \tag{14-3}$$

After dividing both sides of this equality by the price level, we can express the money-market equilibrium condition in terms of aggregate real money demand as

$$\frac{M^s}{P} = L(R, Y). \tag{14-4}$$

Given the price level and output, the equilibrium interest rate is the one at which aggregate real money demand equals the real money supply.

In Figure 14-3, the aggregate real money demand schedule intersects the real money supply schedule at point 1 to give an equilibrium interest rate of

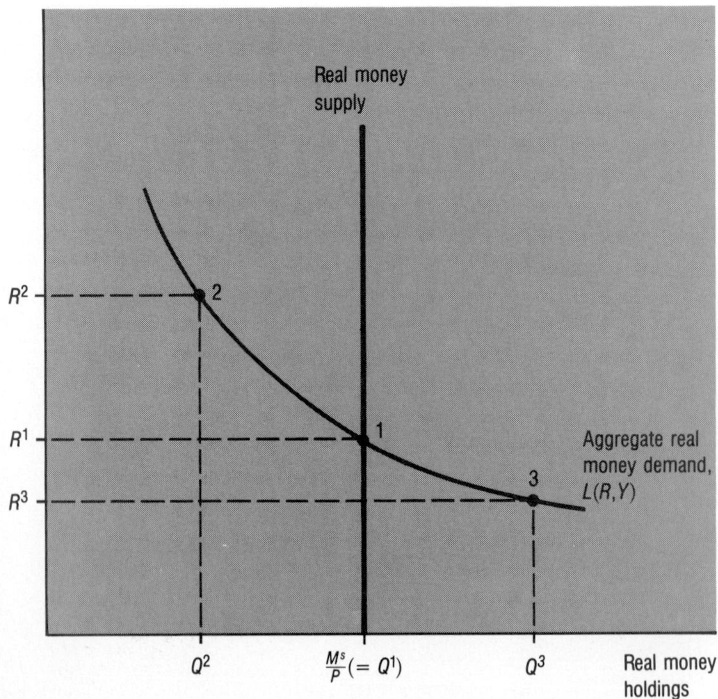

FIGURE 14-3 Determination of the equilibrium interest rate by the equality of aggregate real money demand and the real money supply (with P and Y given). With a real money supply of M^s/P, money-market equilibrium is at point 1 and the equilibrium interest rate is R^1.

R^1. The money supply schedule is vertical at M^s/P because M^s is set by the central bank while P is taken as given.

Let's see why the interest rate tends to settle at its equilibrium level by considering what happens if the market is initially at point 2, with an interest rate, R^2, that is greater than R^1.

At point 2 the demand for real money holdings falls short of the supply by $Q^1 - Q^2$, so there is an excess supply of money. If individuals are holding more money than they desire given the interest rate of R^2, they will attempt to reduce their money holdings by using some money to purchase interest-bearing assets. In other words, individuals will attempt to get rid of their excess money by lending it to others. Since there is an excess supply of money at R^2, however, not everyone can succeed in doing this; there are more people who would like to lend money than there are people who would like to borrow money to increase their real money holdings. Those who cannot unload their extra money try to tempt potential borrowers by lowering the interest rate they charge for lending money to an interest rate less than R^2. The downward pressure on the interest rate continues until the rate reaches R^1. At this interest rate, anyone wishing to lend money can do so because the aggregate excess supply of money has disappeared; that is, supply once again equals demand. Once the market reaches point 1, there is therefore no further tendency for the interest rate to drop.[5]

Similarly, if the interest rate is initially at a level R^3 below R^1, it will tend to rise. As Figure 14-3 shows, there is excess demand for money equal to $Q^3 - Q^1$ at point 3. Individuals therefore attempt to sell interest-bearing assets such as bonds to increase their money holdings (that is, they sell bonds for cash). At point 3, however, not everyone can sell enough interest-bearing assets to satisfy his demand for money. Thus, people bid for money by offering to borrow at progressively higher interest rates and push the interest rate upward toward R^1. Only when the market has reached point 1 and the excess demand for money has been eliminated does the interest rate stop rising.

We can summarize our findings as follows: *The market always moves toward an interest rate at which the real money supply equals aggregate real money demand. If there is initially an excess supply of money the interest rate falls, and if there is initially an excess demand, it rises.*

INTEREST RATES AND THE MONEY SUPPLY

The effect of increasing the money supply at a given price level is illustrated in Figure 14-4. Initially the money market is in equilibrium at point 1, with a

[5]Another way to view this process is as follows: We saw in the last chapter that an asset's rate of return falls when its current price rises relative to its future value. When there is an excess supply of money, the current money prices of illiquid assets that pay interest will be bid up as individuals attempt to reduce their money holdings. This rise in current asset prices lowers the rate of return on nonmoney assets, and since this rate of return is equal to the interest rate (after adjustment for risk), the interest rate also must fall.

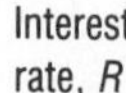

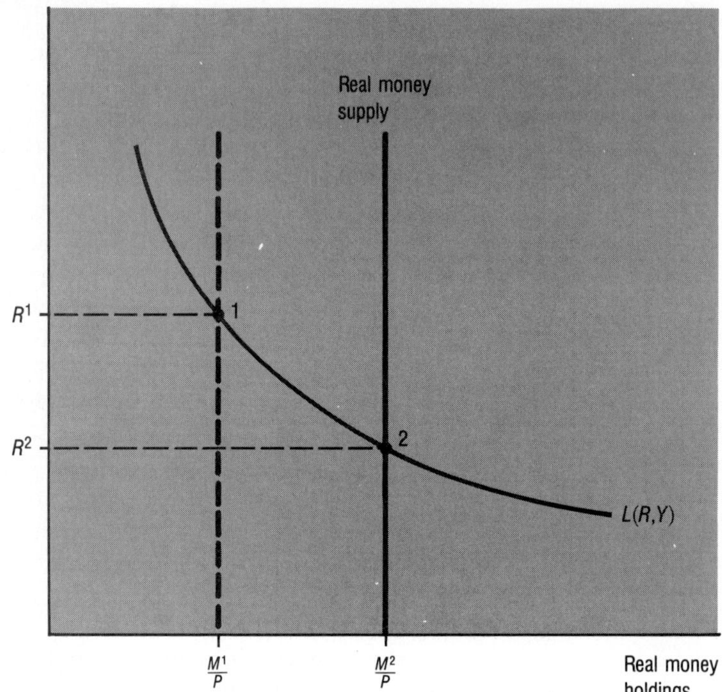

FIGURE 14-4 Effect of an increase in the money supply on the interest rate for a given price level, *P*, and real income level, *Y*. An increase in the money supply from M^1 to M^2 reduces the interest rate from R^1 (point 1) to R^2 (point 2).

money supply M^1 and an interest rate R^1. Since we are holding P constant, a rise in the money supply to M^2 increases the real money supply from M^1/P to M^2/P. With a real money supply of M^2/P, point 2 is the new equilibrium and R^2 is the new, lower interest rate that induces people to hold the increased available real money supply.

The process through which the interest rate falls is by now familiar. Once M^s is increased by the central bank, there is initially an excess supply of real money at the old equilibrium interest rate, R^1, which previously balanced the market. Since people are holding more money than they desire, they use their surplus funds to bid for assets that pay interest. The economy as a whole cannot reduce its money holdings, so interest rates are driven down as unwilling money holders compete to lend out their excess cash balances. At point 2 in Figure 14-4, the interest rate has fallen sufficiently to induce an increase in real money demand equal to the increase in the real money supply.

By running the above policy experiment in reverse, we can see how a reduction of the money supply forces interest rates upward. A fall in M^s causes an excess demand for money at the interest rate that previously balanced supply and demand. People attempt to sell interest-bearing assets—that is, to borrow—in order to rebuild their depleted real money holdings. Since they cannot all be successful when there is excess money demand, the interest rate is pushed upward until everyone is content to hold the smaller real money stock.

We conclude that: *An increase in the money supply lowers the interest rate, while a fall in the money supply raises the interest rate, given the price level and output.*

OUTPUT AND THE INTEREST RATE

Figure 14-5 shows the effect on the interest rate of a rise in the level of output from Y^1 to Y^2, given the money supply and the price level. As we saw earlier, an increase in output causes the entire aggregate real money demand schedule to shift to the right, shifting the equilibrium away from point 1. At the old equilibrium interest rate, R^1, there is initially an excess demand for money equal to $Q^2 - Q^1$ (point 1′). Since the real money supply is given, the interest rate is bid up until it reaches the higher, new equilibrium level R^2 (point 2). A fall in output has opposite effects, causing the aggregate real money demand schedule to shift to the left and therefore causing the equilibrium interest rate to fall.

We conclude that an increase in real output raises the interest rate, while a fall in real output lowers the interest rate, given the price level and the money supply.

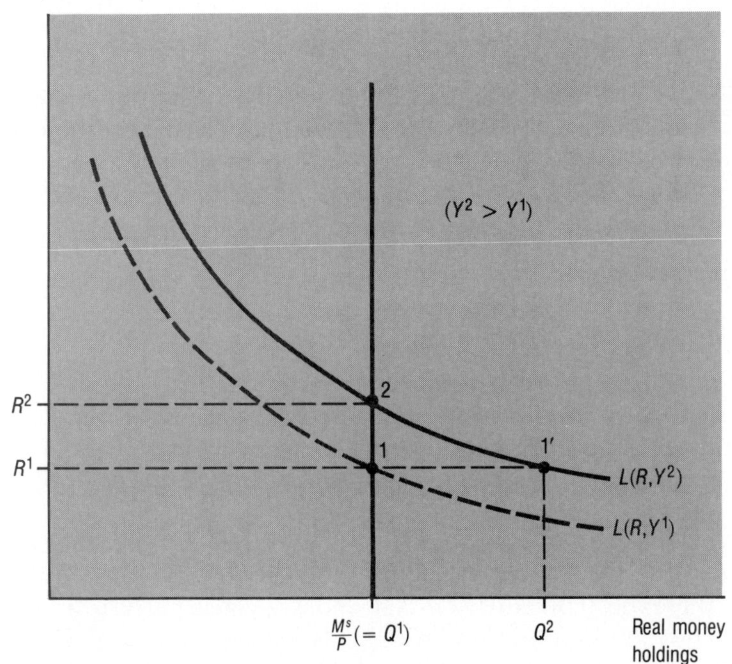

FIGURE 14-5 Effect on the interest rate of a rise in real income from Y^1 to Y^2, given the real money supply. By shifting the real money-demand function to the right, a rise in real income raises the interest rate from R^1 (point 1) to R^2 (point 2).

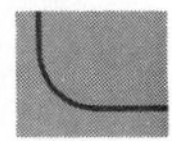

THE MONEY SUPPLY AND THE EXCHANGE RATE IN THE SHORT RUN

In Chapter 13 we learned about the interest parity condition, which predicts how interest-rate movements influence the exchange rate, given expectations about the exchange rate's future level. Now that we know how shifts in a country's money supply affect the interest rate on nonmoney assets denominated in its currency, we can see how monetary changes affect the exchange rate. We will discover that an increase in a country's money supply causes its currency to depreciate in the foreign-exchange market, while a reduction in its money supply causes its currency to appreciate.

In this section we continue to take the price level as given, and for that reason we label the analysis of this section **short run.** The **long-run** analysis of an economic event allows for the complete adjustment of the price level (which may take a long time) and for full employment of all factors of production. Later in this chapter we examine the long-run effects of money-supply changes on the price level, the exchange rate, and other macroeconomic variables. Our long-run analysis will show how the money supply influences exchange-rate expectations, which we also continue to take as given for now.

LINKING MONEY, THE INTEREST RATE, AND THE EXCHANGE RATE

To analyze the relation between money and the exchange rate in the short run, we combine two diagrams that we have already studied separately. The first of these (introduced as Figure 13-4 on p. 331), shows how the equilibrium exchange rate is determined in the foreign-exchange market, given interest rates and expectations about future exchange rates. The second diagram, introduced as Figure 14-3, shows how a country's equilibrium interest rate is determined in its money market. Let's assume once again that the exchange rate we are studying is the dollar/DM exchange rate, that is, the price of DM in terms of dollars.

Figure 14-6 combines the diagrams we used earlier to show equilibrium in the foreign exchange and U.S. money markets. The lower part of Figure 14-6 reproduces the depiction of money-market equilibrium we studied in the previous section of this chapter. For convenience, the diagram we used earlier has here been rotated clockwise by 90°: we now measure dollar interest rates on the horizontal axis starting at point 0; and the U.S. real money supply is measured from 0 on the descending vertical axis. Money-market equilibrium is shown at point 1, where the dollar interest rate $R^1_\$$ induces people to demand real balances equal to the U.S. real money supply, M^s_{US}/P_{US}.

The upper part of Figure 14-6 shows equilibrium in the foreign-exchange market. As you will remember from Chapter 13, the downward-sloping schedule shows the expected return on DM deposits, measured in terms of dollars. The schedule slopes downward because of the effect of current exchange-rate changes on expectations of future depreciation: a strengthening of the dollar today (a fall in $E_{\$/DM}$) relative to its *given* expected future

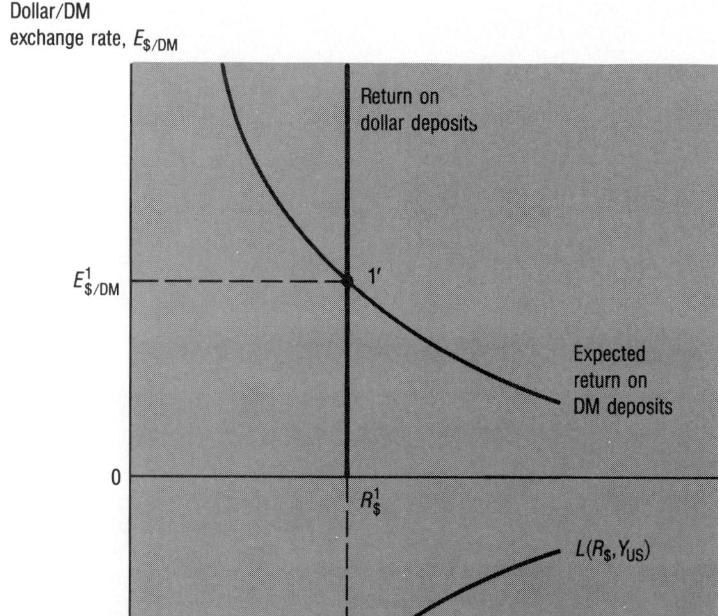

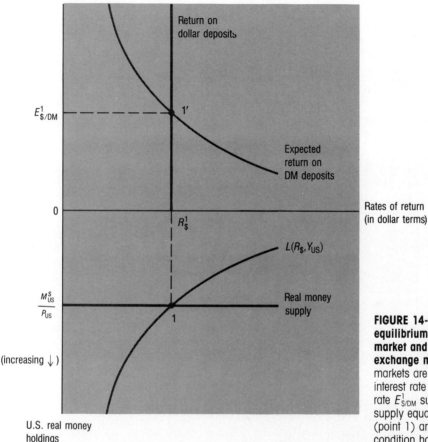

FIGURE 14-6 Simultaneous equilibrium in the U.S. money market and the foreign-exchange market. Both asset markets are in equilibrium at the interest rate $R^1_\$$ and exchange rate $E^1_{\$/DM}$ such that money supply equals money demand (point 1) and the interest parity condition holds (point 1′).

level makes DM deposits more attractive by leading people to anticipate a sharper dollar depreciation in the future. The dollar interest rate determined in the money market, $R^1_\$$, defines the vertical schedule in the figure's upper portion. At the intersection of the two schedules (point 1′), the expected rates of return on dollar and DM deposits are equal, and therefore interest parity holds. $E^1_{\$/DM}$ is the equilibrium exchange rate.

Figure 14-6 emphasizes the link between the U.S. money market (bottom) and the foreign-exchange market (top)—the U.S. money market determines the dollar interest rate, which in turn affects the exchange rate that maintains interest parity. (Of course, there is a similar link between the German money market and the foreign-exchange market that operates through changes in the DM interest rate.)

Figure 14-7 illustrates these linkages. The U.S. and German central banks, the Federal Reserve and the Bundesbank, determine the U.S. and German money supplies, M^s_{US} and M^s_G. Given the price levels and national

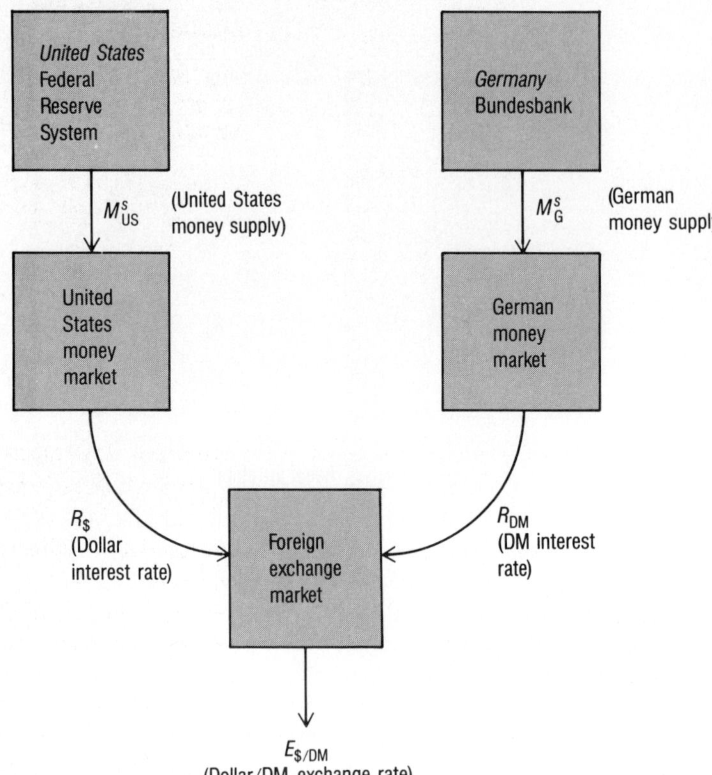

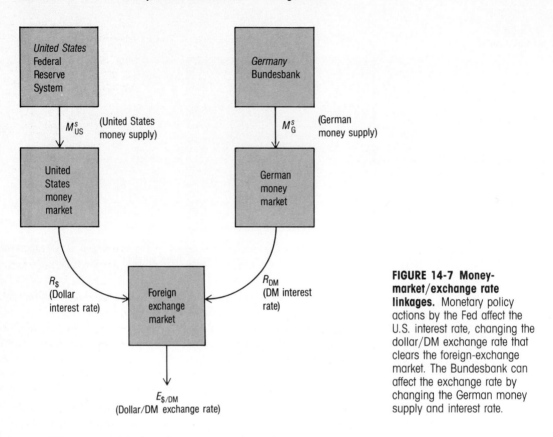

FIGURE 14-7 Money-market/exchange rate linkages. Monetary policy actions by the Fed affect the U.S. interest rate, changing the dollar/DM exchange rate that clears the foreign-exchange market. The Bundesbank can affect the exchange rate by changing the German money supply and interest rate.

incomes of the two countries, equilibrium in national money markets leads to the dollar and DM interest rates $R_\$$ and R_{DM}. These interest rates feed into the foreign-exchange market where, given expectations about the future dollar/DM exchange rate, the current rate $E_{\$/DM}$ is determined by the interest parity condition.

U.S. MONEY SUPPLY AND THE DOLLAR/DM EXCHANGE RATE

We now use our model of asset-market linkages to ask how the dollar/DM exchange rate changes when the Federal Reserve changes the U.S. money supply M^s_{US}. The effects of this change are summarized in Figure 14-8.

At the initial money supply M^1_{US}, the money market is in equilibrium at point 1 with an interest rate $R^1_\$$. Given the DM interest rate and the expected future exchange rate, a dollar interest rate of $R^1_\$$ implies that foreign-exchange market equilibrium occurs at point 1′, with an exchange rate equal to $E^1_{\$/DM}$.

What happens when the Federal Reserve raises the U.S. money supply from M^1_{US} to M^2_{US}? This increase sets in train the following sequence of events: (1) At the initial interest rate $R^1_\$$ there is an excess supply of money in the U.S. money market; so the dollar interest rate falls to $R^2_\$$ as the money

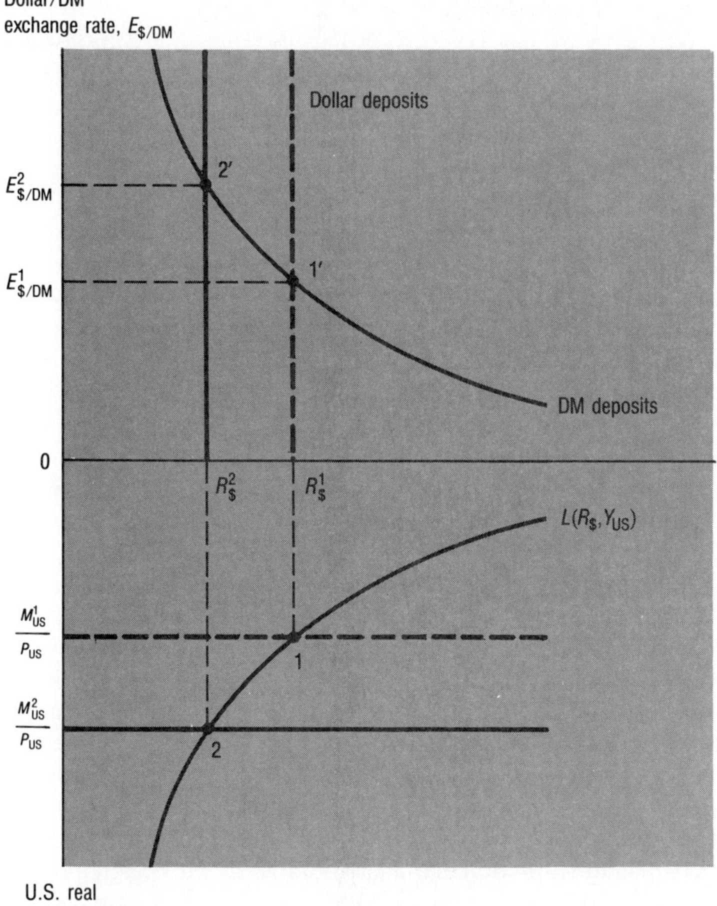

FIGURE 14-8 Effect on the dollar/DM exchange rate and dollar interest rate of an increase in the U.S. money supply (given P_{US} and Y_{US}). When the money supply rises from M^1_{US} to M^2_{US}, the dollar interest rate declines (as money-market equilibrium is reestablished at point 2) and the dollar depreciates against the DM (as foreign-exchange market equilibrium is reestablished at point 2′).

market reaches its new equilibrium position (point 2). (2) Given the initial exchange rate $E^1_{\$/DM}$ and the new, lower interest rate on dollars, $R^2_\$$, the expected return on DM deposits is greater than that on dollar deposits. Holders of dollar deposits therefore try to sell them for DM deposits, which are momentarily more attractive. (3) The dollar depreciates to $E^2_{\$/DM}$ as holders of dollar deposits bid for DM deposits. The foreign-exchange market is once again in equilibrium at point 2′ because the depreciation of the dollar to $E^2_{\$/DM}$ causes a fall in that currency's expected future depreciation rate sufficient to offset the fall in the dollar interest rate.

We conclude that an increase in a country's money supply causes its currency to depreciate in the foreign-exchange market. By running Figure 14-8 in reverse, you can see that a reduction in a country's money supply causes its currency to appreciate in the foreign-exchange market.

GERMAN MONEY SUPPLY AND THE DOLLAR/DM EXCHANGE RATE

The conclusions that we have just reached also apply when the Bundesbank changes Germany's money supply. An increase in M^s_G causes a depreciation of the DM (that is, an appreciation of the dollar, or a fall in $E_{\$/DM}$), while a reduction in M^s_G causes an appreciation of the DM (that is, a depreciation of the dollar, or a rise in $E_{\$/DM}$). The mechanism, running from the German interest rate to the exchange rate, is the same as the one we have analyzed. It is a good exercise to verify these assertions by drawing figures similar to Figures 14-6 and 14-8 that illustrate the linkage between the German money market and the foreign-exchange market.

Here we use a different approach to show how changes in the German money supply affect the dollar/DM exchange rate. In Chapter 13 we learned that a fall in the DM interest rate, R_{DM}, shifts the downward-sloping schedule in the upper part of Figure 14-6 to the left. The reason is that for any level of the exchange rate, a fall in R_{DM} lowers the expected rate of return on DM deposits. Since a rise in the German money supply M^s_G lowers R_{DM}, we can see its effect on the exchange rate by shifting the appropriate schedule in Figure 14-6 to the left.

The result of an increase in the German money supply is shown in Figure 14-9. Initially the U.S. money market is in equilibrium at point 1 and the foreign-exchange market is in equilibrium at point 1′, with an exchange rate $E^1_{\$/DM}$. An increase in Germany's money supply lowers R_{DM} and therefore shifts to the left the schedule linking the expected return on DM deposits to the exchange rate. Foreign-exchange market equilibrium is restored at point 2′, with an exchange rate of $E^2_{\$/DM}$. The increase in German money causes the DM to depreciate against the dollar (that is, causes a fall in the dollar price of DM). Similarly, a fall in Germany's money supply would cause the DM to appreciate against the dollar ($E_{\$/DM}$ would rise). The change in the German money supply does not disturb the U.S. money-market equilibrium, which remains at point 1.[6]

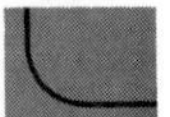

MONEY, THE PRICE LEVEL, AND THE EXCHANGE RATE IN THE LONG RUN

Our short-run analysis of the link between countries' money markets and the foreign-exchange market rested on the simplifying assumptions that price levels and exchange-rate expectations were given. To extend our understanding of how money supply and money demand affect exchange rates, we must examine how monetary factors affect a country's price level in the long run. Our main tool will once again be the theory of aggregate money demand we have developed.

[6]The U.S. money-market equilibrium remains at point 1 because the price adjustments that equilibrate the German money market and the foreign-exchange market after the increase in Germany's money supply do not change either the money supply or money demand in the United States, given Y_{US} and P_{US}.

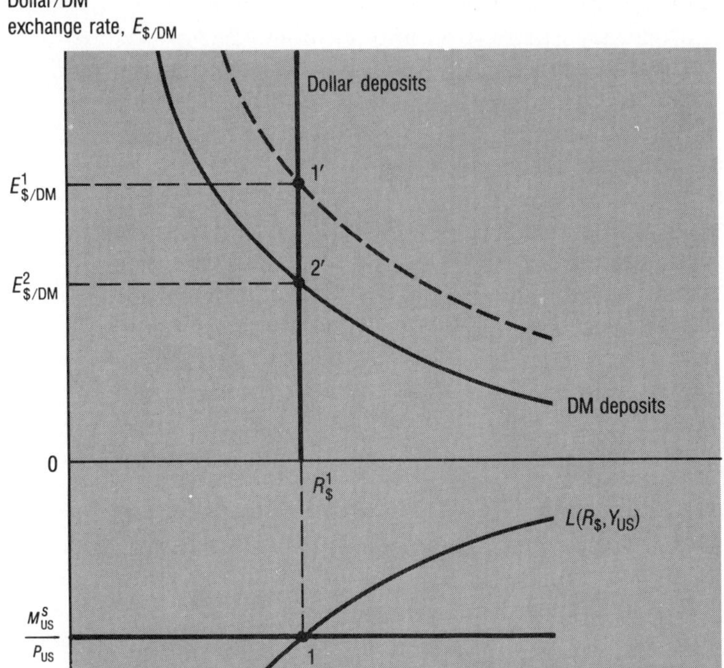

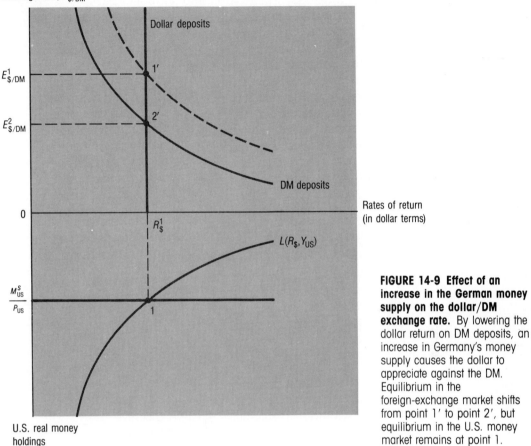

FIGURE 14-9 Effect of an increase in the German money supply on the dollar/DM exchange rate. By lowering the dollar return on DM deposits, an increase in Germany's money supply causes the dollar to appreciate against the DM. Equilibrium in the foreign-exchange market shifts from point 1′ to point 2′, but equilibrium in the U.S. money market remains at point 1.

MONEY AND MONEY PRICES

If the price level and output are fixed in the short run, the condition (14-4) of money-market equilibrium,

$$\frac{M^s}{P} = L(R, Y),$$

determines the domestic interest rate, R. The money market always moves to equilibrium, however, even if we drop our "short-run" assumption and think of periods of time over which P and Y, as well as R, can vary. The above equilibrium condition can therefore be rearranged to give

$$P = M^s/L(R, Y), \qquad \textbf{(14-5)}$$

which shows how the price level depends on the interest rate, real output, and the domestic money supply.

The most important prediction of our equation for P concerns the relationship between a country's price level and its money supply, M^s: *All else equal, an increase in a country's money supply causes a proportional increase in its price level.* If, for example, the money supply doubles (to $2M^s$) but output and the interest rate do not change, the price level must also double (to $2P$) to maintain equilibrium in the money market.

The economic reasoning behind this very precise prediction follows from our observation above that the demand for money is a demand for *real* money holdings: Real money demand is not altered by an increase in M^s that leaves R and Y [and thus aggregate real money demand $L(R, Y)$] unchanged. If aggregate real money demand does not change, however, the money market will remain in equilibrium only if the real money supply also stays the same. To keep the real money supply M^s/P constant, P must rise in proportion to M^s.

THE LONG-RUN EFFECTS OF MONEY-SUPPLY CHANGES

Our theory of how the money supply affects the price level *given* the interest rate and output is not yet a theory of how money-supply changes affect the price level in the long run. To develop such a theory, we still have to determine the long-run effect of the money supply on the interest rate and output. This turns out to be easier than you might think. *As we now argue, money-supply changes have no long-run effect on the interest rate or real output.*[7]

The easiest way to understand the long-run effects of money supply on the interest rate and output is to think first about a *currency reform,* in which a country's government simply redefines the national currency unit. For example, the government of France reformed its currency in 1960 simply by issuing "new" French francs, each equal to 100 "old" French francs. The effect of this reform was to lower the number of currency units in circulation, and all franc prices, to 1/100 of their old-franc values. But the redefinition of the monetary unit had no effect on real output, the interest rate, or the relative prices of goods: all that occurred was a one-shot change in all values measured in francs.

An increase in the supply of a country's currency has the same effect in the long run as a currency reform. A doubling of the money supply, for example, has the same effect in the long run as a currency reform in which each unit of currency is replaced by two units of "new" currency. If the economy is initially fully employed, every money price in the economy eventually doubles, but real GNP, the interest rate, and all relative prices return to their long-run or full-employment levels.

[7]The preceding statement refers only to *permanent* changes in the *level* of the nominal money supply, and not, for example, to changes in the rate at which the money supply is growing over time. The proposition that one-time changes in the level of the money supply have no long-run real effects is often called the *long-run neutrality of money.* In contrast, changes in the money-supply growth rate need not be neutral in the long run.

Why is a money-supply change just like a currency reform in its long-run effects? The full-employment output level is determined by the economy's endowments of labor and capital; so in the long run, real output does not depend on the money supply. Similarly, the interest rate is also independent of the money supply in the long run. If the money supply and all prices double permanently, there is no reason why people previously willing to exchange \$1 today for \$1.10 in a year should not be willing afterward to exchange \$2 today for \$2.20 in a year; so the interest rate will remain at 10 percent per annum. Relative prices also remain the same if all money prices double, since relative prices are just ratios of money prices. Thus, money-supply changes do not change the allocation of resources in the long run. Only the absolute level of money prices changes.

When studying the effect of an increase in the money supply over long time periods, we are therefore justified in concluding that R and Y will not change if they were initially at levels consistent with full employment. Thus, we can conclude from equation (14-5) that: *For an economy initially at full employment, a permanent increase in the money supply will eventually be followed by a proportional increase in the price level.*

EMPIRICAL EVIDENCE ON MONEY SUPPLIES AND PRICE LEVELS

In looking at actual data on money and prices, we should not expect to see an exact proportional relationship over long periods, partly because output, the interest rate, and the aggregate real money demand function can shift for reasons that have nothing to do with the supply of money. Output changes as a result of capital accumulation and technological advance, for example, and money-demand behavior may change as a result of financial innovations such as electronic cash transfer facilities. Nonetheless, we should expect the data to show a strong and clear-cut association between money supplies and price levels. If real-world data did not provide strong evidence that money supplies and price levels move together in the long run, the usefulness of the theory of money demand we have developed would be in severe doubt.

Figure 14-10, which shows the relation between the U.S. money supply and the U.S. price level between 1964 and 1983, gives empirical support to the theory's prediction that the money supply and the price level will show a strong positive association over long periods of time. The increase in the U.S. price level over the period is just about proportional to the increase in the money supply. Between the end of 1964 and the end of 1983, the U.S. money supply grew from \$166.4 billion to \$525.3 billion, an increase of 216 percent. Over the same period the consumer price index rose from 37.7 to 120.4, or 219 percent—a percentage increase very nearly equal to the increase in the supply of money.

Evidence on the money-supply/price-level linkage for the world's seven largest industrial countries is shown in Figure 14-11. The horizontal axis in

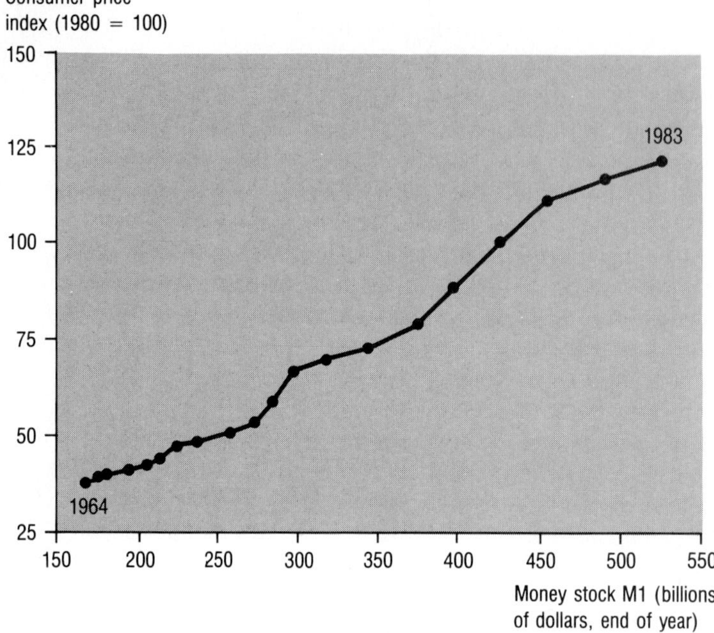

FIGURE 14-10 Money and the price level in the United States, 1964–1983. Source: OECD, *Main Economic Indicators.*

this figure measures percentage increases in money supplies between 1973 and 1983, the vertical axis measures percentage increases in price levels. As you can see, there is a strong positive relation between money growth and the price level in all seven countries. In countries plotted close to the 45° line, money supplies and price levels increased more or less in proportion over 1973–1983. In France, for example, both the money supply and the price level rose by about 300 percent. In some cases, however, the observations stray from the 45° line along which increases in money and prices are proportional. Germany's price level, for example, rose by a much smaller percentage than its money supply, as indicated by that country's position below the 45° line.

As we observed above, we should expect these discrepancies because the theory of money demand predicts exactly proportional increases in money and price levels only when no other factors affecting the money market change at the same time. These other factors, however, have not remained constant in the countries shown. Countries close to the 45° line in Figure 14-11 are those in which the effects on money-market equilibrium of factors other than money supply roughly offset each other. A similar canceling out of factors other than money supply occurred in the United States over the 1964–1983 period described by Figure 14-10. The main lesson to be drawn from Figures 14-10 and 14-11 is that the data confirm the strong long-run link between national money supplies and national price levels predicted by economic theory.

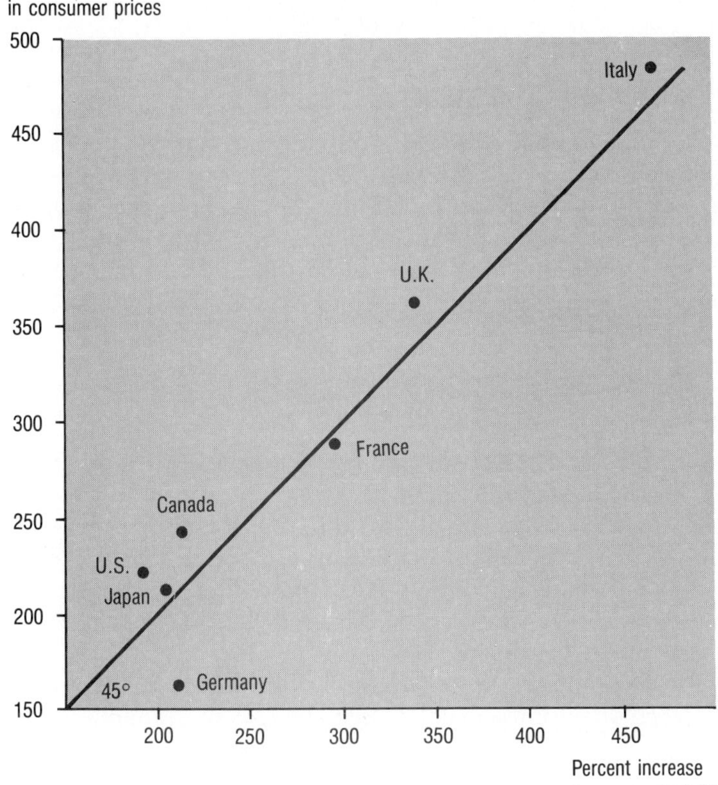

FIGURE 14-11 Monetary growth and price-level change in the seven main industrial countries, 1973–1983. Source: OECD, *Main Economic Indicators.*

MONEY AND THE EXCHANGE RATE IN THE LONG RUN

The domestic-currency price of foreign currency is one of the many prices in the economy that rise in the long run after a permanent increase in the money supply. If you think again about the effects of a currency reform, you will see how the exchange rate moves in the long run. Suppose, for example, that the United States government replaced every pair of "old" dollars by one "new" dollar. Then if the dollar/DM exchange rate had been 0.30 *old* dollars per DM before the reform, it would change to 0.15 *new* dollars per DM immediately after the reform. In much the same way, a halving of the U.S. money supply would eventually lead the dollar to appreciate from an exchange rate of 0.30 dollars/DM to one of 0.15 dollars/DM. Since the dollar prices of all U.S. goods and services would also fall by a half, this 50 percent appreciation of the dollar leaves the *relative* prices of all U.S. and foreign goods and services unchanged.

We conclude that in the long run, a permanent increase in a country's money supply causes a proportional depreciation of its currency against foreign currencies. Simi-

larly, a permanent decrease in a country's money supply causes a proportional long-run appreciation of its currency against foreign currencies.

INFLATION AND EXCHANGE-RATE DYNAMICS

In this section we tie together our short-run and long-run findings about the effects of monetary changes by examining the process through which the price level adjusts to its long-run position. An economy is experiencing **inflation** when its price level is rising (and it is experiencing **deflation** when its price level is falling). Our examination of inflation will give us a deeper understanding of how the exchange rate adjusts to monetary disturbances in the economy.

SHORT-RUN PRICE RIGIDITY VS. LONG-RUN PRICE FLEXIBILITY

Our analysis of the short-run effects of monetary changes assumed that a country's price level, unlike its exchange rate, does not jump immediately. This assumption cannot be exactly correct, because many commodities, such as agricultural products, are traded in markets where prices adjust sharply every day as supply or demand conditions shift. In addition, exchange-rate changes themselves may affect the prices of some of the foreign goods and services that domestic residents consume.

Many prices in the economy, however, are written into long-term contracts and cannot be changed immediately when changes in the money supply occur. The most important prices of this type are workers' wages, which are negotiated only periodically in many industries. Wages do not directly enter the price level, but they make up a very large fraction of the cost of producing goods and services. Since output prices depend heavily on production costs, the behavior of the overall price level is influenced by the sluggishness of wage movements. We will therefore continue to assume that the price level is given in the short run and does not take significant jumps in response to monetary changes.[8]

[8]This assumption would not be reasonable, however, for all countries at all times. In extremely inflationary conditions, such as those seen recently in some less-developed countries, long-term contracts specifying money payments may go out of use. This development makes the price level much less rigid than it would be under moderate inflation, and large price-level jumps become possible. Our analysis assuming short-run price rigidity is therefore most applicable to countries with histories of relative price-level stability, such as the United States. Some econometric evidence on price-level stickiness for the United States is presented by Robert J. Gordon, "Price Inertia and Policy Ineffectiveness in the United States, 1890–1980," *Journal of Political Economy* 90 (December 1982), pp. 1087–1117; and by Julio J. Rotemberg, "Sticky Prices in the United States," *Journal of Political Economy* 90 (December 1982), pp. 1187–1221. For evidence on Germany, see Alberto Giovannini and Julio J. Rotemberg, "Exchange Rate Dynamics with Sticky Prices: The Deutsche Mark, 1974–1982," Working Paper, Columbia University, January 1986. A study of individual U.S. industries by Dennis W. Carlton also finds evidence of significant price rigidity. See Carlton, "The Rigidity of Prices," *American Economic Review* 76 (September 1986), pp. 637–658.

Even in the short run, however, a change in the money supply creates pressures that lead to *future* increases in the price level. These pressures come from three main sources:

1. *Excess demand for output and labor.* An increase in the money supply has an expansionary effect on the economy, raising the total demand for final goods and services. To meet this demand, producers of goods and services must put their workers on overtime and take on new workers. Even if wages are given in the short run, the additional demand for labor allows workers to demand higher wages in the next round of wage negotiations. Producers are not too reluctant to pay these higher wages, for they know that with a booming economy it will be easy to pass the higher wage costs to consumers in the form of higher product prices.

2. *Inflationary expectations.* If everyone expects the price level to rise in the future, their expectation will increase the pace of inflation today. Workers bargaining over wage contracts will insist on higher money wages to counteract the effect on their *real* wages of the anticipated general increase in prices. Producers, once again, will give in to these wage demands if they expect product prices to rise and cover the additional wage costs.

3. *Raw materials prices.* Many raw materials used in the production of final goods, for example, petroleum products and metals, are sold in markets where prices may adjust sharply even in the short run. By causing the prices of such materials to jump upward, a money-supply increase raises production costs in industries using raw materials. This cost increase eventually leads producers in those industries to raise product prices.

PERMANENT MONEY-SUPPLY CHANGES AND THE EXCHANGE RATE

We now apply our analysis of inflation to study the adjustment of the dollar/DM exchange rate following a *permanent* increase in the U.S. money supply. Figure 14-12 shows both the short-run (Figure 14-12a) and long-run (Figure 14-12b) effects of this disturbance. We assume here, as before, that output is given.

Figure 14-12a assumes that the U.S. price level is initially given at P^1_{US}. An increase in the nominal money supply from M^1_{US} to M^2_{US} therefore raises the real money supply from M^1_{US}/P^1_{US} to M^2_{US}/P^1_{US} in the short run, lowering the interest rate from $R^1_\$$ (point 1) to $R^2_\$$ (point 2). So far our analysis goes through exactly as it did earlier in the chapter.

The first change in our analysis comes when we ask how the American money-supply change affects the foreign-exchange market. As before, the fall in the U.S. interest rate is shown as a leftward shift in the vertical schedule giving the dollar return on dollar deposits. This is no longer the whole story, however, for the money-supply increase now affects *exchange-rate expectations.* Because the U.S. money-supply change is permanent, people expect that there will be a long-run increase in all dollar prices, including the ex-

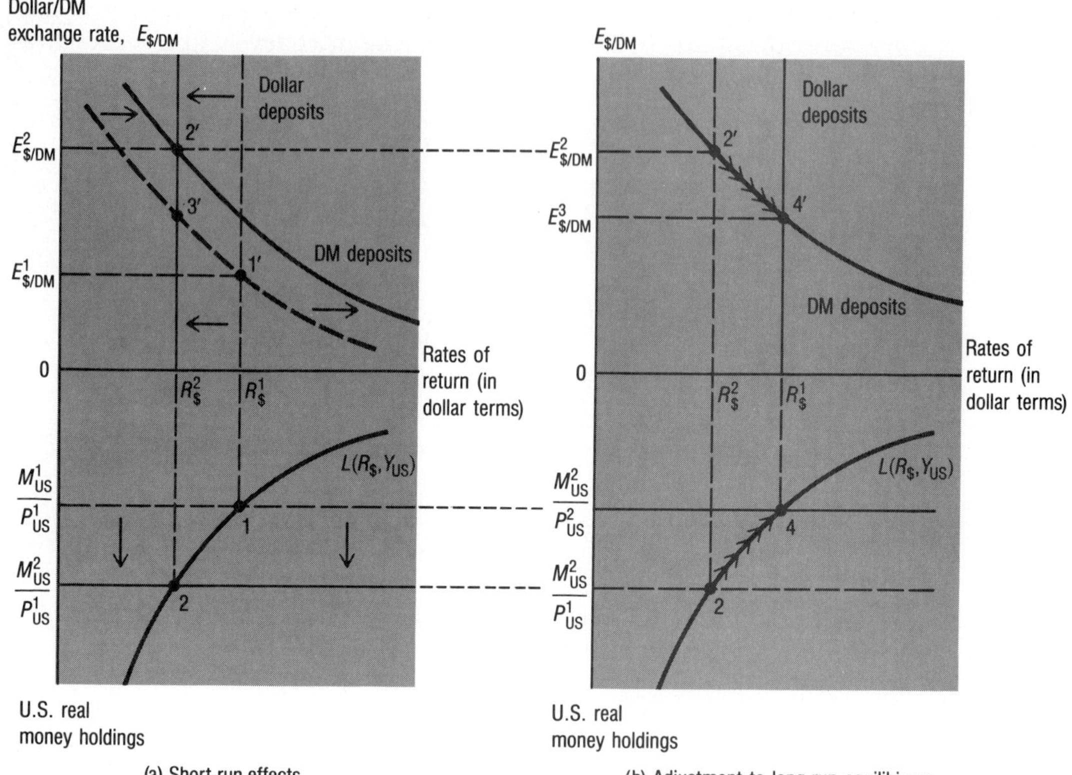

FIGURE 14-12 Short-run and long-run effects of an increase in the U.S. money supply (given real output, *Y*). (a) Short-run adjustment of the asset markets. (b) How the interest rate, price level, and exchange rate move over time as the economy approaches its long-run equilibrium.

change rate, which is the dollar price of DM. As you will recall from Chapter 13, a rise in the expected future dollar/DM exchange rate raises the dollar return on DM deposits and thus shifts the downward-sloping schedule in the top part of Figure 14-12a to the right. The dollar depreciates against the DM, moving from an exchange rate of $E^1_{\$/DM}$ (point 1′) to $E^2_{\$/DM}$ (point 2′). Notice that the dollar depreciation is *greater* than it would be if the expected future dollar/DM exchange rate stayed fixed (as it might if the money-supply increase were temporary rather than permanent). If the expectation $E^e_{\$/DM}$ did not change, the new short-run equilibrium would be at point 3′ rather than at point 2′.

Figure14-12b shows how the interest rate and exchange rate behave as the price level rises during the economy's adjustment to its long-run equilibrium. The price level begins to rise from the initially given level P^1_{US}, eventually reaching P^2_{US}. Because the long-run increase in the price level must be proportional to the increase in the money supply, the final *real* money supply, M^2_{US}/P^2_{US}, is shown equal to the initial real money supply, M^1_{US}/P^1_{US}. Since output is given and the real money supply has returned to its original level, the equilibrium interest rate must again equal $R^1_\$$ in the long run (point 4). The interest rate therefore rises from $R^2_\$$ (point 2) to $R^1_\$$ (point 4) as the price level rises from P^1_{US} to P^2_{US}.

The rising U.S. interest rate has exchange-rate effects that can also be seen in Figure 14-12b: the dollar *appreciates* against the DM in the process of adjustment. If exchange-rate expectations do not change further during the adjustment process, the foreign-exchange market moves to its long-run position along the downward-sloping schedule defining the dollar return on DM deposits. The market's path is just the path traced out by the vertical dollar interest rate schedule as it moves rightward because of the price level's gradual rise. In the long run (point 4′) the equilibrium exchange rate $E^3_{\$/DM}$ is higher than at the original equilibrium, point 1′. Like the price level, the dollar/DM exchange rate has risen in proportion to the increase in the money supply.

Figure 14-13 shows the time paths described for the U.S. money supply, the dollar interest rate, the U.S. price level, and the dollar/DM exchange

FIGURE 14-13 Time paths of U.S. economic variables after a permanent increase in the U.S. money supply. After the money supply increases at time t_0, the interest rate, price level, and exchange rate move as shown toward their long-run levels. The exchange rate overshoots in the short-run.

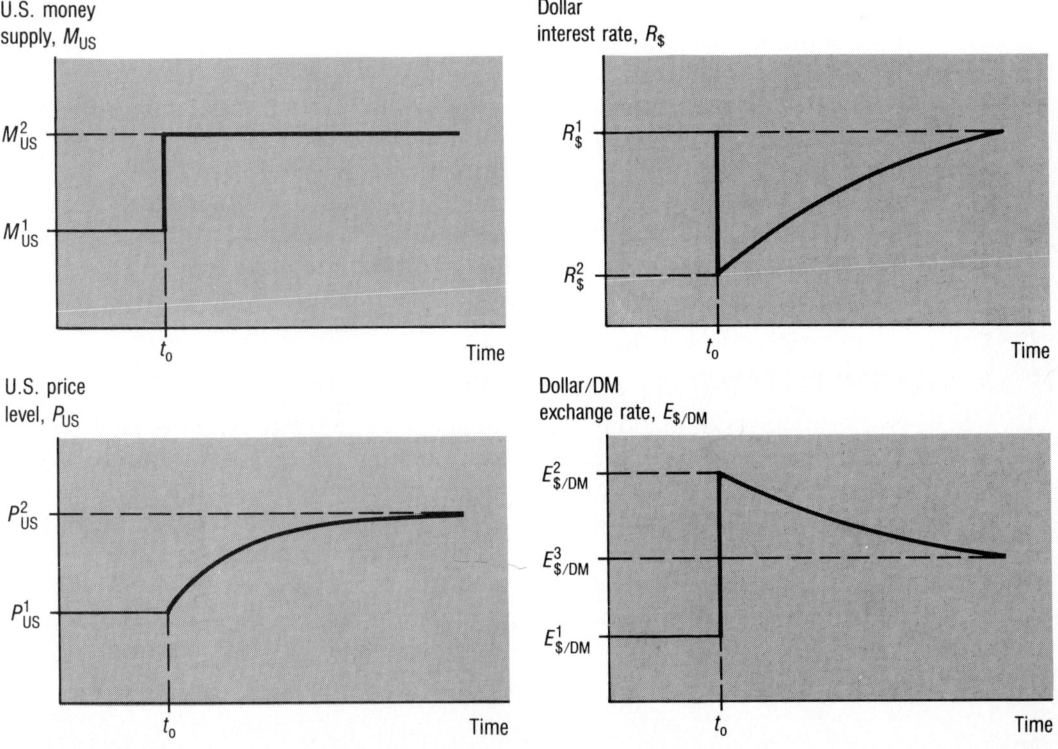

rate. The figure is drawn so that the long-run increases in the price level and exchange rate are proportional to the increase in the money supply.

EXCHANGE-RATE OVERSHOOTING

In its initial depreciation after the money-supply rise, the exchange rate depreciates from $E^1_{\$/DM}$ to $E^2_{\$/DM}$, a depreciation greater than its *long-run* depreciation from $E^1_{\$/DM}$ to $E^3_{\$/DM}$ (see Figure 14-13). The exchange rate is said to overshoot when its short-run response to a disturbance is greater than its long-run response. **Exchange-rate overshooting** is an important phenomenon because it helps explain why exchange rates move so sharply from day to day.

The economic explanation of overshooting comes from the interest parity condition. The explanation is easiest to grasp if we assume that before the money-supply increase first occurs, no change in the dollar/DM exchange rate is expected, so that $R^1_\$$ equals R_{DM}, the given interest rate on DM deposits. A permanent increase in the U.S. money supply doesn't affect R_{DM}, so it causes $R^1_\$$ to fall below R_{DM} and remain below that interest rate until the U.S. price level has completed the long-run adjustment to P^2_{US} shown in Figure 14-13. For the foreign-exchange market to be in equilibrium during this adjustment process, however, the interest difference in favor of DM deposits must be offset by an expected *appreciation* of the dollar against the DM, that is, by an expected fall in $E_{\$/DM}$. Only if the dollar/DM exchange rate overshoots $E^3_{\$/DM}$ in the short run will market participants expect a subsequent appreciation of the dollar against the DM.

Overshooting is a direct consequence of the short-run rigidity of the price level. In a hypothetical world where the price level could adjust immediately to its new long-run level after a money-supply increase, the dollar interest rate would not fall because prices *would* adjust immediately and the real money supply would therefore not rise. Thus, there would be no need for overshooting to maintain equilibrium in the foreign-exchange market. The exchange rate would maintain equilibrium simply by jumping to its new long-run level right away.

INFLATION EXPECTATIONS AND THE INTEREST RATE–EXCHANGE RATE LINK

So far in our examination of how monetary factors influence exchange rates, we have always found that a fall in a country's interest rate causes its currency to depreciate in the foreign-exchange market and that a rise in its interest rate causes its currency to appreciate. As we remarked at the end of the last chapter, however, this relationship between interest rates and exchange rates is by no means a hard-and-fast rule: the effect of an interest-rate change on the exchange rate depends on *why* the interest rate has moved. A rising interest rate, for example, may well be associated with a *depreciating* currency.

We have now developed the tools that will allow us to understand why exchange rates can respond differently to interest-rate movements in different circumstances. Our analysis is based on a phenomenon called the **Fisher effect,** which is a tendency for interest rates to rise when expected inflation is high and fall when expected inflation is low.[9]

NOMINAL INTEREST RATES, REAL INTEREST RATES, AND THE FISHER EFFECT

To understand the effect of inflation on interest rates, we must recall the last chapter's distinction between expected rates of return measured in terms of money and expected rates of return measured in terms of output. As we saw in the last chapter, the interest rate on a deposit is equal to the deposit's rate of return expressed in terms of the currency in which the deposit is denominated. An interest rate expressed in terms of some currency is called a **nominal interest rate.** The interest rates that appeared in our discussions of the foreign exchange and money markets were all nominal interest rates.

By measuring the value of a deposit in terms of goods and services rather than money, however, we can compute its *real* rate of return, that is, the rate at which its value in terms of output rises. This rate of return is the *real interest rate* offered by the deposit. The real interest rate equals the nominal interest rate—the deposit's money rate of return—less the inflation rate—the rate at which the money prices of goods and services rise. Because the future price level cannot be predicted with certainty, we usually speak of the *expected* real interest rate, that is, the nominal interest rate less the *expected* rate of inflation.[10]

Suppose, for example, that a \$1 deposit pays you \$1.10 after a year but that you expect the U.S. price level to rise by 4 percent over the year. Then the nominal interest rate on dollar deposits is 10 percent per year, while the expected real interest rate is 10 percent per year − 4 percent per year = 6 percent per year.

Some notation will help us relate the concepts of nominal and real interest rates to the Fisher effect. Let P^e be the price level expected for a year from now. Then the expected rate of inflation over the year is defined as

$$\pi^e = \frac{P^e - P}{P},$$

where P is today's price level. We can now express the expected real interest rate, r^e, as the nominal interest rate less expected inflation:

$$r^e = R - \pi^e.$$

[9]The Fisher effect is named after Irving Fisher, one of the great American economists of the early twentieth century. The effect is discussed at length in his book, *The Theory of Interest* (New York: Macmillan, 1930). Fisher, incidentally, was one of the early discoverers of the interest parity condition on which we have based our theory of foreign-exchange market equilibrium.

[10]Chapter 7 examined the role of real interest rates in international borrowing and lending.

By writing this equation in a slightly different form, we can see that the nominal interest rate is the sum of the expected real interest rate and the expected inflation rate:

$$R = r^e + \pi^e. \tag{14-6}$$

Equation (14-6) is the key to understanding the Fisher effect of inflation on nominal interest rates. *It tells us that a rise in expected inflation that does not change the expected real interest rate will cause an equal rise in the nominal interest rate.* All else equal, therefore, an increase in expected inflation will cause a point-for-point increase in the nominal interest rate. If the U.S. nominal interest rate is 10 percent per year, for example, and expected U.S. inflation rises by 2 percent per year, then the nominal interest rate will rise to 12 percent per year if the expected U.S. real interest rate does not change.[11]

Real interest rates need not be constant, of course; so data from the real world do not show a one-for-one link between nominal interest rates and expected inflation. The important lesson of the Fisher effect, however, is that nominal interest rates are likely to rise when expected future inflation rises.

This lesson is borne out by recent experience, as Figure 14-14 shows. The figure plots inflation rates and nominal interest rates for three countries that have had somewhat different inflationary experiences since the mid-1960s, Switzerland, the United States, and Italy. In each country, nominal interest rates tend to rise after inflation rises as people come to expect high inflation in the future; reductions in inflation eventually reduce nominal interest rates for the same reason. Moreover, the average level of nominal interest rates is lowest in Switzerland, which has the lowest average inflation rate, and highest in Italy, which has the highest average inflation rate. The Fisher effect's prediction of a positive association between nominal interest rates and expected inflation comes out quite strongly in comparing data from these three countries.

INTEREST RATES AND EXCHANGE RATES, REVISITED

Our breakdown of the nominal interest rate into the expected real interest rate and expected inflation (the Fisher effect) gives us a better understanding of how interest-rate changes affect the exchange rate. The outcome depends on how the two components of the nominal interest rate change.

Let's look first at how an interest-rate increase induced by heightened expectations of future U.S. inflation would affect the dollar/DM exchange rate. Suppose people learn that the Federal Reserve plans to increase the U.S.

[11]The decomposition of the nominal interest rate into the expected real interest rate and the expected inflation rate gives us another way of seeing why the *nominal* interest rate is the opportunity cost of holding money. To hold money you must sacrifice the real return you could earn on bonds. In addition, your money yields a real rate of return equal to *minus* the inflation rate. The expected real rate-of-return difference between bonds and money is thus $r^e - (-\pi^e) = r^e + \pi^e = R$.

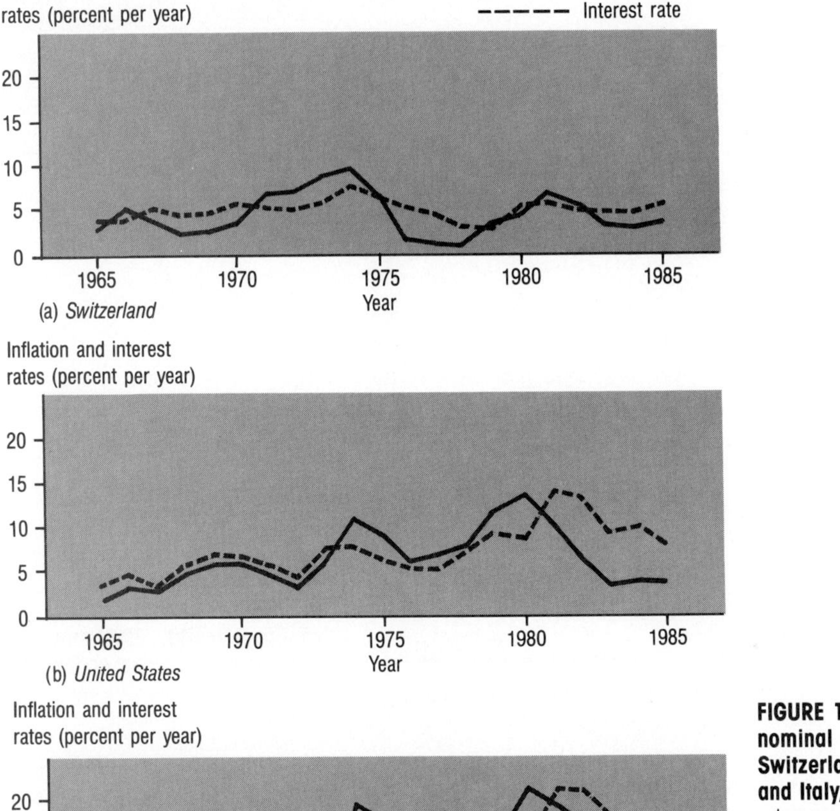

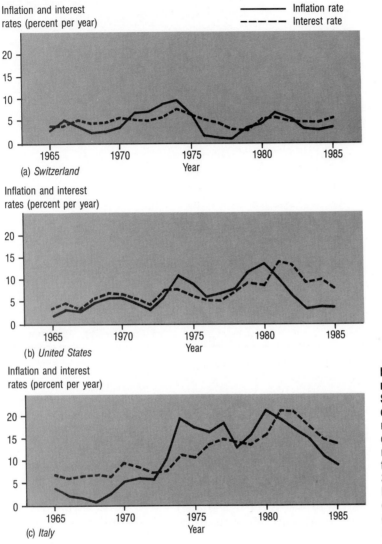

FIGURE 14-14 Inflation and the nominal interest rate in Switzerland, the United States, and Italy, 1965–1986. Inflation rates are year-to-year changes in consumer price indexes. Interest rates: Switzerland, yield of confederation bonds; United States, 3-month Treasury bill rate; Italy, bond yields of credit institutions; all measured at end of second quarter. Source: OECD, *Main Economic Indicators.*

money supply in the near future. Since this future money-supply increase will ultimately push the U.S. price level upward, the inflation rate expected for the future rises. As we saw above, higher inflationary expectations will cause the price level to begin rising as workers demand higher money wages and producers pass the resulting cost increases along to consumers by raising product prices. The lower section of Figure 14-15 shows the result of this inflationary process as a rise in the price level from P^1_{US} to P^2_{US}. Because the nominal money supply has not yet changed from its initial level of M^s_{US}, the real money supply falls and the U.S. nominal interest rate is pushed upward from $R^1_\$$ (point 1) to $R^2_\$$ (point 2).

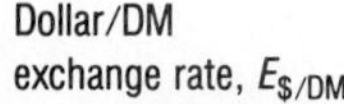

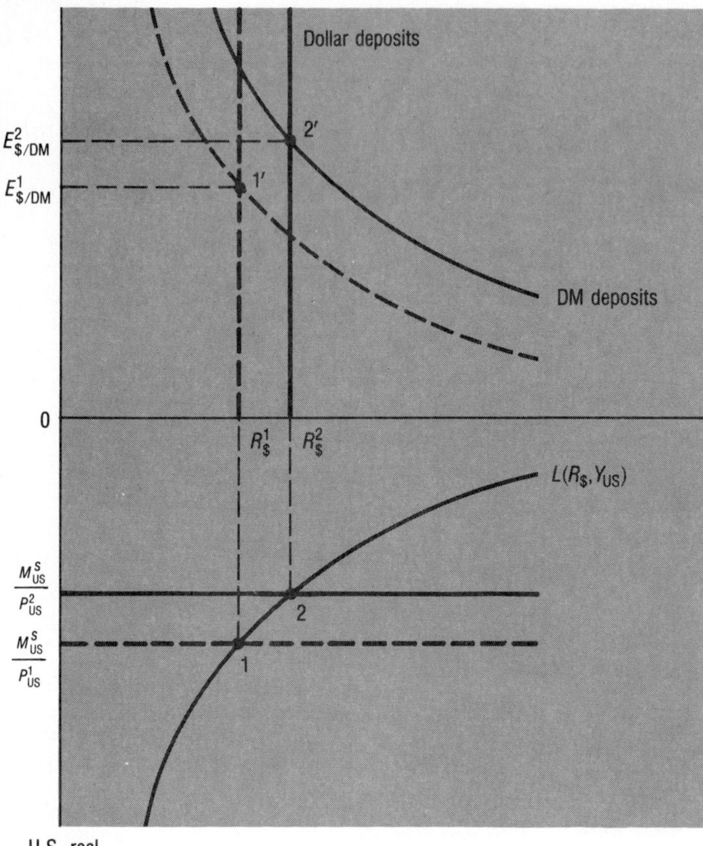

FIGURE 14-15 An increase in expected U.S. inflation raises the nominal dollar interest rate and causes the dollar to depreciate in the foreign-exchange market. Over time, expected inflation pushes the U.S. price level upward from P^1_{US} to P^2_{US}. Expected inflation therefore causes the dollar interest rate to rise, but because higher anticipated inflation also raises the expected future dollar/DM exchange rate, the dollar depreciates against the DM.

The upper section of Figure 14-15 shows the effect of these changes on the foreign-exchange market. The expectation of future money-supply growth that pushes the interest rate upward also leads people to revise their expectations about the future dollar/DM exchange rate. Because future U.S. money-supply growth is expected to raise all dollar prices—including the dollar price of DM—everyone now expects a greater future depreciation of the dollar against the DM. This change in exchange-rate expectations shifts the downward-sloping schedule to the right. The exchange rate jumps from its initial equilibrium level $E^1_{\$/DM}$ (point 1′) to $E^2_{\$/DM}$ (point 2′); so there is a *depreciation* of the dollar against the DM in spite of the rise in the dollar interest rate. The reason, of course, is that the rise in $R_\$$ has been accompanied by a change in expectations about the future exchange rate.[12]

[12]The diagram suggests that if the rise in the dollar interest rate is large relative to the rise in the expected future dollar/DM exchange rate, the dollar could still appreciate (though by a

RUNAWAY INFLATION AND THE FISHER EFFECT IN ARGENTINA

Countries with high and variable inflation provide striking examples of the close connection between nominal interest rates and expected inflation. One such country is Argentina, which has been struggling for years to control its inflation rate. After an unsuccessful war with Britain over the Falkland Islands in mid-1982, Argentina's inflation rate began moving upward. By early 1985, inflation was around 25 percent *per month,* which translates into an annual inflation rate of close to 1400 percent! In June 1985, the government introduced a stabilization program called the "austral plan." The plan consisted of a government-imposed freeze on wages and prices, a sharp slowdown in the growth of the money supply, and a currency reform that replaced the old currency, the peso, with a new one, the austral.

As Irving Fisher would have predicted, interest rates in Argentina over the past 10 years have reflected the vicissitudes of inflation. Figure 14-16, which shows monthly data, indicates that interest-rate swings have followed, and at times overshot, the broad swings in inflation. At the height of the runaway inflation in 1985, the nominal interest rate approached 35 percent per month, or around 3600 percent per year. Evidently, people at the time expected inflation to rise quickly to even higher levels.

Inflation and the interest rate both dropped precipitously when the austral plan was introduced. As this book is being written, the ultimate success of the austral plan in taming inflation remains to be seen.

Now let's think about an increase in the nominal interest rate that is associated with a fall in expected inflation and an increase in the real interest rate. Such a change can be visualized by reversing the action in Figure 14-12, which shows the dynamic effects of a current increase in the U.S. money supply. A *decrease* in today's M^s_{US} raises the nominal dollar interest rate $R_\$$; and because a fall in today's money supply leads people to expect a lower future price level, the expected inflation rate falls. The expected real interest rate in the United States, however, is

$$r^e_\$ = R_\$ - \pi^e_{US},$$

smaller amount than if expectations did not change). This is an extremely unlikely outcome, but for reasons that will become clear only in Chapter 16. Briefly, an appreciation of the dollar would make U.S. products more expensive relative to foreign products and thus reduce the demand for them. By lowering the demand for U.S. output, a dollar appreciation would thus prevent the rise in the U.S. price level that reduces the real money supply and pushes the dollar interest rate upward. If this interest-rate rise does not occur, however, the dollar cannot possibly appreciate.

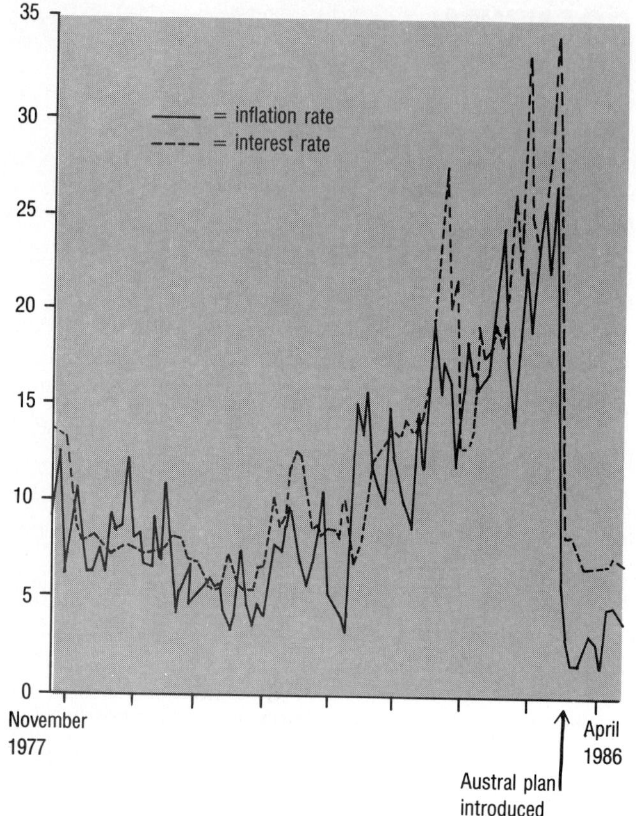

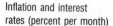

FIGURE 14-16 Inflation and the nominal interest rate in Argentina. To proxy expected inflation, the figure shows as time-t inflation $\pi_{t+1} = (P_{t+1} - P_t)/P_t$. Source: Data courtesy of Carlos Alfredo Rodríguez, Centro de Estudios Macroeconómicos de Argentina, Buenos Aires.

which must *rise* if both $R_\$$ rises and π^e_{US} falls. At the same time, the dollar *appreciates* against the DM. The appreciation occurs for two reasons: the nominal dollar interest rate has risen relative to the nominal DM interest rate, and the expected future price of DM in terms of dollars has fallen.

Our examination of how nominal interest-rate changes affect the exchange rate leads us to the following conclusion: *A nominal interest-rate increase caused by a rise in expected inflation causes the currency to depreciate in the foreign-exchange market, while a nominal interest-rate increase associated with a fall in expected inflation (and thus with a rise in the expected real interest rate) causes the currency to appreciate.* Similarly, lower nominal interest rates due to lower inflation expectations cause currency appreciation, while lower nominal interest rates associated with higher expected inflation and thus with lower expected real interest rates cause currency depreciation.

SUMMARY

1. Money is held because of its liquidity. When considered in real terms, *aggregate money demand* is not a demand for a certain number of currency units

but is instead a demand for a certain amount of purchasing power. Aggregate real money demand depends negatively on the opportunity cost of holding money (measured by the domestic interest rate) and positively on the volume of transactions in the economy (measured by real GNP).

2. The money market is in equilibrium when the real *money supply* equals aggregate real money demand. With the *price level* given in the short run, a rise in the money supply lowers the interest rate and a fall in the money supply raises the interest rate. A rise in real output raises the interest rate, while a fall in real output has the opposite effect.

3. By lowering the domestic interest rate, an increase in the money supply causes the domestic currency to depreciate in the foreign-exchange market (even when expectations of future exchange rates do not change). Similarly, a fall in the domestic money supply causes the domestic currency to appreciate against foreign currencies.

4. The assumption that the price level is given in the *short run* is a good approximation to reality in countries with moderate *inflation.* Over the *long run,* however, permanent changes in the money supply push the price level proportionally in the same direction but do not influence output, the interest rate, or any relative prices. One important money price that eventually rises in proportion to a permanent money-supply increase is the exchange rate, the domestic-currency price of foreign currency.

5. An increase in the money supply can cause the exchange rate to overshoot its long-run level in the short run. If output is given, a permanent money-supply increase, for example, causes a more-than-proportional short-run depreciation of the currency, followed by an appreciation of the currency to its long-run exchange rate. *Exchange-rate overshooting,* which heightens the volatility of exchange rates, is a direct result of sluggish short-run price-level adjustment and the interest parity condition.

6. A country's *nominal interest rate* is the sum of its expected real interest rate and its expected inflation rate. The effect on the exchange rate of a nominal interest-rate change depends on how these two components have changed. Increases in nominal interest rates associated with reductions in expected inflation (and thus with increases in real interest rates) cause the currency to appreciate in the foreign-exchange market. Increases in nominal interest rates due to increases in expected inflation (the Fisher effect) cause the currency to depreciate.

KEY TERMS

money supply
aggregate money demand
price level
short run
long run
inflation
deflation
exchange-rate overshooting
Fisher effect
nominal interest rate

PROBLEMS

1. Suppose there is a reduction in aggregate real money demand, that is, a negative shift in the aggregate real money demand function. Trace through the short-run and long-run effects on the exchange rate, interest rate, and price level.

2. What is the short-run effect on the exchange rate of an increase in domestic real GNP, given expectations about future exchange rates?

3. If in the long run the actual exchange rate also equals the expected future exchange rate, how would you expect an increase in domestic real GNP to change the economy's long-run equilibrium?

4. Does our discussion of money's usefulness as a medium of exchange and unit of account suggest reasons why some currencies become vehicle currencies for foreign-exchange transactions? (The concept of a vehicle currency was discussed in Chapter 13.)

5. If a currency reform has no effects on the economy's real variables, why do governments typically institute currency reforms in connection with broader programs aimed at halting runaway inflation? (There are many instances beside the French case mentioned in the text. Examples from the 1980s include Argentina's switch from the peso to the austral and Brazil's switch from the cruzeiro to the cruzado.)

6. Imagine that the central bank of an economy with unemployment doubles its money supply. In the long run, full employment is restored and output returns to its full employment level. On the assumption that the interest rate before the money-supply increase equals the long-run interest rate, is the long-run increase in the price level more than proportional or less than proportional to the money-supply change? What if the interest rate was initially below its long-run level?

7. In our discussion of short-run exchange-rate overshooting, we assumed that real output was given. Assume instead that an increase in the money supply raises real output in the short run (an assumption that will be justified in Chapter 16). How does this affect the extent to which the exchange rate overshoots when the money supply first increases? Is it likely that the exchange rate *under*shoots? (Hint: In Figure 14-12a, allow the aggregate real money demand schedule to shift in response to the increase in output.)

8. If the nominal interest rate is 10 percent per year and people expect the price level to rise by 8 percent over the coming year, what is the expected real interest rate?

9. Every week the Federal Reserve announces how quickly the money supply grew in the week ending 10 days previously. (There is a 10-day delay because it takes that long to assemble data on bank deposits.) Economists have noticed that when the announced increase in the money supply is greater than expected, nominal interest rates *rise* just after the announcement; and interest rates *fall* when the market learns that the money supply grew more slowly than expected. Two competing explanations of this phenomenon are: (1) Unexpectedly high money growth, for example, raises expected inflation and thus raises nominal interest rates through the Fisher effect. (2) Unexpectedly high money growth leads the market to expect future Fed action to reduce the money supply, causing a decrease in the amount of deposits supplied by banks but no increase in expected inflation. How would you use data from the foreign-exchange market to distinguish between these two hypotheses? (For an answer, see the paper by Engel and Frankel suggested for Further Reading below.)

10. The difference between the nominal interest rate and the actual inflation rate is often called the ex post real interest rate (as opposed to the ex ante, or expected real interest rate). Figure 14-14 shows that between 1976 and 1980, the ex post real interest rate in Switzerland was usually positive while that in the United States was usually negative. Assume that people were able to forecast inflation accurately in both countries during these years. What would you guess about the dollar's strength against the Swiss franc in the foreign-exchange market between 1976 and 1980? What do you think happened to the dollar/Swiss franc exchange rate in 1981–1982? Check your answer by looking up the history of this exchange rate. (See, for example, the International Monetary Fund's publication, *International Financial Statistics.*)

FURTHER READING

Rudiger Dornbusch. "Expectations and Exchange Rate Dynamics." *Journal of Political Economy* 84 (December 1976), pp. 1161–1176. A theoretical analysis of exchange-rate overshooting.

Rudiger Dornbusch and Stanley Fischer. *Macroeconomics,* 4th edition, Chapter 14. New York: McGraw-Hill, 1987. Contains a detailed discussion of the inflation process for a closed economy.

Charles Engel and Jeffrey Frankel. "Why Money Announcements Move Interest Rates: An Answer from the Foreign Exchange Market," in *Sixth West Coast Academic/Federal Reserve Economic Research Seminar* (Economic Review Conference Supplement). San Francisco: Federal Reserve Bank of San Francisco, 1983, pp. 1–26. Studies the link between Fed money announcements, interest rates, and the exchange rate.

Jacob A. Frenkel and Michael L. Mussa. "The Efficiency of Foreign Exchange Markets and Measures of Turbulence." *American Economic Review* 70 (May 1980), pp. 374–381. Contrasts the behavior of national price levels with that of exchange rates and other asset prices.

Richard M. Levich. *"Overshooting" in the Foreign Exchange Market*. Occasional Paper 5. New York: Group of Thirty, 1981. An examination of the theory and evidence on exchange-rate overshooting.

Frederic S. Mishkin. *The Economics of Money, Banking and Financial Markets,* Chapter 6. Boston: Little, Brown and Company, 1986. Discusses interest rates and the Fisher effect.

15 PRICE LEVELS AND THE EXCHANGE RATE IN THE LONG RUN

In 1968, 1 Deutschemark cost 25 cents; by 1978, the price of a DM had more than doubled to 55 cents. In the spring of 1985, however, the dollar/DM exchange stood at around 32 cents per DM, far below its 1978 level. What economic factors can explain such long-term movements in exchange rates?

We have seen that exchange rates are determined by interest rates and expectations about the future, which are, in turn, affected by conditions in national money markets. The next step in building a complete model of exchange-rate determination is to examine how demand and supply shifts in countries' output markets influence exchange rates. Such output-market disturbances cause short-run employment fluctuations that alter interest rates and, with them, exchange rates. Shifts in output markets, however, also have long-run effects on exchange rates—effects that persist even after all prices have adjusted and all productive factors are again fully employed. This chapter develops a framework to examine how exchange rates' long-run levels are affected by events in national output markets.

In the long run, national price levels play a key role in determining both interest rates and the relative prices of national outputs. Thus, to understand why exchange rates can change dramatically over periods of several years, we must study the interdependence of national price levels and exchange rates. We begin our analysis by discussing the famous theory of **purchasing power parity (PPP),** which states that the exchange rate between two countries' currencies equals the ratio of the currencies' purchasing powers, as measured by national price levels. Next, we examine reasons why PPP may fail to give accurate long-run predictions, and show how the theory must sometimes be modified to account for supply or demand shifts in countries' output markets. Finally, we look at what our extended PPP theory predicts about how changes in money and output markets affect exchange rates.

Our analysis of *long-run* exchange-rate determination shows how economic events affect peoples' expectations of future exchange rates. We therefore draw heavily on this chapter's conclusions when we analyze the *short-run* interaction of exchange rates and output in Chapter 16.

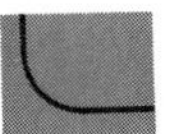

THE LAW OF ONE PRICE

To understand the market forces that might give rise to the results predicted by the purchasing power parity theory, we discuss first a related but distinct proposition known as the **law of one price.** The law of one price states that in competitive markets free of transportation costs and official barriers to trade (such as tariffs), identical goods sold in different countries must sell for the same price when their prices are expressed in terms of the same currency. For example, if the dollar/pound exchange rate is \$1.50 per pound, a sweater that sells for \$45 in New York must sell for £30 in London. The dollar price of the sweater when sold in London is then (\$1.50 per pound) × (£30 per sweater) = \$45 per sweater, the same as its price in New York.

Let's continue with this example to see why the law of one price must hold when trade is free and there are no transport costs or trade barriers. If the dollar/pound exchange rate were \$1.45 per pound, you could buy a sweater in London by converting \$43.50 (= 1.45 \$/£ × £30) into £30 in the foreign-exchange market. Thus, the dollar price of a sweater in London would be only \$43.50. If the same sweater were selling for \$45 in New York, U.S. importers and British exporters would have an incentive to buy sweaters in London and ship them to New York, pushing the London price up and the New York price down until prices were equal in the two locations. Similarly, at an exchange rate of \$1.55 per pound, the dollar price of sweaters in London would be \$46.50 (= 1.55 \$/£ × £30), \$1.50 more than in New York. Sweaters now would be shipped from west to east until the same price prevailed in the two markets.

The law of one price is a restatement, in terms of currencies, of a principle that was important in the trade theory portion of this book: when trade is open and costless, identical goods must trade at the same relative prices regardless of where they are sold. We remind you of that principle here because it provides one link between the domestic prices of goods and exchange rates. We can state the law of one price formally as follows: Let P^i_{US} be the dollar price of good i when sold in the U.S. and let P^i_G be the corresponding DM price in Germany. Then the law of one price implies that the dollar price of good i is the same wherever it is sold,

$$P^i_{US} = (E_{\$/DM}) \times (P^i_G).$$

Equivalently, the dollar/DM exchange rate is the ratio of good i's U.S. and German money prices,

$$E_{\$/DM} = P^i_{US}/P^i_G.$$

PURCHASING POWER PARITY

The theory of purchasing power parity (PPP) states that the exchange rate between two countries' currencies equals the ratio of the two currencies' purchasing powers. Recall from Chapter 14 that the purchasing power of a country's currency is reflected in the country's price level, the money price of a typical basket of consumption goods. The currency of a country with a high price level has low purchasing power because the "cost of living" is high when measured in domestic currency. The PPP theory predicts that a fall in a currency's domestic purchasing power (as indicated by an increase in the domestic price level) will cause a proportional currency depreciation in the foreign-exchange market. Symmetrically, PPP predicts that an increase in the currency's domestic purchasing power will cause a proportional currency appreciation.

The basic idea of PPP was put forth in the writings of nineteenth century British economists, among them David Ricardo (the originator of the theory of comparative advantage). Gustav Cassel, a Swedish economist writing in the first third of this century, popularized PPP by making it the centerpiece of a theory of exchange rates. While there has been much controversy about the usefulness of PPP, the PPP theory does highlight important factors behind long-term exchange-rate movements.

To express the PPP theory in symbols, let P_{US} be the United States price level and P_G the German price level. Then PPP predicts a dollar/DM exchange rate of

$$E_{\$/DM} = P_{US}/P_G. \quad \textbf{(15-1)}$$

If, for example, the typical consumption basket costs \$200 in the United States and DM600 in Germany, PPP predicts a dollar/DM exchange rate of \$0.33 per DM (= \$200 per consumption basket/DM600 per consumption basket).

According to PPP, *a rise in the U.S. price level, P_{US}, must lead to a proportional depreciation of the dollar against the DM, while a rise in Germany's price level, P_G, must lead to a proportional appreciation of the dollar against the DM.* In terms of our previous example, a doubling of the U.S. price level from \$200 per consumption basket to \$400 per basket would cause the dollar to depreciate by 100 percent, that is, to a rate of \$0.67 per DM. A doubling of the German price level would result in an exchange rate of \$0.17 per DM.

By rearranging equation (15-1) to read

$$P_{US} = (E_{\$/DM}) \times (P_G),$$

we get an alternative interpretation of PPP. The left-hand side of this equation is the dollar price of a typical U.S. consumption basket; the right-hand side is the dollar price of a typical German consumption basket (that is, the DM price multiplied by the dollar price of a DM). These two prices are the same if PPP holds. *PPP thus asserts that all countries' price levels are equal when measured in terms of the same currency.*

THE RELATION BETWEEN PPP AND THE LAW OF ONE PRICE

Superficially, the statement of PPP given by equation (15-1) looks like the law of one price, which says that $E_{\$/DM} = P^i_{US}/P^i_G$ for any commodity i. There is an important difference between PPP and the law of one price, however: the law of one price applies to an individual commodity (commodity i), while PPP applies to the general price level, which is a composite of the prices of all the commodities that enter into a typical consumption basket.

Nonetheless, the reasoning behind the PPP theory builds on the law of one price. If the law of one price holds for all commodities individually, prices and exchange rates should not stray from the relation predicted by PPP. When a country's goods become temporarily more expensive than similar goods produced abroad, the demand for domestic goods falls, pushing their prices back into line with foreign prices. When a country's goods become temporarily cheap relative to foreign goods, the demand for domestic goods rises and pushes prices and exchange rates back toward PPP. PPP asserts that the economic forces behind the law of one price tend to equalize the cost of living in all countries.

ABSOLUTE PPP AND RELATIVE PPP

The statement that exchange rates equal relative price levels [equation (15-1)] is sometimes referred to as *absolute* PPP. Absolute PPP implies a theory known as *relative* PPP, which states that the percentage change in the exchange rate between two currencies over some period equals the difference between the percentage changes in national price levels. If the U.S. price level rises by 10 percent over a year while Germany's rises by 5 percent, for example, relative PPP predicts a 5 percent depreciation of the dollar against the DM. More formally, relative PPP between the U.S. and Germany would be written as

$$(E_{\$/DM,t} - E_{\$/DM,t-1})/E_{\$/DM,t-1} = \pi_{US,t} - \pi_{G,t}, \qquad (15\text{-}2)$$

where π_t denotes an inflation rate [that is, $\pi_t = (P_t - P_{t-1})/P_{t-1}$].[1] Unlike absolute PPP, relative PPP can be defined only with respect to the time period over which price levels and the exchange rate change.

Relative PPP is important because it may be valid even when absolute PPP is not. Provided the factors causing deviations from absolute PPP are rather stable over time, percentage *changes* in relative price levels can still approximate percentage *changes* in exchange rates.

EMPIRICAL EVIDENCE ON PPP AND THE LAW OF ONE PRICE

How well does the PPP theory explain actual data on exchange rates and national price levels? A brief answer is that while PPP is sometimes a good approximation to the data, changes in national price levels often tell us little about exchange-rate movements.

Figure 15-1 illustrates these points by plotting both the dollar/DM exchange rate, $E_{\$/DM}$, and the ratio of the U.S. and German price levels, P_{US}/P_G, between 1964 and 1986. The price ratios that appear in the figure are relative consumer price indexes (CPIs). Because the CPI attempts to measure the price of a typical consumption basket, the CPI is an appropriate price index for PPP calculations.[2]

Relative PPP predicts that $E_{\$/DM}$ and P_{US}/P_G should move proportionally, and as you can see in the figure, this was more or less so through 1970. But PPP broke down dramatically after 1970, with the dollar depreciating sharply between 1970 and 1973 even though U.S. prices *fell* relative to German prices in those years. From 1973 through 1979, PPP is somewhat more successful, as U.S. prices rise relative to German prices and the dollar (in all but one of these years) depreciates against the DM. But the magnitude of the dollar's depreciation between 1973 and 1979 is far greater than relative PPP would predict.

The most dramatic breakdown of PPP occurs in the years after 1979. In those years the dollar first sustained a massive appreciation against the DM

[1]More precisely, equation (15-1) implies a close approximation to equation (15-2) when rates of change are not too large.

[2]Price indexes like the CPI are not reported as dollar amounts but rather as index numbers relative to some base year. Thus, data published by the U.S. government show that the U.S. CPI was 100 in the base year 1967 and 298.4 in 1983, from which we can infer that the dollar price of a typical consumption basket (the price level) nearly tripled between 1967 and 1983. To highlight the failure of relative PPP, the base years for the U.S. and German price indexes in Figure 15-1 have been chosen so that their ratio in 1964 equals the 1964 exchange rate. Clearly, this equality does *not* mean that absolute PPP held in 1964. Governments generally report an array of different price indexes covering different commodity groups, and there is some controversy over which index should be used for PPP calculations. That controversy is discussed by Lawrence Officer in a paper listed in this chapter's Further Reading.

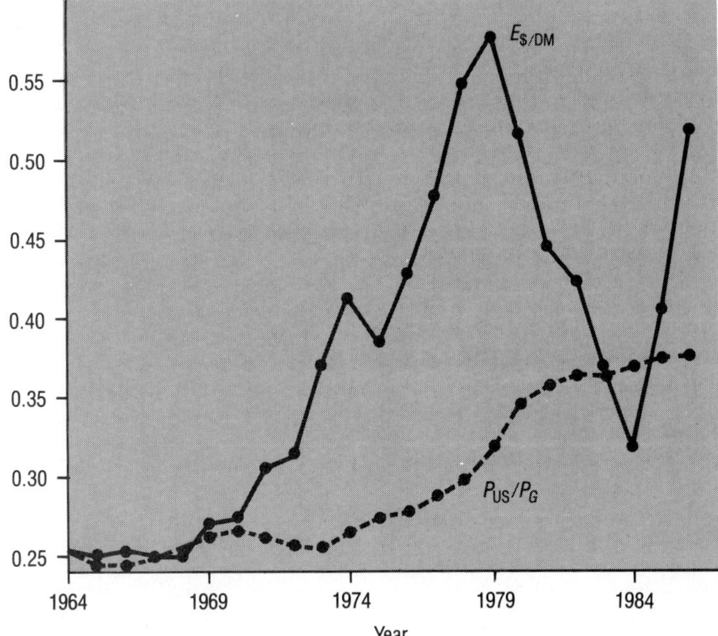

FIGURE 15-1 The dollar/DM exchange rate and relative U.S./German price levels, 1964–1986. The graph shows that relative PPP does not explain the dollar/DM exchange rate after 1970. Source: OECD, *Main Economic Indicators.* Exchange rates and price levels are end-of-year data.

even though the U.S. price level continued to rise relative to that of Germany; subsequently the dollar depreciated by far more than PPP would predict. Relative PPP does hold over the period 1964–1983 taken as a whole: over those two decades, the percentage rise in the dollar/DM exchange rate is very close to the percentage increase in the U.S. price level relative to the German price level. In view of the wide departures from relative PPP over long subperiods of the 1964–1983 span and after 1983, however, PPP appears to be of limited use even as a long-run explanation of exchange-rate movements.

Studies of other currencies largely confirm the lessons of Figure 15-1. PPP has not held up well since the early 1970s, but in the 1960s it is a more reliable guide to the relationship among exchange rates and national price levels.[3] As you will learn later in this book, the period between the end of World War II in 1945 and the early 1970s was also a period in which ex-

[3]See, for example, Jacob A. Frenkel, "The Collapse of Purchasing Power Parities during the 1970s," *European Economic Review* 16 (1981), pp. 145–165; Hans Genberg, "Purchasing Power Parity under Fixed and Flexible Exchange Rates," *Journal of International Economics* 8 (May 1978), pp. 247–276; and Robert E. Cumby and Maurice Obstfeld, "International Interest Rate and Price Level Linkages under Flexible Exchange Rates," in John F. O. Bilson and Richard C. Marston, eds., *Exchange Rate Theory and Practice* (Chicago: University of Chicago Press, 1984), pp. 121–151.

change rates were fixed within narrow internationally agreed margins through the intervention of central banks in the foreign-exchange market. During the first half of the 1920s, when many exchange rates were market-determined as in the 1970s and 1980s, important deviations from PPP also occurred.[4]

Even the law of one price does not fare well in some careful recent studies of price data broken down by commodity type.[5] Manufactured goods that are very similar to each other have sold at quite disparate prices in various international markets since the early 1970s. Because the argument leading to PPP builds on the law of one price, it is not surprising that the PPP theory does not stand up well to the data.

As you will recall, the law of one price assumes that there are no significant trade barriers. That assumption is certainly wrong. Several factors in addition to trade barriers, however, help explain the limited applicability of PPP. A detailed discussion of the factors causing departures from PPP will help us build on the PPP theory to develop a more realistic long-run model of exchange rates.

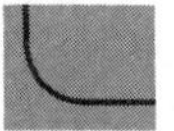

PROBLEMS WITH PPP

There are several immediate problems with our rationale for the PPP theory of exchange rates, which was based on the law of one price:

1. Contrary to the assumption of the law of one price, transport costs and restrictions on trade do exist, as we noted above. These trade barriers may prevent some goods and services from being traded between countries.
2. Because consumption baskets in different countries are not the same, there is no reason for the consumption baskets of different countries to have the same price, even when there are no barriers to trade.
3. Monopolistic or oligopolistic practices in goods markets may interact with transport costs and other trade barriers to further weaken the link between the prices of similar goods sold in different countries.

All three of these factors work against the central idea of absolute PPP that the cost of living should be the same everywhere. They may also invalidate relative PPP, which predicts constant percentage cost-of-living differences between countries.

[4]See Paul R. Krugman, "Purchasing Power Parity and Exchange Rates: Another Look at the Evidence," *Journal of International Economics* 8 (August 1978), pp. 397–407; and Paul De Grauwe, Marc Janssens, and Hilde Leliaert, *Real-Exchange-Rate Variability from 1920 to 1926 and 1973 to 1982,* Princeton Studies in International Finance 56 (International Finance Section, Department of Economics, Princeton University, September 1985).

[5]See Peter Isard, "How Far Can We Push the Law of One Price?" *American Economic Review* 67 (December 1977), pp. 942–948; and Irving B. Kravis and Robert E. Lipsey, "Price Behavior in the Light of Balance of Payments Theories," *Journal of International Economics* 8 (May 1978), pp. 193–246.

SOME MEATY EVIDENCE ON THE LAW OF ONE PRICE

In the summer of 1986, the *Economist* magazine conducted an extensive survey on the prices of Big Mac hamburgers at McDonald's restaurants throughout the world. This apparently whimsical undertaking was not the result of an outbreak of editorial giddiness. The magazine wanted to poke fun at economists who confidently declare exchange rates to be "overvalued" or "undervalued" on the basis of PPP comparisons. Since Big Macs are "sold in 41 countries, with only the most trivial changes of recipe," the magazine argued, a comparison of hamburger prices should serve as a "medium-rare guide to whether currencies are trading at the right exchange rates."*

One way of interpreting the *Economist* survey is as a test of the law of one price. Viewed in this way, the results of the test are quite startling. The dollar prices of Big Macs turned out to be wildly different in different countries. The price of a Big Mac in the United States was 50 percent higher than in Australia and 64 percent higher than in Hong Kong. In contrast, a Parisian Big Mac cost 54 percent more than its American counterpart; a Tokyo Big Mac cost 50 percent more. Only in Britain and Ireland were the dollar prices of the burgers close to their U.S. levels.

How can this dramatic violation of the law of one price be explained? As the *Economist* noted, transport costs and government regulations are part of the explanation. If trade impediments such as these were the whole story, however, Big Mac prices would have been more uniform within the European Economic Community than they were. Product differentiation is probably an important additional element of the explanation. In many countries, relatively few close substitutes for Big Macs are available. This factor gives McDonald's varying degrees of power to tailor its prices to the local market.

*"On the Hamburger Standard," *Economist,* September 6–12, 1986.

TRADE BARRIERS AND NONTRADABLES

Transport costs and trade restrictions make it expensive to move goods between markets located in different countries, and therefore weaken the law-of-one-price mechanism underlying PPP. Suppose once again that a sweater sells for \$45 in New York and for £30 in London, but that it costs \$2 to ship a sweater between the two cities. At an exchange rate of \$1.45 per pound, the dollar price of a London sweater is (\$1.45 per pound) × (£30) = \$43.50, but an American importer would have to pay \$43.50 + \$2 = \$45.50 to purchase the sweater in London and get it to New York. At an exchange rate of \$1.45 per pound, it therefore would not pay to ship sweaters from London to New York, even though their dollar price would be higher in the latter location. Similarly, at an exchange rate of $1.55 per pound, an American exporter would lose money by shipping sweaters from New York to London even though the New York price of $45 would then be below the dollar price of the sweater in London, $46.50.

The lesson of this example is that transport costs sever the close link between exchange rates and goods prices implied by the law of one price. The greater the transport costs, the greater the range over which the exchange rate can move, given goods' prices in different countries. Official trade restrictions like tariffs have a similar effect, because a fee paid to the customs inspector affects the importer's profit in the same way as an equivalent shipping fee. Either type of trade impediment weakens the basis of PPP by allowing national price levels (expressed in a common currency) to differ more widely from each other.

While transport costs pose an obvious problem for the absolute version of PPP, *relative* PPP may still hold closely if transport costs don't change much over time and are small enough that most goods and services are tradable. As you will recall from Chapter 2, however, transport costs may be so large a part of the cost of producing some goods and services that they can never be traded internationally at a profit. Such goods and services are called *nontradables.* The time-honored classroom example of a nontradable is the haircut. A Frenchman desiring an American haircut would have to transport himself to the United States or transport an American barber to France; in either case, the cost of transport is so large relative to the price of the service being purchased that (tourists excepted!) French haircuts are consumed only by residents of France while American haircuts are consumed only by residents of the United States.

The existence in all countries of nontraded goods and services whose prices are not linked internationally allows systematic deviations even from relative PPP. Because the price of a nontradable is determined entirely by its *domestic* supply and demand curves, shifts in those curves may cause the domestic price of a typical consumption basket to change relative to the foreign price of the same basket. This price behavior contradicts relative PPP, which predicts that the prices of any two countries' consumption baskets will move in proportion to each other when the prices are measured in the same currency.

Each country's consumption basket includes a wide variety of nontradables, including (along with haircuts) routine medical treatment, aerobic dance instruction, and housing, among others. Broadly speaking, we can identify traded goods with manufactured products, raw materials, and agricultural products. Nontradables are primarily services and the output of the construction industry.[6] We can get a rough idea of the importance of non-

[6]There are naturally exceptions to this rule. For example, some financial services provided by banks and brokerage houses can be traded internationally. In addition, trade restrictions, if sufficiently severe, can cause goods that would normally be traded to become nontraded. Thus, in most countries some manufactures are nontraded. Remember also that the retail prices of many "tradables" reflect costs of retailing services that can vary sharply from country to country.

tradables in the American economy by looking at the contribution of the service and construction industries to U.S. GNP. In 1984, the output of these industries accounted for 57.9 percent of U.S. GNP. Nontradables help explain the wide departures from relative PPP illustrated by Figure 15-1.

INTERNATIONAL DIFFERENCES IN CONSUMPTION PATTERNS

People living in different countries spend their income in different ways. The Italians consume more olive oil than Americans, the Japanese consume more rice, and the British consume more tea. Even when competition is free and there are no trade impediments, PPP may be violated simply because national price levels do not place the same weights on the prices of different goods.

These differences point to a general difficulty with attempts to apply absolute PPP to the real world: How do we define a "typical" consumption basket? Even within a single country, the typical consumption baskets of different households may differ widely according to their income, location, and so on. Our judgments about the validity of absolute PPP will therefore be quite sensitive to the consumption baskets we choose to regard as "typical" in various countries. For this reason, applied comparisons of international price levels try to calculate the prices of the same quality-adjusted commodity basket in different countries.

Because relative PPP makes predictions about price *changes* rather than price *levels,* it can hold regardless of the baskets used to define price levels in the countries being compared. Change in the relative prices of basket components, however, may cause violations of relative PPP.

DEPARTURES FROM FREE COMPETITION

When trade barriers and imperfectly competitive market structures occur together, linkages between national price levels are weakened further. An extreme case occurs when a commodity is produced by a single producer who sells it for different prices in different markets. (Recall the analysis of dumping in Chapter 6.) The prices of Mercedes-Benz autos, for example, were higher in the United States than in Germany in the mid-1980s.

Such discriminatory pricing would be difficult to enforce if it were not costly for drivers to buy autos in Germany and ship them to the United States. Similarly, if consumers viewed Volvos and Acuras as good substitutes for Mercedes, competition among producers would keep both the U.S. and German prices of the German cars from getting too far out of line with production costs. The combination of product differentiation and segmented markets, however, leads to departures from the law of one price and absolute PPP. Shifts over time in market structure and demand can also invalidate relative PPP.

PPP IN THE SHORT RUN AND IN THE LONG RUN

The three factors we have examined so far in explaining the PPP theory's poor performance—trade barriers, international differences in consumption patterns, and imperfect competition—can cause national price levels to diverge even in the long run, after all prices have had time to adjust to their market-clearing levels. As you will recall from Chapter 14, however, many prices in the economy are sticky and take time to adjust fully. Departures from PPP will therefore be even greater in the short run than in the long run.

An abrupt depreciation of the dollar against foreign currencies, for example, makes farm equipment in the United States cheaper relative to similar equipment produced abroad. As farmers throughout the world shift their demand for tractors and reapers to U.S. producers, the price of American farm equipment tends to rise to reduce the divergence from the law of one price caused by the dollar's depreciation. It takes time, however, before buyers abandon long-standing business relationships with their previous suppliers and establish new relationships with U.S. firms. The prices of U.S. and foreign farm equipment may differ considerably while markets adjust to the exchange-rate change.

You might suspect that short-run price stickiness and exchange-rate volatility help explain a phenomenon we noted in discussing Figure 15-1, that violations of PPP have been much more flagrant over periods when exchange rates have floated. Recent empirical research supports this interpretation of the data. In a careful study covering many countries and historical episodes, Michael Mussa of the University of Chicago compared the extent of short-run deviations from PPP under fixed and floating exchange rates. He found that floating exchange rates systematically lead to much larger and more frequent short-run deviations from PPP.[7]

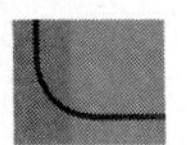

GENERALIZING PURCHASING POWER PARITY: A MODEL OF EXCHANGE RATES IN THE LONG RUN

Why devote so much discussion to the purchasing power parity theory when it is fraught with exceptions and apparently contradicted by the data? We examined the PPP theory so closely because its basic idea of relating long-run exchange rates to long-run national price levels is correct. While the version of PPP presented above is too simple to give accurate predictions about the real world, we can generalize PPP by taking account of some of the reasons why that theory predicts badly in practice. In this section we develop this generalized model of long-run exchange-rate determination, which is more complicated than the simple PPP model but also better at explaining how exchange rates really behave.

[7]See Mussa, "Nominal Exchange Rate Regimes and the Behavior of Real Exchange Rates: Evidence and Implications," in Karl Brunner and Allan H. Meltzer, eds., *Real Business Cycles, Real Exchange Rates and Actual Policies,* Carnegie-Rochester Conference Series on Public Policy 25. Amsterdam: North-Holland, 1986, pp. 117–214.

The last section's discussion of problems with the PPP theory gives us an important clue about the factors we should incorporate in extending it. A common thread running through that discussion was the failure of simple PPP to come to grips with different supply and demand conditions in countries' output markets. In generalizing PPP, our strategy will therefore be to model the characteristics of country's output markets that influence the interaction of exchange rates and price levels. This generalization will equip us to study how output-market disturbances can cause exchange-rate changes that do not conform to PPP.

Our generalized model provides another reason why PPP remains a useful concept, for the model shows that in some important situations, the predictions of the simple PPP theory *are* accurate for the long run.

The long-run analysis below avoids the short-run complications caused by sticky prices which, as we have seen, help magnify deviations from PPP. An understanding of how exchange rates behave in the long run is, however, a prerequisite for the more complicated short-run analysis that we undertake in the next chapter.

TAKING ACCOUNT OF NONTRADED GOODS AND SERVICES

As the first step in extending the PPP theory, we study how the existence of nontraded goods and services affects the long-run relation between exchange rates and national price levels. The model we develop classifies all goods and services as either *nontradables* or *tradables*. We begin by studying the influence of nontradables because they are probably the most important reason for the failure of PPP.

As usual, we sacrifice some realism to highlight how the nontradable-tradable distinction alters the PPP theory of exchange rates. We therefore assume for now that PPP holds in the long run for countries' tradables, but not necessarily for their nontradables. As we saw earlier, this assumption is not quite right because PPP can fail to hold even when all products are traded. Later in this section, the assumption that tradables' prices obey PPP will be relaxed so that we can examine how output-market factors other than the supply and demand for nontradables affect the exchange rate.

We start by defining *separate* price levels for a country's consumption of tradables and nontradables. Just as we defined a country's overall price level, P, to be the cost of a typical consumption basket, we now define the *price of tradables, P^T*, to be the cost of the tradables included in the consumption basket, and the *price of nontradables, P^N*, to be the cost of the nontradables included in the basket. Because all goods in the typical consumption basket are either tradable or nontradable, the overall price level within a country is an average of the prices of tradables and nontradables. If a typical family spends a fraction γ of its income on nontradables and a fraction $1 - \gamma$ on tradables, the overall price level can be expressed in terms of the prices of tradables and nontradables as

$$P = \gamma P^N + (1 - \gamma)P^T.$$

If a country's residents consume only haircuts (a nontradable) and wheat (a tradable), for example, its price level is a weighted average of the prices of haircuts and wheat, with the weights depending on the relative importance of the two in the consumption basket.

Let's suppose again that we are interested in explaining the long-run dollar/DM exchange rate. Because we have assumed that PPP between U.S. and German *tradables* holds in the long run, we can express the exchange rate as

$$E_{\$/DM} = P^{T}_{US}/P^{T}_{G}. \qquad \textbf{(15-3)}$$

Equation (15-3) differs from the statement of PPP in equation (15-1),

$$E_{\$/DM} = P_{US}/P_{G},$$

because equation (15-3) involves the prices of tradables in the United States and Germany rather than those countries' overall price levels. Equation (15-3) will allow us to generalize PPP because it recognizes that only some commodities consumed within a country have prices directly linked to those of foreign goods through international trade.

We generalize PPP by first writing the overall U.S. price level as an average of the U.S. prices of nontradables and tradables. Let

α = share of nontradables in U.S. consumption,

$1 - \alpha$ = share of tradables in U.S. consumption.

Then the overall price level in the United States is

$$P_{US} = \alpha P^{N}_{US} + (1 - \alpha)P^{T}_{US}.$$

We can give a similar breakdown of Germany's overall price level into price levels for nontradables and tradables. If we let

β = share of nontradables in German consumption,

$1 - \beta$ = share of tradables in German consumption,

then the corresponding equation for Germany's overall price level is

$$P_{G} = \beta P^{N}_{G} + (1 - \beta)P^{T}_{G}.$$

It is the ratio of these two overall price levels that our generalization of PPP relates to the exchange rate. The expressions above show that the price-level ratio is

$$\frac{P_{US}}{P_{G}} = \frac{\alpha P^{N}_{US} + (1 - \alpha)P^{T}_{US}}{\beta P^{N}_{G} + (1 - \beta)P^{T}_{G}}.$$

By combining the expression above with the PPP condition for tradables [equation (15-3)], we can derive our basic equation for the long-run exchange rate. Equation (15-3) implies that $P^{T}_{US} = (E_{\$/DM}) \times (P^{T}_{G})$, that is, that the dollar prices of tradables are equal in the United States and in Germany. We can therefore divide the numerator of our expression for P_{US}/P_{G} by the dollar price of U.S. tradables, P^T_{US}, and divide the denominator by the (identical) dollar price of German tradables, $(E_{\$/DM}) \times (P^T_G)$. This step gives us the equation

$$\frac{P_{US}}{P_G} = E_{\$/DM} \times \frac{\alpha(P^N_{US}/P^T_{US}) + (1 - \alpha)}{\beta(P^N_G/P^T_G) + (1 - \beta)},$$

which we solve for the long-run dollar/DM exchange rate,

$$E_{\$/DM} = \frac{P_{US}}{P_G} \times \frac{\beta(P^N_G/P^T_G) + (1 - \beta)}{\alpha(P^N_{US}/P^T_{US}) + (1 - \alpha)}. \quad \textbf{(15-4)}$$

Equation (15-4) generalizes the PPP theory of the exchange rate by taking into account the relative price of nontradables and tradables in each of the two countries being compared. Our generalized model asserts that the long-run exchange rate is determined as the multiplicative product of two factors. The first of these factors, the ratio of national price levels (P_{US}/P_G), is the one emphasized by the simple version of PPP. The second factor, the last fraction in equation (15-4), depends on output-market conditions specific to Germany or the United States. This second factor tells us that for given overall national price levels, a rise in the price of German nontradables relative to German tradables (P^N_G/P^T_G) causes the dollar to depreciate against the DM (a rise in $E_{\$/DM}$). Similarly, a rise in the price of U.S. nontradables relative to U.S. tradables (P^N_{US}/P^T_{US}), other things equal, causes the dollar to appreciate against the DM.

TAKING ACCOUNT OF DEPARTURES FROM PPP FOR TRADABLES

We have generalized PPP to account for nontradables but have maintained the assumption that for tradable goods, PPP does hold. Our earlier discussion of problems with PPP showed, however, that PPP fails even if we restrict our attention to tradable goods. So our long-run exchange-rate equation (15-4), which was based on the assumption that PPP holds for tradables,

$$E_{\$/DM} = P^T_{US}/P^T_G,$$

must be modified if we want an exchange-rate theory that accounts for such factors as non-prohibitive trade barriers as well as for nontradables.

To generalize our long-run exchange-rate model further, we replace the PPP assumption for tradables with the condition

$$E_{\$/DM} = \tau_{G,US} \times (P^T_{US}/P^T_G), \quad \textbf{(15-5)}$$

where $\tau_{G,US}$ is a variable reflecting factors that influence the relation among the exchange rate and the home prices of U.S. and German tradables in the long run. By rewriting equation (15-5) as

$$\tau_{G,US} = \frac{(E_{\$/DM} \times P^T_G)}{P^T_{US}},$$

we can interpret $\tau_{G,US}$ as the ratio between the dollar price of German tradables and the dollar price of U.S. tradables. A rise in $\tau_{G,US}$ therefore means that Germany's typical consumption basket of tradables has become more expensive relative to the typical basket of tradables consumed in the United States.

Suppose, for example, that the dollar depreciates against the DM but that the dollar prices of Mercedes-Benz autos sold in the United States are held fixed by the manufacturer to avoid losing sales to American competitors. If the German prices of those cars don't change either, the price of a Mercedes purchased in Germany rises relative to the price of one purchased in the United States. All else equal, this relative price movement raises $\tau_{G,US}$ by making German tradables more expensive in terms of American tradables ($E_{\$/DM}$ rises but P^T_G and P^T_{US} don't change).

If you retrace the steps leading to the exchange-rate equation (15-4) using equation (15-5) instead of the PPP assumption for tradables [equation (15-3)], you find that instead of equation (15-4) we now get

$$E_{\$/DM} = \frac{P_{US}}{P_G} \times \frac{\beta(P^N_G/P^T_G) + (1 - \beta)}{\alpha(P^N_{US}/P^T_{US}) + (1 - \alpha)} \times \tau_{G,US}, \tag{15-6}$$

which differs from (15-4) because the right-hand side is now multiplied by $\tau_{G,US}$, the price of German tradables in terms of U.S. tradables.

The model of the long-run exchange rate described by equation (15-6) now provides an additional prediction: all else equal, any change that raises $\tau_{G,US}$, the price of German tradables relative to U.S. tradables, causes the dollar to depreciate against the DM (a rise in $E_{\$/DM}$). Symmetrically, any factor that raises the price of U.S. tradables relative to German tradables (and thus lowers $\tau_{G,US}$) causes the dollar to appreciate against the DM.

THE REAL EXCHANGE RATE

The generalization of PPP described by equation (15-6) appears quite complicated. Our ultimate goal is to use equation (15-6) to understand how specific supply and demand shifts in countries' output markets affect the exchange rate. It will be easiest, however, to proceed in steps and look first at the effect of output-market changes on a relative price known as the **real exchange rate.** The *real* dollar/DM exchange rate is the number of typical U.S. consumption baskets needed to purchase a typical German consumption basket.

We can express the real exchange rate as the dollar value of Germany's price level divided by the dollar value of the U.S. price level or, in symbols, as

$$\begin{aligned} \textit{Real} \text{ dollar/DM exchange rate} &= (E_{\$/DM} \times P_G)/P_{US} \\ &= (\$/\text{DM}) \times (\text{DM/German output}) \\ &\quad \div (\$/\text{U.S. output}) \\ &= (\text{U.S. output/German output}). \end{aligned}$$

We denote the real dollar/DM exchange rate by $q_{\$/DM}$, so

$$q_{\$/DM} = \frac{(E_{\$/DM} \times P_G)}{P_{US}}.$$

The real exchange rate is important because it measures the cost of living in the United States relative to Germany. A rise in the real dollar/DM exchange rate $q_{\$/DM}$ (which we call a **real depreciation** of the dollar against the DM) indicates a relative increase in Germany's cost of living. A fall in the real dollar/DM exchange rate (a **real appreciation** of the dollar against the DM) indicates a relative increase in America's cost of living.

According to the absolute PPP theory, the real exchange rate must always equal 1 [that is, $E_{\$/DM} = P_{US}/P_G$, so $q_{\$/DM} = (E_{\$/DM} \times P_G)/P_{US} = 1$]. According to relative PPP, the real exchange rate may not equal 1, but its value, whatever it is, never changes. Equation (15-6) allows for the real appreciations and depreciations (the deviations from PPP) that occur in reality, explaining them by changes in (1) the relative price of nontraded goods and services and (2) changes in the ratio of tradable-goods prices in different countries. The implications of equation (15-6) for real exchange rates become apparent after dividing both sides by the price-level ratio P_{US}/P_G to derive an equation for the long-run *real* dollar/DM exchange rate,

$$q_{\$/DM} = \frac{(E_{\$/DM} \times P_G)}{P_{US}} = \frac{\beta(P^N_G/P^T_G) + (1 - \beta)}{\alpha(P^N_{US}/P^T_{US}) + (1 - \alpha)} \times \tau_{G, US}. \tag{15-7}$$

Equation (15-7) should clarify the economic factors behind the important role that the relative price of nontradables plays in exchange-rate determination. All else equal, a rise in the relative price of German nontradables (P^N_G/P^T_G) raises the cost of living in Germany relative to the United States, thereby causing a real depreciation of the dollar against the DM. In general, this real exchange-rate change may be brought about through changes in any of the three prices $E_{\$/DM}$, P_G, and P_{US} that enter into the definition of the real exchange rate; but if we hold P_G and P_{US} constant, as in equation (15-6), a rise in P^N_G/P^T_G must cause $E_{\$/DM}$ to rise. Similarly, a rise in P^N_{US}/P^T_{US}, by raising the cost of living in the United States relative to Germany, causes a real appreciation of the dollar against the DM (and causes $E_{\$/DM}$ to fall if P_G and P_{US} do not change).

The cost of living in Germany will also rise relative to the cost of living in the United States if German tradables become more expensive relative to U.S. tradables. Equation (15-7) therefore predicts a real depreciation of the dollar when $\tau_{G, US}$ rises, a real appreciation when $\tau_{G, US}$ falls.

Real exchange rates will be important in the chapters that follow, and we sometimes refer to the relative price of two currencies as a **nominal exchange rate** to distinguish it from the corresponding real exchange rate. When there is no risk of confusion, however, we continue to use the shorter term "exchange rate" to refer to nominal exchange rates.

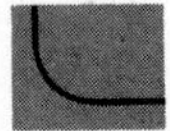

HOW OUTPUT-MARKET CHANGES AFFECT THE REAL EXCHANGE RATE

Now that we understand how the real exchange rate depends on the relative prices of nontradables and on international differences in the prices of tradables, we study how changes in output markets move those prices and the real exchange rate. Our conclusions will be useful later in this chapter when we examine how specific output-market changes affect the long-run *nominal* exchange rate.

As usual in economics, we analyze disturbances to a country's output markets in terms of their effects on demand and supply. We examine the price effects of (1) demand changes due to shifts in private or government consumption patterns and (2) supply changes due to productivity change in nontradable- or tradable-producing industries.

1. A shift in private or government demand away from tradables and toward nontradables *raises* the relative price of nontradables. As you might expect, the relative-price change causes factors of production to move out of the tradables sector and into the nontradables sector, increasing the supply of nontradables and helping to bring the market for nontradables into equilibrium. Less obviously, an increase in spending on *both* tradables and nontradables is *also* likely to raise the relative price of nontradables. While the increased demand for tradables can be satisfied by importing more tradables from abroad, the increased demand for nontradables can be satisfied only by producing more nontradables at home. The relative price of nontradables, P^N/P^T, will therefore generally rise.

The long-run effects of these demand shifts on the real exchange rate follow from equation (15-7):

$$q_{\$/DM} = \frac{\beta(P_G^N/P_G^T) + (1 - \beta)}{\alpha(P_{US}^N/P_{US}^T) + (1 - \alpha)} \times \tau_{G,US}.$$

Suppose, for example, that the demand shifts just considered occur in the United States. The resulting increase in the relative price of U.S. nontradables (P_{US}^N/P_{US}^T) tends to reduce the real exchange rate $q_{\$/DM}$ in both cases (a real appreciation of the dollar). In the case of an increase in U.S. spending on both nontradables and tradables, $\tau_{G,US}$, the ratio of the German and U.S. price levels for tradables, falls, strengthening the dollar's real appreciation. In the case of a switch in U.S. spending from tradables to nontradables, however, $\tau_{G,US}$ will rise instead, and the extent of the dollar's real appreciation could be reduced. Because the prices of tradables are determined in part in world markets, these prices are likely to be less responsive to purely domestic demand disturbances than the prices of nontradables. We therefore assume that a U.S. demand shift away from tradables and toward nontradables, like an increase in overall domestic spending, causes a real appreciation of the dollar.

A more complicated demand change is a shift in German spending away from German output and toward U.S. tradables. The analysis of this shift is so complicated because it simultaneously causes a fall in the relative prices of nontradables in *both* Germany and the United States, and a rise in the price of U.S. tradables relative to German tradables. The most likely outcome, however, is that a shift in German spending in favor of American tradables causes a real appreciation of the dollar against the DM.

2. An increase in productivity in nontradables causes factors of production to migrate from the tradables sector to the nontradables sector. As the supply of nontradables expands relative to the demand for them, their price in terms of tradables falls to maintain market equilibrium. An increase in productivity in the tradables industries causes capital and labor to move in the opposite direction, out of nontradables and into tradables. The supply of nontradables therefore shrinks, and as a result, their relative price rises.

To determine the effects of these supply disturbances on the real exchange rate, we once again assume that the disturbances occur in the United States and use our real-exchange-rate equation [equation (15-7)].

A productivity increase in U.S. nontradables, by lowering P^N_{US}/P^T_{US}, tends to depreciate the real dollar/DM exchange rate; but if it simultaneously causes the U.S. price level for tradables to rise relative to the price level for tradables consumed in Germany, a productivity increase in U.S. nontradables may cause a real dollar appreciation. The effect of this supply disturbance on the real exchange rate is therefore ambiguous in principle, but we assume that any resulting fall in $\tau_{G,US}$ is secondary and that the outcome of a productivity increase in nontradables is a real depreciation of the dollar.

A productivity increase in U.S. tradables has a similarly ambiguous effect on the real exchange rate. This disturbance causes P^N_{US}/P^T_{US} to rise, but it may also cause $\tau_{G,US}$ to rise by making U.S. tradables cheaper relative to those consumed by Germans. If the prices of tradables are set largely in world markets in the long run, however, the likely result is a real appreciation of the dollar. We assume that this is the case. (See the box for some relevant evidence.)

Our discussion of how shifts in output markets affect the real exchange rate is summarized by Table 15-1.[8]

[8]Our analysis of productivity changes is somewhat oversimplified because we have ignored the *demand* effects that inevitably accompany productivity changes. In fact, an increase in productivity in either industry raises domestic income and, with it, domestic spending. If the productivity increase is in tradables, our analysis of demand changes shows that these additional spending effects reinforce the rise in the relative price of nontradables. Thus, the conclusion in the text is strengthened if we take account of the spending effects of the productivity change. If the productivity increase is in nontradables, however, the increase in spending works to reduce the fall in the relative price of nontradables. But our conclusion that the relative price of nontradables falls cannot be overturned by spending effects. At the initial relative price, national income and spending rise by less than the increased supply of nontradables (since the supply of tradables shrinks), and in addition, only part of the spending increase is devoted to nontradables. Therefore, the supply of nontradables still rises relative to demand and the relative price of nontradables falls. In both cases, demand effects increase the likelihood of a real appreciation of the domestic currency.

PRODUCTIVITY GROWTH AND THE REAL DOLLAR/YEN EXCHANGE RATE

The theory we have developed suggests that, all else equal, a productivity increase in tradables should cause a country's real exchange rate to appreciate. Results in agreement with the theory come from a recent study of the dollar/yen real exchange rate by University of Pennsylvania economist Richard Marston.*

Marston used industry-level data for the United States and Japan to calculate the growth of labor productivity in tradables and nontradables over the years 1973–1983. He found that in the United States, productivity increased by 13.2 percent more in tradables than in nontradables. In Japan, however, productivity growth in tradables outstripped that in nontradables by a massive 73.2 percent.

Our earlier reasoning implies that the price of nontradables in terms of tradables should have risen in both countries but that the increase should have been greater in Japan. If relative tradables prices do not vary much in the long run, we'd expect this pattern of relative price changes within the two countries to cause a real appreciation of the yen against the dollar.

This reasoning fits the facts quite well. Marston found that the relative price of nontradables rose by 12.3 percent in the United States; the corresponding number for Japan was 56.9 percent. While the price of Japanese tradables did fall sharply relative to that of American tradables, the end result was still a 9 percent real appreciation of the yen against the dollar.

*Richard C. Marston, "Real Exchange Rates and Productivity Growth in the United States and Japan," Working Paper 1922, National Bureau of Economic Research, May 1986.

TABLE 15-1 Effects of output-market changes on the long-run real dollar/DM exchange rate, $q_{\$/DM}$

Change	Effect on real dollar/DM exchange rate
1. Changes in demand for U.S. output	
a. Shift in domestic demand from tradables to nontradables	Appreciation ($q_{\$/DM} \downarrow$)
b. Increase in overall domestic demand	Appreciation ($q_{\$/DM} \downarrow$)
c. Increase in German demand for tradables	Appreciation ($q_{\$/DM} \downarrow$)
2. U.S. productivity increases	
a. In nontradables	Depreciation ($q_{\$/DM} \uparrow$)
b. In tradables	Appreciation ($q_{\$/DM} \downarrow$)

Note: The corresponding changes in Germany's output markets have the opposite effects on the long-run real dollar/DM exchange rate.

Case Study WHY PRICE LEVELS ARE LOWER IN POORER COUNTRIES

Research on international price-level differences has uncovered a striking empirical regularity: when expressed in terms of a single currency, countries' price levels are positively related to the level of real income per capita. The last section's analysis of the role of nontraded goods in the determination of national price levels suggests that the price of nontradables relative to tradables may contribute to price-level discrepancies between rich and poor nations. Figure 15-2 shows that when nontradables are defined as services and construction, the relative price of nontradables does rise systematically with per capita real output. Higher prices for nontradables in richer countries therefore contribute to those countries' higher overall price levels.[9]

One reason for the lower relative price of nontradables in poor countries has been suggested by Bela Balassa of Johns Hopkins University

FIGURE 15-2 Ratio of price indexes for nontradable and tradable goods and services, 1975. The relative price of a country's nontradables tends to rise as its real per capita income rises.

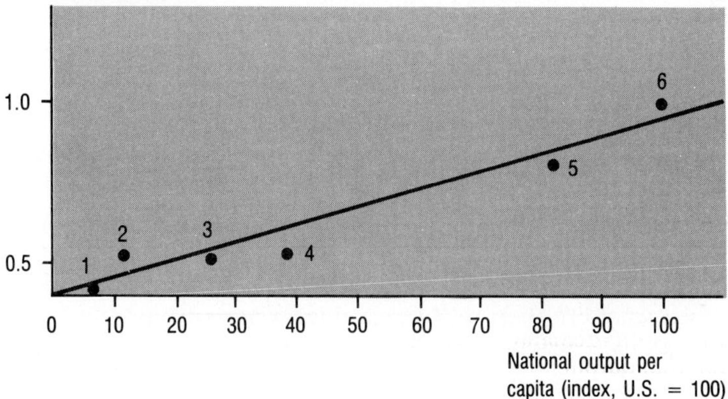

Horizontal axis measures average per capita levels of national output for the following 6 income groups:
1. Malawi, Kenya, India, Pakistan, Sri Lanka, Zambia, Thailand, Philippines
2. Korea, Malaysia, Colombia, Jamaica, Syria, Brazil
3. Romania, Mexico, Yugoslavia, Iran, Uruguay, Ireland
4. Hungary, Poland, Italy, Spain
5. U.K., Japan, Austria, Netherlands, Belgium, Luxembourg, France, Denmark, Germany
6. U.S.

Source: Irving B. Kravis and Robert E. Lipsey, *Toward an Explanation of National Price Levels* (Princeton Studies in International Finance 52, November 1983), table 2.

[9]The price indexes for tradable goods underlying Figure 15-2 show, however, that tradables as well as nontradables tend to be cheaper in poorer countries.

and by Paul Samuelson.[10] The Balassa-Samuelson theory postulates that the labor forces of poor countries are less productive than those of rich countries in the tradables sector, but that international productivity differences in nontradables are negligible. If the prices of traded goods are roughly equal in all countries, the lower labor productivity in the tradables industries of poor countries implies lower wages there than abroad and so a lower price of nontradables. The detailed reasoning leading to this conclusion is the same we used above to show that an increase in productivity in tradables must raise the relative price of nontradables, and it implies that countries with higher labor productivity in the tradables sector will tend to have higher price levels. Productivity statistics give some empirical support to the Balassa-Samuelson differential productivity postulate. And it is plausible on theoretical grounds that international productivity differences are sharper in traded than in nontraded goods. Whether a country is rich or poor, a barber can give only so many haircuts in a week, but there may be significant scope for productivity differences between advanced and developing countries in the manufacture of traded goods like home computers.

An alternative theory that attempts to explain the lower price levels of poor countries has been put forth by Jagdish Bhagwati and by Irving Kravis of the University of Pennsylvania and Robert Lipsey of the City University of New York.[11] The Bhagwati-Kravis-Lipsey view relies on differences in endowments of capital and labor rather than productivity differences, but it also predicts that the relative price of nontradables increases as real per capita income increases. Rich countries have high capital-labor ratios, while poor countries have more labor relative to capital. Because rich countries have higher capital-labor ratios, the marginal productivity of labor is greater in rich countries than in poor countries, and the former will therefore have a higher wage level than the latter.[12] Nontradables, which consist largely of services, are naturally labor-intensive relative to tradables. Because labor is cheaper in poor countries and this factor is used intensively in producing nontradables, nontradables also will be cheaper there than in the rich, high-wage countries. Once again, this international difference in the relative price of nontradables suggests that

[10]See Balassa, "The Purchasing Power Parity Doctrine: A Reappraisal," *Journal of Political Economy* 72 (December 1964), pp. 584–596, and Samuelson, "Theoretical Notes on Trade Problems," *Review of Economics and Statistics* 46 (May 1964), pp. 145–154. The Balassa-Samuelson theory was foreshadowed by some observations of Ricardo. See Jacob Viner, *Studies in the Theory of International Trade* (New York: Harper & Brothers, 1937), p. 315.

[11]See Kravis and Lipsey, *Toward an Explanation of National Price Levels,* Princeton Studies in International Finance 52 (International Finance Section, Department of Economics, Princeton University, November 1983); and Bhagwati, "Why Are Services Cheaper in the Poor Countries?" *Economic Journal* 94 (June 1984), pp. 279–286.

[12]This argument assumes that factor-endowment differences between rich and poor countries are sufficiently great that factor-price equalization cannot hold.

overall price levels should be higher in rich countries than in poor countries when measured in a single currency.

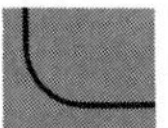

MONETARY CHANGES, OUTPUT-MARKET CHANGES, AND THE LONG-RUN NOMINAL EXCHANGE RATE

We now pull together what we have learned in this chapter and the last one to show how nominal exchange rates are determined in the long run. We see that in the long run, changes in national money supplies give rise to the proportional movements in exchange rates and international price-level ratios predicted by the relative purchasing power parity theory. Changes in output markets, however, cause deviations from relative PPP, as we saw earlier. Below, we use our knowledge of how national price levels are determined by monetary factors to examine how these deviations from PPP affect long-run nominal exchange rates.[13]

MONETARY CHANGES AND THE EXCHANGE RATE IN THE LONG RUN

To study how the nominal exchange rate is set in the long run, we will combine our model of long-run price-level determination from Chapter 14 with the model of the long-run *real* exchange rate developed in this chapter. Recall that we defined the real dollar/DM exchange rate as

$$q_{\$/DM} = \frac{(E_{\$/DM} \times P_G)}{P_{US}}.$$

If we now solve this equation for the nominal exchange rate, we get an equation stating that the nominal dollar/DM exchange rate equals the U.S.–German price-level ratio times the real dollar/DM exchange rate:

$$E_{\$/DM} = \frac{P_{US}}{P_G} \times q_{\$/DM}. \qquad \textbf{(15-8)}$$

Using this equation, it is easy to see how increases in the U.S. and German money supplies affect the nominal dollar/DM exchange rate in the long run.

As you will remember from the last chapter, a permanent increase in a country's money supply has no effect on the long-run levels of output, the interest rate, or any relative price. The only long-run effect of the money-supply change is to raise all *money* prices, including the nominal exchange rate, in proportion to the increase in the money supply. Equation (15-8) also leads to the conclusion that a permanent increase in the U.S. money supply

[13]Many of the points of this section can be made more formally by adapting the framework developed in Appendixes I and II to this chapter.

causes proportional increases in the long-run levels of the U.S. price level and the nominal dollar/DM exchange rate. Because a U.S. money-supply increase has no permanent effect on the real exchange rate $q_{\$/DM}$ (which depends only on *relative* prices), and no permanent effect on P_G (which depends on German money-market conditions in the long run), $E_{\$/DM}$ and P_{US} must eventually rise in proportion to each other. For example, if the U.S. money supply rises permanently by 10 percent, the U.S. price level and the nominal dollar/DM exchange rate will both rise by 10 percent in the long run, resulting in a nominal dollar depreciation proportional to the increases in the U.S. price level and U.S. money supply.

The analysis of an increase in the German money stock is similar. In the long run, an increase in German money causes only a proportional increase in P_G and therefore a proportional decrease in $E_{\$/DM}$. For example, a 10 percent increase in the German money supply causes Germany's price level to rise eventually by 10 percent and the dollar to appreciate against the DM by 10 percent. The monetary disturbance has no effect on the real dollar/DM exchange rate.

Our analysis shows that monetary changes cause proportional long-run movements in nominal exchange rates and in the ratios of national price levels. Monetary changes, however, never affect *real* exchange rates in the long run. We therefore reach the following conclusion about the response of nominal exchange rates and national price levels to purely monetary changes: *When all disturbances are monetary in nature, exchange rates obey relative PPP in the long run.* In the long run, a monetary disturbance affects only the purchasing power of a currency, and this change in purchasing power changes equally the currency's value in terms of domestic and foreign goods. When disturbances occur in output markets, however, the exchange rate may not obey relative PPP, even in the long run.

OUTPUT-MARKET CHANGES AND THE EXCHANGE RATE IN THE LONG RUN

We consider the effects of four output-market disturbances on the long-run nominal exchange rate: (1) an increase in U.S. demand for nontradables, (2) an increase in German demand for U.S. tradables, (3) an increase in productivity in U.S. nontraded goods, and (4) an increase in productivity in U.S. traded goods. (For brevity, the corresponding events in Germany are not discussed in detail, as their effect on the nominal exchange rate is the same, but in the opposite direction.)

1. An increase in demand for U.S. nontradables will cause the relative price of nontradables to increase. As Table 15-1 shows, this price change causes a real appreciation of the dollar against the DM (a fall in $q_{\$/DM}$), regardless of whether the change results from a demand switch from tradables to nontradables (case 1a) or an increase in American spending on all goods (case 1b). Equation (15-8) shows that in the long run, the dollar appreciates against the DM in *nominal* terms (that is, $E_{\$/DM}$ falls) if the overall U.S.–German price-

level ratio, P_{US}/P_G, does not change. Because the U.S. and German money supplies are constant and the demand shift leads to no long-run change in either country's real money demand, however, there is no reason for a significant change in the long-run ratio of the U.S. and German price levels. We therefore conclude that the nominal dollar/DM exchange rate falls in the long run. Notice how relative PPP is violated in this case: the dollar appreciates against the DM while price levels in the U.S. and Germany do not change.

2. An increase in German demand for U.S. tradables also causes a real appreciation of the dollar against the DM (see case 1c in Table 15-1). As in the last case, however, the change has little or no permanent impact on the ratio of the U.S. and German price levels. Equation (15-8) therefore implies a long-run nominal appreciation of the dollar against the DM and a departure from relative PPP.

3. An increase in productivity in U.S. nontradables has two effects that tend to move the nominal dollar/DM exchange rate in opposite directions. First, the rise in real national income caused by the productivity increase tends to push P_{US} down in the long run (since it raises the demand for real money holdings). Second, $q_{\$/DM}$ rises as the supply of nontradables expands (see case 2a in Table 15-1). Because the German price level does not change significantly in the long run, equation (15-8) shows that $E_{\$/DM}$ can rise or fall, depending on whether the rise in $q_{\$/DM}$ or the fall in P_{US} is proportionally greater. Equation (15-8) also shows that in any event, relative PPP will not be satisfied: even if the dollar appreciates nominally in the long run, the accompanying rise in $q_{\$/DM}$ makes that nominal appreciation proportionally smaller than the fall in P_{US}.

4. An increase in productivity in the U.S. tradables sector has two effects that move the nominal dollar/DM exchange rate in the same direction. First, there is an increase in U.S. real income, a development that raises the demand for real money balances and tends, therefore, to lower the long-run price level P_{US}. Second, the real exchange rate $q_{\$/DM}$ falls (case 2b in Table 15-1) as the supply of nontradables falls. Equation (15-8) shows that both effects work together to cause a nominal long-run appreciation of the dollar against the DM. Because $q_{\$/DM}$ falls, equation (15-8) also shows that the long-run appreciation of the dollar against the DM is proportionally greater than the long-run fall in P_{US}. Once again, relative PPP does not accurately predict the extent of the exchange rate's change.

Our discussion in this section is summarized in Table 15-2, where the corresponding results for disturbances in the German economy are also shown.

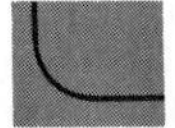

SUMMARY

1. The *purchasing power parity* theory, in its absolute form, asserts that the exchange rate between two countries' currencies equals the ratio of their price levels. An alternative but equivalent statement of PPP is that when measured

TABLE 15-2 Effects of monetary and output-market changes on the long-run nominal dollar/DM exchange rate, $E_{\$/DM}$

Change	Effect on $E_{\$/DM}$
Monetary changes	
1. Increase in U.S. money supply	Proportional increase (nominal depreciation of \$)
Increase in German money supply	Proportional decrease (nominal depreciation of DM)
Output-market changes	
1. Increase in demand for U.S. nontradables	Decrease (nominal appreciation of \$)
Increase in demand for German nontradables	Increase (nominal appreciation of DM)
2. Increase in German demand for U.S. tradables	Decrease (nominal appreciation of \$)
Increase in U.S. demand for German tradables	Increase (nominal appreciation of DM)
3. Productivity increase in U.S. nontradables	Ambiguous
Productivity increase in German nontradables	Ambiguous
4. Productivity increase in U.S. tradables	Decrease (nominal appreciation of \$)
Productivity increase in German tradables	Increase (nominal appreciation of DM)

in a single currency, the "cost of living" is the same in all countries. Absolute PPP implies a second version of the PPP theory, relative PPP, which predicts that percentage changes in exchange rates are completely explained by differences in national inflation rates.

2. A building block of PPP theory is the *law of one price,* which states that under free competition and in the absence of trade impediments, a good must sell for a single price regardless of where in the world it is sold.

3. The empirical support for PPP and the law of one price is weak in recent data. The failure of these propositions in the real world is related to trade barriers, different definitions of price levels in different countries, and departures from free competition. For some products, including many services, international transport costs are so steep that these products become nontradable.

4. The existence in all countries of nontraded goods and services whose prices are not linked internationally allows systematic deviations from PPP, even in the long run. Deviations from PPP can also arise from differences in the prices of countries' tradables. These deviations are equivalent to changes

in a country's *real exchange rate,* the price of a typical foreign consumption basket in terms of the typical domestic consumption basket. All else equal, a country's currency undergoes a *real depreciation* against foreign currencies when the price of its nontradables in terms of its tradables falls or when the price of its tradables in terms of foreign tradables falls. The home currency undergoes a *real appreciation* against foreign currencies when either of the opposite relative price changes occurs.

5. The long-run determination of *nominal exchange rates* can be analyzed by combining two theories: the theory of the long-run *real* exchange rate and the theory of how domestic monetary factors determine long-run price levels. An increase in a country's money stock ultimately leads to a proportional increase in its price level and a proportional depreciation of its currency in the foreign-exchange market, just as relative PPP predicts. However, disturbances due to supply or demand changes in output markets cause long-run nominal exchange-rate movements that do not conform to PPP.

KEY TERMS

purchasing power parity (PPP)	real depreciation
law of one price	real appreciation
real exchange rate	nominal exchange rate

PROBLEMS

1. Suppose that Brazil's inflation rate is 100 percent over a year but that the inflation rate in Holland is only 5 percent. According to relative PPP, what should happen over the year to the Dutch guilder's exchange rate against the Brazilian cruzado?

2. It is often asserted that exporters suffer when their home currencies appreciate in real terms against foreign currencies and prosper when their home currencies depreciate in real terms. Discuss.

3. Assume that Americans and Japanese spend half their income on tradables and half on nontradables. If the law of one price holds for tradables consumed in the U.S. and Japan, what is the value of the real dollar/yen exchange rate when the price of nontradables in terms of tradables is 4 in the United States and 2 in Japan? What happens to the real exchange rate if Japanese spending rises and the relative price of Japanese nontradables increases to 3?

4. Large-scale wars typically bring a suspension of international trading and financial activities. Exchange rates lose their relevance under these conditions, but once the war is over, central banks wishing to fix exchange rates face the problem of deciding what the new exchange rates should be. The PPP theory has often been applied to this problem of postwar exchange-rate realignment. Imagine that you are a British central banker and that World War II has just ended. Explain how you would figure out the dollar/pound exchange rate implied by PPP. When might it be a bad idea to use the PPP theory in this way?

5. In the late 1970s Britain seemed to have struck it rich. Having developed its North Sea oil-producing fields in earlier years, Britain suddenly found its real income higher as a result of a dramatic increase in world oil prices in 1979–1980. In the early 1980s, however, oil prices receded as the world economy slid into a deep recession and world oil demand faltered.

Below, we show index numbers for the average real exchange rate of the pound against several foreign currencies. (Such average index numbers are called real *effective* exchange rates.) A rise in one of these numbers indicates a real *appreciation* of the pound, that is, an increase in Britain's cost of living relative to the average cost of living abroad measured in pounds. A fall is a real depreciation.

Real effective exchange rate of the pound sterling, 1976–1984 (1980 = 100)

1976	1977	1978	1979	1980	1981	1982	1983	1984
68.3	66.5	72.2	81.4	100.0	102.8	100.0	92.5	89.8

(Data come from International Monetary Fund, *International Financial Statistics*. The real exchange rate measures are based on indexes of net output prices called value-added deflators.)

Use the clues we have given about the British economy to explain the rise and fall of the pound's real effective exchange rate between 1978 and 1984. Pay particular attention to the role of nontradables.

6. How would you expect an increase in the world price of oil to affect the real exchange rate of an oil-importing country?

7. Explain how permanent shifts in national real money-demand functions affect real and nominal exchange rates in the long run.

8. In Chapter 5 we discussed the effects of transfers between countries, such as the indemnity imposed on Germany after World War I. Use the theory developed in the present chapter to discuss the mechanisms through which a permanent transfer from Germany to France would affect the real French franc/DM exchange rate in the long run.

9. Continuing with the preceding problem, discuss how the transfer would affect the long-run *nominal* exchange rate between the two currencies.

10. A country imposes a tariff on imports from abroad. How does its action change the long-run real exchange rate between home and foreign currency? How is the long-run nominal exchange rate affected?

11. Suppose that the expected real interest rate in the United States is 9 percent per year while that in Germany is 3 percent per year. What do you expect to happen to the real dollar/DM exchange rate over the next year?

FURTHER READING

Gustav Cassel. *Post-war Monetary Stabilization*. New York: Columbia University Press, 1928. Applies the purchasing power parity theory of exchange rates in analyzing the monetary problems that followed World War I.

Robert E. Cumby and Frederic S. Mishkin. "The International Linkage of Real Interest Rates: The U.S.–European Connection." *Journal of International Money and Finance* 5 (March 1986), pp. 5–23. An econometric study of the relationship between real interest rates in the United States and Europe.

Rudiger Dornbusch. "The Theory of Flexible Exchange Rate Regimes and Macroeconomic Policy," in Jan Herin, Assar Lindbeck, and Johan Myhrman, eds. *Flexible Exchange Rates and Stabilization Policy.* Boulder, CO: Westview Press, 1977, pp. 123–143. Develops a long-run model of exchange rates incorporating traded and nontraded goods and services.

Rudiger Dornbusch. "Purchasing Power Parity," in *The New Palgrave Dictionary of Economics.* London: Stockton-Macmillan, 1987. Examines the role of the purchasing power parity theory in international macroeconomics.

Irving B. Kravis. "Comparative Studies of National Incomes and Prices." *Journal of Economic Literature* 22 (March 1984), pp. 1–39. An account of the findings of a United Nations–sponsored research project that compared the real incomes and price levels of more than 100 countries.

Robin Marris. "Comparing the Incomes of Nations: A Critique of the International Comparison Project." *Journal of Economic Literature* 22 (March 1984), pp. 40–57. A critical appraisal of the research described in the previous reading by Kravis.

Lloyd A. Metzler. "Exchange Rates and the International Monetary Fund," in *International Monetary Policies,* Postwar Economic Studies 7. Washington, D.C.: Board of Governors of the Federal Reserve System, 1947, pp. 1–45. The author applies purchasing power parity with skill and skepticism to evaluate the fixed exchange rates established by the International Monetary Fund after World War II.

Lawrence Officer. "The Purchasing-Power-Parity Theory of Exchange Rates: A Review Article." *International Monetary Fund Staff Papers* 23 (March 1976), pp. 1–61. A comprehensive review of the history of the purchasing power parity doctrine.

APPENDIX I TO CHAPTER 15
International Interest-Rate Differences and Real Exchange Rates

In this appendix we apply what we have learned about real exchange rates to analyze the relationship between nominal and real interest rates in different countries. As you will recall from Chapter 14, the expected real interest rate, denoted r^e, is just the nominal interest rate, R, less the expected inflation rate, π^e:

$$r^e = R - \pi^e.$$

We will see that when the nominal interest parity condition equates nominal interest-rate differences between currencies to expected changes in *nominal* exchange rates, a *real* interest parity condition equates expected real interest-rate differences to expected changes in *real* exchange rates. If relative purchasing power parity is expected to hold, no real exchange-rate change is anticipated and expected real interest rates on all currencies are therefore the same (assuming nominal interest parity).

To start, recall the nominal interest parity condition, which states that the difference between the nominal interest rates on two currencies, the dollar and the DM, for example, must equal the expected rate of nominal depreciation of the dollar against the DM:

$$R_{\$} - R_{DM} = (E^e_{\$/DM} - E_{\$/DM})/E_{\$/DM}.$$

If we subtract the expected U.S. inflation rate π^e_{US} and add the expected German inflation rate π^e_G to both sides of this equation, we get an equation explaining the expected real interest differential between dollar and DM deposits:

$$\begin{aligned} r^e_{\$} - r^e_{DM} &= (R_{\$} - \pi^e_{US}) - (R_{DM} - \pi^e_G) \\ &= (E^e_{\$/DM} - E_{\$/DM})/E_{\$/DM} - (\pi^e_{US} - \pi^e_G). \end{aligned}$$

To interpret this equation, recall that an expected inflation rate, π^e, is defined as $(P^e - P)/P$, while the real dollar/DM exchange rate, $q_{\$/DM}$, is defined as $(E_{\$/DM} \times P_G)/P_{US}$. The lower line of the above equation is therefore (approximately) equal to the expected change in the real dollar/DM exchange rate. Thus, the expected real interest rate difference between dollars and DM can be identified with the expected change in the real dollar/DM exchange rate:

$$r^e_{\$} - r^e_{DM} = (q^e_{\$/DM} - q_{\$/DM})/q_{\$/DM}.$$

The equation above looks much like the usual interest parity condition from which it is derived, but it explains the difference in expected *real* interest between dollar and DM deposits by expected movements in the *real* exchange rate between those currencies.

When people expect relative PPP to hold, the real exchange rate is not expected to change. In terms of our notation, the expectation that relative PPP will hold implies that

$$\begin{aligned} (q^e_{\$/DM} - q_{\$/DM})/q_{\$/DM} &= (E^e_{\$/DM} - E_{\$/DM})/E_{\$/DM} - (\pi^e_{US} - \pi^e_G) \\ &= 0. \end{aligned}$$

[Recall the statement of relative PPP given in equation (15-2).] Therefore, when no changes in the real exchange rate are expected, expected real interest rates are the same internationally, that is,

$$r^e_{\$} = r^e_{\text{DM}}.$$

By using the definition of the expected real interest rate as the nominal interest rate less expected inflation, we can rewrite this equality as

$$R_{\$} - R_{\text{DM}} = \pi^e_{\text{US}} - \pi^e_{\text{G}}.$$

The equation above states that when relative PPP holds, international differences between nominal interest rates are explained completely by differences between expected national inflation rates.

In general, however, expected real interest rates for different countries need not be equal, even in the long run, if continuing change in output markets is expected.[1] Suppose, for example, that productivity in the U.S. nontradables sector is expected to rise relative to productivity in U.S. tradables over the next two decades. At the same time, productivity in Korean tradables industries is expected to rise over the same two decades relative to productivity in Korean nontradables. As the analysis summarized in Table 15-1 showed, these persistently growing intersectoral productivity differences in the two countries should lead people to expect that the U.S. dollar will depreciate in real terms against Korea's currency, the won, for many years. Our equation for the expected real interest-rate difference thus implies that the expected real interest rate should be higher in the United States than in Korea over the same period.[2]

[1]The two-country, two-period analysis of international borrowing and lending in Chapter 7 assumed that both countries face the same real interest rate. PPP must hold in that analysis, however, because there is only one consumption good in each period.

[2]A cross-border real interest difference implies that residents of two countries perceive different real rates of return on wealth. Interest parity still implies that any one investor expects the same real return on domestic- and foreign-currency assets. Two investors residing in different countries need not calculate this single real rate of return in the same way, however, if relative PPP does not link the prices of their consumption baskets.

APPENDIX II TO CHAPTER 15

The Monetary Approach to Exchange-Rate Determination

When all changes are monetary and relative purchasing power parity therefore holds, a simple model of long-run interest-rate differences and exchange rates applies. Because the resulting theory emphasizes the importance of monetary factors and downplays changes in output markets, it is often called the *monetary approach to exchange-rate determination.* In this appendix, we briefly review the most important implications of the monetary approach.

Long-run real exchange rates are constant when all changes are monetary; so, as we saw in Appendix I, long-run expected real interest rates are equal in all countries and long-run nominal interest-rate differences equal expected inflation-rate differences. If we again consider the United States and Germany, for example, and denote the worldwide expected real interest rate by r^e_w, we can therefore express the nominal interest rates on dollars and DM as

$$R_{\$} = r^e_w + \pi^e_{\mathrm{US}},\ R_{\mathrm{DM}} = r^e_w + \pi^e_{\mathrm{G}}.$$

The monetary approach uses these expressions, together with the money-market equilibrium conditions in the United States and Germany, to arrive at an equation in which the long-run nominal exchange rate is expressed directly in terms of money-market conditions. As you will recall from the last chapter, the money-market equilibrium conditions for the United States and Germany are that the real money supply equal aggregate real money demand in each country,

$$\frac{M^s_{\mathrm{US}}}{P_{\mathrm{US}}} = L(R_{\$}, Y_{\mathrm{US}}),$$

$$\frac{M^s_{\mathrm{G}}}{P_{\mathrm{G}}} = L(R_{\mathrm{DM}}, Y_{\mathrm{G}}).$$

To simplify the notation, we have assumed that the same aggregate real money demand function $L(R, Y)$ describes the behavior of households and firms in both countries. These two equilibrium conditions and the interest-rate relations given in the last paragraph tell us that the long-run U.S. and German price levels are

$$P_{\mathrm{US}} = M^s_{\mathrm{US}}/L(r^e_w + \pi^e_{\mathrm{US}}, Y_{\mathrm{US}}),$$

$$P_{\mathrm{G}} = M^s_{\mathrm{G}}/L(r^e_w + \pi^e_{\mathrm{G}}, Y_{\mathrm{G}}).$$

If we substitute these expressions for P_{US} and P_{G} into equation (15-8),

$$E_{\$/\mathrm{DM}} = \frac{P_{\mathrm{US}}}{P_{\mathrm{G}}} \times q_{\$/\mathrm{DM}},$$

we get the long-run exchange-rate equation basic to the monetary approach:

$$E_{\$/\mathrm{DM}} = (M^s_{\mathrm{US}}/M^s_{\mathrm{G}}) \times [L(r^e_w + \pi^e_{\mathrm{G}}, Y_{\mathrm{G}})/L(r^e_w + \pi^e_{\mathrm{US}}, Y_{\mathrm{US}})] \times q_{\$/\mathrm{DM}}.$$

This equation's implications about money-supply changes agree with what we found earlier: a permanent increase in a country's money supply causes a proportional long-run nominal depreciation of its currency. The equation yields some additional predictions, however, about the effects of inflationary expectations. A rise in expected German inflation, for example, reduces real money demand in Germany by raising the nominal interest rate there, and thus causes a depreciation of the DM (a fall in $E_{\$/DM}$). Similarly, the dollar depreciates ($E_{\$/DM}$ rises) when U.S. expected inflation rises. In Chapter 14, we learned that the dollar depreciates in nominal terms when $R_{\$} - R_{DM}$ rises because of a rise in U.S. inflationary expectations (the Fisher effect). In contrast, the dollar appreciates in nominal terms when an increase in $R_{\$} - R_{DM}$ reflects a fall in the expected U.S. inflation rate relative to German inflation, and thus a rise in the expected real interest rate on dollars relative to that on DM. Because the monetary approach assumes that expected real interest rates are always equal across countries, however, that theory's predictions about changes in nominal interest-rate differences presuppose that those changes are caused by the Fisher effect.

The monetary approach stresses factors that affect national money markets. It doesn't attempt to explain the real exchange rate and regards that rate as a constant. The monetary approach therefore analyzes output changes entirely in terms of their effects on aggregate money demand, predicting that a rise in U.S. output, Y_{US}, causes a nominal dollar appreciation while a rise in German output, Y_G, causes a nominal DM appreciation. The more detailed discussion given in this chapter shows that these conclusions may be reversed if we take account of how the real exchange rate responds to output changes (see Table 15-2). Usually, the sector of the economy in which an output change occurs matters for determining how the exchange rate responds.

The monetary approach to the exchange rate is a long-run theory that has been most successful empirically when applied to situations dominated by monetary change. Data from the 1970s and 1980s, however, give little support to the monetary approach. This poor empirical performance is due to both short-run output-price rigidity and large changes in long-run real exchange rates, neither of which is modeled by the monetary approach.[1]

[1]For an empirical application of the monetary approach to the German hyperinflation of the 1920s, see Jacob A. Frenkel, "A Monetary Approach to the Exchange Rate: Doctrinal Aspects and Empirical Evidence," in Jan Herin, Assar Lindbeck, and Johan Myhrman, eds., *Flexible Exchange Rates and Stabilization Policy* (Boulder, CO: Westview Press, 1977), pp. 68–92. The failure of the monetary approach when applied to more recent data is documented in Rudiger Dornbusch, "Exchange Rate Economics: Where Do We Stand?" *Brookings Papers on Economic Activity* 1:1980, pp. 143–185.

16 OUTPUT AND THE EXCHANGE RATE IN THE SHORT RUN

When the real gross national product of the United States fell by 2.5 percent in 1982, many observers blamed the slump on the sharp appreciation of the dollar that had occurred since 1980. In 1984, however, U.S. real GNP *rose* by a whopping 6.4 percent in spite of another sizable appreciation of the dollar. This chapter will help us understand the complicated factors that cause output and exchange-rate changes by completing the macroeconomic model built up in the last two chapters.

Chapters 14 and 15 explained the connections among exchange rates, interest rates, and price levels but always assumed that output levels were given. Those chapters give us only a partial picture of how macroeconomic changes affect an open economy because events that change exchange rates, interest rates, and price levels also change output. In this chapter we fill in the picture by examining how output and the exchange rate are determined in the short run.

Our discussion combines what we have learned about asset markets and the long-run behavior of exchange rates with a new element, a theory of how the output market adjusts to demand changes when commodity and factor prices in the economy are themselves slow to adjust. As we learned in Chapter 14, institutional factors like long-term nominal contracts can give rise to "sticky" or slowly adjusting output-market prices. By putting a short-run model of the output market together with our models of the foreign exchange and money markets (the asset markets), we build a model explaining all the important macroeconomic variables in an open economy. The long-run exchange-rate model of the last chapter provides the framework that participants in the asset markets use to form their expectations about future exchange rates.

Output changes may push the economy away from full employment; so the links among output and other macroeconomic variables are of great concern to economic policymakers. We will use this chapter's model to examine how macroeconomic policy tools affect the economy and how those tools can be used to maintain full employment.

DETERMINANTS OF AGGREGATE DEMAND IN AN OPEN ECONOMY

To analyze how a country's output is determined in the short run, we introduce the concept of **aggregate demand** for its output. Aggregate demand is the amount of a country's goods and services demanded by households and firms throughout the world. Just as the output of an individual good or service depends in part on the demand for it, a country's overall short-run output level depends on the aggregate demand for its products. The economy is at full employment in the long run (by definition); so in the long run, a country's output depends only on the available domestic supplies of factors of production such as labor and capital. As we will see, however, these productive factors may be over- or underemployed in the short run as a result of shifts in aggregate demand that have not yet had their full long-run effects on prices.

In Chapter 12 we learned that an economy's output could be divided among the four different types of expenditure that generate national income: consumption, investment, government purchases, and the current account. Correspondingly, aggregate demand for an open economy's output is the sum of consumption demand (C), investment demand (I), government demand (G), and *net* export demand, that is, the current account (CA). Each of these components of aggregate demand depends on different factors. In this section we examine the factors that determine consumption demand and the current account. Government demand will be discussed later in this chapter when we examine the effects of fiscal policy, and for now we assume that G is given. To avoid complicating our model, we also assume that investment demand is given. The determinants of investment demand are incorporated into the model in Appendix I to this chapter.

DETERMINANTS OF CONSUMPTION DEMAND

In this chapter we view the amount that a country's residents wish to consume as a function of national income less taxes ($Y - T$), or disposable income (Y^d).[1] (C, Y, and T are all measured in terms of domestic output units.) With this assumption, a country's desired consumption level can be written as a function of disposable income:

$$C = C(Y^d).$$

Because each consumer naturally demands more goods and services as her real income rises, we expect consumption to increase as disposable income increases at the aggregate level, too. Thus, consumption demand and disposable income are positively related. When disposable income rises, however, consumption demand will generally rise by *less* because part of the income increase is saved.

DETERMINANTS OF THE CURRENT ACCOUNT

The current account is determined by two factors: the domestic currency's real exchange rate against foreign currency (that is, the price of a typical foreign consumption basket in terms of domestic consumption baskets) and domestic disposable income. (In reality, a country's current account depends on many other factors, such as the level of foreign expenditure, but for now we regard these other factors as being held constant.)[2]

As we saw in the previous chapter, the domestic-currency prices of a representative foreign consumption basket and a representative domestic consumption basket are, respectively, EP^* and P, where E (the nominal exchange rate) is the price of foreign currency in terms of domestic currency, P^* is the foreign price level, and P is the home price level. The *real* exchange rate, defined as the price of foreign output in terms of domestic output, is therefore EP^*/P. If, for example, the representative basket of German goods and services costs DM100 (P^*), the representative U.S. basket costs \$50 (P),

[1]A more complete model would allow other factors, such as real wealth and the real interest rate, to affect consumption plans. This chapter's Appendix I takes account of the real interest rate's effect on consumption demand.

[2]In Chapter 19 we study a two-country model that takes account of how events in the domestic economy affect foreign output, and how these changes in foreign output, in turn, feed back to the domestic economy. As the previous footnote observed, we are ignoring a number of factors other than disposable income (such as wealth and interest rates) which affect consumption. Since some part of any consumption change goes into imports, these omitted determinants of consumption are also determinants of the current account.

and the dollar/DM exchange rate is \$0.40 per DM (E), then the price of the German basket in terms of U.S. baskets is

$$\begin{aligned} EP^*/P &= (0.40\ \$/\text{DM}) \times (100\ \text{DM/German basket}) \\ &\quad \div (50\ \$/\text{U.S. basket}) \\ &= (40\ \$/\text{German basket}) \div (50\ \$/\text{U.S. basket}) \\ &= 0.8\ \text{U.S. basket/German basket.} \end{aligned}$$

The domestic current account, then, is a function of the real exchange rate, EP^*/P, and domestic disposable income, Y^d:

$$CA = CA(EP^*/P, Y^d).$$

Real exchange-rate changes affect the current account by changing the relative prices of domestic and foreign goods and services, while disposable income affects the current account through its effect on total domestic spending.[3] To understand how these real exchange rate and disposable-income effects work, it is helpful to look separately at the demand for the country's exports, EX, and the demand for imports by the country's residents, IM. As we saw in Chapter 12, the current account is related to exports and imports by the identity

$$CA = EX - IM$$

when CA, EX, and IM are all measured in terms of domestic output.

HOW REAL EXCHANGE RATE CHANGES AFFECT THE CURRENT ACCOUNT

To determine how a real exchange-rate change affects the current account, we must ask how it affects both EX and IM. If EP^*/P rises, for example, foreign products have become more expensive relative to domestic products: each unit of domestic output now purchases fewer units of foreign output. Foreign consumers will respond to this price shift by demanding more of our exports. This response by foreigners will therefore raise EX and will tend to improve the domestic country's current account.

The effect of the real exchange-rate increase on IM is more complicated. Domestic consumers respond to the price shift by purchasing fewer units of the more expensive foreign products. Their response does not imply, however, that IM must fall. IM denotes the value of imports *measured in terms of*

[3]As we saw in the last chapter, the price indexes that are used to calculate the real exchange rate are the prices of *consumption* baskets that already include some imports as well as nontradables. The real exchange rate is used here as a convenient summary measure of the relative price of domestic and foreign products. Our assumption that the current account depends on the real exchange rate will be a good one when most tradables consumed by a country are also produced there and when demand and supply shifts tend to have proportional (i.e., unbiased) effects on countries' tradable and nontradable sectors.

domestic output, and not the volume of foreign products imported: because a rise in EP^*/P tends to raise the value of each unit of imports in terms of domestic-output units, imports measured in domestic-output units may rise as a result of a rise in EP^*/P even if imports decline when measured in foreign-output units. IM can therefore rise or fall when EP^*/P rises, so the effect of real exchange-rate changes on the current account is ambiguous.

Whether the current account itself improves or worsens depends on which effect of a real exchange-rate change is dominant, the *volume* effect of consumer spending shifts on export and import volumes, or the *value* effect, which changes the domestic-output value of a given volume of foreign imports. We assume for now that the volume effect of a real exchange-rate change always outweighs the value effect, so that a real depreciation of the currency improves the current account and a real appreciation of the currency worsens the current account.[4]

HOW DISPOSABLE-INCOME CHANGES AFFECT THE CURRENT ACCOUNT

The second factor influencing the current account is domestic disposable income. Since a rise in Y^d causes domestic consumers to increase their spending on *all* goods, including imports from abroad, an increase in disposable income worsens the current account. (An increase in Y^d has no effect on export demand because we are holding foreign income constant and not allowing Y^d to affect it.)

The table below summarizes our discussion of how real exchange-rate and disposable-income changes influence the domestic current account:

Change	Effect on *CA*
$EP^*/P\uparrow$	$CA\uparrow$
$EP^*/P\downarrow$	$CA\downarrow$
$Y^d\uparrow$	$CA\downarrow$
$Y^d\downarrow$	$CA\uparrow$

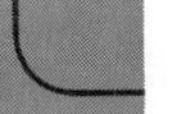

THE EQUATION OF AGGREGATE DEMAND

We now combine the four components of aggregate demand to get an expression for total aggregate demand, D:

$$D = C(Y - T) + I + G + CA(EP^*/P, Y - T),$$

[4]This assumption requires that import and export demands be relatively *elastic* with respect to the real exchange rate. Appendix II to this chapter works out precise conditions, called the Marshall-Lerner conditions, under which the assumption in the text will be valid. The appendix also examines empirical evidence on the time horizon over which the Marshall-Lerner condition holds.

where we have written disposable income Y^d as output Y less taxes T. This equation shows that aggregate demand can be written as a function of the real exchange rate, disposable income, investment demand, and government spending:

$$D = D(EP^*/P, Y - T, I, G).$$

We now want to see how overall aggregate demand depends on the real exchange rate and domestic GNP given the level of taxes, T, investment demand, I, and government purchases, G.

THE REAL EXCHANGE RATE AND AGGREGATE DEMAND

A rise in EP^*/P makes domestic goods and services cheaper relative to foreign goods and services and shifts both domestic *and* foreign spending from foreign goods to domestic goods. As a result, CA rises, and, in turn, aggregate demand D goes up. *A real depreciation of the home currency raises aggregate demand for home output; a real appreciation lowers aggregate demand for home output.*

REAL INCOME AND AGGREGATE DEMAND

The effect of domestic real income on aggregate demand is slightly more complicated. If taxes are fixed at a given level, a rise in Y represents an equal rise in disposable income Y^d. While this rise in Y^d raises consumption, it worsens the current account by raising home spending on foreign imports. The first of these effects raises aggregate demand, but the second lowers it. Since increases in consumption are generally divided between spending on home products and spending on foreign imports, however, the first effect (the effect of disposable income on total consumption) is greater than the second (the effect of disposable income on import spending). *Therefore, a rise in domestic real income raises aggregate demand for home output, and a fall in domestic real income lowers aggregate demand for home output.*

Figure 16-1 shows the relation between aggregate demand and real income Y for fixed values of the real exchange rate, taxes, investment demand, and government spending. As Y rises, consumption rises by a fraction of the increase in income. Part of this increase in consumption, moreover, goes into import spending. The effect of an increase in Y on the aggregate demand for home output is therefore smaller than the accompanying rise in consumption demand, which is smaller, in turn, than the increase in Y. We show this in Figure 16-1 by drawing the aggregate demand schedule with a slope less than 1.

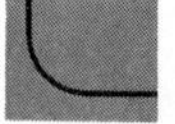

HOW OUTPUT IS DETERMINED IN THE SHORT RUN

Having discussed the factors that influence the demand for an open economy's output, we now study how output is determined in the short run. We show in this section that the output market is in equilibrium when real out-

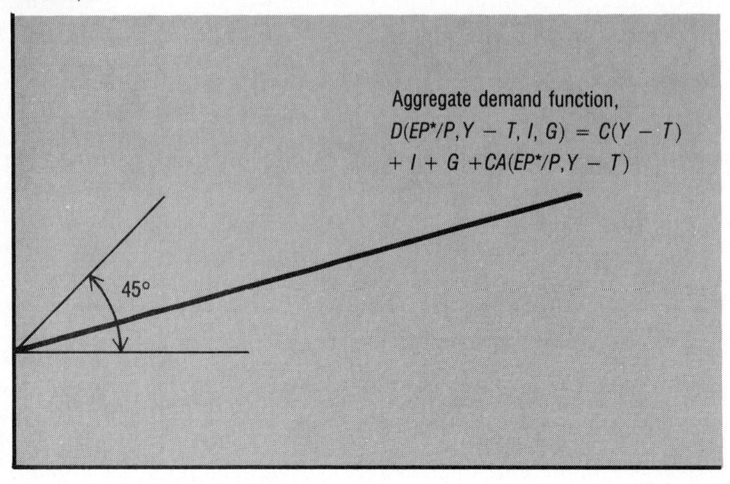

FIGURE 16-1 Aggregate demand as a function of income. Given taxes, a rise in income raises aggregate demand, but by a smaller amount.

put Y equals the aggregate demand for domestic output:

$$Y = D(EP^*/P, Y - T, I, G). \tag{16-1}$$

The equality of aggregate supply and demand therefore determines the short-run equilibrium output level.[5]

Our analysis of real output determination applies to the short run because we assume that the money prices of goods and services are *temporarily fixed.* As we will see later in the chapter, the short-run real output changes allowed by temporarily fixed prices eventually cause price-level changes that move the economy to its long-run equilibrium. In long-run equilibrium, factors of production are fully employed, the level of real output is completely determined by factor supplies, and the real exchange rate has adjusted to equate that long-run real output level to aggregate demand.[6]

The determination of national output in the short run is illustrated in Figure 16-2, where we again graph aggregate demand as a function of output for fixed levels of the real exchange rate, taxes, investment demand, and

[5]Superficially, equation (16-1), which may be written as $Y = C(Y^d) + I + G + CA(EP^*/P, Y^d)$, looks like the GNP identity we discussed in Chapter 12, $Y = C + I + G + CA$. How do the two equations differ? They differ in that (16-1) is an equilibrium condition, not an identity. As you will recall from Chapter 12, the investment quantity I appearing in the GNP identity includes *undesired* or involuntary inventory accumulation by firms, so that the GNP identity always holds as a matter of definition. The investment demand appearing in equation (16-1), however, is *desired* or planned investment. Thus, the GNP identity always holds but equation (16-1) holds only if firms are not building up or drawing down unwanted inventories of goods.

[6]Thus, equation (16-1) also holds in long-run equilibrium, but the equation determines the long-run real exchange rate when Y equals its long-run value.

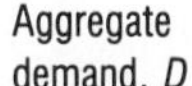

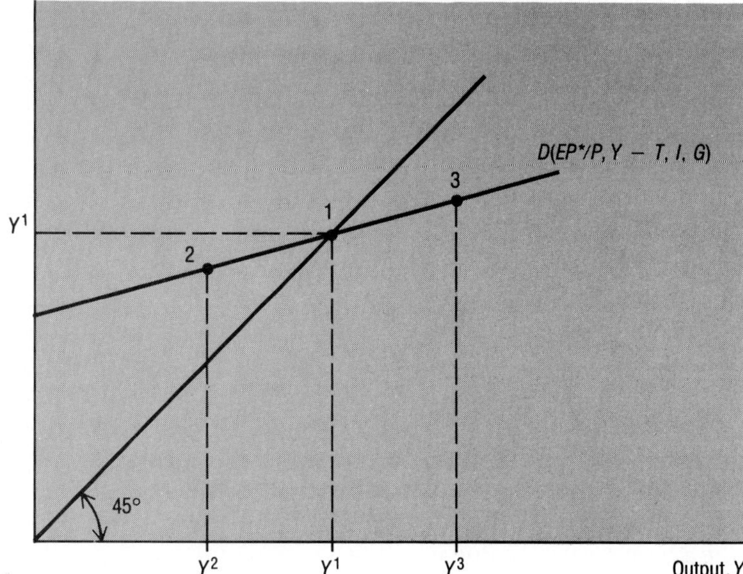

FIGURE 16-2 The determination of output in the short run.
In the short run output settles at Y^1 (point 1), where aggregate demand equals aggregate supply.

government spending. The intersection (at point 1) of the aggregate demand schedule and a 45° line drawn from the origin gives us the unique output level Y^1 at which output equals aggregate demand (that is, $Y = D$).

Let's use Figure 16-2 to see why output tends to settle at Y^1 in the short run. At an output level of Y^2, aggregate demand (point 2) exceeds output. Firms therefore increase their production to meet this excess demand. (If they did not, they would have to meet the excess demand out of inventories, reducing investment below the desired level I.) Thus, output expands until national income reaches Y^1.

At point 3 there is an excess supply of domestic output and firms find themselves involuntarily accumulating inventories (involuntarily raising their investment spending above its desired level). As inventories start to build up, firms cut back on production; only when output has fallen to Y^1 will firms be content with their level of production. Once again, output settles at point 1, the point at which output exactly equals aggregate demand. In this short-run equilibrium, consumers, firms, the government, and foreign buyers of domestic products are all able to realize their desired expenditures.

OUTPUT-MARKET EQUILIBRIUM IN THE SHORT RUN: THE *DD* SCHEDULE

Now that we understand how output is determined for a given real exchange rate EP^*/P, let's look at how the exchange rate and output are simultaneously determined in the short run. To understand this process, we need two elements. The first element, developed in this section, is the relationship between output and the exchange rate (the *DD* schedule) that must hold when the output market is in equilibrium. The second element, developed in the next section, is the relationship between output and the exchange rate that must hold when the home money market and the foreign-exchange market (the asset markets) are in equilibrium. As we will see, both elements are necessary because the economy as a whole is in equilibrium only when both the output market and the asset markets are in equilibrium.

OUTPUT, THE EXCHANGE RATE, AND OUTPUT-MARKET EQUILIBRIUM

Figure 16-3 illustrates the relationship between the exchange rate and output. Specifically, the figure illustrates the effect of a depreciation of the domestic currency against foreign currency (that is, a rise in E from E^1 to E^2) for fixed values of the domestic price level P and the foreign price level P^*. With fixed price levels at home and abroad, the rise in the exchange rate makes foreign goods and services more expensive relative to domestic goods and services. This relative price change shifts the aggregate demand schedule upward.

The fall in the relative price of domestic output shifts the aggregate demand schedule upward because for each level of domestic output, the demand for domestic products is higher after the depreciation. Output

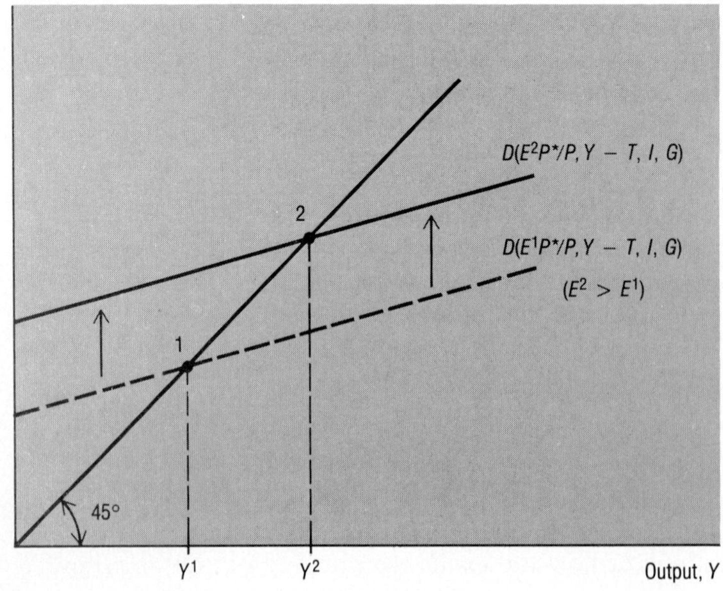

FIGURE 16-3 Output effect of a currency depreciation with fixed output prices. A rise in the exchange rate from E^1 to E^2 raises aggregate demand and output, all else equal.

expands from Y^1 to Y^2 as firms find themselves faced with excess demand at initial production levels.

Although we have considered the effect of a change in E with P and P^* held fixed it is straightforward to analyze the effect of changes in P or P^* on output. *Any rise in the real exchange rate EP^*/P (whether due to a rise in E, a rise in P^*, or a fall in P) will cause an upward shift in the aggregate demand function and an expansion of output, all else equal.* (A rise in P^*, for example, has effects qualitatively identical to those of a rise in E.) *Similarly, any fall in EP^*/P, regardless of its cause (a fall in E, a fall in P^*, or a rise in P), will cause output to contract, all else equal.* (A rise in P, with E and P^* held fixed, for example, makes domestic products more expensive relative to foreign products, reduces aggregate demand for domestic output, and causes output to fall.)

DERIVING THE *DD* SCHEDULE

If we assume that P and P^* are fixed in the short run, a depreciation of the domestic currency (a rise in E) is associated with a rise in domestic output, Y, while an appreciation (a fall in E) is associated with a fall in Y. This association provides us with one of the two relationships between E and Y needed to describe the short-run macroeconomic behavior of an open economy. We summarize this relationship by the *DD* schedule, which shows all combinations of output and the exchange rate such that the output market is in short-run equilibrium with aggregate demand equal to aggregate supply.

Figure 16-4 shows how to derive the *DD* schedule, which relates E and Y when P and P^* are fixed. The upper part of the figure reproduces the result of Figure 16-3 (a depreciation of the domestic currency shifts the aggregate demand function upward, causing output to rise). The *DD* schedule in the lower part shows the resulting relationship between the exchange rate and output (given that P and P^* are held constant). Point 1 on the *DD* schedule gives the output level Y^1 at which aggregate demand equals aggregate supply when the exchange rate is E^1. A depreciation of the currency to E^2 leads to the higher output level Y^2 according to the upper part, and this information allows us to locate point 2 on *DD*.

FACTORS THAT SHIFT THE *DD* SCHEDULE

A number of factors affect the position of the *DD* schedule: the levels of government demand, taxes, and investment; the domestic and foreign price levels; the stability of domestic consumption behavior; and the foreign demand for home output. To understand the effects of shifts in these factors, we must study how the *DD* schedule shifts when they change.

1. *A change in G.* Figure 16-5 shows the effect on *DD* of a rise in government purchases, G. Before the increase in G, the relevant *DD* curve is D^1D^1 in the lower part of the figure. As shown in the upper part, the exchange rate E^0

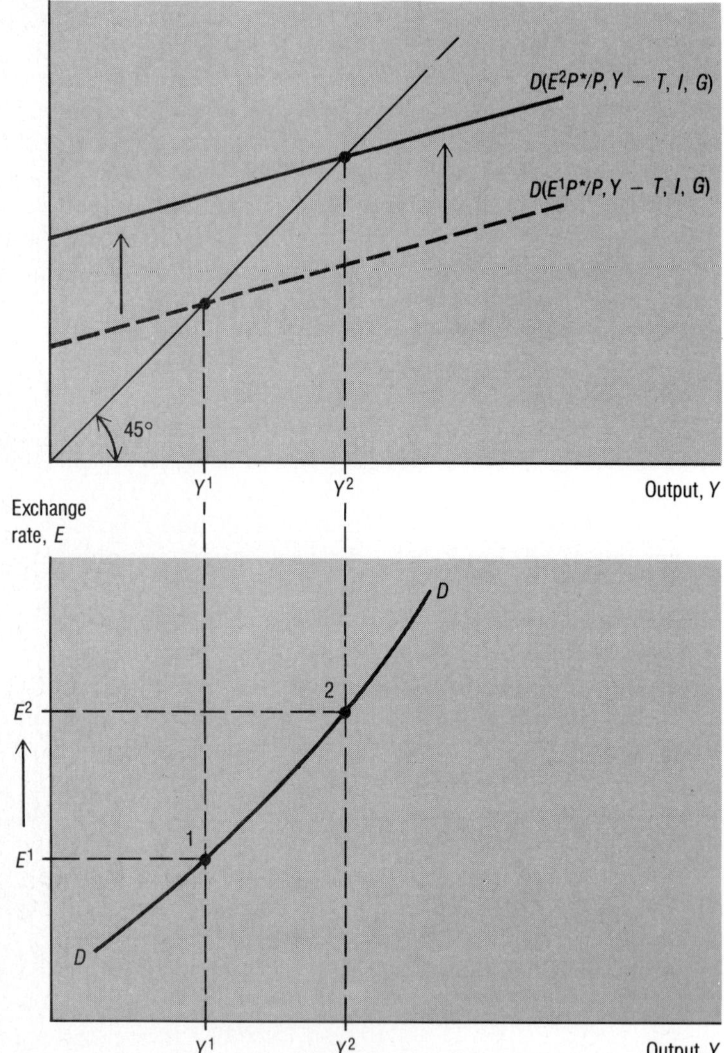

FIGURE 16-4 Deriving the *DD* schedule. The *DD* schedule slopes upward because a rise in the exchange rate from E^1 to E^2, all else equal, causes output to rise from Y^1 to Y^2.

leads to an equilibrium output level Y^1 at the initial level of government demand; so point 1 is one point on D^1D^1.

An increase in G causes the aggregate demand schedule in the upper part of the figure to shift upward. Everything else remaining unchanged, output increases. Point 2 in the bottom part shows the higher level of output Y^2 at which aggregate demand and supply are now equal, given an unchanged exchange rate of E^0. Point 2 is on the new DD curve, D^2D^2.

For any level of the exchange rate, the level of output equating aggregate demand and supply is higher after the increase in G. This implies that

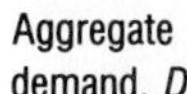

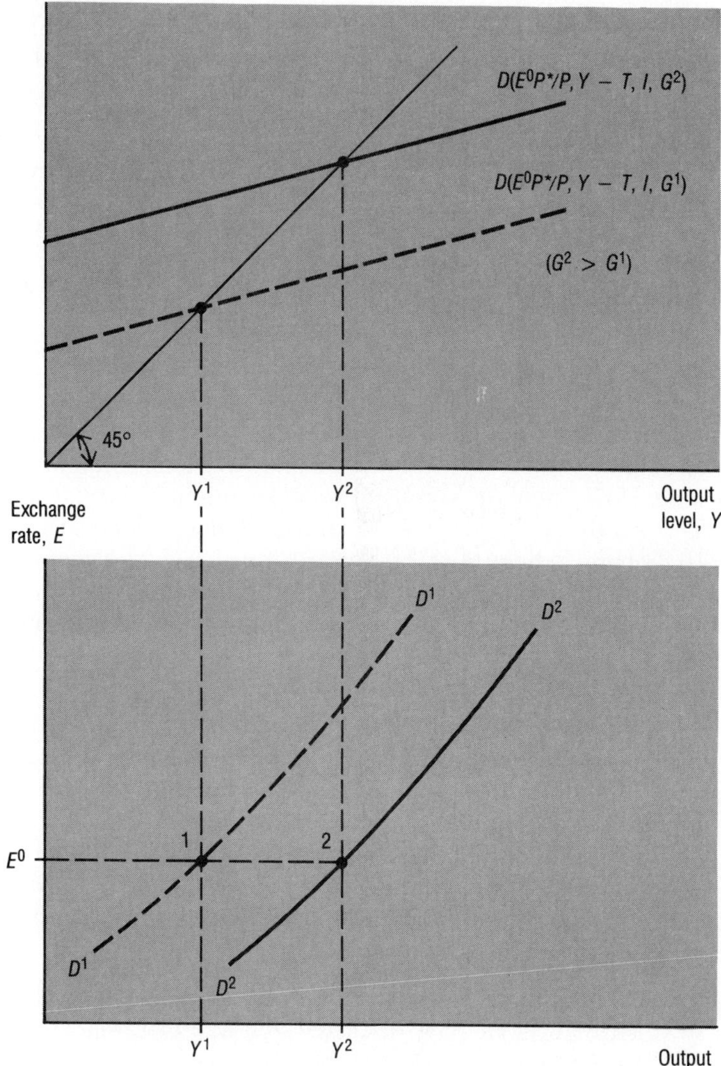

FIGURE 16-5 Government demand and the position of the *DD* schedule. A rise in government demand from G^1 to G^2 raises output at every level of the exchange rate. The change therefore shifts *DD* to the right.

an increase in G causes DD to shift to the right, as shown in Figure 16-5. Similarly, *a decrease in G causes DD to shift to the left.*

The method and reasoning we have just used to study the effect of an increase in G on the position of the *DD* curve can be applied to all the cases that follow. So we give only a brief summary of the results, leaving it to you to provide a more detailed analysis using diagrams similar to Figure 16-5.

2. *A change in T.* Taxes, T, affect aggregate demand by changing disposable income, and thus consumption, for any level of GNP, Y. It follows that an increase in taxes causes the aggregate demand function of Figure 16-1 to shift

downward given the exchange rate E. Since this effect is the opposite of that of an increase in G, an increase in T must cause the DD schedule to shift leftward. Similarly, a fall in T causes a rightward shift of DD.

3. *A change in I.* An increase in investment demand has the same effect as an increase in G: the aggregate demand schedule shifts upward and DD shifts to the right. A fall in investment demand shifts DD to the left.

4. *A change in P.* Given E and P^*, an increase in P makes domestic output more expensive relative to foreign output and lowers net export demand. The DD schedule shifts to the left as aggregate demand falls. A fall in P makes domestic goods cheaper and causes a rightward shift of DD.

5. *A change in P*.* Given E and P, a rise in P^* makes foreign goods and services relatively more expensive. Aggregate demand for domestic output therefore rises and DD shifts to the right. Similarly, a fall in P^* causes DD to shift to the left.

6. *A change in the consumption function.* Suppose residents of the home economy suddenly decide they want to consume more and save less at each level of disposable income. If the increase in consumption spending is not devoted entirely to imports from abroad, aggregate demand for domestic output rises and the aggregate demand schedule shifts upward for any given exchange rate E. This implies a shift to the right of the DD schedule. An autonomous fall in consumption (if it is not entirely due to a fall in import demand) shifts DD to the left.

7. *A demand shift between foreign and domestic goods.* Suppose that there is no change in the domestic consumption function but that domestic and foreign residents suddenly decide to devote more of their spending to goods and services produced in the home country. If home disposable income and the real exchange rate remain the same, this shift in demand *improves* the current account by raising exports and lowering imports. The aggregate demand schedule shifts upward, and DD therefore shifts to the right. The same reasoning shows that a shift in world demand away from domestic products and toward foreign products causes DD to shift to the left.

You may have noticed that a simple rule allows you to predict the effect on DD of any of the disturbances we have discussed: *Any disturbance that raises aggregate demand for domestic output shifts the DD schedule to the right; any disturbance that lowers aggregate demand for domestic output shifts the DD schedule to the left.*

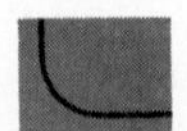

ASSET-MARKET EQUILIBRIUM IN THE SHORT RUN: THE *AA* SCHEDULE

We have now derived the first element in our account of short-run exchange-rate and income determination, the relation between the exchange rate and output consistent with the equality of aggregate demand and supply. This relation is summarized by the DD schedule, which shows all exchange-rate and output levels that lead to short-run equilibrium in the output market. As we noted at the beginning of the last section, however, equilibrium in the economy as a whole requires equilibrium in the asset markets as well as in the output market, and there is no reason in general why points on the *DD* schedule should lead to asset-market equilibrium.

To complete the story of short-run equilibrium, we therefore introduce a second element to ensure that the exchange rate and output level consistent with output-market equilibrium are also consistent with asset-market equilibrium. The schedule of exchange rates and output levels consistent with equilibrium in the domestic money market and the foreign-exchange market is called the *AA* schedule.

OUTPUT, THE EXCHANGE RATE, AND ASSET-MARKET EQUILIBRIUM

In Chapter 13 we studied the interest parity condition, which states that the foreign-exchange market is in equilibrium only when the expected rates of return on domestic- and foreign-currency deposits are equal. In Chapter 14 we learned how the interest rates that enter the interest-parity relationship are determined by the equality of real money supply and real money demand in national money markets. Now we combine these asset-market equilibrium conditions to see how the exchange rate and output must be related when all asset markets simultaneously clear. Because the focus for now is on the domestic economy, the foreign interest rate is taken as given.

For a given expected future exchange rate E^e, the interest parity condition describing foreign-exchange market equilibrium is

$$R = R^* + (E^e - E)/E,$$

where R is the interest rate on domestic-currency deposits and R^* is the interest rate on foreign-currency deposits. In Chapter 14 we saw that the domestic interest rate satisfying the interest-parity condition must also equate the real domestic money supply (M^s/P) to aggregate real money demand:

$$\frac{M^s}{P} = L(R, Y).$$

You will recall that aggregate real money demand $L(R, Y)$ rises when the interest rate falls because a fall in R makes interest-bearing assets less attractive to hold. (Conversely, a rise in the interest rate lowers real money demand.) A rise in real output increases real money demand by raising the volume of monetary transactions that people must carry out (and a fall in real output reduces real money demand by reducing transactions needs).

We now use the diagrammatic tools developed in Chapter 14 to study the changes in the exchange rate that must accompany output changes so that asset markets remain in equilibrium. Figure 16-6 shows the equilibrium domestic interest rate and exchange rate associated with the output level Y^1

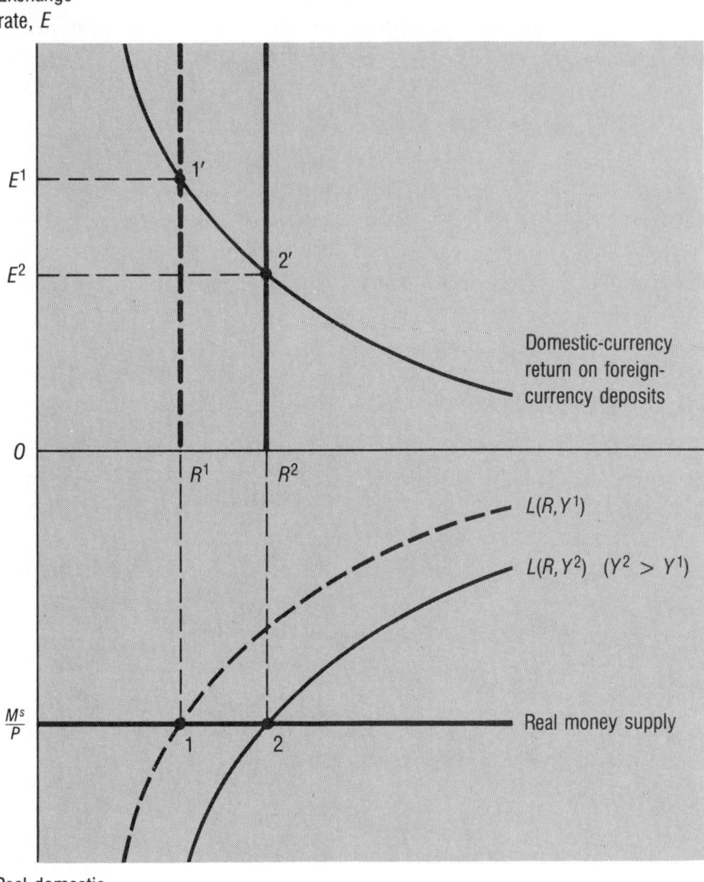

FIGURE 16-6 Output and the exchange rate in asset-market equilibrium. For the asset markets to remain in equilibrium, a rise in output must be accompanied by an appreciation of the currency, all else equal.

for a given nominal money supply, M^s, a given domestic price level, P, a given foreign interest rate, R^*, and a given value of the expected future exchange rate, E^e. In the lower part of the figure, we see that with real output at Y^1 and the real money supply at M^s/P, the interest rate R^1 clears the home money market (point 1) while the exchange rate E^1 clears the foreign-exchange market (point 1′). The equilibrium exchange rate E^1 clears the foreign-exchange market because it equates the expected rate of return on foreign deposits, measured in terms of domestic currency, to R^1.

As we saw in Chapter 14, a rise in output from Y^1 to Y^2 raises aggregate real money demand from $L(R, Y^1)$ to $L(R, Y^2)$. This, in turn, raises the equilibrium domestic interest rate to R^2 (point 2). With E^e and R^* fixed, the domestic currency must appreciate from E^1 to E^2 to bring the foreign-exchange market back into equilibrium at point 2′. The domestic currency appreciates by just enough so that the increase in the rate at which it is expected to depreciate in the future offsets the increased interest-rate advantage of home-currency deposits. *For asset markets to remain in equilibrium, a rise in domestic output must be accompanied by an appreciation of the domestic currency, all else equal, and a fall in domestic output must be accompanied by a depreciation.*

DERIVING THE *AA* SCHEDULE

While the *DD* schedule plots exchange rates and output levels at which the output market is in equilibrium, the *AA* schedule relates exchange rates and output levels that keep the money and foreign-exchange markets in equilibrium. Figure 16-7 shows the *AA* schedule. From Figure 16-6 we see that for any output level Y^1, there is a unique exchange rate E^1 satisfying the interest parity condition (given the real money supply, the foreign interest rate, and the expected future exchange rate). Our previous reasoning tells us that a rise in Y^1 to Y^2 will produce an appreciation of the domestic currency, that is, a fall in the exchange rate from E^1 to E^2. The *AA* schedule therefore has a negative slope, as shown.

FACTORS THAT SHIFT THE *AA* SCHEDULE

Five factors cause the *AA* schedule to shift: changes in the domestic money supply, M^s; changes in the domestic price level, P; changes in the expected

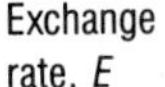

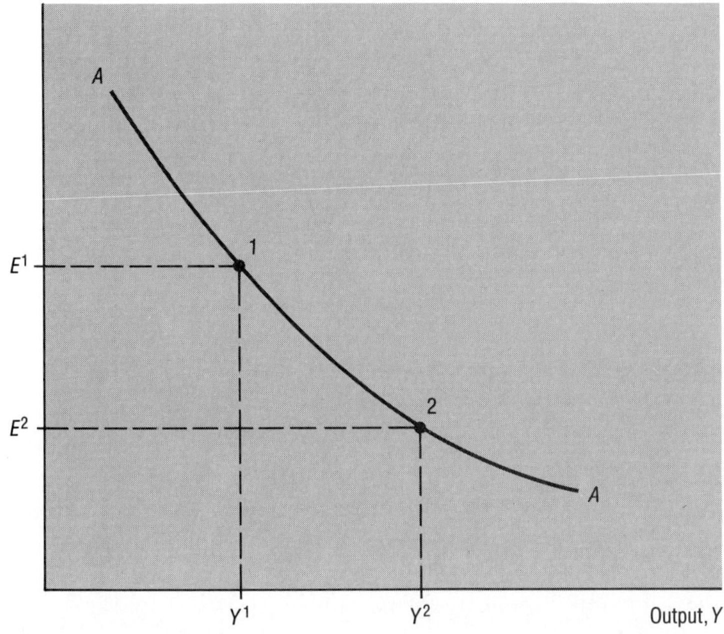

FIGURE 16-7 The *AA* schedule. The asset-market equilibrium schedule *AA* slopes downward because a rise in output, all else equal, causes a rise in the home interest rate and a domestic currency appreciation.

future exchange rate, E^e; changes in the foreign interest rate R^*; and shifts in the aggregate money demand schedule.

1. *A change in* M^s. For a fixed level of output, an increase in M^s causes the domestic currency to depreciate in the foreign-exchange market, all else equal (that is, E rises). Since for each level of output the exchange rate E is higher after the rise in M^s, the rise in M^s causes AA to shift *upward.* Similarly, a fall in M^s causes AA to shift *downward.*

2. *A change in* P. An increase in P reduces the *real* money supply and drives the interest rate upward. Other things equal, this rise in the interest rate causes E to fall, given Y. The effect of a rise in P is therefore a downward shift of AA. A fall in P results in an upward shift of AA.

3. *A change in* E^e. Suppose participants in the foreign-exchange market suddenly revise their expectations about the exchange rate's future value so that E^e rises. Such a change shifts the curve in the top part of Figure 16-6 (which measures the expected domestic-currency return on foreign-currency deposits) to the right. The rise in E^e therefore causes the domestic currency to depreciate, other things being equal. Because the exchange rate producing equilibrium in the foreign-exchange market is higher after a rise in E^e, given output, AA shifts upward when a rise in the expected future exchange rate occurs. It shifts downward when the expected future exchange rate falls.

4. *A change in* R^*. A rise in R^* raises the return on foreign-currency deposits and therefore shifts the downward-sloping schedule at the top of Figure 16-6 to the right. Given output, the domestic currency must depreciate to restore interest parity. A rise in R^* therefore has the same effect on AA as a rise in E^e: it causes an upward shift. A fall in R^* results in a downward shift of AA.

5. *A change in money demand.* Suppose domestic residents decide they would prefer to hold lower real money balances at each output level and interest rate. (Such a change in asset-holding preferences is a *reduction in money demand.*) A reduction in money demand implies an inward shift of the aggregate real money demand function $L(R, Y)$ for any fixed level of Y, and it thus results in a lower interest rate and a rise in E. A reduction in money demand therefore has the same effect as an increase in the money supply, in that it shifts AA upward. The opposite disturbance of an increase in money demand would shift AA downward.

SHORT-RUN EQUILIBRIUM FOR THE ECONOMY: PUTTING THE *DD* AND *AA* SCHEDULES TOGETHER

By assuming that output prices are temporarily fixed, we have derived two separate schedules of exchange-rate and output levels: the DD schedule, along which the output market is in equilibrium, and the AA schedule, along which the asset markets are in equilibrium. A short-run equilibrium for the economy as a whole must lie on *both* schedules because such a point must bring about equilibrium simultaneously in the output and asset markets. We can therefore find the economy's short-run equilibrium by finding the intersection of the *DD* and *AA* schedules. Once again, it is the assumption that output prices are temporarily fixed that makes this intersection a *short-run* equilibrium. The analysis in this section continues to assume that the foreign interest rate R^* and the expected future exchange rate E^e are fixed.

Figure 16-8 combines the *DD* and *AA* schedules to locate short-run equilibrium. The intersection of *DD* and *AA* at point 1 is the only point consistent with both the equality of aggregate demand and aggregate supply and asset-market equilibrium. The short-run equilibrium levels of the exchange rate and output are therefore E^1 and Y^1.

To convince yourself that the economy will indeed settle at point 1, imagine that the economy is instead at a position like point 2 in Figure 16-9. At point 2, which lies above *AA* and *DD*, both the output and asset markets are out of equilibrium. Because *E* is so high relative to *AA*, the rate at which *E* is expected to fall in the future is also high relative to the rate that would maintain interest parity. The high expected future appreciation rate of the domestic currency implies that the expected domestic-currency return on foreign deposits is below that on domestic deposits, so there is an excess demand for the domestic currency in the foreign exchange market. The high level of *E* at point 2 also makes domestic goods cheap (given prices), causing an excess demand for domestic output at that point.

The excess demand for domestic currency leads to an immediate fall in the exchange rate. This appreciation equalizes the expected returns on

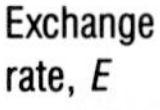
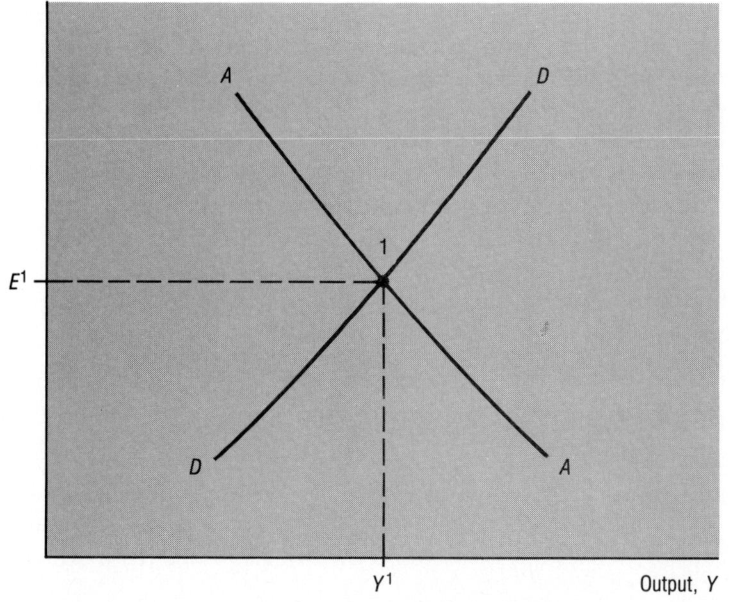

FIGURE 16-8 Short-run equilibrium: The intersection of *DD* and *AA*. The short-run equilibrium of the economy occurs at point 1, where the output and asset markets simultaneously clear.

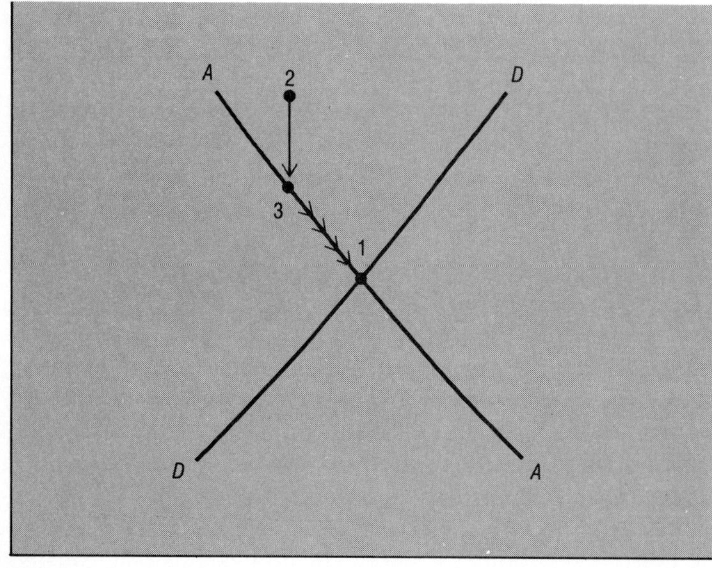

FIGURE 16-9 How the economy reaches its short-run equilibrium. Because asset markets adjust very quickly, the exchange rate jumps immediately from point 2 to point 3 on *AA*. The economy then moves to point 1 along *AA* as output rises to meet aggregate demand.

domestic and foreign deposits and places the economy at point 3 on the asset-market equilibrium curve *AA*. But since point 3 is above the *DD* schedule, there is still excess demand for domestic output. As firms raise production to avoid depleting their inventories, the economy travels along *AA* to point 1, where aggregate demand and supply are equal. Because asset prices can jump immediately while changes in production plans take some time, the asset markets remain in continual equilibrium even while output is changing.

The exchange rate falls as the economy approaches point 1 along *AA* because rising national output causes money demand to rise, pushing the interest rate steadily upward. (The currency must appreciate steadily to lower the expected rate of future domestic currency appreciation and maintain interest parity.) Once the economy has reached point 1 on *DD*, aggregate demand equals output and producers no longer face involuntary inventory depletion. The economy therefore settles at point 1, the only point at which the output *and* asset markets clear.

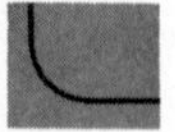

TEMPORARY CHANGES IN MONETARY AND FISCAL POLICY

Now that we have seen how the economy's short-run equilibrium is determined, we can study how shifts in government macroeconomic policies affect output and the exchange rate. Our interest in the effects of macroeconomic policies stems from their usefulness in counteracting economic disturbances that cause fluctuations in output, employment, and inflation. In this section we learn how government policies can be used to maintain full employment in open economies.

We concentrate on two types of government policy, **monetary policy,** which works through changes in the money supply, and **fiscal policy,** which works through changes in government spending or taxes.[7]

In this section we examine *temporary* policy shifts, shifts that the public expects to be reversed in the future. The expected future exchange rate E^e is now assumed to equal the long-run exchange rate discussed in Chapter 15, that is, the exchange rate that prevails once full employment is reached and domestic prices have adjusted fully to past disturbances in the output and asset markets. In line with this interpretation, a temporary policy change does *not* affect the long-run expected exchange rate E^e.

We assume throughout that events in the economy we are studying do not influence the foreign interest rate R^* or price level P^*, and that the domestic price level P is fixed in the short run.

MONETARY POLICY

The short-run effect of a temporary increase in the domestic money supply is shown in Figure 16-10. An increased money supply shifts A^1A^1 upward to A^2A^2 but does not affect the position of DD. The upward shift of the asset-market equilibrium schedule moves the economy from point 1, with exchange rate E^1 and output Y^1, to point 2, with exchange rate E^2 and output Y^2. An increase in the money supply causes a depreciation of the domestic currency, an expansion of output, and therefore an increase in employment.

We can understand the economic forces causing these results by recalling our earlier discussions of asset-market equilibrium and output determination. At the initial output level Y^1 and given the fixed price level, an increase in money supply must push down the home interest rate R. We have been assuming the monetary change is temporary and does not affect the expected future exchange rate E^e; so to preserve interest parity in the face of a decline in R (given that R^* does not change), the exchange rate must depreciate immediately, from E^1 to E^2, to create the expectation that the home currency will appreciate in the future at a greater rate than was expected before R fell. This depreciation of the domestic currency, however, makes home products cheaper relative to foreign products. There is therefore an increase in aggregate demand, which must be matched by an increase in output.

[7]Other policies, such as commercial policies, can also have macroeconomic effects. Such policies, however, are usually adopted to attain sectoral goals rather than for purposes of macroeconomic stabilization; so we do not discuss them in this chapter. (A problem at the end of this chapter does ask you to look at the macroeconomic effects of a tariff.) The connection between macroeconomic events and commercial policies is discussed in Chapters 18 and 19.

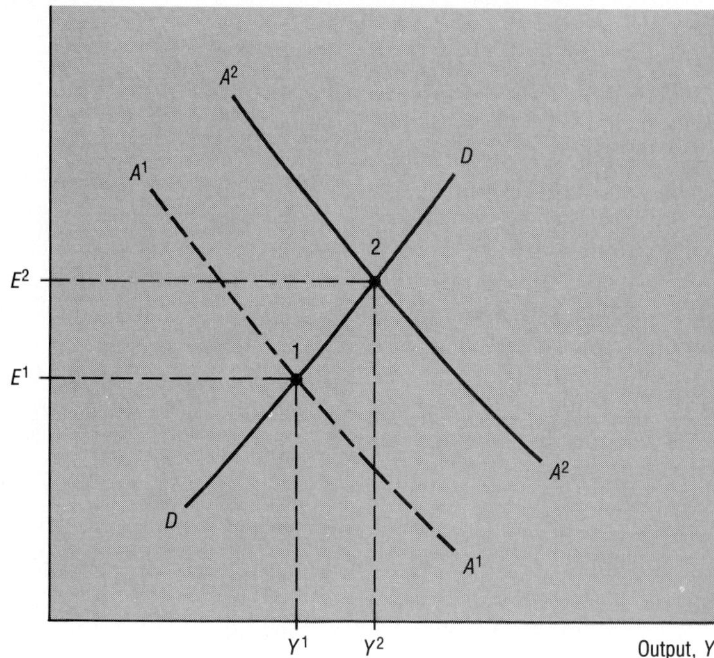

FIGURE 16-10 Effects of a temporary increase in the money supply. By shifting A^1A^1 to the right, a temporary increase in the money supply causes a currency depreciation and a rise in output.

FISCAL POLICY

As we saw earlier, expansionary fiscal policy can take the form of an increase in government demand, a cut in taxes, or some combination of the two that raises aggregate demand. A temporary fiscal expansion (which does not affect the expected future exchange rate) therefore shifts the *DD* schedule to the right but does not move *AA*.

Figure 16-11 shows how expansionary fiscal policy affects the economy in the short run. Initially the economy is at point 1, with an exchange rate E^1 and output Y^1. Suppose the government decides to spend $5 billion to develop a new space shuttle. This one-time increase in government purchases moves the economy to point 2, causing the currency to appreciate to E^2 and output to expand to Y^2. The economy would respond in a similar way to a temporary cut in taxes.

What economic forces produce the movement from point 1 to point 2? The increase in output caused by the increase in government spending raises the transactions demand for real money holdings. Given the fixed price level, this increase in money demand pushes the interest rate *R* upward. Because the expected future exchange rate E^e and the foreign interest rate R^* have not changed, the currency must therefore appreciate to create the expectation of a subsequent depreciation just large enough to offset the higher in-

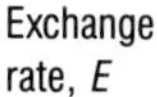

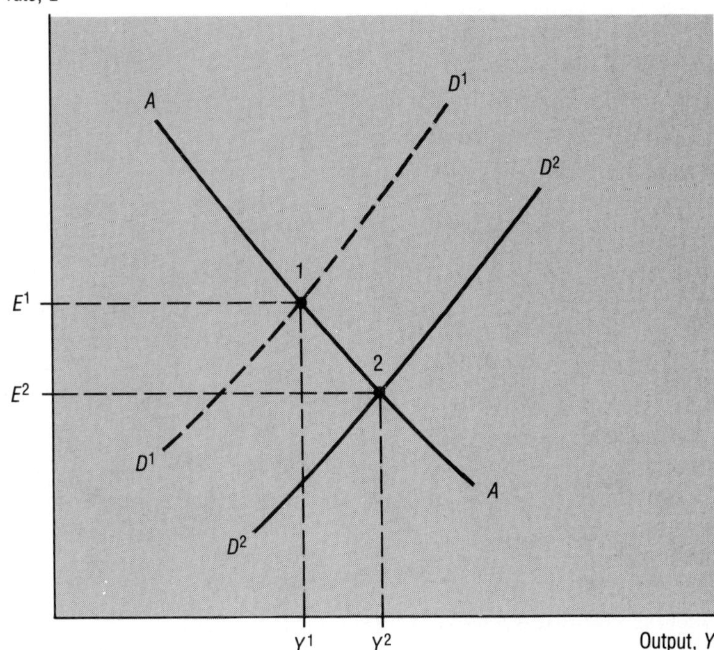

FIGURE 16-11 Effects of a temporary fiscal expansion. By shifting D^1D^1 to the right, a temporary fiscal expansion causes a currency appreciation and a rise in output.

ternational interest-rate differential between domestic- and foreign-currency deposits.

POLICIES TO MAINTAIN FULL EMPLOYMENT

The analysis of this section can be applied to the problem of maintaining full employment in open economies. Because temporary monetary expansion and temporary fiscal expansion both raise output and employment, they can be used to counteract the effects of temporary disturbances that lead to recession. Similarly, disturbances that lead to overemployment can be offset through contractionary macroeconomic policies.

Figure 16-12 illustrates this use of macroeconomic policy. Suppose that the economy's initial equilibrium is at point 1, where output equals its full-employment level, denoted Y^f. Suddenly there is a temporary shift in consumer tastes away from domestic products. As we saw earlier in this chapter, such a shift is a decrease in aggregate demand for domestic goods, and it causes the curve D^1D^1 to shift leftward, to D^2D^2. At point 2, the new short-run equilibrium, the currency has depreciated to E^2 and output, at Y^2, is below its full-employment level. Because the shift in preferences is assumed to be temporary, it does not affect E^e; so there is no change in the position of A^1A^1.

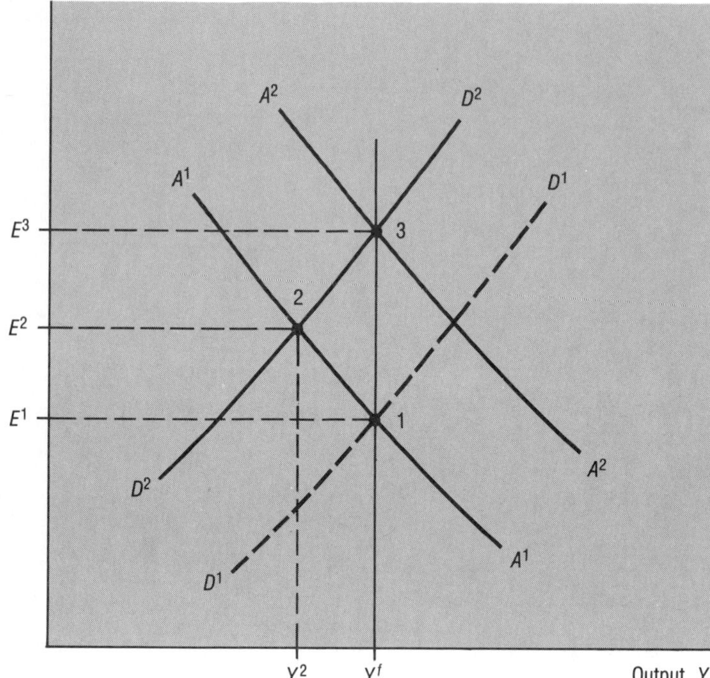

FIGURE 16-12 Policies to maintain full employment after a temporary fall in world demand for domestic products. A temporary fall in world demand shifts D^1D^1 to the left, reducing output (point 2). Temporary fiscal expansion can restore full employment (point 1) by shifting the *DD* schedule back to its original position. Temporary monetary expansion restores full employment (point 3) by shifting A^1A^1 to A^2A^2. The two policies differ in their exchange-rate effects.

To restore full employment, the government may use either monetary or fiscal policy, or both. A temporary fiscal expansion shifts D^2D^2 back to its original position, restoring full employment and returning the exchange rate to E^1. A temporary money-supply increase shifts the asset-market equilibrium curve to A^2A^2 and moves the economy to point 3, a move that restores full employment but causes the home currency to depreciate even further.

Another possible cause of recession is a temporary increase in the demand for money, illustrated in Figure 16-13. An increase in money demand pushes up the domestic interest rate and appreciates the currency, thereby making domestic goods more expensive and causing output to contract. Figure 16-13 shows this asset-market disturbance as the downward shift of A^1A^1 to A^2A^2, which moves the economy from its initial full-employment equilibrium at point 1 to point 2.

Expansionary macroeconomic policies can again restore full employment. A temporary money-supply increase moves the economy back to its initial position at point 1, completely offsetting the increase in money demand by giving domestic residents the additional money they desire to hold. Temporary fiscal expansion shifts D^1D^1 to D^2D^2 and restores full em-

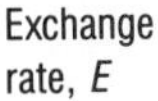

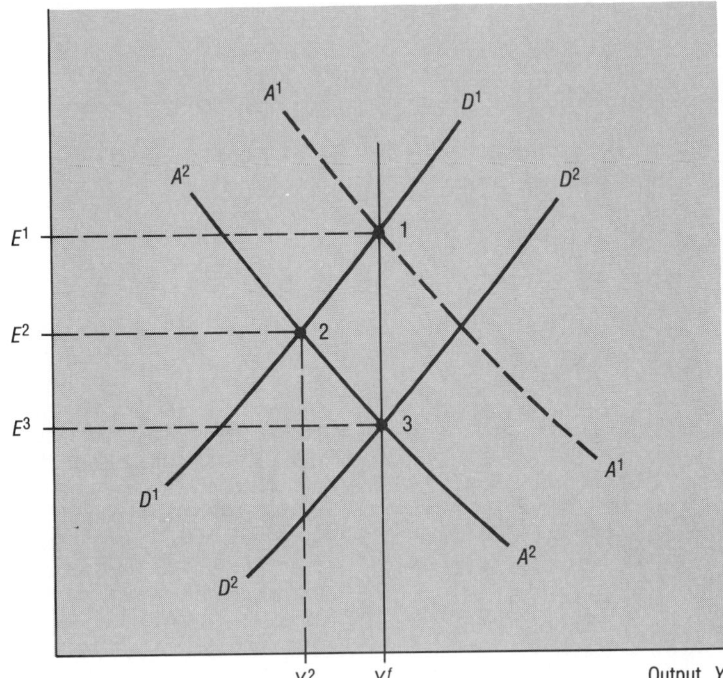

FIGURE 16-13 Policies to maintain full employment after a money-demand increase. After a temporary money-demand increase, either an increase in the money supply or temporary fiscal ease can be used to maintain full employment. The two policies have different exchange-rate effects.

ployment at point 3. But the move to point 3 involves an even greater appreciation of the currency.

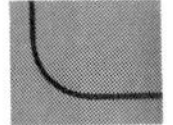

PERMANENT SHIFTS IN MONETARY AND FISCAL POLICY

A permanent policy shift affects not only the current value of the government's policy instrument (the money supply, government spending, or taxes) but also affects the *long-run* exchange rate. This change in the long-run exchange rate, in turn, affects expectations about future exchange rates. Because these changes in expectations have a major influence on the exchange rate prevailing in the short run, the effects of permanent policy shifts differ from those of temporary shifts. In this section we look at the effects of permanent changes in monetary and fiscal policy, in both the short run and the long run.

A PERMANENT INCREASE IN THE MONEY SUPPLY

Figure 16-14 shows the short-run effects of a permanent increase in the money supply on an economy initially at its full-employment output level Y^f

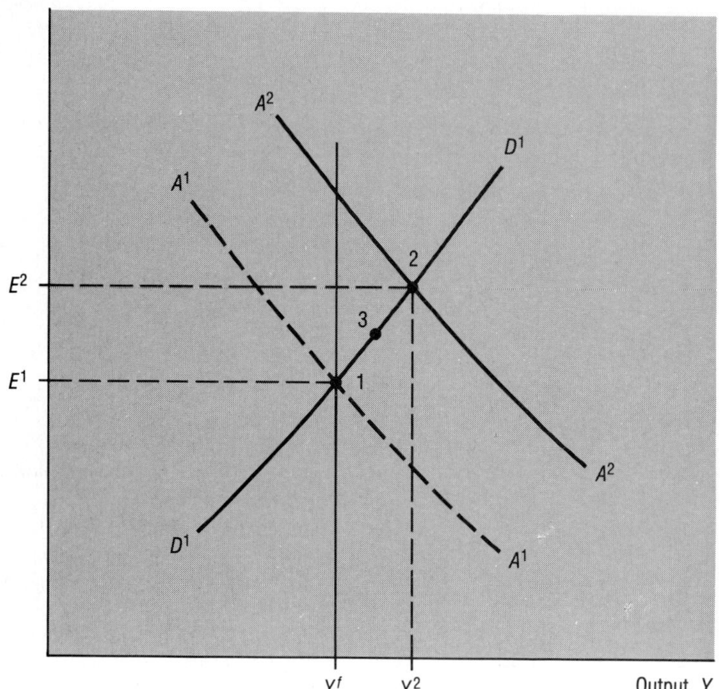

FIGURE 16-14 Short-run effects of a permanent increase in the money supply. A permanent increase in the money supply, which moves the economy from point 1 to point 2, has stronger effects on the exchange rate and output than a temporary increase, which moves the economy to point 3.

(point 1). As we saw earlier, an increase in M^s causes the asset-market equilibrium schedule A^1A^1 to shift upward. Because the increase in M^s is permanent, however, it also affects the exchange rate expected for the future, E^e. Chapter 14 showed how a permanent increase in the money supply affects the long-run exchange rate: a permanent increase in M^s must ultimately lead to a proportional rise in E. Therefore, the rise in M^s causes E^e, the expected future exchange rate, to rise.

Because a rise in E^e accompanies a *permanent* increase in the money supply, the upward shift of A^1A^1 to A^2A^2 is greater than that caused by an equal, but transitory, increase. At point 2, the economy's new short-run equilibrium, Y and E are both higher than they would be were the change in the money supply temporary. (Point 3 shows the equilibrium that might result from a temporary increase in M^s.)

ADJUSTMENT TO A PERMANENT INCREASE IN THE MONEY SUPPLY

Because the increase in the money supply shown in Figure 16-14 is not reversed by the central bank, it is natural to ask how the economy is affected *over time.* At the short-run equilibrium shown as point 2 in Figure 16-14, output is above its full-employment level, so labor and machines are working overtime. There is therefore upward pressure on the price level as workers demand higher wages and producers raise prices to cover their increasing production costs. Chapter 14 showed that while an increase in the money supply must eventually cause all money prices to rise in proportion, it has no lasting effect on output, relative prices, or interest rates. Over time, the inflationary pressure that follows a permanent money-supply expansion pushes the price level to its new long-run value and returns the economy to full employment.

Figure 16-15 will help you visualize the adjustment back to full employment. Whenever output is greater than its full-employment level Y^f and productive factors are working overtime, the price level P is rising to keep up with rising production costs. Although the DD and AA schedules are drawn for a constant price level P, we have seen how increases in P cause them to shift. A rise in P makes domestic goods more expensive relative to foreign goods, discouraging exports and encouraging imports. A rising domestic price level therefore causes D^1D^1 to shift to the left over time. Because a rising price level reduces the real money supply steadily over time, A^2A^2 also travels to the left as prices rise.

The DD and AA schedules stop shifting only when they intersect at the full-employment output level Y^f; as long as output differs from Y^f, the price

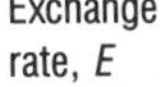

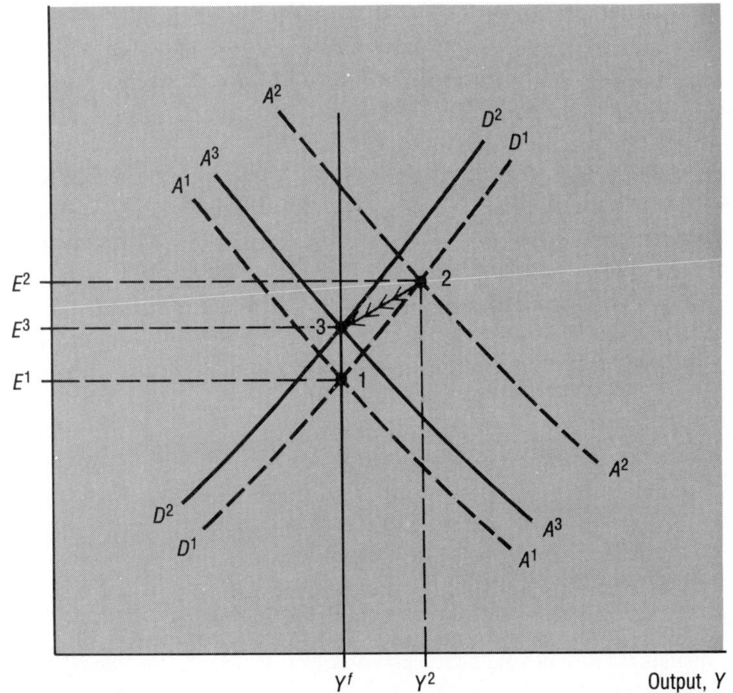

FIGURE 16-15 Long-run adjustment to a permanent increase in the money supply. After a permanent money-supply increase, a steadily increasing price level shifts the *DD* and *AA* schedules to the left until long-run equilibrium (point 3) is reached.

level will change and the two schedules will continue to shift. The schedules' final positions are shown as D^2D^2 and A^3A^3 in Figure 16-15. At point 3, their intersection, the exchange rate, E, and the price level, P, have risen in proportion to the increase in the money supply, as required by the long-run neutrality of money. (A^2A^2 does not shift all the way back to its original position because E^e is permanently higher after a permanent increase in the money supply.)

Notice that along the adjustment path between the initial short-run equilibrium (point 2) and the long-run equilibrium (point 3), the domestic currency actually appreciates (from E^2 to E^3) following its initial sharp depreciation (from E^1 to E^2). This exchange-rate behavior is an example of the *overshooting* phenomenon that we discussed in Chapter 14, in which the exchange rate's initial response to some change is greater than its long-run response. While the exchange rate initially overshoots in the case shown in Figure 16-15, overshooting does not have to occur in all circumstances.

A PERMANENT FISCAL EXPANSION

A permanent fiscal expansion has an immediate impact in the output market but also affects the asset markets through its impact on long-run exchange-rate expectations. Figure 16-16 shows the short-run effects of a government decision to spend an extra $5 billion a year on its space-travel program forever. As before, the direct effect of this rise in G on aggregate demand causes D^1D^1 to shift to the right. But because the increase in government demand for domestic goods and services is permanent in this case, it causes a long-run appreciation of the currency, as we saw in Chapter 15. The resulting fall in E^e pushes the asset-market equilibrium schedule A^1A^1 downward. Point 2, where the new schedules D^2D^2 and A^2A^2 intersect, is the economy's short-run equilibrium.

The important result illustrated in Figure 16-16 is that when a fiscal expansion is permanent, the additional currency appreciation caused by the shift in exchange-rate expectations reduces the policy's expansionary effect on output. Without this additional expectations effect due to the permanence of the fiscal change, output would initially be at point 3, with higher output and a smaller appreciation. The greater the downward shift of the asset-market equilibrium schedule, the greater is the appreciation of the currency. This appreciation "crowds out" aggregate demand for domestic products by making them more expensive relative to foreign products.

If the shift from A^1A^1 to A^2A^2 is sufficiently large, output may not rise at all. In such a situation, any output effect of expansionary fiscal policy is completely frustrated by the currency's appreciation.[8]

[8]This outcome occurs if the exchange rate is initially at its long-run level and (as we have assumed) people change their expectations immediately so that the new expected future exchange rate equals the new long-run equilibrium exchange rate. You can verify this statement by writing down the equations of output- and asset-market equilibrium when $Y = Y^f$. (See the problem at the end of the chapter.)

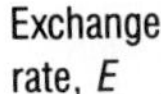

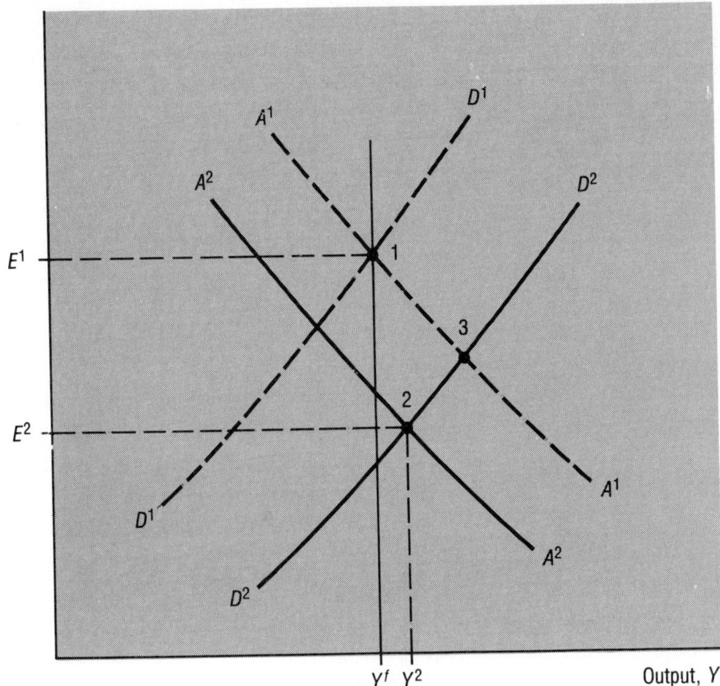

FIGURE 16-16 Effects of a permanent fiscal expansion. Because a permanent fiscal expansion changes exchange-rate expectations, it shifts A^1A^1 leftward as it shifts D^1D^1 to the right. The effect on output (which may be nil) is smaller than that of a comparable temporary fiscal expansion.

The results of Chapter 14 tell us that output will eventually return to its full-employment level and that the overall price level P will not change in the long run. The ultimate effect of the fiscal expansion on the relative prices of domestic tradables, foreign tradables, and nontradables—and thus on the real exchange rate—depends on how the increase in government spending is divided between nontradables and tradables.

MAINTAINING FULL EMPLOYMENT WHEN PERMANENT CHANGES OCCUR

Choosing the proper policy response to a *permanent* disturbance is often more difficult for policymakers than choosing the response to a temporary disturbance. Because the monetary or fiscal policy that offsets the employment effect of a permanent disturbance cannot be reversed quickly, the policy's long-term consequences must be taken into account.

A permanent fall in world demand for domestic products, for example, has effects opposite to those of a permanent fiscal expansion (see Figure 16-16). If the domestic currency depreciates sufficiently, the disturbance may have little effect on output and employment. Should significant unemployment occur, however, the government may find itself in a quandary. A money-supply expansion alleviates unemployment in the short run, but since the policy cannot be reversed later without reducing employment, the economy may eventually pass through a bout of inflation as the price level catches up with the higher money supply. Permanent fiscal expansion, which can offset the shifts in *DD* and *AA* perfectly, has problems of its own, however. A tax cut or spending increase may lead to a government budget deficit that must sooner or later be closed by a fiscal reversal.

The proper response to permanent shifts in money demand is more clear cut. A permanent increase in money demand, for example, can be offset with a permanent increase in the money supply of equal magnitude. Such a policy maintains full employment; but because the price level would fall in the absence of the policy, it will have no inflationary consequences. Instead, monetary expansion can move the economy immediately to its long-run, full-employment position.

A government's decision problem is complicated in practice by the difficulty of evaluating the permanence of the economic fluctuations that dislodge the economy from its full-employment path. In addition, real-world choices between monetary and fiscal policy are frequently determined by political necessities rather than by detailed consideration of whether shocks to the economy are real or monetary, permanent or transitory. Shifts in fiscal policy can often be made only after lengthy legislative deliberation, while monetary policy, in contrast, is fully controlled by the central bank. To avoid procedural delays, governments are likely to respond to disturbances by changing monetary policy even when a shift in fiscal policy would be more appropriate.

MACROECONOMIC POLICIES AND THE CURRENT ACCOUNT

Policymakers are often concerned about the level of the current account. As we will discuss more fully in Chapter 18, an excessive imbalance in the current account—either a surplus or a deficit—may have undesirable long-run effects on national welfare. Large external imbalances may also generate international pressures for government restrictions on trade. It is therefore important to know how monetary and fiscal policies aimed at domestic objectives affect the current account.

Figure 16-17 shows how the *DD-AA* model can be extended to illustrate the effects of macroeconomic policies on the current account. In addition to the *DD* and *AA* curves, the figure contains a new curve, labelled *XX*, which shows combinations of the exchange rate and output at which the current account is equal to some desired level, say *X*. The curve slopes upward because, other things equal, a rise in output worsens the current account if it is not accompanied by a currency depreciation.

The central feature of Figure 16-17 is that *XX* is *flatter* than *DD*. The reason is seen by asking how the current account changes as we move up along

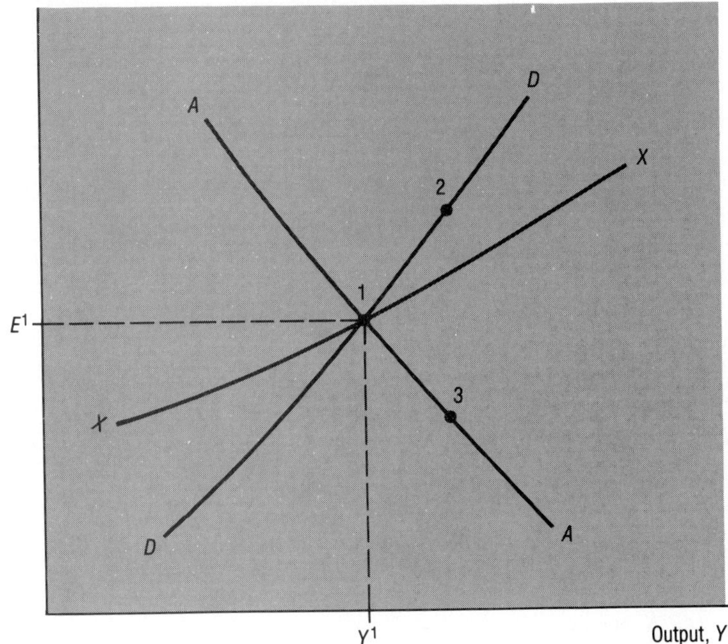

FIGURE 16-17 How macroeconomic policies affect the current account. Along the curve XX, the current account is constant at the level $CA = X$. Monetary expansion moves the economy to point 2 and thus raises the current account balance. Temporary fiscal expansion moves the economy to point 3, lowering the current account balance.

the DD curve from point 1, where all three curves intersect (so that, initially, $CA = X$). As we move up along DD, domestic consumption demand increases by less than the increase in output (since some income is saved). Thus, to maintain equilibrium in the home output market, net foreign demand–the current account–must improve. To the right of point 1, therefore, DD is in the region above XX, where $CA > X$; and similar reasoning shows that DD lies below XX (where $CA < X$) to the left of point 1.

The current-account effects of macroeconomic policies can now be examined. As shown earlier, an increase in the money supply, for example, shifts the economy to a position like point 2, expanding output and depreciating the currency. Since point 2 lies above XX, the current account has improved as a result of the policy action. *Monetary expansion causes the current account balance to increase in the short run.*

Consider next a temporary fiscal expansion. This action shifts DD to the right and moves the economy to a position like point 3 in the figure. Because the currency appreciates and income rises, there is a deterioration in the current account. *Expansionary fiscal policy reduces the current account balance.*

Case Study U.S. MONETARY AND FISCAL POLICY IN ACTION, 1979–1983

The effects of monetary and fiscal policy we have just studied are illustrated by U.S. macroeconomic policy between 1979 and 1983. Table 16-1 summarizes the courses of monetary policy, measured by the growth rate of the money supply, and of fiscal policy. Because fiscal policy may operate through a change in government spending or taxes, Table 16-1 measures the extent to which fiscal policy is contractionary by the size of the government budget surplus, $T - G$. The higher the budget surplus, the more contractionary is fiscal policy. A negative value of $T - G$ indicates a government deficit.

The two major U.S. policy initiatives taken in the years 1979–1983 were a contractionary shift in monetary policy in late 1979 and a drastic cut in taxes legislated in 1981. These policy actions preceded the sharpest U.S. (and indeed, worldwide) recession since the Great Depression, a recession that reached its low point in the United States in 1982. Together with a buildup of military spending, the tax cut led to a sharply increased government budget deficit. Between 1981 and 1983 the deficit rose from 1.0 to 3.8 percent of GNP. (The relation of the government deficit to the large current-account deficit that also emerged in the early 1980s was discussed in the case study in Chapter 12.)

TABLE 16-1 U.S. macroeconomic data, 1979–1983

	1979	1980	1981	1982	1983
Annualized growth rate of money supply (M1) (percent per year)	7.1	6.5	5.1	8.7	10.4
Government surplus (as a percent of GNP)	0.5	−1.3	−1.0	−3.5	−3.8
Annualized growth rate of real GNP (percent per year)	2.5	−0.2	1.9	−2.5	3.6
Dollar interest rate (percent per year, average for year)	12.1	14.3	16.6	13.3	9.9
Dollar/DM exchange rate (dollars per DM, average for year)	0.5456	0.5501	0.4436	0.4124	0.3924

Note: Data on money growth come from Tables 19-2 and 19-5. Government surplus is from Table 19-6. GNP growth rate is from International Monetary Fund, *World Economic Outlook*, April 1987. Interest rate is 6-month London interbank offered rate, from World Bank, *World Development Report 1986*. Exchange rate is from *Economic Report of the President, 1985*.

Table 16-1 also shows the slowdown in monetary growth after 1979. The analysis of the previous section suggests that monetary contraction should result in a rise in the dollar interest rate, a fall in output, and a currency appreciation. The interest rate did, in fact, rise from 12.1 to 14.3 percent per year, while the growth rate of real GNP became negative (−0.2 percent per year in 1980).[9]

The table shows little change in the average dollar/DM exchange rate between 1979 and 1980. In fact, the large appreciation of the dollar against foreign currencies between 1980 and 1981 began at the end of 1980 as monetary growth became particularly restrictive and participants in the foreign exchange market became convinced that slow monetary growth would continue into the future.

Although the data show a relatively small change in the government surplus as a fraction of GNP between 1979 and 1981, the tax cuts legislated in 1981 affected expectations about future government deficits and exchange rates, and therefore moved the exchange rate immediately. The dollar appreciated in 1981, as our model would predict. As already noted, tight monetary policy also pushed the dollar in this direction.

The dollar's appreciation, which came before the legislated fiscal expansion had come fully into force, reduced aggregate demand for U.S. output and helped contribute to a sharp decline in GNP in 1982 (when output fell by 2.5 percent). The other factor contributing to this fall in output was the continuing restrictive stance of monetary policy in the first half of the year. For 1982, we must be careful about interpreting the sharp increase in the government deficit ratio as indicating expansionary fiscal policy only. The high ratio of the deficit to GNP also reflects the fall in GNP as well as the fall in government tax receipts that always occurs in recessions when national income falls.

Responding to the deep slump, the Federal Reserve adopted a more expansionary monetary policy in the second half of 1982 and in 1983. As our theory would predict, the interest rate fell sharply (from 13.3 to 9.9 percent) and output expanded (at a 3.6 percent rate) in 1983. Continuing fiscal expansion strengthened the dollar further, but because monetary growth was so rapid, the dollar appreciated by an amount far smaller than in the previous two years.[10]

[9]The growth rate of output in 1980 was so low in part because of a series of oil price increases sparked by the Iranian revolution. These events are discussed more fully in Chapter 19.

[10]The expansion of 1983 helped set off a 1984 boom in investment demand. The resulting increase in aggregate demand helps explain a fact mentioned earlier in this chapter—the rapid rise in U.S. GNP that accompanied the dollar's further 1984 appreciation. A slump accompanied the dollar's 1980–1982 appreciation because the appreciation was caused by different factors than the appreciation of 1984—tight money and expected *future* fiscal expansion.

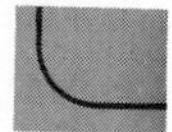

GRADUAL CURRENT-ACCOUNT ADJUSTMENT AND THE J-CURVE

An important assumption underlying our *DD-AA* model of short-run exchange-rate determination is that a real depreciation of the home currency improves the current account while a real appreciation causes the current account to worsen. In reality, however, it is often observed that a country's current account *worsens* immediately after a currency depreciation, and only begins to improve some months later. The resulting path of the current account, shown in Figure 16-18, has an initial segment that looks like a "J" and is therefore called the **J-curve**. In this section we look at the factors that give rise to the J-curve and the modifications they imply for the *DD-AA* model.

The current account is likely to deteriorate sharply immediately after a currency depreciation (the move from point 1 to point 2 in the figure) because most import and export orders are placed several months in advance. In the first few months after the depreciation, export and import volumes therefore reflect buying decisions that were made on the basis of the old real exchange rate: the only effect of the depreciation is to raise the value of the precontracted level of imports in terms of domestic products. Because exports measured in domestic output do not change while imports measured in domestic output rise, there is an initial fall in the current account, as shown.

Even after the old export and import contracts have been fulfilled, it still takes time for new orders to adjust fully to the relative-price change. On the

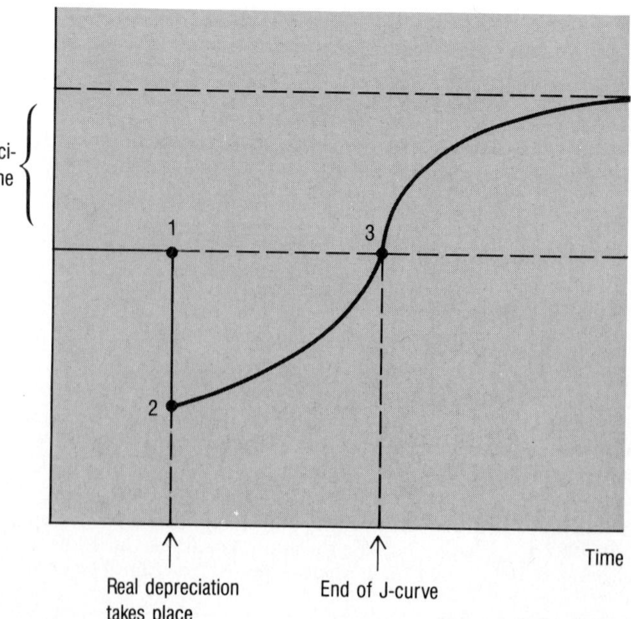

FIGURE 16-18 The J-curve. The J-curve describes the time lag with which a real currency depreciation improves the current account.

production side, producers of exports may have to install additional plant and equipment and hire new workers. To the extent that imports represent materials used in producing domestic products, such as petroleum, import adjustment will also occur gradually as importers switch to new production techniques that economize on imported materials. There are lags on the consumption side as well. To expand significantly foreign consumption of domestic exports, for example, it may be necessary to build new retailing outlets abroad, a time-consuming process.[11]

The result of these lags in adjustment is the gradually improving current account shown in Figure 16-18. Only after point 3 does the current account exceed its predepreciation level. Eventually, the increase in the current account tapers off as the adjustment to the real depreciation is completed.

Empirical evidence indicates that for most industrial countries, the J-curve lasts for more than 6 months but for less than a year. Thus, point 3 in the figure is typically reached within a year of the real depreciation and the current account continues to improve afterward.[12]

The existence of a significant J-curve effect implies that some of our earlier conclusions need to be modified for the very short run of a year or less. By depreciating the home currency, monetary expansion, for example, can have a depressing initial effect on output. In this case, it may take some time before an increase in the money supply results in an improved current account and therefore in higher aggregate demand.

SUMMARY

1. The *aggregate demand* for an open economy's output consists of four components, corresponding to the four components of GNP: consumption demand, investment demand, government demand, and the current account (net export demand). An important determinant of the current account is the real exchange rate, the ratio of the foreign price level (measured in domestic currency) to the domestic price level.

2. Output is determined in the short run by the equality of aggregate demand and aggregate supply. When aggregate demand is greater than output, firms increase production to avoid unintended inventory depletion. When aggregate demand is less than output, firms cut back production to avoid unintended accumulation of inventories.

3. The economy's short-run equilibrium occurs at the exchange rate and output level such that, given the price level and the expected future ex-

[11]An implication of this analysis is that *permanent* real exchange-rate changes are likely to have stronger current-account effects than *temporary* changes. No one will make long-term investments on the basis of a real exchange-rate change he views as temporary. A more sophisticated model than the one we have analyzed would therefore add the expected long-run real exchange rate to the list of determinants of the current account.

[12]See the discussion of Table 16AII-1 in Appendix II.

change rate, aggregate demand equals aggregate supply and the asset markets are in equilibrium. In a diagram with the exchange rate and real output on its axes, the short-run equilibrium can be visualized as the intersection of an upward-sloping *DD* schedule, along which the output market clears, and a downward-sloping *AA* schedule, along which the asset markets clear.

4. A temporary increase in the money supply, which does not alter the long-run expected exchange rate, causes a depreciation of the currency and a rise in output. Temporary fiscal expansion also results in a rise in output, but it causes the currency to appreciate. *Monetary policy* and *fiscal policy* can be used by the government to offset the effects of disturbances to output and employment.

5. Permanent shifts in the money supply, which do alter the long-run expected exchange rate, cause sharper exchange-rate movements and therefore have stronger short-run effects on output than transitory shifts. If the economy is at full employment, a permanent increase in the money supply leads to a rising price level that ultimately reverses the effect of the nominal exchange rate's initial depreciation on the real exchange rate. In the long run, output returns to its initial level and all money prices rise in proportion to the increase in the money supply.

6. Permanent fiscal expansion has a weaker effect on output than an equal temporary expansion. Because permanent fiscal expansion changes the long-run expected exchange rate, it causes a sharper currency appreciation than a transitory expansion. The additional appreciation makes domestic goods and services more expensive, thereby "crowding out" some aggregate demand and dampening the policy's effect on output and employment. It is possible that a permanent fiscal expansion has no effect at all on output.

7. If export and import demands adjust gradually to real exchange-rate changes, the current account may follow a *J-curve* pattern after a real currency depreciation, first worsening and then improving. If such a J-curve exists, currency depreciation may have a contractionary initial effect on output.

KEY TERMS

aggregate demand
monetary policy
fiscal policy
J-curve

PROBLEMS

1. How does the *DD* schedule shift if there is a decline in investment demand?

2. Suppose that the government imposes a tariff on all imports. Use the *DD-AA* model to analyze the effects this measure would have on the economy. Analyze both temporary and permanent tariffs.

3. Imagine that Congress passes a constitutional amendment requiring the U.S. government to maintain a balanced budget at all times. Thus, if the government wishes to change government spending, it must always change taxes by the same amount, that is, $\Delta G = \Delta T$ always. Does the constitutional amendment imply that the government can no longer use fiscal policy to affect employment and output? (Hint: Analyze a "balanced-budget" increase in government spending, one that is accompanied by an equal tax hike.)

4. Examine the effect of a permanent increase in government spending under the assumption that the expected future exchange rate always equals the long-run exchange rate.

5. How does a permanent cut in taxes affect the current account? What about a permanent increase in government spending? Now reread the case study in Chapter 12 and see if your answer accurately reflects the U.S. experience in the early 1980s.

6. If a government initially has a balanced budget but then cuts taxes, it is running a deficit which it must somehow finance. Suppose people think that the government will finance its deficit by printing the extra money it now needs to cover its expenditures. Would you still expect the tax cut to cause a currency appreciation?

7. You observe that a country's currency depreciates but that its current account worsens at the same time. What data might you look at to decide whether you are witnessing a J-curve effect? What other macroeconomic change might bring about a currency depreciation coupled with a deterioration of the current account, even if there is no J-curve?

8. A new government is elected and announces that once it is inaugurated, it will increase the money supply. Use the *DD-AA* model to study the economy's response to this announcement.

9. When the home country's currency depreciates, foreign firms that sell goods there often do not raise the home-currency prices of those goods by the full amount of the depreciation. Instead, they trim profit margins in the hope of maintaining their share in the home country's markets. How does this practice affect the speed of current-account adjustment to a nominal currency depreciation?

10. How would you draw the *DD-AA* diagram when the current account's response to exchange rate changes follows a J-curve? Use this modified diagram to examine the effects of temporary and permanent changes in monetary and fiscal policy.

11. What does the Marshall-Lerner condition look like if the country whose real exchange rate changes does *not* start out with a current account of zero? (The Marshall-Lerner condition is derived in Appendix II under the "standard" assumption of an initially balanced current account.)

FURTHER READING

Victor Argy and Michael G. Porter. "The Forward Exchange Market and the Effects of Domestic and External Disturbances under Alternative Exchange Rate Systems." *International Monetary Fund Staff Papers* 19 (November 1972), pp. 503–532. Advanced analysis of a macroeconomic model similar to the one studied in this chapter.

Victor Argy and Joanne K. Salop. "Price and Output Effects of Monetary and Fiscal Policy under Flexible Exchange Rates." *International Monetary Fund Staff Papers* 26 (June 1979), pp. 224–256. The effects of macroeconomic policies under alternative institutional assumptions about the wage-price adjustment process.

Rudiger Dornbusch. "Exchange Rate Expectations and Monetary Policy." *Journal of International Economics* 6 (August 1976), pp. 231–244. A formal analysis of monetary policy and the exchange rate in a model with a J-curve.

Rudiger Dornbusch and Paul Krugman. "Flexible Exchange Rates in the Short Run." *Brookings Papers on Economic Activity* 3:1976, pp. 537–575. Theory and evidence on short-run macroeconomic adjustment under floating exchange rates.

Morris Goldstein and Mohsin S. Khan. "Income and Price Effects in International Trade," in Ronald W. Jones and Peter B. Kenen, eds. *Handbook of International Economics.* Vol. 2. Amsterdam: North-Holland Publishing Company, 1985. Surveys empirical work on the macroeconomic determinants of trade balances.

Paul R. Krugman and Richard E. Baldwin. "The Persistence of the U.S. Trade Deficit." *Brookings Papers on Economic Activity,* 1:1987, pp. 1–43. An analysis of why the dollar's depreciation after early 1985 was slow to reduce the large American current-account deficit that had emerged by then.

Robert A. Mundell. *International Economics,* Chapter 17. New York: Macmillan, 1968. A classic account of macroeconomic policy effects under floating exchange rates.

APPENDIX I TO CHAPTER 16

The *IS-LM* Model and the *DD-AA* Model

In this appendix we examine the relationship between the *DD-AA* model of the chapter and another model frequently used to answer questions in international macroeconomics, the *IS-LM* model. The *IS-LM* model generalizes the *DD-AA* model by allowing the real domestic interest rate to affect aggregate demand.

The diagram usually used to analyze the *IS-LM* model has the nominal interest rate and output, rather than the nominal exchange rate and output, on its axes. Like the *DD-AA* diagram, the *IS-LM* diagram determines the short-run equilibrium of the economy as the intersection of two individual market-equilibrium curves, called *IS* and *LM*. The *IS* curve is the schedule of nominal interest rates and output levels at which the output and foreign-exchange markets are in equilibrium, while the *LM* curve shows points at which the money market is in equilibrium.[1]

The *IS-LM* model assumes that investment, and some forms of consumer purchases (such as purchases of autos and other durable goods), are related to the expected real interest rate. When the expected real interest rate is low, firms find it profitable to borrow and undertake investment plans. (The appendix to Chapter 7 presented a model of this link between investment and the real interest rate.) A low expected real interest rate also makes it more profitable to carry inventories rather than alternative assets. For both these reasons, we would expect investment to increase when the expected real interest rate falls. Similarly, because consumers find borrowing cheaper and saving less attractive when the real interest rate is low, interest-responsive consumer purchases also rise when the real interest rate falls.

In the *IS-LM* model, aggregate demand is therefore written as a function of the real exchange rate, disposable income, *and* the real interest rate,

$$D(EP^*/P, Y - T, R - \pi^e) = C(Y - T, R - \pi^e) + I(R - \pi^e) + G + CA(EP^*/P, Y - T),$$

where π^e is the expected inflation rate and $R - \pi^e$ is therefore the expected real interest rate. The model assumes that P, P^*, G, T, R^*, and E^e are all given. (To simplify the notation, we've left G out of the aggregate demand function D.)

To find the *IS* curve of R and Y combinations such that aggregate demand equals output,

$$Y = D(EP^*/P, Y - T, R - \pi^e),$$

we must first write this output-market equilibrium condition so that it does not depend on E.

We solve out for E using the interest parity condition, $R = R^* + (E^e - E)/E$. If we solve this equation for E, the result is

$$E = E^e/(1 + R - R^*).$$

[1]In a closed-economy context, the original exposition of the *IS-LM* model is in J. R. Hicks, "Mr. Keynes and the 'Classics': A Suggested Interpretation," *Econometrica* 5 (April 1937), pp. 147–159. Hicks's article still makes enjoyable and instructive reading today. The name *IS* comes from the fact that in a closed economy (but not necessarily in an open economy!) the output market is in equilibrium when investment (I) and saving (S) are equal. Along the *LM* schedule, real money demand (L) equals the real money supply (M^s/P in our notation).

Substitution of this expression into the aggregate-demand function shows that we can express the condition for output-market equilibrium as

$$Y = D[E^eP^*/P(1 + R - R^*), Y - T, R - \pi^e].$$

To get a complete picture of how output changes affect goods market equilibrium, we must remember that the inflation rate in the economy depends positively on the gap between actual output, Y, and full employment output, Y^f. We therefore write π^e as an increasing function of that gap:

$$\pi^e = \pi^e(Y - Y^f).$$

Under this assumption on expectations, the goods market is in equilibrium when

$$Y = D[E^eP^*/P(1 + R - R^*), Y - T, R - \pi^e(Y - Y^f)].$$

This condition shows that a fall in the nominal interest rate R raises aggregate demand through two channels: (1) Given the expected future exchange rate, a fall in R causes a domestic currency depreciation that improves the current account. (2) Given expected inflation, a fall in R directly encourages consumption and investment spending.

The *IS* curve is found by asking how output must respond to such a fall in the interest rate to maintain output-market equilibrium. Since a fall in R raises aggregate demand, the output market will remain in equilibrium after R falls only if Y rises. The *IS* curve therefore slopes downward, as shown in Figure 16AI-1. Even though

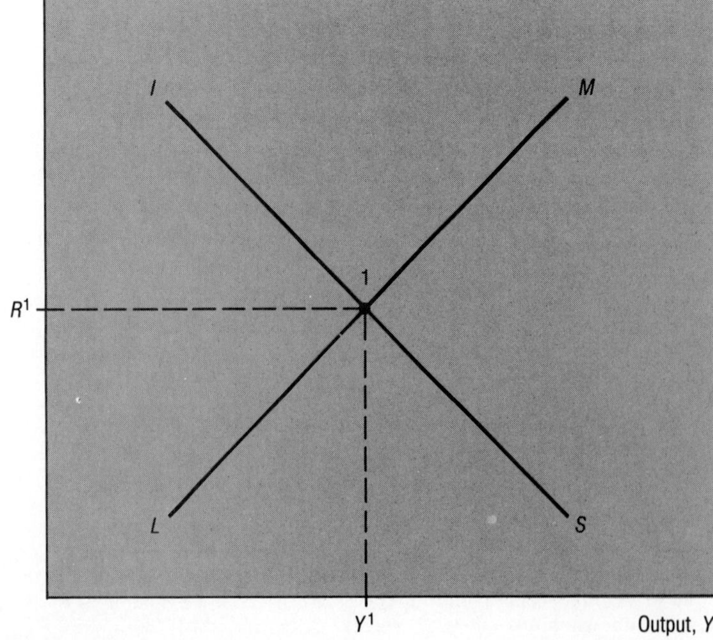

FIGURE 16AI-1 Short-run equilibrium in the IS-LM model. Equilibrium is at point 1, where the output and asset markets simultaneously clear.

the *IS* and *DD* curves both reflect output-market equilibrium, *IS* slopes downward while *DD* slopes upward. The reason for this difference is that the interest rate and the exchange rate are inversely related by the interest parity condition, given the expected future exchange rate.[2]

The slope of the *LM* (or money-market equilibrium) curve is much easier to derive. Money-market equilibrium holds when $M^s/P = L(R, Y)$. Because a rise in the interest rate reduces money demand, it results in an excess supply of money for a given output level. To maintain equilibrium in the money market after R rises, Y must therefore rise also (because a rise in output stimulates the transactions demand for money). The *LM* curve thus has a positive slope as shown in Figure 16AI-1. The intersection of the *IS* and *LM* curves at point 1 determines the short-run equilibrium

FIGURE 16AI-2 Effects of permanent and temporary increases in the money supply in the IS-LM model. A temporary increase in the money supply shifts the *LM* curve alone to the right, but a permanent increase shifts both the *IS* and *LM* curves in that direction.

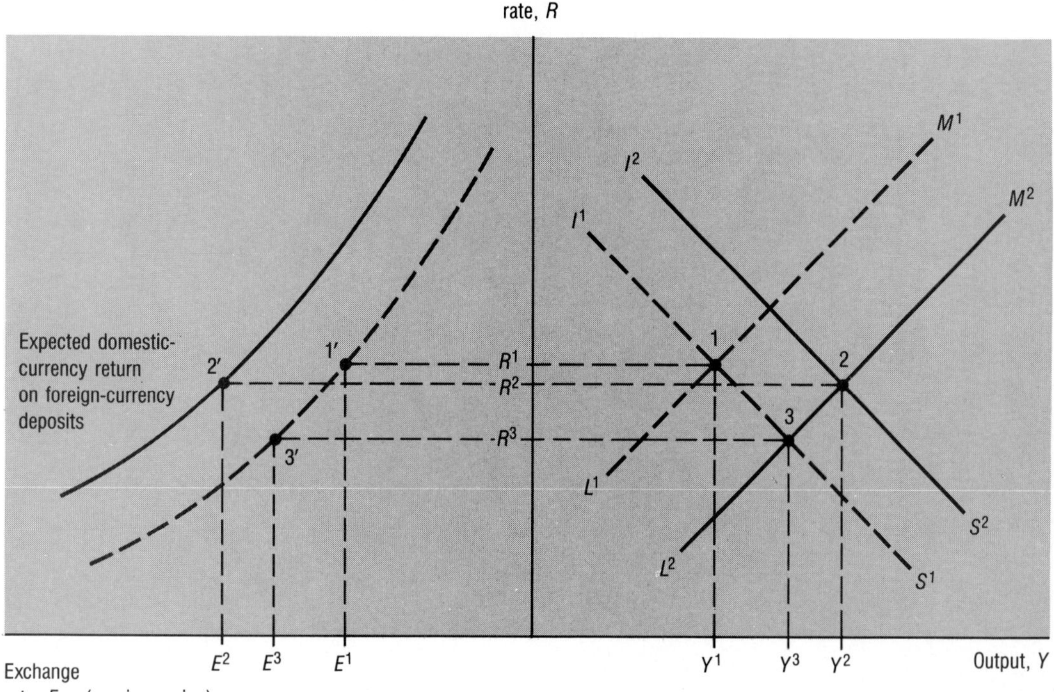

[2]In concluding that *IS* has a negative slope, we have argued that a rise in output reduces the excess demand for output caused by a fall in R. This reduction in excess demand occurs because while consumption demand rises with a rise in output, it rises by less. Notice, however, that a rise in output also raises expected inflation and thus stimulates demand. So it is conceivable that a fall in output, not a rise, eliminates excess demand in the output market. We assume that this perverse possibility (which would give an upward-sloping *IS* curve) does not arise.

values of output, Y^1, and the nominal interest rate, R^1. The equilibrium interest rate, in turn, determines a short-run equilibrium exchange rate through the interest parity condition.

The *IS-LM* model can be used to analyze the effects of monetary and fiscal policies. A temporary increase in the money supply, for example, shifts *LM* to the right, lowering the interest rate and expanding output. A *permanent* increase in the money supply, however, shifts *LM* to the right but also shifts *IS* to the right, since that schedule depends on E^e, which now rises. The right-hand side of Figure 16AI-2 shows these shifts. At the new short-run equilibrium following a permanent increase in the money supply (point 2), output and the interest rate are higher than at the short-run equilibrium (point 3) following an equal temporary increase. The nominal interest rate can even be higher at point 2 than at point 1. This possibility provides another example of how the Fisher expected-inflation effect of Chapter 14 can push the nominal interest rate upward after a monetary expansion.

The left-hand side of Figure 16AI-2 shows how the monetary changes affect the exchange rate. This is our usual picture of equilibrium in the foreign-exchange market, but it has been rotated counterclockwise so that a movement to the left along the horizontal axis is an increase in E (a depreciation of the home currency). The interest rate R^2 following a permanent increase in the money supply implies foreign-ex-

FIGURE 16AI-3 Effects of permanent and temporary fiscal expansions in the IS-LM model. Temporary fiscal policy has a stronger effect on output than permanent fiscal policy.

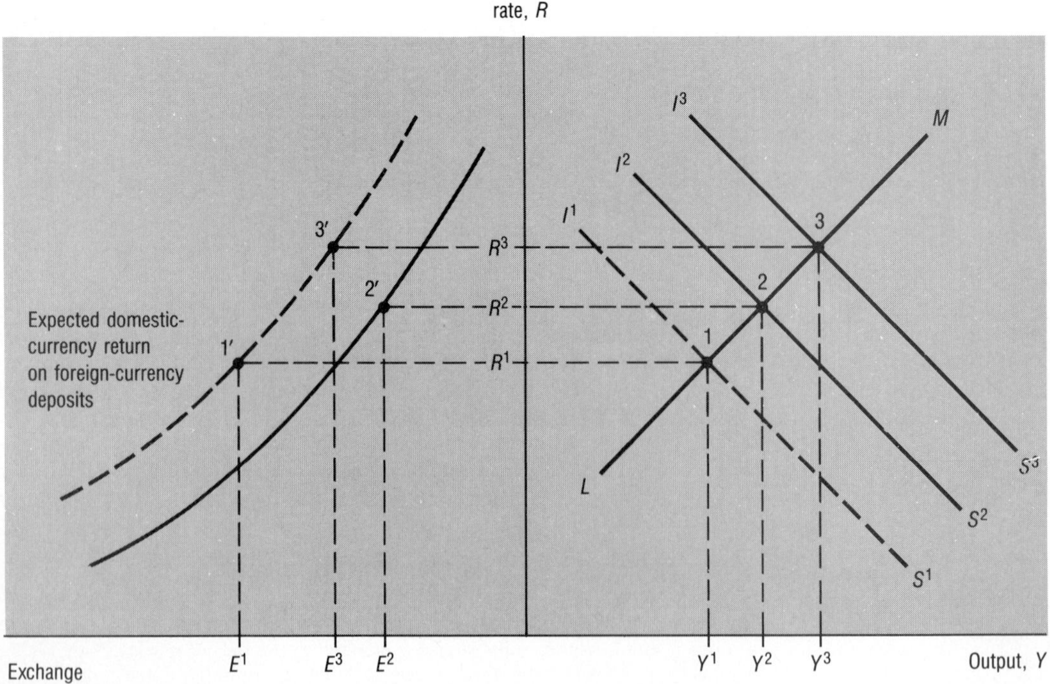

change market equilibrium at point 2′, since the accompanying rise in E^e shifts the curve that measures the expected domestic-currency return on foreign deposits. That curve does not shift if the money-supply increase is temporary; so the equilibrium interest rate R^3 that results in this case leads to foreign-exchange equilibrium at point 3′.

Fiscal policy is analyzed in Figure 16AI-3. A temporary increase in government spending, for example, shifts I^1S^1 to the right but has no effect on *LM*. The new short-run equilibrium at point 3 shows a rise in output and a rise in the nominal interest rate, while the foreign-exchange market equilibrium at point 3′ indicates a currency appreciation. A permanent increase in government spending causes a fall in the long-run equilibrium exchange rate and thus a fall in E^e. The *IS* curve therefore does not shift out as much as in the case of a temporary policy (and it may not shift at all). At the short-run equilibrium point 2, the expansion in output and the rise in the nominal interest rate are smaller than at point 3. The reason why permanent fiscal policy moves are weaker can be seen in the figure's left-hand side: the accompanying change in exchange-rate expectations generates a sharper currency appreciation and thus a greater "crowding out" effect on aggregate demand.

APPENDIX II TO CHAPTER 16

The Marshall-Lerner Condition and Empirical Estimates of Trade Elasticities

The chapter assumed that a real depreciation of a country's currency improves its current account. As we noted, however, the validity of this assumption depends on the response of export and import volumes to real exchange-rate changes. In this appendix we derive a condition on those responses for the assumption in the text to be valid. The condition, called the *Marshall-Lerner condition,* states that, all else equal, a real depreciation improves the current account if export and import volumes are sufficiently elastic with respect to the real exchange rate. (The condition is named after two of the economists who discovered it, Alfred Marshall and Abba Lerner.) After deriving the Marshall-Lerner condition, we look at empirical estimates of trade elasticities and analyze their implications for actual current-account responses to real exchange rate changes.

To start, write the current account, measured in domestic output units, as the difference between exports and imports of goods and services similarly measured:

$$CA(EP^*/P, Y^d) = EX(EP^*/P) - IM(EP^*/P, Y^d).$$

Above, export demand is written as a function of EP^*/P alone because foreign income is being held constant.

Let q denote the real exchange rate EP^*/P (as in the last chapter) and let EX^* denote domestic imports measured in terms of *foreign,* rather than domestic, output. The notation EX^* is used because domestic imports from abroad, measured in foreign output, equal the volume of foreign exports to the home country. If we identify q with the price of foreign products in terms of domestic products, then IM and EX^* are related by

$$IM = q \times EX^*,$$

that is, imports measured in domestic output = (domestic output units/foreign output unit) × (imports measured in foreign output units).[1]

The current account can therefore be expressed as

$$CA(q, Y^d) = EX(q) - q \times EX^*(q, Y^d).$$

Now let EX_q stand for the effect of a rise in q (a real depreciation) on export demand and let EX^*_q stand for the effect of a rise in q on import volume. Thus,

$$EX_q = \Delta EX/\Delta q, EX^*_q = \Delta EX^*/\Delta q.$$

As we saw in the chapter, EX_q is positive (a real depreciation makes home products relatively cheaper and stimulates exports) while EX^*_q is negative (a relative cheapen-

[1]As footnote 3 in the chapter warned, the identification of the real exchange rate with relative output prices is not quite correct since, as we defined it, the real exchange rate is the relative price of consumption baskets. For most practical purposes, however, the discrepancy is not qualitatively important. To avoid the additional complexity that would result from a more detailed treatment of the composition of national outputs, we therefore use the real exchange rate in our derivation of the Marshall-Lerner condition.

ing of home products reduces domestic import demand). Using these definitions, we can now ask how a rise in q affects the current account, all else equal.

If superscript 1 indicates the initial value of a variable while superscript 2 indicates its value after q has changed by $\Delta q = q^2 - q^1$, then the change in the current account caused by a real exchange-rate change Δq is

$$\begin{aligned}\Delta CA &= CA^2 - CA^1 = (EX^2 - q^2 \times EX^{*2}) - (EX^1 - q^1 \times EX^{*1}) \\ &= \Delta EX - (q^2 \times \Delta EX^*) - (\Delta q \times EX^{*1}).\end{aligned}$$

Dividing through by Δq gives the current account's response to a change in q,

$$\frac{\Delta CA}{\Delta q} = EX_q - (q^2 \times EX_q^*) - EX^{*1}.$$

This equation summarizes the two current-account effects of a real depreciation discussed in the text, the *volume* effect and the *value* effect. The terms involving EX_q and EX_q^* represent the volume effect, the effect of the change in q on the number of output units exported and imported. These terms are always positive because $EX_q > 0$ and $EX_q^* < 0$. The last term above, EX^{*1}, represents the value effect, and it is preceded by a negative sign. This last term tells us that a rise in q worsens the current account to the extent that it raises the domestic-output value of the initial volume of imports.

We are interested in knowing when the right-hand side of the equation above is positive, so that a real depreciation causes the current account balance to increase. To answer this question, we first define the elasticity of export demand with respect to q,

$$\eta = (q^1/EX^1)EX_q,$$

and the elasticity of import demand with respect to q,

$$\eta^* = -(q^1/EX^{*1})(EX_q^*).$$

(The definition of η^* involves a negative sign because $EX_q^* < 0$ and we are defining trade elasticities as positive numbers.) Returning to our equation for $\Delta CA/\Delta q$, we multiply its right-hand side by (q^1/EX^1) to express it in terms of trade elasticities. Then if the current account is initially zero (that is, $EX^1 = q^1 \times EX^{*1}$), this last step shows that $\Delta CA/\Delta q$ is positive when

$$\eta + (q^2/q^1)\eta^* - 1 > 0.$$

If the change in q is assumed to be small, so that $q^2 \approx q^1$, the condition for an increase in q to improve the current account is

$$\eta + \eta^* > 1.$$

This is the *Marshall-Lerner condition.* The condition states that if the current account is initially zero, a real currency depreciation causes a current-account surplus if the sum of the relative-price elasticities of export and import demand exceeds 1. (If the current account is not zero initially, the condition becomes substantially more complex.) In applying the Marshall-Lerner condition, you should remember that its derivation assumes that disposable income is held constant when q changes.

Now that we have the Marshall-Lerner condition, we can ask whether empirical estimates of trade equations imply price elasticities consistent with the chapter's assumption that a real exchange-rate depreciation improves the current account.

TABLE 16AII-1 Estimated price elasticities for international trade in manufactured goods

	η			η^*		
Country	**Impact**	**Short-run**	**Long-run**	**Impact**	**Short-run**	**Long-run**
Austria	0.39	0.71	1.37	0.03	0.36	0.80
Belgium	0.18	0.59	1.55	—	—	0.70
Britain	—	—	0.31	0.60	0.75	0.75
Canada	0.08	0.40	0.71	0.72	0.72	0.72
Denmark	0.82	1.13	1.13	0.55	0.93	1.14
France	0.20	0.48	1.25	—	0.49	0.60
Germany	—	—	1.41	0.57	0.77	0.77
Italy	—	0.56	0.64	0.94	0.94	0.94
Japan	0.59	1.01	1.61	0.16	0.72	0.97
Netherlands	0.24	0.49	0.89	0.71	1.22	1.22
Norway	0.40	0.74	1.49	—	0.01	0.71
Sweden	0.27	0.73	1.59	—	—	0.94
Switzerland	0.28	0.42	0.73	0.25	0.25	0.25
United States	0.18	0.48	1.67	—	1.06	1.06

Note: Estimates are taken from Jacques R. Artus and Malcolm D. Knight, *Issues in the Assessment of the Exchange Rates of Industrial Countries,* Occasional Paper 29. Washington, D.C.: International Monetary Fund, July 1984, table 4. Unavailable estimates are indicated by dashes.

Table 16AII-1 presents International Monetary Fund elasticity estimates for trade in manufactured goods. The table reports export- and import-price elasticities measured over three successively longer time horizons, and thus allows for the possibility that export and import demands adjust gradually to relative price changes, as in our discussion of the J-curve. "Impact" elasticities measure the response of trade flows to relative price changes in the first 6 months after the change; "short-run" elasticities apply to a 1-year adjustment period; and "long-run" elasticities measure the response of trade flows to the price change over a hypothetical infinite adjustment period.

For most countries, the impact elasticities are so small that the sum of the impact export and import elasticities is less than 1. Since the impact elasticities usually fail to satisfy the Marshall-Lerner condition, the estimates support the existence of an initial J-curve effect that causes the current account to deteriorate immediately following a real depreciation.

It is also true, however, that most countries in the table satisfy the Marshall-Lerner condition in the short run and that virtually all do so in the long run. The evidence is therefore consistent with the assumption made in the chapter: except over very short time periods, a real depreciation is likely to improve the current account while a real appreciation is likely to worsen it.

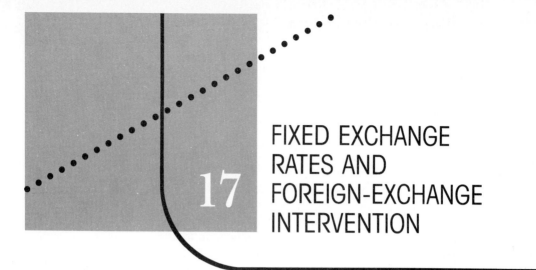

17 FIXED EXCHANGE RATES AND FOREIGN-EXCHANGE INTERVENTION

In the past several chapters we have developed a model that helps us understand how a country's exchange rate and national income are determined by the interaction of asset and output markets. Using that model, we saw how monetary and fiscal policies can be used to maintain full employment and a stable price level.

To keep our discussion simple, we assumed that exchange rates are *completely* flexible, that is, that central banks themselves do not trade in the foreign-exchange market to influence exchange rates. In reality, however, the assumption of complete exchange-rate flexibility is rarely accurate. As we mentioned earlier, the world economy operated under a system of *fixed* dollar exchange rates between the end of World War II and 1973, with central banks routinely trading foreign exchange to hold their exchange rates at internationally agreed levels. Industrialized countries now operate under a hybrid system of **managed floating exchange rates**—a system in which central banks may attempt to moderate exchange-rate movements without keeping exchange rates rigidly fixed. Most developing countries have retained fixed exchange rates, for reasons that we discuss in Chapter 20.

In this chapter we study how central banks intervene in the foreign-exchange market to fix exchange rates and how macroeconomic policies work when exchange rates are fixed. The chapter will help us understand the role of central-bank foreign-exchange intervention in the determination of exchange rates under a system of managed floating.

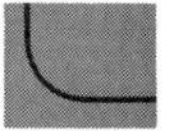

WHY STUDY FIXED EXCHANGE RATES?

A discussion of fixed exchange rates may seem outdated in an era when newspaper headlines regularly highlight sharp changes in the exchange rates of the major industrial-country currencies. Our interest in fixed exchange rates, however, is not the result of nostalgia, antiquarianism, or an unhealthy obsession with hypothetical worlds. There are four reasons why we must understand fixed exchange rates before analyzing contemporary macroeconomic policy problems:

1. *Managed floating.* As noted above, central banks often intervene in currency markets to influence exchange rates. So while the dollar exchange rates of the industrial countries' currencies are not fixed by central banks, they are not left to fluctuate freely either. The system of floating dollar exchange rates is often referred to as a *dirty float,* to distinguish it from a *clean float* in which central banks make no direct attempts to influence foreign-currency values. (The model of the exchange rate developed in earlier chapters assumed a cleanly floating, or completely flexible, exchange rate.)[1] Because the present monetary system is a hybrid of the "pure" fixed and floating rate systems, an understanding of fixed exchange rates gives us insight into the effects of foreign-exchange intervention when it occurs under floating rates.

2. *Regional currency arrangements.* Some countries belong to *exchange-rate unions,* organizations whose members agree to fix their mutual exchange rates while allowing their currencies to fluctuate in value against the currencies of nonmember countries. The most important exchange-rate union is the **European Monetary System (EMS),** which began operating in 1979 and whose largest members are France, Germany, and Italy. As a result of the EMS rules, the DM and the French franc, for example, have a fixed relative price, but the prices of both of those currencies in terms of dollars can change from day to day. To analyze macroeconomic interactions between France and Germany, we need to know how fixed exchange rates work.

3. *Less-developed countries.* While industrial countries generally allow their currencies to float against the dollar, these economies account for less than a sixth of the world's countries. Almost all less-developed countries peg the values of their currencies in terms of the dollar, some other currency, or some

[1]It is questionable if a truly clean float has ever existed in reality. Most government policies affect the exchange rate, and governments rarely undertake policies without considering their exchange-rate implications.

"basket" of currencies chosen by the central bank. Thailand pegs its currency to a basket, for example, while Colombia pegs to the U.S. dollar and Senegal pegs to the French franc. No examination of the problems of developing countries would get very far without taking into account the implications of fixed exchange rates.

4. *Lessons of the past for the future.* Fixed exchange rates were the norm in many periods, such as the decades before World War I, between 1918 and 1931, and again between 1945 and 1973. Today, many economists and policymakers dissatisfied with floating exchange rates are proposing a new international agreement that would resurrect the fixed-rate system. Would this plan benefit the world economy? Who would gain or lose from such a system? In order to compare the merits of fixed and floating exchange rates (the topic of Chapter 19), the functioning of fixed rates must be understood.

CENTRAL-BANK INTERVENTION AND THE MONEY SUPPLY

In Chapter 14 we defined an economy's money supply as the total amount of currency and checking deposits held by its households and firms and assumed that the central bank determined the amount of money in circulation. To understand the effects of central-bank intervention in the foreign-exchange market, we need to look first at how central-bank financial transactions affect the money supply.

THE CENTRAL-BANK BALANCE SHEET

The main tool we will use in studying central-bank transactions in asset markets is the **central-bank balance sheet,** which records both the assets held by the central bank and its liabilities. Like any other balance sheet, the central-bank balance sheet is organized according to the principles of double-entry bookkeeping. Any acquisition of an asset by the central bank results in a positive change on the "Assets" side of the balance sheet, while any increase in the bank's liabilities results in a positive change on the balance sheet's "Liabilities" side.[2]

A balance sheet for the central bank of the imaginary country of Pecunia is shown below.

Central-bank balance sheet

Assets		*Liabilities*	
Foreign assets	$1000	Deposits held by private banks	$500
Domestic assets	$1500	Currency in circulation	$2000

[2]Since the central-bank balance sheet is concerned with measuring *stocks* of assets and liabilities rather than payments *flows* (such as the balance of payments accounts measure), entries are not classified as "credit" and "debit" items, as they are in balance of payments accounting.

The "Assets" side of the Bank of Pecunia's balance sheet lists two types of assets, *foreign assets* and *domestic assets.* Foreign assets consist mainly of foreign-currency bonds owned by the central bank. These foreign assets make up the central bank's official international reserves, and their level changes when the central bank intervenes in the foreign-exchange market by buying or selling foreign exchange. For historical reasons to be discussed later in this chapter, a central bank's international reserves also include any gold that it owns. The defining characteristic of international reserves is that they be either claims on foreigners or (like gold) a universally acceptable means of making international payments. In the present example, the central bank's holdings of foreign assets are worth $1000.

Domestic assets are central-bank holdings of claims to future payments by its own citizens and domestic institutions. These claims usually take the form of domestic government bonds and loans to domestic private banks.[3] The Bank of Pecunia owns $1500 in domestic assets. Its total assets therefore equal $2500, the sum of foreign and domestic asset holdings.

The "Liabilities" side of the balance sheet lists as liabilities the deposits of private banks and currency in circulation, both notes and coin. (Nonbank firms and households generally cannot deposit money at the central bank, while banks are generally required by law to hold central-bank deposits to partially back up their own liabilities.) Private-bank deposits are liabilities of the central bank because the money may be withdrawn whenever private banks need it. Currency in circulation is considered a central-bank liability mainly for historical reasons: at one time, many central banks were obliged to give a certain amount of gold or silver to anyone wishing to exchange domestic currency for one of those precious metals. The balance sheet above shows that Pecunia's private banks have deposited $500 at the central bank. Currency in circulation equals $2000, so the central bank's total liabilities amount to $2500.

The central bank's total assets equal its total liabilities because any change in the central bank's assets *automatically* causes an equal change in its liabilities. When the central bank purchases an asset, for example, it can pay for it in one of two ways. A cash payment raises the supply of currency in circulation by the amount of the bank's asset purchase. A payment by check promises the check's owner a central-bank deposit equal in value to the asset's price. When the recipient of the check deposits it in her account at a private bank, the private bank's claims on the central bank (and thus the central bank's liabilities to private banks) rise by the same amount. In either case, the central bank's purchase of assets automatically causes an equal increase in its liabilities. Similarly, asset sales by the central bank involve either the withdrawal of currency from circulation or the reduction of private banks'

[3]If you have studied money and banking, you will recall that central banks often lend to domestic private banks through the central-bank discount window.

claims on the central bank, and thus a fall in central-bank liabilities to the private sector.

THE CENTRAL-BANK BALANCE SHEET AND THE MONEY SUPPLY

The central-bank balance sheet is so important because changes in the central bank's assets cause the domestic money supply to move in the same direction. Our discussion of the equality between central bank assets and liabilities illustrates the mechanism at work.

When the central bank buys an asset from the public, for example, its payment—whether cash or check—directly enters the money supply. The increase in central-bank liabilities associated with the asset purchase thus causes the money supply to expand. The money supply shrinks when the central bank sells an asset to the public because the cash or check that the central bank receives in payment goes out of circulation, reducing the central bank's liabilities to the public. Changes in the level of central-bank asset holdings thus cause the money supply to change in the same direction because they require equal changes in the central bank's liabilities.

The process we have described will be familiar to you from studying central-bank open-market operations in earlier courses. By definition, open-market operations involve the purchase or sale of domestic assets, but official transactions in foreign assets have the same direct effect on the money supply. You will also recall that when the central bank buys assets, for example, the accompanying increase in the money supply is generally *larger* than the initial asset purchase because of multiple deposit creation within the private banking system. The existence of this *money multiplier* effect, which amplifies the impact of central-bank transactions on the money supply, reinforces our main conclusion: *Any central-bank purchase of assets automatically results in an increase in the domestic money supply, while any central-bank sale of assets automatically causes the money supply to decline.*[4]

FOREIGN-EXCHANGE INTERVENTION AND THE MONEY SUPPLY

To see in greater detail how foreign-exchange intervention affects the money supply, let's look at an example. Suppose that the Bank of Pecunia goes to the foreign-exchange market and sells \$100 worth of foreign bonds for Pecunian money. The sale reduces official holdings of foreign assets from \$1000 to \$900, causing the "Assets" side of the central-bank balance sheet to shrink from \$2500 to \$2400.

The payment the Bank of Pecunia receives for these foreign assets automatically reduces its liabilities by \$100 as well. If the Bank of Pecunia is paid

[4]For a detailed description of multiple deposit creation and the money multiplier, see Frederic S. Mishkin, *The Economics of Money, Banking, and Financial Markets* (Boston: Little, Brown and Company, 1986), chapter 12.

with domestic currency, the currency goes into its vault and out of circulation. Currency in circulation therefore falls by $100. As a result of the foreign-asset sale, the central bank's balance sheet changes as follows:

Central-bank balance sheet after $100 foreign asset sale (buyer pays with currency)

Assets		*Liabilities*	
Foreign assets	$900	Deposits held by private banks	$500
Domestic assets	$1500	Currency in circulation	$1900

After the sale, assets still equal liabilities, but both have declined by $100, equal to the amount of currency that the Bank of Pecunia has taken out of circulation through its intervention in the foreign-exchange market. The change in the central bank's balance sheet implies a decline in the Pecunian money supply.

What happens if the buyer of the foreign assets pays the Bank of Pecunia with a $100 check drawn on his account at Pecuniacorp, a private domestic bank? Pecuniacorp debits $100 from the buyer's checking account and the Bank of Pecunia settles with Pecuniacorp by debiting $100 from Pecuniacorp's central-bank account. Private-bank deposits with the central bank fall by $100, and the Bank of Pecunia's balance sheet becomes:

Central-bank balance sheet after $100 foreign asset sale (buyer pays with a check)

Assets		*Liabilities*	
Foreign assets	$900	Deposits held by private banks	$400
Domestic assets	$1500	Currency in circulation	$2000

Once again, the Bank of Pecunia's liabilities fall by $100 and the Pecunian money supply shrinks.

A $100 *purchase* of foreign assets by the Bank of Pecunia would cause its liabilities to increase by $100. If the central bank paid for its purchase in cash, currency in circulation would rise by $100. If it paid by writing a check on itself, private-bank deposits at the Bank of Pecunia would ultimately rise by $100. In either case, there would be a rise in the domestic money supply.

STERILIZATION

Central banks sometimes carry out equal foreign- and domestic-asset transactions in opposite directions to nullify the impact of their foreign-exchange operations on the domestic money supply. This type of policy is called **sterilized foreign-exchange intervention.** We can understand how sterilized foreign-exchange intervention works by considering the following example.

Suppose once again that the Bank of Pecunia sells $100 of its foreign assets and receives as payment a $100 check on the private bank Pecuniacorp. This transaction causes the central bank's foreign assets and its liabilities to decline simultaneously by $100, and there is therefore a fall in the domestic money supply. If the central bank wishes to negate the effect of its foreign-asset sale on the money supply, it can turn around and *buy* $100 of domestic assets, such as government bonds. This second action increases the Bank of Pecunia's domestic assets *and* its liabilities by $100 and so completely offsets the money-supply effect of the $100 sale of foreign assets. If the central bank buys the government bonds with a check, for example, the two transactions (a $100 sale of foreign assets and a $100 purchase of domestic assets) have the following net effect on its balance sheet:

Central-bank balance sheet before sterilized $100 foreign-asset sale

Assets		*Liabilities*	
Foreign assets	$1000	Deposits held by private banks	$500
Domestic assets	$1500	Currency in circulation	$2000

Central-bank balance sheet after sterilized $100 foreign-asset sale

Assets		*Liabilities*	
Foreign assets	$900	Deposits held by private banks	$500
Domestic assets	$1600	Currency in circulation	$2000

The $100 decrease in the central bank's foreign assets is matched with a $100 increase in domestic assets, and the "Liabilities" side of the balance sheet does not change. The sterilized foreign-exchange sale therefore has no effect on the money supply.

THE BALANCE OF PAYMENTS AND THE MONEY SUPPLY

In our discussion of balance of payments accounting in Chapter 12, we defined a country's balance of payments (or official settlements balance) as the balance of official reserve transactions: purchases of foreign assets by the home central bank less purchases of domestic assets by foreign central banks. What we have learned in this section illustrates the important connection between the balance of payments and the growth of money supplies at home and abroad. *If central banks are not sterilizing and the home country has a balance of payments surplus, for example, any associated increase in the home central bank's foreign assets implies an increased home money supply. Similarly, any associated decrease in a foreign central bank's claims on the home country implies a decreased foreign money supply.*

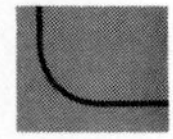

HOW THE CENTRAL BANK FIXES THE EXCHANGE RATE

Having seen how central-bank foreign-exchange transactions affect the money supply, we can now look at how a central bank fixes the domestic currency's exchange rate through foreign-exchange intervention.

In order to hold the exchange rate constant, a central bank must be willing to trade any amounts of domestic and foreign currency at the fixed exchange rate with the private actors in the foreign-exchange market. For example, to fix the DM/dollar rate at DM2.00 per dollar, the German Bundesbank must be willing to buy DM with its dollar reserves, and in any amount the market desires, at a rate of DM2.00 per dollar. The bank must also be willing to use DM to buy any amount of dollar assets that the market wants to sell at that exchange rate. If the Bundesbank did not remove such excess supplies or demands for DM by intervening in the market, the exchange rate would have to change to restore equilibrium in asset markets.

The central bank can succeed in holding the exchange rate fixed only if its financial transactions ensure that asset markets remain in equilibrium when the exchange rate is at its fixed level. The process through which asset-market equilibrium is maintained is illustrated by the model of simultaneous foreign-exchange and money-market equilibrium used in previous chapters.

FOREIGN-EXCHANGE MARKET EQUILIBRIUM UNDER A FIXED EXCHANGE RATE

To begin, we consider how equilibrium in the foreign-exchange market can be maintained when the central bank fixes the exchange rate at the level E^0. The foreign-exchange market is in equilibrium when the interest parity condition holds, that is, when the domestic interest rate, R, equals the foreign interest rate, R^*, plus $(E^e - E)/E$, the expected rate of depreciation of the domestic currency against foreign currency. When the exchange rate is fixed at E^0, however, and market participants expect it to remain fixed, the expected rate of domestic currency depreciation is zero. The interest parity condition therefore implies that E^0 is today's equilibrium exchange rate only if

$$R = R^*.$$

Because no exchange-rate change is expected by participants in the foreign-exchange market, they are content to hold the available supplies of domestic- and foreign-currency deposits only if these offer the same interest rate.[5]

To ensure equilibrium in the foreign-exchange market when the exchange rate is fixed at E^0, the central bank must therefore hold R equal to

[5]Even when an exchange rate is currently fixed at some level, market participants may expect the central bank to change it. In such situations the home interest rate must equal the foreign interest rate plus the expected depreciation rate of the domestic currency (as usual) for the foreign-exchange market to be in equilibrium. We examine this type of situation later in this chapter, but for now we assume that no one expects the central bank to alter the exchange rate.

R^*. Because the domestic interest rate is determined by the interaction of real money demand and the real money supply, we must look at the money market to complete our analysis of exchange-rate fixing.

MONEY-MARKET EQUILIBRIUM UNDER A FIXED EXCHANGE RATE

To hold the domestic interest rate at R^*, the central bank's foreign-exchange intervention must adjust the money supply so that R^* equates aggregate real domestic money demand and the real money supply:

$$\frac{M^s}{P} = L(R^*, Y).$$

Given P and Y, the above equilibrium condition tells what the money supply must be if a fixed exchange rate is consistent with asset-market equilibrium.

When the central bank intervenes to hold the exchange rate fixed, it is *automatically* adjusting the domestic money supply so that money-market equilibrium is maintained with $R = R^*$. Let's look at an example to see how this process works. A rise in output, Y, raises the demand for domestic money, and this increase in money demand tends to push the domestic interest rate upward. To prevent the appreciation of the home currency that would otherwise occur, the central bank must intervene in the foreign-exchange market by buying foreign assets. This foreign-asset purchase eliminates the excess demand for money because the central bank issues money to pay for the foreign assets it buys and thus automatically increases the money supply until asset markets are again in equilibrium with $E = E^0$ and $R = R^*$.

If the central does *not* purchase foreign assets when output increases but instead holds the money stock constant, can it still keep the exchange rate fixed at E^0? The answer is no. If the central bank did not satisfy the excess demand for money caused by a rise in output, the domestic interest rate would begin to rise above the foreign rate R^* to balance the home money market. Traders in the foreign-exchange market, perceiving that domestic-currency deposits were offering a higher rate of return, would begin to bid up the price of domestic currency in terms of foreign currency. In the absence of central-bank intervention, the exchange rate would appreciate from E^0. To prevent this appreciation, the bank must sell domestic currency and buy foreign assets, thereby increasing the money supply and preventing any excess money demand from pushing the home interest rate above R^*.

A DIAGRAMMATIC ANALYSIS

The preceding mechanism of exchange-rate fixing can be pictured using a diagrammatic tool developed earlier. Figure 17-1 shows the simultaneous equilibrium of the foreign exchange and domestic money markets when the exchange rate is fixed at E^0 and is expected to remain fixed.

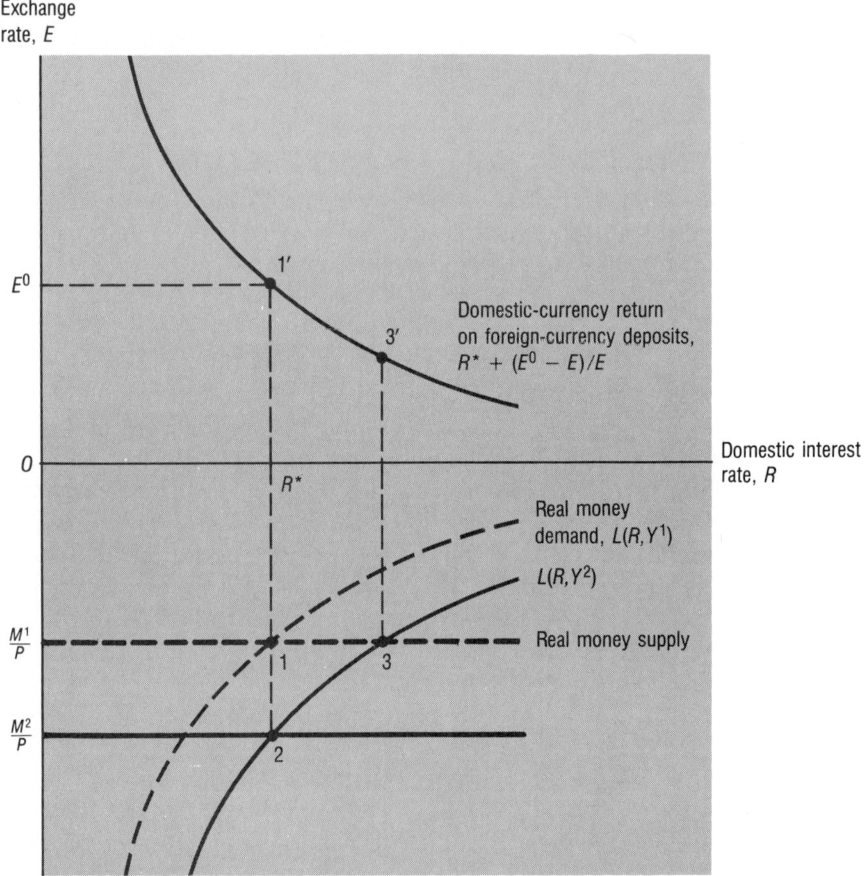

FIGURE 17-1 Asset-market equilibrium with a fixed exchange rate, E^0. To hold the exchange rate fixed at E^0 when output rises from Y^1 to Y^2, the central bank must purchase foreign assets and thereby raise the money supply from M^1 to M^2.

Money-market equilibrium is initially at point 1 in the lower part of the figure. The diagram shows that for a given price level P and a given national income level Y^1, the money supply must equal M^1 when the domestic interest rate equals the foreign rate R^*. The upper part of the figure shows the equilibrium of the foreign-exchange market at point 1′. If the expected future exchange rate is E^0, the interest parity condition holds when $R = R^*$ only if today's exchange rate also equals E^0.

To see how the central bank must react to macroeconomic changes in order to hold the exchange rate at E^0, let's look again at the example of an increase in income. A rise in income (from Y^1 to Y^2) raises the demand for real money holdings at every interest rate, thereby shifting the aggregate money demand function in Figure 17-1 downward.

If the central bank were to take no action, the new money-market equilibrium would be at point 3. Because the domestic interest rate is above R^* at point 3, the currency would have to appreciate to bring the foreign-exchange market to equilibrium at point 3′.

The central bank cannot allow this appreciation of the domestic currency to occur if it is fixing the exchange rate; so it will buy foreign exchange. As we have seen, the increase in the central bank's foreign assets is accompanied by an expansion of the domestic money supply. The central bank will continue to purchase foreign assets until the domestic money supply has expanded to M^2. At the resulting money-market equilibrium (point 2 in the figure), the domestic interest rate again equals R^*. Given this domestic interest rate, the foreign-exchange market equilibrium remains at point 1′ with the equilibrium exchange rate still equal to E^0.

STABILIZATION POLICIES WITH A FIXED EXCHANGE RATE

Having seen how the central bank uses foreign-exchange intervention to fix the exchange rate, we can now analyze the effects of various macroeconomic policies. In this section we consider three possible policies, monetary policy, fiscal policy, and an abrupt change in the exchange rate's fixed level, E^0.

The stabilization policies we studied in the last chapter have surprisingly different effects when the central bank is fixing the exchange rate rather than allowing the foreign-exchange market to determine it. By fixing the exchange rate, the central bank may give up its ability to influence the economy through monetary policy. Fiscal policy, however, becomes a more potent tool for affecting output and employment.

As in the last chapter, we use the *DD-AA* model to describe the economy's short-run equilibrium. You will recall that the *DD* schedule shows combinations of the exchange rate and output for which the output market is in equilibrium, that the *AA* schedule shows combinations of the exchange rate and output for which the asset markets are in equilibrium, and that the short-run equilibrium of the economy as a whole is at the intersection of *DD* and *AA*. To apply the model to the case of a fixed exchange rate, we add the assumption that the expected future exchange rate, E^e, equals the rate E^0 at which the central bank is pegging.

MONETARY POLICY

Figure 17-2 shows the economy's short-run equilibrium as point 1 when the central bank fixes the exchange rate at the level E^0. Output equals Y^1 at point 1, and, as in the last section, the money supply is at the level where a domestic interest rate equal to the foreign rate (R^*) clears the domestic money market. Suppose now that in order to increase output, the central bank decides to increase the money supply through a purchase of domestic assets.

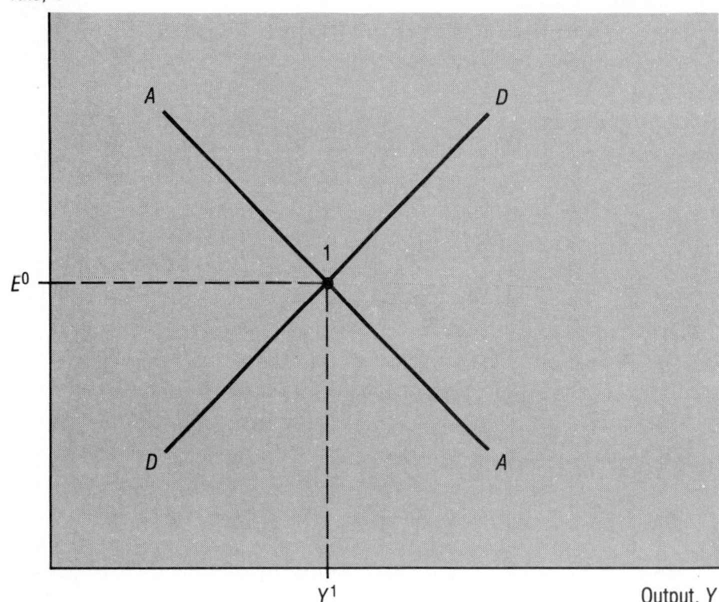

FIGURE 17-2 Short-run equilibrium in the *DD-AA* model with a fixed exchange rate, E^0. Equilibrium is shown at point 1, where the output and asset markets simultaneously clear at an exchange rate of E^0 and output level of Y^1.

Figure 17-3 shows the effect of such a policy action. In the absence of foreign-exchange intervention, the increase in the central bank's domestic assets would push the original asset-market equilibrium curve A^1A^1 rightward to A^2A^2 and would therefore result in a new equilibrium at point 2 and a currency depreciation. To prevent this depreciation, the central bank sells foreign assets in the foreign-exchange market. The money the bank receives for its foreign assets goes out of circulation, and the asset-market equilibrium curve shifts back toward its initial position as the home money supply falls. Only when the money supply has returned to its original level, so that the asset-market schedule is again A^1A^1, is the exchange rate no longer under upward pressure. The attempt to increase the money supply under a fixed exchange rate thus leaves the economy at its initial equilibrium (point 1). *Under a fixed exchange rate, central-bank monetary policy tools are powerless to affect the economy's money supply or its output.*

This result is very different from our finding in Chapter 16 that a central bank can use monetary policy to raise the money supply and output when the exchange rate floats; so it is instructive to ask just why the difference arises. By purchasing domestic assets under floating, the central bank causes an initial excess supply of domestic money that simultaneously pushes the domestic interest rate downward and weakens the currency. Under a fixed exchange rate, however, the central bank will resist any tendency for the currency to depreciate by selling foreign assets for domestic money and so

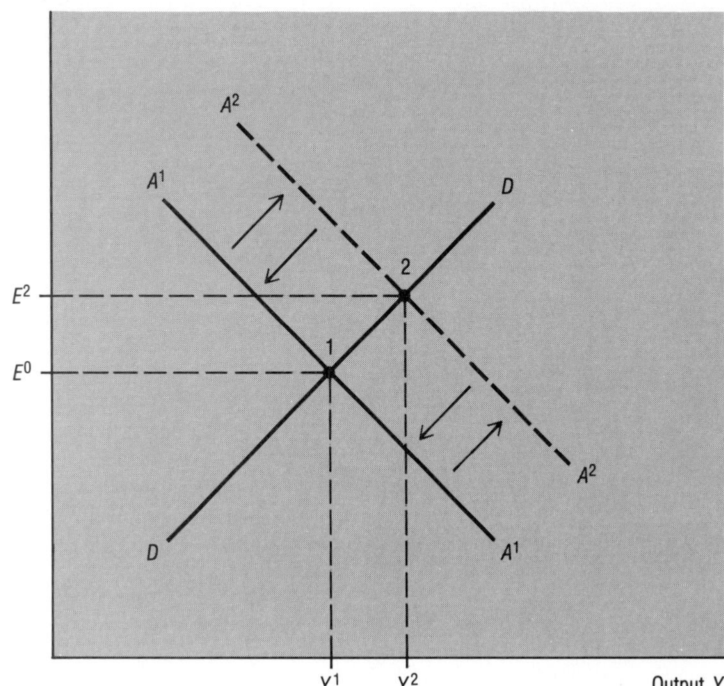

FIGURE 17-3 Monetary expansion is ineffective under a fixed exchange rate. The initial shift of A^1A^1 to A^2A^2 is reversed immediately, and the economy's equilibrium remains at point 1.

removing the initial excess supply of money its policy move has caused. Because any increase in the domestic money supply, no matter how small, will cause the domestic currency to depreciate, the central bank must continue selling foreign assets until the money supply has returned to its original level. In the end, the increase in the central bank's domestic assets is exactly offset by an equal *decrease* in the bank's official international reserves. Similarly, an attempt to decrease the money supply through a sale of domestic assets would cause an equal *increase* in reserves that would keep the money supply as a whole from changing. Under fixed rates, monetary policy can affect international reserves but nothing else.

By fixing the exchange rate, then, the central bank loses its ability to use monetary policy for the purpose of macroeconomic stabilization. However, the government's second key stabilization tool, fiscal policy, is more effective under a fixed rate than under a floating rate.

FISCAL POLICY

Figure 17-4 illustrates the effects of expansionary fiscal policy when the economy's initial equilibrium is at point 1. As we saw in Chapter 16, fiscal ex-

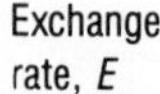

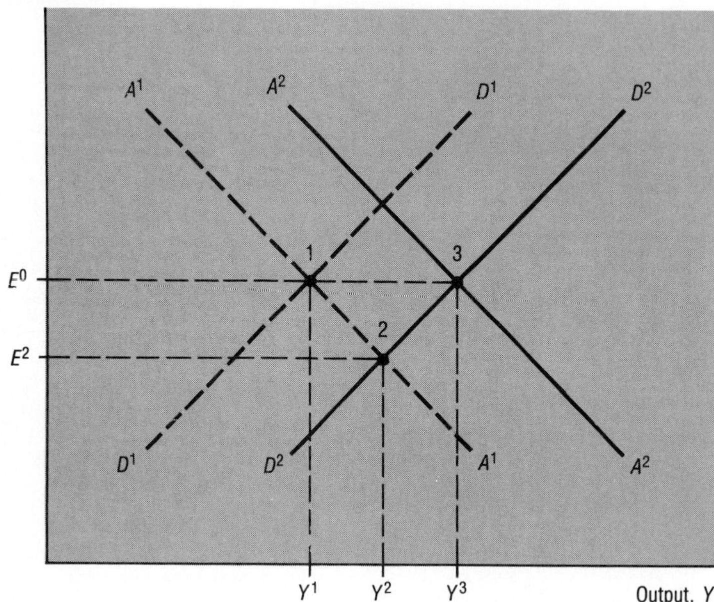

FIGURE 17-4 Fiscal expansion under a fixed exchange rate. Fiscal expansion and the intervention that accompanies it move the economy from point 1 to point 3 by causing both the *DD* and *AA* schedules to shift.

pansion shifts the output-market equilibrium schedule to the right. D^1D^1 therefore shifts to D^2D^2 in the figure. If the central bank refrained from intervening in the foreign-exchange market, output would rise to Y^2 and the exchange rate would fall to E^2 (a currency appreciation) as a result of a rise in the home interest rate.

How does central-bank intervention hold the exchange rate fixed after the fiscal expansion? Initially, there is an excess demand for money because the rise in output raises money demand. To prevent the excess money demand from pushing up the home interest rate and appreciating the currency, the central bank must buy foreign assets with money, thereby increasing the money supply. Intervention holds the exchange rate at E^0 by shifting A^1A^1 rightward to A^2A^2. At the new equilibrium (point 3), output is higher than originally, the exchange rate is unchanged, and official international reserves (and the money supply) are higher.

Unlike monetary policy, fiscal policy can be used to affect output under a fixed exchange rate. Indeed, it is even more effective than under a floating rate! Under a floating rate, fiscal expansion is accompanied by an appreciation of the domestic currency that makes domestic goods and services more expensive and so tends to counteract the policy's positive effect on aggregate demand. To prevent this appreciation, a central bank that is fixing the exchange rate is forced to expand the money supply through foreign-exchange purchases. The additional expansionary effect of this involuntary increase in the money supply explains why fiscal policy is more potent than under a floating rate.

CHANGES IN THE EXCHANGE RATE

A central bank that is fixing its exchange rate sometimes decides on a sudden change in the foreign-currency value of the domestic currency. A **devaluation** occurs when the central bank raises the domestic-currency price of foreign currency, E, and a **revaluation** occurs when the central bank lowers E. All the central bank has to do to devalue or revalue is announce its willingness to trade domestic and foreign currency, in unlimited amounts, at the new exchange rate.[6]

Figure 17-5 shows how a devaluation affects the economy. A rise in the level of the fixed exchange rate, from E^0 to E^1, makes domestic goods and services cheaper relative to foreign goods and services (given that P and P^* are fixed in the short run). Output therefore moves to the higher level Y^2 shown by point 2 on the DD schedule. Point 2, however, does not lie on the initial asset-market equilibrium schedule A^1A^1: at point 2, there is initially an excess demand for money due to the rise in the transactions demand for money caused by the output increase. This excess demand would push the interest rate above the world interest rate if the central bank did not intervene in the foreign-exchange market. To maintain the exchange rate at its new fixed level E^1, the central bank must therefore buy foreign assets and expand the money supply until the asset-market curve reaches A^2A^2 and passes through point 2. Devaluation therefore causes a rise in output, a rise in official reserves, and an expansion of the money supply. A private capital inflow matches the central bank's reserve gain (an official outflow) in the balance of payments accounts.[7]

The effects of devaluation illustrate the three main reasons why governments sometimes choose to devalue their currencies. First, devaluation allows the government to fight unemployment in spite of the unavailability of effec-

[6]We observe a subtle distinction between the terms "devaluation" and "depreciation" (and between "revaluation" and "appreciation"). Depreciation (appreciation) is a rise in E (a fall in E) under floating, while devaluation (revaluation) is a rise in E (a fall in E) when the exchange rate is pegged. Depreciation (appreciation) thus involves the active voice (as in "the currency appreciated"), while devaluation (revaluation) involves the passive voice (as in "the currency was devalued"). Put another way, devaluation (or revaluation) reflects a government decision while depreciation (or appreciation) reflects the outcome of market forces.

[7]After the exchange rate is devalued, market participants expect that the new higher exchange rate, rather than the old rate, will prevail in the future. The change in expectations alone shifts A^1A^1 to the right, but without central-bank intervention, this by itself is insufficient to move A^1A^1 all the way to A^2A^2. At point 2, as at point 1, $R = R^*$ if the foreign-exchange market clears. Because output is higher at point 2 than at point 1, however, real money demand is also higher at the former point. With P fixed, an expansion of the money supply is therefore necessary to make point 2 a position of money-market equilibrium, that is, a point on the new AA schedule. Central-bank purchases of foreign assets are therefore a necessary part of the economy's shift to its new fixed-exchange-rate equilibrium.

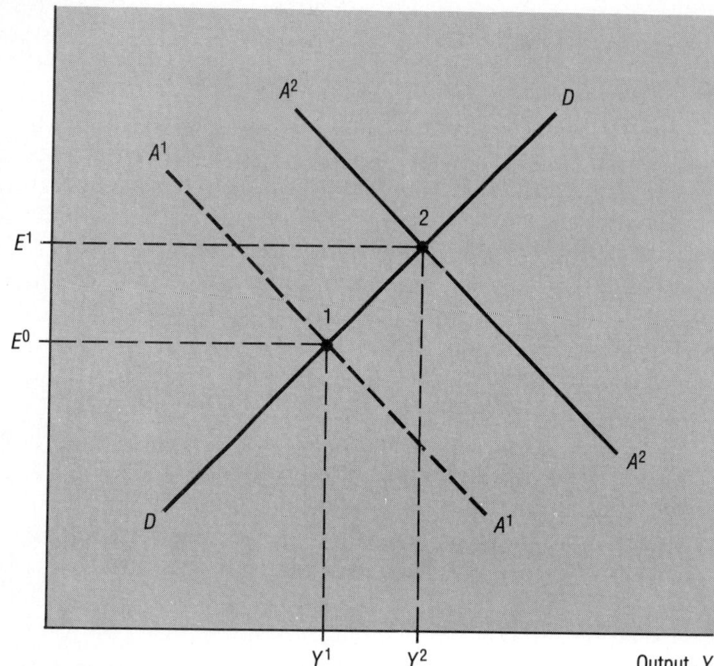

FIGURE 17-5 Effect of a currency devaluation from E^0 to E^1. The economy's equilibrium moves from point 1 to point 2 as both output and the money supply expand.

tive monetary policy. If government budget deficits are politically unpopular, for example, or if the legislative process is slow, a government may opt for devaluation as the most convenient way of boosting aggregate demand. A second reason for devaluing is the resulting improvement in the current account, a development the government may feel to be desirable. The third motive behind devaluations is their effect on the central bank's foreign reserves. If the central bank is running low on reserves, a sudden, one-time devaluation can be used to draw in more reserves.[8]

ADJUSTMENT TO FISCAL POLICY AND EXCHANGE-RATE CHANGES

If fiscal and exchange-rate changes occur when there is full employment and the policy changes are maintained indefinitely, they will ultimately cause the domestic price level to move in such a way that full employment is restored. To understand this dynamic process, we discuss the economy's adjustment to fiscal expansion and devaluation in turn.

[8]Because an unexpected devaluation lowers the foreign-currency value of the government's domestic-currency liabilities to the private sector, the initial reserve gain by the central bank is being financed essentially by a surprise tax on holders of government bonds and money.

If the economy is initially at full employment, fiscal expansion raises output, and this rise in output above its full-employment level causes the domestic price level, P, to begin rising. As P rises home output becomes more expensive, and so aggregate demand gradually falls, returning output to the initial, full-employment level. Once this point is reached, the upward pressure on the price level comes to an end. There is no real appreciation in the short run, as there is with a floating exchange rate, but regardless of whether the exchange rate is floating or fixed, the real exchange rate appreciates *in the long run* by the same amount.[9]

At first glance, the long-run price level increase caused by a fiscal expansion under fixed rates seems inconsistent with the conclusion of Chapter 14 that for a given output level and interest rate, the price level and the money supply move proportionally in the long run. There is no inconsistency because fiscal expansion *does* cause a money-supply increase by forcing the central bank to intervene in the foreign-exchange market. To fix the rate throughout the adjustment process, the central bank ultimately must increase the money supply through intervention in proportion to the long-run increase in P.

The adjustment to a devaluation is similar. In fact, since a devaluation does not change long-run demand or supply conditions in the output market, the long-run increase in the price level caused by a devaluation is proportional to the increase in the exchange rate. A devaluation under a fixed rate has the same long-run effect as a proportional increase in the money supply under a floating rate. Like the latter policy, devaluation is neutral in the long run, in the sense that its only long-run effect is a proportional rise in all nominal prices and in the domestic money supply.

BALANCE OF PAYMENTS CRISES AND CAPITAL FLIGHT

Until now we have assumed that participants in the foreign-exchange market believe that a fixed exchange rate will be maintained at its current level forever. In many practical situations, however, the central bank may find it undesirable or infeasible to maintain the current fixed exchange rate. The central bank may be running short on foreign reserves, for example, or it may face high unemployment. Because market participants know that the central bank may respond to such situations by devaluing the currency, it would be unreasonable for them to expect the current exchange rate to be maintained forever, come what may.

The market's belief in an impending change in the exchange rate gives rise to a **balance of payments crisis,** a sharp change in official foreign reserves sparked by a change in expectations about the future exchange rate.

[9]To see this, just observe that the long-run real exchange rate, EP^*/P, must in either case satisfy the same equation $Y^f = D(EP^*/P, Y^f - T, I, G)$ where Y^f, as in Chapter 16, is the full-employment output level.

In this section we use our model of asset-market equilibrium to examine how balance of payments crises can occur under fixed exchange rates.

Figure 17-6 shows the asset markets in equilibrium at points 1 (the money market) and 1′ (the foreign-exchange market) with the exchange rate fixed at E^0 and expected to remain there indefinitely. M^1 is the money supply consistent with this initial equilibrium. Suppose that a sudden deterioration in the current account, for example, leads the foreign-exchange market to expect the government to devalue and adopt a new fixed exchange rate $E^1 > E^0$. The figure's upper part shows this change in expectations as a rightward shift in the downward-sloping curve measuring the expected

FIGURE 17-6 Capital flight, the money supply, and the interest rate. To hold the exchange rate fixed at E^0 after the market decides it will be devalued to E^1, the central bank must use its reserves to finance a capital outflow that shrinks the money supply and raises the home interest rate.

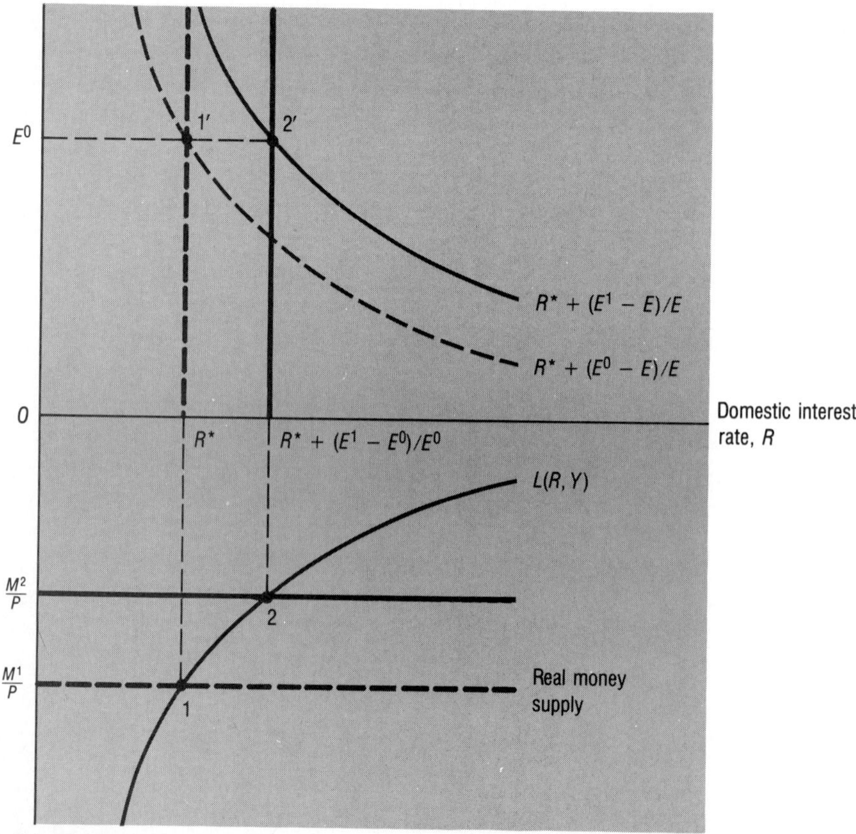

domestic-currency return on foreign-currency assets. Equilibrium in the foreign-exchange market (point 2′) requires a rise in the domestic interest rate to $R^* + (E^1 - E^0)/E^0$, which now equals the expected domestic-currency return on foreign-currency assets.

Initially, however, the domestic interest rate remains at R^*, which is below the new expected return on foreign assets. This differential causes an excess demand for foreign-currency assets in the foreign-exchange market; to continue holding the exchange rate at E^0 the central bank must sell foreign reserves and thus shrink the domestic money supply. The bank's intervention comes to an end once the money supply has fallen to M^2, so that the money market is in equilibrium at the interest rate $R^* + (E^1 - E^0)/E^0$ that clears the foreign-exchange market (point 2). *The expectation of a future devaluation causes a balance of payments crisis marked by a sharp fall in reserves and a rise in the home interest rate above the world interest rate. Similarly, an expected revaluation causes an abrupt rise in foreign reserves together with a fall in the home interest rate below the world rate.*

The reserve loss accompanying a devaluation scare is often labeled **capital flight** because the associated debit in the balance of payments accounts is a private capital outflow. Residents flee the domestic currency by selling it to the central bank for foreign exchange; they then invest the proceeds abroad. Capital flight is of particular concern to the government when fears of devaluation have arisen because the central bank's reserves are low to begin with. By pushing reserves even lower, capital flight may force the central bank to devalue sooner and by a larger amount than planned.[10]

For the rest of this chapter we continue to assume that no exchange-rate changes are expected by the market when exchange rates are fixed. But we draw on the preceding analysis repeatedly in later chapters when we discuss various countries' experiences with fixed exchange rates.

MANAGED FLOATING AND STERILIZED INTERVENTION

Previous sections argued that a central bank gives up its ability to influence output through monetary policy when it adopts a fixed exchange rate. Under managed floating, however, monetary policy is influenced by exchange-rate changes without being completely subordinate to the requirements of a fixed exchange rate. Instead, the central bank faces a trade-off between domestic objectives such as employment or the inflation rate and exchange-rate stability. Suppose that the central bank tries to expand the money supply to fight domestic unemployment, for example, but at the same time carries out foreign-asset sales to restrain the resulting depreciation of the home currency. The foreign-exchange intervention will tend to *reduce* the money supply, hindering the central bank's pursuit of a reduction in unemployment.

[10] If aggregate demand depends on the real interest rate (as in the *IS-LM* model), capital flight reduces output by shrinking the money supply and raising the real interest rate. This possibly contractionary effect of capital flight is another reason why policymakers hope to avoid it.

Discussions of central-bank foreign-exchange intervention in policy forums and newspapers often appear to ignore the intimate link between intervention and the money supply that we explored in detail above. In reality, however, these discussions are often assuming that foreign-exchange intervention is being *sterilized,* so that opposite domestic-asset transactions prevent it from affecting the money supply. Empirical studies of central-bank behavior confirm this assumption and consistently show central banks to have practiced sterilized intervention all through the twentieth century and before.[11]

In spite of widespread sterilization by central banks, there is considerable disagreement among economists about its effects. In this section we study the role of sterilized intervention in central-bank exchange-rate management.

PERFECT ASSET SUBSTITUTABILITY AND THE INEFFICACY OF STERILIZED INTERVENTION

When a central bank carries out a sterilized foreign-exchange intervention, its transactions leave the domestic money supply unchanged. A rationale for such a policy is difficult to find using the model of exchange-rate determination developed above, for the model predicts that without an accompanying change in the money supply, the central bank's intervention, all else equal, will not affect the domestic interest rate and therefore will not affect the exchange rate.

Our model also predicts that sterilization will be fruitless under a fixed exchange rate. The example of a fiscal expansion illustrates why a central bank might wish to sterilize under a fixed rate and why our model says the policy will fail. You will recall that to hold the exchange rate constant when fiscal policy becomes more expansive, the central bank must buy foreign assets and expand the home money supply. The policy expands output but also causes inflation, which the central bank may try to avoid by sterilizing the increase in the money supply that its fiscal policy has induced. But as quickly as the central bank sells domestic assets to reduce the money supply, it will have to *buy* more foreign assets to keep the exchange rate fixed. The ineffectiveness of monetary policy under a fixed exchange rate implies that sterilization is a self-defeating policy.

The key feature of our model that leads to these results is the assumption that the foreign-exchange market is in equilibrium only when the ex-

[11]Three recent studies are Leroy O. Laney and Thomas D. Willett, "The International Liquidity Explosion and Worldwide Inflation: The Evidence from Sterilization Coefficient Estimates," *Journal of International Money and Finance* 1 (August 1982), pp. 141–152; Maurice Obstfeld, "Exchange Rates, Inflation, and the Sterilization Problem: Germany, 1975–1981," *European Economic Review* 21 (March/April 1983), pp. 161–189; and Robert E. Cumby and Maurice Obstfeld, "Capital Mobility and the Scope for Sterilization: Mexico in the 1970s," in Pedro Aspe Armella, Rudiger Dornbusch, and Maurice Obstfeld, eds., *Financial Policies and the World Capital Market: The Problem of Latin American Countries* (Chicago: University of Chicago Press, 1983), pp. 245–269.

pected returns on domestic- and foreign-currency bonds are the same.[12] This assumption is often called **perfect asset substitutability.** Two assets are perfect substitutes when, as our model assumed, investors don't care how their portfolios are divided between them provided both yield the same expected rate of return. With perfect asset substitutability in the foreign-exchange market, the exchange rate is therefore determined so that the interest parity condition holds.

In contrast to perfect asset substitutability, **imperfect asset substitutability** exists when assets' expected returns can differ in equilibrium. As we saw in Chapter 13, the main factor that may lead to imperfect asset substitutability in the foreign-exchange market is *risk.* If bonds denominated in different currencies have different degrees of risk, investors may be willing to earn lower expected returns on bonds that are less risky. Correspondingly, they will hold a very risky asset only if the expected return it offers is relatively high.

In a world of perfect asset substitutability, participants in the foreign-exchange market care only about expected rates of return, and since these rates are determined by monetary policy, actions such as sterilized intervention which do not affect the money supply also do not affect the exchange rate. Under imperfect asset substitutability both risk *and* return matter; so central-bank actions that alter the riskiness of domestic-currency assets can move the exchange rate even when the money supply does not change. To understand how sterilized intervention can alter the riskiness of domestic-currency assets, however, we must modify our model of equilibrium in the foreign-exchange market.

FOREIGN-EXCHANGE MARKET EQUILIBRIUM UNDER IMPERFECT ASSET SUBSTITUTABILITY

When domestic- and foreign-currency bonds are perfect substitutes, the foreign-exchange market is in equilibrium only if the interest parity condition holds:

$$R = R^* + (E^e - E)/E. \tag{17-1}$$

When domestic- and foreign-currency bonds are *imperfect* substitutes, the condition above does not hold in general. Instead, equilibrium in the foreign-exchange market requires that the domestic interest rate equal the expected domestic-currency return on foreign bonds *plus* a **risk premium,** ρ, that reflects the difference between the riskiness of domestic and foreign bonds:

$$R = R^* + (E^e - E)/E + \rho. \tag{17-2}$$

[12]We are assuming that all interest-bearing assets denominated in *the same* currency, whether deposits or government bonds, are perfect substitutes in portfolios. The single term "bonds" will generally be used to refer to all these assets.

Appendix I to this chapter develops a detailed model of foreign-exchange market equilibrium with imperfect asset substitutability. The main conclusion of that model is that the risk premium on domestic assets rises when the stock of domestic government bonds available to be held by the public rises, and falls when the central bank's domestic assets rise. It is not hard to grasp the economic reasoning behind this result. Private investors become more vulnerable to unexpected changes in the home currency's exchange rate as the stock of domestic government bonds they hold rises. Investors will be unwilling to assume the increased risk of holding more domestic-government debt, however, unless they are compensated by a higher expected rate of return on domestic-currency assets. An increased stock of government debt will therefore raise the difference between the expected returns on domestic- and foreign-currency bonds. Similarly, when the central bank buys domestic assets, the market need no longer hold them; private vulnerability to home-currency exchange-rate risk is thus lower, and the risk premium on home-currency assets falls.

This alternative model of foreign-exchange market equilibrium implies that the risk premium depends positively on the stock of government debt, denoted B, less the domestic assets of the central bank, denoted by A:

$$\rho = \rho(B - A). \tag{17-3}$$

The risk premium on domestic bonds therefore rises when $B - A$ rises. This relation between the risk premium and the central bank's domestic-asset holdings allows the bank to affect the exchange rate through sterilized foreign-exchange intervention.[13]

THE EFFECTS OF STERILIZED INTERVENTION WITH IMPERFECT ASSET SUBSTITUTABILITY

Figure 17-7 modifies our earlier picture of asset-market equilibrium by adding imperfect asset substitutability to illustrate how sterilized intervention can affect the exchange rate.

The lower part of the figure, which shows the money market in equilibrium at point 1, does not change. The upper part of the figure is also much the same as before, except that the downward-sloping schedule now shows how the *sum* of the expected domestic-currency return on foreign assets *and* the risk premium depends on the exchange rate. The curve continues to slope downward because the risk premium itself is assumed not to depend on the exchange rate. Equilibrium in the foreign-exchange market is at point 1′, which corresponds to a domestic government debt of B and central-bank domestic-asset holdings of A^1. At that point, the domestic interest rate equals the risk-adjusted domestic-currency return on foreign deposits [equation (17-2)].

[13]The stock of central-bank domestic assets is often called domestic *credit*.

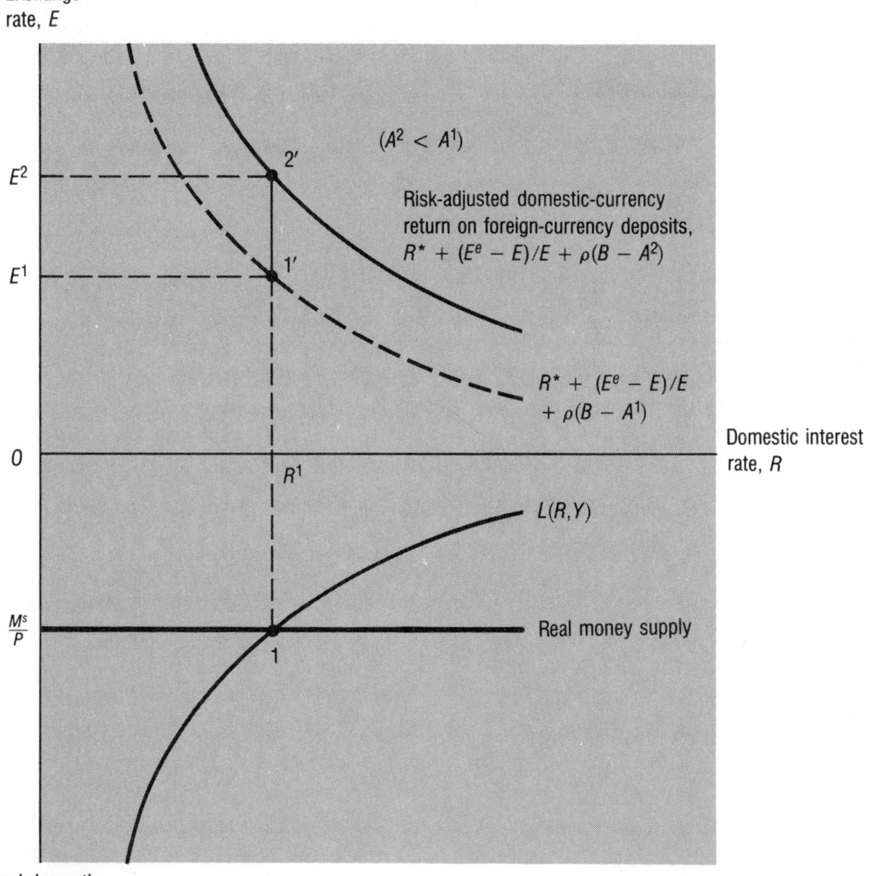

FIGURE 17-7 Effect of a sterilized central-bank purchase of foreign assets under imperfect asset substitutability. A sterilized purchase of foreign assets leaves the money supply unchanged but raises the risk-adjusted return that domestic-currency deposits must offer in equilibrium. Other things equal, this depreciates the domestic currency.

Let's use the diagram to examine the effects of a sterilized purchase of foreign assets by the central bank. By matching its purchase of foreign assets with a sale of domestic assets, the central bank holds the money supply constant at M^s and avoids any change in the lower part of Figure 17-7. As a result of the domestic-asset sale, however, the central bank's domestic assets are lower (they fall to A^2) and the stock of domestic assets that the market must hold, $B - A^2$, is therefore higher than the initial level $B - A^1$. This increase pushes the risk premium ρ upward and shifts to the right the negatively sloped schedule in the upper part of the figure. The foreign-exchange market now settles at point 2′, and the domestic currency depreciates.

With imperfect asset substitutability, even sterilized purchases of foreign exchange cause the home currency to depreciate. Similarly, sterilized sales of foreign exchange cause the home currency to appreciate. A slight modification of our analysis shows that the central bank can also use sterilized intervention to hold the exchange rate fixed as it varies the money supply to achieve domestic objectives such as full employment. In effect, the exchange rate and monetary policy can be managed independently of each other in the short run when sterilized intervention is effective.

EVIDENCE ON THE EFFECTS OF STERILIZED INTERVENTION

In the early 1980s, European countries called on the United States to intervene systematically in the foreign-exchange market and resist sharp movements in the dollar's exchange rate against other currencies. Leaders of the seven largest industrial economies discussed intervention at an economic summit meeting held at Versailles in June 1982.[14] As a result of the discussion, researchers in the central banks of the summit countries were asked to prepare a study of the effects of alternative intervention practices.

The conclusions of the central-bank study were published in 1983 as the "Report of the Working Group on Exchange Market Intervention." The report asked in particular if sterilized intervention might allow central banks to manage exchange rates without corresponding adjustments in domestic monetary policies. Little evidence was found to support the idea that sterilized intervention had been a major factor influencing exchange rates.

This conclusion agrees with the one reached by most academic studies of sterilized intervention.[15] As we will discuss at greater length in Chapter 21, however, there is also considerable evidence against the view that bonds denominated in different currencies are perfect substitutes. Some economists conclude from these conflicting results that while risk premiums are important, they do not depend on central-bank asset transactions in the simple way our model assumes.[16] Others contend that the tests that have been used to detect the effects of sterilized intervention are flawed.[17] Given the meager evidence that sterilized intervention has a reliable effect on exchange rates, however, a skeptical attitude is probably in order.

[14]The countries represented were Britain, Canada, France, Germany, Italy, Japan, and the United States.

[15]An article by Kenneth Rogoff analyzes Canadian data and surveys results for other countries. See Rogoff, "On the Effects of Sterilized Intervention: An Analysis of Weekly Data," *Journal of Monetary Economics* 14 (September 1984), pp. 133–150. The findings of the Federal Reserve participants in the Versailles project are summarized in the piece by Henderson and Sampson in this chapter's Further Reading.

[16]For this view, see Robert J. Hodrick and Sanjay Srivastava, "An Investigation of Risk and Return in Forward Foreign Exchange," *Journal of International Money and Finance* 3 (April 1984), pp. 5–29.

[17]See, for example, Richard N. Cooper, "Comment," *Brookings Papers on Economic Activity,* 2:1985, pp. 451–456.

THE SIGNALING EFFECT OF INTERVENTION

A phenomenon sometimes referred to as the **signaling effect of foreign-exchange intervention** is an important complicating factor in econometric efforts to study sterilization's effects. Our discussion of sterilized intervention has assumed that it does not change the market's exchange-rate expectations. If market participants are unsure about the future direction of macroeconomic policies, however, sterilized intervention may give an indication of where the central bank expects the exchange rate to move. This signal, in turn, can alter the market's view of the future and cause an immediate exchange-rate change even when bonds denominated in different currencies are perfect substitutes.

The signaling effect is most important when the central bank is unhappy with the exchange rate's level and declares in public that it will alter monetary or fiscal policies to bring about a change. By simultaneously intervening on a sterilized basis, the bank sometimes lends credibility to its announcement. A sterilized purchase of foreign assets, for example, may convince the market that the central bank intends to bring about a home-currency depreciation because the bank will lose money if an appreciation occurs instead. Even central banks must watch their budgets!

A central bank may be tempted to exploit the signaling effect for temporary benefits, however, even when it has no intention of changing monetary or fiscal policy to bring about a different long-run exchange rate. The result of crying "Wolf!" too often is the same in the foreign-exchange market as elsewhere. If central banks do not follow up on their exchange-market signals, these too become ineffective. The box on page 480 gives examples of how the signaling effect can work—or backfire.

RESERVE CURRENCIES IN THE WORLD MONETARY SYSTEM

Up until now, we have studied a single country that fixes its exchange rate in terms of a hypothetical single foreign currency by trading domestic for foreign assets when necessary. In the real world there are many currencies, and it is possible for a country to fix the exchange rates of its domestic currency against some foreign currencies while allowing it to float against others. This is the case in the European Monetary System, whose members hold their mutual exchange rates fixed but allow their currencies' dollar prices to fluctuate.

This section and the next adopt a global perspective and study the macroeconomic behavior of the world economy under two possible systems for fixing the exchange rates of *all* currencies against each other.

The first such fixed-rate system is very much like the one we have been studying; in it, one currency is singled out as a **reserve currency,** the currency central banks hold in their international reserves, and each nation's central bank fixes its currency's exchange rate against the reserve currency

GAMES GOVERNMENTS PLAY

Faced with accelerating inflation and a sharply depreciating dollar, U.S. President Jimmy Carter announced on November 1, 1978, that the dollar's foreign-exchange value was too low and that the U.S. Treasury and Federal Reserve were taking actions to strengthen the currency. A week earlier the president had announced another anti-inflation program to halt the dollar's slide but had mentioned no specifics about monetary policy. As a result of this vagueness, the dollar had plummeted against the yen and DM, despite massive sterilized dollar purchases by the Bank of Japan and the Bundesbank.

Having previously disappointed the market, President Carter was more specific on November 1. Two main policy shifts were announced. First, the United States would borrow Swiss francs, marks, and yen (in the market and from central banks) and use the proceeds to buy dollars in the foreign-exchange market. Whether these dollar purchases would be sterilized or allowed to reduce the U.S. money supply was not stated. Second, the Federal Reserve would take contractionary monetary measures—an increase in the discount rate at which it lends money to U.S. banks and a rise in required reserves on some bank deposits.

The foreign-exchange market's initial reaction to this second announcement was favorable, and the dollar soon appreciated by 7.5 percent against the Swiss franc, 7 percent against the DM, and 5 percent against the yen. By the summer of 1979, however, the U.S. money supply was ballooning and the dollar once again took a nosedive. Substantial sterilized intervention by the Fed and foreign central banks made little apparent difference: the markets no longer believed that the United States seriously intended to slow down monetary growth.

The dollar firmed only in October 1979 when a new Federal Reserve chairman known for his monetary conservatism, Paul A. Volcker, announced a credible program of money-supply control.

by standing ready to trade domestic money for reserve assets at that rate. Between the end of World War II and 1973, the U.S. dollar was the main reserve currency and almost every country pegged the dollar exchange rate of its currency.[18]

The second fixed-rate system (studied in the next section) is a **gold standard.** Under a gold standard, central banks peg the prices of their currencies

[18]As noted in Chapter 12, the U.S. dollar has remained the world's principal reserve currency under the present floating exchange rate system.

in terms of gold, and hold gold as official international reserves. The heyday of the international gold standard was between 1870 and 1914, although many countries attempted unsuccessfully to restore a permanent gold standard after the end of World War I in 1918.

Both reserve-currency standards and the gold standard result in fixed exchange rates between *all* pairs of currencies in the world. But the two systems have very different implications about the growth and control of national money supplies.

THE MECHANICS OF A RESERVE-CURRENCY STANDARD

The workings of a reserve-currency system are illustrated by the system based on the U.S. dollar set up at the end of World War II. Under that system, every central bank fixed the dollar exchange rate of its currency through foreign-exchange market trades of domestic currency for dollar assets. The frequent need to intervene meant that each central bank had to have on hand sufficient dollar reserves to meet any excess supply of its currency that might arise. Central banks therefore held a large portion of their international reserves in the form of U.S. Treasury bills and short-term dollar deposits, which pay interest and can be turned into cash at relatively low cost.

Because each currency's dollar price was fixed by its central bank, the exchange rate between any two currencies was automatically fixed as well because of arbitrage in the foreign-exchange market. How did this process work? Let's suppose that the French franc price of dollars was fixed at FFr5 per dollar while the DM price of dollars was fixed at DM4 per dollar. The exchange rate between the franc and the DM had to remain constant at DM0.80 per franc = (DM4 per dollar) ÷ (FFr5 per dollar), even though no central bank was directly trading francs for DM to hold the relative price of those two currencies fixed. At a DM/FFr rate of DM0.85 per franc, for example, you could have made a sure profit of $6.25 by taking $100, selling them to the French central bank, the Bank of France, for ($100) × (FFr5 per dollar) = FFr500, selling your FFr500 in the foreign-exchange market for (FFr500) × (DM0.85 per franc) = DM425, and then selling the DM to the German Bundesbank for (DM425) ÷ (DM4 per dollar) = $106.25. With everyone trying to exploit this profit opportunity by selling francs for DM in the foreign-exchange market, however, the DM would have appreciated against the franc until the DM/FFr rate reached DM0.80 per franc. Similarly, at a rate of DM0.75 per franc, pressure in the foreign-exchange market would have forced the DM to depreciate against the franc until the rate of DM0.80 per franc was reached.

Even though each central bank tied its currency's exchange rate only to the dollar, market forces automatically held all other exchange rates—called cross rates—constant at the values implied by the dollar rates. Thus, the post–World War II exchange-rate system was one in which exchange rates between any two currencies were fixed.[19]

THE ASYMMETRIC POSITION OF THE RESERVE CENTER

In a reserve-currency system the country whose currency is held as reserves occupies a special position because it never has to intervene in the foreign-exchange market. The reason is that if there are N countries with N currencies in the world, there are $N - 1$ exchange rates against the reserve currency. If the $N - 1$ non-reserve-currency countries fix their exchange rates against the reserve currency, there is no exchange rate left over for the reserve center to fix.

This set of arrangements puts the reserve-issuing country in a privileged position because it can use its monetary policy for macroeconomic stabilization even though it has fixed exchange rates. We saw earlier in this chapter that when a country must intervene to hold its exchange rate constant, an attempt to expand its money supply is bound to be frustrated by central-bank losses of international reserves. But because the reserve center is the one country in the system that can enjoy fixed exchange rates without the need to intervene, it is still able to use monetary policy for stabilization purposes.

What would be the effect of a purchase of domestic assets by the central bank of the reserve-currency country? The resulting expansion in its money supply would momentarily push its interest rate below those prevailing abroad, and thereby cause an excess demand for foreign currencies in the foreign-exchange market. To prevent their currencies from appreciating against the reserve currency, *all* other central banks in the system would be forced to buy reserve assets with their own currencies, expanding their money supplies and pushing their interest rates down to the level established by the reserve center. Output throughout the world, as well as at home, would expand after a purchase of domestic assets by the reserve country.

Our account of monetary policy under a reserve-currency system points to a basic asymmetry. The reserve country has the power to affect its own economy, as well as foreign economies, by using monetary policy. Other central banks are forced to relinquish monetary policy as a stabilization tool, and instead must passively "import" the monetary policy of the reserve center because of their commitment to peg their currencies to the reserve currency.

This inherent asymmetry of a reserve system places immense economic power in the hands of the reserve country and is therefore likely to lead eventually to policy disputes within the system. Such problems helped lead to the breakdown of the "dollar standard" in 1973, a topic we discuss in detail in Chapter 18.

[19]The rules of the postwar system actually allowed currencies' dollar values to move as much as 1 percent above or below the "official" values. This meant that cross rates could fluctuate by as much as 4 percent.

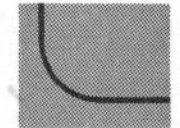

THE GOLD STANDARD

An international gold standard avoids the asymmetry inherent in a reserve-currency standard by avoiding the "*N*th currency" problem. Under a gold standard, each country fixes the price of its currency in terms of gold by standing ready to trade domestic currency for gold whenever necessary to defend the official price. Because there are *N* currencies and *N* prices of gold in terms of those currencies, no single country occupies a privileged position within the system: each is responsible for pegging its currency's price in terms of the official international reserve asset, gold.

THE MECHANICS OF A GOLD STANDARD

Because countries tie their currencies to gold under a gold standard, official international reserves take the form of gold. Gold standard rules also require each country to allow imports and exports of gold across its borders. Under these arrangements, a gold standard, like a reserve-currency system, results in fixed exchange rates between all currencies. For example, if the dollar price of gold is pegged at $35 per ounce by the Federal Reserve while the pound price of gold is pegged at £14.58 per ounce by Britain's central bank, the Bank of England, the dollar/pound exchange rate must be constant at ($35 per ounce) ÷ (£14.58 per ounce) = $2.40 per pound. The same arbitrage process that holds cross exchange rates fixed under a reserve currency system keeps exchange rates fixed under a gold standard as well.[20]

SYMMETRIC MONETARY ADJUSTMENT UNDER A GOLD STANDARD

Because of the inherent symmetry of a gold standard, no country in the system occupies a privileged position by being relieved of the commitment to intervene. By considering the international effects of a purchase of domestic assets by one central bank, we can see in more detail how monetary policy works under a gold standard.

Suppose that the Bank of England decides to increase its money supply through a purchase of domestic assets. The initial increase in Britain's money supply will put downward pressure on British interest rates and make foreign-currency assets more attractive than British assets. Holders of pound deposits will attempt to sell them for foreign deposits, but no *private* buyers will come forward. Under floating exchange rates, the pound would depreciate against foreign currencies until interest parity had been reestablished. This depreciation cannot occur when all currencies are tied to gold, however. What happens? Because central banks are obliged to trade their currencies for gold at fixed rates, unhappy holders of pounds can sell these to the Bank

[20]In practice, the costs of shipping gold and insuring it in transit determined narrow "gold points" within which currency exchange rates could fluctuate.

INTERVENTION ARRANGEMENTS IN THE EUROPEAN MONETARY SYSTEM

In March 1979, eight members of the European Economic Community—France, Germany, Italy, Belgium, Denmark, Ireland, Luxembourg, and the Netherlands—agreed to fix their mutual exchange rates and float jointly against the U.S. dollar. This European Monetary System (EMS) has survived only with the aid of several internal exchange-rate readjustments. But its proponents view the EMS as an important further step toward European economic integration, and the possibility of British membership in the system's exchange-rate mechanism is being actively debated.

Exchange rates within the EMS are not literally fixed; rather, they are allowed to fluctuate within specified narrow limits called margins. Each participating currency is also assigned a "central" exchange rate against the European Currency Unit, or ECU, a basket containing specified amounts of EEC currencies. (Not coincidentally, "écu" is the name of an ancient French silver coin.) When a currency's market exchange rate against the ECU diverges sufficiently from its central rate, the central bank that issues the currency is expected to intervene and possibly take other policy actions to correct the situation.

In return for contributing 20 percent of their gold and dollar holdings to a European Monetary Cooperation Fund, central banks in the EMS receive equivalent holdings of ECUs. ECUs can be used, along with other types of international re-

of England for gold, sell the gold to other central banks for their currencies, and use these currencies to purchase deposits that offer interest rates higher than the interest rate on pounds. Britain therefore experiences a private capital outflow, foreign countries experience an inflow.

This process reestablishes equilibrium in the foreign-exchange market. The Bank of England loses foreign reserves since it is forced to buy pounds and sell gold to keep the pound price of gold fixed. Foreign central banks gain reserves as they *buy* gold with their currencies. Because official foreign reserves are declining in Britain and increasing abroad, the British money supply is falling, pushing the British interest rate back up, and foreign money supplies are rising, pushing foreign interest rates down. Once interest rates have again become equal across countries, asset markets are in equilibrium and there is no further tendency for the Bank of England to lose gold or for foreign central banks to gain it.

Our example illustrates the symmetric nature of international monetary adjustment under a gold standard. Whenever a country is losing reserves

serves, to purchase domestic currency from member central banks that acquire it in intervention operations but do not wish to hold it.

International monetary adjustment may be symmetric within the EMS, but it need not be. If the French franc depreciates to its upper limit against the DM, for example, the French central bank must rectify the situation by selling DM reserves; at the same time, the German central bank must lend the necessary DM to the Bank of France. EMS rules thus call for a symmetric intervention procedure when an exchange rate reaches the limit of its range, one in which the weak-currency country loses reserves and the other gains.

Much intervention takes place *within* the EMS exchange-rate margins, however, and such intervention does not oblige other central banks to take action. If the Bank of France buys DM assets and adds them to its reserves, for example, the Bundesbank is not required to intervene as long as the franc stays within its margins.

In addition, the symmetry of intervention at the margins is no guarantee that the resulting adjustments in national money supplies are symmetric. There is little to prevent a central bank from trying to shift the burden of monetary adjustment onto its EMS partners by sterilizing its foreign-exchange intervention.

and seeing its money supply shrink as a consequence, foreign countries are gaining reserves and seeing their money supplies expand. In addition, a given purchase of domestic assets has a positive effect on the world money supply regardless of where it originates. In contrast, monetary adjustment under a reserve-currency standard is highly asymmetric. Countries can gain or lose reserves without inducing any change in the money supply of the reserve-currency country, and only the latter country has the ability to influence domestic and world monetary conditions.[21]

[21]Originally, gold coins were a substantial part of the currency in gold-standard countries. A country's gold losses to foreigners therefore did not have to take the form of a fall in central-bank gold holdings: private citizens could melt gold coins into ingots and ship them abroad, where they were either reminted as foreign gold coins or sold to the foreign central bank for paper currency. In terms of our earlier analysis of the central-bank balance sheet, circulating gold coins are considered to make up a component of the monetary base that is not a central-bank liability. Either form of gold export would thus result in a fall in the domestic money supply and an increase in foreign money supplies.

BENEFITS AND DRAWBACKS OF THE GOLD STANDARD

Advocates of the gold standard argue that it has another desirable property besides symmetry. Because central banks throughout the world are obliged to fix the money price of gold, they cannot allow their money supplies to grow more rapidly than real money demand, since such rapid monetary growth eventually raises the money prices of all goods and services, including gold. A gold standard therefore places automatic limits on the extent to which central banks can cause increases in national price levels through expansionary monetary policies. These limits make the real values of national monies more stable and predictable, thereby enhancing the transactions economies arising from the use of money (see Chapter 14). No such limits to money creation exist under a reserve-currency system; the reserve-currency country faces no automatic barrier to unlimited money creation.

Offsetting this benefit of a gold standard are some drawbacks:

1. The gold standard places undesirable constraints on the use of monetary policy to fight unemployment. In a worldwide recession, it might be desirable for all countries to expand their money supplies jointly even if this were to raise the price of gold in terms of national currencies.

2. Tying currency values to gold ensures a stable overall price level only if the *relative* price of gold and other goods and services is stable. For example, suppose that the dollar price of gold is \$35 per ounce while the relative price of gold and a typical output basket is ⅓ basket per ounce of gold. This implies a price level of \$105 per output basket. Now suppose that there is a major gold discovery in South America and the relative price of gold in terms of output falls to ¼ basket per ounce. With the dollar price of gold unchanged at \$35 per ounce, the price level would have to rise from \$105 to \$140 per basket. In fact, studies of the gold standard era do reveal surprisingly large price-level fluctuations arising from such changes in gold's relative price.[22]

3. An international payments system based on gold is problematic because central banks cannot increase their holdings of international reserves as their economies grow unless there are continual new gold discoveries. Every central bank would need to hold some gold reserves to fix its currency's gold price and as a buffer against unforeseen economic mishaps; so central banks might bring about world unemployment as they attempted to compete for reserves by selling domestic assets and thus shrinking their money supplies.

4. A final problem of the gold standard is that it gives countries with large gold production, such as the Soviet Union and South Africa, considerable ability to influence macroeconomic conditions throughout the world through market sales of gold.

Because of these drawbacks, few economists favor a return to the gold standard today. As early as 1923, the British economist John Maynard

[22]See, for example, Richard N. Cooper, "The Gold Standard: Historical Facts and Future Prospects," *Brookings Papers on Economic Activity,* 1:1982, pp. 1–45.

Keynes characterized gold as a "barbarous relic" of an earlier international monetary system.[23] After coming to office in 1981, President Ronald Reagan set up a special commission directed by the monetary economist Anna Jacobson Schwartz to study whether the United States should return to the gold standard. The commission recommended against a return to gold. While most central banks continue to hold some gold as part of their international reserves, the price of gold now plays no special role in influencing countries' monetary policies.

THE GOLD-EXCHANGE STANDARD

Halfway between the gold standard and a pure reserve-currency standard is the **gold-exchange standard.** Under a gold-exchange standard central banks' reserves consist of gold *and* currencies whose prices in terms of gold are fixed, and each central bank fixes its exchange rate to a currency with a fixed gold price. A gold-exchange standard can operate like a gold standard in restraining excessive monetary growth throughout the world, but it allows more flexibility in the growth of international reserves, which can consist of other assets besides gold. A gold-exchange standard is, however, subject to the other limitations of a gold standard listed above.

The post–World War II reserve-currency system centered on the dollar was, in fact, originally set up as a gold-exchange standard. While foreign central banks did the job of pegging exchange rates, the United States Federal Reserve was responsible for holding the dollar price of gold at $35 an ounce. By the mid-1960s, the system operated in practice more like a pure reserve-currency system than a gold standard. For reasons examined in the next chapter, President Richard Nixon unilaterally severed the dollar's link to gold in August 1971, shortly before the system of fixed dollar exchange rates was abandoned.

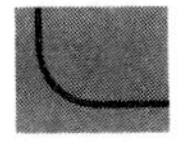

SUMMARY

1. There is a direct link between central-bank intervention in the foreign-exchange market and the domestic money supply. When a country's central bank purchases foreign assets, the country's money supply automatically increases. Similarly, a central-bank sale of foreign assets automatically lowers the money supply. The *central-bank balance sheet* shows how foreign-exchange intervention affects the money supply because the central bank's liabilities, which rise or fall when its assets rise or fall, are part of the money supply. The central bank can negate the money-supply effect of intervention through *sterilization.*

[23]See Keynes, "Alternative Aims in Monetary Policy," reprinted in his *Essays in Persuasion* (New York: W. W. Norton & Company, 1963). For a recent dissenting view on the gold standard, see Robert A. Mundell, "International Monetary Reform: The Optimal Mix in Big Countries," in James Tobin, ed., *Macroeconomics, Prices and Quantities* (Washington, D.C.: Brookings Institution, 1983), pp. 285–293.

2. A central bank can fix the exchange rate of its currency against foreign currency if it is willing to trade unlimited amounts of money and foreign assets at that rate. To fix the exchange rate, the central bank must intervene in the foreign-exchange market whenever this is necessary to prevent the emergence of an excess demand or supply of domestic money. In effect, the central bank adjusts its foreign assets—and so, the domestic money supply—to ensure that asset markets are always in equilibrium under the fixed exchange rate.

3. A commitment to fix the exchange rate forces the central bank to sacrifice its ability to use monetary policy for stabilization purposes. A purchase of domestic assets by the central bank causes an equal fall in its official international reserves, leaving the money supply and output unchanged. Similarly, a sale of domestic assets by the bank causes foreign reserves to rise by the same amount but has no other effects.

4. Fiscal policy, unlike monetary policy, has a more powerful effect on output under fixed exchange rates than under floating rates. Under a fixed exchange, fiscal expansion does not, in the short run, cause a real appreciation that "crowds out" aggregate demand. Instead, it forces central-bank purchases of foreign assets and an expansion of the money supply. *Devaluation* also raises aggregate demand and the money supply in the short run. (*Revaluation* has opposite effects.) In the long run, fiscal expansion causes a real appreciation, an increase in the money supply, and a rise in the home price level, while devaluation causes money and prices to rise eventually in proportion to the exchange-rate change.

5. *Balance of payments crises* occur when market participants expect the central bank to change the exchange rate from its current level. If the market decides a devaluation is coming, for example, the domestic interest rate rises above the world interest rate and foreign reserves drop sharply as private capital flows abroad.

6. A system of *managed floating* allows the central bank to retain some ability to control the domestic money supply, but at the cost of greater exchange-rate instability. If domestic and foreign bonds are *imperfect substitutes,* however, the central bank may be able to control both the money supply and the exchange rate through sterilized foreign-exchange intervention. Empirical evidence provides little evidence that sterilized intervention has a significant direct effect on exchange rates. Sterilized intervention may operate indirectly and change market views of future government policies even when domestic and foreign assets are *perfect substitutes.*

7. A world system of fixed exchange rates in which countries peg the prices of their currencies in terms of a *reserve currency* involves a striking asymmetry. The reserve-currency country, which does not have to fix any exchange rate, can influence economic activity both at home and abroad through its monetary policy. In contrast, all other countries are unable to influence their output or foreign output through monetary policy.

8. A *gold standard,* in which all countries fix their currencies' prices in terms of gold, avoids the asymmetry inherent in a reserve-currency standard and also places constraints on the growth of countries' money supplies. But the gold standard has serious drawbacks that make it impractical as a way of organizing today's international monetary system. Even the dollar-based *gold-exchange standard* set up after World War II ultimately proved unworkable.

KEY TERMS

managed floating exchange rates
European Monetary System (EMS)
central-bank balance sheet
sterilized foreign-exchange intervention
devaluation
revaluation
balance of payments crisis
capital flight
perfect asset substitutability
imperfect asset substitutability
risk premium
signaling effect of foreign-exchange intervention
reserve currency
gold standard
gold-exchange standard

PROBLEMS

1. Show how an expansion in the central bank's domestic assets ultimately affects its balance sheet under a fixed exchange rate. How are the central bank's transactions in the foreign-exchange market reflected in the balance of payments accounts?

2. Do the same exercises as in the previous question for an increase in government spending.

3. Describe the effects of an unexpected devaluation on the central bank's balance sheet and on the balance of payments accounts.

4. The following paragraphs appeared in the *New York Times* on September 22, 1986 (see "Europeans May Prop the Dollar," p. D1):

> To keep the dollar from falling against the West German mark, the European central banks would have to sell marks and buy dollars, a procedure known as intervention. But the pool of currencies in the marketplace is vastly larger than all the governments' holdings.
>
> Billions of dollars worth of currencies are traded each day. Without support from the United States and Japan, it is unlikely that market intervention from even the two most economically influential members of the European Community—Britain and West Germany—would have much impact on the markets. However, just the stated intention of the Community's central banks to intervene could disrupt the market with its psychological effect.
>
> Economists say that intervention works only when markets turn unusually erratic, as they have done upon reports of the assassination of a Presi-

dent, or when intervention is used to push the markets along in a direction where they are already headed anyway.

a) Do you agree with the statement in the article that West Germany has little ability to influence the exchange rate of the DM?

b) Do you agree with the last paragraph's evaluation of the efficacy of intervention?

c) Describe how "just the stated intention" to intervene could have a "psychological effect" on the foreign-exchange market.

d) Try your hand at rewriting the above paragraphs in more precise language so that they agree with what you learned in this chapter.

5. Can you think of reasons why a government might willingly sacrifice some of its ability to use monetary policy so that it can have more stable exchange rates?

6. How does fiscal expansion affect a country's current account under a fixed exchange rate?

7. Devaluation is often used by countries to improve their current accounts. Since the current account equals national saving less domestic investment, however (see Chapter 12), this improvement can occur only if investment falls, saving rises, or both. How might devaluation affect national saving and domestic investment?

8. Using the *DD-AA* model, analyze the output and balance of payments effects of an import tariff under fixed exchange rates. What would happen if all countries in the world simultaneously tried to improve employment and the balance of payments by imposing tariffs?

9. When a central bank devalues after a balance of payments crisis, it usually gains foreign reserves. Can this capital inflow be explained using our model? What would happen if the market believed that *another* devaluation was to occur in the near future?

10. Suppose that under the postwar "dollar standard" system foreign central banks had held dollar reserves in the form of green dollar bills hidden in their vaults rather than U.S. Treasury bills. Would the international monetary adjustment mechanism have been symmetric or asymmetric? (Hint: Think about what happens to the U.S. and German money supplies, for example, when the German Bundesbank sells DM for dollar bills that it then keeps.)

11. To avoid deflation due to insufficient gold supplies, countries have sometimes adopted a "bimetallic" monetary standard in which the currency has a fixed relative price in terms of both gold *and* silver. (The United States was technically on a bimetallic standard until 1873.) Can you see any special problems that a bimetallic standard can cause?

FURTHER READING

Anatol Balbach. "The Mechanics of Intervention in Exchange Markets." *Federal Reserve Bank of St. Louis Review* 60 (February 1978), pp. 2–7. A detailed account of central-bank intervention procedures.

William H. Branson. "Causes of Appreciation and Volatility of the Dollar," in *The U.S. Dollar—Recent Developments, Outlook, and Policy Options.* Kansas City: Federal Reserve Bank of Kansas City, 1985, pp. 33–52. Develops and applies a model of exchange-rate determination with imperfect asset substitutability.

Dale W. Henderson and Stephanie Sampson. "Intervention in Foreign Exchange Markets: A Summary of Ten Staff Studies." *Federal Reserve Bulletin* 69 (November 1983), pp. 830–836. Presents the major findings of the Federal Reserve intervention study that followed the June 1982 Versailles economic summit meeting.

Ronald I. McKinnon. *A New Tripartite Monetary Agreement or a Limping Dollar Standard?* Princeton Essays in International Finance 106. International Finance Section, Department of Economics, Princeton University, October 1974. Critical analysis of intervention arrangements under the post–World War II fixed-exchange-rate system.

Robert A. Mundell. "Capital Mobility and Stabilization Policy under Fixed and Flexible Exchange Rates." *Canadian Journal of Economics and Political Science* 29 (November 1963), pp. 475–485. Reprinted as Chapter 18 in Mundell's *International Economics.* New York: Macmillan, 1968. Classic account of the effects of monetary and fiscal policies under alternative exchange-rate regimes.

Michael Mussa. "The Exchange Rate, the Balance of Payments and Monetary and Fiscal Policy under a Regime of Controlled Floating," in Jan Herin, Assar Lindbeck, and Johan Myhrman, eds. *Flexible Exchange Rates and Stabilization Policy.* Boulder, CO: Westview Press, 1977, pp. 97–116. An exposition of the monetary approaches to the balance of payments and the exchange rate.

Michael Mussa. *The Role of Official Intervention.* Occasional Paper 6. New York: Group of Thirty, 1981. Discusses the theory and practice of central-bank foreign-exchange intervention under a dirty float.

Maurice Obstfeld. "Can We Sterilize? Theory and Evidence." *American Economic Review* 72 (May 1982), pp. 45–50. A review of research on sterilized foreign-exchange intervention under fixed and floating exchange rates.

APPENDIX I TO CHAPTER 17
Equilibrium in the Foreign-Exchange Market with Imperfect Asset Substitutability

This appendix develops a model of the foreign-exchange market in which risk factors may make domestic-currency and foreign-currency assets imperfect substitutes. The model gives rise to a risk premium that can separate the expected rates of return on domestic and foreign assets.[1]

DEMAND

Because individuals dislike risky situations in which their wealth may vary greatly from day to day, they decide how to allocate wealth among different assets by looking at the riskiness of the resulting portfolio as well as at the expected return it offers. Someone who puts her wealth entirely into British pounds, for example, may expect a high return but can be wiped out if the pound unexpectedly depreciates. A more sensible strategy is to invest in several currencies, even if some have lower expected returns than the pound, and thus reduce the impact on wealth of bad luck with any one single currency. By spreading risk in this way among several currencies, an individual can reduce the variability of her wealth.

Considerations of risk make it reasonable to assume that an individual's demand for interest-bearing domestic-currency assets increases when the interest they offer (R) rises relative to the domestic-currency return on foreign-currency assets $[R^* + (E^e - E)/E]$. Put another way, an individual will be willing to increase the riskiness of her portfolio by investing more heavily in domestic-currency assets only if she is compensated by an increase in the relative expected return on those assets.

We summarize this assumption by writing individual i's demand for domestic-currency bonds, B_i^d, as an increasing function of the rate-of-return difference between domestic and foreign bonds,

$$B_i^d = B_i^d[R - R^* - (E^e - E)/E].$$

Of course, B_i^d also depends on other factors specific to individual i, such as her wealth and income. The demand for domestic-currency bonds can be negative or positive, and in the former case individual i is a net borrower in the home currency, that is, a *supplier* of domestic-currency bonds.

To find the *aggregate* private demand for domestic-currency bonds, we need only add up individual demands B_i^d for all individuals i in the world. This summation gives the aggregate demand for domestic-currency bonds, B^d, which is also an increasing function of the expected rate of return difference in favor of domestic-currency assets. Therefore,

$$\text{Demand} = B^d[R - R^* - (E^e - E)/E]$$
$$= \text{sum (for all } i\text{) of } B_i^d[R - R^* - (E^e - E)/E].$$

[1]The Mathematical Postscript to Chapter 21 develops a microeconomic model of individual demand for risky assets.

Since some private individuals may be borrowing, and therefore supplying bonds, B^d should be interpreted as the private sector's *net* demand for domestic-currency bonds.

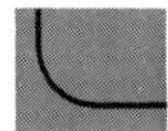

SUPPLY

Since we are interpreting B^d as the private sector's *net* demand for domestic-currency bonds, the appropriate supply variable to define market equilibrium is the net supply of domestic-currency bonds to the public, that is, the supply of bonds that are not the liability of any private person. Net supply therefore equals the value of domestic-currency government bonds held by the public, B, less the value of domestic-currency assets held by the central bank, A:

$$\text{Supply} = B - A.$$

A must be subtracted from B to find the net supply of bonds because purchases of bonds by the central bank reduce the supply available to private investors.

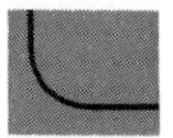

EQUILIBRIUM

The risk premium, ρ, is determined by the interaction of supply and demand. The risk premium is defined as

$$\rho = R - R^* - (E^e - E)/E,$$

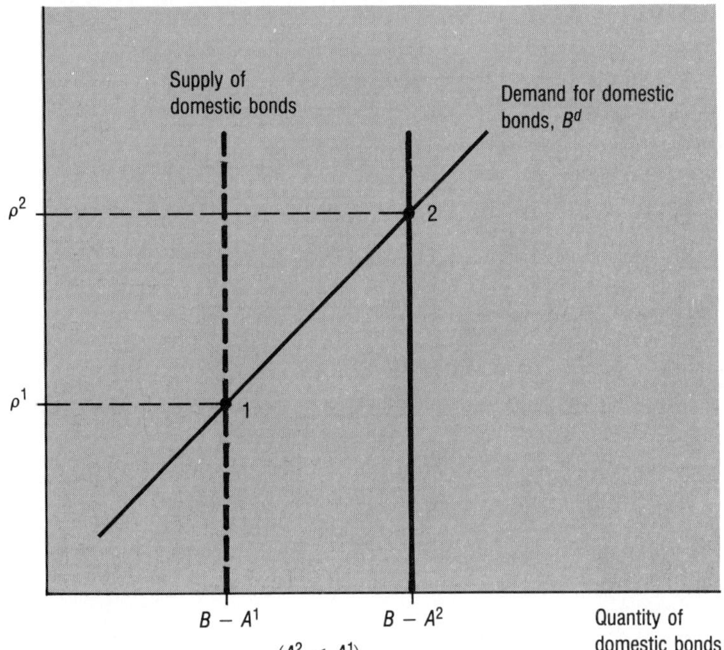

FIGURE 17AI-1 The domestic bond supply and the foreign-exchange risk premium under imperfect asset substitutability. An increase in the supply of domestic-currency bonds that the public must hold raises the risk premium on domestic-currency assets.

that is, as the expected return difference between domestic and foreign bonds. We can therefore write the private sector's net demand for domestic-currency bonds as an increasing function of ρ. Figure 17AI-1 shows this relationship by drawing the demand curve for domestic-currency bonds with a positive slope.

The bond supply curve is vertical at $B - A^1$ because the net supply of bonds to the market is determined by decisions of the government and central bank and is independent of the risk premium. Equilibrium occurs at point 1 (at a risk premium of ρ^1), where the private sector's net demand for domestic-currency bonds equals the net supply. Notice that for given values of R, R^*, and E^e, the equilibrium shown in the diagram can also be viewed as determining the exchange rate, since $E = E^e/(1 + R - R^* - \rho)$.

Figure 17AI-1 shows the effect of a central-bank sale of domestic assets that lowers its domestic asset holdings to $A^2 < A^1$. This sale raises the net supply of domestic-currency bonds to $B - A^2$ and shifts the supply curve to the right. The new equilibrium occurs at point 2, at a risk premium of $\rho^2 > \rho^1$. Similarly, an increase in the domestic-currency government debt, B, would also raise the risk premium.

The model therefore establishes that the risk premium is an increasing function of $B - A$, as we assumed in the discussion of sterilized intervention above [equation (17-3)].

APPENDIX II TO CHAPTER 17
The Monetary Approach to the Balance of Payments

The close link discussed above between a country's balance of payments and its money supply suggests that fluctuations in central-bank reserves can be thought of as the result of changes in the money market. This method of analyzing the balance of payments is called the *monetary approach to the balance of payments.* The monetary approach was developed in the 1950s and 1960s by the International Monetary Fund's research department under Jacques J. Polak, and by Harry G. Johnson, Robert A. Mundell, and their students at the University of Chicago.[1]

The monetary approach can be illustrated through a simple model linking the balance of payments to developments in the money market. To begin, recall that the money market is in equilibrium when the real money supply equals real money demand, that is, when

$$\frac{M^s}{P} = L(R, Y). \qquad \textbf{(17AII-1)}$$

Now let F denote the central bank's foreign assets and A its domestic assets (domestic credit). If μ is the *money multiplier* that defines the relation between central-bank assets $(F + A)$ and the money supply, then

$$M^s = \mu(F + A). \qquad \textbf{(17AII-2)}$$

The change in central-bank foreign assets over any time period, ΔF, equals the balance of payments (for a non-reserve currency country). By combining (17AII-1) and (17AII-2), we can express the central bank's foreign assets as

$$F = (1/\mu)PL(R, Y) - A.$$

If we assume that μ is a constant, the balance of payments surplus is

$$\Delta F = (1/\mu)\Delta[PL(R, Y)] - \Delta A. \qquad \textbf{(17AII-3)}$$

The last equation summarizes the monetary approach. The first term on its right-hand side reflects changes in nominal money demand and tells us that, all else equal, an increase in money demand will bring about a balance of payments surplus and an accompanying increase in the money supply that maintains money-market equilibrium. The second term in the balance of payments equation reflects supply factors in the money market. An increase in domestic credit raises money supply relative to money demand, all else equal; so the balance of payments must go into deficit to reduce the money supply and restore money-market equilibrium.

Because the balance of payments equals the sum of the current- and (non-central bank) capital-account surpluses (see Chapter 12), much of the economics literature that appeared before the monetary approach explained balance of payments movements as the result of current- or capital-account changes. An important contribution

[1]Many original articles using the monetary approach are collected in Jacob A. Frenkel and Harry G. Johnson, eds., *The Monetary Approach to the Balance of Payments* (London: George Allen and Unwin, 1976), and International Monetary Fund, *The Monetary Approach to the Balance of Payments* (Washington, D.C.: International Monetary Fund, 1977).

of the monetary approach was to stress that in many situations, balance of payments problems result directly from imbalances in the money market and a policy solution that relies on monetary policy is therefore most appropriate. A large balance of payments deficit may be the result of excessive domestic credit creation, for example. Even though the balance of payments deficit will generally involve deficits in both the current and private capital accounts, it would be misleading to view the balance of payments deficit as fundamentally due to an exogenous fall in relative world demand for domestic goods or assets.

There are many realistic cases, however, in which a balance of payments analysis based on the monetary approach is roundabout and possibly misleading as a guide to policy. Suppose, for example, that a temporary fall in foreign demand for domestic products does occur. This change will cause a fall in the current account and in the balance of payments, but these effects can be counteracted (when rigid capital-account restrictions are not in place) by a temporarily expansionary fiscal policy.

Because output and thus money demand fall, the monetary approach also predicts that a balance of payments deficit will result from a fall in export demand. It would be wrong, however, for policymakers to conclude that because the balance of payments deficit is associated with a fall in money demand, a contraction of domestic credit is the best response. If the central bank were to restrict domestic credit to improve the balance of payments, unemployment would remain high and might even rise.

While the monetary approach is an extremely useful analytical tool, it must be applied with caution in seeking solutions to macroeconomic problems. It is most useful for formulating policies when policy problems are a direct result of shifts in domestic money demand or supply.

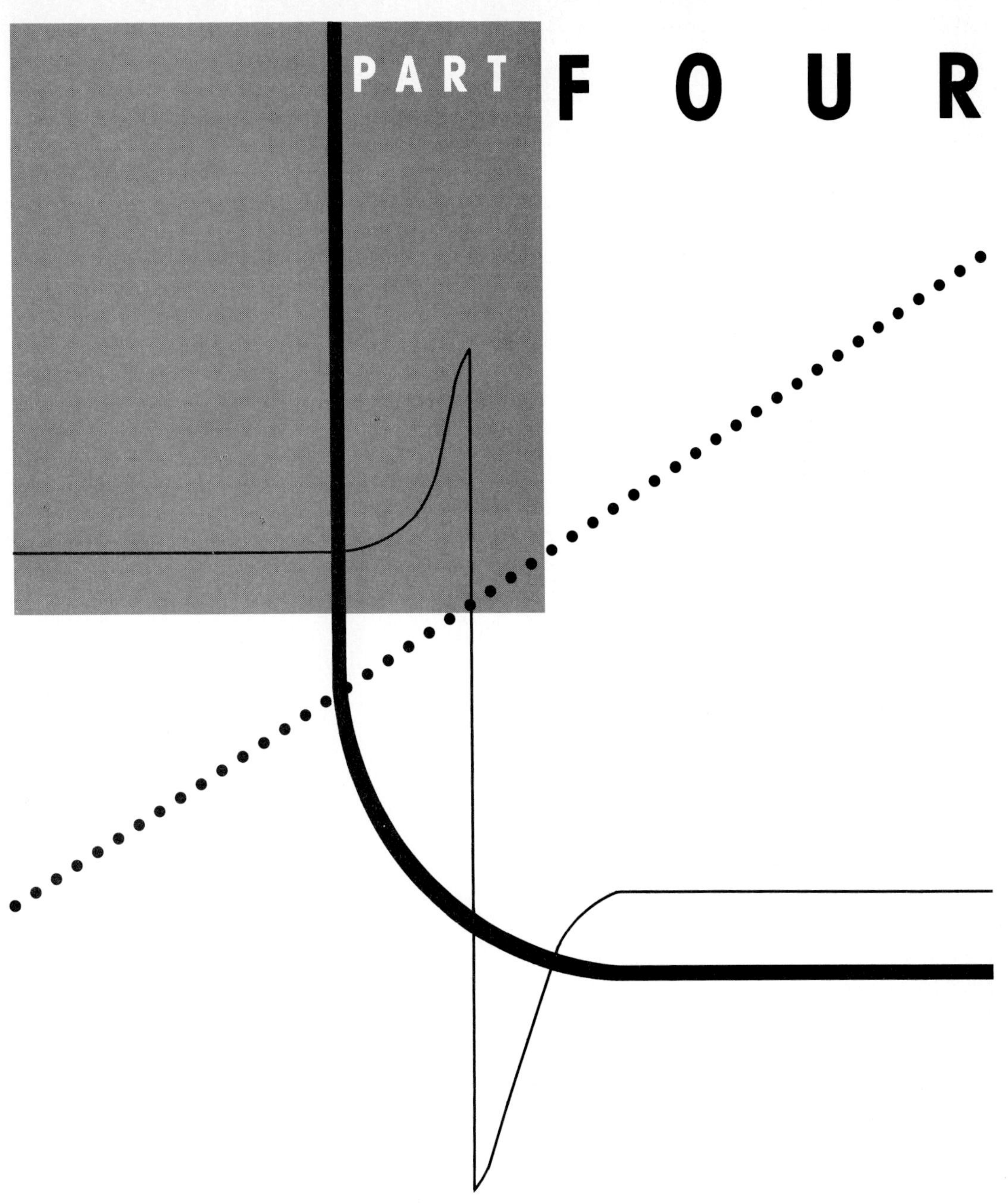

PART FOUR

INTERNATIONAL MACROECONOMIC POLICY

18 THE INTERNATIONAL MONETARY SYSTEM, 1870–1973

In the previous two chapters we saw how a single country can use monetary, fiscal, and exchange-rate policy to change the levels of employment and production within its borders. Although the analysis assumed that macroeconomic conditions in the rest of the world were not affected by the actions of the country we were studying, this assumption is not, in general, a valid one: any change in the home country's real exchange rate automatically implies an opposite change in foreign real exchange rates, and any shift in overall domestic spending is likely to change domestic demand for foreign goods. Unless the home country is insignificantly small, developments within its borders affect macroeconomic conditions abroad and therefore complicate the task of foreign policymakers.

The inherent interdependence of open national economies has sometimes made it more difficult for governments to achieve such policy goals as full employment and price-level stability. The channels of interdependence depend, in turn, on the monetary and exchange-rate arrangements that countries adopt—a set of institutions called the *international monetary system*.

This chapter examines how the international monetary system influenced macroeconomic policymaking and performance during three periods: the gold-standard era (from 1870 to 1914), the interwar period (from 1918 to 1939), and the post–World War II years during which exchange rates were fixed under the Bretton Woods agreement (1945 to 1973).

In an open economy, macroeconomic policy has two basic goals, internal balance (full employment with price stability) and external balance (avoiding excessive imbalances in international payments). Because a country cannot alter its international payments position without automatically causing an opposite change of equal magnitude in the payments position of the rest of the world, one country's pursuit of its macroeconomic goals inevitably influences how well other countries attain their goals. The goal of external balance therefore offers a clear illustration of how policy actions taken abroad may change an economy's position relative to the position its government prefers.

Throughout the period 1870–1973, with its various international currency arrangements, how did countries try to attain internal and external balance, and how successful were they? Did policymakers worry about the foreign repercussions of their actions, or did each adopt nationalistic measures that were self-defeating for the world economy as a whole? The answers to these questions depend on the international monetary system in effect at the time.

MACROECONOMIC POLICY GOALS IN AN OPEN ECONOMY

In open economies, policymakers are motivated by the goals of internal and external balance. Simply defined, **internal balance** requires the full employment of a country's resources and domestic price-level stability. **External balance** is attained when a country's current account is neither so deeply in deficit that the country may be unable to repay its foreign debts in the future nor so strongly in surplus that foreigners are put in that position.

In practice, neither of these definitions captures the full range of potential policy concerns. Along with full employment and stability of the overall price level, for example, policymakers may have a particular domestic distribution of income as an additional internal target. Depending on exchange-rate arrangements, policymakers may worry about swings in balance of payments accounts other than the current account. To make matters even more complicated, the line between external and internal goals can be a fuzzy one. How should one classify an employment target for export industries, for example, when export growth influences the economy's ability to repay its foreign debts?

The simple definitions of internal and external balance given above, however, capture the goals that most policymakers share regardless of the particular economic environment. We therefore organize our analysis around these definitions and discuss possible additional aspects of internal or external balance when they are relevant.

INTERNAL BALANCE: FULL EMPLOYMENT AND PRICE-LEVEL STABILITY

When a country's productive resources are fully employed and its price level is stable, the country is in internal balance. The waste and hardship that occur when resources are underemployed is clear. If a country's economy is "overheated" and resources are *over*employed, however, waste of a different (though probably less harmful) kind occurs. For example, workers on overtime might prefer to be working less and enjoying leisure, but their contracts require them to put in longer hours during periods of high demand. Machines that are being worked more intensely than usual will tend to suffer more frequent breakdowns and to depreciate more quickly.

Under- and overemployment also lead to general price-level movements that reduce the economy's efficiency by making the real value of the monetary unit less certain and thus a less useful guide for economic decisions. Since domestic wages and prices rise when the demands for labor and output exceed full-employment levels, and fall in the opposite case, the government must prevent substantial movements in aggregate demand relative to its full-employment level to maintain a stable, predictable price level.

Inflation or deflation can occur even under conditions of full employment, of course, if the expectations of workers and firms about future monetary policy lead to an upward or downward wage-price spiral. Such a spiral can continue indefinitely, however, only if the central bank fulfills expectations through continuing injections or withdrawals of money (Chapter 14).

One particularly disruptive effect of an unstable price level is its effect on the real value of loan contracts. Because loans tend to be denominated in the monetary unit, unexpected price-level changes cause income to be redistributed between creditors and debtors. A sudden increase in the U.S. price level, for example, makes those with dollar debts better off, since the money they owe to lenders is now worth less in terms of goods and services. At the same time, the price-level increase makes lenders worse off. Because such accidental income redistribution can cause considerable distress to those who are hurt, governments have another reason to maintain price-level stability.[1]

Theoretically, a perfectly predictable trend of rising or falling prices would not be too costly, since everyone would be able to calculate easily the real value of money at any point in the future. But in the real world, there appears to be no such thing as a predictable inflation rate. Indeed, experience shows that the unpredictability of the general price level is magnified tremendously in periods of rapid price-level change. The costs of inflation

[1]The situation is somewhat different when the government itself is a major debtor in domestic currency. In such cases, a surprise inflation that reduces the real value of government debt may be a convenient way of taxing the public. This method of taxation has been quite common in less-developed countries (Chapter 20), but elsewhere it has generally been applied with reluctance and in extreme situations (for example, during wars). A policy of trying to surprise the public with inflation undermines the government's credibility and, through the Fisher effect, worsens the terms on which the government can borrow.

have been most apparent recently in countries like Argentina and Israel, where astronomical price-level increases caused the domestic currencies practically to stop functioning as units of account. (Both countries had currency reforms as a result of the public's flight from domestic money.)

To avoid price-level instability, therefore, the government must prevent excessive fluctuations in output, which are also undesirable in themselves. In addition, it must avoid continuing inflation and deflation by ensuring that the domestic money supply does not grow too quickly or too slowly.

EXTERNAL BALANCE: THE OPTIMAL LEVEL OF THE CURRENT ACCOUNT

The notion of external balance is more difficult to define than internal balance because there are no natural benchmarks like "full employment" or "stable prices" to apply to an economy's external transactions. Whether an economy's trade with the outside world poses macroeconomic problems depends on several factors, including the economy's particular circumstances, conditions in the outside world, and the institutional arrangements governing its economic relations with foreign countries. A country that is committed to fix its exchange rate against a foreign currency, for example, may well adopt a different definition of external balance than one whose currency floats.

International economics textbooks often identify external balance with balance in a country's current account. While this definition is appropriate in some circumstances, it is not helpful as a general rule. Recall from Chapter 12 that a country with a current-account deficit is borrowing resources from the rest of the world that it will have to pay back in the future. This situation is not necessarily undesirable. For example, the country's opportunities for investing the borrowed resources may be attractive relative to the opportunities available in the rest of the world. In this case, paying back loans from foreigners poses no problem because a profitable investment will generate a return high enough to cover the interest and principal on those loans. Similarly, a current-account surplus may pose no problem if domestic savings are being invested more profitably abroad than they would be at home.

More generally, we may think of current-account imbalances as providing another example of how countries gain from trade. The trade involved is what we have called *intertemporal trade,* that is, the trade of consumption over time (Chapter 7). Just as countries with differing abilities to produce goods at a single point in time gain from concentrating their production on what they do best and trading, countries can gain from concentrating the world's investment in those economies best able to turn current output into future output. Countries with weak investment opportunities should invest little at home and channel their savings into more productive investment activity abroad. Put another way, countries where investment is relatively unproductive should be net exporters of currently available output (and thus have current-account surpluses), while countries where investment is relatively productive should be net importers of current output (and have current-account deficits). To pay off their foreign debts when the investments mature, the latter countries export output to the former countries and thereby complete the exchange of present output for future output.

Other considerations may also justify an unbalanced current account. A country where output drops temporarily (for example, because of an unusually bad crop failure) may wish to borrow from foreigners to avoid the sharp temporary fall in its consumption that would occur otherwise. In the absence of this borrowing the price of present output in terms of future output would be higher in the low-output country than abroad; so the intertemporal trade that eliminates this price difference leads to mutual gains.

Insisting that all countries be in current-account equilibrium makes no allowance for these important gains from trade over time. Thus, no realistic policymaker would want to adopt a balanced current account as a policy target appropriate in all circumstances.

At a given point, however, policymakers generally adopt *some* current-account target as an objective, and this target defines their external-balance goal. While the target level of the current account is generally not zero, governments usually try to avoid extremely large external surpluses or deficits unless they have clear evidence that large imbalances are justified by potential intertemporal trade gains. (After the sharp rise in oil prices in the early 1970s, for example, Norway's government allowed extensive foreign borrowing to fund the development of the country's North Sea oil reserves.) Governments are cautious because the exact current-account balance that maximizes the gains from intertemporal trade is difficult if not impossible to figure out. In addition, this optimal current-account balance can change unpredictably over time as conditions in the economy change. Current-account balances that are very wide of the mark can, however, cause serious problems.

Problems with Excessive Current-Account Deficits. Why do governments prefer to avoid current-account deficits that are too large? As noted, a current-account deficit (which means that the economy is borrowing from abroad) may pose no problem if the borrowed funds are channeled into productive domestic investment projects that pay for themselves with the revenue they generate in the future. Sometimes, however, large current-account deficits represent temporarily high consumption resulting from misguided government policies or some other malfunction in the economy. At other times, the investment projects that draw on foreign funds may be badly planned and based on overoptimistic expectations about future profitability. In such cases, the government might wish to reduce the current-account deficit immediately rather than face problems in repaying debts to foreigners later. In particular, a large current-account deficit caused by an expansionary fiscal policy that does not simultaneously make domestic investment opportunities more profitable may signal a need for the government to restore external balance by changing its economic course.

At times the external target is imposed from abroad rather than chosen by the domestic government. When countries begin to have trouble meeting their payments on past foreign loans, foreigners become reluctant to lend them new funds and may even demand immediate repayment of the earlier loans. Since 1982, many developing economies (particularly those in Latin America) have faced this problem of a limited ability to borrow abroad. In such cases, the home government may have to take severe action to reduce the country's desired borrowing from foreigners to feasible levels.

Problems with Excessive Current-Account Surpluses. An excessive current-account surplus poses problems that are different from those posed by deficits. A surplus in the current account implies that a country is accumulating assets located abroad. Why are growing domestic claims to foreign wealth ever a problem? One potential reason stems from the fact that, for a given level of national saving, an increased current-account surplus implies lower investment in domestic plant and equipment. (This follows from the national income identity, $S = CA + I$, which says that total domestic saving, S, is divided between foreign asset accumulation, CA, and domestic investment, I.) Several factors might lead policymakers to prefer that domestic savings be devoted to higher levels of domestic investment and lower levels of foreign investment. First, the returns on domestic capital may be easier to tax than those on assets located abroad. Second, an addition to the home capital stock may reduce domestic unemployment and therefore lead to higher national income than an equal addition to foreign assets.

If a large home current-account surplus reflects excessive external borrowing by foreigners, the home country may be unable to collect the funds it is owed in the future. Put another way, the home country may lose part of its foreign wealth if foreigners find they have borrowed more than they can repay. In contrast, nonrepayment of a loan between domestic residents leads to a redistribution of national wealth within the home country but causes no change in the level of national wealth.

Excessive current-account surpluses may also be inconvenient for political reasons. Countries with large surpluses can become targets for discriminatory protectionist trade measures taken by trading partners with external deficits. To avoid such damaging restrictions, surplus countries may try to keep their surpluses from becoming too large. In the mid-1980s, for example, Japan was running a large and growing current-account surplus with the United States. Threatened by moves in the U.S. Congress to bar imports of Japanese products, the Japanese authorities eventually agreed to ease fiscal policy to reduce their country's current-account surplus.

To summarize, the goal of external balance is a level of the current account that allows the most important gains from trade over time to be realized without risking the problems discussed above. Because governments do not know this current-account level exactly, they usually try to avoid large deficits or surpluses unless there is clear evidence of potential gains from intertemporal trade.

INTERNATIONAL MACROECONOMIC POLICY UNDER THE GOLD STANDARD, 1870–1914

The gold-standard period between 1870 and 1914 was based on ideas about international macroeconomic policy very different from those that have formed the basis of international monetary arrangements in the second half of the twentieth century. Nevertheless, the period warrants attention because subsequent attempts to reform the international monetary system on the basis of fixed exchange rates can be viewed as attempts to build on the strengths of the gold standard while avoiding its weaknesses. (Some of the strengths and weaknesses were examined in Chapter 17.) This section looks at how the gold standard functioned in practice before World War I and examines how well it enabled countries to attain goals of internal and external balance.

ORIGINS OF THE GOLD STANDARD

The gold standard has its origin in the use of gold coins as a medium of exchange, unit of account, and store of value. While gold has been used in this way since ancient times, the gold standard as a legal institution dates from 1819, when the British Parliament passed the Resumption Act. This law derived its name from its requirement that the Bank of England *resume* its practice—discontinued 4 years after the outbreak of the Napoleonic wars (1793–1815)—of exchanging currency notes for gold on demand at a fixed rate. The Resumption Act marks the first adoption of a true gold standard because it simultaneously repealed long-standing restrictions on the export of gold coins and bullion from Britain.

Later in the nineteenth century, Germany, Japan, and other countries also adopted the gold standard. At the time, Britain was the world's leading economic power, and other countries hoped to achieve similar economic success by copying British institutions. The United States effectively joined the gold standard in 1879 when it pegged the paper "greenbacks" issued during the Civil War to gold. The U.S. Gold Standard Act of 1900 institutionalized the dollar-gold link. Given Britain's preeminence in international trade and the advanced development of its financial institutions, London naturally became the center of the international financial system built on the gold standard.

EXTERNAL BALANCE UNDER THE GOLD STANDARD

Under the gold standard, the primary responsibility of a central bank was to preserve the official parity between its currency and gold; to maintain this price, the central bank needed an adequate stock of gold reserves. Policymakers therefore viewed external balance not in terms of a current-account target but as a situation in which the central bank was neither gaining gold from abroad nor (more important) losing gold to foreigners at too rapid a rate.

In the modern terminology of Chapter 12, central banks tried to avoid excessive movements in the *balance of payments* (or official settlements balance), the sum of the current-account balance and the non-central-bank component of the capital-account balance. Because international reserves took the form of gold during this period, the surplus or deficit in the balance of payments had to be financed by gold shipments between central banks.[2] So to avoid sharp gold movements, central banks adopted policies that pushed the current-account surplus (or deficit) into line with the non-central-bank component of the capital-account deficit (or surplus). A country is said to be in **balance of payments equilibrium** when the sum of its current account and its non-central-bank capital account equals zero, so that the current-account balance is financed entirely by international lending without reserve movements.

Many governments took a "laissez-faire" attitude toward the current account. Britain's current-account surplus between 1870 and the First World War averaged 5.2 percent of its GNP, a figure that is remarkably high by post-1945 standards. (Today, a current-account/GNP ratio half that size would be considered sizable.) Several borrowing countries, however, did experience difficulty at one time or another in paying their foreign debts. Perhaps because Britain was the world's leading exporter of international economic theory as well as of capital during these years, the economic writing of the gold-standard era places little emphasis on problems of current-account adjustment. A factor contributing to the neglect of the current account was the greater difficulty (compared with today) of assembling reliable estimates of the current account and other components of the national income accounts. In contrast, it was a relatively simple matter for central banks to keep track of their gold reserves.[3]

THE PRICE-SPECIE-FLOW MECHANISM

The gold standard contains some powerful automatic mechanisms that contribute to the simultaneous achievement of balance of payments equilibrium by all countries. The most important of these, the **price-specie-flow mechanism,** was recognized by the eighteenth century (when precious metals were referred to as "specie"). David Hume, the Scottish philosopher, described the price-specie-flow mechanism as follows in 1752:

> Suppose four-fifths of all the money in Great Britain to be annihilated in one night, and the nation reduced to the same condition, with regard to

[2]In reality, central banks had begun to hold foreign currencies in their reserves even before 1914. (The pound sterling was the leading reserve currency.) It is still true, however, that the balance of payments was financed mainly by gold shipments during this period.

[3]While the economic consequences of the current account were often ignored, governments sometimes restricted international lending by their residents to put political pressure on foreign governments. The political dimensions of international capital flows before World War I are examined in a famous study by Herbert Feis, *Europe, the World's Banker* (New Haven: Yale University Press, 1930).

> specie, as in the reigns of the Harrys and the Edwards, what would be the consequence? Must not the price of all labour and commodities sink in proportion, and everything be sold as cheap as they were in those ages? What nation could then dispute with us in any foreign market, or pretend to navigate or to sell manufactures at the same price, which to us would afford sufficient profit? In how little time, therefore, must this bring back the money which we had lost, and raise us to the level of all the neighbouring nations? Where, after we have arrived, we immediately lose the advantage of the cheapness of labor and commodities; and the farther flowing in of money is stopped by our fulness and repletion.
>
> Again, suppose that all the money in Great Britain were multiplied fivefold in a night, must not the contrary effect follow? Must not all labour and commodities rise to such an exorbitant height, that no neighbouring nations could afford to buy from us; while their commodities, on the other hand, became comparatively so cheap, that, in spite of all the laws which could be formed, they would run in upon us, and our money flow out; till we fall to a level with foreigners, and lose that great superiority of riches which had laid us under such disadvantages?[4]

It is easy to translate Hume's description of the price-specie-flow mechanism into more modern terms. Suppose that Britain's current-account surplus is greater than its non-central-bank capital-account deficit. Because foreigners' net imports from Britain are not being financed entirely by British loans, the balance must be matched by flows of international reserves—that is, of gold—into Britain. These gold flows automatically reduce foreign money supplies and swell Britain's money supply, pushing foreign prices downward and British prices upward. (Notice that Hume fully understood the lesson of Chapter 14 that price levels and money supplies move proportionally in the long run.)[5]

The simultaneous rise in British prices and fall in foreign prices—a real appreciation of the pound, given the fixed exchange rate—reduces foreign demand for British goods and services and at the same time increases British demand for foreign goods and services. These demand shifts work in the direction of reducing Britain's current-account surplus and reducing the foreign current-account deficit. Eventually, therefore, reserve movements stop and both countries reach balance of payments equilibrium. The same process also works in reverse, eliminating an initial situation of foreign surplus and British deficit.

[4]Hume, "Of the Balance of Trade," reprinted (in abridged form) in Barry Eichengreen, ed., *The Gold Standard in Theory and History* (London: Methuen, 1985), pp. 39–48.

[5]As mentioned in the footnote on p. 485, there are several ways in which the reduction in foreign money supplies, and the corresponding increase in Britain's money supply, might have occurred in Hume's day. Foreign residents could have melted gold coins into bars and used them to pay for imports. The British recipients of the gold bars could have then sold them to the Bank of England for British coins or paper currency. Alternatively, the foreign residents could have sold paper money to their central banks in return for gold and shipped this gold to Britain. Since gold coins were then part of the money supply, both transactions would have affected money supplies in the same way.

HUME VS. THE MERCANTILISTS

David Hume's forceful account of the price-specie-flow mechanism is another example of the skillful use of economic theory to mold economic policy. An influential school of economic thinkers called *mercantilists* held that without severe restrictions on international trade and payments, Britain might find itself impoverished and without an adequate supply of circulating monetary gold as a result of balance of payments deficits. Hume refuted their arguments by demonstrating that the balance of payments would automatically regulate itself to ensure an adequate supply of money in every country.

Mercantilism, which originated in the seventeenth century, held that silver and gold were the mainstays of national wealth and essential to vigorous commerce. Mercantilists therefore viewed specie outflows with alarm and had as a main policy goal a continuing surplus in the balance of payments (that is, a continuing inflow of precious metals). As the mercantilist writer Thomas Mun put it around 1630: "The ordinary means therefore to increase our wealth and treasure is by foreign trade, wherein we must ever observe this rule: to sell more to strangers yearly than we consume of theirs in value."

Hume's reasoning showed that a perpetual surplus is impossible: since specie inflows drive up domestic prices and restore equilibrium in the balance of payments, any surplus eventually eliminates itself. Similarly, a shortage of currency leads to low domestic prices and a foreign payments surplus that eventually brings into the country as much money as needed. Government interference with international transactions, Hume argued, would harm the economy without bringing about the ongoing increase in "wealth and treasure" that the mercantilists favored.

Hume pointed out that the mercantilists overemphasized a single and relatively minor component of national wealth, precious metals, while ignoring the nation's main source of wealth, its productive capacity. In making this observation Hume was putting forth a very modern view. Well into this century, however, policymakers concerned with external balance often focused on international gold flows at the expense of broader indicators of changes in national wealth. Since the mercantilists were discredited by the attacks of Hume and like-minded thinkers, this relative neglect of the current account and its relation to domestic investment and productivity is puzzling. Some possible explanations were suggested earlier in the text. In addition, mercantilistic instincts may have survived in the hearts of central bankers.

THE GOLD STANDARD "RULES OF THE GAME": MYTH AND REALITY

The price-specie-flow mechanism could operate automatically under the gold standard to bring countries' current and capital accounts into line and eliminate international gold movements. But the reactions of central banks to gold flows across their borders furnished another potential mechanism to help restore balance of payments equilibrium. Central banks that were persistently losing gold faced the risk of becoming unable to meet their obligation to redeem currency notes. They were therefore motivated to contract their domestic asset holdings when gold was being lost, pushing domestic interest rates upward and attracting inflows of capital from abroad. Central banks gaining gold had much weaker incentives to eliminate their own imports of gold. The main incentive was the greater profitability of interest-bearing domestic assets compared with "barren" gold. A central bank that was accumulating gold might be tempted to purchase domestic assets, thereby increasing capital outflows and driving gold abroad.

These domestic-credit measures, if undertaken by central banks, reinforced the price-specie-flow mechanism in pushing all countries toward balance of payments equilibrium. After World War I, the practices of selling domestic assets in the face of a deficit and buying domestic assets in the face of a surplus came to be known as the gold standard "rules of the game"—a phrase apparently coined by Keynes. Because such measures speeded the movement of all countries toward their external-balance goals, they increased the efficiency of the automatic adjustment processes inherent in the gold standard.

Later research has shown that the supposed "rules of the game" of the gold standard were frequently violated before 1914. As noted, the incentives to obey the rules applied with greater force to deficit than to surplus countries; so in practice it was the deficit countries that bore the burden of bringing the payments balances of *all* countries into equilibrium. By hoarding gold, the surplus countries worsened a problem of international policy coordination inherent in the system: deficit countries competing for a limited supply of gold reserves might adopt overcontractionary monetary policies that harmed employment while doing little to improve their reserve positions.

In fact, many countries reversed the rules and *sterilized* gold flows, that is, sold domestic assets when foreign reserves were rising and bought domestic assets in the opposite case. Widespread government interference with private gold exports also undermined the system. The picture of smooth and automatic balance of payments adjustment before World War I therefore does not match reality. When their policy goals were at stake, governments often ignored both the "rules of the game" and the effects of their actions on other countries.[6]

[6]An influential modern study of central-bank practices under the gold standard is Arthur I. Bloomfield, *Monetary Policy under the International Gold Standard: 1880–1914* (New York: Federal Reserve Bank of New York, 1959).

INTERNAL BALANCE UNDER THE GOLD STANDARD

By fixing the prices of currencies in terms of gold, the gold standard aimed to limit monetary growth in the world economy and thus to ensure stability in world price levels. While price levels within gold-standard countries did not rise as much between 1870 and 1914 as over the period after World War II, national price levels moved unpredictably over shorter horizons as periods of inflation and deflation followed each other. The gold standard's mixed record on price stability reflected a problem discussed in the last chapter, change in the relative prices of gold and other commodities.

In addition, the gold standard does not seem to have done much to ensure full employment. The U.S. unemployment rate, for example, averaged 6.8 percent between 1890 and 1913, but it averaged only 5.5 percent between 1946 and 1985.[7]

A fundamental cause of short-term internal instability under the pre-1914 gold standard was the subordination of economic policy to external objectives. Before the First World War, governments had not assumed responsibility for maintaining internal balance as fully as they did after the Second World War. The importance of internal policy objectives increased after World War I as a result of the worldwide economic instability of the interwar years, 1918–1939. And the unpalatable internal consequences of attempts to restore the gold standard after 1918 helped mold the thinking of the architects of the fixed-exchange-rate system adopted after 1945. To understand how the post–World War II international monetary system tried to reconcile the goals of internal and external balance, we therefore must examine the economic events of the period between the two world wars.

THE INTERWAR YEARS, 1918–1939

Governments abandoned the gold standard during World War I and financed a large fraction of their massive military expenditures by printing money. As a result, price levels were higher everywhere at the war's conclusion in 1918. Further, labor forces and productive capacity had been reduced sharply through war losses.

Several countries experienced runaway inflation as their governments attempted to aid the reconstruction process through public expenditures. These governments financed their purchases simply by printing the money they needed, as they sometimes had during the war. The result was an explosion in some countries' money supplies and price levels.

[7]Data on price levels are given by Cooper (cited on p. 486 in Chapter 17), and data for U.S. unemployment are adapted from the same source. Caution should be used in comparing gold-standard and post-World War II unemployment data because the methods used to assemble the earlier data were much cruder. A critical study of pre-1930 U.S. unemployment data is Christina Romer, "Spurious Volatility in Historical Unemployment Data," *Journal of Political Economy* 94 (February 1986), pp. 1–37.

THE GERMAN HYPERINFLATION

The most celebrated episode of interwar inflation is the German hyperinflation, during which Germany's price index rose from a level of 262 in January 1919 to a level of 126,160,000,000,000 in December 1923—a factor of 481.5 billion!

The Versailles Treaty ending World War I saddled Germany with a huge burden of reparations payments to the Allies. Rather than raising taxes to meet these payments, the German government ran its printing presses. The inflation accelerated most dramatically in January 1923 when France, citing lagging German compliance with the Versailles terms, sent its troops into Germany's industrial heartland, the Ruhr. German workers went on strike to protest the French occupation, and the German government supported their action by issuing even more money to pay them. Within the year, the price level rose by a factor of 452,998,200. Under these conditions, people were unwilling to hold the German currency, which became all but useless.

The hyperinflation was ended toward the end of 1923 as Germany instituted a currency reform, obtained some relief from its reparations burdens, and moved toward a balanced government budget.

THE FLEETING RETURN TO GOLD

The United States returned to gold in 1919. By the early 1920s, European countries yearned increasingly for the comparative financial stability of the gold-standard era. In 1922, at a conference in Genoa, Italy, a group of countries including Britain, France, Italy, and Japan agreed on a program calling for a general return to the gold standard and cooperation among central banks in attaining external and internal objectives. Realizing that gold supplies might be inadequate to meet central banks' demands for international reserves (a problem of the gold standard noted in Chapter 17), the Genoa Conference sanctioned a partial gold *exchange* standard in which smaller countries could hold as reserves the currencies of several large countries whose own international reserves would consist entirely of gold.

In 1925, Britain returned to the gold standard by pegging the pound to gold at the prewar price. Chancellor of the Exchequer Winston Churchill, a champion of the return to the old parity, argued that any deviation from the prewar price would undermine world confidence in the stability of Britain's financial institutions, which had played the leading role in international finance during the gold-standard era. Though Britain's price level had been falling since the war, in 1925 it was still much higher than in the days of the prewar gold standard. To maintain the pound price of gold at its prewar level, the Bank of England was therefore forced to adopt contractionary monetary policies that contributed to severe unemployment.

The depression in Britain that followed the return to gold had been predicted by Keynes and others, but it was not unprecedented. More than a century earlier, Britain's return to the gold standard at the parity prevailing before the Napoleonic Wars had also set off a sustained and deep depression. In both cases, the return to an exchange rate made obsolete by wartime price-level increases amounted to a massive *revaluation* of the pound against foreign currencies, a move that shifted world demand away from British products.

Britain's stagnation in the 1920s accelerated London's decline as the world's leading financial center. Britain's economic weakening proved problematic for the stability of the restored gold standard. In line with the recommendations of the Genoa Conference, many countries held international reserves in the form of pound deposits in London. Britain's gold reserves were limited, however, and the country's persistent stagnation did little to inspire confidence in its ability to meet its foreign obligations. The onset of the Great Depression in 1929 led to bank failures throughout the world, and Britain was forced off gold in 1931 when foreign holders of pounds (including several central banks) suddenly panicked and began to convert their pound holdings to gold.

INTERNATIONAL ECONOMIC DISINTEGRATION

As the Depression continued, many countries renounced their gold-standard obligations and allowed their currencies to float in the foreign-exchange market. The United States left the gold standard in 1933 but returned to it in 1934, having raised the dollar price of gold from $20.67 to $35 per ounce. Several other countries also returned to some form of gold standard after devaluation. These "competitive depreciations" were undertaken by each country in the hope of shifting world demand toward its output, but they largely offset each other and thus did not help countries overcome unemployment (except to the extent that worldwide monetary expansion was encouraged by higher money prices of gold).

Major economic damage was done by restrictions on international trade and payments, which proliferated as countries attempted to discourage imports and keep aggregate demand bottled up at home. The Smoot-Hawley tariff imposed by the United States in 1930 had a damaging effect on employment abroad. The foreign response involved retaliatory trade restrictions and preferential trading agreements among groups of countries.

Uncertainty about government policies led to sharp reserve movements for countries with pegged exchange rates and sharp exchange-rate movements for those with floating rates. Prohibitions on private capital-account transactions were used by many countries to limit these effects of foreign-exchange market developments. Some governments also used administrative methods or multiple exchange rates to allocate scarce foreign-exchange reserves among competing uses. Trade barriers and deflation in the industrial economies of America and Europe led to widespread repudiations of international debts, particularly by Latin American countries, whose export markets were disappearing. In short, the world economy disintegrated into increasingly autarkic national units as the 1930s progressed.

Currency depreciation, like tariff policy, is called a *beggar-thy-neighbor policy* when it benefits the home country only because it worsens economic conditions abroad (Chapter 11). During the worldwide depression, beggar-thy-neighbor policies inevitably provoked foreign retaliation and often left all countries worse off in the end.

Considerable turbulence in world markets continued until the beginning of World War II in 1939, in spite of limited moves toward international economic cooperation in the late 1930s. In the face of the Great Depression, many countries had resolved the choice between external and internal balance by curtailing their trading links with the rest of the world and eliminating, by government decree, the possibility of any significant external imbalance. But this path, by reducing the gains from trade, imposed extremely high costs on the world economy and contributed to the slow recovery from depression which in many countries was still incomplete in 1939. All countries would have been better off in a world with unrestricted international trade, provided international cooperation had helped each country preserve its external balance and financial stability without sacrificing internal policy goals. It was this realization that inspired the blueprint for the postwar international monetary system, the **Bretton Woods agreement.**

THE BRETTON WOODS SYSTEM AND THE INTERNATIONAL MONETARY FUND

In July 1944, representatives of 44 countries meeting in Bretton Woods, New Hampshire, drafted and signed the Articles of Agreement of the **International Monetary Fund (IMF).** Even as the war continued, statesmen in the Allied countries were looking ahead to the economic needs of the postwar world. Remembering the disastrous economic events of the interwar period, they hoped to design an international monetary system that would foster full employment and price stability while allowing individual countries to attain external balance without imposing restrictions on international trade.[8]

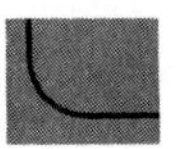

The system set up by the Bretton Woods agreement called for fixed exchange rates against the U.S. dollar and an unvarying dollar price of gold—$35 an ounce. Member countries held their official international reserves largely in the form of gold or dollar assets and had the right to sell dollars to

[8]The same conference set up a second institution, the World Bank, whose goals were to help the belligerents rebuild their shattered economies and to help the former colonial territories develop and modernize theirs. Only in 1947 was the General Agreement on Tariffs and Trade (GATT) inaugurated as a forum for multilateral reduction of the trade barriers set up before and during the war. The GATT was meant as a prelude to the creation of an International Trade Organization (ITO) whose goals in the trade area would parallel those of the IMF in the financial area. Unfortunately, the ITO was doomed by the failures of Congress and Parliament to ratify its charter.

the Federal Reserve for gold at the official price. The system was thus a gold-exchange standard, in which the dollar was the principal reserve currency. In the terminology of Chapter 17, the dollar was the "*N*th currency" in terms of which the $N - 1$ exchange rates of the system were defined. The United States itself intervened only rarely in the foreign-exchange market. Usually, the $N - 1$ foreign central banks intervened when necessary to fix the system's $N - 1$ exchange rates, while the United States was responsible in theory for fixing the dollar price of gold.

GOALS AND STRUCTURE OF THE IMF

The IMF Articles of Agreement were heavily influenced by the disastrous interwar experience of financial and price-level instability, unemployment, and international economic disintegration. The articles tried to avoid a repetition of those events through a mixture of discipline and flexibility.

The major discipline on monetary management was the requirement that exchange rates be fixed to the dollar, which, in turn, was tied to gold. If a central bank other than the Federal Reserve pursued excessive monetary expansion, it would lose international reserves and eventually become unable to maintain the fixed dollar exchange rate of its currency. Since high U.S. monetary growth would lead to dollar accumulation by foreign central banks, the Fed itself was constrained in its monetary policies by its obligation to redeem those dollars for gold. The official gold price of $35 an ounce served as a further brake on American monetary policy, since that price would be pushed upward if too many dollars were created. Fixed exchange rates were viewed as more than a device for imposing monetary discipline on the system, however. Rightly or wrongly, the interwar experience had convinced the Fund's architects that floating exchange rates were a cause of speculative instability and were harmful to international trade.

The interwar experience had shown also that national governments would not be willing to maintain both free trade and fixed exchange rates at the price of long-term domestic unemployment. After the experience of the Great Depression, governments were widely viewed as responsible for maintaining full employment. The IMF agreement therefore tried to incorporate sufficient flexibility to allow countries to attain external balance in an orderly fashion without sacrificing internal objectives or fixed exchange rates.

Two major features of the IMF Articles of Agreement helped promote this flexibility in external adjustment:

1. *IMF lending facilities*. The IMF stood ready to lend foreign currencies to its members to tide them over periods during which their current accounts were in deficit but a tightening of monetary or fiscal policy would have had an adverse effect on domestic employment. A pool of gold and currencies contributed by IMF members provided the IMF with the resources to be used in these lending operations.

How did IMF lending work? Upon joining the Fund, a new member was assigned a *quota*, which determined both its contribution to the reserve pool and its right to draw on IMF resources. Each member contributed to the Fund an amount of gold equal in value to one-fourth of its quota. The remaining three-fourths of its quota took the form of a contribution of its own national currency. A member was entitled to use its own currency to purchase temporarily from the Fund gold or foreign currencies equal in value to its gold subscription. Further gold or foreign currencies (up to a limit) could be borrowed from the Fund, but only under increasingly stringent Fund supervision of the borrower's macroeconomic policies. **IMF conditionality** is the name of this surveillance over the policies of member countries who are heavy borrowers of Fund resources.

2. *Adjustable parities.* While each country's exchange rate was fixed, it could be changed—devalued or revalued against the dollar—if the IMF agreed that the country's balance of payments was in a situation of "fundamental disequilibrium." The term "fundamental disequilibrium" was not defined in the Articles of Agreement, but the clause was meant to cover countries that suffered permanent adverse international shifts in the demand for their products. Without a devaluation, such a country would experience higher unemployment and a higher current-account deficit until the domestic price level fell enough to restore internal and external balance. A devaluation, on the other hand, could simultaneously improve employment and the current account, thus sidestepping a long and painful adjustment process during which international reserves might in any case run out. Remembering Britain's experience with an overvalued currency after 1925, the IMF's founders built in the flexibility of (hopefully infrequent) exchange-rate changes. This flexibility was not available, however, to the "*N*th currency" of the Bretton Woods system, the United States dollar.

CONVERTIBILITY

Just as the general acceptability of national currency eliminates the costs of barter within a single economy, the use of national currencies in international trade makes the world economy function more efficiently. To promote efficient multilateral trade, the IMF Articles of Agreement urged IMF members to make their national currencies convertible as soon as possible. A **convertible currency** is one that may be freely used in international transactions by citizens of any country. The U.S. and Canadian dollars became convertible in 1945. This meant that a Canadian resident who acquired U.S. dollars could use them to make purchases in the United States or could sell them in the foreign-exchange market for Canadian dollars or could sell them to the Bank of Canada, which then had the right to sell them to the Federal Reserve (at the fixed U.S.–Canadian exchange rate) in return for Canadian dollars or gold. General *in*convertibility would make international trade extremely difficult. For example, a French citizen might be unwilling to sell goods to a German in return for inconvertible DM because these DM would then be usable only subject to restrictions imposed by the German government. With no market in inconvertible francs, the German would be unable to obtain French currency to pay for the French goods. The only way of trading would therefore be through barter, the direct exchange of goods for goods.

The IMF articles called for convertibility on *current* account only: countries were explicitly allowed to restrict capital-account transactions provided they allowed the free use of their currencies for transactions entering the current acount. The experience of 1918–1939 had led policymakers to view private-capital movements as a factor leading to economic instability, and they feared that speculative movements of "hot money" across national borders might sabotage their goal of free trade based on fixed exchange rates. By insisting on convertibility for current-account transactions only, the designers of the Bretton Woods system hoped to facilitate free trade while avoiding the possibility that private capital flows might tighten the external constraints faced by policymakers.[9]

Most countries in Europe restored convertibility only by the end of 1958, with Japan following in 1964. Germany also allowed substantial capital-account convertibility in 1958, although this was not required by the IMF articles. Prior to that date, a European Payments Union had functioned as a clearinghouse for inconvertible European currencies, performing some of the functions of a foreign-exchange market and thus facilitating intra-European trade. Britain had made an early "dash for convertibility" in 1947 but had retreated in the face of large foreign reserve losses.

The early convertibility of the U.S. dollar, together with its special position in the Bretton Woods system, made it the postwar world's key currency. Because dollars were freely convertible, much international trade tended to be invoiced in dollars and importers and exporters held dollar balances for transactions. In effect, the dollar became an international money—a universal medium of exchange, unit of account, and store of value. Also contributing to the dollar's dominance was the strength of the American economy relative to the devastated economies of Europe and Japan: dollars were attractive because they could be used to purchase badly needed goods and services that only the United States was in a position to supply. Central banks naturally found it advantageous to hold their international reserves in the form of interest-bearing dollar assets.

INTERNAL AND EXTERNAL BALANCE UNDER THE BRETTON WOODS SYSTEM

How did the international monetary system created at Bretton Woods allow its members to reconcile their external commitments with the internal goals of full employment and price stability? As the world economy evolved in the years after World War II, the meaning of "external balance" changed and conflicts between internal and external goals increasingly threatened the

[9]It was hoped that official capital flows such as reserve movements and World Bank lending would allow countries to reap most gains from intertemporal trade.

fixed-exchange-rate system. The special external-balance problem of the United States, the issuer of the principal reserve currency, was a major concern that led to proposals to reform the system.

THE CHANGING MEANING OF EXTERNAL BALANCE

In the first decade of the Bretton Woods system, many countries ran current-account deficits as they reconstructed their war-torn economies. Since the main external problem of these countries, taken as a group, was to acquire enough dollars to finance necessary purchases from the United States, these years are often called the period of "dollar shortage." The United States helped limit the severity of this shortage through the Marshall Plan, a program of dollar grants from the United States to European countries initiated in 1948.

Individually, each country's overall current-account deficit was limited by the difficulty of borrowing any foreign currencies in an environment of heavily restricted capital-account transactions. With virtually no private-capital movements, current-account imbalances had to be financed almost entirely through official reserve transactions and government loans. (The current-account deficit equals the sum of the private and official capital-account surpluses.) Without access to foreign credit, countries could therefore run current-account deficits only if their central banks were willing to reduce their foreign-exchange reserves. Central banks were unwilling to let reserves fall to low levels, in part because their ability to fix the exchange rate would be endangered.

The restoration of convertibility in 1958 gradually began to change the nature of policymakers' external constraints. As foreign-exchange trading expanded, financial markets in different countries became more tightly integrated—an important step toward the creation of today's worldwide foreign-exchange market. With growing opportunities to move funds across borders, national interest rates became more closely linked and the speed with which policy changes might cause a country to lose or gain international reserves increased. After 1958, and increasingly over the next 15 years, central banks had to be attentive to foreign financial conditions or take the risk that sudden reserve losses might leave them without the resources needed to peg exchange rates. Faced with a sudden rise in foreign interest rates, for example, a central bank would be forced to sell domestic assets and raise the domestic interest rate to hold its international reserves steady.

The restoration of convertibility did not result in immediate and complete international financial integration, as assumed in the model of fixed exchange rates set out in Chapter 17. On the contrary, most countries continued to maintain restrictions on capital-account transactions, as noted above. But the opportunities for *disguised* capital flows increased dramatically. For example, importers within a country could effectively purchase foreign assets by accelerating payments to foreign suppliers relative to actual shipments of goods; they could effectively borrow from foreign suppliers by delaying payments. These trade practices—known, respectively, as "leads" and "lags"—provided two of many ways through which official barriers to private capital movements could be evaded. Even though the condition of international interest-rate equality assumed in the last chapter did not hold exactly, the links among countries' interest rates tightened as the Bretton Woods system matured.

SPECULATIVE CAPITAL FLOWS AND CRISES

Current-account deficits and surpluses took on an added significance under the new conditions of increased private-capital mobility. A country with a large and persistent current-account deficit might be suspected of being in "fundamental disequilibrium," under the IMF Articles of Agreement, and thus ripe for a currency devaluation. Suspicion of an impending devaluation could, in turn, spark a balance of payments crisis (Chapter 17).

Anyone holding pound deposits during a devaluation of the pound, for example, would suffer a loss, since the foreign-currency value of pound assets would decrease suddenly by the amount of the exchange-rate change. If Britain had a current-account deficit, therefore, holders of pounds would become nervous and shift their assets into other currencies. To hold the pound's exchange rate against the dollar pegged, the Bank of England would have to buy pounds and supply the foreign assets that market participants wished to hold. This loss of foreign reserves, if large enough, might force a devaluation by leaving the Bank of England without enough reserves to prop up the exchange rate.

Similarly, countries with large current-account surpluses might be viewed by the market as candidates for revaluation. In this case their central banks would find themselves swamped with official reserves, the result of selling the home currency in the foreign-exchange market to keep it from appreciating. A country in this situation would face the problem of having its money supply grow uncontrollably, a development that could push the price level up and upset internal balance.

Balance of payments crises became increasingly frequent and violent throughout the 1960s and early 1970s. A record British trade-balance deficit in early 1964 led to a period of intermittent speculation against the pound that complicated British policymaking until November 1967, when the pound was finally devalued. France devalued its franc and Germany revalued its DM in 1969 after similar speculative attacks. These crises became so massive by the early 1970s that they eventually brought down the Bretton Woods structure of fixed exchange rates. The events leading up to the system's collapse are covered later in this chapter.

The possibility of a balance of payments crisis therefore lent increased importance to the external goal of a current-account target. Even current-account imbalances justified by differing international investment opportunities or caused by purely temporary factors might fuel market suspicions of an impending parity change. In this environment, policymakers had additional incentives to avoid sharp current-account changes.

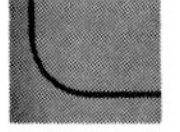

ANALYZING POLICY OPTIONS UNDER THE BRETTON WOODS SYSTEM

To describe the problem an individual country (other than the United States) faced in pursuing internal and external balance under the Bretton Woods system of fixed exchange rates, let's return to the framework used in Chapter 17. Assume that domestic and foreign interest rates are always equal,

$$R = R^*,$$

where R is the domestic interest rate and R^* the foreign interest rate. As noted above, this equality does not fit the Bretton Woods facts exactly (particularly just after 1958), but it leads to a fairly accurate picture of the external constraints policymakers then faced in using their macroeconomic tools. The framework will show how a country's position with respect to its internal and external goals depends on the level of its fixed exchange rate, E, and on its fiscal policy. Throughout, E is the domestic-currency price of the dollar. The analysis applies to the short run because the home and foreign price levels (P and P^*, respectively) are assumed to be fixed.[10]

MAINTAINING INTERNAL BALANCE

First consider internal balance. If both P^* and E are permanently fixed, domestic inflation depends primarily on the amount of aggregate demand pressure in the economy, not on expectations of future inflation. Internal balance therefore requires only full employment, that is, that aggregate demand equal the full-employment level of output, Y^f.[11]

Recall that aggregate demand is the sum of consumption, C, investment, I, government purchases, G, and the current account, CA. Consumption is an increasing function of disposable income, $Y - T$, where T denotes net taxes. The current account surplus is a decreasing function of disposable income and an increasing function of the real exchange rate, EP^*/P (Chapter 16). Finally, investment is assumed constant. The condition of internal balance is therefore

$$Y^f = C(Y^f - T) + I + G + CA(EP^*/P, Y^f - T). \quad \textbf{(18-1)}$$

Equation (18-1) shows the policy tools that affect aggregate demand and that therefore affect output in the short run. Fiscal expansion (a rise in G or

[10]By assumption there is no ongoing balance of payments crisis, that is, no expectation of a future exchange-rate change. The point of this assumption is to highlight the difficult choices policymakers faced even under favorable conditions.

[11]If P^* is unstable because of foreign inflation, for example, full employment alone will not guarantee price stability under a fixed exchange rate. This complex problem is considered below when worldwide inflation under fixed exchange rates is examined.

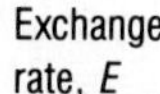

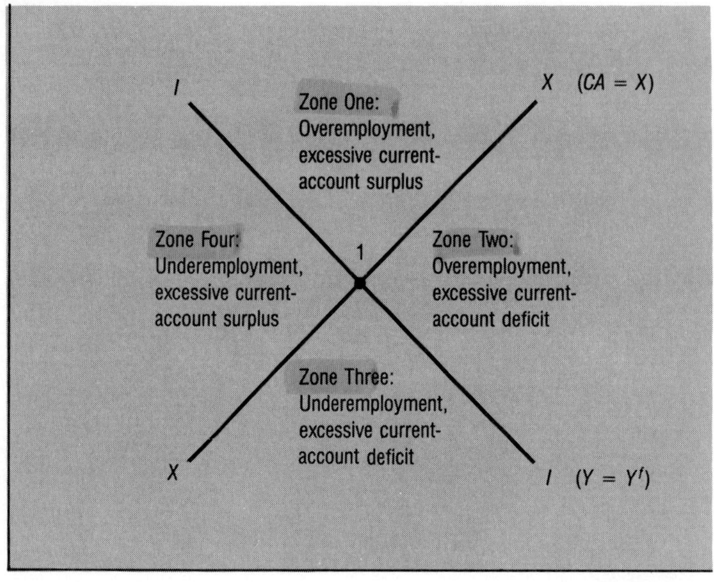

FIGURE 18-1 Internal balance (II), external balance (XX), and the "four zones of economic discomfort." The diagram shows what different levels of the exchange rate and fiscal ease imply for employment and the current account. Along *II*, output is at its full-employment level, Y^f. Along *XX*, the current account is at its target level, *X*.

a fall in T) stimulates aggregate demand and causes output to rise. Similarly, a devaluation of the currency (a rise in E) makes domestic goods and services cheaper relative to those sold abroad and also increases demand and output. The policymaker can hold output steady at its full employment level, Y^f, through fiscal-policy or exchange-rate changes.

Notice that monetary policy is not a policy tool under fixed exchange rates. It is not a tool because, as shown in Chapter 17, an attempt by the central bank to alter the money supply by buying or selling domestic assets will cause an offsetting change in foreign reserves, leaving the domestic money supply unchanged. Domestic-asset transactions by the central bank can be used to alter the level of foreign reserves but not to affect the state of employment and output.

The *II* schedule in Figure 18-1 shows combinations of exchange rates and fiscal policy that hold output constant at Y^f and thus maintain internal balance. The schedule is downward-sloping because currency devaluation (a rise in E) and fiscal expansion (a rise in G or fall in T) both tend to raise output. To hold output constant, a revaluation of the currency (which reduces aggregate demand) must therefore be matched by fiscal expansion (which increases aggregate demand). Schedule *II* shows precisely how the fiscal stance must change as E changes to maintain full employment. To the right of *II* fiscal policy is more expansionary than needed for full employment; so the economy's productive factors are overemployed. To the left of *II* fiscal policy is too restrictive, and there is unemployment.

MAINTAINING EXTERNAL BALANCE

We have seen how fiscal-policy or exchange-rate changes can be used to influence output, and thus to help the government achieve its internal goal of full employment. How do these policy tools affect the economy's external balance? To answer this question, let's assume that the government has a target value, X, for the current-account surplus. The goal of external balance requires the government to manage fiscal policy and the exchange rate so that the equation

$$CA(EP^*/P, Y - T) = X \tag{18-2}$$

is satisfied.

Given P and P^*, a rise in E makes domestic goods cheaper and improves the current account. Fiscal expansion, however, has the opposite effect on the current account. A fall in T raises output, Y; the resulting increase in disposable income raises home spending on foreign goods and worsens the current account. Similarly, a rise in G causes CA to fall by increasing Y.

To maintain its current account at X as it devalues the currency (that is, as it raises E), the government must expand its purchases or lower taxes. Figure 18-1 therefore shows that the XX schedule, along which external balance holds, is positively sloped. The XX schedule shows how much fiscal expansion is needed to hold the current account surplus at X as the currency is devalued by a given amount. Since a rise in E raises net exports, the current account is in surplus, relative to its target level X, above XX. Similarly, below XX the current account is in deficit relative to its target level.[12]

EXPENDITURE-CHANGING AND EXPENDITURE-SWITCHING POLICIES

The *II* and *XX* schedules divide the diagram into four regions, sometimes called the "four zones of economic discomfort." Each of these zones represents the effects of different policy settings. In Zone One the level of em-

[12]Since the central bank does not affect the economy when it raises its foreign reserves by an open-market sale of domestic assets, no separate reserve constraint is shown in Figure 18-1. In effect, the bank can borrow reserves freely from abroad by selling domestic assets to the public. (During a devaluation scare this tactic would not work because no one would want to sell the bank foreign assets for domestic money.) Our analysis, however, assumes perfect asset substitutability between domestic and foreign bonds (Chapter 17). Under imperfect asset substitutability, central-bank domestic-asset sales to attract foreign reserves would drive up the domestic interest rate relative to the foreign rate. Thus, while imperfect asset substitutability would give the central bank an additional policy tool (monetary policy), it would also make the bank responsible for an additional policy target (the domestic interest rate). If the government is concerned about the domestic interest rate because it affects investment, for example, the additional policy tool would not necessarily increase the set of attractive policy options. Imperfect substitutability was exploited by central banks under Bretton Woods, but it did not get countries out of the policy dilemmas illustrated in the text.

ployment is too high and the current-account surplus too great; in Zone Two the level of employment is too high but the current-account deficit is too great; in Zone Three there is underemployment and an excessive deficit; and in Zone Four underemployment is coupled with a current-account surplus greater than the target level. Employed together, fiscal and exchange-rate policy can place the economy at the intersection of *II* and *XX* (point 1), the point at which both internal and external balance hold. Point 1 shows the policy setting that places the economy in the position that the policymaker would prefer.

If the economy is initially away from point 1, appropriate adjustments in fiscal policy and the exchange rate are needed to bring about internal and external balance. The change in fiscal policy that moves the economy to point 1 is called an **expenditure-changing policy** because it alters the *level* of the economy's total demand for goods and services. The accompanying exchange-rate adjustment is called an **expenditure-switching policy** because it changes the *direction* of demand, shifting it between domestic output and imports. In general, both expenditure changing and expenditure switching are needed to reach internal and external balance.

Under the Bretton Woods rules, exchange-rate changes (expenditure-switching policy) were supposed to be infrequent. This left fiscal policy as the main tool for moving the economy toward internal and external balance. But as Figure 18-1 shows, one instrument, fiscal policy, is generally insufficient to attain the two goals of internal and external balance. Only if the economy had been displaced horizontally from point 1 would fiscal policy be able to do the job alone. In addition, fiscal policy is an unwieldy tool, since it often cannot be implemented without legislative approval. Another drawback is that a fiscal expansion, for example, might have to be reversed after some time if it leads to chronic government budget deficits.

As a result of the exchange rate's inflexibility, policymakers sometimes found themselves in dilemma situations. With the fiscal policy and exchange rate indicated by point 2 in Figure 18-2, for example, there is underemployment and an excessive current-account deficit. Only the combination of devaluation and fiscal expansion indicated in the figure moves the economy to internal and external balance (point 1). Expansionary fiscal policy, acting alone, can eliminate the unemployment by moving the economy to point 3, but the cost of reduced unemployment is a larger external deficit. While contractionary fiscal policy alone can bring about external balance (point 4), output falls as a result and the economy moves farther from internal balance. It is no wonder that policy dilemmas such as the one at point 2 gave rise to suspicions that the currency was about to be devalued. Devaluation improves the current account and aggregate demand by raising the real exchange rate EP^*/P in one stroke; the alternative is a long and politically unpalatable period of unemployment to bring about an equal rise in the real exchange rate through a fall in P.[13]

[13]As an exercise to test understanding, show that a fall in P, all else equal, lowers both *II* and *XX*, moving point 1 vertically downward.

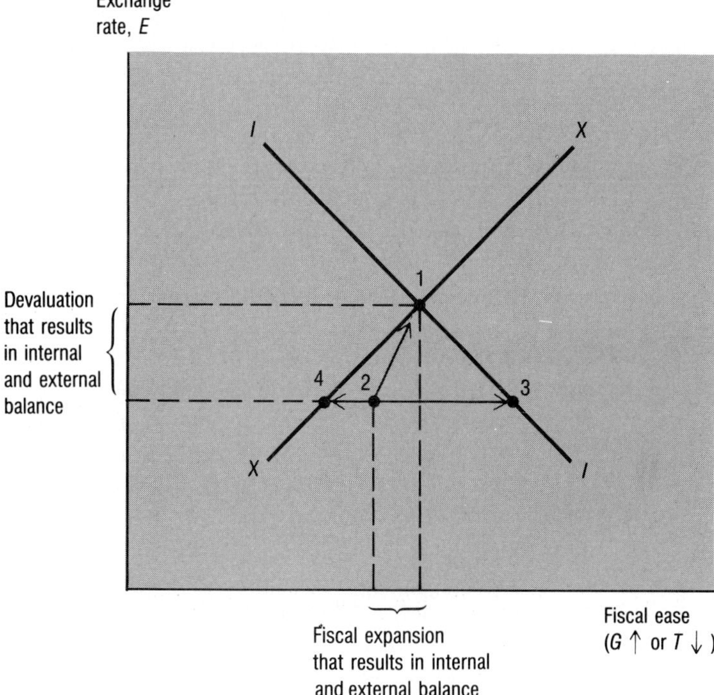

FIGURE 18-2 Policies to bring about internal and external balance. Unless the currency is devalued and the degree of fiscal ease increased, internal and external balance (point 1) cannot be reached. Acting alone, fiscal policy can attain *either* internal balance (point 3) *or* external balance (point 4), but only at the cost of increasing the economy's distance from the goal that is sacrificed.

In practice, countries did sometimes use changes in their exchange rates to move closer to internal and external balance, although the changes were typically accompanied by balance of payments crises. Many countries also tightened controls on capital-account transactions in order to sever the links between domestic and foreign interest rates and make monetary policy more effective. In this they were only partly successful, as the events leading to the breakdown of the system were to prove.

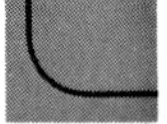

THE EXTERNAL-BALANCE PROBLEM OF THE UNITED STATES

The external-balance problem of the United States was different from the one faced by other countries in the Bretton Woods system. As the issuer of the "*N*th currency," the United States was not responsible for pegging dollar exchange rates. Its main responsibility was to hold the dollar price of gold at $35 an ounce, and in particular, to guarantee that foreign central banks could convert their dollar holdings into gold at that price. For this purpose it had to hold sufficient gold reserves.

Because the United States was required to trade gold for dollars with foreign central banks, the possibility that other countries might convert their dollar reserves into gold was a potential external constraint on U.S. macroeconomic policy. In practice, however, foreign central banks were willing to hold on to the dollars they accumulated, since these paid interest and represented an international money *par excellence.* And the logic of the gold-exchange standard dictated that foreign central banks should continue to accumulate dollars. World gold supplies were not growing quickly enough to keep up with world economic growth; so the only way central banks could maintain adequate international reserve levels (barring deflation) was by accumulating dollar assets. Official gold conversions did occur on occasion, and these depleted the American gold stock and caused concern. But as long as most central banks were willing to add dollars to their reserves and forgo the right of redeeming those dollars for American gold, the U.S. external constraint appeared looser than that faced by other countries in the system.[14]

In an influential book that appeared in 1960, the economist Robert Triffin of Yale University called attention to a fundamental long-run problem of the Bretton Woods system, the **confidence problem.**[15] At the time Triffin wrote, the U.S. gold stock exceeded its dollar liabilities to foreign central banks. But Triffin realized that as central banks' international reserve needs grew over time, their holdings of dollars would necessarily grow until they exceeded the U.S. gold stock. Since the United States had promised to redeem these dollars at $35 an ounce, it would no longer have the ability to meet its obligations should all dollar holders simultaneously try to convert their dollars into gold. This would lead to a confidence problem: central banks, knowing that their dollars were no longer "as good as gold," might become unwilling to accumulate more dollars and might even bring down the system by attempting to cash in the dollars they already held. There was a historical precedent for Triffin's prediction. Recall that in 1931, official holders of pounds, aware how meager Britain's gold holdings were, helped bring down the gold-standard system by suddenly attempting to redeem their pounds for gold.

One possible solution suggested at the time was an increase in the official price of gold in terms of the dollar and all other currencies. But such an increase would have been inflationary and would have had some unattractive political consequences as well. Further, an increase in gold's price would have caused central banks to expect further decreases in the gold value of their dollar reserve holdings in the future, thus possibly worsening the confidence problem rather than solving it!

Triffin himself proposed a plan in which the IMF issued its own currency, which central banks would hold as international reserves in place of dollars. According to this plan, the IMF would ensure adequate growth of the supply of international reserves in much the same way as a central bank

[14]France, in particular, was *not* willing to continue accumulating dollars. President Charles de Gaulle, criticizing the Bretton Woods system for the "exorbitant privilege" it allowed the United States to enjoy, converted a large portion of France's dollar holdings into gold in 1965. But de Gaulle's aggressive action, part of his broader campaign against the alleged "Anglo-Saxon" dominance of the Western alliance, was atypical of the behavior of most countries.

[15]See Triffin, *Gold and the Dollar Crisis* (New Haven: Yale University Press, 1960).

ensures adequate growth of the domestic money supply. In effect, Triffin's plan would have transformed the IMF into a world central bank.[16]

In 1967, IMF members agreed to the creation of the **Special Drawing Right (SDR),** an artificial reserve asset similar to the IMF currency Triffin had envisioned. SDRs are used in transactions between central banks, but their creation had relatively little impact on the functioning of the international monetary system. Their impact was limited partly because by the late 1960s, the system of fixed exchange rates was beginning to show strains that would soon lead to its collapse. These strains were closely related to the special position of the United States.

Case Study

THE DECLINE AND FALL OF THE BRETTON WOODS SYSTEM

The system of fixed parities made it difficult for countries to attain simultaneous internal and external balance without discrete exchange-rate adjustments. As it became easier to transfer funds across borders, however, the very possibility that exchange rates *might* be changed set off speculative capital movements that made the task facing policymakers even harder. The history of the Bretton Woods system's breakdown is the history of countries' unsuccessful attempts to reconcile internal and external balance under its rules.

THE CALM BEFORE THE STORM: 1959–1965

In 1958, the same year currency convertibility was restored in Europe, the U.S. current-account surplus fell sharply. In 1959, it moved into deficit. Although the current account improved in 1960 as the U.S. economy entered a recession, foreign central banks converted nearly $2 billion of their dollar holdings into gold in that year, after having converted around $3 billion in 1958 and 1959. The year 1960 marked the end of the period of "dollar shortage" and the beginning of a period dominated by fears that the United States might devalue the dollar relative to gold. The price of gold in the London market, where most trading then took place, reflected these worries about the dollar's future. Late in the year, the price of gold rose from its official price of $35 an ounce. Only after central-bank intervention in the gold market and a statement from presidential candidate John F. Kennedy ruling out a devaluation did gold's price return to the official level.

[16]Triffin's plan was similar to one Keynes had advanced while the IMF was first being designed in the early 1940s. Keynes's blueprint was not adopted, however.

On the whole, the period from 1961 to 1965 was a calm one for the United States, although some other countries, most notably Britain, faced external problems. The U.S. current-account surplus widened and the threat of large-scale conversions of dollars into gold by foreign central banks receded. Continuing private capital outflows from the United States, which augmented the dollar component of foreign official reserves, were, however, a source of concern to the Kennedy and Johnson administrations. In 1963, therefore, the United States moved to discourage capital outflows by imposing a tax on purchases of foreign assets by Americans. In 1965, further measures to discourage capital outflows were taken.

Early in this period, Germany faced a dilemma between internal and external balance that was to recur more dramatically toward the end of the decade. In 1960, Germany experienced an employment boom coupled with large inflows of international reserves. In terms of Figure 18-1, the German authorities found themselves in Zone One. Attempts to restrain the boom through contractionary monetary policy only succeeded in increasing the Bundesbank's international reserves more quickly as the central bank was forced to sell DM for dollars to keep the DM from appreciating. A small revaluation of the DM (5 percent) in March 1961 moved the economy closer to internal and external balance as output growth slowed and the current-account surplus declined. Although the system successfully avoided a major crisis in this case, this was in part due to the foreign-exchange market's perception that the DM revaluation reflected German macroeconomic problems rather than American problems. That perception was to change over the next decade.

THE VIETNAM MILITARY BUILDUP AND THE GREAT SOCIETY: 1965–1968

Many economists view the U.S. macroeconomic policy package of 1965–1968 as a major blunder that helped unravel the system of fixed exchange rates. In 1965, government military purchases began rising as President Lyndon B. Johnson widened America's involvement in the Vietnam conflict. At the same time, other categories of government spending also rose dramatically as the president's "Great Society" programs (which included funds for public education and urban redevelopment) were expanded. Figure 18-3 shows how the growth rate of nominal government purchases began to rise, slowly in 1965 and then quite sharply the next year. These increases in government expenditures were not matched by a prompt increase in taxes: 1966 was an election year, and President Johnson was reluctant to invite close congressional scrutiny of his expenditures by asking for a tax increase.

The result was a substantial fiscal expansion that helped set U.S. prices rising and caused a sharp deterioration in the U.S. current-account surplus. Although monetary policy (as measured by the growth rate of the money supply) initially turned contractionary as output expanded, the negative

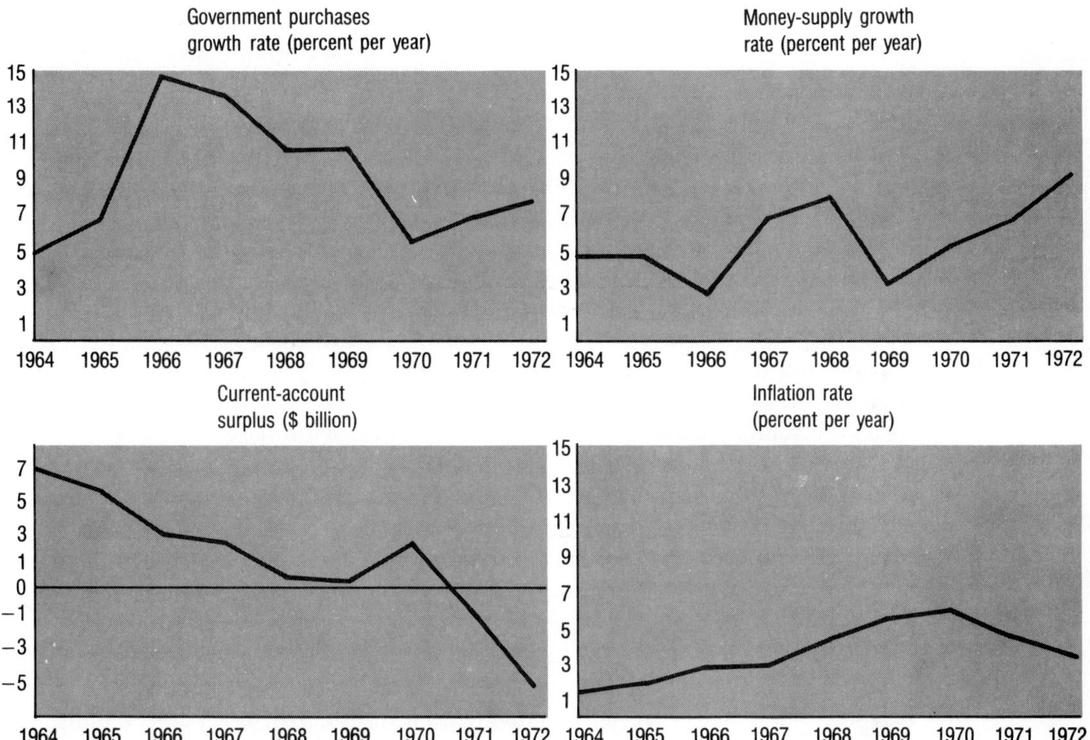

FIGURE 18-3 U.S. macroeconomic data, 1964–1972.
Source: *Economic Report of the President, 1985.* Money-supply growth rate is the December to December percentage increase in M1. Inflation rate is the percentage increase in each year's average consumer price index over the average consumer price index for the previous year.

effect of the resulting high interest rates on the construction industry led the Federal Reserve to choose a much more expansionary monetary course in 1967 and 1968. As Figure 18-3 shows, this further push to the domestic price level left the United States with an inflation rate near 6 percent per year by the end of the decade. Only in June 1968 was a tax increase signed into law. But by then, considerable damage had been done to the U.S. economy and to the international monetary system.

FROM THE GOLD CRISIS TO THE COLLAPSE: 1968–1973

Early signals of future problems came from the London gold market. In late 1967 and early 1968, private speculators began buying gold in anticipation of a rise in its dollar price. It was thought at the time that the speculation had been triggered by the British pound's devaluation in November 1967, but the sharp U.S. monetary expansion over 1967 and rising U.S. inflation probably influenced speculative sentiments as well.

After massive gold sales by the Federal Reserve and European central banks, the Bank of England closed the gold market on March 15, 1968. Two days later the central banks announced the creation of a *two-tier* gold market, with one tier private and the other official. Private gold traders would continue to trade on the London gold market, but the gold price set there would be allowed to fluctuate. In contrast, central banks would continue to transact with each other in the official tier at the official gold price of $35 an ounce.

The creation of the two-tier market was a turning point for the Bretton Woods system. A prime goal of the gold-exchange standard created at Bretton Woods was to prevent inflation by tying down gold's dollar price. By severing the link between the supply of dollars and a fixed *market* price of gold, the central banks had jettisoned the system's built-in safeguard against inflation. The new arrangements did not eliminate the external constraint on the United States altogether, because foreign central banks retained the right to purchase gold for dollars from the Federal Reserve. But the *official* price of gold had been reduced to a fictitious device for squaring accounts among central banks; it no longer placed an automatic constraint on worldwide monetary growth.

The June 1968 tax increase helped push the U.S. economy into a recession by 1970, but, as Figure 18-3 shows, inflation rose in that year. By then, inflationary expectations had become entrenched in the economy and were affecting wage settlements even in the face of recession. Falling aggregate demand did, however, contribute to an improvement in the U.S. current account in 1970.

The improvement in the U.S. current account proved transitory. Adverse balance of payments figures released in early 1971 helped set off massive private purchases of DM in the foreign-exchange market, motivated by expectations that the DM would be revalued against the dollar. On a single day, May 4, 1971, the Bundesbank had to buy $1 billion to hold its dollar exchange rate fixed in the face of the great demand for its currency. On the morning of May 5, the Bundesbank purchased $1 billion during the first hour of foreign-exchange trading alone! At that point the Bundesbank gave up and allowed its currency to float. The alternative was to see the German money supply balloon even further as a result of Bundesbank dollar purchases.

As the weeks passed, the markets became increasingly convinced that the dollar would have to be devalued against all the major European currencies. U.S. unemployment was still high in 1971 and the U.S. price level had risen substantially over the previous years. To restore full employment and a balanced current account, the United States had to somehow bring about a real depreciation of the dollar.

That real depreciation could be brought about in two ways. The first option was a fall in the U.S. price level in response to domestic unemployment, coupled with a rise in foreign price levels in response to continuing purchases of dollars by foreign central banks. The second option was a fall in the dollar's nominal value in terms of foreign currencies. The first route—unemployment in the United States and inflation abroad—seemed a painful one for policymakers to follow. The markets rightly guessed that a change in the dollar's value was inevitable. Their realization led to renewed sales of dollars in the foreign-exchange market that reached a climax in August.

Devaluation was no easy matter for the United States, however. Any other country could change its exchange rates against all currencies simply by fixing its *dollar* rate at a new level. But as the "*N*th currency," the dollar could be devalued only if foreign governments agreed to peg their currencies against the dollar at new rates. In effect, all countries had to agree to simultaneously *revalue* their currencies against the dollar. Dollar devaluation could therefore be accomplished only through extensive multilateral negotiations. And some foreign countries were not anxious to revalue because revaluation would make their goods more expensive relative to U.S. goods and would therefore hurt their export industries.

President Nixon forced the issue on August 15, 1971. First, he ended U.S. gold losses by announcing that the United States would no longer automatically sell gold to foreign central banks for dollars. This action effectively cut the remaining link between the dollar and gold. Second, the president announced a 10 percent tax on all imports into the United States, to remain effective until America's trading partners agreed to revalue their currencies against the dollar. A number of domestic stabilization measures were also announced at the same time, including a freeze on wages and prices aimed at reducing U.S. inflation.

An international agreement on exchange-rate realignment was reached in December 1971 at the Smithsonian Institution in Washington, D.C. On average, the dollar was devalued against foreign currencies by about 8 percent, and the 10 percent import surcharge that the United States had imposed to force the realignment was removed. The official gold price was raised to $38 an ounce, but the move had no economic significance because the United States did not agree to resume sales of gold to foreign central banks. The Smithsonian agreement made clear that the last remnant of the gold standard had been abandoned.

The Smithsonian realignment, although hailed at the time by President Nixon as "the most significant monetary agreement in the history of the world," was in shambles less than 15 months later. A sharp deterioration of the U.S. current account in 1972, together with sharply higher U.S. monetary growth, contributed to market sentiment that the Smithsonian devaluation of the dollar had been insufficient. Throughout 1972 there were further speculative capital flows out of dollars and into other currencies, particularly the DM and the yen. Germany tightened controls on capital inflows to impede reserve movements that were bloating Germany's money supply.

Early in February 1973, another massive speculative attack on the dollar started and the foreign-exchange market was closed down while the United States and its main trading partners negotiated on dollar support measures.

A further 10 percent devaluation of the dollar was announced on February 12, but speculation against the dollar resumed as soon as governments allowed the foreign-exchange market to reopen. After European central banks purchased $3.6 billion on March 1 to prevent their currencies from appreciating, the foreign-exchange market was closed down once again.

When the foreign-exchange market reopened on March 19, the currencies of Japan and most European countries were floating against the dollar.[17] The floating of the industrialized countries' dollar exchange rates was viewed at the time as a temporary response to unmanageable speculative capital movements. But the interim arrangements adopted in March 1973 turned out to be permanent and marked the end of fixed exchange rates and the beginning of a turbulent new period in international monetary relations.

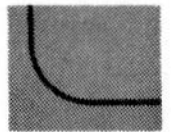

WORLDWIDE INFLATION AND THE TRANSITION TO FLOATING RATES

The acceleration of American inflation in the late 1960s, shown in Figure 18-3, was a worldwide phenomenon. Table 18-1 shows that, by the end of the 1960s, inflation had also speeded up in European economies. The theory in Chapter 17 predicts that when the reserve-currency country speeds up its monetary growth, as the United States did in the second half of the 1960s, one effect is an automatic increase in monetary growth rates and inflation abroad as foreign central banks purchase the reserve currency to maintain their exchange rates and expand their money supplies in the process. One interpretation of the Bretton Woods system's collapse is that foreign countries were forced to *import* U.S. inflation through the mechanism described in

TABLE 18-1 Inflation rates in European countries, 1966–1972 (percent per year)

Country	1966	1967	1968	1969	1970	1971	1972
Britain	3.6	2.6	4.6	5.2	6.5	9.7	6.9
France	2.8	2.8	4.4	6.5	5.3	5.5	6.2
Germany	3.4	1.4	2.9	1.9	3.4	5.3	5.5
Italy	2.1	2.1	1.2	2.8	5.1	5.2	5.3

Source: Organization for Economic Cooperation and Development. *Main Economic Indicators: Historical Statistics, 1964–1983.* Paris: OECD, 1984. Figures are percentage increases in each year's average consumer price index over the average consumer price index for the previous year.

[17]Many developing countries continued to peg to the dollar, and a number of European countries were continuing to peg their mutual exchange rates as part of an informal arrangement called the "snake." This arrangement ultimately evolved into the European Monetary System.

Chapter 17: to stabilize their price levels and regain internal balance, they had to abandon fixed exchange rates and allow their currencies to float. How much blame for the system's breakdown can be placed on U.S. macroeconomic policies?

To understand how inflation can be imported from abroad unless exchange rates are adjusted, look again at the graphical picture of internal and external balance shown in Figure 18-1. Let's suppose that the home country is faced with foreign inflation. Above, the foreign price level, P^*, was assumed to be given; now, however, P^* rises as a result of inflation abroad. Figure 18-4 shows the effect on the home economy.

To understand how the two schedules shift, ask what would happen if the nominal exchange rate were to fall in proportion to the rise in P^*. In this case, the real exchange rate EP^*/P would be unaffected (given P), and the economy would remain in internal balance or in external balance if either of these conditions originally held. Figure 18-4 therefore shows that for a given initial exchange rate, a rise in P^* shifts both I^1I^1 and X^1X^1 downward by the same distance (equal to the proportional increase in P^* times the initial exchange rate). The intersection of the new schedules I^2I^2 and X^2X^2 (point 2) lies directly below point 1.

If the economy is at point 1, a rise in P^*, *given* the fixed exchange rate and the domestic price level, therefore strands the economy in Zone One

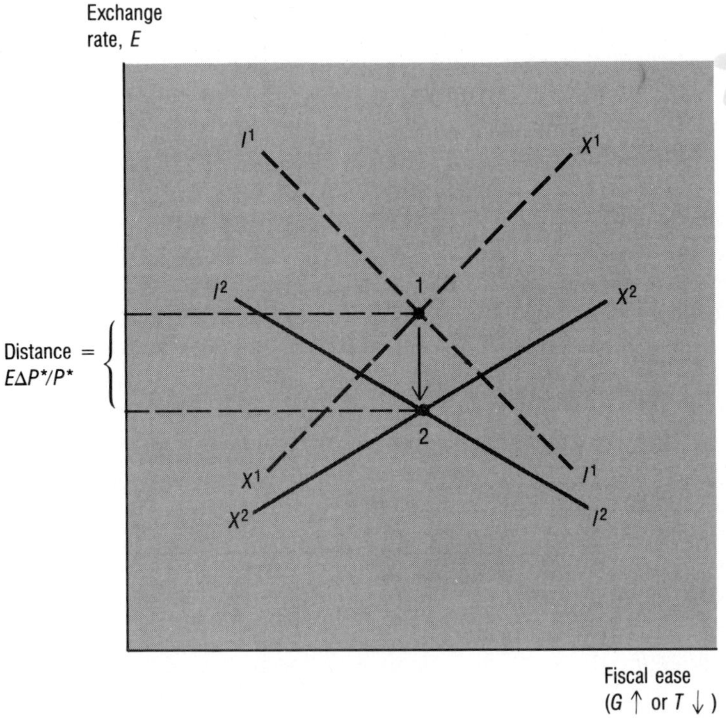

FIGURE 18-4 Effect on internal and external balance of a rise in the foreign price level, P^*. After P^* rises, point 1 is in Zone One (overemployment and an excessive surplus). Revaluation (a fall in E) restores balance immediately by moving the policy setting to point 2.

with overemployment and an undesirably high surplus in its current account. The factor that causes this outcome is a real currency depreciation that shifts world demand toward the home country (EP^*/P rises because P^* rises).

If nothing is done by the government, overemployment puts upward pressure on the domestic price level and this pressure gradually shifts the two schedules back to their original positions. The schedules stop shifting once P has risen in proportion to P^*. At this stage the real exchange rate, employment, and the current account are at their initial levels; so point 1 is once again a position of internal and external balance.

The way to avoid the imported inflation is to revalue the currency (that is, lower E) and move to point 2. A revaluation restores internal and external balance immediately, without domestic inflation, by using the nominal exchange rate to offset the effect of the rise in P^* on the real exchange rate. Only an expenditure-switching policy is needed to respond to an increase in foreign prices.

The rise in domestic prices that occurs when no revaluation takes place requires a rise in the domestic money supply, since prices and the money supply move proportionally in the long run. The mechanism that brings this rise about is foreign-exchange intervention by the home central bank. As domestic output and prices rise after the rise in P^*, the real money supply shrinks and the demand for real money holdings increases. To prevent the resulting upward pressure on the home interest rate from appreciating the currency, the central bank must purchase international reserves and expand the home money supply. In this way, inflationary policies pursued by the reserve center spill over into foreign countries' money supplies.

The close association between U.S. and foreign inflation evident in Figure 18-3 and Table 18-1 suggests that some European inflation was imported from the United States. But the timing of the inflationary surges in different countries suggests that factors peculiar to individual economies also played a role. In Britain, for example, inflation speeds up markedly in 1968, the year following the pound's devaluation. Since (as in the last chapter) devaluation is neutral in the long run, it must eventually raise the domestic price level proportionally. The devaluation is therefore part of the explanation for the rise in British inflation. Strikes in France in 1968 led to large wage increases, a French-German currency crisis, and a devaluation of the franc in 1969. These events partly explain the sharp increase in French inflation in 1968–1969. The role of imported inflation was probably greatest in Germany, where the painful earlier experience with hyperinflation had made policymakers determined to resist price-level increases.

Evidence on money supplies confirms that European and Japanese monetary growth accelerated in the late 1960s, as our theory predicts. Table 18-2 shows the evolution of the international reserves and money supply of West Germany over the years 1968–1972. The table shows how monetary growth

TABLE 18-2 Germany's money supply and international reserves, 1968–1972

Growth rate of	1968	1969	1970	1971	1972
Money supply	6.4	6.3	8.9	12.3	14.7
Official international reserves	37.8	−43.6	215.7	36.1	35.8

Source: Organization for Economic Cooperation and Development. *Main Economic Indicators: Historical Statistics, 1964–1983.* Paris: OECD, 1984. Figures are percentage increases in each year's end-of-year money supply or international reserves over the level at the end of the previous year. Official reserves are measured net of gold holdings.

rose dramatically after 1969 as the Bundesbank's international reserves expanded.[18] This evidence is consistent with the view that American inflation was imported into Germany through the Bundesbank's purchases of dollars in the foreign-exchange market.

The acceleration of German money growth can probably not be explained entirely as a direct consequence of the acceleration in U.S. monetary growth, however. A comparison of Figure 18-3 and Table 18-2 shows that German monetary growth accelerated by much more than U.S. monetary growth after 1969. This difference suggests that much of the growth in Germany's international reserves reflected speculation on a possible dollar devaluation in the early 1970s, and the resulting shift by market participants away from dollar assets and into DM assets. U.S. monetary policy certainly contributed to inflation abroad by its direct effect on prices and money supplies. It helped wreck the fixed-rate system by confronting foreign policymakers with a choice between fixed rates and imported inflation. But the U.S. fiscal policy that helped make a dollar devaluation necessary also contributed to foreign inflation by giving further encouragement to speculative capital flows out of dollars. U.S. fiscal policy in the late 1960s must be viewed as an additional cause of the Bretton Woods system's demise.

Thus, the collapse of the Bretton Woods system was, in part, due to the lopsided macroeconomic power of the United States. But it was also due to the fact that the key expenditure-switching tool needed for internal and external balance—discrete exchange-rate adjustment—inspired speculative attacks that made both internal and external balance progressively more difficult to achieve. The architects of the Bretton Woods system had hoped that its most powerful member would see beyond purely domestic goals and adopt policies geared to the welfare of the world economy as a whole. When the United States proved unwilling to shoulder this responsibility after the mid-1960s, the fixed-exchange-rate system came apart.

[18]The behavior of reserves in 1968 and 1969—a large increase followed by a large decrease—reflects speculation on a DM revaluation against the franc during the French-German currency crisis of those years.

SUMMARY

1. In an open economy, policymakers try to maintain *internal balance* (full employment and a stable price level) and *external balance* (a current account level that is neither so negative that the country may be unable to repay its foreign debts nor so positive that foreigners are put in that position). The definition of external balance depends on a number of factors, including the exchange-rate regime and world economic conditions. Because each country's macroeconomic policies have repercussions abroad, a country's ability to reach internal and external balance depends on the policies other countries adopt.

2. The gold-standard system contains a powerful automatic mechanism for assuring external balance, the *price-specie-flow mechanism.* The flows of gold accompanying deficits and surpluses cause price changes that reduce current-account imbalances and therefore tend to return all countries to external balance. The system's performance in maintaining internal balance was mixed, however. With the eruption of World War I in 1914, the gold standard was suspended.

3. Attempts to return to the prewar gold standard after 1918 were unsuccessful. As the world economy moved into general depression after 1929, the restored gold standard fell apart and international economic integration weakened. In the turbulent economic conditions of the period, governments made internal balance their main concern and tried to avoid the external-balance problem by partially shutting their economies off from the rest of the world. The result was a world economy in which all countries' situations could have been bettered through international cooperation.

4. The architects of the *International Monetary Fund* hoped to design a fixed-exchange-rate system that would encourage growth in international trade while making the requirements of external balance sufficiently flexible that they could be met without sacrificing internal balance. To this end, the IMF charter provided financing facilities for deficit countries and allowed exchange-rate adjustments in conditions of "fundamental disequilibrium." All countries pegged their currencies to the dollar. The United States pegged to gold and agreed to exchange gold for dollars with foreign central banks at a price of $35 an ounce.

5. After *currency convertibility* was restored in Europe in 1958, countries' financial markets became more closely integrated, monetary policy became less effective (except for the United States), and movements in international reserves became more volatile. These changes revealed a key weakness in the system. To reach internal and external balance at the same time, *expenditure-switching* as well as *expenditure-changing* policies were needed. But the possibility of expenditure-switching policies (exchange-rate changes) could give rise to speculative capital flows that undermined fixed exchange rates. As the main reserve-currency country, the United States faced a unique external-balance problem: the *confidence problem* that would arise as foreign official dollar holdings inevitably grew to exceed U.S. gold holdings.

6. U.S. macroeconomic policies in the late 1960s helped caused the breakdown of the Bretton Woods system by early 1973. Overexpansionary U.S. fiscal policy contributed to the need for a devaluation of the dollar in the early 1970s, and fears that this would occur touched off speculative capital flows out of dollars that caused foreign money supplies to balloon. Higher U.S. money growth fueled inflation at home and abroad, making foreign policymakers increasingly reluctant to continue importing U.S. inflation through fixed exchange rates. A series of international crises beginning in the spring of 1971 led in stages to the abandonment of both the dollar's link to gold and of fixed dollar exchange rates for the industrialized countries.

KEY TERMS

internal balance
external balance
balance of payments equilibrium
price-specie-flow mechanism
Bretton Woods agreement

International Monetary Fund (IMF)
IMF conditionality
convertible currency
expenditure-changing policy
expenditure-switching policy
confidence problem
Special Drawing Right (SDR)

PROBLEMS

1. If you were in charge of macroeconomic policies in a small open economy, what qualitative effect would each of the following events have on your target for external balance?

a) Large deposits of uranium are discovered in the interior of your country.
b) The world price of your main export good, copper, rises permanently.
c) The world price of copper rises temporarily.
d) There is a temporary rise in the world price of oil.

2. Under a gold standard of the kind analyzed by Hume, describe how balance of payments equilibrium between two countries, A and B, would be restored after a transfer of income from B to A.

3. In spite of the flaws of the pre-1914 gold standard, exchange-rate changes were rare. In contrast, such changes became quite frequent in the interwar period. Can you think of reasons for this contrast?

4. Under a gold standard, countries may adopt excessively contractionary monetary policies as all scramble in vain for a larger share of the limited supply of world gold reserves. Can the same problem arise under a reserve-currency standard when bonds denominated in different currencies are all perfect substitutes?

5. A central bank that adopts a fixed exchange rate may sacrifice its autonomy in setting domestic monetary policy. It is sometimes argued that when this is the case, the central bank also gives up the ability to use monetary policy to combat the wage-price spiral. The argument goes like this: "Suppose workers demand higher wages and employers give in, but that the employers then raise output prices to cover their higher costs. Now the price level is higher and real balances are momentarily lower, so to prevent an interest-rate rise that would appreciate the currency, the central bank must buy foreign exchange and expand the money supply. This action accommodates the initial wage demands by monetary growth and the economy moves permanently to a higher level of wages and prices. With a fixed exchange rate there is thus no way of keeping wages and prices down." What is wrong with this argument?

6. Economists have long debated whether the growth of dollar reserve holdings in the Bretton Woods years was "demand-determined" (that is, determined by central banks' desire to add to their international reserves) or "supply-determined" (that is, determined by the speed of U.S. monetary growth). What would your answer be? What are the consequences for analyzing the relationship between growth in the world stock of international reserves and worldwide inflation?

7. Suppose the central bank of a small country is faced by a rise in the world interest rate, R^*. What is the effect on its foreign reserve holdings? On its money supply? Can it offset either of these effects through domestic open-market operations?

8. How might restrictions on private capital-account transactions alter the problem of attaining internal and external balance with a fixed exchange rate? What costs might such restrictions involve?

FURTHER READING

W. Max Corden. "The Geometric Representation of Policies to Attain Internal and External Balance," in Richard N. Cooper, ed. *International Finance.* Harmondsworth, England: Penguin Books, 1969, pp. 256–290. A classic diagrammatic analysis of expenditure-switching and expenditure-changing macroeconomic policies.

Barry Eichengreen, ed. *The Gold Standard in Theory and History.* London: Methuen, 1985. A valuable collection of readings on the performance of the gold standard in different historical periods.

Richard N. Gardner. *Sterling-Dollar Diplomacy in Current Perspective.* New York: Columbia University Press, 1980. Readable account of the negotiations that established the IMF, World Bank, and GATT.

Charles P. Kindleberger. *The World in Depression 1929–1939.* Berkeley and Los Angeles: University of California Press, 1975. A leading international economist examines the causes and effects of the Great Depression.

Ragnar Nurkse. *International Currency Experience: Lessons of the Inter-war Period.* Geneva: League of Nations, 1944. Classic critique of the nationalistic macroeconomic policies many countries adopted between the world wars.

Maurice Obstfeld. "International Finance," in *The New Palgrave Dictionary of Economics.* London: Stockton-Macmillan, 1987. Discusses changing conceptions of internal and external balance.

Michael Parkin. "A 'Monetarist' Analysis of the Generation and Transmission of World Inflation: 1958–71." *American Economic Review* 67 (February 1977), pp. 164–171. Proposes a monetary explanation of world inflation under the Bretton Woods system.

Robert Solomon. *The International Monetary System, 1945–1981.* New York: Harper & Row, 1982. Chapters 1–14 chronicle international monetary relations between World War II and the early 1970s. The author was chief of the Federal Reserve's international finance division during the period leading up to the breakdown of fixed exchange rates.

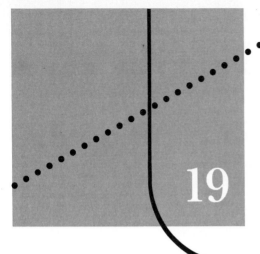

19 MACROECONOMIC POLICY AND COORDINATION UNDER FLOATING EXCHANGE RATES

As the Bretton Woods system of fixed exchange rates began to show signs of strain in the late 1960s, many economists recommended that countries allow currency values to be determined freely in the foreign-exchange market. When the governments of the industrialized countries adopted floating exchange rates early in 1973, they viewed their step as a temporary emergency measure and were not consciously following the advice of the economists then advocating a permanent floating-rate system. So far, however, it has proved impossible to put the fixed-rate system back together again: the dollar exchange rates of the industrialized countries have continued to float since 1973.

The advocates of floating saw it as a way out of the conflicts between internal and external balance that often arose under the rigid Bretton Woods exchange rates. By the mid-1980s, however, economists and policymakers had become more skeptical about the benefits of an international monetary system based on floating rates. Some critics describe the post-1973 currency arrangements as an international monetary "nonsystem," a free-for-all in which national macroeconomic policies are continually at odds. Many observers now feel that the current exchange-rate system is badly in need of reform.

Why has the performance of floating rates been so disappointing, and what direction should reform of the current system take? In this chapter our models of fixed and floating exchange rates are applied to examine the recent performance of floating rates and to compare the macroeconomic policy problems of different exchange-rate regimes.

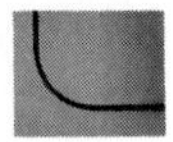

THE CASE FOR FLOATING EXCHANGE RATES

As international currency crises of increasing scope and frequency erupted in the late 1960s, most economists began advocating greater flexibility of exchange rates. Many of them argued that a system of floating exchange rates (one in which central banks did not intervene in the foreign-exchange market to fix rates) would not only automatically ensure exchange-rate flexibility but would also produce several other benefits for the world economy. The case for floating exchange rates rested on three major claims:

1. *Monetary policy autonomy.* If central banks were no longer obliged to intervene in currency markets to fix exchange rates, governments would be able to use monetary policy to reach internal and external balance. Further, no country would be forced to "import" inflation (or deflation) from abroad.

2. *Symmetry.* Under a system of floating rates the inherent asymmetries of Bretton Woods would disappear and the United States would no longer be able to set world monetary conditions all by itself. At the same time, the United States would have the same opportunity as other countries to influence its exchange rate against foreign currencies.

3. *Exchange rates as automatic stabilizers.* Even in the absence of an active monetary policy, the swift adjustment of market-determined exchange rates would help countries maintain internal and external balance in the face of changes in aggregate demand. The long and agonizing periods of speculation preceding exchange-rate realignments under the Bretton Woods rules would not occur under floating.

MONETARY POLICY AUTONOMY

Under the Bretton Woods fixed-rate system, countries other than the United States had little scope to use monetary policy to attain internal and external balance. Monetary policy was weakened by the mechanism of offsetting capital flows (discussed in Chapter 17). A central-bank purchase of domestic assets, for example, would put temporary downward pressure on the domestic interest rate and cause the domestic currency to weaken in the foreign-exchange market. The exchange rate then had to be propped through central-bank sales of official foreign reserves. Pressure on the interest and exchange rates disappeared, however, only when official reserve losses had driven the domestic money supply back down to its original level. Thus, in the closing years of fixed exchange rates, central banks imposed increasingly stringent restrictions on international payments to keep control over their money supplies. These restrictions were only partially successful in strengthening monetary policy, and they had the damaging side effect of distorting international trade.

Advocates of floating rates pointed out that removal of the obligation to peg currency values would restore monetary control to central banks. If, for example, the central bank faced unemployment and wished to expand its money supply in response, there would no longer be any legal barrier to the resulting fall in the home interest rate and the currency depreciation this would cause. As in the analysis of Chapter 16, the currency depreciation would reduce unemployment by lowering the relative price of domestic products and increasing world demand for them. Similarly, the central bank of an overheated economy could cool activity down by contracting the money supply without worrying that undesired reserve inflows would undermine its stabilization effort. Enhanced control over monetary policy would allow countries to dismantle their distortionary barriers to international payments.

Advocates of floating also argued that floating rates would allow each country to choose its own desired long-run inflation rate rather than passively importing the inflation rate established abroad. We saw in the last chapter that a country faced with a rise in the foreign price level will be thrown out of balance and eventually will import the foreign inflation if it holds its exchange rate fixed: by the end of the 1960s many countries felt that they were importing inflation from the United States. By revaluing its currency—that is, by lowering the domestic-currency price of foreign currency—a country can insulate itself completely from an increase in foreign prices, and so remain in internal and external balance. One of the most telling arguments in favor of floating rates was their automatic ability, in theory, to bring about exchange-rate changes that insulate economies from foreign inflation.

The mechanism behind this insulation is purchasing power parity (Chapter 15). Recall that when all changes in the world economy are monetary, exchange rates move in the long run to offset exactly national differences in inflation. If U.S. monetary growth leads to a doubling of the U.S. price level, while Germany's price level remains constant, for example, PPP predicts that the DM price of the dollar will ultimately be halved. This nominal exchange-rate change leaves the *real* exchange rate betweeen the dollar and DM unchanged and thus maintains Germany's internal and external balance. In other words, the long-run exchange-rate change predicted by PPP is exactly the change that insulates Germany from U.S. inflation.

A money-induced increase in U.S. prices also causes an *immediate* appreciation of foreign currencies against the dollar when the exchange rate floats. In the short run, the size of this appreciation can differ from what

PPP predicts, but the foreign-exchange speculators who might have mounted an attack on fixed dollar exchange rates play a beneficial role in speeding the adjustment of floating rates. Since they know that foreign currencies will appreciate according to PPP in the long run, they act on their expectations and push exchange rates quickly to long-run levels.

Countries operating under the Bretton Woods rules were forced to choose between matching U.S. inflation to hold their dollar exchange rates fixed or deliberately revaluing their currencies in proportion to the rise in U.S. prices. Under floating, however, the foreign-exchange market automatically brings about the exchange-rate changes that shield countries from U.S. inflation. Since this outcome does not require any government policy decisions, the revaluation crises that would have occurred under fixed rates are avoided.[1]

SYMMETRY

The second argument put forward by the advocates of floating was that abandonment of the Bretton Woods system would remove the asymmetries that caused so much international disagreement in the 1960s and early 1970s. There were two main asymmetries, both the result of the dollar's central role in the international monetary system. First, because central banks pegged their currencies to the dollar and accumulated dollars as international reserves, the United States Federal Reserve played the leading role in determining the world money supply and central banks abroad had little scope to determine their own domestic money supplies. Second, any foreign country could devalue its currency against the dollar in conditions of "fundamental disequilibrium," but the system's rules did not give the United States the option of devaluing against foreign currencies. Thus, when the dollar was at last devalued in August 1971, it was only after a long and economically disruptive period of multilateral negotiation.

A system of floating exchange rates, its proponents argued, would do away with these asymmetries. Since countries would no longer peg dollar exchange rates or need to hold dollar reserves for this purpose, each would be in a position to guide monetary conditions at home. For the same reason, the United States would not face any special obstacle to altering its exchange rate through monetary or fiscal policies. All countries' exchange rates would be determined symmetrically by the foreign-exchange market, not by government decisions.[2]

[1]Countries can also avoid importing undesired *deflation* by floating, since the analysis above goes through, in reverse, for a fall in the foreign price level.

[2]The symmetry argument is not an argument against fixed-rate systems in general, but an argument against the specific type of fixed-exchange-rate system that broke down in the early 1970s. As we saw in Chapter 17, a fixed-rate system based on a gold standard can be completely symmetric. The creation of an artificial reserve asset, the SDR, in the late 1960s was an attempt to attain the symmetry of a gold standard without the other drawbacks of that system.

EXCHANGE RATES AS AUTOMATIC STABILIZERS

The third argument in favor of floating rates concerned their ability, theoretically, to promote swift and relatively painless adjustment to certain types of economic changes. One such change, discussed above, is foreign inflation. Figure 19-1, which uses the *DD-AA* model, examines another type of change by comparing the economy's response under a fixed and a floating exchange rate to a temporary fall in foreign demand for its exports.

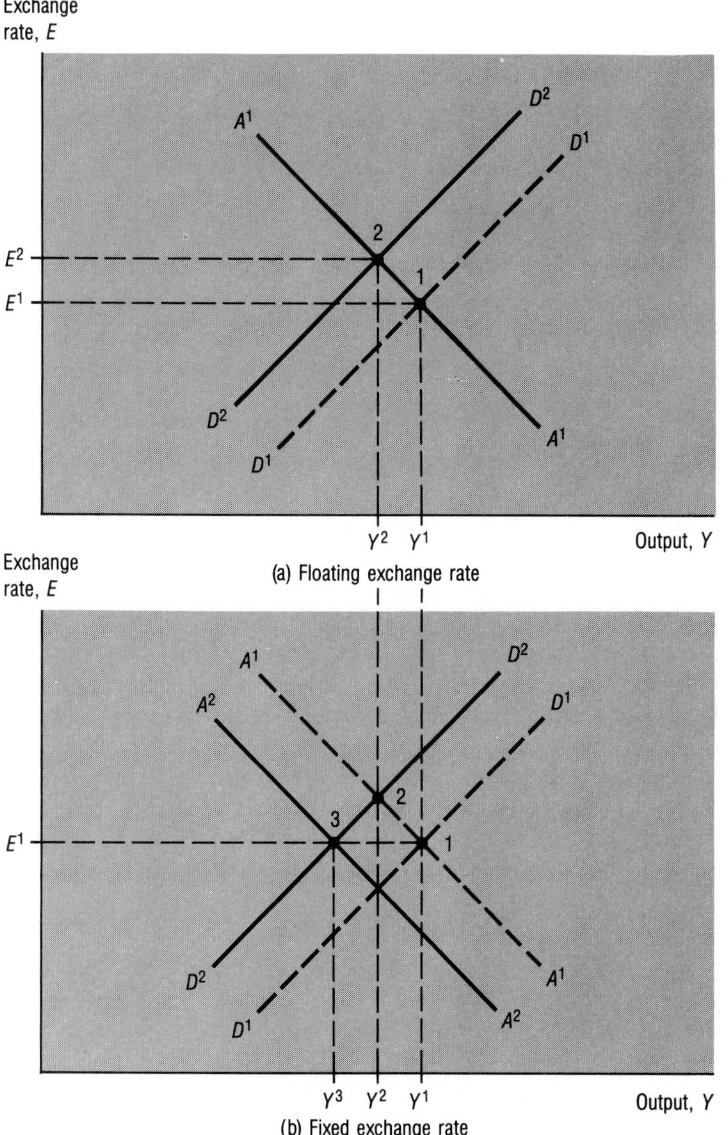

FIGURE 19-1 Effects of a fall in export demand under floating and fixed exchange rates. With a floating rate (a), output falls only to Y^2 as the currency's depreciation shifts demand back toward domestic goods. With a fixed rate (b), output falls all the way to Y^3 as the central bank reduces the money supply.

A fall in demand for the home country's exports reduces aggregate demand for every level of the exchange rate, E, and so shifts the DD schedule leftward from D^1D^1 to D^2D^2. (Recall that the DD schedule shows exchange rate and output pairs for which aggregate demand equals aggregate supply.) Figure 19-1a shows how this shift affects the economy's equilibrium when the exchange rate floats. Because the demand shift is assumed to be temporary, it does not change the long-run expected exchange rate and so does not move the asset-market equilibrium schedule A^1A^1. (Recall that the AA schedule shows exchange rate and output pairs at which the foreign-exchange market and the domestic money market are in equilibrium.) The economy's short-run equilibrium is therefore at point 2; compared with the initial equilibrium at point 1, the currency depreciates (E rises) and output falls. Why does the exchange rate rise from E^1 to E^2? As demand and output fall, reducing the transactions demand for money, the home interest rate must also decline to keep the money market in equilibrium. This fall in the home interest rate causes the domestic currency to depreciate in the foreign-exchange market, and the exchange rate therefore rises from E^1 to E^2.

The effect of the same export-demand disturbance under a fixed exchange rate is shown in Figure 19-1b. Since the central bank must prevent the currency depreciation that occurs under a floating rate, it buys domestic money with foreign currency, an action that contracts the money supply and shifts A^1A^1 left to A^2A^2. The new short-run equilibrium of the economy under a fixed exchange rate is at point 3, where output equals Y^3.

Figure 19-1 shows that output actually falls more under a fixed rate than under a floating rate, dropping all the way to Y^3 rather than Y^2. In other words, the movement of the floating exchange rate stabilizes the economy by reducing the shock's effect on employment relative to its effect under a fixed rate. Currency depreciation in the floating-rate case makes domestic goods and services cheaper when the demand for them falls, partially offsetting the initial reduction in demand. In addition to reducing the departure from internal balance caused by the fall in export demand, the depreciation also reduces the current-account deficit that occurs under fixed rates by making domestic products more competitive in international markets.

We have considered the case of a transitory fall in export demand, but even stronger conclusions can be drawn when there is a *permanent* fall in export demand. In this case, the expected exchange rate E^e also rises and AA shifts upward as a result. A permanent shock causes a greater depreciation than a temporary one, and the movement of the exchange rate therefore cushions domestic output more when the shock is permanent.

Under the Bretton Woods system, a fall in export demand such as the one shown in Figure 19-1b would, if permanent, have led to a situation of "fundamental disequilibrium" calling for a devaluation of the currency or a long period of domestic unemployment as export prices fell. In addition, uncertainty about the government's intentions would have encouraged speculative capital outflows under fixed rates, further worsening the situation by depleting central-bank reserves and contracting the domestic money supply at a time of unemployment. Advocates of floating rates pointed out that the foreign-exchange market would automatically bring about the necessary *real* currency depreciation through a movement in the nominal exchange rate. This exchange-rate change would make it unnecessary to push the price level down through unemployment; and because it would occur immediately, there would be no risk of speculative disruption, as there would be under a fixed rate.

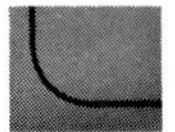

THE CASE AGAINST FLOATING EXCHANGE RATES

The experience with floating exchange rates between the world wars had left many doubts about how they would function in practice if the Bretton Woods rules were scrapped. Some economists were skeptical of the claims advanced by the advocates of floating, and predicted instead that floating rates would have adverse consequences for the world economy. The case against floating rates rested on five main arguments:

1. *Discipline.* Central banks freed from the obligation to fix their exchange rates might embark on inflationary policies. In other words, the "discipline" imposed on individual countries by a fixed rate would be lost.

2. *Destabilizing speculation and money-market disturbances.* Speculation on changes in exchange rates could lead to tremendous instability in foreign-exchange markets, and this instability, in turn, might have negative effects on countries' internal and external balances. Further, disturbances to the home money market could be more disruptive under floating than under a fixed rate.

3. *Injury to international trade and investment.* Floating rates would make relative international prices more unpredictable and thus injure international trade and investment.

4. *Uncoordinated economic policies.* If the Bretton Woods rules on exchange-rate adjustment were abandoned, the door would be opened to competitive currency practices harmful to the world economy. As happened during the interwar years, countries might adopt policies without considering their possible beggar-thy-neighbor aspects. All countries would suffer as a result.

5. *The illusion of greater autonomy.* Floating exchange rates would not really give countries more policy autonomy. Changes in exchange rates would have such pervasive macroeconomic effects that central banks would feel compelled to intervene heavily in foreign-exchange markets even without a formal commitment to peg. Thus, floating would increase the uncertainty in the economy without really giving macroeconomic policy greater freedom.

DISCIPLINE

Proponents of floating rates argue they give governments more freedom in the use of monetary policy. Some critics of floating rates believed that floating rates would lead to license rather than liberty: freed of the need to worry about losses of foreign reserves, governments might embark on overexpansionary fiscal or monetary policies. Factors ranging from political objectives (such as stimulating the economy in time to win an election) to simple incompetence might set off an inflationary spiral. In the minds of those who made the discipline argument, the German hyperinflation of the 1920s epitomized the kind of monetary instability that floating rates might allow.

The pro-floaters' response to the discipline criticism was that a floating exchange rate would bottle up inflationary disturbances within the country whose government was misbehaving; it would then be up to its voters, if they wished, to elect a government with better policies. Besides, the Bretton Woods arrangements ended up imposing relatively little discipline on the United States, which certainly contributed to the acceleration of worldwide inflation in the late 1960s. Unless a sacrosanct link between currencies and a commodity such as gold were at the center of a system of fixed rates, the system would remain susceptible to human tampering. As discussed in Chapter 17, however, commodity-based monetary standards suffer from difficulties that make them undesirable in practice.

DESTABILIZING SPECULATION AND MONEY-MARKET DISTURBANCES

An additional concern arising out of the experience of the interwar period was the possibility that speculation in currency markets might fuel wide gyrations in exchange rates. If foreign-exchange traders saw that a currency was depreciating, it was argued, they might sell the currency in the expectation of future depreciation regardless of the currency's longer-term prospects; and as more traders "jumped on the bandwagon" by selling the currency, the expectations of depreciation would be realized. Such **destabilizing speculation** would tend to accentuate the fluctuations around the exchange rate's long-run value that would occur normally as a result of unexpected economic disturbances. Aside from interfering with international trade, destabilizing sales of a weak currency might encourage expectations of future inflation and set off a domestic wage-price spiral that would encourage further depreciation. Countries could be caught in a "vicious circle" of depreciation and inflation that might be difficult to escape.

Advocates of floating questioned whether destabilizing speculators could stay in business. Anyone who persisted in selling a currency after it had depreciated below its long-run value or in buying a currency after it had appreciated above its long-run value was bound to lose money over the long term. Destabilizing speculators would thus be driven from the market, the pro-floaters argued, and the field would be left to speculators who had avoided long-term losses by speeding the adjustment of exchange rates *toward* their long-run values.

Proponents of floating also pointed out that capital flows could behave in a destabilizing manner under fixed rates. An unexpected central-bank reserve loss might set up expectations of a devaluation and spark a reserve hemorrhage as speculators dumped domestic-currency assets. Such capital flight might actually force an unnecessary devaluation if government measures to restore confidence proved insufficient.

A more telling argument against floating rates was that they make the economy more vulnerable to shocks coming from the domestic money market. Figure 19-2 uses the *DD-AA* model to illustrate this point. The figure shows the effect on the economy of a rise in real domestic money demand (that is, a rise in the real balances people desire to hold at each level of the interest rate and income) under a floating exchange rate. Because a lower level of income is now needed (given E) for people to be willing to hold the real money supply, A^1A^1 shifts leftward to A^2A^2: income falls from Y^1 to Y^2 as the currency appreciates from E^1 to E^2. The rise in money demand works exactly like a fall in the money supply, and if it is permanent it will lead eventually to a fall in the home price level. Under a fixed exchange rate, however, the change in money demand does not affect the economy at all. To prevent the home currency from appreciating, the central bank buys foreign reserves with domestic money until the real money supply rises by an amount equal to the rise in real money demand. This intervention has the effect of keeping A^1A^1 in its original position, preventing any change in output or inflation.

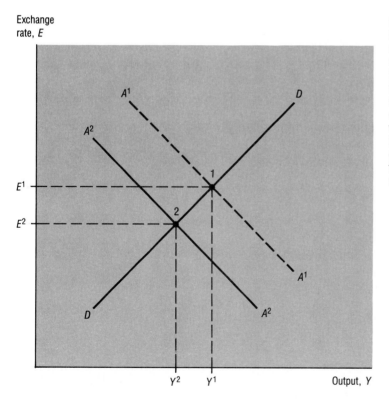

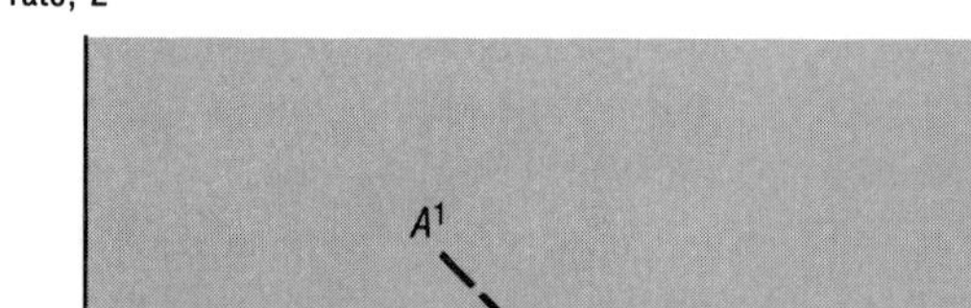

FIGURE 19-2 A rise in money demand under a floating exchange rate. A rise in money demand works exactly like a fall in the money supply, causing the currency to appreciate and output to fall. Under a fixed exchange rate the central bank would prevent A^1A^1 from shifting by purchasing foreign exchange and thus automatically expanding the money supply to meet the rise in money demand.

A fixed exchange rate therefore automatically prevents instability in the domestic money market from affecting the economy. This is a powerful argument in favor of fixed rates *if* most of the shocks that buffet the economy come from the home money market (that is, if they result from shifts in *AA*). But as we saw in the previous section, fixing the exchange rate will worsen macroeconomic performance on average if output-market shocks (that is, shocks involving shifts in *DD*) predominate.

INJURY TO INTERNATIONAL TRADE AND INVESTMENT

Critics of floating also charged that the inherent variability of floating exchange rates would injure international trade and investment. Fluctuating currencies make importers more uncertain about the prices they will have to pay for goods in the future, and make exporters more uncertain about the prices they will receive. This uncertainty, it was claimed, would make it more costly to engage in international trade, and as a result, trade volumes—and with them, the gains countries realize through trade—would shrink. Similarly, uncertainty about the payoff on investments might interfere with productive international capital flows.

Supporters of floating countered that international traders could avoid exchange-rate uncertainty through transactions in the forward exchange market (see Chapter 13), which would grow in scope and efficiency in a floating-rate world. The skeptics replied that forward exchange markets would be expensive to use and that it was doubtful that forward transactions could be used to cover all risks. A long-term investment abroad yielding payoffs over a period of 10 years, for example, could not be covered in the forward market, where the maturities of the contracts available are typically much shorter than 10 years.

At a more general level, opponents of floating rates feared that the usefulness of each country's money as a guide to rational planning and calculation would be reduced. Residents of Germany, for example, would find their currency less useful as a unit of account if its purchasing power over imports became less predictable.

UNCOORDINATED ECONOMIC POLICIES

Some defenders of the Bretton Woods system felt that its rules had helped promote orderly international trade by outlawing the competitive currency depreciations that occurred during the Great Depression. With countries once again free to alter their exchange rates at will, they argued, history might repeat itself. Countries might again follow self-serving macroeconomic policies that hurt all countries and benefit none.

In rebuttal, the pro-floaters replied that the Bretton Woods rules for exchange-rate adjustment were cumbersome. In addition, the rules were inequitable because, in practice, it was deficit countries that came under pressure to adopt restrictive macroeconomic policies or devalue. The fixed-rate system had "solved" the problem of international cooperation on monetary policy only by giving the United States a dominant position that it ultimately abused.

THE ILLUSION OF GREATER AUTONOMY

A final line of criticism held that the policy autonomy promised by the advocates of floating rates was, in part, illusory. True, a floating rate could in theory shut out foreign inflation over the long haul and allow central banks to set their money supplies as they pleased. But, it was argued, the exchange rate is such an important macroeconomic variable that policymakers would find themselves unable to take domestic monetary policy measures without considering their effects on the exchange rate.

Particularly important to this view was the role of the exchange rate in the domestic inflationary process. A currency depreciation that raised import prices might induce workers to demand higher wages in order to maintain their customary standard of living. Higher wage settlements would then feed into final goods prices, fueling price-level inflation and further wage hikes. In addition, currency depreciation would immediately raise the prices of imported goods used in the production of domestic output. Therefore, floating rates could be expected to quicken the pace at which the price level responded to increases in the money supply. While floating rates implied greater central-bank control over the nominal money supply, M^s, they did not necessarily imply correspondingly greater control over the policy instrument that affects employment and other real economic variables, the *real* money supply, M^s/P. The response of domestic prices to exchange-rate changes would be particularly rapid in economies where imports make up a large share of the domestic consumption basket: in such countries, currency changes have significant effects on the purchasing power of workers' wages.

The skeptics also maintained that the insulating properties of a floating rate are very limited. They conceded that the exchange rate would adjust *eventually* to offset foreign price inflation due to excessive monetary growth. In a world of sticky prices, however, countries are nonetheless buffeted by foreign monetary developments, which affect real interest rates and real exchange rates in the short run. Further, there is no reason, even in theory, why one country's fiscal policies cannot have repercussions abroad.

Critics of floating thus argued that its potential benefits had been oversold relative to its costs. Macroeconomic policymakers would continue to labor under the constraint of avoiding excessive exchange-rate fluctuations. But by abandoning fixed rates, they would have forgone the benefits for world trade and investment of predictable currency values.

Case Study EXCHANGE-RATE EXPERIENCE BETWEEN THE OIL SHOCKS, 1973–1980

Who was right, the advocates of floating rates or the critics? In this case study and the next we survey the experience with floating exchange rates since 1973 in an attempt to answer this question. To avoid future disappointment, however, it is best to state up front that, as is often the case in economics, the data do not yield a clear verdict. Although a number of predictions made by the critics of floating were borne out by subsequent events, it is also unclear whether a regime of fixed exchange rates would have survived the series of economic storms that has shaken the world economy since 1973.

THE FIRST OIL SHOCK AND ITS EFFECTS, 1973–1975

As the industrialized countries' exchange rates were allowed to float in March 1973, an official group representing all IMF members was preparing plans for a new world monetary system. Formed in the fall of 1972, this group, called the Committee of Twenty, had been assigned the job of designing a new system of fixed exchange rates free of the asymmetries of Bretton Woods. By the time the committee issued its final "Outline of Reform" in July 1974, however, an upheaval in the world petroleum market had made an early return to fixed exchange rates unthinkable.

Energy Prices And The 1974–1975 Recession. In October 1973, war broke out between Israel and the Arab countries. To protest support of Israel by the United States and the Netherlands, Arab members of the Organization of Petroleum Exporting Countries (OPEC), an international cartel including most large oil producers, imposed an embargo on oil shipments to those two countries (Chapter 10). Fearing more general disruptions in oil shipments, buyers bid up market oil prices as they tried to build precautionary inventories. Encouraged by these developments in the oil market, OPEC countries began raising the price they charged to their main customers, the large oil companies. By March 1974, the oil price had quadrupled from its prewar price of $3 per barrel to $12 per barrel.

The massive increase in the price of oil raised the energy prices paid by consumers and the operating costs of energy-using firms, and also fed into the prices of nonenergy petroleum products, such as plastics. To understand the impact of these price increases, think of them as a large tax on oil importers imposed by the oil producers of OPEC. The oil shock had the same macroeconomic effect as a simultaneous increase in consumer and business taxes: consumption and investment slowed down everywhere, and the world economy was thrown into recession.

TABLE 19-1 Inflation rates in major industrialized countries, 1973–1980 (percent per year)

Country	1973	1974	1975	1976	1977	1978	1979	1980
United States	6.1	11.1	9.0	5.8	6.5	7.6	11.3	13.5
Britain	8.3	15.8	24.1	15.9	15.9	8.3	13.4	18.0
Canada	7.6	11.0	10.8	7.4	8.0	8.9	9.1	10.2
France	7.2	13.8	11.8	9.7	9.4	9.1	10.8	13.6
Germany	7.0	7.1	6.0	4.5	3.7	2.7	4.1	5.4
Italy	10.4	19.5	17.3	16.5	17.0	12.1	14.8	21.2
Japan	11.7	23.3	11.7	9.4	8.0	3.8	3.6	8.0

Source: Organization for Economic Cooperation and Development. *Main Economic Indicators: Historical Statistics, 1964–1983.* Paris: OECD, 1984; and International Monetary Fund, *World Economic Outlook,* April 1985 and April 1986. Figures are percentage increases in each year's average consumer price index over the average consumer price index for the previous year.

Because the price rise raised the import bills of oil importers, it worsened the current-account deficits of many countries. The overall current-account balance of the industrialized countries, taken as a group, went from $20.3 billion in 1973 to −$10.8 billion in 1974, while the overall current account of the less-developed countries that were not major oil exporters moved from −$11.3 billion to −$37.0 billion. The increased current-account deficits of these two groups corresponded to a greater current-account surplus for the main oil exporters. The total current-account surplus of those countries rose from $6.7 billion to $68.3 billion between 1973 and 1974. (Data on 1973–1985 current-account balances for the three major groups of countries described here are given in Table 20-2.)[3]

The Acceleration Of Inflation. The model of Chapter 16 predicted that inflation tends to rise in booms and fall in recessions. As the world went into deep recession in 1974, however, inflation accelerated in most countries. Table 19-1 shows how inflation in the seven largest industrial rates jumped upward in that year. In a number of these countries inflation rates came close to doubling in spite of rising unemployment.

What happened? An important contributing factor was the oil shock itself: by directly raising the prices of petroleum products and the costs of energy-using industries, the increase in the oil price caused the price level to jump upward. Further, the worldwide inflationary pressures that had built up since the end of the 1960s had become entrenched in the

[3]The fall in the U.S. current-account surplus, from $9.1 billion in 1973 to $7.6 billion in 1974, was relatively minor. This was because the United States, itself an oil producer, was less dependent on oil imports than many other countries. In contrast, Japan, which is heavily dependent on energy imports, moved from a surplus of $0.1 billion to a deficit of $4.5 billion.

wage-setting process and were continuing to contribute to inflation in spite of the deteriorating employment picture. The same inflationary expectations that were driving new wage contracts were also putting additional upward pressure on commodity prices as speculators built up stocks of commodities whose prices they expected to rise.

Finally, the oil crisis, as luck would have it, was not the only supply shock troubling the world economy at the time. From 1972 on, a coincidence of adverse supply disturbances pushed farm prices upward and thus contributed to the general inflation. These supply disturbances included poor harvests in the United States and the Soviet Union; shortages of sugar and cocoa; and the mysterious disappearance of the Peruvian anchovies from their customary feeding grounds. Although you may think that anchovies are important only to consumers of pizza and Caesar salad, anchovies are also important to farmers since they are used in the fish meal that is fed to livestock. The precipitous drop in the anchovy catch led to sharp increases in the prices of competing feed grains (mainly corn and soybeans).

Stagflation. To describe the unusual macroeconomic conditions of 1974–1975, economists coined a new word that has since become commonplace: **stagflation**, a combination of stagnating output and high inflation. Stagflation was the result of two factors:

1. Increases in commodity prices that directly raised inflation while at the same time depressing aggregate demand and supply.
2. Expectations of future inflation that fed into wages and other prices in spite of recession and rising unemployment.

Even before the oil shock hit, the move to floating rates had allowed the industrialized countries to adopt more restrictive monetary and fiscal policies aimed at restraining the accelerating inflation. The slowdown in money growth was most dramatic in Germany, where the Bundesbank used its new-found control over the money supply to reduce its annual monetary growth rate from 14.7 percent in 1972 to a mere 2.6 percent in 1973 (compare Tables 18-2, p. 533, and 19-2). A significant monetary slowdown also took place in the United States, where the Fed allowed the money supply to grow by only 5.5 percent in 1973 and 4.4 percent in 1974, as compared with 9.2 percent in 1972 (see Figure 18-3, p. 527, and Table 19-2). These initially restrictive policies helped deepen the 1974–1975 slump.

Regaining Internal And External Balance. The commodity shocks left most oil importers farther from both internal and external balance than they were at the commencement of floating in early 1973. In these unfavorable circumstances, it was inconceivable that countries would sacrifice the expenditure-switching advantages of exchange-rate flexibility and burden monetary policy with the job of defending a fixed rate. No commitment to fixed exchange rates would have been credible in a period when countries were experiencing different inflation rates and suffering from shocks that permanently altered production costs. The speculative attacks that had brought the fixed-rate system down would have quickly undermined any attempt to fix parities anew.

How did countries use their policy tools to regain internal and external balance? As the recession deepened over 1974 and early 1975, most governments shifted to expansionary fiscal and monetary policies. Table 19-2 shows that in the seven largest industrial countries, monetary growth rates rose between 1974 and 1975 as central banks reacted to rising unemployment. As a result of these policy actions, recovery was underway in most industrialized countries by the second half of 1975. At the same time inflation was falling (see Table 19-1). Unfortunately, however, the unemployment rates of industrialized countries failed to return to prerecession levels even as output recovered.

The 1974 current-account deficit of the industrial countries, taken as a group, turned to a surplus in 1975 as spending fell, and was near zero in 1976. The OPEC countries, which could not raise spending quickly enough to match their increased income, were running a substantial current-account surplus in 1975 and 1976, but this was matched by the deficit of the oil-importing less-developed countries (LDCs). Because the non-oil LDCs did not cut their spending as sharply as industrial countries, GNP growth in LDCs as a group did not become negative in 1975, as it did in many developed countries. The LDCs financed their oil deficits in part by borrowing funds that the OPEC countries had deposited in the industrial countries' financial centers. This "recycling" of the OPEC surplus,

TABLE 19-2 Monetary growth rates in major industrialized countries, 1973–1980 (percent per year)

Country	1973	1974	1975	1976	1977	1978	1979	1980
United States	5.5	4.4	4.8	6.6	8.0	8.2	7.1	6.5
Britain	5.1	10.8	18.0	11.2	21.7	16.3	9.1	4.0
Canada	11.1	5.8	23.1	2.0	11.6	8.5	3.6	10.7
France	9.8	11.6	16.7	7.8	11.6	11.1	12.2	7.0
Germany	2.6	8.5	13.6	3.9	11.3	14.3	4.2	3.8
Italy	24.1	10.4	12.2	19.7	21.6	26.4	23.5	13.4
Japan	16.8	8.6	11.2	13.0	7.1	10.8	7.9	−1.5

Source: Organization for Economic Cooperation and Development. *Main Economic Indicators: Historical Statistics, 1964–1983*. Paris: OECD, 1984. Figures are percentage increases in the end-of-year money stock M1 over the corresponding value for the previous year.

which took place over the years 1974–1977, is an important element in our examination of the LDC debt crisis and the growth of international capital markets (Chapters 20 and 21).

Most economists and policymakers viewed the international adjustment to the first oil shock as a success for floating exchange rates. Freed of the need to defend a fixed exchange rate, each government had chosen the monetary and fiscal response that best suited its goals. The United States and Germany had even been able to relax the capital controls they had set up before 1974. This relaxation eased the adjustment problem of the LDCs, which were able to borrow more easily from developed-country financial markets to maintain their own spending and economic growth. In turn, the relative strength of LDC demand for imports from the industrial countries helped mitigate the severity of the 1974–1975 recession.

RAMBOUILLET AND JAMAICA: REVISING THE IMF'S CHARTER, 1975–1976

Because floating rates had seemed to function well in conditions of adversity, the governments of the industrialized countries acknowledged in late 1975 that they were prepared to live with floating exchange rates for the indefinite future. Meeting at the Chateau de Rambouillet, near Paris, in the first in a series of annual economic summit meetings, leaders of the main industrial countries called on the IMF to revise its Articles of Agreement to take account of the reality of floating exchange rates. The participating governments committed themselves to countering "erratic fluctuations" in exchange rates but made no provision for a return to fixed parities.

In response to the Rambouillet decisions, the IMF's directors met at Kingston, Jamaica, in January 1976 to approve a revision of the fourth IMF Article of Agreement, which covered exchange-rate arrangements. The new Article IV implicitly endorsed floating rates by freeing each member country to choose any exchange-rate system it preferred. Governments were urged to follow macroeconomic policies that would promote price stability and growth; and they were to avoid "manipulating exchange rates... to gain an unfair competitive advantage over other members," as had occurred during the interwar period when many countries engineered beggar-thy-neighbor currency depreciations. But more detailed restrictions were not placed on IMF members' policies.

The amended Article IV called on the IMF to monitor members' exchange-rate policies to ensure compliance with the new guidelines. Although this "surveillance" of exchange-rate policies went beyond IMF conditionality in that it applied even to countries not borrowing from the Fund, no mechanism was created to give the Fund clout in influencing nonborrowers' policies. In practice, therefore, the new article did no more than sanction what had already existed for nearly 3 years: a scheme of decentralized policymaking in which each country pursued what it perceived as its own interest.

THE WEAK DOLLAR, 1976–1979

As the recovery from the 1974–1975 recession slowed in late 1976 and unemployment remained persistently high, the United States urged the two other industrial giants, Germany and Japan, to join it in adopting expansionary policies that would pull the world economy out of its doldrums. Only at the Bonn economic summit of July 1978 did Germany and Japan, less fearful of inflation than 2 years earlier, agree to join the United States as "locomotives" of world economic growth. Up until then, the United States had been attempting to go it alone, and its policies, while causing a sharp drop in the U.S. unemployment rate (to 6.1 percent in 1978 from a recession high of 8.5 percent in 1975), had reignited inflation and pushed the U.S. current account into deficit. In contrast, inflation in Germany and Japan had reached relatively low levels by 1978. (See Table 19-1.)

The result of this policy imbalance—vigorous expansion in the United States unmatched by expansion abroad—was a steep depreciation of the dollar starting in 1976. The depreciation of the dollar in these years is evident in Figure 19-3, which shows both **nominal and real effective exchange-rate indexes** of the dollar. These indexes measure, respectively, the price of a dollar in terms of a basket of foreign currencies and the price of U.S. output in terms of a basket of foreign outputs. Thus, a rise in either index is a (nominal or real) dollar appreciation, while a fall is a depreciation.

The dollar's depreciation was an *ap*preciation of the DM and yen, a development that put deflationary pressure on the German and Japanese economies by deflecting aggregate demand away from their exports and toward U.S. exports. To offset this negative stimulus to their economies, the Bundesbank and Bank of Japan intervened heavily in the foreign-exchange market, buying dollars and issuing their own currencies in exchange. This foreign-exchange intervention helps explain Germany's rapid money-supply growth in 1977–1978 and Japan's in 1978 (see Table 19-2). In 1979, after the adoption of the expansionary measures promised at the Bonn summit, unemployment fell in Japan and fell sharply in Germany.

International investors had little confidence in the dollar's future value in view of the widening gap between U.S. and foreign inflation rates. In addition, the weakening dollar helped fuel U.S. inflation by raising import prices and the inflation expectations of wage setters. To restore confidence in the dollar, President Carter appointed a new Federal Reserve Board chairman with broad experience in international financial affairs, Paul A. Volcker. The dollar remained weak in the foreign-exchange market until October 1979, when Volcker announced a sharp tightening of U.S.

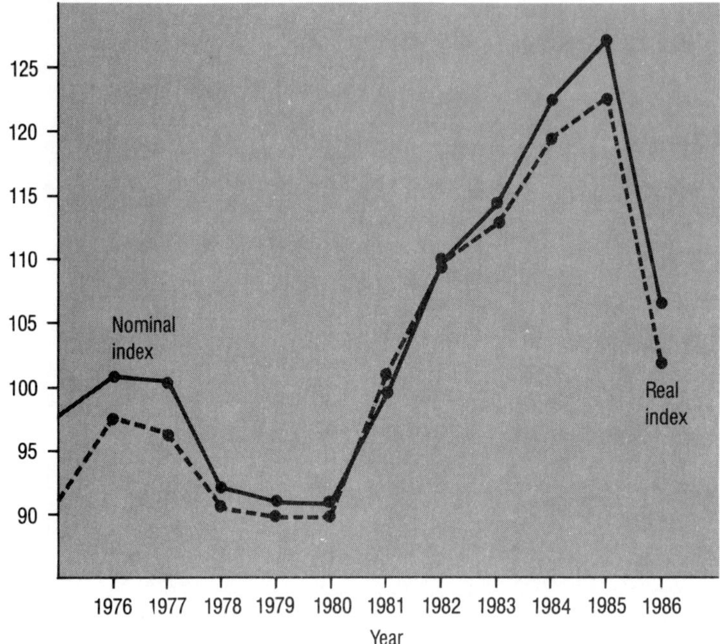

FIGURE 19-3 Nominal and real effective dollar exchange rate indexes, 1976–1986. The indexes are measures of the nominal and real value of the U.S. dollar in terms of a basket of 15 industrial-country currencies. An increase is a dollar appreciation, a decrease a dollar depreciation. For both indexes, the 1980–1982 average value is 100.
Source: Morgan Guaranty Trust Company of New York, *World Financial Markets,* 1986. Indexes for 1986 are averages for January–November.

monetary policy and the adoption by the Fed of more rigorous procedures for controlling money-supply growth.

The German and Japanese foreign-exchange intervention of 1977–1978, along with the sharp U.S. monetary turnaround of 1979, illustrated the truth of one point made by the critics of floating exchange rates. Governments could not be indifferent to the behavior of exchange rates, and inevitably surrendered some of their policy autonomy in other areas to prevent exchange-rate movements they viewed as harmful to their economies.

THE SECOND OIL SHOCK, 1979–1980

The fall of the Shah of Iran in 1979 sparked a second round of oil price increases by disrupting oil exports from that country. Oil prices rose from around $13 per barrel in 1978 to nearly $32 per barrel in 1980 as importers stockpiled oil to guard against possible supply cutoffs. And once again, oil-importing economies faced stagflation as they had after the 1973-1974 episode. Table 19-1 shows that inflation accelerated sharply in all the industrialized economies between 1978 and 1980. Output growth slowed and unemployment rose, particularly in 1980. The oil-importing LDCs were similarly affected by the oil shock.

TABLE 19-3 Unemployment rates in major industrialized countries, 1979–1986 (percent)

Country	1979	1980	1981	1982	1983	1984	1985	1986
United States	5.9	7.2	7.6	9.7	9.6	7.5	7.2	7.0
Britain	5.4	6.5	10.1	11.8	11.4	11.4	11.3	11.6
Canada	7.4	7.4	7.5	11.1	11.9	11.3	10.5	9.6
France	6.2	6.6	7.7	8.4	8.6	10.0	10.4	10.7
Germany	3.3	3.4	4.9	6.8	8.2	8.1	8.2	7.9
Italy	7.7	7.6	7.9	8.6	9.4	9.9	10.3	11.1
Japan	2.1	2.0	2.2	2.4	2.7	2.7	2.6	2.8

Source: International Monetary Fund. *World Economic Outlook,* April 1987.

As in the earlier oil shock, the industrial countries as a group ran a current-account deficit that declined quickly, while the non-oil-producing LDCs ran persistent high deficits rather than adjusting spending downward (see Table 20-2, p. 597). But in contrast to what happened after the first round of oil price hikes, the LDC deficits caused serious problems for the world financial system later in the 1980s. This LDC debt crisis is discussed in Chapter 20.

In 1975, macroeconomic policymakers in the industrial countries had responded to the first oil shock with expansionary monetary and fiscal policies. They responded very differently to the second oil shock. Over 1979 and 1980, monetary growth was actually *restricted* in most major industrial countries in an attempt to offset the rise in inflation accompanying the oil-price increase. Several countries undertook contractionary fiscal measures at the same time. After struggling to reduce the higher inflation of the early 1970s, central banks were now worried that the 1979–1980 upswing in inflation might be hard to reverse later if it were allowed to be built into inflationary expectations and the wage-setting process. The sharp depreciation of the U.S. dollar after 1976 provided an additional motive for restrictive American monetary policy, as we have seen.

The fight against inflation had a high price in terms of employment and output. Unemployment appeared to take a ratchet step upward by early 1981 (see Table 19-3), and restrictive macroeconomic policies ensured that the recovery of output from the shock was feeble compared with the recovery of late 1975 and 1976. In fact, the recovery from the oil shock hardly had time to start up before the world economy, in 1981, plunged into the deepest recession since the Great Depression of the 1930s.

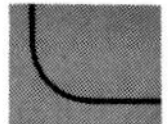

A TWO-COUNTRY MODEL OF MACROECONOMIC INTERACTIONS UNDER A FLOATING RATE

Before discussing macroeconomic interactions between the United States and the rest of the world in the years 1980–1987, we develop a model to analyze transmission of policies between countries linked by a floating exchange rate. The model is applied to the short run in which output prices can be assumed to be fixed.

Imagine a world of two countries, Home and Foreign. In previous models the home country's current-account balance has been written as a function of its real exchange rate and its income. In reality, however, the level of GNP abroad influences foreign demand for the home country's exports, and therefore the home current-account balance. The model of Chapters 16 and 17 implicitly assumed that the home country was too small to influence foreign income, the level of which we took as fixed. The model cannot adequately illuminate recent international macroeconomic developments unless it is extended to apply to large economies like the United States.

As the first step in this extension, we now assume that Home's current account is a function of the real exchange rate, EP^*/P, its own disposable income, $Y - T$, *and* Foreign's disposable income, $Y^* - T^*$, where Y^* denotes Foreign's output and T^* Foreign's taxes. E is the Home-currency price of Foreign's currency and EP^*/P is the price of foreign output in terms of domestic output. Home's current account is therefore

$$CA = CA(EP^*/P, Y - T, Y^* - T^*).$$

A real depreciation of Home's currency (a rise in EP^*/P) is assumed to cause an increase in its current-account balance while a rise in Home disposable income leads to a fall. Our previous model ignored the effect of *Foreign* disposable income on Home's current account, but in a model of two interacting economies we must ask how a rise in $Y^* - T^*$ affects CA. Because a rise in Foreign disposable income raises Foreign spending on Home products, it raises Home exports. A rise in Foreign disposable income therefore causes an increase in Home's current-account balance.

Aggregate demand for Home output is, as always, the sum of Home's spending, $C + I + G$, and its current account, CA. Aggregate supply and demand are therefore equal in Home when

$$Y = C(Y - T) + I + G + CA(EP^*/P, Y - T, Y^* - T^*). \qquad \textbf{(19-1)}$$

Foreign's current account, CA^*, also depends on the relative price of Home and Foreign products, EP^*/P, and on disposable income in the two countries. In fact, in a world of two countries, Home's current-account surplus must exactly equal Foreign's current-account deficit when both balances are measured in terms of a common unit. Since Home exports are Foreign imports and Home imports are Foreign exports, any Home export surplus is necessarily matched by a corresponding Foreign import surplus. In terms of Foreign output, Foreign's current account is

$$CA^* = -CA(EP^*/P, Y - T, Y^* - T^*) \div (EP^*/P).$$

(CA is divided by the real exchange rate EP^*/P, the price of Foreign output in terms of Home output, to convert it into the Foreign output units used to measure CA^*.)

Clearly, a rise in Home income, by worsening Home's current account CA, improves CA^*; in the same way, a rise in Foreign income worsens CA^*. Although the effect of a change in EP^*/P on CA^* is more complicated, we assume that a rise in EP^*/P (a relative cheapening of Home output) causes CA^* to fall at the same time that it causes CA to rise.[4] In the Foreign output market demand equals supply when

$$Y^* = C^*(Y^* - T^*) + I^* + G^* - (P/EP^*) \times CA(EP^*/P, Y - T, Y^* - T^*). \qquad \textbf{(19-2)}$$

Assuming temporarily that the real exchange rate EP^*/P is constant at a given level, Figure 19-4 shows how the Home and Foreign output levels are determined. The HH schedule shows the Home and Foreign output levels at which aggregate demand equals aggregate supply *in Home*. HH slopes upward because a rise in Y^* increases Home exports, raising aggregate demand and calling forth a higher level of Home output, Y. The FF schedule shows the Home and Foreign output levels at which aggregate demand equals aggregate supply *in Foreign*. Like HH, FF has a positive slope, and for the same reason: a rise in Y raises demand for Foreign exports, and Foreign output, Y^*, must rise to meet this increase in aggregate demand. At the intersection of HH and FF (point 1), aggregate demand and supply are equal in *both* countries, given the real exchange rate.

Notice that HH is drawn to be steeper than FF. The slopes of the two schedules differ in this way because a rise in a country's output has a greater effect on its own output market than on the foreign one. To remain on HH, then, a large increase in Y^* is needed to remove the excess supply of Home output caused by a rise in Y. Likewise, to remain on FF, a large increase in Y is needed to restore balance in the Foreign output market after a rise in Y^*.[5]

Changes in fiscal policy at home or abroad shift the schedules by altering government purchases, G and G^*, and net taxes, T and T^*. In addition, fiscal policies also affect HH and FF by altering the exchange rate, E (Chapter 16). Home fiscal expansion causes E to fall (an appreciation of Home

[4]The complication behind this assumption is related to the one behind the Marshall-Lerner condition (see Chapter 16, Appendix II). We have already assumed that a rise in EP^*/P causes CA to rise. But this is not always sufficient to imply that CA^* falls at the same time, even though $CA^* = -CA \div (EP^*/P)$. For example, if Home has a current-account surplus ($CA > 0$), a rise in EP^*/P pushes CA further away from zero, tending to make CA^* more negative than it was, but at the same time pushes CA^* closer to zero by increasing the denominator of $-CA \div (EP^*/P)$—that is, by making Foreign's exports more expensive relative to its imports from Home. These two effects work in opposite directions, but the second will be small if current accounts are initially near zero.

[5]More formally, let s be the fraction of any increase in Home income that goes into saving and m the fraction that is spent on imports from Foreign. Let s^* and m^* denote the corresponding fractions for Foreign. Then an increase ΔY in Home output leads to an excess supply $(s + m)\Delta Y$ in Home's output market, which must be matched by an increase in Foreign demand equal to $(EP^*/P)m^*\Delta Y^*$ along HH. The slope of HH is therefore $\Delta Y^*/\Delta Y = (s + m)/[(EP^*/P)m^*]$. An identical argument shows that the slope of FF is $\Delta Y^*/\Delta Y = m/[(EP^*/P)(s^* + m^*)]$. From these equations, the slope of HH is greater than that of FF when $(s + m)/m^* > m/(s^* + m^*)$, that is, when $(s + m)(s^* + m^*) > mm^*$. This last inequality is always true, however, when none of the fractions that appear in it is a negative number.

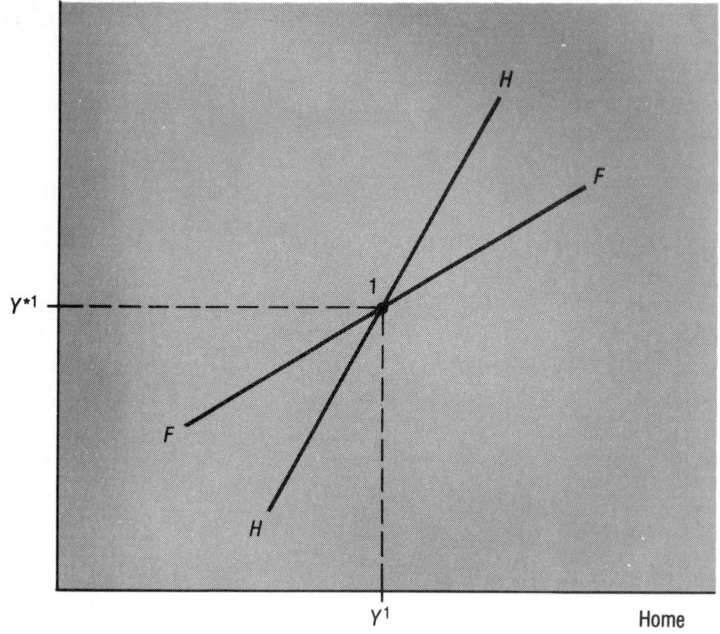

FIGURE 19-4 Output determination in a two-country world. For a given real exchange rate, the intersection of HH (along which the Home output market clears) and FF (along which the Foreign output market clears) determines short-run equilibrium output levels in the two countries.

currency against Foreign currency), while Foreign fiscal expansion causes E to rise (a depreciation of Home currency against Foreign currency). Monetary policies can also move the two schedules by influencing the exchange rate. Both monetary and fiscal policies are at the heart of the 1980s exchange-rate experience, and we now apply our two-country framework to these recent events.

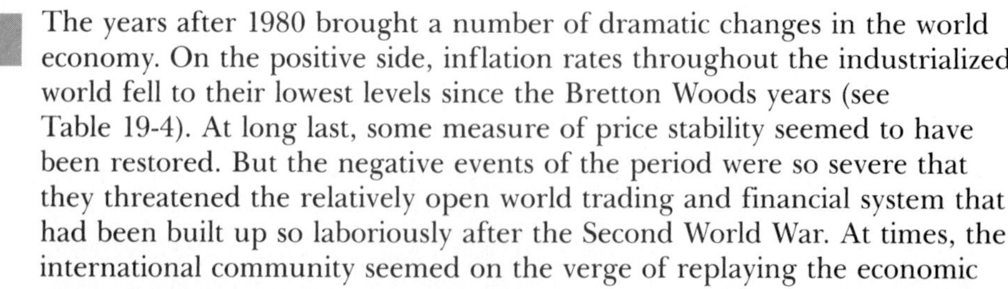

Case Study U.S. POLICIES, THE GREAT RECESSION, AND THE DOLLAR, 1980–1987

The years after 1980 brought a number of dramatic changes in the world economy. On the positive side, inflation rates throughout the industrialized world fell to their lowest levels since the Bretton Woods years (see Table 19-4). At long last, some measure of price stability seemed to have been restored. But the negative events of the period were so severe that they threatened the relatively open world trading and financial system that had been built up so laboriously after the Second World War. At times, the international community seemed on the verge of replaying the economic

TABLE 19-4 Inflation rates in major industrialized countries, 1981–1986, and 1961–1971 average (percent per year)

Country	1981	1982	1983	1984	1985	1986	1961–1971 Average
United States	10.4	6.1	3.2	4.3	3.6	1.9	3.1
Britain	11.9	8.6	4.6	5.0	6.1	3.4	4.6
Canada	12.5	10.8	5.8	4.3	4.0	4.2	2.9
France	13.4	11.8	9.6	7.4	5.8	2.2	4.3
Germany	6.3	5.3	3.3	2.4	2.2	−0.3	3.0
Italy	18.7	16.3	14.6	10.8	9.2	5.9	4.2
Japan	4.9	2.7	1.9	2.3	2.0	0.6	5.9

Source: Organization for Economic Cooperation and Development. *Economic Outlook;* and International Monetary Fund. *World Economic Outlook,* April 1987. Figures are percentage increases in each year's average consumer price index over the average consumer price index for the previous year.

tragedy of the interwar years. Many economists and policymakers began to see floating exchange rates as a major cause of the world economy's problems, and urged a return to more limited exchange-rate flexibility.

DISINFLATION AND THE RECESSION OF 1981–1983

In October 1979, Federal Reserve Chairman Volcker announced an abrupt change in U.S. monetary policy aimed at fighting domestic inflation and stemming the dollar's fall. The slowdown in U.S. monetary growth under Volcker convinced the foreign-exchange market that the Fed chairman would make good his promise to wring inflation out of the American economy. With the November 1980 election of President Ronald Reagan, who had campaigned on an anti-inflation platform, the dollar's value soared upward. Between the end of 1979 and the end of 1981, the dollar appreciated against the DM by 23.2 percent. U.S. interest rates also rose sharply in late 1979; by 1981, short-term interest rates in the United States were nearly double their 1978 levels.

Figure 19-5, which shows the effect of a Home monetary slowdown in the two-country model, will help you understand the effects of the Volcker policy change both in the United States and abroad. By pushing up the U.S. interest rate and causing investors to expect a stronger dollar in the future, the U.S. action led to an immediate appreciation of the dollar. This appreciation made U.S. (Home) goods more expensive relative to Foreign goods, thereby raising the level of Foreign output, Y^*, needed to maintain the demand for Home output at any given level Y. Figure 19-5 shows this change as an upward shift of H^1H^1 to H^2H^2. The appreciation of the dollar (the Home currency) affects Foreign's output market as well; since Foreign output becomes relatively cheaper, F^1F^1 shifts leftward, to F^2F^2.

As a result of the two shifts, Home output falls, Foreign output rises, and the world economy moves from its initial equilibrium at point 1 to a

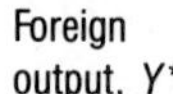

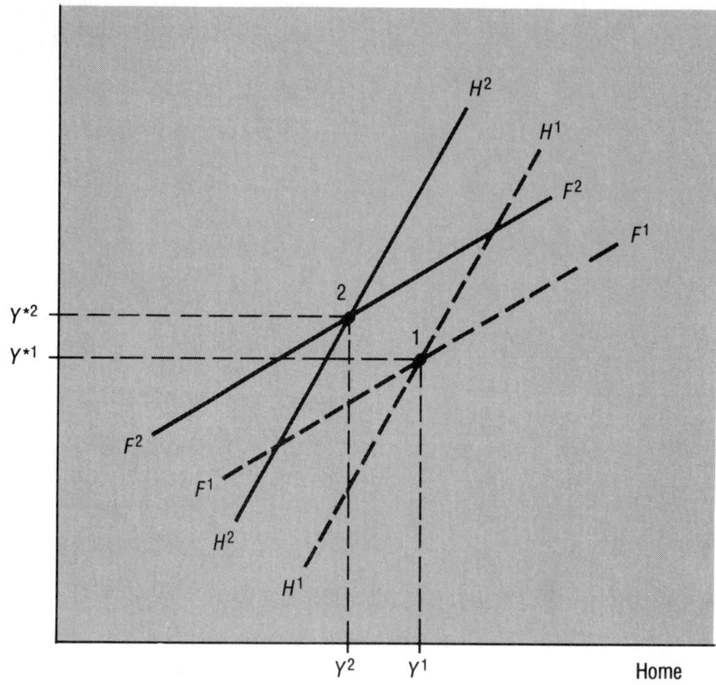

FIGURE 19-5 Monetary contraction in Home. Monetary contraction in Home, by appreciating its currency relative to Foreign's, causes Home output to fall (from Y^1 to Y^2) and Foreign output to rise (from Y^{*1} to Y^{*2}).

new equilibrium at point 2. It may seem surprising at first that monetary contraction at Home raises output abroad, since the fall in Home output causes a direct reduction in Home's demand for imports. This last reduction in Home's import demand is, however, a secondary effect of the initial switch in world spending from Home to Foreign goods.[6]

[6]You may be wondering if it can ever happen that Home output *rises*, which is what would occur if the upward shift of H^1H^1 were less than that of F^1F^1. To see that this outcome is impossible, let Z (a positive quantity measured in Home output units) equal the switch in aggregate demand from Home to Foreign products caused by the Home currency's appreciation and recall the notation introduced in the last footnote. If Foreign demand for Home goods rises by $Z = (EP^*/P)m^*\Delta Y^*$ (where EP^*/P is the new real exchange rate), Home output Y does not change. The upward shift of H^1H^1 is therefore $Z/[(EP^*/P)m^*]$. How must Y^* change to maintain goods-market equilibrium in Foreign, given Y? Since world demand for Foreign products rises by $Z/(EP^*/P)$, a Foreign output increase given by $Z/(EP^*/P) + (1 - s^* - m^*)\Delta Y^* = \Delta Y^*$ leaves aggregate demand and supply equal in Foreign for a given value of Y. The solution of this last equation is $\Delta Y^* = Z/[(EP^*/P)(s^* + m^*)]$, which equals the upward shift of F^1F^1. This number is smaller than the upward shift of H^1H^1. Thus, Home monetary contraction must cause a fall in Home's output.

A similar argument shows that the leftward shift of F^1F^1 always exceeds that of H^1H^1, so that Foreign output always rises. (See problem 6 at the end of this chapter.) The model's predictions would be somewhat more complicated if real interest rates influenced spending decisions (as in Chapter 16, Appendix I).

As the model suggests, the Fed's monetary slowdown did have a negative effect on America's output and employment. The dollar's appreciation was not welcomed abroad, however, even though it may have lent foreign economies some positive stimulus in a period of slow growth. The reason was that a stronger dollar hindered foreign countries in their own fights against inflation, both by raising the import prices they faced and by encouraging higher wage demands by their workers. A stronger dollar had the opposite effect in the United States, hastening the decline of inflation there. The tight U.S. monetary policy therefore had a beggar-thy-neighbor effect on foreign economies, in that it lowered American inflation in part by exporting inflation to foreign economies.

Foreign central banks responded by intervening in the foreign-exchange market to slow the dollar's rise. Through the process of selling dollar reserves and buying their own currencies, the central banks reduced their monetary growth rates and drove domestic interest rates upward. Sales of dollars in the foreign-exchange market contributed to the foreign monetary growth reductions for 1980 and 1981 shown in Tables 19-2 and 19-5.

Synchronized monetary contraction in the United States and abroad, following fast on the heels of the second oil shock, threw the world economy into a deep recession, the most severe since the Great Depression of the 1930s. Table 19-3 shows how unemployment rates moved in the major industrial countries. In 1982 and 1983, unemployment rates throughout the world rose to levels unprecedented in the post–World War II period. You can appreciate the severity of the unemployment rates shown in the table by comparing them with the average unemployment rate for the same seven countries over the years 1963–1972 (a mere 3.2 percent). As Table 19-4 shows, however, monetary contraction and the recession it brought did lead to a dramatic drop in the inflation rates of industrialized countries.

TABLE 19-5 Monetary growth rates in major industrialized countries, 1981–1986 (percent per year)

Country	1981	1982	1983	1984	1985	1986
United States	5.1	8.7	10.4	5.3	11.9	16.5
Britain	10.3	12.3	11.4	15.6	17.5	21.5
Canada	1.1	3.3	8.6	0.3	9.4	14.9
France	14.5	10.5	11.7	9.5	10.0	—
Germany	−0.8	6.6	8.1	5.9	5.3	8.2
Italy	10.2	16.7	12.9	12.2	12.9	—
Japan	10.0	5.7	−0.1	6.9	4.5	10.1

Source: International Monetary Fund. *World Economic Outlook,* April 1986 (table 25), and *International Financial Statistics,* June 1987. Figures are percentage increases in the end-of-year money stock M1 over the corresponding value for the previous year. Dashes indicate figures unavailable as this book went to press.

FISCAL POLICIES, THE DOLLAR, AND THE CURRENT ACCOUNT, 1981–1987

During his election campaign, President Reagan had promised to lower taxes and balance the federal budget. He made good on the first of these promises in 1981 when Congress approved legislation lowering personal taxes and providing fiscal investment incentives to businesses. At the same time, the Reagan administration pushed for an acceleration of defense spending, accompanied by cuts in government spending on domestic programs. The net result of these and subsequent congressional actions was a ballooning U.S. government budget deficit and a sharp fiscal stimulus to the economy. Table 19-6 shows the U.S. government budget surplus, as a percentage of GNP, between 1979 and 1986.

Figure 19-6 illustrates the effects of this fiscal expansion in the two-country world-economy model. Because fiscal expansion by Home causes its currency (the dollar) to appreciate, Foreign products become relatively cheap and world demand for them rises. Foreign output, Y^*, therefore must rise for every level of home output, Y, as represented by the upward shift of F^1F^1 to F^2F^2. The impact of Home fiscal expansion on Home aggregate demand is positive, in spite of the domestic currency's appreciation, and so Y must rise for every value of Y^*. This rise in Home aggregate demand implies that H^1H^1 shifts rightward to H^2H^2. Output goes up both in Home and in Foreign as the world economy moves to point 2 from its initial position at point 1.

The U.S. fiscal expansion did encourage further dollar appreciation (see Figure 19-3), and by February 1985, the dollar's cumulative appreciation against the DM since the end of 1979 was 47.9 percent. The recession reached its low point in the United States in December 1982, and output began to recover both there and abroad as the U.S. fiscal stimulus was transmitted to foreign countries through the dollar's appreciation. Also contributing to the recovery was a looser Federal Reserve monetary policy.

Foreign central banks remained fearful of encouraging inflation through expansionary policies of their own. As easier U.S. money brought dollar interest rates down in the second half of 1982, however, some foreign central banks began to feel they could ease their monetary policies without causing their currencies to depreciate too sharply (see Table 19-5). By early 1984, U.S. unemployment had fallen and U.S. output was growing rapidly. Unemployment remained high in other industrialized countries, however, and the growth of output was slow by historical standards.

TABLE 19-6 U.S. government budget surplus as a percent of GNP, 1979–1986 (percent)

1979	1980	1981	1982	1983	1984	1985	1986
0.5	−1.3	−1.0	−3.5	−3.8	−2.9	−3.5	−3.2

Source: International Monetary Fund. *World Economic Outlook,* April 1987.

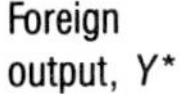

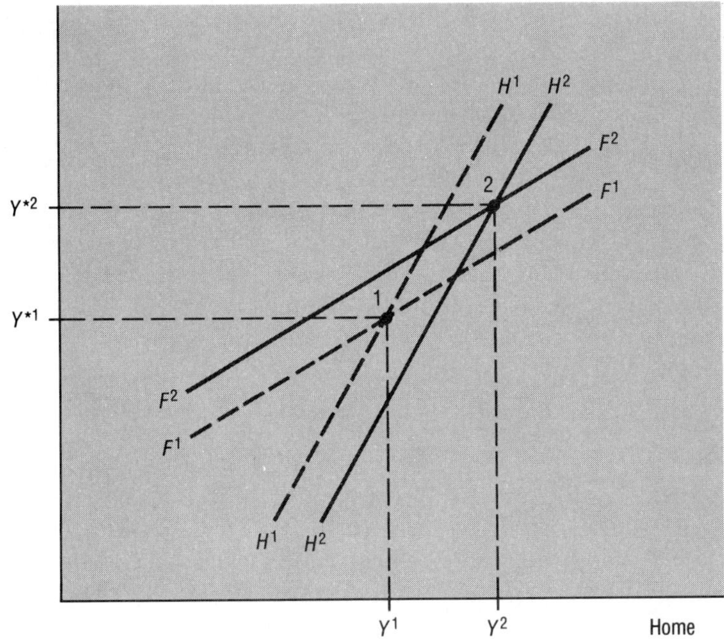

FIGURE 19-6 Fiscal expansion in Home. A Home fiscal expansion raises output at home and abroad.

While the U.S. fiscal expansion contributed to world recovery, growing federal budget deficits raised serious worries about the future stability of the world economy. Increasing government deficits were not met with offsetting increases in private saving or decreases in investment; so the American current-account balance deteriorated sharply (recall Chapter 12's case study of the link between the government deficit and the current account, pp. 293–295). By the end of 1985, the United States had become a net debtor to foreign countries, and in 1986, its current-account deficit was at a record level, equal to around 3.3 percent of GNP. Some analysts worried that foreign creditors would lose confidence in the future value of the dollar assets they were accumulating and sell them, causing a sudden, precipitous dollar depreciation.

Equally worrisome was the strong dollar's impact on the distribution of income within the United States. The dollar's appreciation had reduced U.S. inflation and allowed consumers to purchase imports more cheaply, but those hurt by the terms-of-trade change were better organized and more vocal than those who had benefited. Persistently poor economic performance in the 1980s had led to increased pressures on governments to protect declining industries in the exporting and import-competing sectors. As the U.S. recovery slowed late in 1984, protectionist pressures snowballed.

THE RESURGENCE OF PROTECTIONISM, 1984–1987

By making American exports more expensive for foreigners while cheapening foreign imports, the dollar's real appreciation had reduced demand in several sectors of the American economy, for example, agriculture, textiles, steel, and autos. In late 1984, these sectors stepped up their demands for protective legislation, and an avalanche of protectionist trade bills was the result. As the threat of American trade restrictions grew, foreign governments vowed to retaliate against any restrictive trade measures the United States might take.

The Reagan administration had, from its start, adopted a policy of "benign neglect" toward the exchange rate, opposing any intervention in the foreign-exchange market by the United States. Administration officials took the position that the market was best able to determine the appropriate level of the exchange rate, and the president himself appeared to view the dollar's strength as a market vote of confidence in his economic policies. By 1985, however, the link between the strong dollar and the gathering protectionist storm became impossible to ignore.

Faster U.S. monetary growth in 1985 caused some depreciation of the dollar but failed to reverse Congressional sentiment in favor of restricting imports. Fearing a disaster for the international trading system, economic officials of the Group of Five (G5) countries—the United States, Britain, France, Germany, and Japan—announced on September 22, 1985, that they would jointly intervene in the foreign-exchange market to bring about a dollar depreciation. The dollar dropped sharply the next day and continued to decline through 1986 and much of 1987 as the United States maintained its loose monetary policy. (See Figure 19-3 and Table 19-5.)

The G5 announcement represented a sharp change in the policy of the Reagan administration, a reversal of its opposition to foreign-exchange intervention. As such, the announcement was a strong indication of growing dissatisfaction in government circles with the performance of floating exchange rates. The dollar's subsequent sharp decline helped temporarily to avert a generalized disaster in international trade relations.

The dollar moved differently against different currencies during its 1986 depreciation. The dollar's value against the currencies of some major trading partners (such as Canada and South Korea) changed very little over the year. Against the currencies of Japan and Germany, however, the dollar depreciated by around 30 percent.

Although the dollar depreciated sharply against the yen and the DM, the current-account surpluses of Japan and Germany continued to rise (when measured in dollars) and the U.S. deficit rose substantially. Congress failed to make a dramatic dent in the federal budget deficit in 1985–1986, and without the necessary expenditure-changing policy of fiscal contraction, it is no surprise that the U.S. external balance problem worsened. As a result, the pressures for protection remained a threat. By April 1987, the United States and Japan were engaged in a mini-trade-war over semiconductor chips. This development was in part a Reagan administration effort to head off more wide-ranging congressional action by assuming a "tough" posture in U.S.-Japan trade talks.

On the macroeconomic front, the Reagan administration urged Japan and Germany to adopt more expansionary monetary and fiscal policies. American policymakers hoped that increased demand from those countries would help shrink the U.S. current-account deficit and resolve the trade problem. German officials were unsympathetic, but the Japanese, more vulnerable than the Germans to U.S. protectionist measures, agreed in late 1986 to take stimulative macroeconomic steps. Japanese export industries were suffering from the yen's sharp appreciation, and in return for the Japanese promise of macroeconomic expansion the U.S. tacitly agreed not to seek a further depreciation of the dollar against the yen. Within 3 months the United States–Japanese agreement fell apart as a result of an unexpected drop in the U.S. trade balance. The foreign-exchange market was in turmoil as U.S. officials predicted further dollar depreciation while the Japanese central bank intervened heavily to prevent the yen from appreciating. In early 1987, history repeated itself as the United States and Japan competitively manipulated exchange rates to protect their export industries.

To stabilize the foreign-exchange market, financial officials from the main industrial countries hinted that existing dollar exchange rates would be defended by coordinated intervention. At the same time, Japan advanced a new plan for domestic macroeconomic expansion. These announcements did not stop the dollar from falling further. In the spring of 1987, it became painfully apparent that the market was waiting for concrete policy changes, not communiqués.

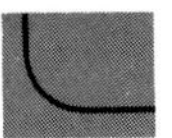

WHAT HAS BEEN LEARNED SINCE 1973?

The first two sections of this chapter outlined the main elements of the cases for and against floating exchange rates. Having examined the events of the recent floating-rate period, we now compare experience with the predictions made before 1973 by the proponents and opponents of floating and ask whether recent history supports a definitive judgment about reforming the current exchange-rate system.

MONETARY POLICY AUTONOMY

There is no question that floating gave central banks the ability to control their money supplies and to choose their preferred rates of trend inflation. A comparison of Tables 19-1 and 19-4 (which show inflation rates over the floating-rate period) with Table 18-1 and Figure 18-3 (which apply to the fixed-rate period) shows that floating rates allowed a much larger international divergence in inflation rates. Did exchange depreciation offset inflation differentials between countries over the floating-rate period? Figure 19-7 compares exchange-rate depreciation against the dollar with the difference between domestic and U.S. consumer-price inflation for the six largest industrial countries beside the United States. The PPP theory predicts that the points in the figure should lie along the 45° line, but this is not the case. While Figure 19-7 therefore confirms the lesson of Chapter 15 that PPP has not held closely, it does show that on balance, high-inflation countries have tended to have weaker currencies than their low-inflation neighbors.

While the inflation-insulation part of the policy autonomy argument is broadly supported as a *long-run* proposition, economic analysis and experience both show that in the short run, the effects of monetary as well as fiscal changes are transmitted across national borders under floating rates. The two-country macroeconomic model developed earlier, for example, shows that monetary policy affects output in the short run both at home and abroad as long as it alters the real exchange rate. The critics of floating were therefore right in claiming that floating rates would not insulate countries completely from foreign policy shocks.

Experience has also given dramatic support to the skeptics who argued that no central bank can be indifferent to its currency's value in the foreign-exchange market. After 1973, central banks intervened repeatedly in the foreign-exchange market to alter currency values, and even the Reagan

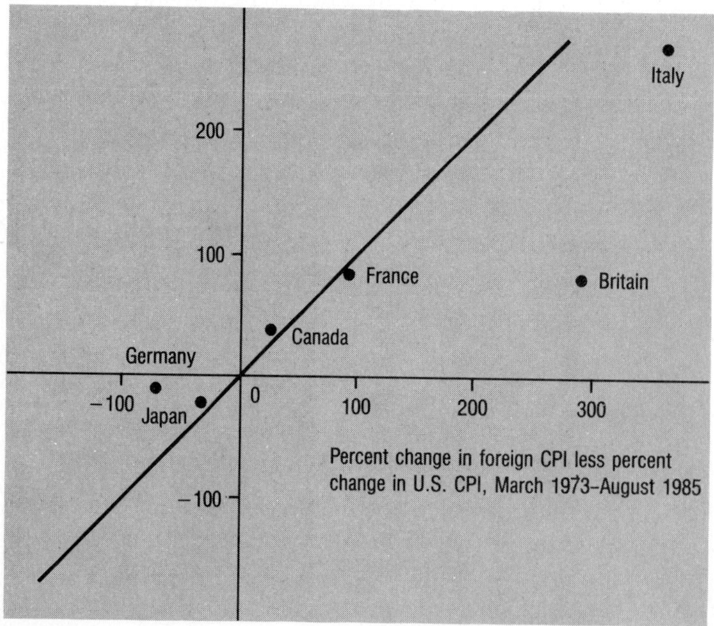

FIGURE 19-7 Exchange-rate depreciation and inflation differentials, 1973–1985. Over the floating-rate period as a whole, higher inflation has been associated with greater currency depreciation. The exact relationship predicted by relative PPP, however, has not held for most countries.
Source: OECD, *Main Economic Indicators.*

administration's laissez-faire policy on exchange rates was abandoned when the G5 initiative of September 1985 was launched. The post-1973 floating of exchange rates is often characterized as a "dirty float" rather than a "clean float" because central banks intervened on a discretionary basis and continued to hold foreign-exchange reserves (Chapter 17). Advocates of floating had argued that central banks would not need to hold foreign reserves, but between 1972 and November 1986, the international reserves of the industrial countries' central banks rose in value from $120 billion to $332 billion.

Why did central banks continue to intervene even in the absence of any formal obligation to do so? As we saw in the example of a change in domestic money demand, intervention to fix the exchange rate can stabilize output and the price level when certain disturbances occur, and central banks sometimes felt that exchange-rate movements were due to such factors. But even in the presence of output-markets disturbances, central banks often slowed exchange-rate changes to prevent sharp changes in the international competitiveness of their tradable-goods sectors. Such changes, if they were reversed later, might generate excessive employment fluctuations, and they could also lead to pressures for protection. Finally, central banks often worried that even temporary exchange-rate changes might have medium-term inflationary effects that would be hard to wring out of the economy.

Those skeptical of the autonomy argument had also predicted that while floating would allow central banks to control nominal money supplies, their ability to affect output would still be limited by the price level's tendency to respond more quickly to monetary changes under a floating rate. This prediction was partially borne out by experience. Monetary changes clearly had a much greater short-run effect on the *real* exchange rate under a floating nominal exchange rate than under a fixed one, and this factor increased the short-run influence of money on output in some countries. In many cases, however, this influence turned out to be short-lived. The quick response of the exchange rate to money-supply changes affected import prices and wage settlements, shortening the time span over which money could alter real economic activity without changing nominal output prices. The link between exchange depreciation and inflation was illustrated by the U.S. experience of 1976–1979 and by the rapid inflation that resulted from attempts by Britain, France, and Italy, at various times, to encourage output growth through monetary expansion. The U.S. disinflation after 1979 illustrated that a floating rate could also speed the translation of monetary contraction into lower inflation.

SYMMETRY

Because central banks continued to hold dollar reserves and intervene, the international monetary system did not become symmetric after 1973. The DM gained in importance as an international reserve currency (and the British pound declined), but the dollar remained the primary component of most central banks' official reserves.

Economist Ronald McKinnon of Stanford University has argued that the current floating-rate system is similar in some ways to the asymmetric reserve-currency system underlying the Bretton Woods arrangements.[7] When Germany and Japan intervened in 1977–1978 to prevent their currencies from appreciating in the face of rapid U.S. monetary growth, their own money supplies expanded with no offsetting reduction in U.S. money. McKinnon suggests that this increase in the world money supply, which would have been dampened under a more symmetric monetary adjustment mechanism, helped fuel the synchronized upswing in industrial-country inflation rates at the end of the 1970s. Similarly, foreign intervention to slow the dollar's rise after 1979 led to monetary contraction abroad with no symmetric increase in the U.S. money supply. The resulting world monetary crunch was harsher because of this asymmetry, which therefore helped deepen the recession that followed.

THE EXCHANGE RATE AS AN AUTOMATIC STABILIZER

The world economy has undergone major structural changes since 1973. Because these shifts changed relative national output prices (Figure 19-7), it is doubtful that any pattern of fixed exchange rates would have been viable without some significant parity changes. The industrial economies certainly wouldn't have weathered the two oil shocks as well as they did while defending fixed exchange rates. In the absence of capital controls, speculative attacks similar to those that brought down the Bretton Woods system would have occurred periodically. Under floating, however, many countries were able to relax the capital controls put in place earlier. The progressive loosening of controls spurred the rapid growth of a global financial industry and allowed countries to realize greater gains from intertemporal trade.

The effects of the U.S. fiscal expansion after 1981 illustrate the stabilizing properties of a floating exchange rate. As the dollar appreciated, U.S. inflation was slowed, American consumers enjoyed an improvement in their terms of trade, and economic recovery was spread abroad.

The dollar's appreciation after 1981 also illustrates a problem with the view that floating rates can cushion the economy from real disturbances such as shifts in aggregate demand. Even though *overall* output and the price level may be cushioned, some sectors of the economy may be hurt. For example, while the dollar's appreciation helped transmit U.S. fiscal expansion abroad in the 1980s, it worsened the plight of American agriculture, which did not benefit directly from the higher government demand. Real exchange-rate changes can do damage by causing excessive adjustment problems in some sectors and by generating calls for increased protection.

Permanent changes in goods-market conditions require eventual adjustment in real exchange rates which can be speeded by a floating-rate system.

[7]Ronald I. McKinnon, *An International Standard for Monetary Stabilization*, Policy Analyses in International Economics 8 (Washington, D.C.: Institute for International Economics, 1984).

Foreign-exchange intervention to peg nominal exchange rates cannot prevent this eventual adjustment because money is neutral in the long run and thus is powerless to alter relative prices permanently. The events of the 1980s show, however, that if it is costly for factors of production to move between sectors of the economy there is a case for pegging rates in the face of temporary output-market shocks. Unfortunately, this lesson leaves policymakers with the difficult task of determining which disturbances are temporary and which are permanent.

An indictment of floating exchange rates is sometimes based on the poor economic-growth performance of industrial countries in the 1970s and 1980s compared with the 1950s and 1960s. As noted above, unemployment rates in industrial countries rose sharply after the 1960s; in addition, labor productivity and real GNP growth rates dropped. These adverse developments followed the adoption of floating dollar exchange rates, but this coincidence does not prove that floating rates were their cause. Although economists have not yet fully explained the growth slowdown or the rise in unemployment rates, the likely culprits are structural changes that had little to do with floating rates. Examples include the oil price shocks, restrictive labor-market practices, and worker displacement caused by the emergence of several LDCs as major exporters of manufactured goods. Much of the international trade of the European Monetary System takes place at fixed exchange rates, yet the record of EMS countries in generating jobs and keeping down unemployment has been far worse than that of the United States or Japan.

DISCIPLINE

Did countries abuse the autonomy afforded by floating rates? Inflation rates did accelerate after 1973 and remained high through the second oil shock. But the concerted disinflation in industrial countries after 1979 proved that central banks could control inflation under floating rates. On several occasions, voters in industrial countries showed that they viewed a weak currency as a sign of economic mismanagement. For this reason, currency depreciation sometimes brought sharp changes in monetary policies, as in the United States in 1979.

The system placed fewer obvious restraints on unbalanced fiscal policies, for example, the high U.S. government budget deficits of the 1980s. While some observers felt that fixed rates would have forced a more moderate American fiscal stance, their arguments were not compelling. In the late 1960s, fixed rates had failed to restrain the Johnson administration's fiscal expansion, a policy move that contributed to the collapse of Bretton Woods.

DESTABILIZING SPECULATION

Floating exchange rates have exhibited much more day-to-day volatility than the early advocates of floating would have predicted, but as we saw in Chapter 13, exchange rates are asset prices and so considerable volatility is to be expected. The asset-price nature of exchange rates was not well understood by economists before the 1970s.

Even with the benefit of hindsight, however, short-term exchange-rate movements can be quite difficult to relate to actual news about economic events that affect currency values. Part of the difficulty is that government officials often try to influence exchange rates by hinting at intended policy changes, thus making expectations about future macroeconomic policies volatile. The question of whether exchange-rate volatility has been "excessive" relative to the theoretical determinants of exchange rates is a controversial one and provides an active research area for academic economists (Chapter 21).

Over the longer term, however, exchange rates have roughly reflected fundamental changes in monetary and fiscal policies, and their broad movements do not appear to be the result of destabilizing speculation. The decline of the dollar in the late 1970s (Figure 19-3) coincides with loose U.S. monetary policies, while its steep ascent between 1980 and 1985 occurred as the United States embarked on disinflation and a fiscal expansion of a size unprecedented in peacetime. While most economists agree that the direction of these exchange-rate swings was appropriate, there is continuing debate about their magnitude. Some feel that the foreign-exchange market overreacted to government actions and that more systematic foreign-exchange intervention would have been beneficial.

The experience with floating rates has not supported the idea that arbitrary exchange-rate movements can lead to "vicious circles" of inflation and depreciation. Britain, Italy, and to a lesser extent, France experienced inflationary spirals similar to those predicted by the vicious-circle theory. But the currency depreciation that accompanied these spirals was not the arbitrary result of destabilizing exchange-rate speculation. As Figure 14-11 (p. 363) shows, industrial countries with poor inflation performances under floating exchange rates have also tended to have relatively rapid rates of monetary growth.

INTERNATIONAL TRADE AND INVESTMENT

Critics of floating had predicted that international trade and investment would suffer as a result of increased uncertainty. The prediction was certainly wrong on the investment side, for international financial intermediation expanded strongly after 1973 as countries lowered barriers to capital movement (Chapter 21).

There is more controversy about the effect of floating rates on international trade. The use of forward markets expanded dramatically, just as advocates of floating had foreseen, and innovative financial instruments were developed to help traders avoid exchange-rate risk. But some economists contend that the costs of avoiding exchange-rate risk have had an effect similar to increased international transport costs in reducing the available gains from trade. They argue that as a result of these costs, international trade has grown more slowly than it would have under a hypothetical fixed-exchange-rate regime.

A very direct measure of the extent of a country's international trade is the average of its imports and exports of goods and services, divided by its real output. Figure 19-8 plots this number for the seven main industrial economies over the period from the early 1950s to the early 1980s. For most countries, the extent of trade shows a rising trend over the whole period,

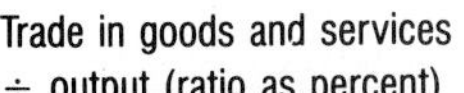

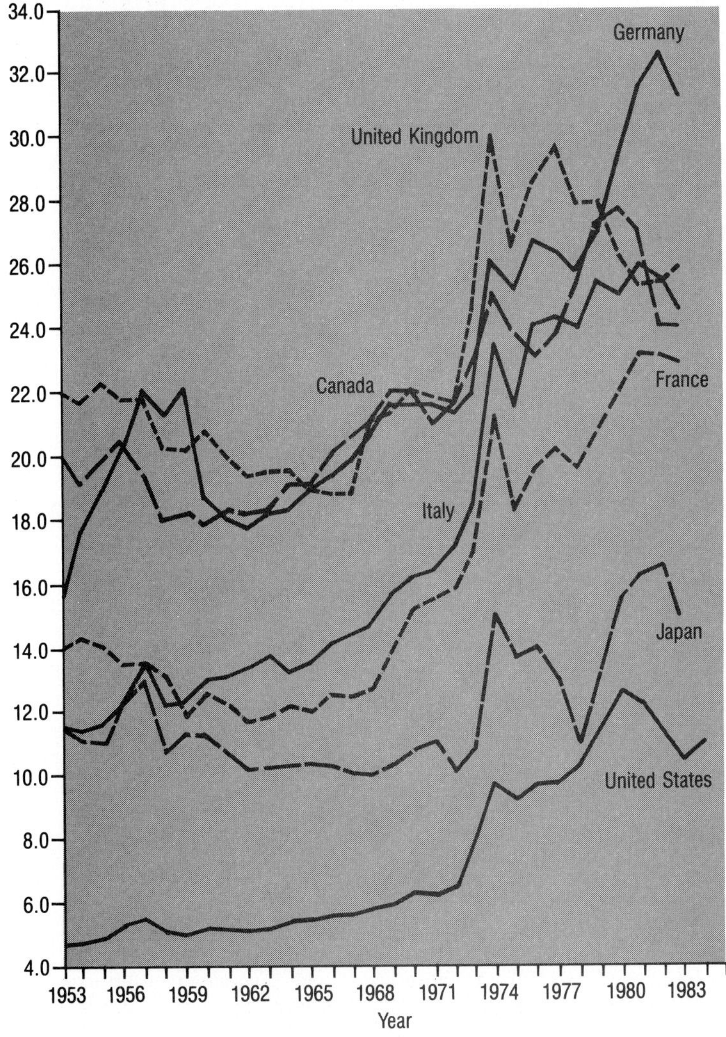

FIGURE 19-8 Trade in goods and services as a proportion of the output of major industrial countries, 1953–1983. Floating exchange rates do not appear to have reduced the trend growth rate of world trade. Source: IMF, *International Financial Statistics.* From Ralph C. Bryant, "International Financial Intermediation: Underlying Trends and Implications for Government Policies" (Washington: The Brookings Institution, 1985). Reprinted by permission.

with no marked slowdown in trend after the move to floating. The figure probably exaggerates the growth of world trade in the decade after 1973 because a number of factors (notably the two OPEC shocks, whose effects are easily seen) caused the prices of tradable goods to rise relative to the prices of those that do not enter trade. Even after correcting for the resulting bias, however, it is difficult to make a case that the volume of world trade has grown more slowly since the move to floating exchange rates. Further, to compare world trade growth before and after the early 1970s is to stack the deck against floating rates because the 1950s and 1960s were periods of dramatic trade liberalization.

Evaluation of the effects of floating rates on world trade is complicated further by the activities of multinational firms, many of which expanded their international production operations in the years after 1973. Facing a more turbulent economic environment, multinationals may have spread their activities over more countries in the hope of reducing their dependence on any individual government's macroeconomic policies. Because trade and capital movements can substitute for each other, however, the displacement of some trade by multinational firms' overseas production does not necessarily imply that welfare-improving trade gains have been lost.[8]

After 1980, international trade was threatened by the resurgence of protectionism, a symptom of slower economic growth and wide swings in real exchange rates. It is not clear, however, that pressures to limit trade would not have emerged also under fixed exchange rates.

POLICY COORDINATION

The floating-rate system has been a disappointment in terms of promoting better international coordination of macroeconomic policies. On several occasions, for example, during the disinflation of the early 1980s, industrial countries as a group could have attained their macroeconomic goals more effectively by negotiating a joint approach to common objectives. The appendix to this chapter presents a formal model that illustrates the gains from international policy coordination.

While beggar-thy-neighbor policies remain a problem, critics of floating have not made a strong case that the problem would disappear under an alternative currency regime. Under fixed rates, for example, countries can always devalue their currencies unilaterally to attain nationalistic goals.

Governments, like people, are motivated by their own interest rather than that of the community. Legal penalties discourage antisocial actions by individuals, but it is a more difficult matter to design sanctions that bind sovereign governments. It seems doubtful that an exchange-rate system

[8]A recent study documenting the growth of U.S. multinationals' foreign exporting activities is Robert E. Lipsey and Irving B. Kravis, "The Competitiveness and Comparative Advantage of U.S. Multinationals, 1957–1984," *Banca Nazionale del Lavoro Quarterly Review,* no. 161 (June 1987), pp. 147–165.

LESSONS OF THE EMS EXPERIENCE, 1979–1987

The eight participants in the European Monetary System have maintained mutually fixed exchange rates since March 1979. What lessons does the EMS experience offer concerning the workability of a broader area of fixed exchange rates that would include the United States and Japan as well as Europe?

When the EMS was founded at the initiative of France and Germany, skeptics argued that the system would soon be shattered by speculative attacks on its exchange parities. The prospects for a successful fixed-rate system within Europe indeed seemed bleak in early 1979, when recent annual inflation rates ranged from Germany's 2.7 percent to Italy's 12.1 percent (Table 19-1). Through a mixture of policy cooperation and frequent exchange-rate adjustment, however, the EMS has somehow survived. In the mid-1980s, the system was strengthened by shrinking inflation-rate differences between its three largest members, France, Germany, and Italy (Table 19-4).

The EMS has relied on the help of several expedients. Most EMS exchange rates may fluctuate 2.25 percent above or below their central parities, but the Italian lira has a band of plus or minus 6 percent. This arrangement gives Italy greater latitude than other EMS countries in choosing its monetary policies. In addition, both Italy and France have maintained strict exchange controls during most of the years of the system's operation.

Despite these safety valves, the IMF has identified 18 distinct "periods of strain" within the EMS between March 1979 and August 1986, defined as "periods with reports of substantial interference in the exchange market by intervention, capital and exchange controls, or measures of monetary policy motivated by exchange rate developments."* Ten of these speculative episodes led to exchange-rate realignments. An eleventh realignment occurred in January 1987 after student demonstrations and strikes in France set off a speculative run out of the French franc and into the DM. On average, therefore, realignments have taken place about once every 10 months.

The continuing operation of the EMS is often credited to monetary cooperation among its members, in particular the extension of credit from strong- to weak-currency members. Cynical observers, however, argue that the tone of monetary policy within the EMS is really set by the powerful German economy, which occupies a leadership position analogous to the one occupied by the United States in the Bretton Woods system.

The durability and partial success of the EMS are of limited relevance in judging the viability of a broader zone of exchange-rate stability. EMS members are probably more similar to each other than any is to the United States or Japan. Structural demand shifts are therefore less likely to occur within the EMS than within a broader area comprising all major industrial countries. In addition, the EMS members are also members of the European Economic Community. Thus, even before 1979, EMS members had developed the habit of delegating some control over economic policy to a supranational agency representing the community's interests.

*See Horst Ungerer, Owen Evans, Thomas Mayer, and Philip Young. *The European Monetary System: Recent Developments,* Occasional Paper 48. Washington, D.C.: International Monetary Fund, December 1986, pp. 32–33.

alone can restrain a government from following its own perceived interest when it formulates macroeconomic policies.[9]

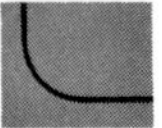

DIRECTIONS FOR REFORM

The recent experience with floating exchange rates shows that neither side in the debate over floating was entirely right in its predictions. The floating-rate system has not been free of serious problems, but it has not been the fiasco that its opponents predicted it would be.

An important lesson of this chapter and the previous one is that no exchange-rate system—fixed or floating—works well when countries "go it alone" and act on the basis of narrowly perceived self-interest. The Bretton Woods system functioned reasonably well until the United States unilaterally adopted overexpansionary policies under President Johnson. Similarly, the worst problems of the floating-rate system occurred when the industrial countries failed to take coordinated action on common macroeconomic problems. Internationally balanced and stable policies are a prerequisite for the successful performance of any international monetary system.

Current proposals to reform the exchange-rate system run the gamut from the creation of wide "target zones" for exchange rates to the resurrection of fixed rates to the introduction of a single world currency. Because countries seem unwilling to give up the autonomy floating rates have given them, it appears unlikely that any of these changes is in the cards.[10]

With greater cooperation among the main players, there is no reason why floating exchange rates should not function tolerably well in the future. International policy cooperation is not unprecedented, as the GATT rounds of tariff reduction and the founding of the IMF indicate. Cooperation should be sought as an end in itself, however, and not as the indirect result of exchange-rate rules that eventually are discredited through repeated amendment or violation.

SUMMARY

1. The weaknesses of the Bretton Woods system led many economists to advocate floating exchange rates before 1973. They made three main arguments in favor of floating. First, they argued that floating rates would give

[9]At their annual economic summit meeting in Tokyo in May 1986, the leaders of the Big Seven industrial countries agreed to the "close and continuous coordination" of economic policies and asked the IMF to construct a set of quantitative measures of economic policy stance to help in monitoring individual countries. As this book was being completed, the concrete implications of the Tokyo agreement remained to be seen.

[10]The target zone proposal is outlined in John Williamson, *The Exchange Rate System*, Policy Analyses in International Economics 5 (Washington, D.C.: Institute for International Economics, 1983). McKinnon, op. cit., presents a program for reestablishing fixed rates for the dollar, yen, and DM. The case for a single world currency is made by Richard N. Cooper, "A Monetary System for the Future," *Foreign Affairs* 63 (1984), pp. 166–184.

national macroeconomic policymakers greater autonomy in managing their economies. Second, they predicted that floating rates would remove the asymmetries of the Bretton Woods arrangements. Third, they pointed out that floating exchange rates would quickly eliminate the "fundamental disequilibriums" that had led to parity changes and speculative attacks under fixed rates.

2. Critics of floating rates advanced several counterarguments. Some feared that floating would encourage monetary and fiscal excesses and beggar-thy-neighbor policies. Other lines of criticism asserted that floating rates would be subject to *destabilizing speculation* and that uncertainty over exchange rates would retard international trade and investment. Finally, a number of economists questioned whether countries would be willing in practice to disregard the exchange rate in formulating their monetary and fiscal policies. The exchange rate, they felt, was an important enough price that it would become a target of macroeconomic policy in its own right.

3. The period between 1973 and 1980 was one in which floating rates seemed on the whole to function well. In particular, it is unlikely that the industrial countries could have maintained fixed exchange rates in the face of the *stagflation* caused by two oil shocks. The dollar suffered a sharp depreciation after 1976, however, as the United States adopted macroeconomic policies more expansionary than those of other industrial countries.

4. A sharp turn toward slower monetary growth in the United States, coupled with a rising U.S. government budget deficit, contributed to massive dollar appreciation between 1980 and early 1985. Other industrial economies pursued disinflation along with the United States, and the resulting worldwide monetary slowdown, coming soon after the second oil shock, led to the deepest recession since the 1930s. As the recovery from the recession slowed in late 1984 and the U.S. current account began to register record deficits, political pressure for wide-ranging trade restrictions gathered momentum in Washington. The drive for protection was slowed (but not defeated) by the decision of the Group of Five countries to take concerted action to bring down the dollar.

5. The experience of floating does not fully support either the early advocates of that exchange-rate system or its critics. One unambiguous lesson of experience, however, is that no exchange-rate system functions well when international economic cooperation breaks down. Severe limits on exchange-rate flexibility are unlikely to be reinstated in the near future. But increased consultation among policymakers in the industrial countries should improve the performance of floating rates.

KEY TERMS

destabilizing speculation

stagflation

nominal and real effective exchange-rate indexes

PROBLEMS

1. Use the *DD-AA* model to examine the effects of a one-time rise in the foreign price level, P^*. If the expected future exchange rate E^e rises immediately in proportion to P^* (in line with PPP), show that the exchange rate will also appreciate immediately in proportion to the rise in P^*. If the economy is initially in internal and external balance, will its position be disturbed by such a rise in P^*?

2. Analyze a transitory increase in the foreign interest rate, R^*. Under which type of exchange rate is there a smaller effect on output, fixed or floating?

3. Suppose now that R^* rises permanently. What happens to the economy, and how does your answer depend on whether the change reflects a rise in the foreign real interest rate or in foreign inflation expectations (the Fisher effect)?

4. If the foreign *inflation rate* rises permanently, would you expect a floating exchange rate to insulate the domestic economy in the short run? What would happen in the long run? In answering the latter question, pay attention to the long-run relationship between domestic and foreign nominal interest rates.

5. Imagine that domestic- and foreign-currency bonds are imperfect substitutes and that investors suddenly shift their demand toward foreign-currency bonds, raising the risk premium on domestic assets (Chapter 17). Which exchange-rate regime minimizes the effect on output, fixed or floating?

6. In the two-country model of this chapter, show that Foreign output must rise as a result of monetary contraction in Home.

7. How would you analyze the use of monetary and fiscal policy to maintain internal and external balance under a floating exchange rate?

8. The chapter described how the United States tried after 1985 to reduce its current-account deficit by accelerating monetary growth and depreciating the dollar. Assume that the United States was in internal balance but that external balance called for an expenditure-reducing policy (a cut in the government budget deficit) as well as the expenditure switching caused by currency depreciation. How would you expect the use of monetary expansion alone to affect the U.S. economy in the short and long runs?

9. After 1985 the United States asked Germany and Japan to adopt fiscal and monetary expansion as ways of increasing foreign demand for U.S. output and reducing the American current-account deficit. Would fiscal expansion by Germany and Japan have accomplished these goals? What about monetary expansion?

10. Suppose that the United States and Japanese governments both want to depreciate their currencies to help their export industries but fear the resulting inflation. The two policy choices available to them are (1) expansionary monetary policy and (2) no change in monetary policy. Develop an analysis like the one in the appendix to show the consequences of different policy choices. Can Japan and the United States do better by cooperating than by acting individualistically?

FURTHER READING

Richard N. Cooper. "Economic Interdependence and Coordination of Economic Policies," in Ronald W. Jones and Peter B. Kenen, eds. *Handbook of International Eco-*

nomics. Vol. 2. Amsterdam: North-Holland Publishing Company, pp. 1195–1234. Examines the interaction among national economic policies and the scope for international coordination.

Andrew Crockett and Morris Goldstein. *Strengthening the International Monetary System*, Occasional Paper 50. Washington, D.C.: International Monetary Fund, 1987. Up-to-date review of the performance of floating exchange rates, the IMF's role in the current international monetary system, and options for reform.

Milton Friedman. "The Case for Flexible Exchange Rates," in *Essays in Positive Economics*. Chicago: University of Chicago Press, 1953, pp. 157–203. A classic exposition of the merits of floating exchange rates.

Harry G. Johnson. "The Case for Flexible Exchange Rates, 1969." *Federal Reserve Bank of St. Louis Review* 51 (June 1969), pp. 12–24. An influential treatment of the case for replacing the Bretton Woods system by floating rates.

Charles P. Kindleberger. "The Case for Fixed Exchange Rates, 1969," in *The International Adjustment Mechanism*, Conference Series 2. Boston: Federal Reserve Bank of Boston, 1970, pp. 93–108. Prescient analysis of problems with a floating-rate system.

Michael Mussa. "Macroeconomic Interdependence and the Exchange Rate Regime," in Rudiger Dornbusch and Jacob A. Frenkel, eds. *International Economic Policy*. Baltimore: Johns Hopkins University Press, 1979, pp. 160–204. Analyzes macroeconomic policy interactions under fixed and floating exchange rates.

Maurice Obstfeld. "Floating Exchange Rates: Experience and Prospects." *Brookings Papers on Economic Activity*, 2:1985, pp. 369–450. Compares the merits of fixed and floating rates in light of the macroeconomic events of the previous decade.

Robert D. Putnam and Nicholas Bayne. *Hanging Together: The Seven-Power Summits*. Cambridge: Harvard University Press, 1984. Describes the economic summit meetings of the Big Seven industrial countries.

Robert Solomon. *The International Monetary System, 1945–1981*. New York: Harper & Row, 1982. Chapters 15–19 cover the recent period of floating exchange rates.

APPENDIX TO CHAPTER 19
International Policy-Coordination Failures

This appendix illustrates the importance of macroeconomic policy coordination by showing how all countries can suffer as a result of self-centered policy decisions. The phenomenon is another example of the Prisoner's Dilemma of game theory (Chapter 9). Governments can achieve macroeconomic outcomes that are better for all if they choose policies cooperatively.

These points are made using an example based on the disinflation of the early 1980s. Recall that contractionary monetary policies in the industrial countries helped throw the world economy into a deep recession in 1981. Countries hoped to reduce inflation by slowing monetary growth, but the situation was complicated by the influence of exchange rates on the price level. A government that adopts a less restrictive monetary policy than its neighbors is likely to face a currency depreciation that partially frustrates its attempt to disinflate.

Many observers feel that in their individual attempts to resist currency depreciation, the industrial countries as a group adopted overly tight monetary policies that deepened the recession. All governments would have been happier if everyone had adopted looser monetary policies, but given the policies that other governments did adopt, it was not in the interest of any individual government to change course.

The argument above can be made more precise with a simple model. There are two countries, Home and Foreign, and each country has two policy options, a very restrictive monetary policy and a somewhat restrictive monetary policy. Figure 19A-1, which is similar to a diagram we used to analyze trade policies, shows the results in Home and Foreign of different policy choices by the two countries. Each row corresponds to a particular monetary-policy decision by Home and each column to a decision by Foreign. The boxes contain entries giving changes in annual inflation rates ($\Delta\pi$ and $\Delta\pi^*$) and unemployment rates (ΔU and ΔU^*). Within each box, lower-left entries are Home outcomes and upper-right entries are Foreign outcomes.

The hypothetical entries in Figure 19A-1 can be understood in terms of this chapter's two-country model. Under somewhat restrictive policies, for example, inflation rates fall by 1 percent and unemployment rates rise by 1 percent in both countries. If Home suddenly shifts to a very restrictive policy while Foreign stands pat, Home's currency appreciates, its inflation drops further, and its unemployment rises. Home's additional monetary contraction, however, has two effects on Foreign. Foreign's unemployment rate falls, but because Home's currency appreciation is a currency *de*preciation for Foreign, Foreign inflation goes back up to its predisinflation level. In Foreign, the deflationary effects of higher unemployment are offset by the inflationary impact of a depreciating currency on import prices and wage demands. Home's sharper monetary crunch therefore has a beggar-thy-neighbor effect on Foreign, which is forced to "import" some inflation from Home.

To translate the outcomes in Figure 19A-1 into policy payoffs, we assume that each government wishes to get the biggest reduction in inflation at the lowest cost in terms of unemployment. That is, each government wishes to maximize $-\Delta\pi/\Delta U$, the inflation reduction per point of increased unemployment. The numbers in Figure 19A-1 lead to the payoff matrix shown as Figure 19A-2.

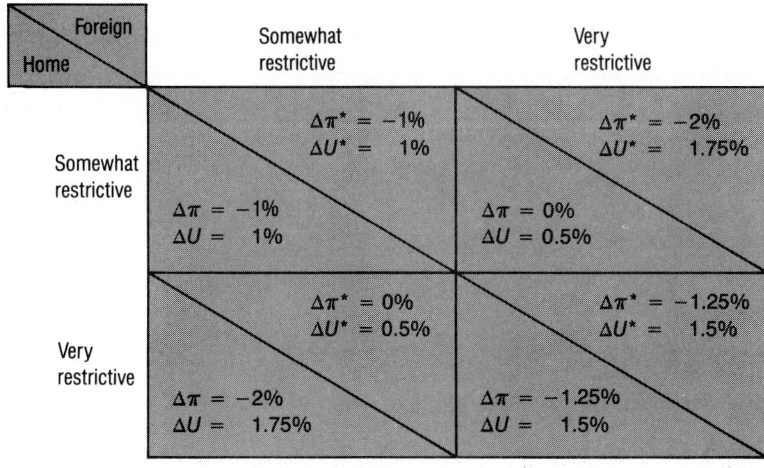

FIGURE 19A-1 Hypothetical effects of different monetary-policy combinations on inflation and unemployment. Monetary-policy choices in one country affect the outcomes of monetary-policy choices made abroad.

How do Home and Foreign behave faced with the payoffs in this matrix? Assume that each government "goes it alone" and picks the policy that maximizes its own payoff given the other player's policy choice. If Foreign adopts a somewhat restrictive policy, Home does better with a very restrictive policy (payoff = 8/7) than with a somewhat restrictive one (payoff = 1). If Foreign is very restrictive, Home still does better by being very restrictive (payoff = 5/6) than by being somewhat restrictive (payoff = 0). So no matter what Foreign does, Home's government will always choose a very restrictive monetary policy.

Foreign finds itself in a symmetric position. It, too, is better off with a very restrictive policy regardless of what Home does. The result is that both countries will choose very restrictive monetary policies, and each will get a payoff of 5/6.

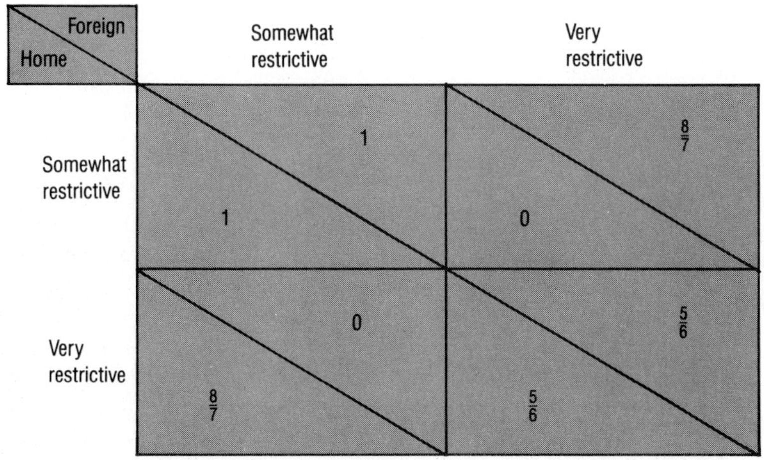

FIGURE 19A-2 Payoff matrix for different monetary-policy moves. Each entry equals the reduction in inflation per unit rise in the unemployment rate (calculated as $-\Delta\pi/\Delta U$). If each country "goes it alone," they both choose very restrictive policies. Somewhat restrictive policies, if adopted by both countries, lead to an outcome better for both.

Notice, however, that *both* countries are actually better off if they simultaneously adopt the somewhat restrictive policies. The resulting payoff for each is 1, which is greater than 5/6. Under this last policy configuration, inflation comes down less in the two countries, but the rise in unemployment is far less than under very restrictive policies.

Since both countries are better off with somewhat restrictive policies, why aren't these adopted? The answer is at the root of the problem of policy coordination. Our analysis assumed that each country "goes it alone" by maximizing its own payoff. Under this assumption, a situation where both countries were somewhat restrictive would not be stable: each country would want to reduce its monetary growth further and use its exchange rate to hasten disinflation at its neighbor's expense.

For the superior outcome in the upper left corner of the matrix to occur, Home and Foreign must reach an explicit agreement, that is, they must *coordinate* their policy choices. Both countries must agree to forgo the beggar-thy-neighbor gains offered by very restrictive policies, and each country must abide by this agreement in spite of the incentive to cheat. If Home and Foreign can cooperate, both end up with a preferred mix of inflation and unemployment.

The reality of policy coordination is more complex than in this simple example because the choices and outcomes are more numerous and more uncertain. These added complexities make policymakers less willing to commit themselves to cooperative agreements and less certain that their counterparts abroad will live up to the agreed terms.

20 DEVELOPING COUNTRIES AND THE INTERNATIONAL DEBT PROBLEM

Until now, we have studied macroeconomic interactions between industrialized market economies like those of the United States, Canada, Japan, and the countries of Europe. Richly endowed with capital and skilled labor, these economies generate high levels of GNP for their populations. And their markets, compared with those of poorer countries, are relatively free of direct government control.

In the 1980s, however, the macroeconomic problems of the world's poorer countries have been at the forefront of concerns about the stability and future of the international economy. Over the past two decades, merchandise trade between less-developed countries (LDCs) and the industrialized nations has expanded, as has LDC borrowing from richer countries. In turn, the more extensive links between the two groups of economies have made each group more dependent than ever before on economic events in the other.

This chapter studies the macroeconomic problems of the LDCs and the repercussions of those problems on the developed countries. Although many of the insights from international macroeconomics gained in previous chapters also apply to the less-developed world, the structures of poorer economies are sufficiently different from those of the rich industrialized countries to warrant separate discussion. In addition, the lower income level of the LDCs means that macroeconomic fluctuations can be even more painful than in developed countries, with consequences that may threaten internal political stability.

The chapter also reviews the history of relations between developed and developing countries in this century. That history culminated in 1982 in a widespread and continuing contraction of rich-country lending to LDCs— an international debt crisis. Below, we apply what we learn about LDC macroeconomics to examine the causes of the debt crisis and policies that might help resolve it.

INCOME AND WEALTH IN THE WORLD ECONOMY

Compared with industrialized countries, LDCs are poor in the factors of production essential to modern industry: capital and skilled labor. The relative scarcity of these productive factors results in low levels of per capita income and often prevents LDCs from realizing economies of scale from which many richer countries benefit.

The world's economies can be divided into six categories according to per capita income levels: low-income economies (including mainland China, India, and much of sub-Saharan Africa); middle-income economies (including the smaller Latin American and Caribbean countries and most of the remaining African countries); upper middle-income countries (including the largest Latin American countries, Hong Kong, Korea, Israel, and the poorest noncommunist European countries); high-income oil exporters (Libya and the OPEC members of the Arabian peninsula); the East European communist economies; and the industrial market economies. The first four of these categories consist of countries at a backward stage of development relative to the industrial economies. Table 20-1 shows 1983 average per capita income levels (measured in dollars) for five of these groups, together with another indicator of economic well-being, average life expectancy at birth.[1]

Table 20-1 illustrates the sharp disparities in international income levels. Average per capita annual GNP in the industrial economies is more than

[1]Chapter 15 showed that an international comparison of *dollar* incomes will portray relative welfare levels inaccurately because countries' price levels measured in terms of a common currency (here U.S. dollars) generally differ. An additional problem with dollar income comparisons is that some LDCs have multiple exchange rates for current-account transactions. A detailed description of how the numbers in Table 20-1 were adjusted is given in their source, the World Bank's *World Development Report 1985*. More reliable real output estimates for 124 countries are reported by Robert Summers and Alan Heston, "Improved International Comparisons of Real Product and Its Composition: 1950–1980," *Review of Income and Wealth* 30 (June 1984), pp. 207–264. The alternative estimates, like those in Table 20-1, show that real output per capita differs widely among countries.

TABLE 20-1 Indicators of economic welfare in six groups of countries, 1983

Income group	GNP per capita (U.S. dollars)	Life expectancy (years)
Low-income developing	260	59
Middle-income developing	1,310	61
Upper middle-income developing	2,050	65
High-income oil exporters	12,370	59
Eastern European communist	n.a.	70
Industrialized market	11,060	76

Source: World Bank. *World Development Report 1985.*

40 times greater than in the poorest LDCs. Even the upper middle-income countries enjoy only about a fifth of the annual per capita GNP of the industrial group. The high-income oil-exporting countries are at a low level of industrial development, but because they are richly endowed with a valuable natural resource and their populations are so small, their per capita income level is the highest of all.

The life expectancy figures generally reflect international differences in income levels: average lifespans fall as relative poverty increases. Here again the rich oil exporters are an exception, for life expectancy at birth in these countries is no greater than in the poorest LDCs. Although there are no readily available data on income distribution within the rich oil exporters, a good guess is that average lifespans are short because the oil resources are owned by small fractions of their populations.

MACROECONOMIC FEATURES OF LESS-DEVELOPED COUNTRIES

Five main macroeconomic features of LDCs differentiate them from most developed countries. These features apply to most, but not all, LDCs, and several of them are shared by some industrialized economies. Nonetheless, a broad description of a "typical" LDC's structure is essential to understanding macroeconomic relationships between the developed and less-developed areas of the world economy.

1. Domestic financial markets in LDCs are undeveloped and subject to heavy government control. Governments tend to keep interest rates below the level that would equalize demand and supply for loans; so loans are typically rationed.

2. Direct government involvement in the economy extends beyond the financial markets. Governments own a significant portion of the economy's firms, and government spending is a very high percentage of GNP.
3. The government finances much of its budget deficit by printing money. This practice results in high average inflation rates and, sometimes, in the indexation of wages, other money prices, and loan contracts to the general price level.
4. Exchange rates are set by the central bank rather than determined in the foreign-exchange market. Private international borrowing and lending are heavily restricted, and the government may allow residents to purchase foreign exchange only for certain purposes.
5. Natural resources or agricultural commodities make up a large fraction of exports for many LDCs.

UNDEVELOPED FINANCIAL MARKETS

On the whole, LDCs lack the broad and rapidly adjusting financial markets characteristic of the main industrial countries. Stock markets are usually rudimentary or nonexistent and the flow of lending from banks to businesses is determined in large part by government fiat. Lending often takes place at artificially low interest rates decreed by the government.

Developing-country governments tend to exercise direct control over credit markets because it is one way of channeling funds at reduced interest rates to favored industries or sectors of the economy. Governments often find such a method preferable to outright subsidies because subsidies would show up in the government's budget and increase its measured deficit. Thus, official credit diversion represents an implicit subsidy to the recipients of artificially cheap loans and an implicit tax on the banking system, which could earn higher profits in a less heavily regulated national capital market. Low domestic interest rates also help the government finance its budget deficit.

The absence of the higher-yielding assets available in industrial economies means that the few assets that are available to savers in LDCs are not very attractive as stores of wealth. Strict government controls generally prevent domestic savers from holding foreign assets; so the main financial assets available are money and time deposits. Low rates of return on these assets discourage saving and contribute to a vicious cycle in which low saving levels make the introduction of new financial instruments and institutions unprofitable. Saving is low in many LDCs also because income is low. Once households take care of their basic consumption needs, little or nothing is left over to be put in the bank.

GOVERNMENT'S PERVASIVE ROLE

To a greater extent than in most industrial countries, LDC governments are involved in the day-to-day management of the economy. Government regulations abound, and many firms are state companies run directly by the government. Partly as a result, the share of government purchases in GNP is very high. In Brazil, for example, government purchases are reckoned to exceed 50 percent of output once purchases by state-owned companies are taken into account. The corresponding figure for the United States was about 20 percent in 1985.

INFLATION AND THE GOVERNMENT BUDGET

In the undeveloped domestic financial markets of LDCs, governments sometimes find it difficult to issue bonds to finance their deficits. This difficulty results in extensive direct government borrowing from foreigners. LDC governments are also led to rely on an additional instrument of public finance: they run the printing presses and use newly created money to purchase goods and services.

The real output that a government obtains by printing money and spending it is called **seigniorage**. Seigniorage is a component of government revenue everywhere, but it is particularly important in the finances of LDC governments.

Money creation leads to inflation, which erodes the real value of nominal money holdings. This "inflation tax" paid by money holders is the counterpart of the real resources the government obtains by printing money. The inflation rates attained by some LDCs seem spectacular compared with the low (usually less than double-digit) rates seen recently in the industrial economies. In the mid-1980s, for example, Brazil's monthly inflation rate reached 400 percent per year, Israel's and Argentina's exceeded 1500 percent per year, and Bolivia's, at *24,000* percent per year, topped them all. Such rapid rates of price increase reflect continuing attempts by governments to extract seigniorage from their economies by printing money.

As a result of chronically high inflation, nominal wages are indexed to the price level in many LDCs. When wages are indexed, they are adjusted frequently in response to inflation rather than set, once and for all, until the next contract negotiation. This procedure is meant to prevent the large fluctuations in workers' real wages that would otherwise occur over the life of labor contracts.

Wage indexation has two major drawbacks that have contributed to macroeconomic instability in LDCs. First, changes in real wages are sometimes necessary to maintain full employment, but indexation makes these changes difficult if not impossible to achieve. If real wages do not fall when the terms of trade deteriorate, for example, export industries are forced to lay off workers and shut down plants.

The second problem with indexation is that wages are often linked to *past* price-level increases. If a government decides to reduce a rapid inflation rate, for example, real wages may rise as nominal wages continue to be adjusted upward to compensate for earlier inflation. Rising real wage bills, however, lead to layoffs and put additional upward pressure on product

HOW IMPORTANT IS SEIGNIORAGE?

According to some accounts, the use of inflation as a tax on money holders was discovered by the ancient Romans, who first hit upon the idea of debasing their coinage to raise revenue. The word "seigniorage" refers to a tax that feudal princes would levy for turning nonmonetary gold into coins at their mints.

Seigniorage has remained important in the modern world of paper money. Stanley Fischer, an economist at the Massachusetts Institute of Technology, put together estimates of the importance of seigniorage as a source of government revenue in various countries.* Roughly speaking, Fischer estimated the annual flow of seigniorage by summing the cash and checks issued by the central bank during the year and dividing the result by the price level.†

Data for a selection of countries from Fischer's sample are shown below. Reported are his calculations of period averages for (1) seigniorage as a fraction of total real government revenue (including seigniorage) and (2) inflation.

It may be misleading to compare the below industrial-country and developing-country numbers below because they cover different time periods. Nonetheless, Fischer's calculations give the impression that seigniorage is less important in the government finances of industrial countries. In those countries, it is unusual to find seigniorage amounting to more than 10 percent of government revenue. This is not true in LDCs.

*Fischer, "Seigniorage and the Case for a National Money," *Journal of Political Economy* 90 (April 1982), pp. 295–313.

†This is an oversimplified description of how seigniorage is measured. In some LDCs seigniorage is extracted in subtle ways, for example, by requiring private banks to hold government debt that pays below-market interest rates.

	Period	(Seigniorage) ÷ (Revenue)	Inflation (percent per year)
Industrial countries			
United States	1960–1973	0.021	3.18
Britain	1960–1973	0.019	5.00
France	1960–1973	0.051	4.57
Germany	1960–1973	0.063	3.33
Italy	1960–1973	0.098	4.66
Japan	1960–1973	0.107	6.12
Developing countries			
Argentina	1960–1975	0.459	57.22
Chile	1960–1977	0.183	88.95
Ghana	1960–1974	0.107	20.14
India	1960–1976	0.104	6.83
Korea	1960–1978	0.127	13.78
Pakistan	1960–1978	0.106	7.61

prices. An LDC government that contemplates disinflation may therefore be discouraged by the prospect of a long and painful adjustment to a lower inflation rate. LDC governments have recently coupled disinflation programs with direct wage controls, but such "incomes policies" are politically unpopular and cannot be sustained unless the government's program improves economic conditions very quickly.[2]

PEGGED EXCHANGE RATES, EXCHANGE CONTROLS, AND INCONVERTIBLE CURRENCIES

Most developing-country governments set the exchange rate and strictly control financial transactions involving foreign currencies. Foreign-exchange controls prevent LDC residents from legally purchasing foreign currencies without government permission, and someone who earns foreign currency abroad may be required to sell it to the government for domestic currency. In addition, foreigners holding an LDC currency are not generally entitled to exchange it for foreign currencies with the LDC central bank or with LDC residents. Thus, developing-country currencies are often *inconvertible,* even for current-account transactions.

Why do LDC governments peg exchange rates and supervise foreign transactions? One main reason is the government's desire to use exchange-rate arrangements as a tool of commercial policy. Many LDC governments maintain different exchange rates for different types of current-account transaction. For example, the government may subsidize imports of investment goods by selling dollars cheaply to firms that import machinery, while taxing luxury consumption goods by selling dollars at a higher price to individuals who import limousines.[3]

Such multiple exchange-rate systems clearly cannot be enforced unless the government itself buys and sells foreign currencies at the rates it wishes to maintain and prevents the private sector from transacting at any other rates. Exchange controls also help the central bank prevent sharp reductions in its foreign-exchange reserves, which might eventually leave it unable to peg rates. Finally, by preventing the public from holding foreign rather than domestic money, the government is able to collect more seigniorage through its inflation tax.

Even if considerations of commercial and macroeconomic policy did not lead LDCs to peg exchange rates, financial restrictions would make private foreign-exchange trading very time-consuming and costly under a floating exchange rate. Because LDC currencies are typically inconvertible, they are not traded on a significant scale by financial institutions in the developed

[2]Some industrial countries that experienced double-digit inflation, such as Italy, also indexed wages. LDC governments sometimes index their bonds by adjusting interest and principal payments upward in line with domestic inflation. Once again, some industrial countries (such as Britain) also issue indexed government debt.

[3]Chapter 10 examined in detail the commercial policies of LDCs.

world. In addition, LDC financial institutions face burdensome restrictions that prevent them from trading freely. The actors who normally would be at the center of a market in LDC currencies—domestic and foreign financial institutions—are therefore unable to participate, leaving the LDC's central bank as the main trader in its currency. Transaction costs for the economy are reduced if the central bank fixes the exchange rate and "makes a market" at that rate for individuals authorized to trade foreign exchange.

It is not surprising that strict foreign-exchange controls lead to illegal black markets for foreign exchange in most developing countries. In these black markets, foreign currencies smuggled into the country generally command a higher domestic-currency price than the one offered by the central bank. As a tourist, you can often take advantage of the black market rate simply by selling dollars to one of the dealers stationed in front of your hotel. The dollars you sell will probably be used by a resident of the LDC to purchase goods or assets abroad without government approval.

Since high inflation in LDCs makes it impossible to maintain absolutely rigid exchange rates for long, many LDCs have used an exchange-rate system called the **crawling peg.** Under a crawling peg, the central bank always fixes the domestic-currency price of foreign exchange but allows that price to "crawl" upward over time, so that the home currency is being devalued continuously against foreign currencies. The central bank's mini-devaluations take place quite frequently, sometimes even daily.

Until the early 1970s, LDCs generally pegged their currencies to a single major industrial-country currency—usually the dollar, but sometimes the British pound or French franc. Since then, in response to floating dollar exchange rates among the industrialized countries, some LDCs have pegged their currencies to *baskets* of industrialized-country currencies. An example shows that floating rates make it riskier for LDCs to peg to a single foreign currency. An LDC pegging to the dollar would find itself forced to revalue its currency against nondollar currencies if the dollar appreciated sharply in the foreign-exchange market. By pegging to a basket instead, the LDC can reduce the effect on its international trade of large swings in the values of the individual currencies in the basket.

THE STRUCTURE OF LDC EXPORTS

Many LDCs rely for their export earnings on a small number of natural resources or agricultural products—sometimes only one. Nigeria depends heavily on oil exports, Chile on copper, Colombia on coffee (and cocaine), and Malaysia on rubber.

Dependence on such commodity exports poses a macroeconomic problem for LDCs because commodity prices are highly variable relative to those of manufactured goods. In turn, drastic shifts in the prices of a country's most important export goods cause corresponding shifts in real income and the current account. A fall in export prices, for example, simultaneously causes a slump in the economy and a current-account deficit. The government may find it impossible to regain internal and external balance until export prices recover.

LDC export prices are particularly sensitive to the macroeconomic policies adopted in the industrialized world. A reduction in aggregate demand in the industrialized countries is quickly transmitted to LDCs as commodity prices plummet and LDC real incomes fall.

LDC BORROWING AND DEBT

One further feature of LDCs is crucial to understanding their macroeconomic problems: LDCs rely largely on capital inflows from abroad to finance their domestic investment. In recent years, LDCs have borrowed on a large scale from richer countries and have built up a large debt to the rest of the world (nearly $1 trillion at the beginning of 1987). This debt has been at the center of a crisis in international lending that has preoccupied macroeconomic policymakers throughout the world since 1982.

THE ECONOMICS OF LDC BORROWING

Most LDCs have borrowed extensively abroad over the period since World War II and now have substantial debts to foreigners. Why has this borrowing occurred?

Recall the identity (analyzed in Chapter 12) that links national saving, S, domestic investment, I, and the current-account balance, CA: $S - I = CA$. If national saving falls short of domestic investment, the difference equals the current-account deficit. As observed earlier, saving levels are quite low in many LDCs. But because these same countries are relatively poor in capital, the opportunities for introducing profitable plant and equipment can be abundant. Such opportunities justify a high level of investment, and by running a deficit in its current-account balance, an LDC can obtain resources to invest even if its domestic saving level is low. A deficit in the current account implies, however, that the LDC is borrowing abroad. In return for being able to import more foreign goods today than it exports today, the LDC must promise to repay in the future the interest and principal on the loan foreigners are making.

Thus, much LDC borrowing from more developed countries results from the incentives for *intertemporal trade* examined in Chapter 7. Low-income countries generate too little saving of their own to take advantage of all their opportunities for investment; so they must borrow abroad. In capital-rich countries, on the other hand, the most productive investment opportunities have been exploited already but saving levels are relatively high. To take advantage of the higher returns available in LDCs, savers in developed countries willingly finance LDC investments by lending the funds LDCs wish to borrow.

Notice that when developing countries borrow to undertake productive investments that they could not undertake otherwise, both they and the lenders reap gains from trade. Borrowers gain because they can build up their capital stocks in spite of limited national saving levels. Lenders gain because they earn higher returns on their investments than they could earn at home.

While the reasoning above provides a rationale for LDC external deficits and debt, it does not say that *any* loan from developed to developing countries is justified. Loans made to finance unprofitable investments or to finance the import of consumption goods may result in debts that the LDC cannot repay. In addition, because low LDC saving rates are due in part to faulty government policies, those policies may have led to excessive foreign borrowing.

ALTERNATIVE FORMS OF CAPITAL INFLOW

When a developing country has a current-account deficit, it is selling assets to foreigners to finance the difference between its spending and its income. While we have lumped these asset sales together under the catch-all term "borrowing," the capital inflows that finance LDC deficits (and indeed, any country's deficit) can take several forms. Different types of capital inflow have predominated in different historical periods; and because different types of inflow give rise to different LDC obligations to foreign lenders, an understanding of the macroeconomic problems of LDCs requires a careful analysis of the four major channels through which they have financed their external deficits.

1. *Bond finance.* LDCs have sometimes sold bonds to private foreign citizens to finance their current-account deficits. Bond finance was important in the period up to 1914 and in the interwar years but has been a relatively insignificant component of LDC external financing since the Second World War. The trend away from bond finance accelerated after 1970. Bond financing was equal to 1.5 percent of the 1970 aggregate LDC deficit but had sunk to only 0.5 percent by 1983.[4]

2. *Bank loans.* Since the early 1970s, LDCs have increasingly borrowed directly from commercial banks in the financial centers of the developed countries. In 1970, roughly 26 percent of LDC external finance was provided by banks, while in 1983 the corresponding percentage was 42. These aggregate figures conceal large differences in the experiences of individual LDCs. Some Latin American countries, for example, became much more dependent on bank finance by the 1980s than average figures indicate. These countries' sharp shift toward bank finance was an important element in the post-1982 debt crisis.

[4]See World Bank, *World Development Report 1985,* table 2.3, p. 21, for a summary of LDC external finance since 1970. For the purposes of these numbers, the current-account deficit is measured net of transfers.

3. *Direct foreign investment.* In direct foreign investment, a firm largely owned by foreign residents acquires or expands a subsidiary firm or factory located domestically (Chapter 7). A loan from IBM to its plant in Mexico, for example, would be a direct investment by the United States in Mexico. Similarly, Japanese stockholders financing the construction of a Toyota plant in the United States are carrying out direct investment. The first of these direct investments would enter the Mexican balance of payments accounts as a capital inflow (and the U.S. balance of payments accounts as an equal capital outflow); the second would enter Japan's balance of payments accounts as a capital outflow (and the U.S. balance of payments accounts as an equal capital inflow).

Direct investment is often the only way for foreigners to acquire substantial direct claims on plant and equipment operating within an LDC economy. Residents of any country can easily buy shares of stock on the New York, London, or Frankfurt stock exchanges, but LDCs generally do not have extensive organized stock markets in which domestic firms can sell shares of ownership in their productive assets. Thus, foreign firms wishing to operate in LDC economies typically invest directly by building and running their own factories there. The combination of ownership and control is the characteristic feature of direct foreign investment in LDCs.

While direct investment was an important source of developing-country external finance in the 25 years after World War II, its importance has declined recently. Between 1970 and 1983, the percentage of LDC external finance coming from direct investment inflows dropped from around 19 percent to just under 8 percent.

4. *Official lending.* LDCs sometimes borrow from international agencies like the International Monetary Fund and the World Bank, and from the governments of other countries. Such loans can be made on a "concessional" basis—that is, at interest rates below market rates—or on a market basis that allows the lender to earn the market rate of return. Official lending flows to LDCs have shrunk relative to total flows over the post–World War II period.

DEBT VS. EQUITY FINANCE

The four types of finance just describe can be classified into two categories: **debt finance** and **equity finance.** Bond, bank, and official finance are all forms of debt finance. The debtor must repay the face value of the loan, plus interest, regardless of its own economic circumstances. Direct investment, on the other hand, is a form of equity finance. Foreign owners of a direct investment have a claim to a share of its net output, not a claim to a fixed stream of money payments. Therefore, adverse economic events in the LDC result in an automatic fall in the earnings of direct investments and in the dividends paid out to foreigners.

The distinction between debt and equity finance is useful in analyzing how LDC payments to foreigners adjust in response to unforeseen economic disturbances such as world recessions and terms-of-trade changes. When an

LDC has a large debt burden, its payments to creditors do not fall if its real income falls; so it may become extremely painful for the country to continue honoring its foreign obligations. The problem does not arise with equity finance. In that case, a fall in LDC income simply reduces the earnings of foreign shareholders. But this reduction does not involve the violation of any loan agreement, as it would under debt finance, since foreigners, by acquiring equity, have in effect agreed to share in both the bad and the good times of the economy.

GOVERNMENT AND PUBLICLY GUARANTEED BORROWING

It is important to realize that most LDC debt finance represents either direct loans to governments or government-owned firms, or publicly guaranteed loans to the private sector, that is, loans for which the LDC government agrees to be responsible in case of private nonpayment. In the presence of exchange controls and undeveloped domestic financial markets, LDC authorities more or less automatically become involved in any borrowing agreement between domestic residents and foreigners. The government's ultimate responsibility for paying the country's foreign debts implies that external payments problems usually reflect government budgetary difficulties and affect most of an LDC's external debt at the same time.

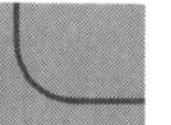

LDC BORROWING IN HISTORICAL PERSPECTIVE

With this background on the general features of LDC macroeconomic structure and on the long-run factors behind LDC foreign borrowing, we now turn to the role LDCs have played in the world economy over the last century. From the late nineteenth century to the early 1980s, lending to LDCs first boomed, then disappeared as the world slid into the Great Depression, and finally reappeared and expanded quickly. Events of 1982 led to a sharp contraction in lending to LDC debtors and an international debt crisis that still threatens the prosperity of developed and developing nations alike. The events of the pre-1982 period provide valuable historical lessons that help illuminate the recent debt crisis and the steps international policymakers can take to resolve it.

CAPITAL FLOWS TO DEVELOPING COUNTRIES BEFORE 1914

The period ending with World War I was one of substantial capital flow from Europe to developing areas, much of it in the form of loans. Between 1870 and 1914, Britain, on average, invested more than 5 percent of its GNP abroad. The corresponding numbers for France and Germany, the other two leading foreign lenders, were between 2 and 3 percent. In this period London, the hub of the gold-standard system, was the main international financial center. Many developing countries borrowed by selling bonds in London, usually through syndicates of London financial brokers and banks.

From the vantage point of an international economy shattered by World War I, the pre-1914 period appeared to be a paradise for international investors. The international capital market centered in London certainly did thrive up to 1914, but conditions were not as tranquil as nostalgic descriptions penned during the interwar period (and after) might lead you to believe. As we saw in Chapter 18, economic fluctuations were severe under the gold standard, and fluctuations in Europe had a major impact on the prosperity of developing borrowers. Faced with sudden declines in export earnings, debtor countries were sometimes forced to suspend payments of interest and principal on their debt. In addition, domestic economic mismanagement sometimes contributed to the interruption of payments to foreign creditors.

Whenever a borrower does not make the payments specified in the loan contract, the loan is said to be in **default**. Defaults by less-developed debtors were not at all uncommon before 1914—in fact, several American states defaulted on foreign loans in that period. The losers in cases of default were the individuals who had purchased bonds from LDC borrowers. Even though a defaulting borrower sometimes resumed payments after its economic circumstances had improved, the immediate effect of default was a sharp fall in the value of its outstanding bonds, and therefore a sharp capital loss for bondholders. Bondholders could do little to prevent LDC governments from defaulting.

Why did international lending to LDCs boom before 1914 in spite of the very real possibility of default? Three factors appear to have been particularly important:

1. Foreign investment opportunities appeared very profitable. Resource-rich areas were relatively unexploited, and the payoffs expected from building factories, railways, and utilities were immense.

2. Countries like the United States, Canada, Argentina, and Australia, which absorbed most of the funds lent by Europe before 1914, had low population densities and were therefore attracting a large immigration of Europeans, including skilled workers and entrepreneurs. In a famous article, the economist Ragnar Nurkse of Columbia University pointed out that flows of labor and capital from Europe were mutually reinforcing. European lenders felt confident that European immigrants moving to "regions of recent settlement" would successfully transplant the achievements of the Industrial Revolution; and a shared cultural heritage made the negotiation of international loans easier. European countries invested in more densely populated areas like India and Southeast Asia largely by acquiring direct investments in mines, plantations, or other resource-based ventures rather than by buying bonds. Unlike bond lending, direct investments run by European owners could be profitable even in the absence of local entrepreneurial talent.[5]

[5]See Nurkse, "International Investment Today in the Light of Nineteenth-Century Experience," *Economic Journal* 64 (1954), pp. 134–150.

3. Britain's leadership of the world economy played a key role in promoting a hospitable environment for international investment. As a champion of free trade and capital movements, Britain provided a ready source of savings for the rest of the world and a ready market in which LDC exporters could earn the money needed to meet payments on their foreign debts. Because investment opportunities within Britain were relatively sparse by the end of the nineteenth century, anywhere from 25 to 40 percent of Britain's savings flowed abroad between 1870 and 1914. London's financial houses therefore had strong incentives to seek investment opportunities overseas, and foreign investment made up a large part of their activities. In addition, British loans to LDCs allowed those countries to import machinery and other goods from Britain. Recognizing foreign lending as crucial to domestic prosperity, the British government played an active role in assuring that LDC defaults were quickly settled and did not lead to a breakdown of international lending and trade.

THE INTERWAR PERIOD AND ITS AFTERMATH: 1918–1972

London lost its position as the world's leading financial center after World War I, and the United States emerged as the major lender to the less-developed world. Britain and France had incurred large war debts to the United States, while Germany was saddled with reparations. None of these European countries, which had been the main foreign lenders before 1914, was now in a position to play a major role in LDC lending. To bolster its weak balance of payments, Britain prohibited foreign lending by its residents at several points during the interwar years.

During the 1920s, many LDC governments floated bonds in the United States, and American direct investment in LDCs grew. No LDC governments defaulted in the 1920s, but signs of trouble appeared as the decade drew to a close. After the mid-1920s, world prices for agricultural products, a main source of export revenue for many LDCs, declined. And after 1928, U.S. lending abroad fell as Americans diverted their savings from foreign investments to the booming New York stock market.

The New York stock market crash of October 1929 and the ensuing worldwide depression caused the LDCs' sources of foreign finance to dry up almost entirely. Unable to borrow from industrial countries, the LDCs were forced to cut their imports, a move that accentuated the decline in aggregate demand in the developed world. As industrialized countries erected higher barriers to imports, it became nearly impossible for LDCs to earn the export revenues they needed to meet debt payments. Bolivia defaulted on January 1, 1931, and it was followed, within 3 years, by almost every other country in Latin America. Most of these countries simultaneously left the gold standard, adopted floating exchange rates, and pursued expansionary monetary and fiscal policies to combat the effects of the worldwide depression.

The United States was not in a position to avert the worldwide financial collapse, as Britain might have been before 1914. Only a small fraction of

U.S. saving was lent abroad and exports were a relatively small part of U.S. GNP. Therefore, the American government and financial community did not perceive a well-functioning international trade and financial system as crucial to U.S. economic health.

Also in contrast to Britain before 1914, the United States failed to shoulder its responsibility as an international creditor of providing a ready market for debtor exports. As countries throughout the world raised tariffs in the early 1920s to combat recession or protect new industries that had grown up during the war, the United States, rather than setting an example of free trade, enacted the Fordney-McCumber tariff in 1922. Many economists think that the subsequent Smoot-Hawley tariff of 1930 was particularly damaging to the world economy (Chapters 9 and 18). The latter measure aggravated the plunge in LDC agricultural export prices at the beginning of the Great Depression.

While LDC default had occurred in the years before 1914, the widespread and synchronized default of the early 1930s was unprecedented. The nearly universal LDC default was accompanied by that of a major developed country, Germany, after Adolf Hitler's accession to power. Under the pressure of these shocks, the flow of international lending that had encouraged world economic growth during the 1920s shrank to a trickle in the 1930s. Before 1914, individual countries in default generally were able to resume borrowing once their economic prospects brightened and their previous foreign debts were settled. After the defaults of the 1930s, however, the international capital market showed no such resilience. The generalized nature of the interwar debt crisis helped deepen the Great Depression. The Depression and the trade restrictions it inspired, in turn, encouraged default and discouraged a return to normal international lending. At the outbreak of World War II, LDCs remained largely shut out of the international capital market; private lending to LDCs on the scale seen before the Depression did not revive until the 1970s.

From 1945 to the early 1970s, most capital flows to LDCs took one of three forms: official lending, short-term trade credit granted to LDCs by foreign exporters, or direct foreign investment. Many trade-related loans to LDCs became official loans when lender governments guaranteed them as a way of indirectly subsidizing their countries' exports. Because individual LDCs sometimes encountered difficulties in paying their debts during this period, governments and international institutions lending to LDCs established the **Paris Club** in 1956 as a framework for rescheduling debts to official creditors (see the box). **Debt rescheduling** occurs when some or all of the principal payments on the debt are postponed, subject to the provision that interest is paid on the postponed payments.

Direct investments were subject to a threat different from default, the threat of nationalization (that is, expropriation) by the host government. The period following World War II was one of rising nationalism as former colonial territories became independent. In this environment, some governments did not stop at taxing the profits of foreign-owned firms but instead simply

THE PARIS CLUB

In 1956, Argentine debt difficulties prompted the formation of the Paris Club, a forum for negotiations on countries' debts to government creditors. The club has no set membership. Instead, the participants in any Paris Club negotiation are the debtor government and its creditors, who traditionally meet under the chairmanship of a senior French Treasury official.

An important principle governing Paris Club rescheduling negotiations is the symmetric treatment of all creditors. Prior to the conclusion of an agreement, debtor countries approaching the Paris Club are usually required to conclude an agreement with the International Monetary Fund providing for an IMF loan together with an IMF-approved program of economic-policy measures. The IMF adjustment program, an example of Fund conditionality, is typically aimed at restricting aggregate demand in the debtor country and raising its exports. Creditors view the IMF stabilization package as essential for attaining a current-account path that allows the debtor to resume payment on its foreign debt.*

*Brazil, which concluded a Paris Club negotiation in 1986 *without* agreeing to an IMF program, is the exception. By early 1987, however, Brazil's domestic economic problems had led it to suspend interest payments on its foreign commercial-bank debt.

seized their assets. Disputes over compensation for such seizures were resolved on a case-by-case basis, but companies whose assets were seized usually had little power to influence the outcome. In spite of the risk of nationalization or heavy taxation, direct investment flows to LDCs grew quickly in the 1950s and 1960s, in part because many developing countries offered abundant supplies of valuable raw materials.

LDC BORROWING AFTER 1973: OIL SHOCKS AND FLOATING INTEREST RATES

The OPEC oil shock of 1973–1974 marked the beginning of a surge in private commercial bank lending to LDCs that was to last nearly a decade. Banks in the industrialized world had not previously played a dominant role in lending to developing countries, but the huge OPEC current-account surplus that followed the rise in oil prices had to be "recycled" to finance the current-account deficits of the rest of the world. The OPEC countries placed their surplus funds in developed-country banks, and these banks found they could earn high returns by relending the funds to LDCs.

TABLE 20-2 Current-account balances of major oil exporters, other developing countries, and industrial countries, 1973–1985 (billions of dollars)

Year	Major oil exporters	Other developing countries	Industrial countries
1973	6.7	−11.3	20.3
1974	68.3	−37.0	−10.8
1975	35.4	−46.3	19.8
1976	40.3	−32.6	0.5
1977	29.4	−29.6	−2.4
1978	−1.3	−33.2	14.6
1979	56.8	−49.7	−25.6
1980	102.4	−74.4	−61.8
1981	45.8	−95.0	−18.9
1982	−17.8	−73.2	−22.2
1983	−18.0	−40.9	−23.0
1984	−10.0	−25.0	−64.2
1985	−5.5	−28.7	−54.2

Source: International Monetary Fund. *World Economic Outlook,* 1983, 1985, 1986. The current-account balances reported above do not include official transfers. The countries included as major oil exporters are those whose oil exports are at least two-thirds of overall exports and at least 100 million barrels per year. Global current accounts may not sum to zero because of errors, omissions, and the exclusion of some countries (for example, members of the Soviet bloc).

Table 20-2 shows the global pattern of current-account balances for the period between 1973 and 1985. An immediate effect of the oil-price rise was a tenfold increase in the current-account surplus of the major oil exporters between 1973 and 1974. These countries could not raise their spending quickly enough in the short run to keep pace with their skyrocketing export earnings, so they ran large but declining surpluses until 1978, when their expenditure finally caught up with their income. As a group, the industrial countries ran a short-lived deficit after the first OPEC shock. In contrast, the current-account deficit of the nonoil LDCs rose sharply in 1974 and remained high through 1978. Why did nonoil LDC current accounts fail to adjust quickly to the oil shock? As the industrial countries slipped into the recession of 1974–1975, LDC governments adopted and maintained expansionary policies that spurred domestic investment and helped keep LDC output growth rates high relative to those in the industrialized world. The cost of these measures was the large and persistent LDC deficit: LDCs were borrowing heavily abroad and building up foreign debt to maintain spending levels in excess of their incomes. The total debt of the nonoil developing countries at the end of 1978 ($336 billion) was nearly three times its 1973 level ($130 billion).[6]

[6]See International Monetary Fund, *World Economic Outlook,* 1983, table 32.

In most of the years between 1974 and 1978, the deficits of the nonoil LDCs shown in Table 20-2 correspond closely to the surpluses of the major oil producers. The oil producers were not lending directly to the other LDCs but instead were depositing the oil earnings they could not spend in industrial-country banks, which then turned around and lent these funds to LDC borrowers. This recycling was necessary because oil exporters did not want to assume the risks of direct lending to LDCs but preferred to acquire safer assets located in developed countries. At the same time, banks in developed countries faced interest rates that were low; in fact, when measured in real terms, that is, in terms of output, interest rates in developed countries were negative.[7] It is no wonder that when faced with negative real interest rates at home, developed-country banks were eager to lend to LDCs, who were willing to pay somewhat higher rates than the banks' local customers. Even after the addition of a borrowing premium, LDCs faced historically low real interest rates, which naturally encouraged them to borrow abroad.

The second oil shock brought a renewed surge in the current-account surpluses of the main oil exporters in 1979; at the same time, it worsened the deficits of other countries. Oil producers' earnings were once again recycled to LDC borrowers, but while the industrial countries as a group were much closer to current-account balance by 1981, the nonoil LDCs borrowed almost $100 billion in that year to finance their overall current-account deficit. From a year-end level of $336 billion in 1978, the indebtedness of these countries rose to $662 billion by the end of 1982. By 1982, however, the oil exporters were themselves running a deficit, and therefore were not providing the funds to finance the still-large deficit of the other LDCs. As a result, LDCs were encountering increased difficulty in borrowing from developed-country banks even before the debt crisis erupted in the second half of 1982.

The severity of the LDC debt crisis is closely tied to a major institutional feature of bank lending to LDCs in the late 1970s. That feature is the use of loan contracts with adjustable interest rates, called **floating-rate loan contracts.** Under a floating-rate loan contract, the lender is allowed to change the interest rate you pay on the loan as market interest rates change. As an example, suppose that you borrow from a bank for a year at a rate of 5 percentage points above the rate on U.S. Treasury bills, adjustable every 6 months. If the Treasury bill rate is 5 percent per annum when you take out your loan, you pay interest at a rate of 10 percent during the loan's first 6 months; but if the Treasury bill rate rises to 9 percent within the first 6 months, you must pay interest at a rate of 14 percent for the next 6 months. Typically, the interest charged on floating-rate dollar loans from banks to LDCs was tied to the London Interbank Offered Rate (LIBOR), the interest rate London commerical banks charge each other for dollar loans.

[7]In 1976, for example, the interest rate on 3-month U.S. Treasury bills averaged 4.9 percent per year, while the consumer price index rose by 6.7 percent over the same year. These figures tell us that a U.S. bank lending domestically in 1976 would have earned an average real rate of return of 4.9 − 6.7 = −1.8 percent over the year. Econometric studies suggest that *expected* as well as realized U.S. real interest rates were negative in the mid-1970s.

Banks favored the use of floating-rate contracts because adjustable interest rates protected them from being "locked in" to low-interest-rate loans when the interest rates they themselves had to pay to depositors rose. By the late 1970s, a large portion of LDC debt (particularly that of Latin American countries) carried floating interest rates. Heavy borrowing on a floating-rate basis left LDCs exposed to the danger that a sharp rise in U.S. interest rates would increase their interest burden dramatically. Such an increase did occur in the late 1970s, and that increase, together with the events that caused it, set the stage for a widespread LDC debt crisis comparable only with that of the 1930s.

THE LDC DEBT CRISIS: 1982 TO THE PRESENT

In the years 1981–1983, the world economy suffered the worst recession since the 1930s. Just as the Great Depression made it hard for LDCs to pay interest and principal on foreign loans—quickly causing an almost universal default—the great recession of the 1980s also sparked a crisis over LDC debt.

LEADING UP TO THE CRISIS

Chapter 19 described how the U.S Federal Reserve adopted a tough anti-inflationary monetary policy at the end of 1979 that helped propel the world economy into a profound recession by 1981. Even before the recession hit, however, the U.S monetary shift had direct adverse effects on the real income of LDCs.

Adverse effects came through two principal channels, U.S. interest rates and the dollar's exchange rate. The Fed's monetary changes were followed by sharp rises in dollar interest rates and in the dollar's value in the foreign-exchange market. LIBOR, to which interest rates on many LDC loans are tied, rose sharply in 1979 (Figure 20-1a).[8] This rise in LIBOR made new LDC borrowing more expensive, but because much LDC debt had been contracted at floating interest rates, the interest payments due on *previous* loans also rose. The foreign interest burden of LDCs therefore took an immediate upward jump.

The interest-rate effect was reinforced by the behavior of the dollar. Since much LDC debt was denominated in dollars, the dollar's appreciation increased the *real* value of LDC **debt service**—the flow of interest payments and principal to foreign creditors. Table 20-3 shows a partial measure of the dollar value of LDC debt service payments from 1977 to 1985. In reading this table, keep in mind that the dollar's appreciation after 1980 caused the real value of these payments to rise by more than their dollar value. Thus,

[8]Through asset-market arbitrage, LIBOR is determined mainly by interest rates on dollar assets located in the United States. The shift in U.S. monetary policy in 1979 therefore had a direct and immediate impact on LIBOR.

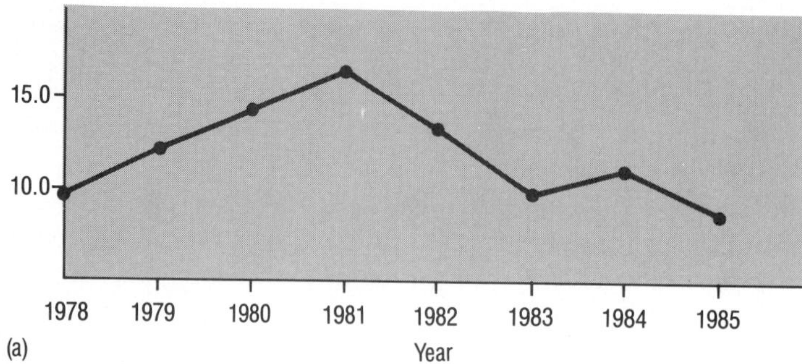

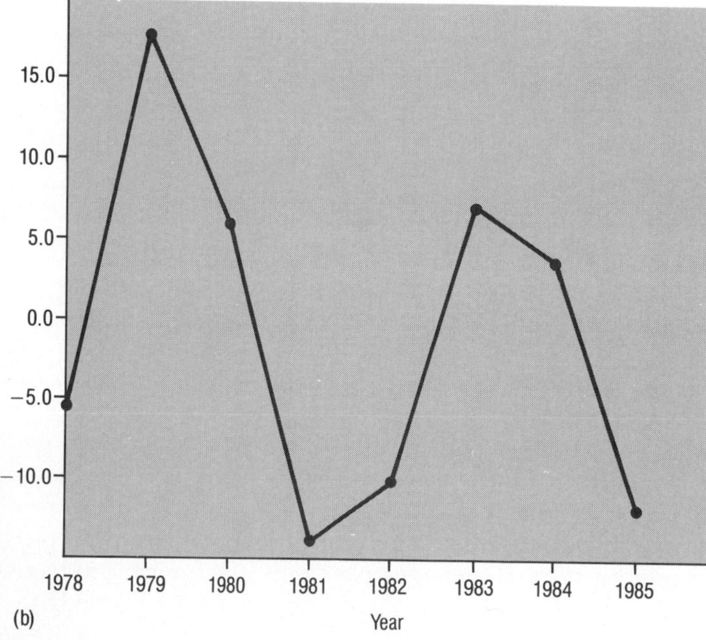

FIGURE 20-1 LIBOR and LDC commodity export prices, 1978–1985. In 1981, dollar interest rates reached a historic high point, worsening LDC debt-service burdens. At the same time, LDC commodity export prices (and LDC terms of trade) plunged. In 1985, the favorable effect of lower dollar interest rates on debt-service burdens was offset by another decline in commodity export prices.
Source: (a) World Bank, *World Development Report 1986,* table 2.10. (b) International Monetary Fund, *World Economic Outlook,* April 1986, table A29.

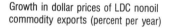

TABLE 20-3 Debt service payments of LDC debtors, 1977–1985 (billions of dollars)

1977	1978	1979	1980	1981	1982	1983	1984	1985
39.5	57.2	75.3	87.9	110.2	119.5	110.7	126.2	131.4

Source: International Monetary Fund, *World Economic Outlook,* April 1985, April 1986, tables 44 and A46. The debt-service payments reported here include all interest payments plus principal payments on debt with a maturity exceeding 1 year.

the rise in dollar payments between 1980 and 1982 understates the increase in the real interest burden of the LDCs.

The reaction of LDCs to the adverse movement in interest rates and their real debt burdens helped set the stage for the crisis to follow. The rise in nonoil LDC borrowing after 1978 (Table 20-2) was a result not only of the oil shock but also of the rise in real debt service burdens. LDCs viewed both these setbacks as partially temporary and hoped to soften their impact by borrowing from foreign banks and maintaining domestic demand until better conditions allowed them to repay their loans. Interest rates did not, however, return quickly to their pre-1979 levels.

In 1981, when the world economy began sliding into recession, LDCs were therefore carrying an unprecedented external debt burden. U.S. interest rates were at a peak, and these rates were reflected in LDC payments on new borrowing and older floating-rate debt (Figure 20-1a). Much of the short-term borrowing of the immediately preceding years was coming due, and LDCs faced the choice of repaying these loans or refinancing them at historically high interest rates. As Table 20-2 shows, the overall current-account surplus of the oil exporters had shrunk by 1981 (it turned to a deficit in 1982); so the ready supply of "petrodollars" that had financed LDC borrowing in earlier years was disappearing. And with inflation falling throughout the industrialized world (see Table 19-4, p. 559), commercial banks in the developed countries found they could now earn high real returns by lending at home. As a result, LDCs were finding it increasingly hard to borrow from the banks that had eagerly financed their earlier current-account deficits.

LDCs AND THE WORLDWIDE RECESSION

The 1981–1983 growth slowdown in industrial countries had two immediate effects on LDC incomes. First, as income fell in the industrialized world, LDCs began to face diminished demand for their exports. This fall in aggregate demand directly reduced the growth rate of output in developing countries. Second, the reduction in demand for LDC products tended to lower their prices. As noted earlier, many LDCs depend on exports of agricultural products or raw materials whose prices are sensitive to demand conditions in world markets. LDCs' real incomes therefore declined not only as a result of the fall in their output but also because the prices of the primary commodities they export fell relative to the prices of their imports. A further negative effect on the LDCs resulted from protectionist pressures in a number of industrialized countries. Such pressures made it harder for LDCs to sell their products in industrial-country markets and contributed to a further worsening of LDCs' terms of trade.

The effect of the world recession on the dollar prices of nonoil primary commodities can be seen in Figure 20-1b. After rising fairly steadily from the mid-1960s to 1980, commodity prices plunged dramatically in 1981 and

TABLE 20-4 Growth rates of output for developed and developing countries, 1978–1985 (percent per year)

Country Group	1978	1979	1980	1981	1982	1983	1984	1985
Industrial countries	4.2	3.3	1.2	1.4	−0.4	2.6	4.7	2.8
Developing countries	5.1	4.3	3.5	2.2	1.6	1.3	4.1	3.2
Regions:								
Africa	1.1	3.2	3.8	1.7	0.8	−1.5	1.6	1.6
Asia	9.1	4.4	5.5	5.5	5.0	7.4	7.9	6.1
Western Hemisphere	4.1	6.0	5.3	0.9	−0.9	−3.1	3.1	3.8

Source: International Monetary Fund, *World Economic Outlook,* April 1986, tables A2 and A5. Output measures are real gross national product for developed countries, real gross domestic product for developing countries.

1982. The fall in prices was not entirely due to the fall in worldwide aggregate demand. The appreciation of the dollar against foreign currencies also put downward pressure on the dollar prices of commodities.[9]

Table 20-4 shows output growth rates between 1978 and 1985 for developed and developing countries. The table indicates a marked reduction in industrial-country growth rates after 1978, with GNP growth actually turning negative around the low point of the recession in 1982. LDCs exhibit a similar fall in growth rates after 1978, reaching their low point in 1982–1983. However, the numbers for LDCs as a group conceal important regional differences. Asian LDCs such as South Korea and Taiwan suffered relatively minor declines in their growth rates as a result of the recession (the 1967–1977 average annual growth rate for these countries was 5.4 percent). LDCs in Africa and the Western Hemisphere did not fare so well. The group of Western Hemisphere LDCs, which includes Latin America, was particularly hard hit, with an output growth rate of only 0.9 percent in 1981 and of *minus* 0.9 percent in 1982. The staggering −3.1 percent growth rate these countries suffered in 1983 was a direct result of the debt crisis, which started in August 1982.

MEXICO: THE BEGINNING OF THE CRISIS

On August 12, 1982, Mexico notified foreign financial officials that its central bank had nearly run out of reserves and that it could no longer meet previously scheduled payments on its external debt. That debt, amounting to

[9]The fall in commodity prices was mirrored in the behavior of the developing countries' terms of trade. The terms of trade of indebted developing countries fell by 3.3 percent in 1981 and by 2.7 percent in 1982. See International Monetary Fund, *World Economic Outlook,* April 1985, table 27.

more than $80 billion, made Mexico, after Brazil, the world's largest LDC debtor. Mexico requested a loan from foreign governments and central banks, a moratorium on payments of principal to commercial banks, and a rescheduling of the principal on debt due to mature in coming months. At the same time, Mexican officials approached the International Monetary Fund with a request for a loan and an IMF-sponsored macroeconomic stabilization plan.

What chain of events had placed Mexico on the brink of default? As was typically the case in countries that experienced debt-servicing problems in the 1980s, both adverse external shocks and internal macroeconomic mismanagement were to blame. In the mid-1970s, Mexico had become a major oil exporter (though not a member of OPEC); by the mid-1980s some 60 percent of Mexico's export revenues came from oil. Since the Mexican oil industry is government-owned, the surge in oil revenues accrued directly to the government, which used the funds to finance subsidies, public works, and social programs. Indeed, government spending rose more quickly than oil revenues: some of this spending was financed through seigniorage—that is, the monetary printing press—while some was financed by borrowing abroad. Money creation sparked rapid inflation and a real appreciation of the Mexican peso, whose nominal exchange rate with the dollar was fixed by the Banco de Mexico, Mexico's central bank. But, helped by the fiscal stimulus, Mexico achieved a high rate of economic growth; and with oil prices high and rising, foreign banks, particularly U.S. banks, competed to lend Mexico money.

Mexico's prospects dimmed in 1981 as the worldwide recession began and oil demand fell. The Mexican government committed the major blunder of not immediately lowering the price of its oil in the face of weakening demand, and it had to borrow abroad to make up for the resulting fall in its oil revenues. The Banco de Mexico's foreign reserves fell as Mexicans, increasingly nervous about a possible peso devaluation, fled from pesos to dollars.

The economic outlook became bleaker as the recession in the United States deepened in early 1982. Closely linked to the United States through international trade, Mexico was bound to suffer a large decline in growth as a result of the fall in U.S. demand. Mexico devalued the peso in February but failed to cut the government budget deficit or adopt other significant expenditure-changing measures that would reduce its current-account deficit and thus reduce the country's need for additional loans from abroad. The devaluation therefore translated quickly into additional domestic inflation, with little benefit to external balance or employment.

Commercial banks began to question Mexico's ability to repay its substantial debt without politically hazardous cuts in domestic consumption and investment: petroleum prices were weak, demand for Mexican exports was down as a result of the recession, high interest rates and the high dollar had increased the country's debt-service burden, and there was no confidence that the government would brake its inflationary fiscal expansion. By the summer of 1982, Mexico found its credit lines drying up. Like many other

LDCs, Mexico had built up a substantial short-term debt whose principal had to be "rolled over" by the banks—that is re-lent to Mexico—or repaid. Any banks still willing to lend to Mexico would now do so only at penalty interest rates that reflected the possibility of default. Anticipating another devaluation, Mexicans had nearly bought out the Banco de Mexico's dollar reserves by mid-August 1982. At that point the Mexican government took its dramatic step of seeking a multilateral international loan package and negotiations with its commercial-bank creditors.

THE DEBT CRISIS IN OTHER COUNTRIES

Even as Mexico began its long and complex debt negotiations, other debtors in Latin America, for example, Brazil (with a 1982 debt of close to $88 billion) and Argentina (with a 1982 debt near $40 billion), found themselves unable to take out new foreign loans or even roll over maturing short-term debt. Bankers saw similarities in the economic circumstances of all the Latin American debtors; and they feared that if Mexico defaulted, other countries might follow its example, as in the 1930s. Banks scrambled to reduce their risks by refusing to extend new credits or renew old ones. By the end of 1986, more than 40 countries in Latin America, Africa, and elsewhere had encountered severe external financing problems. Countries in East Asia (with the exception of the Philippines) maintained high growth rates throughout the recession and avoided the need to reschedule their debts (see Table 20-4).

Much of the debt of African nations was owed to official agencies and governments; the Paris Club therefore provided a ready-made forum for the resolution of African debt issues. A framework for rescheduling Latin America's massive debts to commercial banks, however, did not yet exist. Hundreds of banks around the world had claims on Latin America, and American giants like Citicorp, Bank of America, Manufacturers Hanover, and Chemical had invested significant portions of their loan portfolios in the region. A widespread Latin American default would have threatened the viability of the large banks and some of the smaller banks, endangering the world financial system. The Fed and foreign central banks therefore viewed the task of averting default, even by a single country, as crucial. A Brazilian default, say, could have set off a chain reaction of bank failures involving many countries. No one wanted a replay of the widespread banking crisis that occurred at the beginning of the Great Depression.

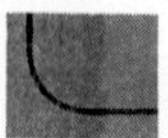

ANALYZING LDC BORROWING AND DEFAULT

The task of averting default was a delicate one that involved cooperation by creditor and debtor governments, the IMF, and the largest private banks holding Latin American loans. Working together, these actors evolved a framework for rescheduling commercial-bank loans to LDCs that has so far avoided a generalized default. To understand why this framework has been effective, we must first examine the theory of international lending in a world of possible default.

THE COSTS OF SOVEREIGN DEFAULT

As noted above, most loans extended to an LDC are either taken out or guaranteed by the LDC's government. This characteristic of lending to LDCs makes an LDC's decision to default essentially a government decision, not a decision by individual resident borrowers. A government decision to default on external obligations is called a **sovereign default** because a defaulting government is not subject to the legal remedies that would usually be invoked in cases of private default. Even a sovereign defaulter would, however, incur significant costs. How does a government measure the costs of sovereign default against its benefits in deciding whether to continue meeting its debt-service obligations?

When a sovereign borrower defaults on its foreign debt, its creditors cannot penalize it as they would penalize defaulting private borrowers resident in their own countries. If you default on a car loan, for example, the lender can take you to court. A bank cannot take Brazil or Mexico to court if those countries fail to live up to the terms of their loan agreements. Nonetheless, even sovereign borrowers cannot default with impunity. There are three main costs a sovereign borrower must consider in deciding whether to default:

1. *Seizure of assets.* Creditors of a sovereign defaulter may be able to persuade their governments to seize any of the debtor's assets located in their jurisdiction. These could include the foreign reserves of the defaulting country's central bank, foreign assets owned by the defaulting country's private citizens, or even goods in international trade owned by the debtor and crossing creditors' borders. Seizure of assets is probably a minor deterrent to default, given the magnitude of LDCs' foreign debts, but the possibility does enter government's calculations. In early 1986, for example, the Peruvian government brought home some $700 million worth of gold and silver it had been holding abroad. The country had fallen into serious arrears in its debt payments, and it feared that its precious metal stocks would be seized by creditors.

2. *Exclusion from future borrowing.* A country that defaulted would be shut out of the international capital market, at least for several years. Once a country has already defaulted on previous debts, prospective lenders will be unwilling to believe promises that it will abide by the terms of new loan contracts. Further, if a sovereign defaulter did succeed in getting a loan abroad, its existing creditors would try to seize the new funds.

The characteristics of LDC borrowing make an exclusion from the international capital market costly. A defaulting LDC would no longer be able to draw on foreign savings to develop profitable domestic investment opportunities; all domestic investment would have to be financed from the possibly meager supply of domestic savings. Further, the country would lose the flexibility to borrow abroad and maintain consumption and investment in the face of temporary fluctuations in its real income. Sharper booms and busts would impose economic costs and might also threaten the country's political stability.

3. *Reduction of the gains from international trade.* The most serious cost of default is a consequence of the first two: sovereign defaulters could find their ability to engage in international trade severely curtailed. As noted above, debtor-country goods involved in international trade would be subject to seizure whenever they crossed a creditor's border. In addition, a defaulter's exclusion from the international capital market might leave it unable to obtain trade credits abroad or even to maintain checking accounts in foreign banks (since these accounts could be seized). Without the ability to make payments in internationally acceptable currencies, a sovereign defaulter could be reduced to barter trade.[10]

For the purposes of the present analysis, we do not need to go into the details behind default costs; it is sufficient to know that sovereign debtors perceive default to be costly.

THE BENEFIT OF SOVEREIGN DEFAULT

The benefit of default is that the debtor escapes the responsibility of paying interest and principal on its foreign debt. A debtor country therefore derives a larger benefit from defaulting the larger the amount of money is that it must pay to its creditors if it does not default.

Factors other than the debt-service burden will affect the benefit from default, however. The most important of these is the country's income level at the time. If a country's income is high, it can service its foreign debt without painful cuts in domestic consumption and investment; but if the economy is in a slump, continuation of debt service may impose severe hardship on the population and court revolution. We therefore assume that the benefit a country derives from default decreases as the country's income rises.

To develop a model with which to analyze the default decision, the arguments in the last two paragraphs can be formalized. Let D stand for the total foreign debt of the country and let $\tilde{D}$ be the amount of principal due for repayment in the current period. If R^L is the interest rate the country must

[10]Conceivably, a country could default on loans to some banks but not to others, and thus maintain its ability to trade. In practice, however, international loans are syndicated so that a country that falls into default with respect to one creditor must be declared in default by other creditors.

pay to foreign lenders, its total debt-service burden equals the interest and principal currently due,

$$\tilde{D} + R^L D \tag{20-1}$$

The above expression does not represent the amount that the LDC must currently hand over to creditors, since it may be receiving new loans as it repays its old ones. If L stands for the level of new loans being extended to the country, the *net* amount it pays to foreign banks when it does not default is its debt service less new loans:

$$\tilde{D} + R^L D - L. \tag{20-2}$$

The quantity above is the amount the debtor saves by defaulting. This quantity is often called the **resource transfer** from debtor to creditor. (When preceded by a minus sign, it is the resource transfer from creditor to debtor.)

The benefit from a decision to default in the current period, B, thus depends on output, Y, and the resource transfer:

$$B = B(Y, \tilde{D} + R^L D - L). \tag{20-3}$$

The benefit of defaulting falls when Y rises, rises when R^L, $\tilde{D}$, or D rises, and falls when L rises.

Assume that for any Y, a country obtains no benefit from defaulting when the resource transfer from debtor to creditor is zero. In other words, a country gains nothing from defaulting when creditors are lending it the funds it needs to service its existing debt. In symbols, the assumption is

$$B(Y, 0) = 0,$$

for any level of Y.

WHEN DOES A COUNTRY DEFAULT?

The decision to default is easy to analyze. A country defaults whenever the benefit of default, B, is greater than the cost of default, denoted by C:

$$B > C.$$

The country continues to meet its debt-service obligations, however, when

$$B \leq C.$$

Figure 20-2 shows how the default decision depends on the loan rate, R^L, and the flow of new bank loans, L, given the initial stock of debt, D, the portion due for immediate repayment, $\tilde{D}$, and real income, Y. The schedule labeled BC shows combinations of R^L and L where the benefit of default just equals its cost:

$$B(Y, \tilde{D} + R^L D - L) = C. \tag{20-4}$$

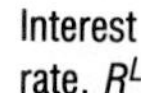

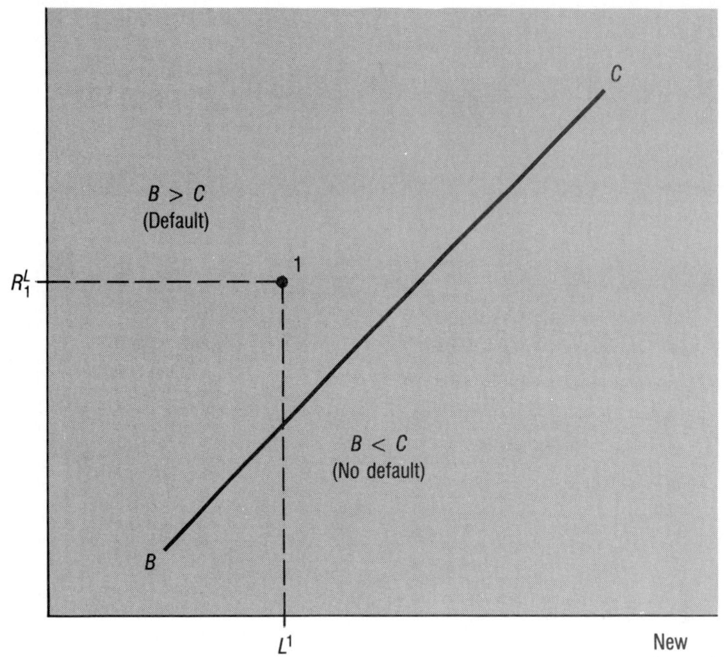

FIGURE 20-2 How the decision to default depends on new loans and their interest cost. The LDC is better off defaulting than taking loan packages above *BC* (such as point 1). Loan packages below *BC* are superior to defaulting in the current period.

Along *BC*, therefore, the resource transfer to creditors is just low enough to keep the debtor from defaulting. *BC* slopes upward because a rise in R^L raises the LDC's debt-service obligation, raising the resource transfer it must make, while a rise in L lowers this resource transfer back to its original level.

At any time, banks in developed countries are willing to lend the LDC a particular amount of new money, L^1, at an interest rate R_1^L. If the resulting combination of new loans and interest rate is above *BC* (for example, point 1 in Figure 20-2), the country will default rather than pay and take the loan. Along *BC* the country is already on the verge of default; so a rise in R^L from any point on *BC* pushes it over the brink. Reversing this argument, the country will not default if the banks offer it a loan-interest-rate package below *BC*.[11]

An additional fact about schedule *BC* is crucial in analyzing the default decision. Along *BC*, the resource transfer from debtor to creditor must be *positive;* that is, the flow of new loans from the banks does not cover the

[11]This discussion implicitly identifies the interest rate on new loans with that on the preexisting debt, *D*. All that is needed for the analysis is that some of the earlier debt was contracted under a floating interest rate tied to the current loan rate. As noted earlier, the widespread extension of loans under floating interest rates was indeed a major factor in the debt crisis; so the assumption of floating-rate loans is realistic.

country's debt service. The reason is that, as observed above, the benefit of default is zero when the resource transfer is zero [that is, $B(Y, 0) = 0$]. Since the cost of default, C, is positive, it is impossible to have $B = C$ when the resource transfer to banks is zero or negative.

THE BEHAVIOR OF BANKS

Figure 20-2 shows the combinations of interest rates and loan levels at which default occurs but does not indicate the supply schedule for loans to the LDC, that is, the interest rates at which banks will be willing to offer various levels of new loans. To complete the analysis of the default decision, we must now examine the motives of banks that lend to LDCs.

When a bank decides how much to lend to an LDC in the current period, and at what interest rate, it must take into account the possibility that the LDC may default on its loans *next* period even if default does not occur *this* period. If the LDC's income is high enough today to deter immediate default, default could still occur tomorrow if an unexpectedly low level of income then suddenly raised the perceived benefit of default above the cost.

Since the possibility that the country may default in the future is a central factor in bank lending decisions, it is a major determinant of the supply of new loans to the country. The supply schedule for new loans and the BC locus determine whether a default takes place in the current period.

The banks face the problem that any amount they lend to an LDC in the current period raises the resource transfer that country must make next period and therefore *raises* the benefit of default then. Paradoxically, a higher flow of new loans this period, while discouraging an immediate default, raises the debt-service burden the country faces in the next period and (other things equal) raises the probability that a default will take place in the future.

The important implication of this apparent paradox is that the interest rate banks require will rise as the flow of new loans to the LDC increases. The more the banks lend to a country, the greater the risk that those loans will not be repaid next period; as a result, banks will be willing to increase the amount of new loans they make only if the interest rate they receive rises sufficiently to compensate them for the increased risk of default. An LDC will therefore face an upward-sloping supply schedule of loans from the banks: the more the LDC wishes to borrow today, the higher the interest rate it must pay. Figure 20-3 shows the supply schedule of new bank loans, labeled SS.

HOW SOVEREIGN DEFAULT OCCURS

To see how a sovereign default can occur, we must combine the BC line of Figure 20-2 with the supply curve for new loans shown in Figure 20-3. Figure 20-4 shows a situation in which SS intersects BC, a situation in which the LDC does *not* default in the current period.

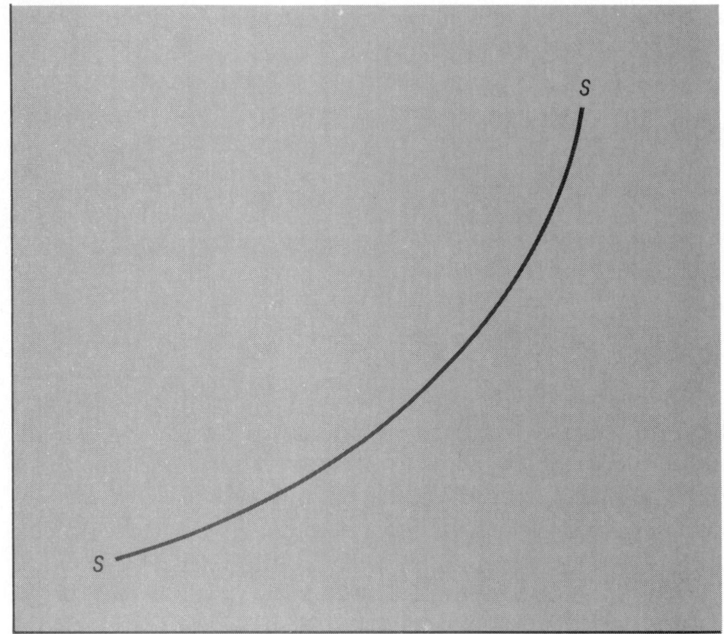

FIGURE 20-3 The supply by banks of new loans to an LDC. The supply curve for loans, *SS*, shows that banks increase the level of new loans they are willing to extend to the LDC only if the loan rate, R^L, rises.

The analysis of this case requires two steps. First, notice that the borrower prefers loan packages on the segment of *SS* between points 1 and 2 to loan packages on *SS* that lie to the left of point 1 or to the right of point 2. This is so because the benefits of default are higher above *BC* than below it; thus, the terms of the loan packages available above *BC* are *always* more burdensome than those of the loan packages between 1 and 2. It follows that the LDC will choose a loan–interest rate combination that lies below *BC*. The second step is now obvious: since the benefits of default are less than its costs at points below the *BC* schedule, the LDC will not default. We have therefore shown that when *SS* intersects *BC*, as in Figure 20-4, it will not be in the borrower's interest to default in the current period (although a default may still occur in some future period).

Now consider the situation shown in Figure 20-5. In that case, *SS* lies above *BC*, so there is no *available* combination of loans and interest rate that is preferable to default from the country's standpoint. If there were such a loan package, the country would take it; but in the situation shown in Figure 20-5, the country immediately defaults on its foreign debt rather than choosing any of the loan packages on *SS*.

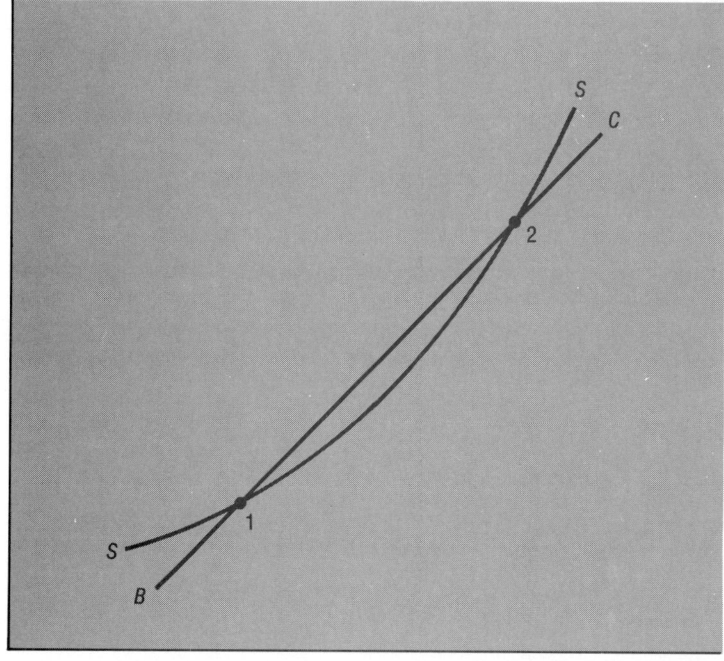

FIGURE 20-4 A situation in which the LDC will not default in the current period. The LDC prefers any loan contract on SS between points 1 and 2 to default.

APPLYING THE MODEL TO THE 1982 CRISIS

We can now use this model to examine why many LDCs were pushed to the brink of default in 1982. The events of that year caused the SS schedule to shift backward (from S^1S^1 to S^2S^2) and the BC schedule to shift downward (from B^1C^1 to B^2C^2), as shown in Figure 20-6.

Consider first the SS schedule describing the supply of new loans. The SS schedule's positive slope reflects the increased risk of higher lending to a sovereign debtor. Two events of the early 1980s contributed to the decrease in the supply of new loans represented by the shift from S^1S^1 to S^2S^2. First, interest rates rose in the industrial countries, making domestic loans more attractive and loans to LDCs less so. Therefore, for any lending rate R^L, the amount of new loans banks were willing to make to LDCs declined. Second, LDC debtors suffered declines in their incomes and terms of trade. These declines made a future default seem more likely, and thus increased the riskiness of loans to LDCs. This second factor also helped shift the loan supply schedule backward.

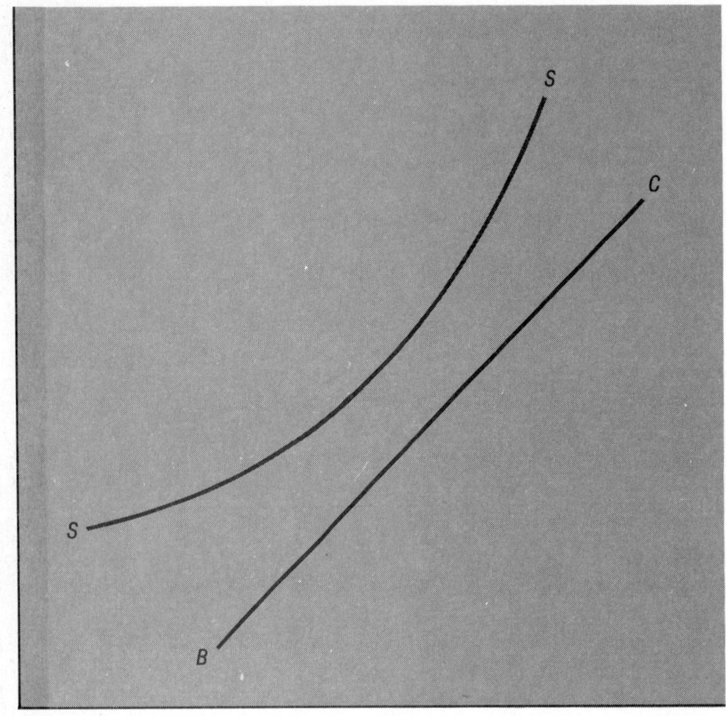

FIGURE 20-5 A situation in which the LDC will default in the current period. Default is preferable to any loan package on the lenders' supply curve.

Consider next the position of BC, along which the benefit of default is just offset by its costs. The position of BC depends on the borrower's income, with a lower income level *raising* the benefit of defaulting for any L and R^L. The fall in many LDCs' real incomes that occurred in 1982 shifted B^1C^1 downward and to the right (to B^2C^2): after the fall in LDC income, deterrence of a default required a smaller resource transfer from debtor countries to the banks, that is, some combination of lower interest rates and higher levels of new lending.

Since the shifts in the two schedules add up to a debt crisis because S^2S^2 and B^2C^2 don't intersect, why hasn't the lending slowdown of 1982 resulted, to date, in a large-scale default by LDCs?

THE CASE FOR COLLECTIVE ACTION BY BANKS

The model developed to show how default can occur also implies that it is in the interest of banks to act collectively by offering to lend at points *to the right* of B^2C^2, thus averting default.

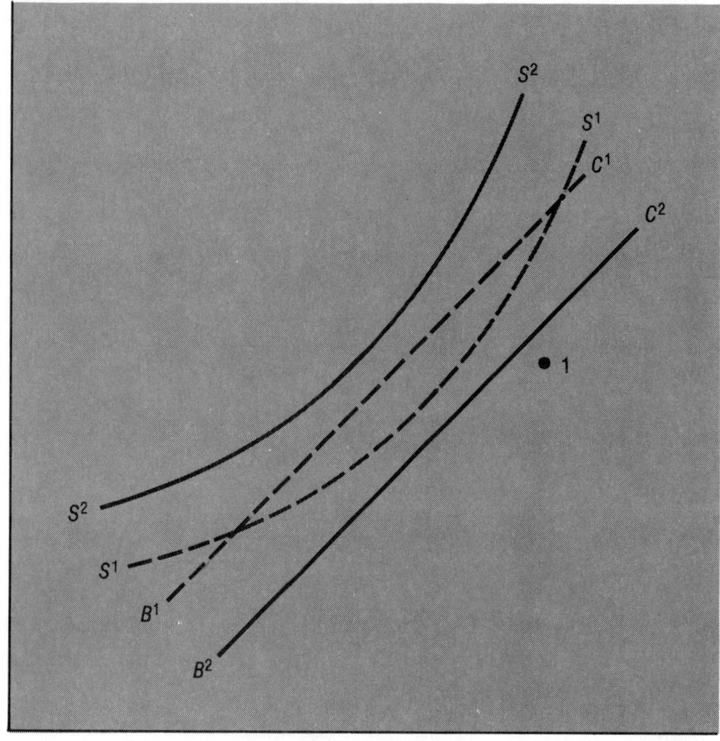

FIGURE 20-6 Effects of the 1982 disturbances. The loan-supply schedule *SS* shifted to the left as industrial-country interest rates rose and future default became more likely. The benefit-cost schedule *BC* shifted downward as LDC output fell and current default became more attractive.

To derive the loan-supply schedule *SS*, we asked the usual question: For a given loan rate R^L, what level of new loans will banks be willing to supply to a sovereign borrower when they act as individual, profit-maximizing units? At points to the right of *SS*, the riskiness of lending to the country is so great relative to the loan rate R^L that each individual bank would prefer to lend nothing; indeed, each will try to reduce its outstanding loans to the country. At points to the left of *SS*, the risk of future default is sufficiently small that, given R^L, each bank would like to lend the country more.

If default is about to occur, however, all banks may benefit if lending to the LDC continues at some level. To see why, consider Figure 20-6 after the shift of the two curves, and imagine that banks offer the loan package described by point 1. If there is an immediate default, banks receive no payments. But by extending new loans, L, to the LDC, they receive the resource transfer $\tilde{D} + R^L D - L$. We saw earlier that the resource transfer from the LDC to its creditors must be positive along B^2C^2. If point 1 is close enough to B^2C^2, the associated resource transfer to banks, $\tilde{D} + R^L D - L$, can be positive but small enough that the debtor does not default. The point is that by continuing to lend, banks as a group are paid the positive amount $\tilde{D} + R^L D - L$, which is certainly better than getting nothing. In effect, banks can bribe the debtor to pay them the debt service $\tilde{D} + R^L D$ by giving them the smaller amount L. This is a good deal for the banks even if the LDC decides to default on some future date.

Why don't market forces automatically ensure that this type of outcome occurs? A standard coordination failure stands in the way. If banks acted cooperatively, they would recognize that it is in their collective interest to continue lending enough to the LDC to avert a default. *Given* that other banks cooperate and offer the loan package 1 in Figure 20-6, however, it is in the interest of each *individual* bank to lend nothing. This is so because point 1 is to the right of S^2S^2, where each individual bank perceives continued lending to the country as too risky relative to the return. Therefore, if banks act as individuals and take the actions of other banks as given, no new loans will be extended and a default will necessarily occur.

The particular coordination problem leading to default is often called a **free-rider problem** in economics. Each bank is better off if all other banks continue lending to the LDC while it lends nothing or reduces its outstanding loans. In other words, each has an incentive to take a "free ride" on the continued lending of other banks. But since every bank has an incentive to a free ride, it is likely that no new lending to the country occurs. In this case all banks suffer by collectively losing the debt service, net of new loans, that they would have been paid by the debtor otherwise.

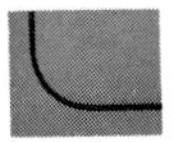

POLICY RESPONSES TO THE DEBT CRISIS

The model presented in the last section shows how dangerous a laissez-faire approach to the international debt problem would have been after 1982. Governments and the IMF intervened, however, to assure that LDCs would not find it attractive to opt out of the international trading and financial system through default. To date, this strategy has staved off a generalized default, but it has also imposed immense costs on the debtor countries in terms of unemployment and slow growth.

GOVERNMENTS, BIG BANKS, AND SMALL BANKS

As a result of the LDC debt problems, individual banks wanted to stop new lending to LDCs and reduce their overall holdings of those countries' obligations. Such a reduction in LDC debts to foreign banks would have required LDCs to run current-account surpluses after 1982 rather than the deficits they actually had. LDCs would have preferred default to the politically unacceptable cuts in domestic expenditure needed to produce external surpluses. The task facing international policymakers was to somehow finance LDC current-account deficits large enough to deter immediate default, even though individual banks preferred not to lend or roll over maturing loans.

When the Mexican crisis began, Mexico and the United States organized a meeting between Mexican financial officials and representatives of the hundreds of banks that had claims on Mexico. Afterward, a steering committee consisting of the largest banks was set up to represent all the banks and to keep banks informed about the progress of negotiations. This steering committee model has served as a pattern for handling the numerous debt problems that arose after the Mexican case. The banks that sit on steering committees have lent too much to LDCs to be able to stop new lending without provoking a default that would threaten their own solvency. These banks are therefore too large to free-ride on the lending of other banks. Smaller banks (which are tempted to free-ride) are coaxed (or pressured) into continued lending by the steering committees and their governments. The IMF has also played a key role in limiting the free-rider problem.

Continued lending to LDCs has taken two forms, rescheduling and the extension of new credits. Rescheduling is one way of rolling over maturing debts: principal payments are postponed, but they are due with additional interest, so that short-term debts are, in effect, changed into longer-term debts. But if banks only rolled over or rescheduled principal on maturing debts, the net foreign liabilities of the debtor would not change, so its current account would have to be in balance. The banks have also provided new loans to cover the smaller current-account deficits that the LDCs have run. Bank finance has been supplemented by loans from some governments and the IMF.

THE ROLE OF THE IMF

IMF lending and conditionality have been more visible during the debt crisis than ever before. Recall that IMF conditionality is the close economic surveillance a country's policymakers may have to accept as a condition for borrow ing Fund resources (Chapter 18). Countries rescheduling debts have in most cases also borrowed from the IMF and agreed to IMF-designed stabilization programs aimed at reducing current-account deficits. Even though the amounts lent by the Fund have been small relative to the debtors' financing needs, the Fund's involvement has been crucial. When a debtor agrees to an IMF stabilization program, banks are reassured that the debtor is taking measures that will eventually allow it to resume normal debt servicing.

In addition, IMF involvement may be politically useful for a debtor government. To reduce current-account deficits to levels that can be financed, debtor governments have been forced to reduce public-sector deficits by removing subsidies, cutting wages in publicly owned industries, and raising the prices of goods and services provided by the government. An expenditure-switching devaluation is often necessary as well. These measures have naturally been unpopular with the sectors of the population that are directly affected. Debtor governments have sometimes shifted public resentment toward the IMF, which can be blamed for "imposing" the restrictive economic measures. In reality, debtor governments that have cooperated with the IMF have viewed the costs of cooperation as outweighing the costs of default.

The IMF has also played a key role in coordinating bank lending to debt-ridden LDCs. In the Mexican case, the IMF's managing director at the time, Jacques de Larosière, shocked the banks by announcing that he would not approve an IMF loan package for Mexico unless banks agreed not only to reschedule existing Mexican debts but to provide Mexico with *additional* funds—that is, to increase their net claims on Mexico. Since an IMF loan and stabilization program were critical to Mexico's future ability to pay its debts, the bank steering committee had no choice but to raise the extra money from the hundreds of banks then holding Mexican loans. De Larosière's tactic of "forced lending" by banks has become the norm in other cases. By making continued bank lending the price of IMF involvement, the Fund has helped discourage smaller banks from free riding on its own lending or that of the larger banks.

LDC ADJUSTMENT IN THE DEBT CRISIS

The effects of the adjustment measures taken in LDCs after 1982 are clearly visible in Tables 20-2 and 20-4. By 1984, LDC current-account deficits had fallen far below their levels of the early 1980s and LDCs were making a substantial resource transfer to creditor countries. This reduction in external deficits was not achieved without cost. As Table 20-4 shows, the regions most affected by the crisis had negative output growth rates in 1983. Sharply lower growth was naturally accompanied by high levels of unemployment, falling real wages, and growing political unrest. Further, low growth in Latin America helped deepen the recession of the early 1980s in the developed world, particularly in the United States.

The recovery of 1984 had a positive effect on LDC growth and employment (see Table 20-4). By early 1985, many observers felt that the worst of the debt crisis was over and that the world economy would simply "grow its way out" of debt problems. These hopes were shown to be premature later in 1985.

The worldwide recovery slowed down in that year, directly reducing foreign demand for LDC exports and contributing to a fall in LDC terms of trade (see Figure 20-1). LDCs derived some benefit from a fall in U.S. interest rates, which slowed the growth of debt-service burdens, but there was no sign that the vigorous developed-country growth that had pushed LDCs closer to internal and external balance in 1984 would soon resume. Equally worrisome was the growing domestic political pressure in industrialized countries (particularly the United States) for restrictive trade measures aimed in part at LDC exports. By closing industrialized-country markets to additional LDC exports, protectionist policies risked pushing debtor countries closer to default, as in the 1930s.

THE ROAD AHEAD

There is now serious question whether the strategy followed since 1982 will suffice to avoid a breakdown. Debtor countries are asking more insistently whether it is reasonable to expect LDCs to shoulder the entire burden of paying their debts to banks. This seems particularly reasonable in cases like that of Mexico, whose terms of trade deteriorated when the world price of oil fell sharply in 1985. Mexico made an enormous economic sacrifice to reach agreement with its debtors and play within the international financial system's rules. It was not responsible for the fall in oil prices, yet that development conferred a tremendous benefit on industrial countries at the same time as it impaired Mexico's ability to meet its foreign commitments. The industrial countries that benefited from the oil-market collapse were in a position to extend debt relief to Mexico and still be better off.

The question of reallocating the burden of external adjustment between debtors and creditors was raised forcefully in a February 1986 meeting of the Cartagena group—a group of the most heavily indebted Latin American countries that derives its name from the location of the group's first meeting (Cartagena, Colombia) in June 1984.[12] The Cartagena group called for a lowering of interest rates on existing debts, and implied that it would support unilateral actions by debtors to reduce debt-service burdens if such actions seemed necessary to avoid severe economic distress. One country, Peru, had already announced unilaterally that it would limit its debt-service payments to 10 percent of its export earnings.

The Cartagena group's declaration raised the more threatening possibility of a joint default by a *debtors' cartel.* A single country can be heavily penalized if it defaults alone, but it is very unlikely that the industrialized world can exclude most of Latin America from the international trading system. The costs of default perceived by members of a debtors' cartel might therefore be significantly lower than those perceived by individual debtors.

The intensification of some countries' debt problems in 1985–1986, by pushing debtors toward joint action, seemed to be making a widespread default more likely. In February 1987, Brazil stunned the world by unilaterally suspending interest payments on its commercial-bank debt for an indefinite period. As of this writing, the ultimate consequences of Brazil's action are still unclear. Other major debtors did not follow Brazil's example. However, some bank creditors (led by Citicorp in May 1987) decided to increase sharply

[12]The members of the Cartagena group are Argentina, Bolivia, Brazil, Chile, Colombia, the Dominican Republic, Ecuador, Mexico, Peru, Uruguay, and Venezuela.

their loan-loss reserves. These actions implied large accounting losses and a tacit admission by the banks that they do not expect to be repaid in full.

An issue central to the future of LDC borrowing is the nature of loan contracts between LDCs and banks. Bank lending is debt finance, and it makes no provision for a sharing of the risks that might make it difficult for LDCs to repay. Equity finance, in contrast, would automatically have shifted some losses onto foreign holders of stocks issued by LDCs. No debt crisis would have arisen—just a reduction in dividends paid abroad. LDCs are now asking in effect that existing loan agreements with banks be rewritten after the fact to contain an equity component. In addition, some countries are reducing their debt burdens through explicit debt-equity swaps.

There is no question that in some cases LDCs borrowed excessively to finance government spending, or invested foreign funds unwisely. Often, however, the funds were unwisely lent. In addition, the LDC debtors were hit by severe macroeconomic shocks that were not of their making. Further international cooperation to redistribute the burden of LDC debt will be needed to ensure lasting stability for the international financial system. To avoid a repeat of the interwar debt disaster, industrialized-country governments will also have to recognize that protectionist measures aimed at imports from LDCs make it impossible for those countries to reach the reduced current-account deficits that banks are currently willing to finance.

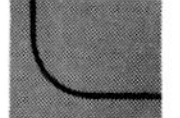

SUMMARY

1. Undeveloped financial markets and heavy government intervention characterize the economies of LDCs. As a result of these characteristics, many LDCs have turned to fixed exchange rates or *crawling pegs,* inflationary finance of government deficits, and widespread wage indexation. The heavy dependence of LDCs on flexible-price primary commodity exports makes them particularly vulnerable to shocks originating in international markets.

2. Because many LDCs have low saving rates but offer rich opportunities for investment, it is natural that they have current-account deficits and borrow from richer countries. Potentially, LDC borrowing from richer countries can lead to gains from intertemporal trade that make all countries better off.

3. LDC borrowing can take a number of forms, including bond finance, bank finance, loans from official entities, and direct foreign investment. Direct foreign investment is a form of *equity finance.* Equity finance differs from *debt finance* in that the outflows of payments it generates are not contractually prespecified but depend on economic conditions within the borrowing country.

4. In the nineteenth and early twentieth centuries, LDCs borrowed heavily from Europe, particularly from Britain. Despite frequent individual episodes of *default* and sharp international business fluctuations, the international capital market thrived up to the outbreak of World War I. This was in part a result of London's leadership of the world economy—its commitment to free

trade and its flexibility in accommodating the temporary difficulties of less-developed debtors. In the interwar period, most LDC loans originated in the United States. When the Great Depression began, there was no internationally recognized authority prepared to ensure a continuing flow of credit to LDCs. As a result, most LDCs defaulted on their foreign debts. Private lending to LDCs on the scale of the 1920s did not resume until the early 1970s.

5. Bank lending to LDCs after 1973 was stimulated by negative real interest rates in industrialized countries and by the need to recycle OPEC's current-account surplus. By borrowing abroad, LDCs were able to sustain high growth rates of spending and output through the 1970s. Heavy borrowing after the second oil shock led to trouble, however, as disinflation in the industrial countries raised interest rates and drove the world economy into recession. In August 1982, Mexico's announcement that it could no longer meet scheduled payments to creditors sparked a generalized slowdown in lending to developing countries.

6. A country contemplating *sovereign default* faces several potential costs, the most serious of which is a virtual exclusion from international trade. The benefit of default is immediate relief from the burden of *debt service.* Economic theory predicts that an LDC defaults when the benefit exceeds the cost, but not otherwise. The disturbances of the early 1980s created circumstances in which LDCs might well have defaulted had governments, banks, and the IMF not joined to ensure a continuing flow of loans. Collective action prevented the complete halt in lending that might have occurred if each bank, acting in its own self-interest, had attempted to *free-ride* on the lending of others by reducing its own LDC claims.

7. LDC attempts to reduce their current-account gaps in 1983 (often the result of IMF stabilization programs) resulted in negative output growth rates in some regions, particularly Latin America. Growth improved as LDC exports picked up in the recovery year 1984. Since then, lackluster growth in industrial countries and growing protectionist pressures have dimmed hopes for an easy solution to the debt problem. There is growing pressure from debtors to write an equity component into existing loan contracts by reducing interest burdens when debtors encounter unavoidable external problems, such as the weak oil prices Mexico faced after 1985.

KEY TERMS

seigniorage
crawling peg
debt finance
equity finance
default
Paris Club
debt rescheduling
floating-rate loan contracts
debt service
sovereign default
resource transfer
free-rider problem

PROBLEMS

1. Can the government always collect more seigniorage simply by letting the money supply grow faster? Discuss factors that might influence the level of *real* resources the government can obtain by printing money.

2. How does an artificially low domestic interest rate help an LDC government finance its budget deficit?

3. Suppose that an economy open to international capital movements has a crawling-peg exchange rate that is continuously devalued at a rate of 10 percent per year. How would the domestic nominal interest rate be related to the foreign nominal interest rate?

4. In the late 1970s, the countries in Latin America's "Southern Cone" (Argentina, Chile, and Uruguay) all tried to reduce domestic inflation by adopting crawling pegs in which the rate of exchange-rate crawl was supposed to fall gradually to zero according to a preannounced schedule. People in those countries believed, however, that the government might deviate from the preannounced schedule at some point and carry out a large surprise devaluation of the domestic currency. How would you expect this belief to affect the behavior of wages and the real exchange rate during the course of disinflation? (Hint: All three countries had massive real currency appreciations as a result of their programs.)

5. The external debt buildup of some LDCs (such as Argentina) is in large part due to (legal or illegal) capital flight in the face of expected currency devaluation. (Governments and central banks borrowed foreign currencies to prop up their exchange rates, and these funds found their way into private hands and into bank accounts in New York and elsewhere.) Since capital flight leaves a government with a large debt but creates an offsetting foreign asset for citizens who take money abroad, the consolidated net debt of the country as a whole does not change. Does this mean that countries whose external government debt is largely the result of capital flight face no debt problem?

6. Much LDC borrowing was carried out by state-owned companies. In some LDCs there is now talk of "privatizing" the economy by selling state companies to private owners. Would LDCs have borrowed more or less if their economies had been privatized?

7. How would an LDC's decision to reduce trade restrictions such as import tariffs affect its ability to borrow in the world capital market?

8. Show that the *BC* schedule of Figure 20-2 is a straight line with slope equal to $1/D$.

9. Given output, a country can improve its current account by either cutting investment or cutting consumption (private or government). Since the debt crisis began, many LDCs have achieved improvements in their current accounts by cutting investment. Is this a sensible strategy?

10. Do you agree that it is a good idea to partially forgive some LDC debt? What problems might arise from such an approach to the debt crisis?

FURTHER READING

Bela Balassa. "Adjustment Policies in Developing Countries: A Reassessment." *World Development* 12 (September 1984), pp. 955–972. A review of trade and macroeconomic policies in LDCs after 1973.

Carlos F. Díaz-Alejandro. "Good-bye Financial Repression, Hello Financial Crash." *Journal of Development Economics* 19 (September–October 1986), pp. 1–24. Discusses linkages between financial liberalization, macroeconomic policy, and external debt problems.

Jonathan Eaton and Mark Gersovitz. *Poor-Country Borrowing in Private Financial Markets and the Repudiation Issue.* Princeton Studies in International Finance 47. International Finance Section, Department of Economics, Princeton University, June 1981. Theoretical and empirical analysis of LDC foreign borrowing with default risk.

Sebastian Edwards. *The Order of Liberalization of the External Sector in Developing Economies.* Princeton Essays in International Finance 156. International Finance Section, Department of Economics, Princeton University, December 1984. Examines problems of liberalizing trade and capital movements in LDCs.

Albert Fishlow. "Lessons from the Past: Capital Markets during the 19th Century and the Interwar Period." *International Organization* 39 (Summer 1985), pp. 383–439. A historical review of international borrowing experience, including comparisons with the post-1982 debt crisis.

David Folkerts-Landau. "The Changing Role of International Bank Lending in Development Finance." *International Monetary Fund Staff Papers* 32 (June 1985), pp. 317–363. A good review of trends in developing-country external finance.

Joseph Kraft. *The Mexican Rescue.* New York: Group of Thirty, 1984. A journalist's account of the 1982 Mexican crisis and the international policy response.

Paul Krugman. "International Debt Strategies in an Uncertain World," in Gordon W. Smith and John T. Cuddington, eds. *International Debt and the Developing Countries.* Washington, D.C.: World Bank, 1985. A more advanced theoretical discussion of sovereign default and bank lending.

Joseph Ramos. *Neoconservative Economics in the Southern Cone of Latin America, 1973–1983.* Baltimore: Johns Hopkins University Press, 1986. An account of plans for economic liberalization and stabilization in Argentina, Chile, and Uruguay.

Jeffrey Sachs. "Managing the LDC Debt Crisis." *Brookings Papers on Economic Activity* 2:1986, pp. 397–431. Examines the case for debt relief as part of a solution to the LDC debt crisis.

21 THE GLOBAL CAPITAL MARKET: PERFORMANCE AND POLICY PROBLEMS

If a financier name Rip van Winkle had gone to sleep in the early 1960s and awakened two decades later, he would have been shocked by changes in both the nature and the scale of international financial activity. In the early 1960s, for example, most banking business was purely domestic, involving the currency and customers of the bank's home country. Two decades later, however, many banks were deriving a large share of their profits from international activities. To his surprise, Rip would have found that he could locate branches of Citibank in São Paulo, Brazil, and branches of Britain's National Westminster Bank in New York. He would also have discovered that by the early 1980s, it had become routine for a branch of an American bank located in London to accept a deposit denominated in Japanese yen from a Swedish corporation, or to lend Swiss francs to a Dutch manufacturer.

The market in which residents of different countries trade assets is called the **international capital market.** The international capital market is not really a single market; it is a group of closely interconnected markets in which asset exchanges with some international dimension take place. International currency trades take place in the foreign-exchange market, which is an important part of the international capital market. The main actors in the international capital market are the same as those in the foreign-exchange market (Chapter 13): commercial banks, large corporations, nonbank financial institutions, central banks, and other government agencies. And, like the foreign-exchange market, the international capital market's activities take place in a network of world financial centers linked by sophisticated communications systems. The assets traded in the international capital market, however, include different countries' stocks and bonds in addition to bank deposits denominated in their currencies.

This chapter discusses three main questions about the international capital market. First, how has this well-oiled global financial network enhanced countries' gains from international trade? Second, what caused the rapid growth in international financial activity that has occurred since the early 1960s? And third, how can policymakers minimize the problems raised by a worldwide capital market without sharply reducing the benefits it provides?

THE INTERNATIONAL CAPITAL MARKET AND THE GAINS FROM TRADE

In earlier chapters, the discussion of gains from international trade concentrated on exchanges involving goods and services. By providing a worldwide payments system that lowers transaction costs, banks active in the international capital market enlarge the trade gains that result from such exchanges. But most deals that take place in the international capital market result in exchanges of *assets* between residents of different countries, for example, the exchange of a share of IBM stock for some British government bonds. Although such asset trades are sometimes derided as unproductive "speculation," they do, in fact, lead to gains from trade that can make consumers everywhere better off.

THREE TYPES OF GAIN FROM TRADE

All transactions between the residents of different countries fall into one of three categories: trades of goods or services for goods or services, trades of goods or services for assets, and trades of assets for other assets. At any moment, a country is generally carrying out trades in each of these categories. Figure 21-1 (which assumes that there are two countries, Home and Foreign) illustrates the three types of international transaction, each of which involves a different type of gain from trade.

So far in this book we have discussed two types of trade gain. Chapters 2 through 6 showed that countries can gain by concentrating on the production activities in which they are most efficient and using some of their output to pay for imports of other goods from abroad. This type of trade gain involves the exchange of goods or services for other goods or services. The top

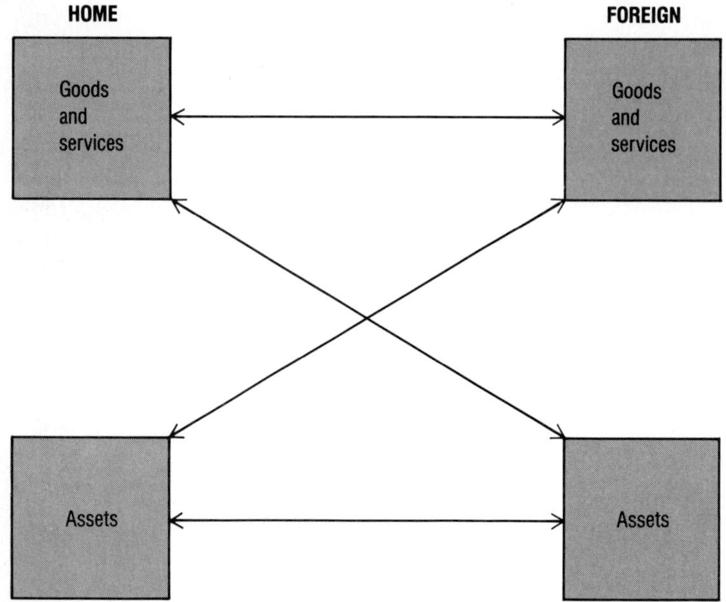

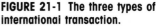

FIGURE 21-1 The three types of international transaction. Residents of different countries can trade goods and services for other goods and services, goods and services for assets (that is, for future goods and services), and assets for other assets. All three types of exchange lead to gains from trade.

horizontal arrow in Figure 21-1 shows exchanges of goods and services between Home and Foreign.

A second type of trade gain results from *intertemporal* trade, which is the exchange of goods and services for claims to future goods and services, that is, for assets (Chapters 7, 18, and 20). When a less-developed country borrows abroad (that is, sells a bond to foreigners) so that it can import materials for a domestic investment project, it is engaging in intertemporal trade. The borrowing country gains from this trade because it can carry out a project that it could not easily finance out of its domestic savings alone; and the lending country gains because it gets an asset that yields a higher return than is available at home. The diagonal arrows in Figure 21-1 indicate trades of goods and services for assets. If Home has a current-account deficit with Foreign, for example, it is a net exporter of assets to Foreign and a net importer of goods and services from Foreign.

The bottom horizontal arrow in Figure 21-1 represents the last category of international transaction, trades of assets for assets, such as the exchange of real estate located in France for U.S. Treasury bonds. In Table 12-3 (p. 297), which shows the 1982 U.S. balance of payments accounts, you will see under the capital account both a \$113.0 billion purchase of foreign assets by private U.S. residents (a capital outflow) and an \$84.7 billion purchase of U.S. assets by private foreign residents (a capital inflow). So while the United States could have financed its \$11.2 billion current-account deficit for 1982 simply by selling to foreigners \$11.2 billion worth of assets, U.S. and foreign residents instead engaged in a volume of asset swapping several times greater than the U.S. current account. Such a large volume of trade in assets between countries occurs because international asset trade, like trades involving goods and services, can yield benefits to all the countries involved.

RISK AVERSION

When individuals select assets, an important factor in their decisions is the riskiness of the asset's return (Chapter 13). Other things equal, people dislike risk. Economists call this property of peoples' preferences **risk aversion.** Chapter 17 showed that risk-averse investors in foreign-currency assets base their demand for a particular asset on its riskiness (as measured by a risk premium) in addition to its expected return.

An example will make the meaning of risk aversion clearer. Suppose you are offered a gamble in which you lose \$1000 half of the time and gain \$1000 half of the time. Since you are as likely to win as to lose the \$1000, the average payoff on this gamble—its *expected value*—is $(1/2) \times (\$1000) + (1/2) \times (-\$1000) = 0$. If you are risk-averse, you will not take the gamble because, for you, the possibility of losing \$1000 more than outweighs the possibility that you will win, even though both outcomes are equally likely. Although some people (called risk lovers) enjoy taking risks and would take the above gamble, there is much evidence that risk-averse behavior is the norm. For example, risk aversion helps explain the profitability of insurance companies, which sell policies that allow people to protect themselves or their families from the financial risks of theft, illness, and other mishaps.

If people are risk-averse, they value a collection (or portfolio) of assets not only on the basis of its expected return but also on the basis of the riskiness of that return. Under risk aversion, for example, people may be willing to hold bonds denominated in several different currencies, even if the interest rates they offer are not linked by the interest parity condition, if the resulting portfolio of assets offers a desirable combination of return and risk. In general, a portfolio whose return fluctuates wildly from year to year is less desirable than one that offers the same average return with only mild year-to-year fluctuations. This observation is basic to understanding why countries exchange assets.

PORTFOLIO DIVERSIFICATION AS A MOTIVE FOR INTERNATIONAL ASSET TRADE

International trade in assets can make both parties to the trade better off by allowing them to reduce the riskiness of the return on their wealth. Trade accomplishes this reduction in risk by allowing both parties to diversify their portfolios—to divide their wealth among a wider spectrum of assets and thus reduce the amount of money they have riding on each individual asset. The economist James Tobin of Yale University, an originator of the theory of portfolio choice with risk aversion, has described the idea of **portfolio diversification** as: "Don't put all your eggs in one basket." When an economy is opened to the international capital market, it can reduce the riskiness of its wealth by placing some of its "eggs" in additional foreign "baskets." This reduction in risk is the basic motive for asset trade.

A simple two-country example illustrates how countries are made better off by trade in assets. Imagine that there are two countries, Home and Foreign, and that residents of each own only one asset, domestic land yielding an annual harvest of kiwi fruit.

The yield of the land is uncertain, however. Half the time, Home's land yields a harvest of 100 tons of kiwi fruit at the same time as Foreign's land yields a harvest of 50 tons. The other half of the time the outcomes are reversed: the Foreign harvest is 100 tons, but the Home harvest is only 50. On average, then, each country has a harvest of $(1/2) \times (100) + (1/2) \times (50) =$ 75 tons of kiwi fruit, but its inhabitants never know whether the next year will bring feast or famine.

Now suppose the two countries can trade shares in the ownership of their respective assets. A Home owner of a 10 percent share in Foreign land, for example, receives 10 percent of the annual Foreign kiwi fruit harvest, and a Foreign owner of a 10 percent share in Home land is similarly entitled to 10 percent of the Home harvest. What happens if international trade in these two assets is allowed? Home residents will buy a 50 percent share of Foreign land, and they will pay for it by giving Foreign residents a 50 percent share in Home land.

To see why this is the outcome, think about the returns to the Home and Foreign portfolios when both are equally divided between titles to Home and Foreign land. When times are good in Home (and therefore bad in Foreign), each country earns the same return on its portfolio: half of the Home harvest (100 tons of kiwi fruit) plus half of the Foreign harvest (50 tons of kiwi fruit), or 75 tons of fruit. In the opposite case—bad times in Home, good times in Foreign—each country *still* earns 75 tons of fruit. If the countries hold portfolios equally divided between the two assets, therefore, each country earns a *certain* return of 75 tons of fruit—the same as the average harvest each faced before international asset trade was allowed.

Since the two available assets—Home and Foreign land—have the same return on average, any portfolio consisting of those assets yields an expected (or average) return of 75 tons of fruit. Since people everywhere are risk-averse, however, all prefer to hold the 50-50 portfolio described above, which gives a sure return of 75 tons of fruit every year. After trade is opened, therefore, residents of the two countries will swap titles to land until the 50-50 outcome is reached. Because this trade eliminates the risk faced by both countries without changing average returns, both countries are clearly better off as a result of asset trade.

The above example is oversimplified because countries can never eliminate *all* risk through international asset trade. (Unlike the model's world, the real world is a risky place even in the aggregate!) The example does demonstrate that countries can nonetheless *reduce* the riskiness of their wealth by diversifying their portfolios internationally. A major function of the international capital market is to make this diversification possible.[1]

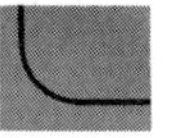

INTERNATIONAL BANKING AND THE INTERNATIONAL CAPITAL MARKET

The Home-Foreign kiwi fruit example portrayed an imaginary world with only two assets. Since the number of assets available in the real world is obviously enormous, specialized institutions have sprung up to bring together buyers and sellers of assets located in different countries.

THE STRUCTURE OF THE INTERNATIONAL CAPITAL MARKET

As we noted above, the main actors in the international capital market include commercial banks, corporations, nonbank financial institutions (such as insurance companies and pension funds), central banks, and other government agencies.

1. *Commercial banks.* Commercial banks are at the center of the international capital market, not only because they run the international payments mechanism but because of the broad range of financial activities they undertake. Bank liabilities consist chiefly of deposits of various maturities, while their assets consist largely of loans (to corporations and governments), deposits at other banks (interbank deposits), and bonds. Multinational banks are also heavily involved in other types of asset transaction. For example, banks may *underwrite* issues of corporate stocks and bonds by agreeing, for a fee, to find buyers for those securities at a guaranteed price. One of the key facts about international banking is that banks are often free to pursue activities abroad that they would not be allowed to pursue in their home countries. This type of regulatory asymmetry has spurred the growth of international banking over the last two decades.

2. *Corporations.* Corporations—particularly those with multinational operations—routinely finance their investment by drawing on foreign sources of funds. To obtain these funds, corporations may sell shares of stock, which give owners an equity claim to the corporation's assets, or they may use debt finance. Debt finance typically takes the form of borrowing from international banks or, when longer-term borrowing is desired, the sale of corporate debt instruments in the international capital market. Corporations frequently denominate their bonds in the currency of the financial center in which the bonds are being offered for sale. Increasingly, however, corporations have been pursuing novel denomination strategies that make their bonds attractive to a wider spectrum of potential buyers. **Eurobonds** are corporate bonds that are *not* denominated in the currency of the financial center in which

[1]The Mathematical Postscript to this chapter develops a detailed model of international portfolio diversification.

they are sold, for example, DM bonds sold in London. Dollar-denominated Eurobonds were most important in the late 1960s, but they have lost some of their predominance since then. (Currently around half of new Eurobond issues are dollar-denominated.) Some Eurobonds are not denominated in a single currency but are multicurrency instruments that give the lender the right to request repayment in one of several currencies. For example, the bond may give its owner the right to be repaid either $1.50 or £1 five years after the date it is issued if the exchange rate on the issue date is $1.50 per pound; because this provision gives the lender the option of being paid £1.20 if the pound has depreciated to $1.25 per pound or $1.75 if the dollar has depreciated to $1.75 per pound, he is partially protected from exchange risk and therefore may be willing to lend to the corporation at a lower interest rate. More complicated denomination schemes, called "currency cocktails," are also available. One of these is a Eurobond denominated in IMF Special Drawing Rights, introduced in 1975. Bonds denominated in the European Currency Unit used by the EMS (Chapter 17) are gaining in popularity.

3. *Nonbank financial institutions.* Nonbank institutions such as insurance companies, pension funds, and mutual funds have become important players in the international capital market as they have moved into foreign assets to diversify their portfolios. Of particular importance are *investment banks* such as First Boston Corporation, Goldman Sachs, and Lazard Frères, which are not banks at all but specialize in underwriting sales of stocks and bonds by corporations and (in some cases) governments. Since Congress enacted the Bank ing Act of 1933, U.S. commercial banks have been barred from investment banking activity within the United States (and from most other domestic transactions involving corporate stocks and bonds). But these banks *are* allowed to participate in investment banking activities overseas, and such banks as Citicorp, Morgan Guaranty, and Bankers Trust have competed vigorously with the more specialized investment banks. Figure 21-2 shows how an international consortium of underwriters—including both investment banks and commercial banks—recently advertised an offering of Chevron Corporation bonds. (Because of American legal restrictions, these bonds could be sold only to non-American buyers located outside the United States, even though Chevron is an American corporation.)

4. *Central banks and other government agencies.* Central banks are routinely involved in the international financial markets through foreign-exchange intervention. In addition, other government agencies frequently borrow abroad. For example, foreigners purchase U.S. government bonds and in the late 1970s, the U.S. Treasury sold bonds denominated in DM in Europe (these were called "Carter bonds"). LDC governments and state-owned enterprises have borrowed substantially from foreign commercial banks. Even the governments of some Soviet-bloc countries such as Poland are heavily indebted to Western capitalist bankers.

New Issue
April 15, 1986

This advertisement appears as a matter of record only. These Notes have not been registered under the United States Securities Act of 1933. Neither these Notes nor any portion thereof may be offered or sold directly or indirectly in the United States of America, or its territories or possessions or to nationals or residents thereof.

Chevron

Chevron Corporation
San Francisco, U.S.A.

U.S. $ 300,000,000
8¼% U.S. Dollar Bearer Notes of 1986/1996

Deutsche Bank Capital Markets Limited

Credit Suisse First Boston Limited	Goldman Sachs International Corp.	Merrill Lynch International & Co.
Morgan Guaranty Ltd	Nomura International Limited	Salomon Brothers International Limited
Swiss Bank Corporation International Limited	Union Bank of Switzerland (Securities) Limited	S. G. Warburg & Co. Ltd.
Bank of America International Limited	Banque Nationale de Paris	Commerzbank Aktiengesellschaft
County Bank Limited	Crédit Lyonnais	Daiwa Europe Limited
Generale Bank	IBJ International Limited	Mitsubishi Finance International Limited

Orion Royal Bank Limited
Wood Gundy Inc.

FIGURE 21-2 Advertising an international bond issue. This April 1986 issue of Chevron Corporation bonds was underwritten by a consortium of financial institutions from the United States, Japan, Germany, France, and other countries.
Source: Courtesy of the Chevron Corporation.

OFFSHORE BANKING AND OFFSHORE CURRENCY TRADING

One of the most pervasive features of the commercial banking industry in the 1980s is that banking activities have become globalized as banks have branched out from their home countries into foreign financial centers. In 1960, only eight American banks had branches in foreign countries, but now more than 200 have such branches. Similarly, the number of foreign bank offices in the United States has risen steadily in recent years.

The term **offshore banking** is used to describe the business that banks' foreign offices conduct outside of their home countries. Banks may conduct foreign business through any one or more of three types of institution:

1. An *agency* office located abroad, which arranges loans and transfers funds but does not accept deposits.
2. A foreign bank that is its *subsidiary*. A subsidiary of a foreign bank differs from a local bank only in that a foreign bank is the controlling owner. Switzerland's Banca del Gottardo, for example, is a susidiary of Japan's Sumitomo Bank, which bought it in 1984. Subsidiaries are

subject to the same regulations as local banks but are not subject to the regulations of the parent bank's country.

3. A foreign *branch,* which is simply an office of the home bank in another country. Branches carry out the same business as local banks and are usually subject to local *and* home banking regulations. Often, however, branches can take advantage of cross-border regulatory differences.

The growth of **offshore currency trading** has gone hand in hand with that of offshore banking. An offshore deposit is simply a bank deposit denominated in a currency other than that of the country in which the bank resides—for example, yen deposits in a London bank or French franc deposits in Zurich. Many of the deposits traded in the foreign-exchange market are offshore deposits. Offshore currency deposits are usually referred to as **Eurocurrencies**, something of a misnomer since much Eurocurrency trading occurs in such non-European centers as Singapore and Hong Kong. Dollar deposits located outside the United States are called **Eurodollars**. Banks that trade in the markets for Eurocurrencies (including Eurodollars) are called **Eurobanks**.

One motivation for the rapid growth of offshore banking and currency trading has been the growth of international trade and the increasingly multinational nature of corporate activity. American firms engaged in international trade, for example, require overseas financial services, and American banks have naturally expanded their domestic business with these firms into foreign areas. By offering more rapid clearing of payments and the flexibility and trust established in previous dealings, American banks compete with the foreign banks that could also serve American customers. Eurocurrency trading is another natural outgrowth of expanding world trade in goods and services. British importers of American goods frequently need to hold dollar deposits, for example, and it is natural for banks based in London to woo their business.

World trade growth alone, however, cannot explain the growth of international banking since the 1960s. Ralph Bryant of the Brookings Institution has estimated that between 1964 and 1983, international trade (measured as the total exports of goods and services by all countries outside the Soviet bloc) grew at a compound rate of 13 percent per year. In contrast, Bryant's measure of international banking transactions grew at a compound annual rate of almost 28 percent per year—more than double the figure for world trade.[2]

[2]See Bryant, "International Financial Intermediation: Underlying Trends and Implications for Government Policies," paper presented at the Second International Conference, Institute for Monetary and Economic Studies, Bank of Japan, May 1985. As Bryant points out, the complex nature of international banking makes any measure of international banking activity somewhat arbitrary and incomplete. The one cited in the text is based on Eurocurrency transactions. The conclusion that international banking has grown much more rapidly than world trade would only be reinforced, however, if a more comprehensive measure of international banking transactions were used.

Two main factors explain the rapid expansion of international banking beyond what would be required by the growth of world trade. The first of these factors is the banks' desire to escape domestic government regulations on financial activity (and sometimes taxes) by shifting some of their operations abroad and into foreign currencies. The second factor is political, the desire by some depositors to hold currencies outside the jurisdictions of the countries that issue them.

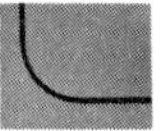

EURODOLLARS AND OTHER EUROCURRENCIES

The large pool of Eurocurrency deposits is often a cause of alarm. Politicians and the press worry that this "stateless money," beyond the control of any national monetary authority, may foil governments' efforts to maintain economic stability and may even set off a worldwide inflation. How are Eurocurrency deposits created, and why has Eurocurrency trading expanded so swiftly since the 1960s? Do Eurocurrencies pose a threat to the world's economic health?

HOW BIG IS THE EUROCURRENCY MARKET?

In June 1986, the size of the Eurocurrency market stood at $3 trillion. That number is the total stock of bank deposit liabilities denominated in foreign currencies. Roughly 20 percent of those deposits were held by private nonbanks. The rest were interbank deposits, held by other banks, or were held by official monetary institutions, primarily central banks. The Eurodollar component of the market is by far the largest. Roughly three-quarters of the Eurocurrency market (about $2.2 trillion) is dollar-denominated. Contrast the market's current size with its size in 1963—just $7 *billion,* of which $5 billion were Eurodollars.

HOW EUROCURRENCIES ARE CREATED

It is easier to understand how Eurocurrency trading came into being once the process of Eurocurrency deposit creation is understood. Discussions of the problems posed by Eurocurrencies are, unfortunately, often clouded by confused notions about the determination of Eurocurrency supplies. As you will see, however, Eurocurrencies should *not* be viewed as portions of national currency supplies that have somehow migrated from their countries of origin.

The typical Eurocurrency deposit is a nonnegotiable time deposit with a fixed term to maturity ranging from overnight to 5 years. The process through which these deposits are created is extremely simple. We deal with the example of Eurodollars; other Eurocurrencies come into being in exactly the same way.

A Eurodollar Deposit Is Born. Let's imagine that the German company Daimler-Benz has just sold a car to an American for $40,000. The American pays with a check on his account at Citibank; so Daimler-Benz ends up holding a check for $40,000 and faces a decision about where to put the money. Suppose the company expects that it will need dollars in a month to pay for some computer components bought in the United States. It may well decide to hold the dollars for a month, in some interest-earning form, until they are needed to pay for the components.

Two ways Daimler-Benz could hold its $40,000 are by buying U.S. Treasury bills or by buying certificates of deposit issued by American banks. But it could also buy a Eurodollar deposit by depositing the check from the American citizen with a British bank, Barclays Bank, in London. (For reasons to be explained later, this last option is attractive because Barclays will typically be offering a higher interest rate on dollar deposits than that available in the United States.) If Daimler-Benz chooses to deposit the dollars at Barclays, a Eurodollar deposit is born.

The Effect on Bank Balance Sheets. A look at the balance sheets of the banks involved will clarify what has happened. Assume that Barclays has a dollar account with Chase Manhattan in New York, in which it deposits any dollars it acquires. Then the sequence of transactions just described affects three banks' balance sheets. First, Barclays' liabilities rise by the amount of Daimler-Benz's $40,000 deposit, and its assets rise by the amount of the $40,000 increase in its deposits at Chase:

Balance sheet of Barclays Bank, London

Assets		*Liabilities*	
Deposits at Chase	+$40,000	Customers' deposits (Daimler-Benz account)	+$40,000

Second, Citibank's checking account at the Federal Reserve Bank of New York is debited by $40,000 as the check used to pay Daimler-Benz clears. The funds a private bank deposits with its home central bank are referred to as the private bank's *reserves,* which are part of its assets. (Private bank reserves should not be confused with the central bank's foreign-exchange reserves.) Citibank's reserves therefore drop by $40,000, but so do its liabilities to the depositor who bought the car:

Balance sheet of Citibank, New York

Assets		*Liabilities*	
Reserves at Fed	−$40,000	Customers' deposits (car buyer's account)	−$40,000

Third, the $40,000 in reserves debited from Citi's account at the New York Fed are credited to Chase's account there. At the same time, Chase's liabilities rise by the $40,000 that Barclays deposits at Chase:

Balance sheet of Chase Manhattan Bank, New York

Assets		*Liabilities*	
Reserves at Fed	+$40,000	Customers' deposits (Barclays account)	+$40,000

Have Any Dollars Escaped Abroad? The $40,000 increase in Barclays Bank's dollar liabilities is the increase in the supply of Eurodollars resulting from Daimler-Benz's decision to hold its dollars in London rather than in the United States. But notice that the company's action has the same effect on the U.S. banking system as would a decision to hold the $40,000 in the form of a deposit at Chase (or some other U.S. bank): a reshuffling of reserves between banks' accounts at the Fed, and a corresponding shift in deposits from the bank losing reserves to the one gaining them. In particular, the U.S. *monetary base* —the sum of the banking system's reserves at the Fed and the currency supply—does not change. *Because the U.S. monetary base makes up the "liabilities" side of the Fed's balance sheet (Chapter 17), no reduction in the U.S. money supply has to occur for the Eurodollar supply to rise.*

These observations are important because Eurodollars are often viewed *incorrectly* as dollars that have somehow "escaped" abroad. In the example, the supply of Eurodollars goes up even though the $40,000 paid to Daimler-Benz is returned to the U.S. banking system when Barclays Bank deposits that sum with Chase.

You may wonder how the picture changes if Barclays does not keep all of the $40,000 in its Chase deposit. Indeed, Barclays is likely to have customers who want to borrow dollars; that is why it accepted the dollar deposit from Daimler-Benz in the first place. If Barclays lends part of the $40,000 to customers, the Eurodollar supply can rise by *more* than $40,000, but there is still no migration of dollars from the United States to Europe.

Secondary Eurodollar Deposit Expansion. Let's see how an additional expansion of the Eurodollar pool can come about if Barclays lends out part of its new $40,000 deposit. To guard against an unexpected need for dollar liquidity, Barclays is likely to keep some fraction of its new $40,000 deposit—$5000, say—in its Chase account. But it can earn a high return by lending the remaining $35,000 to a Dutch multinational corporation, Philips. Barclays balance sheet now becomes:

Balance sheet of Barclays Bank, London

Assets		Liabilities	
Deposits at Chase	+$5000	Customers' deposits (Daimler-Benz account)	+$40,000
Loan to Philips	+$35,000		

After the loan to Philips, the Eurodollar supply is still $40,000 higher than it was before Daimler-Benz deposited its dollars at Barclays.

This may not be the end of the story, however, because Philips has several options for using its newly borrowed $35,000. If Philips spends the money immediately to buy goods from the United States, or if it deposits the money in an onshore U.S. bank, there is no further increase in the Eurodollar supply. The $35,000 is simply shifted from Barclays's account at Chase to some other account within the United States. If Philips does not need to use its loan immediately, it could deposit the $35,000 with Barclays, or with some other European bank. Suppose Philips temporarily places the money with the London branch of Deutsche Bank, which in turn deposits Philips's check at Bankers Trust in New York. The balance sheets of Deutsche Bank and Bankers Trust are affected as follows:

Balance sheet of Deutsche Bank, London

Assets		Liabilities	
Deposits at Bankers Trust	+$35,000	Customers' deposits (Philips account)	+$35,000

Balance sheet of Bankers Trust, New York

Assets		Liabilities	
Reserves at Fed	+$35,000	Customers' deposits (Deutsche Bank account)	+$35,000

In this case, the supply of Eurodollars rises by $75,000—the $40,000 deposited at Barclays by Daimler-Benz, plus the $35,000 deposited at Deutsche Bank by Philips. As before, the U.S. monetary base is unaffected: the net result of the long chain of transactions is simply a transfer of reserves from Citibank's Fed account (which falls by $40,000) to those of Chase and Bankers Trust (which rise by $5000 and $35,000, respectively). Obviously, the process can continue further if Deutsche Bank lends out part of the $35,000 deposited by Philips rather than holding it all in its Bankers Trust account in New York. The $40,000 paid out by the U.S. auto buyer who initiates all this, however, always finds its way back to the U.S. banking system. Once again, the expansion in the volume of Eurodollars can occur without any dollars ever having to "leave" the United States.

Eurodollars and the U.S. Balance of Payments. Another assertion often made about Eurodollars is that growth in the Eurodollar supply requires continuing U.S. balance of payments deficits. The example shows that this statement is also incorrect. The $40,000 paid to import a car from Germany enters the U.S. current account as a debit. Offsetting this debit is a capital-account credit of $40,000, which reflects the $5000 deposit at Chase acquired by Barclays and the $35,000 deposit at Bankers Trust acquired by Deutsche Bank. The net effect on the U.S. balance of payments is nil, even though the Eurodollar supply rises by $75,000.

THE GROWTH OF EUROCURRENCY TRADING

Earlier we outlined the main reasons for the growth of offshore banking activities: (1) the growth of world trade, (2) government financial regulations (including taxes), and (3) political considerations. The growth of Eurocurrency trading illustrates the importance of all three of these factors in the internationalization of banking.

Eurodollars were born in the late 1950s, a response to the needs generated by a growing volume of international trade. European firms involved in trade frequently wished to hold dollar balances or to borrow dollars. In many cases, banks located in the United States could have served these needs, but Europeans often found it cheaper and more convenient to deal with local banks familiar with their circumstances. As currencies other than the dollar became increasingly convertible after the late 1950s, offshore markets for them sprang up also.

While the convenience of dealing with local banks was a key factor inspiring the invention of Eurodollars, the growth of Eurodollar trading was encouraged at an early stage by both of the two other factors we have mentioned, official regulations and political concerns.

In 1957, at the height of a balance of payments crisis, the British government prohibited British banks from lending pounds to finance non-British trade. This lending had been a highly profitable business, and to avoid losing it, British banks began financing the same trade by attracting dollar deposits and lending dollars instead of pounds. Because stringent financial regulations prevented the British banks' nonsterling transactions from affecting Britain's domestic-asset markets, the government was willing to take a laissez-faire attitude toward foreign-currency activities. As a result, London became—and has remained—the leading center of Eurocurrency trading.

The political factor stimulating the Eurodollar market's early growth was a surprising one—the Cold War between the United States and the U.S.S.R. During the 1950s, the Soviet Union acquired dollars (largely through sales of gold and other raw materials) so that it could purchase goods such as grains from the West. The Soviets feared that the United States might confiscate dollars placed in American banks if the Cold War were to heat up. So instead, Soviet dollars were placed in European banks, which had the advantage of residing outside America's jurisdiction.

The Eurodollar system mushroomed in the 1960s as a result of new U.S. restrictions on capital outflows and U.S. banking regulations. As America's balance of payments weakened in the 1960s, the Kennedy and Johnson administrations imposed a series of measures to discourage American lending abroad. The first of these was the Interest Equalization Tax of 1963, which discouraged Americans from buying foreign assets by taxing those assets' returns. Next, in 1965, came "voluntary" guidelines on the amounts U.S. commercial banks could lend abroad, followed 3 years later by a set of wide-ranging mandatory controls. All these measures increased the demand for Eurodollar loans by making it harder for would-be dollar borrowers located abroad to obtain the funds they wanted in the United States.

Federal Reserve regulations on U.S. banks also encouraged the creation of Eurodollars—and new Eurobanks—in the 1960s. The Fed's Regulation Q (which was phased out after 1980) placed a ceiling on the interest rates U.S. banks could pay on time deposits. When U.S. monetary policy was tightened at the end of the 1960s to combat rising inflationary pressures (see Chapter 18), market interest rates were driven above the Regulation Q ceiling and American banks found it impossible to attract time deposits for relending. The banks got around the problem by borrowing funds from their European branches, which faced no restriction on the interest they could pay on Eurodollar deposits and which were able to attract deposits from investors who might have placed their funds with U.S. banks in the absence of Regulation Q. Many American banks that had previously not had foreign branches established them in the late 1960s so that they could end-run Regulation Q.

With the move to floating exchange rates in 1973, the United States and other countries began to dismantle controls on capital flows across their borders, removing an important impetus to the growth of Eurocurrency markets in earlier years. But at that point, the political factor once again came into play in a big way. Arab members of OPEC accumulated vast wealth as a result of the oil shocks of 1973–1974 and 1979–1980 but were reluctant to place most of their money in American banks for fear of possible confiscation. (In 1979, Iranian assets in U.S. banks and their European branches were frozen by President Carter in response to the taking of hostages at the American embassy in Teheran.) Instead, these countries placed funds with Eurobanks.

THE IMPORTANCE OF REGULATORY ASYMMETRIES

The history of Eurocurrencies shows how the growth of world trade, financial regulations, and political considerations helped form the present system. The major factor behind the continuing profitability of Eurocurrency trading is, however, regulatory: In formulating bank regulations, governments in the main Eurocurrency centers discriminate between deposits denominated in the home currency and those denominated in others. Domestic-currency deposits are heavily regulated as a way of maintaining control over the domestic money supply, while banks are given much more freedom in their dealings in foreign currencies.

The example of U.S. *reserve requirements* shows how regulatory asymmetries can operate to enhance the profitability of Eurocurrency trading. Every time a U.S. bank operating "onshore" accepts a deposit, it must place some fraction of that deposit in a non-interest-bearing account at the Fed as part of its required reserves.[3] The British government imposes reserve requirements on *pound sterling* deposits within its borders, but it does not impose reserve requirements on *dollar* deposits within its borders. A London Eurobank therefore has a competitive advantage over a bank in New York in attracting dollar deposits and in attracting dollar borrowers: it can pay more interest to its depositors than the New York bank while still covering its operating costs. The Eurobank's competitive advantage comes from its ability to avoid a "tax" (the reserve requirement) that the Fed imposes on domestic banks' dollar deposits.

To understand this competitive advantage, suppose that the New York bank faces a 10 percent reserve requirement. If the bank receives a $100 deposit, it can relend at most $90 and it is obliged to place $10 in its Fed account, which pays no interest. Suppose the bank has operating costs equal to $1 per $100 of deposits and that the interest rate on bank loans is 10 percent per year. Then the New York bank can offer its depositors an interest rate of at most 8 percent and still cover its costs. At that deposit rate, the bank pays the owner of the $100 dollar deposit (0.08) × ($100) = $8, while earning (0.10) × ($90) = $9 on the fraction of the deposit it can relend. So the bank is just able to cover its $1 operating expense out of the difference between what it gets from the borrower and what it pays to the depositor.

In contrast, a Eurobank can offer a higher interest rate on dollar deposits than the New York bank. The Eurobank, which faces no reserve requirement, can lend out *all* of a $100 deposit, and therefore it can earn (0.10) × ($100) = $10 at a loan rate of 10 percent. If the Eurobank pays its depositors interest of 9 percent, the owner of a $100 deposit gets $9, and the difference, $10 − $9 = $1, just covers the bank's operating cost. Because the Eurobank faces no reserve requirement, it is able to offer its depositors an interest rate that is a full percentage point higher than what the New York bank can offer. Interest rates on Eurodollar deposits are always higher than rates on comparable time deposits located in the United States (in fact as well as in theory), and many depositors have been lured to the Eurocurrency markets by the higher interest rates Eurobanks offer.

Eurobanks can compete with onshore banks on the loan side also by offering lower interest rates to borrowers, but competition in the loan market tends to drive all banks' loan charges to approximate equality. Why are any depositors willing to hold onshore time deposits when they offer lower yields

[3]Alternatively, the bank could add the same amount to its holdings of vault cash, which also pay no interest. The discussion assumes that the bank holds reserves at the Fed.

than Eurocurrency deposits? Part of the reason is that the regulations faced by onshore banks make domestic deposits less susceptible to the risk of bank failure. The risk that depositors' claims will not be honored is greater in the unregulated Eurocurrency market, and the higher deposit rates paid there compensate depositors for bearing this risk.

Freedom from reserve requirements is probably the most important regulatory factor that makes Eurocurrency trading attractive to banks and their customers, but there are others. For example, Eurodollar deposits are available in shorter maturities than the corresponding time deposits banks are allowed to issue in the United States. Regulatory asymmetries like these explain why those financial centers whose governments impose the fewest restrictions on foreign-currency banking have become the main Eurocurrency centers. London is the leader in this respect, but it has been followed by Luxembourg, Bahrain, Hong Kong, and other countries that have competed for international banking business by lowering restrictions and taxes on foreign bank operations within their borders.

Neither the United States nor Germany has attracted a significant share of the world's Eurocurrency business because both countries apply fairly uniform regulations to all domestic deposits, regardless of their currency of denomination. Recently, however, the U.S. government has tried to help the American banking industry get a piece of the action. In 1981, the Fed allowed resident banks to set up **international banking facilities (IBFs)** within the United States for the purpose of accepting time deposits and making loans to foreigners. IBFs are not subject to reserve requirements or interest-rate ceilings, and they are exempt from state and local taxes. But they are prohibited from accepting deposits from Americans or from lending money within the United States. The IBFs provide an excellent example of how countries have attempted to lure lucrative international banking business to their shores while trying to insulate their domestic financial systems from the banks' international activities.

EUROCURRENCIES AND MACROECONOMIC STABILITY

The large pool of Eurocurrency deposits is often viewed with alarm by macroeconomic policymakers. Two related fears appear to be paramount: (1) The unregulated process of Eurocurrency creation has been producing a vast pool of international liquidity that could set off worldwide inflation. (2) The Eurocurrency system makes it more difficult for national monetary authorities to control their money supplies.

1. *Eurocurrencies and world inflation.* In Chapter 14, we linked a country's inflation rate to the growth of its money supply, defined as the stock of currency and checking deposits. Eurocurrency deposits do not fit easily into this definition of money—which corresponds to the Federal Reserve's money measure M1—because they are relatively illiquid. Instead, Eurocurrency de-

posits are much more like time deposits, and the Fed includes Eurodollar deposits held by nonbank U.S. residents in its broader money-stock measures. But the fact that most Eurocurrency deposits are *near-money* rather than money does not mean that their influence on countries' price levels can be ignored. Central banks watch all monetary aggregates because, to the extent that near monies substitute for money as mediums of exchange, they can exert an important influence on the price level. Thus, the possibility that Eurocurrency creation has had some inflationary effect cannot be dismissed.[4]

There is no clear-cut evidence that the inflationary effect of Eurocurrency creation has been important, but this does not mean that the effect could not become important in the future if Eurocurrency growth continues at a rapid clip. Unfortunately, there are few (if any) options individual governments can pursue to limit the growth of offshore deposits of their currencies. If the U.S. government imposed reserve requirements on the dollar liabilities of American banks' foreign branches and subsidiaries, for example, it would succeed only in driving Eurodollar business to banks headquartered in other countries. Eurocurrency growth can be brought under control only if all governments cooperatively impose reserve requirements on the foreign-currency operations of banks within their regulatory jurisdictions. But such cooperation, technically complex and politically difficult, is unlikely to occur in the near future. In particular, international agreement on reserve requirements and other financial regulations would be required.

The inflationary dangers of Eurocurrencies, while real, should not be exaggerated. Financial regulation has always induced markets to create unregulated near monies in the domestic sphere as well as in the international sphere. While such financial innovation causes problems of monetary control in the short run, it has never set off the protracted inflation that some worried observers of the Eurocurrency system appear to fear. The difficulty peculiar to *international* financial innovations like Eurocurrencies is that the creation of near monies by *offshore* institutions is usually beyond the control of any individual government.

2. *Eurocurrencies and monetary control.* Because the monetary base equals the central bank's liabilities, a central bank directly controls the monetary base through its transactions in domestic and foreign assets (Chapter 17). The relationship between the base and various monetary aggregates is through *money multipliers* that tell us what size monetary aggregate a given monetary base can support. Reserve requirements on different categories of deposit are of central importance in determining the size of money multipliers, and

[4]It would be misleading, however, to take the total size of the Eurocurrency market as a measure of the addition to national monetary aggregates from offshore-deposit creation. About four-fifths of the measured Eurocurrency market represents interbank deposits. Domestic interbank deposits are not included in measuring domestic monetary aggregates; so interbank Eurocurrency deposits should not be included in monetary aggregates that take account of offshore activities.

this fact implies that one effect of Eurocurrency trading is to make the multipliers less stable. When people shift their money between domestic deposits subject to reserve requirements and Eurobank liabilities that are not, the quantitative link between the monetary base and monetary aggregates is likely to shift as well. In general, a shift from domestic time deposits to similarly-denominated Eurocurrency deposits increases the multipliers for broadly defined money stocks because only domestic banks face reserve requirements.

To the extent that the existence of Eurocurrencies makes multipliers for the broader monetary aggregates less stable, central banks are prevented from controlling those aggregates as closely as they might like in the short run. Once again, however, the problem is not intrinsic to Eurocurrencies—purely domestic financial innovations also cause multiplier instability—and the effect of such instability over the longer run need not be large. By reducing the cost of international asset trades, the Eurocurrency system certainly encourages portfolio shifts that authorities may find undesirable on macroeconomic grounds. But against any macroeconomic disadvantages must be set the facts that the cost savings are to the advantage of consumers, as are the asset exchanges that the Eurobanks facilitate.

Any monetary instability connected with Eurocurrency markets does not extend to the monetary base, however: that monetary aggregate is firmly under the control of the central bank, which manages the base through its transactions in domestic and foreign assets. When an individual takes dollars out of a time deposit at Citibank in New York and places them in an account at Barclays Bank in London, the Federal Reserve is not involved in the transaction and so no change in its balance sheet need occur. From a balance of payments standpoint, the capital outflow measured when the individual switches funds from New York to London is exactly balanced by the inflow that occurs when Barclays or an ultimate borrower of the dollars uses them to purchase goods and services or assets from the United States. This is just a restatement of the earlier point that Eurocurrency creation is not the result of currencies emigrating from their home countries.

A symmetric argument shows that the U.S. monetary base would not balloon if, for example, a political scare in Europe led to a huge shift out of Eurocurrencies and into onshore dollar assets. In other words, Eurodollars cannot come "flooding back" into the United States, as is sometimes predicted.

REGULATING INTERNATIONAL BANKING

Increased regulation of international banking may be desirable on grounds that have nothing to do with the effectiveness of month-to-month macroeconomic policy. Many observers believe that the largely unregulated nature of global banking activity leaves the world financial system vulnerable to bank failure on a massive scale. Is this a real threat? And if so, what measures have governments taken to reduce it?

THE PROBLEM OF BANK FAILURE

A bank fails when it is unable to meet its obligations to its depositors. Banks use depositors' funds to make loans and to purchase other assets, but some of a bank's borrowers may find themselves unable to repay their loans, or the bank's assets may decline in value for some other reason. In these circumstances the bank may find itself unable to pay off its deposits.

A peculiar feature of banking is that a bank's financial health depends on the confidence of depositors in the value of its assets. If depositors come to believe that many of the bank's assets have declined in value, each has an incentive to withdraw her funds and place them in another bank. A bank faced with the wholesale loss of deposits is likely to close its doors, however, even if the asset side of its balance sheet is fundamentally sound. The reason is that many bank assets are illiquid and cannot be sold quickly to meet deposit obligations without substantial loss to the bank. If an atmosphere of financial panic develops, therefore, bank failure may not be limited to banks that have mismanaged their assets. It is in the interest of each depositor to withdraw her money from a bank if all other depositors are doing the same, even when the bank's assets are sound.

Bank failures obviously inflict serious financial harm on individual depositors who lose their money. But beyond these individual losses, bank failure can harm the economy's macroeconomic stability. One bank's problems may easily spread to sounder banks if they are suspected of having lent to the bank that is in trouble. Such a general loss of confidence in banks undermines the payments system on which the economy runs. And a rash of bank failures can bring a drastic reduction in the banking system's ability to finance investment and consumer-durable expenditure, thus reducing aggregate demand and throwing the economy into a slump. There is evidence that the string of U.S. bank closings in the early 1930s helped start and worsen the Great Depression.[5]

Because the potential consequences of a banking collapse are so harmful, governments attempt to prevent bank failures through extensive regulation of their domestic banking systems. Banks themselves take precautions against failure even in the absence of regulation, but because the costs of failure extend far beyond the bank's owners, some banks might be led by their own self-interest to shoulder a level of risk greater than what is socially optimal. In addition, even banks with cautious investment strategies may fail if rumors of financial trouble begin circulating. Many of the precautionary bank regulation measures taken by governments today are a direct result of their countries' experiences during the Great Depression.

In the United States an extensive "safety net" has been set up since the

[5]For a recent evaluation, see Ben S. Bernanke, "Nonmonetary Effects of the Financial Crisis in the Propagation of the Great Depression," *American Economic Review* 73 (June 1983), pp. 257–276.

1930s to reduce the risk of bank failure; other industrialized countries have taken similar precautions. The main U.S. safeguards are:

1. *Deposit insurance.* The Federal Deposit Insurance Corporation (FDIC) insures bank depositors against losses up to $100,000. Banks are required to make contributions to the FDIC to cover the cost of this insurance. FDIC insurance discourages "runs" on banks because small depositors, knowing that their losses will be made good by the government, no longer have an incentive to withdraw their money just because others are doing so. A separate corporation provides insurance for deposits with savings and loans associations.[6]

2. *Reserve requirements.* Reserve requirements are central to monetary policy as the main channel through which the central bank influences the relation between the monetary base and monetary aggregates. At the same time, reserve requirements force the bank to hold a portion of its assets in a liquid form easily mobilized to meet sudden deposit outflows.

3. *Capital requirements and asset restrictions.* The difference between a bank's assets and its liabilities is called its *bank capital.* Bank capital is essentially the equity that the bank's shareholders acquire when they buy the bank's stock, and since it equals the portion of the bank's assets that is *not* owed to depositors, it gives the bank a margin of safety in case some of its assets go bad. U.S. bank regulators set minimum required levels of bank capital to reduce the system's vulnerability to failure: in 1983, the statutory minimum was set at 5 percent of total assets for large banks (over $1 billion in assets) and 6 percent for small banks (below $1 billion in assets). Other rules prevent banks from holding assets that are "too risky," such as common stocks, whose prices tend to be volatile. Banks also face rules against lending too large a fraction of their assets to a single customer or to a single sovereign borrower.

4. *Bank examination.* The Fed, the FDIC, and the Office of the Comptroller of the Currency all have the right to examine a bank's books to ensure compliance with bank capital standards and other regulations. Banks may be forced to sell assets that the examiner deems too risky or to adjust their balance sheet by writing off loans the examiner thinks will not be repaid.

5. *Lender of last resort facilities.* U.S. banks can borrow from the Fed's discount window. While discounting is a tool of monetary management, the Fed can also use discounting to prevent bank panics. Since the Fed has the ability to create currency, it can lend banks facing massive deposit outflows as much as they need to satisfy their depositors' claims. When the Fed acts in this way, it is acting as a **lender of last resort (LLR)** to the bank. When depositors know

[6]Holders of deposits over $100,000 still have an incentive to run if they scent trouble, of course. When rumors began circulating in May 1984 that the Continental Illinois National Bank had made a large number of bad loans, the bank began rapidly to lose its large, uninsured deposits. As part of its rescue effort, the FDIC extended its insurance coverage to all of Continental Illinois's deposits, regardless of size. Officially, however, FDIC insurance still applies automatically only up to the $100,000 limit.

that the Fed is standing by as the LLR, they have more confidence in the bank's ability to withstand a panic and are therefore less likely to run if financial trouble looms. The administration of LLR facilities is complex, however. If banks think the central bank will *always* bail them out, they will take excessive risks. So the central bank must make access to its LLR services conditional on sound management. To decide when banks in trouble have not brought it on themselves through unwise risk taking, the LLR must be involved in the bank examination process.

DIFFICULTIES IN REGULATING INTERNATIONAL BANKING

Banking regulations of the type used in the United States and other countries become much less effective in an international environment where banks can shift their business among different regulatory jurisdictions. A good way of seeing why an international banking system is harder to regulate than a national one is to look at how the effectiveness of the U.S. safeguards just described is reduced as a result of offshore banking activities.

1. Deposit insurance is essentially absent in international banking. National deposit insurance systems may protect domestic and foreign depositors alike, but the amount of insurance available is invariably too small to cover the size of deposit usual in international banking. In particular, interbank deposits are unprotected.

2. The absence of reserve requirements has been a major factor in the growth of Eurocurrency trading. While Eurobanks derive a competitive advantage from escaping the required-reserve tax, there is a social cost in terms of the reduced stability of the banking system. No country can solve the problem single-handedly by imposing reserve requirements on its own banks' overseas branches. Concerted international action is blocked, however, by the political and technical difficulty of agreeing on an internationally uniform set of regulations and by the reluctance of some countries to drive banking business away by tightening regulations.

3 and 4. Bank examination to enforce capital requirements and asset restrictions becomes more difficult in an international setting. National bank regulators usually monitor the balance sheets of domestic banks and their foreign branches on a consolidated basis. But they are less strict in keeping track of banks' foreign subsidiaries and affiliates, which are more tenuously tied to the parent bank but whose financial fortunes may affect the parent's solvency. Banks have often been able to take advantage of this laxity by shifting risky business that home regulators might question to regulatory jurisdictions where fewer questions are asked. Further, it is often unclear which group of regulators has responsibility for monitoring a given bank's assets. Suppose that the London subsidiary of an Italian bank deals primarily in Eurodollars. Should the subsidiary's assets be the concern of British, Italian, or American regulators?

5. A final difference between national banking safeguards and those available in an international setting is the uncertainty over which central bank, if any, is responsible for providing lender of last resort assistance in international banking. The problem is similar to the one that arises in allocating responsibility for bank supervision. Let's return to the example of the London subsidiary of an Italian bank. Should the Fed bear responsibility for saving the subsidiary from a sudden drain of dollar deposits? Should the Bank of England step in? Or is it the Banca d'Italia that should bear the ultimate responsibility? When central banks provide LLR assistance they increase their domestic money supplies and may compromise domestic macroeconomic objectives. In an international setting, a central bank may also be providing resources to a bank located abroad whose behavior it is not equipped to monitor. Central banks are therefore reluctant to extend the coverage of their LLR responsibilities. The problems surrounding the 1982 failure of Italy's Banco Ambrosiano, discussed in the box, illustrate how international banking can lead to gaps in LLR coverage.

INTERNATIONAL REGULATORY COOPERATION

The internationalization of banking has weakened national safeguards against banking collapse, but at the same time it has made the need for effective safeguards more urgent. Offshore banking involves a tremendous volume of interbank deposits—roughly 80 percent of all Eurocurrency deposits, for example, are owned by private banks. A high level of interbank depositing implies that problems affecting a single bank could be highly contagious and could spread quickly to banks with which it is thought to do business. Through this ripple effect, a localized disturbance could, conceivably, set off a banking panic on a global scale.

This nightmarish scenario has haunted central bankers and other government officials since offshore banking began to grow rapidly in the 1960s. Little was done, however, until 1974. In that year a number of banks failed as a result of foreign-exchange losses, among them the Franklin National Bank in the United States and Germany's Bankhaus I.D. Herstatt. The failures sent tremors through the international financial markets, and the volume of international lending dropped sharply.

In response to the 1974 banking crises, central-bank heads from 11 industrialized countries set up a group called the **Basle Committee** whose job was to achieve "a better co-ordination of the surveillance exercised by national authorities over the international banking system. . . ." (The group was named after Basle, Switzerland, the home of the central bankers' meeting place, the Bank for International Settlements.) The Basle Committee remains the major forum for cooperation among bank regulators from different countries.

In 1975, the Committee reached an agreement, called the Concordat, which allocated responsibility for supervising multinational banking establishments between parent and host countries. (A revised Concordat was

THE BANCO AMBROSIANO COLLAPSE

The collapse of Italy's most important private bank in June 1982 is a vivid illustration of how the intricate cross-border links between financial institutions can frustrate bank supervisors and cause financial crises. The Banco Ambrosiano failure is notorious, however, because of the bank president's close connections with a subversive political group and with the Vatican.

Roberto Calvi, the president of Banco Ambrosiano, stood at the center of a vast international financial network spanning Europe, the Caribbean, and South America. In 1981, Calvi was convicted of violating Italian foreign-exchange regulations. At the same time, government investigators obtained the membership roster of a secret lodge of right-wing freemasons known as Propaganda-2 (or P-2). P-2 numbered Calvi and many other influential Italians among its members, including two cabinet ministers. The government of Prime Minister Arnaldo Forlani was forced to resign, and P-2 was outlawed.

Because Banco Ambrosiano had become the object of such close scrutiny by government and press, it soon became known that some of the bank's loans were weak. This revelation led to a deposit run. Italy's central bank, the Banca d'Italia, set up a consortium of Italy's major banks that took over many of Banco Ambrosiano's assets and liabilities and established a new bank, Nuovo Banco Ambrosiano.

The Banca d'Italia exercised its lender of last resort function by ensuring that Nuovo Banco Ambrosiano repaid domestic and foreign residents who had placed deposits with Banco Ambrosiano itself. The central bank did not, however, guarantee the liabilities of Banco Ambrosiano's foreign subsidiaries. Banco Ambrosiano and its subsidiaries allegedly had extensive financial connections with the Catholic Church's Institute for Religious Works (sometimes called the "Vatican bank"). As a result of the many claims raised by Banco Ambrosiano's failure, the Vatican bank's finances came under investigation.

Calvi himself never saw the ramifications of his bank's collapse. In mid-June 1982 he disappeared from Italy. Shortly afterward he was found dead, hanging from Blackfriars Bridge in London, his pockets stuffed with rocks. It has never been determined if he died by suicide or murder.*

*For a lively account of the Banco Ambrosiano scandal and its background, see Rupert Cornwell. *"God's Banker"*. New York: Dodd, Mead & Company, 1984.

issued in 1983.) In addition, the Concordat called for the sharing of information about banks by parent and host regulators, and for "the granting of permission for inspections by or on behalf of parent authorities on the territory of the host authority."[7] In further work the Basle Committee has located

[7]The Concordat was summarized in these terms by W. P. Cooke of the Bank of England, then chairman of the Basle Committee, in "Developments in Co-operation among Banking Supervisory Authorities," *Bank of England Quarterly Bulletin* 21 (June 1981), pp. 238–244.

loopholes in the supervision of multinational banks and brought these to the attention of national authorities. The committee has recommended, for example, that regulatory agencies monitor the assets of banks' foreign subsidiaries as well as their branches. Much of the group's work has been devoted to developing better data on the balance sheets of multinational banks, a prerequisite to more effective supervision.

While the work of the Basle committee has furthered international cooperation on the supervision of multinational banks, little has been done to clarify the division of lender of last resort responsibilities among countries. Following the 1974 bank failures, central bankers discussed the provision of international LLR facilities but declined to announce any definite agreement. There is speculation that such an agreement exists but that central bankers have kept it secret to avoid suggesting to banks that they will be bailed out if they take risks and get into trouble.

As we saw in the last chapter, the world banking system faced a major crisis after 1982 as a result of less-developed countries' debt-servicing difficulties. Some major banks' holdings of Brazilian or Mexican debt exceeded their capital, and a sovereign default would have called into question the ability of those banks to meet deposit obligations. The International Monetary Fund and the central banks of industrialized countries have played a LLR role in the debt crisis, but with a twist. Rather than lending directly to banks, the IMF and the central banks have protected bank solvency by lending to debtors and pressuring the banks to join in. So far, this strategy has held off the threat to banks' solvency that a generalized LDC default would pose.

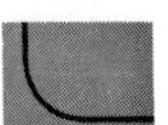

HOW WELL HAS THE INTERNATIONAL CAPITAL MARKET PERFORMED?

The present structure of the international capital market involves risks of financial instability that can be reduced only through the close cooperation of bank supervisors in many countries. But the same profit motive that leads multinational financial institutions to innovate their way around national regulations can also provide important gains for consumers. As we have seen, the international capital market allows residents of different countries to diversify their portfolios by trading risky assets. Further, by ensuring a rapid international flow of information about investment opportunities around the world, the market can help allocate the world's savings to their most productive uses. How well has the international capital market performed in these respects?

THE EXTENT OF INTERNATIONAL PORTFOLIO DIVERSIFICATION

Since data on the overall portfolio positions of different countries' residents are difficult to assemble, it is not feasible to gauge the extent of international portfolio diversification by direct observation. Nonetheless, some U.S. data can be used to get a rough idea about changes in international diversification in recent years.

In 1970, the foreign assets held by U.S. residents were equal in value to 6.2 percent of the U.S. capital stock. Foreign claims on the United States amounted to 4.0 percent of its capital stock. By 1984, U.S.-owned assets abroad equaled 7.9 percent of U.S. capital, while foreign assets in the United States had risen to 7.6 percent of U.S. capital.

These percentages seem small; with full international portfolio diversification, we would expect them to reflect the size of the U.S. economy relative to that of the rest of the world. Thus, in a fully diversified world economy, something like 70 percent of the U.S. capital stock would be owned by foreigners, while U.S. residents' claims on foreigners would equal around 70 percent of the value of the U.S. capital stock.

The data do show, however, that diversification has increased substantially as a result of the growth of the international capital markets in the 1970s and 1980s. Further, international asset holdings are large in absolute terms. At the end of 1984, for example, U.S. claims on foreigners were about $915 billion, equal to 25 percent of U.S. GNP in that year. Other evidence indicates that the trend toward greater international portfolio diversification should continue in future years. Stock exchanges around the world are establishing closer communication links, and companies are showing an increasing readiness to sell shares of stock on foreign exchanges. Japan began a major opening of its financial markets to the world capital market in the mid-1970s, Britain removed restrictions barring its public from international asset trade in 1979, and France began to reduce its capital-account controls in 1986.

There are two complementary explanations for the seemingly low extent of international asset diversification. One is that impediments to asset trade—particularly taxes on international investments, capital-account restrictions, and political risks—have prevented much of the diversification that would otherwise have taken place. The second explanation is more subtle. Macroeconomic cycles of boom and bust have been fairly well synchronized throughout the world economy. Thus, the returns on capital assets located in different countries should be fairly well synchronized too, with most countries' stock markets doing well when the world economy is growing quickly and doing badly when world growth is low. But a high correlation between asset returns in various countries means that the gains from asset trade are low compared with a situation where asset returns are independent or negatively correlated (as in the example in this chapter's first section). The apparently low extent of global diversification may thus reflect the fact that even if asset-trade impediments are low, much asset trade will be discouraged by them if countries have similar "comparative advantages" in producing output in different states of the world.

While the international capital market has not produced full international portfolio diversification, this cannot be viewed as an indictment. The market has certainly contributed to a rise in diversification since the early

1970s, in spite of some impediments to international capital movements. Further, there is no foolproof measure of the socially optimal extent of diversification. What seems certain is that asset trade will expand as barriers to the international flow of capital are progressively dismantled.

ONSHORE-OFFSHORE INTEREST DIFFERENTIALS

Another barometer of the international capital market's performance is the relationship between onshore and offshore interest rates on similar assets denominated in the same currency. If the world capital market is doing its job of communicating information about global investment opportunities, these interest rates should move closely together and not differ too greatly.

Figure 21-3 shows the interest-rate difference between two comparable dollar bank liabilities, 3-month Eurodollar deposits and certificates of deposit issued in the United States. As we saw earlier, these rates should differ mainly by the required-reserve "tax" on domestic banks, provided Eurobanks are competitive and efficient. The solid line in the figure (showing the difference

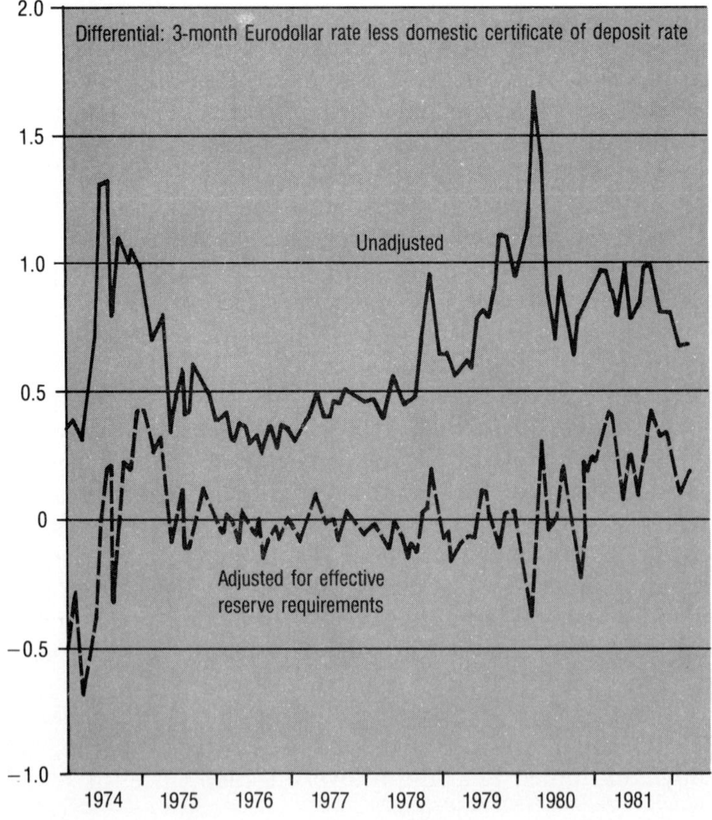

FIGURE 21-3 Comparing Eurodollar and onshore interest rates. When adjusted for the required reserve "tax," the difference between the Eurodollar interest rate and the domestic U.S. certificate of deposit rate is usually very close to zero.
Source: Edward J. Frydl, "The Eurodollar Conundrum," *Federal Bank of New York Quarterly Review* 7 (Spring 1982), p. 13.

between the offshore and onshore rates) confirms that Eurodollar interest rates are always higher than the corresponding domestic rates, as our theory predicts. The dashed line (which adjusts the interest-rate difference to account for the required-reserve tax) shows that the adjusted differential has typically been low since the mid-1970s.

Studies of Germany and the Netherlands, countries with open capital accounts, also show an approximate equality between onshore and offshore interest rates. The same equality has held for Japan since it completed the major step in its capital-account liberalization in December 1980. For France and Italy, which have had strict capital controls, the differences are greater, but there is still a tendency for onshore and offshore rates to move in tandem.[8]

THE EFFICIENCY OF THE FOREIGN-EXCHANGE MARKET

The foreign-exchange market is a central component of the international capital market, and the exchange rates it sets help determine the profitability of international transactions of all types. Exchange rates therefore communicate important economic signals to households and firms engaged in international trade and investment. If these signals do not reflect all available information about market opportunities, a misallocation of resources will result. Studies of the foreign-exchange market's use of available information are therefore potentially important in judging whether the international capital market is sending the right signals to markets.

Studies Based on Interest Parity. The interest parity condition that was the basis of the discussion of exchange-rate determination in Chapter 13 has also been used to study whether market exchange rates incorporate all available information. Recall that interest parity holds when the interest difference between deposits denominated in different currencies is the market's forecast of the percentage by which the exchange rate between those two currencies will change. More formally, if R_t is the date-t interest rate on home-currency deposits, R_t^* the interest rate on foreign-currency deposits, E_t the exchange rate (defined as the home-currency price of foreign currency), and E_{t+1}^e the exchange rate market participants expect when the deposits paying interest R_t and R_t^* mature, the interest parity condition is

$$R_t - R_t^* = (E_{t+1}^e - E_t)/E_t \,. \qquad \textbf{(21-1)}$$

[8]On the European countries, see Francesco Giavazzi and Marco Pagano, "Capital Controls and the European Monetary System," in *Capital Controls and Foreign Exchange Legislation,* Occasional Paper 1. Milan, Italy: Euromobiliare, June 1985, pp. 19–38. The Japanese case is investigated by Takatoshi Ito, "Capital Controls and Covered Interest Parity," *Economic Studies Quarterly* 37 (September 1986), pp. 223–241. A detailed study on the United States is Lawrence L. Kreicher, "Eurodollar Arbitrage," *Federal Reserve Bank of New York Quarterly Review* 7 (1982), pp. 10–21. An examination of Germany between 1970 and 1974, when capital controls were in effect, found large differences between onshore and offshore DM interest rates. See Michael P. Dooley and Peter Isard, "Capital Controls, Political Risk, and Deviations from Interest-Rate Parity," *Journal of Political Economy* 88 (April 1980), pp. 370–384.

Equation (21-1) implies a simple way to test whether the foreign-exchange market is doing a good job of using current information to forecast exchange rates. Since the interest difference, $R_t - R_t^*$, is the market's forecast, a comparison of this *predicted* exchange-rate change with the *actual* exchange-rate change that subsequently occurs indicates the market's skill in forecasting.[9]

Figure 21-4 shows the relationship between the interest difference and later depreciation rates for four currencies over the period 1980–1985. Clearly the interest difference is a very bad predictor, in the sense that it fails to catch any of the large swings in exchange rates. Even worse, over the period shown, the interest difference has been a *biased* predictor; and on average, the interest difference even failed to predict correctly the direction in which the spot exchange rate would change.[10] If the interest-rate difference were a poor, but unbiased, predictor, we could argue that the market is setting the exchange rate according to interest parity and doing the best possible job in a rapidly changing world where prediction is inherently difficult. The finding of bias, however, seems to be at odds with this interpretation of the data.

The interest parity condition also furnishes a test of a second implication of the hypothesis that the market uses all available information in setting exchange rates. Suppose that E_{t+1} is the actual future exchange rate people are trying to guess; then the forecast error they make in predicting future depreciation, u_{t+1}, can be expressed as actual minus expected depreciation:

$$u_{t+1} = (E_{t+1} - E_t)/E_t - (E^e_{t+1} - E_t)/E_t . \qquad \textbf{(21-2)}$$

If the market is making use of all available information, its forecast error, u_{t+1}, should be statistically unrelated to data known to the market on date t, when expectations were formed. In other words, there should be no opportunity for the market to exploit known data to reduce its later forecast errors.

Under interest parity, this hypothesis can be tested by writing u_{t+1} as actual currency depreciation less the international interest difference:

$$u_{t+1} = (E_{t+1} - E_t)/E_t - (R_t - R_t^*) . \qquad \textbf{(21-3)}$$

Statistical methods can be used to examine whether u_{t+1} is predictable, on average, through use of past information. A number of researchers have found

[9]Most studies of exchange-market efficiency study how the forward exchange-rate premium does as a predictor of subsequent spot exchange-rate change. That procedure is equivalent to the one we are following if the *covered* interest parity condition holds, so that the interest difference $R_t - R_t^*$ equals the forward premium (see the appendix to Chapter 13). As noted in Chapter 13, there is strong evidence that covered interest parity holds when the interest rates being compared apply to deposits in the same financial center—for example, London Eurocurrency rates.

[10]Statistical analysis supporting this last statement is in Richard M. Levich, "Gauging the Evidence on Recent Movements in the Dollar," in *The U.S. Dollar—Recent Developments, Outlook, and Policy Options*. Kansas City: Federal Reserve Bank of Kansas City, 1985, 1–27. Similar results are reported in Maurice Obstfeld, "Floating Exchange Rates: Experience and Prospects," *Brookings Papers on Economic Activity* 2:1985, pp. 369–450. The latter paper shows that there is no strong evidence of biased prediction over the floating-rate period prior to 1980.

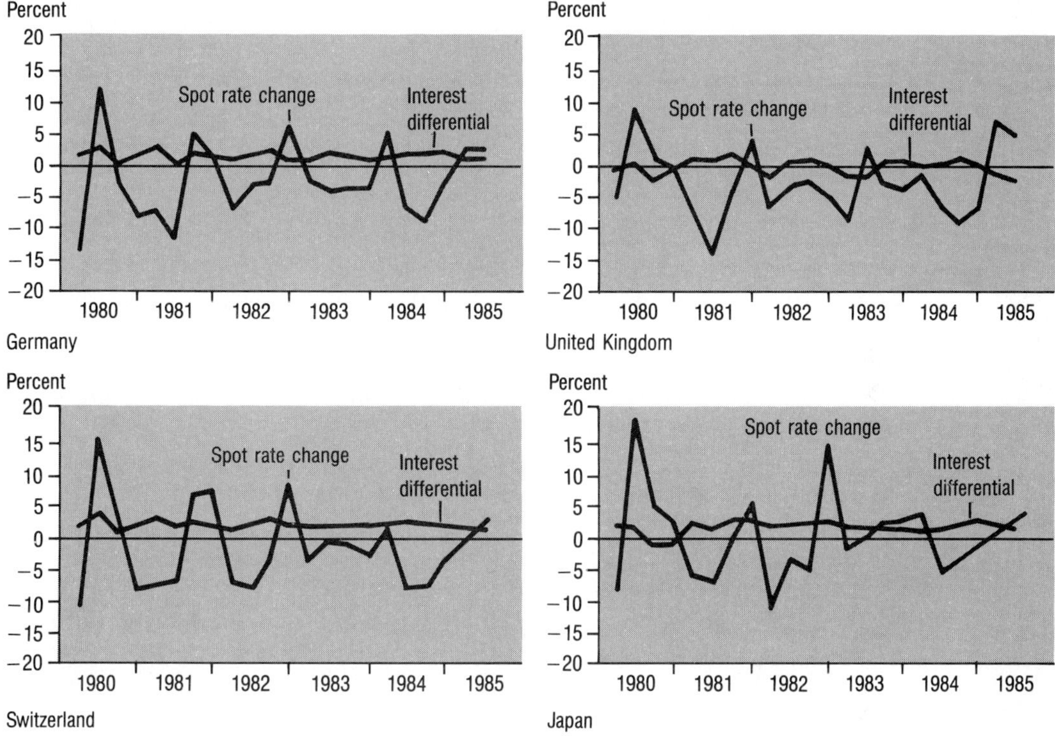

FIGURE 21-4 International interest difference and percentage future spot-rate change. International interest-rate differences have been poor and biased predictors of future movements in exchange rates.

Source: Richard M. Levich, "Gauging the Evidence on Recent Movements in the Dollar," in *The U.S. Dollar–Recent Developments, Outlook, and Policy Options*. Kansas City: Federal Reserve Bank of Kansas City, 1985, p. 20. The interest rates are Euro-currency rates and their differences (3-month dollar rate less 3-month foreign-currency rate) are measured by forward exchange premiums. Exchange rates are dollars per unit of foreign currency. Observations are at 3-month intervals.

that forecast errors, when defined as above, *can* be predicted. For example, past forecast errors, which are widely known, are useful in predicting future errors.[11]

The Role of Risk Premiums. One explanation of the research results described above is that the foreign-exchange market simply ignores easily available information in setting exchange rates. Such a finding would throw doubt on the international capital market's ability to communicate appropri-

[11]For further discussion, see Robert E. Cumby and Maurice Obstfeld, "International Interest Rate and Price Level Linkages under Flexible Exchange Rates: A Review of Recent Evidence," in John F. O. Bilson and Richard C. Marston, eds., *Exchange Rate Theory and Practice* (Chicago: University of Chicago Press, 1984), pp. 121–151; and Lars Peter Hansen and Robert J. Hodrick, "Forward Exchange Rates as Optimal Predictors of Future Spot Rates: An Econometric Analysis," *Journal of Political Economy* 88 (October 1980), pp. 829–853.

ate price signals. Before jumping to this conclusion, however, recall that when people are risk-averse, the interest parity condition may *not* be a complete account of how exchange rates are determined. If, instead, bonds denominated in different currencies are *imperfect* substitutes for investors, the international interest-rate difference equals expected currency depreciation *plus* a risk premium, ρ_t:

$$R_t - R_t^* = (E_{t+1}^e - E_t)/E_t + \rho_t \qquad \textbf{(21-4)}$$

(Chapter 17). In this case, the interest difference is not necessarily the market's forecast of future depreciation. Thus, under imperfect asset substitutability, the empirical results just discussed cannot be used to draw inferences about the foreign-exchange market's efficiency in processing information.

Because people's expectations are inherently unobservable, there is no simple way to decide between equation (21-4) and the interest parity condition, which is the special case that occurs when ρ_t is always zero. Several econometric studies have attempted to explain departures from interest parity on the basis of particular theories of the risk premium, but none has been entirely successful.[12]

The mixed empirical record leaves the following two possibilities: either risk premiums are important in exchange-rate determination, or the foreign-exchange market has been ignoring the opportunity to profit from easily available information. The second alternative seems unlikely in light of foreign-exchange traders' powerful incentives to make profits. The first alternative, however, awaits solid statistical confirmation. It is certainly not supported by the evidence reviewed in Chapter 17, which suggests that sterilized foreign-exchange intervention has not been an effective tool for exchange-rate management. More sophisticated theories show, however, that sterilized intervention may be powerless even under imperfect asset substitutability. Thus, a finding that sterilized intervention is ineffective does not necessarily imply that risk premiums are absent.

Tests for Excessive Volatility. An additional line of research on the foreign-exchange market examines whether exchange rates have been excessively volatile, perhaps because the foreign-exchange market "overreacts" to events. A finding of excessive volatility would prove that the foreign-exchange market is sending confusing signals to traders and investors who base their decisions on exchange rates. But how volatile must an exchange rate be before its volatility becomes excessive? As we saw in Chapter 13, ex-

[12]Among these studies are Lars Peter Hansen and Robert J. Hodrick, "Risk Averse Speculation in the Forward Foreign Exchange Market: An Econometric Analysis of Linear Models," in Jacob A. Frenkel, ed., *Exchange Rates and International Macroeconomics*. (Chicago: University of Chicago Press, 1983), pp. 113–142; Jeffrey A. Frankel, "In Search of the Risk Premium: A Six-Currency Test Assuming Mean-Variance Optimization," *Journal of International Money and Finance* 1 (December 1982), pp. 255–274; and Robert E. Cumby, "Is It Risk? Explaining Deviations from Interest Parity," unpublished manuscript, Graduate School of Business Administration, New York University, October 1985.

change rates *should* be volatile, because to send the correct price signals they must move swiftly in response to news about factors affecting future exchange values. It is possible, though, that exchange rates are substantially more volatile than the underlying factors that move them—such as money supplies, national outputs, and fiscal variables. Attempts to compare exchange rates' volatility with those of their underlying determinants have, however, produced inconclusive results.[13] A basic problem underlying tests for excessive volatility is the impossibility of quantifying exactly all the variables that convey relevant news about the economic future. How does one attach a number to a political assassination attempt or a major bank failure?

The Bottom Line. The ambiguous evidence on the foreign-exchange market's performance warrants an open-minded view. Such a view is particularly advisable because the statistical methods that have been used to study exchange rates are very imperfect. A judgment that the market is doing its job well would support a laissez-faire attitude by governments and a continuation of the present trend toward increased cross-border financial integration in the industrial world. A judgment of market failure, on the other hand, might imply a need for increased foreign-exchange intervention by central banks and a reversal of the trend toward capital-account liberalization. The stakes are high, and more research and experience are needed before a firm conclusion can be reached.

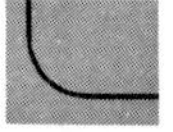

SUMMARY

1. When people are *risk-averse,* countries can gain through the exchange of risky assets. The gains from trade take the form of a reduction in the riskiness of each country's income.

2. The *international capital market* is the market in which residents of different countries trade assets. One of its important components is the foreign-exchange market. Banks are at the center of the international capital market, and many operate offshore, that is, outside the countries where their head offices are based.

3. Regulatory and political factors have encouraged *offshore banking.* The same factors have encouraged *offshore currency trading,* that is, trade in bank deposits denominated in currencies of countries other than the one in which the bank is located. Such *Eurocurrency* trading has received a major stimulus from the absence of reserve requirements on deposits in *Eurobanks.*

4. Creation of a Eurocurrency deposit does not occur because that currency leaves its country of origin; all that is required is that a Eurobank accept a

[13]See, for example, Richard A. Meese, "Testing for Bubbles in Exchange Markets: A Case of Sparkling Rates?" *Journal of Political Economy* 94 (April 1986), pp. 345–373; and Kenneth D. West, "A Standard Monetary Model and the Variability of the Deutschemark-Dollar Exchange Rate," Working Paper 2102, National Bureau of Economic Research, December 1986.

deposit liability denominated in the currency. Eurocurrencies therefore pose no threat for central banks' control over their monetary bases. *Eurodollars,* for example, cannot some day come "flooding in" to the United States. Eurocurrency creation does add to the broader monetary aggregates, however, and may complicate central-bank monetary management by shifting money multipliers unpredictably.

5. Offshore banking is largely unprotected by the safeguards national governments have imposed to prevent domestic bank failures. In addition, the opportunity banks have to shift operations offshore has undermined the effectiveness of national bank supervision. Since 1974, the *Basle Committee* of bank supervisors from 11 industrial countries has worked to enhance regulatory cooperation in the international area. That group's 1975 Concordat allocated national responsibility for monitoring banking institutions and provided for informational exchange.

6. The international capital market has contributed to an increase in international portfolio diversification since 1970, but the extent of diversification still appears rather small. Banks have been effective, however, in keeping deposit rates in different financial centers in line.

7. There is mixed evidence about the foreign-exchange market's record in communicating appropriate price signals to international traders and investors. Tests based on the interest parity condition appear to suggest that the market ignores readily available information in setting exchange rates; but since the interest parity theory ignores risk aversion and the resulting risk premiums, it may be an oversimplification of reality. Attempts to model risk factors empirically have not, however, been very successful. Tests of excessive exchange-rate volatility also yield a mixed verdict on the foreign-exchange market's performance.

KEY TERMS

international capital market
risk aversion
portfolio diversification
Eurobonds
offshore banking
offshore currency trading
Eurocurrencies
Eurodollars
Eurobanks
international banking facilities (IBFs)
lender of last resort (LLR)
Basle Committee

PROBLEMS

1. Which portfolio is better diversified, one that contains stock in a dental supply company and a candy company or one that contains stock in a dental supply company and a dairy-product company?

2. Imagine a world of two countries in which the only causes of fluctuations in stock prices are unexpected shifts in monetary policies. Under which exchange-rate regime would you expect the gains from international asset trade to be greater, fixed or floating?

3. The text points out that covered interest parity holds quite closely for deposits of differing currency denomination issued in a single financial center. Why might covered interest parity fail to hold when deposits issued in *different* financial centers are compared?

4. Show that the competitive advantage of Eurobanks relative to onshore banks rises as domestic interest rates rise. (Hint: Take the example on p. 637 in the text and ask what happens when the U.S. loan rate is 15 percent. You will see that while Eurobanks can offer depositors an interest rate of 14 percent, the best that New York banks can do for their depositors is 12.5 percent—a difference of 1.5 percentage points rather than the 1 percentage point we found assuming a 10 percent loan rate.)

5. Figure 21-3 shows that in 1981 there was an upward jump in the difference between Eurodollar interest rates and interest rates on U.S. certificates of deposit, adjusted for the required-reserve tax. 1981 was also the year in which Poland encountered severe difficulties in servicing a large debt owed to European banks. Can you suggest a link between the two developments?

6. Suppose an English resident holding a dollar deposit in a London bank decides to switch $10,000 to an account in a New York bank. What are the effects on the supply of Eurodollars, the U.S. balance of payments, the British balance of payments, the U.S. monetary base, and Britain's monetary base?

7. The Swiss economist Alexander Swoboda has argued that the Eurodollar market's early growth was fueled by the desire of banks outside the United States to appropriate some of the seigniorage the United States was collecting as issuer of the principal reserve currency. (This argument is made in *The Euro-Dollar Market: An Interpretation,* Princeton Essays in International Finance 64. International Finance Section, Department of Economics, Princeton University, February 1968.) Do you agree with Swoboda's interpretation?

8. After the LDC debt crisis began in 1982, U.S. bank regulators imposed tighter supervisory restrictions on the lending policies of American banks and their subsidiaries. Over the 1980s, the share of U.S. banks in London banking activity declined. Can you suggest a connection between these two developments?

9. In January 1987, American and British bank regulators agreed to a common set of standards for determining the adequacy of bank capital levels. How does this step increase the effectiveness of domestic bank regulation in the two countries?

FURTHER READING

Ralph C. Bryant. *International Financial Intermediation.* Washington, D.C.: Brookings Institution, 1987. A review of the growth and regulation of the international capital market, with emphasis on the interdependence of different governments' regulatory decisions.

Milton Friedman. "The Euro-Dollar Market: Some First Principles." *Morgan Guaranty Survey* (October 1969), pp. 4–14. A classic account of Eurodollar creation.

Edward J. Frydl. "The Eurodollar Conundrum." *Federal Reserve Bank of New York Quarterly Review* 7 (Spring 1982), pp. 11–19. An examination of the Eurodollar market's effect on U.S. monetary policy.

Jack Guttentag and Richard Herring. *The Lender-of-Last-Resort Function in an International Context.* Princeton Essays in International Finance 151. International Finance Section, Department of Economics, Princeton University, May 1983. A study of the need for and the feasibility of an international lender of last resort.

G. G. Johnson (with Richard K. Abrams). *Aspects of the International Banking Safety Net,* Occasional Paper 17. Washington, D.C.: International Monetary Fund, March 1983. Reviews the effectiveness of existing safeguards against international banking problems.

Andrew Lamb. "International Banking in London, 1975–1985." *Bank of England Quarterly Bulletin* 26 (September 1986), pp. 367–378. A detailed description of recent banking developments in the world's leading international financial center.

Warren D. McClam. "Financial Fragility and Instability: Monetary Authorities as Borrowers and Lenders of Last Resort," in Charles P. Kindleberger and Jean-Pierre Laffargue, eds. *Financial Crises: Theory, History, and Policy.* Cambridge, England: Cambridge University Press, 1982, pp. 256–291. Historical overview of instability in the international capital market.

Maurice Obstfeld. "Capital Mobility in the World Economy: Theory and Measurement," in Karl Brunner and Allan H. Meltzer, eds. *The National Bureau Method, International Capital Mobility, and Other Essays,* Carnegie-Rochester Conference Series on Public Policy 24. Amsterdam: North-Holland, 1986, pp. 55–104. An advanced discussion of theory and evidence on the international allocation of capital.

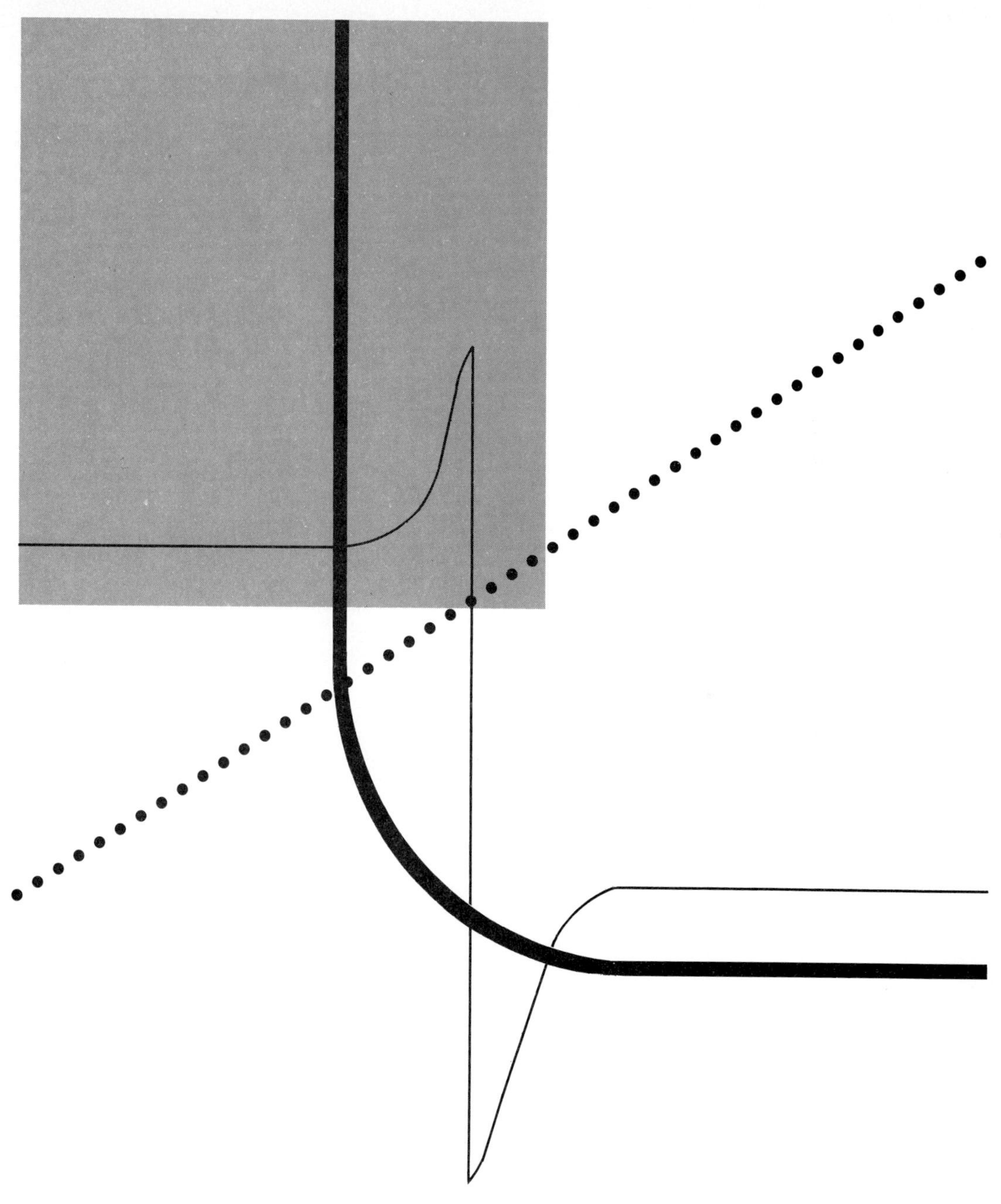

MATHEMATICAL POSTSCRIPTS

POSTSCRIPT to Chapter 3: The Specific Factors Model

In this postscript we set out a formal mathematical treatment of the specific-factors model of production explained in Chapter 3. The mathematical treatment is useful in deepening understanding of the model itself, and it also provides an opportunity to develop concepts and techniques that apply to subsequent models. In particular, it is a good place to introduce an extremely useful tool of analysis, the so-called hat algebra.

FACTOR PRICES, COSTS, AND FACTOR DEMANDS

The specific-factors model has two sectors: Manufactures and Food. In each sector, two factors of production are employed: capital and labor in Manufactures, land and labor in Food. Before turning to the full model, let us examine in general how costs and the demand for factors of production are related to the prices of factors when producers employ two factors.

Consider the production of some good that requires capital and labor as factors of production. Provided that the good is produced with constant returns to scale, the technology of production may be summarized in terms of the *unit isoquant* (*II* in Figure 3S-1), a curve showing all the combinations of capital and labor that can be used to produce one unit of the good. Curve *II* shows that there is a trade-off between the quantity of capital used per unit of output, a_K, and the quantity of labor per unit of output, a_L. The curvature of the unit isoquant reflects the assumption that it becomes increasingly difficult to substitute capital for labor as the capital-labor ratio increases, and conversely.

In a competitive market economy, producers will choose the capital-labor ratio in production that minimizes their cost. Such a cost-minimizing production choice is shown in Figure 3S-1 as point E. It is the point at which the unit isoquant *II* is tan-

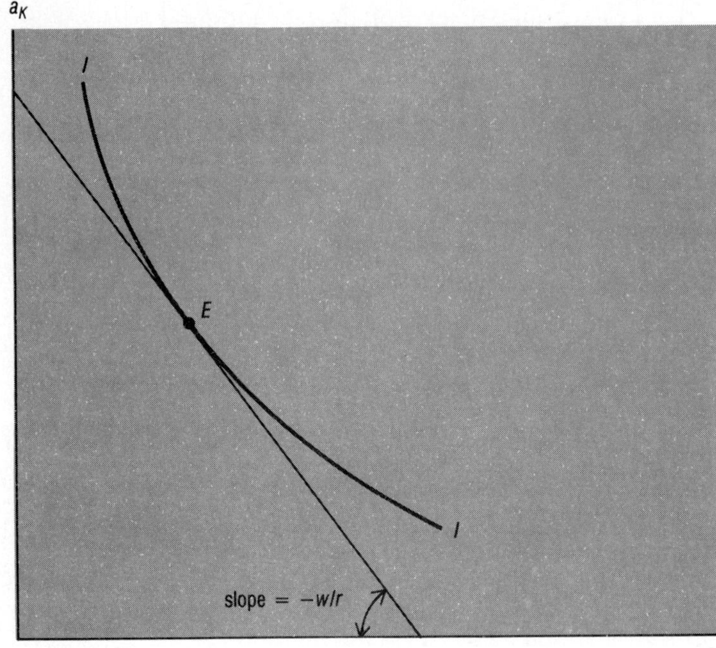

FIGURE 3S-1 Efficient production. The cost-minimizing capital-labor ratio depends on factor prices.

gent to a line whose slope is equal to minus the ratio of the price of labor, w, to the price of capital, r.

The actual cost of production is equal to the sum of the cost of capital and labor inputs,

$$C = a_K r + a_L w\,, \tag{3S-1}$$

where the input coefficients a_K and a_L have been chosen to minimize C.

Because the capital-labor ratio has been chosen to minimize costs, it follows that a change in that ratio cannot reduce costs. Costs cannot be reduced either by increasing a_K while reducing a_L, or conversely. It follows that an infinitesimal change in the capital-labor ratio from the cost-minimizing choice must have no effect on cost. Let da_K, da_L be small changes from the optimal input choices. Then

$$r da_K + w da_L = 0 \tag{3S-2}$$

for any movement along the unit isoquant.

Consider next what happens if the factor prices r and w change. This alteration will have two effects: it will change the choice of a_K and a_L, and it will change the cost of production.

First, consider the effect on the relative quantities of capital and labor used to produce one unit of output. The cost-minimizing labor-capital ratio depends on the ratio of the price of labor to that of capital:

$$\frac{a_K}{a_L} = F\left(\frac{w}{r}\right)$$

The cost of production will also change. For small changes in factor prices dr and dw, the change in production cost is

$$dC = a_K dr + a_L dw + w\,da_K + r\,da_L \tag{3S-4}$$

From equation (3S-2), however, we already know that the last two terms of equation (3S-4) sum to zero. Hence the effect of factor prices on cost may be written

$$dC = a_K dr + a_L dw \tag{3S-4'}$$

It turns out to be very convenient to derive a somewhat different equation from equation (3S-4′). Dividing and multiplying some of the elements of the equation, a new equation can be derived that looks as follows:

$$\frac{dC}{C} = \left(\frac{a_K r}{C}\right)\left(\frac{dr}{r}\right) + \left(\frac{a_L w}{C}\right)\left(\frac{dw}{w}\right) \tag{3S-5}$$

The term dC/C may be interpreted as the *percentage change* in C, and may conveniently be designated as $\hat{C}$; similarly, let $dr/r = \hat{r}$ and $dw/w = \hat{w}$. The term $a_K r/C$ may be interpreted as the *share of capital in total production costs;* it may be conveniently designated θ_K. Thus equation (3S-5) can be compactly written

$$C = \theta_K \hat{r} + \theta_L \hat{w} \tag{3S-5'}$$

where

$$\theta_K + \theta_L = 1\,.$$

This is an example of "hat algebra," an extremely useful way to express mathematical relationships in international economics.

The relationship between factor prices and the capital-labor ratio can also be expressed in hat algebra. A rise in the price of labor relative to the price of capital lowers the ratio of labor to capital; this statement may be written

$$\hat{a}_L - \hat{a}_K = -\sigma(\hat{w} - \hat{r}) \tag{3S-6}$$

where σ is the percentage change in the labor-capital ratio that results from a 1 percent change in the ratio of factor prices, and is known as the *elasticity of substitution.*

FACTOR PRICE DETERMINATION IN THE SPECIFIC-FACTORS MODEL

The specific-factors model has two sectors, each of which is like that just described. Manufactures are produced using capital (the specific factor) and labor:

$$Q_M = M(K, L_M) \tag{3S-7}$$

Food is produced using the specific factor land and labor:

$$Q_F = F(T, L_F) \tag{3S-8}$$

The supplies of capital and land to each sector are simply whatever they are. Labor, however, can be allocated to either sector:

$$L_M + L_F = \overline{L} \tag{3S-9}$$

where $\overline{L}$ is the economy's total supply of labor.

In a perfectly competitive economy, the price of each good must just equal its cost of production. In Manufactures, then,

$$P_M = a_{KM}r_K + a_{LM}w \qquad \textbf{(3S-10)}$$

where r_K is the price of capital, w the wage rate of labor, and a_{KM} and a_{LM} the unit input coefficients. Using the notation introduced in equation (3S-6), it follows that

$$\hat{P}_M = \theta_{KM}\hat{r} + \theta_{LM}\hat{w} \qquad \textbf{(3S-11)}$$

or

$$\hat{r}_K = \left(\frac{1}{\theta_{KM}}\right)(\hat{P}_M - \theta_{LM}\hat{w}) = \hat{P}_M + \left(\frac{\theta_{LM}}{\theta_{KM}}\right)(\hat{P}_M - \hat{w}) \qquad \textbf{(3S-12)}$$

Similarly, with parallel notation, in the Food sector

$$\hat{r}_T = \left(\frac{1}{\theta_{TF}}\right)(\hat{P} - \theta_{LF}\hat{w}) = \hat{P}_M + \left(\frac{\theta_{TF}}{\theta_{LF}}\right)(\hat{P}_M - \hat{w}) \qquad \textbf{(3S-13)}$$

Equations (3S-12) and (3S-13) allow derivation of the change in the prices of capital and land, given the changes in the prices of Manufactures, Food, and labor. The next step is to derive the change in the wage rate, which we do by examining the demand and supply for labor.

Notice first that

$$K = a_{KM}Q_M \qquad \textbf{(3S-14)}$$

and

$$L_M = a_{LM}Q_M \qquad \textbf{(3S-15)}$$

It follows that

$$L_M = \left(\frac{a_{LM}}{a_{KM}}\right)K \qquad \textbf{(3S-16)}$$

Because the supply of the specific-factor capital is fixed, employment of labor in the production of Manufactures can change only through changes in the capital-labor ratio. Using the hat notation, the following can be derived:

$$\hat{L}_M = \hat{a}_{LM} - \hat{a}_{KM} = -\sigma(\hat{w} - \hat{r}_K) \qquad \textbf{(3S-17)}$$

From equation (3S-12), it can be shown that

$$\hat{r}_K - \hat{w} = \left(\frac{1 + \theta_{LM}}{\theta_{KM}}\right)(\hat{P}_M - \hat{w}) \qquad \textbf{(3S-18)}$$

Hence

$$\hat{L}_M = \sigma_M\left(\frac{1 + \theta_{LM}}{\theta_{KM}}\right)(\hat{P}_M - \hat{w}) \qquad \textbf{(3S-19)}$$

where σ_M is the elasticity of substitution in Manufactures and, by analogy

$$\hat{L}_F = \sigma_F\left(\frac{1 + \theta_{LF}}{\theta_{TF}}\right)(\hat{P}_F - \hat{w}) \qquad \textbf{(3S-20)}$$

Now turn to the full-employment condition for labor, equation (3S-9). If total employment is to remain unchanged, an increase in one sector's employment must be offset by a decline in the other sector:

$$dL_M + dL_F = 0 \tag{3S-21}$$

As before, this expression can be transformed into one that uses the hat algebra:

$$\left(\frac{dL_M}{L_M}\right)\left(\frac{L_M}{L}\right) + \left(\frac{dL_F}{L_F}\right)\left(\frac{L_F}{L}\right) = 0 \tag{3S-22}$$

or

$$\alpha_M \hat{L}_M + \alpha_F \hat{L}_F = 0 \tag{3S-22'}$$

where $\alpha_M = L_M/L$ is the share of the labor employed in Manufactures in the economy's total labor supply.

The last step is to substitute the labor-demand equations (3S-19) and (3S-20) into equation (3S-22):

$$\sigma_M\left(\frac{1 + \theta_{LM}}{\theta_{KM}}\right)\hat{P}_M + \sigma_F\left(\frac{1 + \theta_{LF}}{\theta_{TF}}\right)\hat{P}_F = \left[\sigma_M\left(\frac{1 + \theta_{LM}}{\theta_{KM}}\right) + \sigma_F\left(\frac{1 + \theta_{LF}}{\theta_{TF}}\right)\right]\hat{w} \tag{3S-23}$$

or

$$\hat{w} = \frac{[\sigma_M(1 + \theta_{LM}/\theta_{KM})\hat{P}_M + \sigma_F(1 + \theta_{LF}/\theta_{TF})\hat{P}_F]}{[\sigma_M(1 + \theta_{LM}/\theta_{KM}) + \sigma_F(1 + \theta_{LF}/\theta_{TF})]} \tag{3S-23'}$$

That is, the rise in the wage rate is a weighted average of the increases in the prices of Manufactures and Food.

EFFECTS OF A CHANGE IN RELATIVE PRICES

Suppose that the price of Manufactures rises relative to that of Food; that is, $\hat{P}_M > \hat{P}_F$. Then, because the change in the wage rate is a weighted average of the change in the two goods prices,

$$\hat{P}_M > \hat{w} > \hat{P}_F$$

The effect on the allocation of labor is apparent from equations (3S-19) and (3S-20): Because $\hat{P}_M > \hat{w}$, $\hat{L}_M > 0$; since $\hat{P}_F < \hat{w}$, $\hat{L}_F < 0$. Employment in Manufactures rises, employment in Food falls.

The effects on the prices of capital and land may be seen from equations (3S-12) and (3S-13). Again, because $\hat{P}_M > \hat{w}$, r_K must rise by *more* than P_M, while conversely r_T rises by less than P_F. Thus the overall description of the relation of goods price and factor price changes is

$$\hat{r}_K > \hat{P}_M > \hat{w} > \hat{P}_F > \hat{r}_T \tag{3S-24}$$

Because the price of capital rises in terms of both goods, someone who derived her income entirely from capital would be unambiguously better off. Because the price of land falls relative to both goods, someone deriving her income entirely from land would be unambiguously worse off. Someone deriving income from labor would find that the purchasing power of that income had risen in terms of food, fallen in terms of manufactures.

POSTSCRIPT to Chapter 4: The Factor-Proportions Model

The factor-proportions model with flexible coefficients is very similar to the specific-factors model: it has two sectors, each of which uses two factors of production. The only difference is that these are now the *same* factors of production, so that both labor and the other factor (land in this example) can be allocated across sectors.

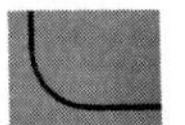

THE BASIC EQUATIONS IN THE FACTOR-PROPORTIONS MODEL

Suppose that a country produces two goods, X and Y, using two factors of production, land and labor. We will assume that X is land intensive. The price of each good must equal its production cost:

$$P_X = a_{TX}r + a_{LX}w \tag{4S-1}$$

$$P_Y = a_{TY}r + a_{LY}w \tag{4S-2}$$

where $a_{TX}, a_{LX}, a_{TY}, a_{LY}$ are the cost-minimizing input choices given the prices of land r and labor w.

Also, the economy's factors of production must be fully employed:

$$a_{TX}Q_X + a_{TY}Q_Y = T \tag{4S-3}$$

$$a_{LX}Q_X + a_{LY}Q_Y = L \tag{4S-4}$$

where T, L, are the total supplies of land and labor.

The factor-price equations (4S-1) and (4S-2) imply hat equations for the rate of change of factor prices, just as in the specific-factors model:

$$\hat{P}_X = \theta_{TX}\hat{r} + \theta_{LX}\hat{w} \tag{4S-5}$$

$$\hat{P}_Y = \theta_{TY}\hat{r} + \theta_{LY}\hat{w} \tag{4S-6}$$

where θ_{TX} is the share of land in the production cost of X, etc. $\theta_{TX} > \theta_{TY}$, and $\theta_{LX} < \theta_{LY}$, because X is more land-intensive than Y.

The quantity equations (4S-3) and (4S-4) must be treated more carefully. The unit inputs a_{TX} etc. can change if factor prices change. If goods prices are held constant, however, then factor prices will not change. Thus for *given* prices of X and Y, it is also possible to write hat equations in terms of factor supplies and outputs:

$$\alpha_{TX}\hat{Q}_X + \alpha_{TY}\hat{Q}_Y = \hat{T} \tag{4S-7}$$

$$\alpha_{LX}\hat{Q}_X + \alpha_{LY}\hat{Q}_Y = \hat{L} \tag{4S-8}$$

where α_{TX} is the share of the economy's land supply that is used in production of X, etc. $\alpha_{TX} > \alpha_{LX}$, and $\alpha_{TY} < \alpha_{LY}$, because of the greater land intensity of X production.

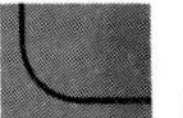

GOODS PRICES AND FACTOR PRICES

The factor-price equations (4S-6) and (4S-7) may be solved together to express factor prices as the outcome of goods prices (these solutions make use of the fact that $\theta_{LX} = 1 - \theta_{TX}$ and $\theta_{LY} = 1 - \theta_{TY}$):

$$\hat{r} = \left(\frac{1}{D}\right)[(1 - \theta_{TY})\hat{P}_X - \theta_{LX}\hat{P}_Y] \tag{4S-9}$$

$$\hat{w} = \left(\frac{1}{D}\right)[-\theta_{TY}\hat{P}_Y + \theta_{TX}\hat{P}_X] \tag{4S-10}$$

where $D = \theta_{TX} - \theta_{TY}$. These may be rearranged in the form

$$\hat{r} = \hat{P}_X + \left(\frac{\theta_{LX}}{D}\right)(\hat{P}_X - \hat{P}_Y) \tag{4S-9$'$}$$

$$\hat{w} = \hat{P}_Y - \left(\frac{\theta_{TY}}{D}\right)(\hat{P}_X - \hat{P}_Y) \tag{4S-10$'$}$$

Suppose that the price of X rises relative to the price of Y, so that $\hat{P}_X > \hat{P}_Y$. Then it follows that

$$\hat{r} > \hat{P}_X > \hat{P}_Y > \hat{w} \tag{4S-11}$$

That is, the real price of land rises in terms of both goods, while the real price of labor falls in terms of both goods. In particular, if the price of X were to rise with no change in the price of Y, the wage rate would actually fall.

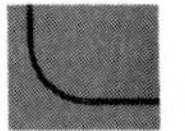

FACTOR SUPPLIES AND OUTPUTS

As long as goods prices may be taken as given, equations (4S-7) and (4S-8) can be solved, using the fact that $\alpha_{TY} = 1 - \alpha_{TX}$ and $\alpha_{LY} = 1 - \alpha_{TX}$, to express the change in output of each good as the outcome of changes in factor supplies:

$$\hat{Q}_X = \left(\frac{1}{D}\right)[\alpha_{LY}\hat{T} - \alpha_{TY}\hat{L}] \tag{4S-12}$$

$$\hat{Q}_Y = \left(\frac{1}{D}\right)[-\alpha_{LX}\hat{T} + \alpha_{TX}\hat{L}] \tag{4S-13}$$

where $D = \alpha_{TX} - \alpha_{LX}$.

These equations may be rewritten

$$\hat{Q}_X = \hat{T} + \left(\frac{\alpha_{TY}}{D}\right)(\hat{T} - \hat{L}) \tag{4S-12'}$$

$$\hat{Q}_Y = \hat{L} - \left(\frac{\alpha_{LX}}{D}\right)(\hat{T} - \hat{L}) \tag{4S-13'}$$

Suppose that P_X and P_Y remain constant, while the supply of land rises relative to the supply of labor—$\hat{T} > \hat{L}$. Then it is immediately apparent that

$$\hat{Q}_X > \hat{T} > \hat{L} > \hat{Q}_Y \tag{4S-14}$$

In particular, if T rises with L remaining constant, output of X will rise more than in proportion while output of Y will actually fall.

POSTSCRIPT
to Chapter 5: The Trading World Economy

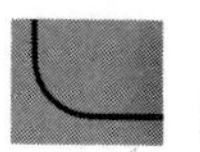

SUPPLY, DEMAND, AND EQUILIBRIUM

WORLD EQUILIBRIUM

Although for graphical purposes it is easiest to express world equilibrium as an equality between relative supply and relative demand, for a mathematical treatment it is preferable to use an alternative formulation. This approach is to focus on the conditions of equality between supply and demand of either one of the two goods Cloth and Food. It does not matter which good is chosen, because equilibrium in the Cloth market implies equilibrium in the Food market and vice versa.

To see this condition, let Q_C, $Q_C{}^*$ be the output of Cloth in Home and Foreign respectively, D_C, $D_C{}^*$ the quantity demanded in each country, and corresponding variables with an F subscript refer to the Food market. Also, let p be the price of Cloth relative to that of Food.

In all cases world expenditure will be equal to world income. World income is the sum of income earned from sales of Cloth and sales of Food; world expenditure is the sum of purchases of Cloth and Food. Thus the equality of income and expenditure may be written

$$p(Q_C + Q_C{}^*) + Q_F + Q_F{}^* = p(D_C + D_C{}^*) + D_F + D_F{}^* \qquad \textbf{(5S-1)}$$

Now suppose that the world market for Cloth is in equilibrium; that is,

$$Q_C + Q_C{}^* = D_C + D_C{}^* \qquad \textbf{(5S-2)}$$

Then from equation (5S-1) it follows that

$$Q_F + Q_F{}^* = D_F + D_F{}^* \qquad \textbf{(5S-3)}$$

That is, the market for Food must be in equilibrium as well. Clearly the converse is also true: if the market for Food is in equilibrium, so too is the market for Cloth.

It is therefore sufficient to focus on the market for Cloth to determine the equilibrium relative price.

PRODUCTION AND INCOME

Each country has a production possibility frontier along which it can trade off between producing Cloth and Food. The economy chooses the point on that frontier which maximizes the value of output at the given relative price of Cloth. This value may be written

$$V = pQ_C + Q_F \tag{5S-4}$$

As in the cost-minimization cases described in earlier postscripts, the fact that the output mix chosen maximizes value implies that a small shift in production along the production-possibility frontier away from the optimal mix has no effect on the value of output:

$$p\,dQ_C + dQ_F = 0 \tag{5S-5}$$

A change in the relative price of Cloth will lead to both a change in the output mix and a change in the value of output. The change in the value of output is

$$dV = Q_C dp + p\,dQ_C + dQ_F; \tag{5S-6}$$

however, because the last two terms are, by equation (5S-5), equal to zero, this expression reduces to

$$dV = Q_C dp \tag{5S-6'}$$

Similarly, in Foreign,

$$dV^* = Q_C^* dp \tag{5S-7}$$

INCOME, PRICES, AND UTILITY

Each country is treated as if it were one individual. The tastes of the country can be represented by a utility function depending on consumption of Cloth and Food:

$$U = U(D_C, D_F) \tag{5S-8}$$

Suppose that a country has an income I in terms of Food. Its total expenditure must be equal to this income, so that

$$pD_C + D_F = I \tag{5S-9}$$

Consumers will maximize utility given their income and the prices they face. Let MU_C, MU_F be the marginal utility that consumers derive from Cloth and Food; then the change in utility that results from any change in consumption is

$$dU = MU_C dD_C + MU_F dD_F \tag{5S-10}$$

Because consumers are maximizing utility given income and prices, there cannot be any affordable change in consumption that makes them better off. This condition implies that at the optimum,

$$\frac{MU_C}{MU_F} = p \tag{5S-11}$$

Now consider the effect on utility of changing income and prices. Differentiating equation (5S-9) yields

$$p\,dD_C + dD_F = dI - D_C\,dp \qquad \textbf{(5S-12)}$$

But from equations (5S-10) and (5S-11),

$$dU = MU_F[p\,dD_C + dD_F] \qquad \textbf{(5S-13)}$$

Thus

$$dU = MU_F[dI - D_C\,dp] \qquad \textbf{(5S-14)}$$

It is convenient to introduce now a new definition: the change in utility divided by the marginal utility of Food, which is the commodity in which income is measured, may be defined as the change in *real income,* and indicated by the symbol dy:

$$dy = \frac{dU}{MU_F} = dI - D_C\,dp \qquad \textbf{(5S-15)}$$

For the economy as a whole, income equals the value of output: $I = V$. Thus the effect of a change in the relative price of Cloth on the economy's real income is

$$dy = [Q_C - D_C]\,dp \qquad \textbf{(5S-16)}$$

The quantity $Q_C - D_C$ is the economy's exports of Cloth. A rise in the relative price of Cloth, then, will benefit an economy that exports Cloth; it is an improvement in that economy's terms of trade. It is instructive to restate this idea in a slightly different way:

$$dy = [p(Q_C - D_C)]\left(\frac{dp}{p}\right) \qquad \textbf{(5S-17)}$$

The term in brackets is the value of exports; the term in parentheses is the percentage change in the terms of trade. The expression therefore says that the real-income gain from a given percentage in terms of trade change is equal to the percentage change in the terms of trade multiplied by the initial value of exports. If a country is initially exporting \$100 billion, and its terms of trade improve by 10 percent, the gain is equivalent to a gain in national income of \$10 billion.

SUPPLY, DEMAND, AND THE STABILITY OF EQUILIBRIUM

In the market for Cloth, a change in the relative price will induce changes in both supply and demand.

On the supply side, a rise in p will lead both Home and Foreign to produce more Cloth. We will denote this supply response as s, s^* in Home and Foreign respectively, so that

$$dQ_C = s\,dp \qquad \textbf{(5S-18)}$$

$$dQ_C^* = s^*\,dp \qquad \textbf{(5S-19)}$$

The demand side is more complex. A change in p will lead to both *income* and *substitution* effects. These effects are illustrated in Figure 5S-1. The figure shows an economy that initially faces a relative price indicated by the slope of the line V^0V^0.

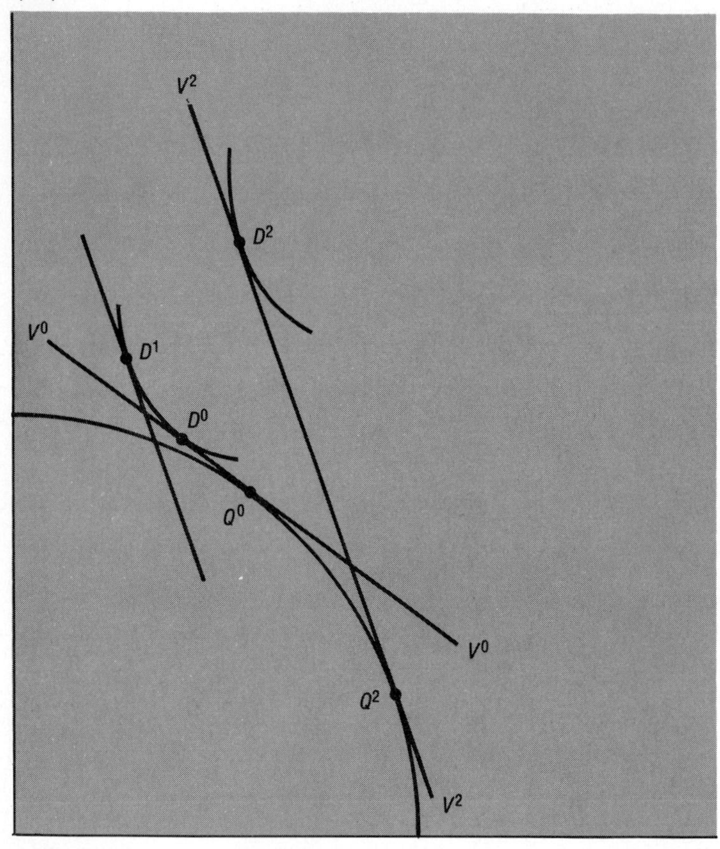

FIGURE 5S-1 Consumption effects of a Price Change. A change in relative prices produces both income and substitution effects.

Given this relative price, the economy produces at point Q^0 and consumes at point D^0. Now suppose that the relative price of Cloth rises, to the level indicated by the slope of V^2V^2. If there were no increase in utility, consumption would shift to D^1, which would involve an unambiguous fall in consumption of Cloth. There is also, however, a change in the economy's real income; in this case, because the economy is initially a net exporter of Cloth, real income rises. This change leads to consumption at D^2 rather than D^1, and this income effect tends to raise consumption of Cloth. To analyze the effect of a change in p on demand requires taking account of both the substitution effect, which is the change in consumption that would take place if real income were held constant, and the income effect, which is the additional change in consumption that is the consequence of the fact that real income changes.

Let the substitution effect be denoted by $-e\,dp$; it is always negative. Also, let the income effect be denoted by $n\,dy$; as long as Cloth is a normal good, for which demand rises with real income, it is positive if the country is a net exporter of Cloth, negative if it is a net importer.[1] Then the total effect of a change in p on Home's demand for Cloth is

$$dD_C = -e\,dp + n\,dy = [-e + n(Q_C - D_C)]\,dp \tag{5S-20}$$

The effect on Foreign's demand similarly is

$$dD_C^* = [-e^* + n^*(Q_C^* - D_C^*)]\,dp \tag{5S-21}$$

Because $Q_C^* - D_C^*$ is negative, the income effect in Foreign is negative.

The demand-and-supply effect can now be put together to get the overall effect of a change in p on the market for Cloth. The *excess supply* of Cloth is the difference between desired world production and consumption:

$$ES_C = Q_C + Q_C^* - D_C - D_C^* \tag{5S-22}$$

The effect of a change in p on world excess supply is

$$dES_C = [s + s^* + e + e^* - n(Q_C - D_C) - n^*(Q_C^* - D_C^*)]\,dp \tag{5S-23}$$

If the market is initially in equilibrium, however, Home's exports equal Foreign's imports, so that $Q_C^* - D_C^* = -(Q_C - D_C)$; the effect of p on excess supply may therefore be written

$$dES_C = [s + s^* + e + e^* - (n - n^*)(Q_C - D_C)]\,dp \tag{5S-23$'$}$$

Suppose that the relative price of Cloth were initially a little higher than its equilibrium level. If the result were an excess supply of Cloth, market forces would push the relative price of Cloth down and thus lead to restoration of equilibrium. On the other hand, if an excessively high relative price of Cloth leads to an excess *demand* for Cloth, the price will rise further, leading the economy away from equilibrium. Thus equilibrium will be *stable* only if a small increase in the relative price of Cloth leads to an excess supply of Cloth; that is, if

$$\frac{dES_C}{dp} > 0 \tag{5S-24}$$

Inspection of equation (5S-23′) reveals the factors determining whether or not equilibrium is stable. Both supply effects and substitution effects in demand work toward stability. The only possible source of instability lies in income effects. The net income effect is of ambiguous sign: it depends on whether $n > n^*$; that is, on whether Home has a higher marginal propensity to consume Cloth when its real income increases than Foreign does. If $n > n^*$, the income effect works against stability, while if $n < n^*$, it reinforces the other reasons for stability.

In what follows it will be assumed that equation (5S-24) holds, so that the equilibrium of the world economy is in fact stable.

[1] If Food is also a normal good, n must be less than $1/p$. To see this effect, notice that if I were to rise by dI without any change in p, spending on Cloth would rise by $np\,dI$. Unless $n < 1/p$, then, more than 100 percent of the increase in income would be spent on Cloth.

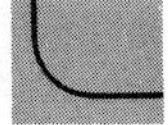

EFFECTS OF CHANGES IN SUPPLY AND DEMAND

THE METHOD OF COMPARATIVE STATICS

To evaluate the effects of changes in the world economy, a method known as *comparative statics* is applied. In each of the cases considered in the text, the world economy is subjected to some change, which will lead to a change in the world relative price of Cloth. The first step in the method of comparative statics is to calculate the effect of the change in the world economy on the excess supply of Cloth *at the original* p. This change is denoted by $dES|_p$. Then the change in the relative price needed to restore equilibrium is calculated by

$$dp = \frac{-dES|_p}{(dES/dp)} \tag{5S-25}$$

where dES/dp reflects the supply, income, and substitution effects described earlier.

The effects of a given change on national welfare can be calculated in two stages. First there is whatever direct effect the change has on real income, which we can denote by $dy|_p$; then there is the indirect effect of the resulting change in the terms of trade, which can be calculated using equation (5S-16). Thus the total effect on welfare is

$$dy = dy|_p + (Q_C - D_C)dp \tag{5S-26}$$

ECONOMIC GROWTH

Consider the effect of growth in the Home economy. As pointed out in the text, by growth we mean an outward shift in the production-possibility frontier. This change will lead to changes in both Cloth and Food output at the initial relative price p; let dQ_C, dQ_F be these changes in output. If growth is strongly biased, one or the other of these changes may be negative, but because production possibilities have expanded, the value of output at the initial p must rise:

$$dV = p\,dQ_C + dQ_F = dy|_p > 0 \tag{5S-27}$$

At the initial p the supply of Cloth will rise by the amount dQ_C. The demand for cloth will also rise, by an amount $n\,dy|_p$. The net effect on world excess supply of Cloth will therefore be

$$dES|_p = dQ_C - n(p\,dQ_C + dQ_F) \tag{5S-28}$$

This expression can have either sign. Suppose first that growth is biased toward Cloth, so that while $dQ_C > 0$, $dQ_F \leq 0$. Then demand for Cloth will rise by

$$dD_C = n(p\,dQ_C + dQ_F) \leq np\,dQ_C < dQ_c$$

(See footnote 1.)

Thus the overall effect on excess supply will be

$$dES|_p = dQ_C - dD_C > 0$$

As a result, $dp = -dES|_p/(dES/dp) < 0$: Home's terms of trade worsen.

On the other hand, suppose that growth is strongly biased toward Food, so that $dQ_C \leq 0$, $dQ_F > 0$. Then the effect on the supply of Cloth at the initial p is negative, but the effect on the demand for Cloth remains positive. It follows that

$$dES|_p = dQ_C - dD_C < 0,$$

so that $dp > 0$. Home's terms of trade improve.

Growth that is less strongly biased can move p either way, depending on the strength of the bias compared with the way Home divides its income at the margin.

Turning next to the welfare effects, the effect on Foreign depends only on the terms of trade. The effect on Home, however, depends on the combination of the initial income change and the subsequent change in the terms of trade, as shown in equation (5S-26). If growth turns the terms of trade against Home, this condition will oppose the immediate favorable effect of growth.

But can growth worsen the terms of trade sufficiently to make the growing country actually worse off? To see that it can, consider first the case of a country that experiences a biased shift in its production possibilities that raises Q_C and lowers Q_F while leaving the value of its output unchanged at initial relative prices. (This change would not necessarily be considered growth, because it violates the assumption of equation (5S-27); but it is a useful reference point). Then there would no change in demand at the initial p, while the supply of Cloth rises; hence p must fall. The change in real income is $dI|_p - (Q_C - D_C)dp$; by construction, however, this is a case in which $dI|_p = 0$, and so dy is certainly negative.

Now this country did not grow, in the usual sense, because the value of output at initial prices did not rise. By allowing the output of either good to rise slightly more, however, we would have a case in which the definition of growth is satisfied. If the extra growth is sufficiently small, however, it will not outweigh the welfare loss from the fall in p. Therefore, sufficiently biased growth can leave the growing country worse off.

THE TRANSFER PROBLEM

Suppose that Home makes a transfer of some of its income to Foreign, say as foreign aid. Let the amount of the transfer, measured in terms of Food, be da. What effect does this alteration have?

At unchanged relative prices there is no effect on supply. The only effect is on demand. Home's income is reduced by da, while Foreign's is raised by the same amount. This adjustment leads to a decline in D by $-n\,da$, while D rises by $n^*\,da$. Thus

$$dES|_p = (n - n^*)\,da \qquad \textbf{(5S-29)}$$

and the change in the terms of trade is

$$dp = -da\frac{(n - n^*)}{(dES/dp)} \qquad \textbf{(5S-30)}$$

Home's terms of trade will worsen if $n > n^*$, which is widely regarded as the normal case; they will, however, improve if $n^* > n$.

The effect on Home's real income combines a direct negative effect from the transfer and an indirect terms-of-trade effect that can go either way. Is it possible for a favorable terms-of-trade effect to outweigh the income loss? In this model it is not. To see the reason, notice that

$$\begin{aligned} dy &= dy|_p + (Q_C - D_C)\,dp \\ &= -da + (Q_C - D_C)\,dp \\ &= -da\left\{1 + \frac{(n - n^*)(Q_C - D_C)}{s + s^* + e + e^* - (n - n^*)(Q_C - D_C)}\right\} \\ &= -da\frac{(s + s^* + e + e^*)}{[s + s^* + e + e^* - (n - n^*)(Q_C - D_C)]} < 0 \end{aligned} \quad \text{(5S-31)}$$

Similar algebra will reveal correspondingly that a transfer cannot make the recipient worse off.

An intuitive explanation of this result is the following. Suppose that p were to rise sufficiently to leave Home as well off as it would be if it made no transfer, and to leave Foreign no better off as a result of the transfer. Then there would be no income effects on demand in the world economy. But the rise in price would produce both increased output of Cloth and substitution in demand away from Cloth, leading to an excess supply that would drive down the price. This result demonstrates that a p sufficiently high to reverse the direct welfare effects of a transfer is above the equilibrium p.

In the text we mention that recent work shows how perverse effects of a transfer are nonetheless possible. This work depends on relaxing the assumptions of this model, either by breaking the assumption that each country may be treated as if it were one individual or by introducing more than two countries.

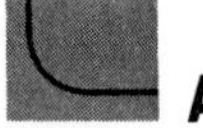

A TARIFF

Suppose that Home places a tariff on imports, imposing a tax equal to the fraction t of the price. Then for a given world relative price of Cloth p, Home consumers and producers will face an internal relative price $\bar{p} = p/(1 + t)$. If the tariff is sufficiently small, the internal relative price will be approximately equal to

$$\bar{p} = p - pt \quad \text{(5S-32)}$$

In addition to affecting p, a tariff will raise revenue, which revenue will be assumed to be redistributed to the rest of the economy.

At the initial terms of trade, a tariff will influence the excess supply of Cloth in two ways. First, the fall in the relative price of Cloth inside Home will lower production of Cloth and induce consumers to substitute away from Food toward Cloth. Second, the tariff may affect Home's real income, with resulting income effects on demand. If Home starts with no tariff and imposes a small tariff, however, the problem may be simplified, because the tariff will have a negligible effect on real income. To see this relation, recall that

$$dy = p\,dD_C + dD_F$$

The value of output and the value of consumption must always be equal at world prices, so that

$$p\,dD_C + dD_F = p\,dQ_C + dQ_F$$

at the initial terms of trade. But because the economy was maximizing the value of output before the tariff was imposed,

$$p\,dQ_C + dQ_F = 0.$$

Because there is no income effect, only the substitution effect is left. The fall in the internal relative price p induces a decline in production and a rise in consumption:

$$dQ_C = -sp\,dt \tag{5S-33}$$

$$dD_C = ep\,dt \tag{5S-34}$$

where dt is the tariff increase. Hence

$$dES|_p = -(s+e)p\,dt < 0 \tag{5S-35}$$

implying

$$\begin{aligned} dp &= \frac{-dES|_p}{(dES/dp)} \\ &= \frac{p\,dt(s+e)}{[s + s^* + e + e^* - (n-n^*)(Q_C - D_C)]} > 0 \end{aligned} \tag{5S-36}$$

This expression shows that a tariff unambiguously improves the terms of trade of the country that imposes it.

Can a tariff actually improve the terms of trade so much that the internal relative price of the imported good falls, and the internal relative price of the exported good rises? The change in $\bar{p}$ is

$$d\bar{p} = dp - p\,dt \tag{5S-37}$$

so that this paradoxical result will occur if $dp > p\,dt$.

By inspecting equation (5S-36) it can be seen that this result, the famous Metzler paradox, is indeed possible. If $s^* + e^* - (n-n^*)(Q_C - D_C) < 0$, there will be a Metzler paradox; this need not imply instability, because the extra terms s and e help give the denominator a positive sign.

POSTSCRIPT to Chapter 21: Risk Aversion and International Portfolio Diversification

This supplement develops a model of international portfolio diversification by a risk-averse investor. The model shows that investors generally care about the risk as well as the return of their portfolios. In particular, people may hold assets whose expected returns are smaller than those of other assets if this strategy reduces the overall riskiness of their wealth.

A representative investor can divide her real wealth, W, between a Home asset and a Foreign asset. Two possible states of nature can occur in the future, and it is impossible to predict which state will occur. In state 1, which occurs with probability q, a unit of wealth invested in the Home asset pays out H_1 units of output and a unit of wealth invested in the foreign asset pays out F_1 units of output. In state 2, which occurs with probability $1 - q$, the corresponding payoffs on the Home and Foreign asset are H_2 and F_2, respectively.

Let α be the share of wealth invested in the Home asset and $1 - \alpha$ the share invested in the Foreign asset. Then if state 1 occurs, the investor will be able to consume the weighted average of her two assets' values,

$$C_1 = [\alpha H_1 + (1 - \alpha)F_1] \times W. \tag{21S-1}$$

Similarly, consumption in state 2 is

$$C_2 = [\alpha H_2 + (1 - \alpha)F_2] \times W. \tag{21S-2}$$

In any state, the investor derives utility $u(C)$ from a consumption level of C. Because the investor does not know beforehand which state will occur, she makes her portfolio decision to maximize the average or *expected* utility from future consumption,

$$qu(C_1) + (1 - q)u(C_2).$$

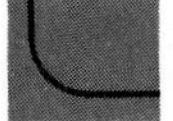

AN ANALYTICAL DERIVATION OF THE OPTIMAL PORTFOLIO

After the state 1 and 2 consumption levels are substituted into the expected utility function above, the investor's decision problem can be expressed as follows: Choose the portfolio share α to maximize expected utility

$$qu\{[\alpha H_1 + (1 - \alpha)F_1] \times W\} + (1 - q)u\{[\alpha H_2 + (1 - \alpha)F_2] \times W\}.$$

This problem is solved by differentiating the expected utility above with respect to α and setting the resulting derivative equal to 0.

Let $u'(C)$ be the derivative of the utility function $u(C)$ with respect to C. Then α maximizes expected utility only if

$$\frac{H_1 - F_1}{H_2 - F_2} = -\frac{(1 - q)u'\{[\alpha H_2 + (1 - \alpha)F_2] \times W\}}{qu'\{[\alpha H_1 + (1 - \alpha)F_1] \times W\}}. \tag{21S-3}$$

This equation can be solved for α, the optimal portfolio share.

For a risk-averse investor, the marginal utility of consumption, $u'(C)$, falls as consumption rises. Declining marginal utility explains why someone who is risk-averse will not take a gamble with an expected payoff of zero: the extra consumption made possible by a win yields less utility than the utility sacrificed if the gamble is lost. If the marginal utility of consumption does not change as consumption changes, we say that the investor is *risk-neutral* rather than risk-averse. A risk-neutral investor is willing to take gambles with a zero expected payoff.

If the investor is risk-neutral so that $u'(C)$ is constant for all C, however, equation (21S-3) becomes

$$qH_1 + (1 - q)H_2 = qF_1 + (1 - q)F_2,$$

which states that *the expected rates of return on Home and Foreign assets are equal.* This result is the basis for the assertion in Chapter 13 that all assets must yield the same expected return in equilibrium when considerations of risk (and liquidity) are ignored. Thus, the interest parity condition of Chapter 13 is valid under risk-neutral behavior but not, in general, under risk aversion.

For the analysis above to make sense, neither of the assets can yield a higher return than the other in *both* states of nature. If one asset did dominate the other in this way, the left-hand side of equation (21S-3) would be positive and its right-hand side would be negative, and there would be no solution. Intuitively, no one wishes to hold an asset if there is another that does better no matter what happens. To be definite, we therefore assume that $H_1 > F_1$ and $H_2 < F_2$, so that the Home asset does better in state 1 but does worse in state 2. This assumption is now used to develop a diagrammatic analysis that helps illustrate additional implications of the model.

A DIAGRAMMATIC DERIVATION OF THE OPTIMAL PORTFOLIO

Figure 21S-1 shows indifference curves for the expected utility function $qu(C_1) + (1 - q)u(C_2)$. The points in the diagram should be thought of as contingency plans showing the level of consumption that will occur in each state of nature. The prefer-

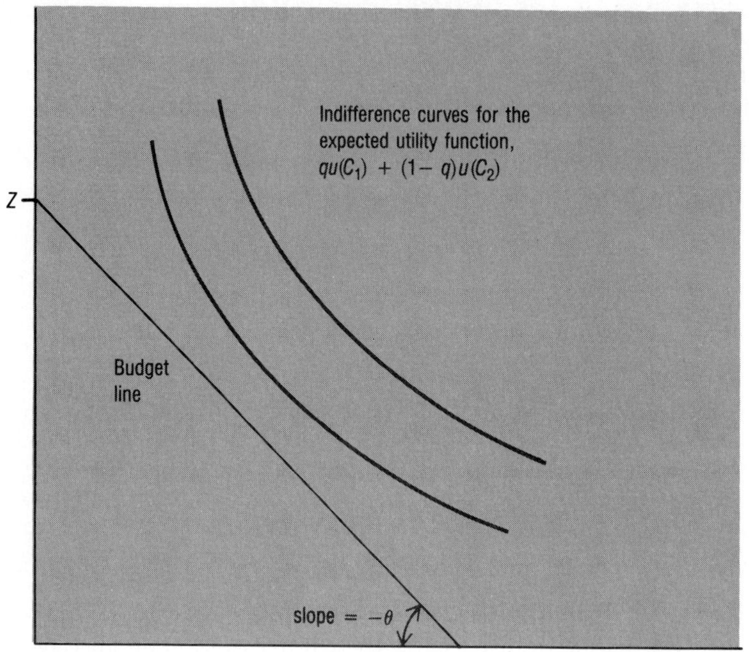

FIGURE 21S-1 Indifference curves and budget line for the portfolio-selection problem. The indifference curves are sets of state-contingent consumption plans with which the individual is equally happy. The budget line describes the trade-off between state 1 and state 2 consumption that results from portfolio shifts between Home and Foreign assets.

ences represented apply to these contingent consumption plans rather than to consumption of different goods in a single state of nature. As with standard indifference curves, however, each curve in the figure represents a set of contingency plans for consumption with which the investor is equally satisfied.

To compensate the investor for a reduction in her consumption in state 1 (C_1), her consumption in state 2 (C_2) must be raised. The indifference curves therefore slope downward. Each curve becomes flatter, however, as C_1 falls and C_2 rises. This property of the curves reflects the property of $u(C)$ that the marginal utility of consumption declines when C rises. As C_1 falls, the investor can be kept on her original indifference curve only by successively greater increments in C_2: additions to C_2 are becoming less enjoyable at the same time as subtractions from C_1 are becoming more painful.

Equations (21S-1) and (21S-2) imply that by choosing the portfolio division given by α, the investor also chooses her consumption levels in the two states of nature. Thus, her problem in choosing an optimal portfolio is equivalent to one of optimally choosing the contingent consumption levels C_1 and C_2. Accordingly, the indifference curves in Figure 21S-1 can be used to determine the optimal portfolio for the investor. All that is needed to complete the analysis is a budget line showing the market trade-off between state 1 consumption and state 2 consumption.

This trade-off is given by equations (21S-1) and (21S-2). If equation (21S-2) is solved for α, the result is

$$\alpha = \frac{F_2 W - C_2}{F_2 W - H_2 W}.$$

After substituting this expression for α into (21S-1), the latter equation becomes

$$C_1 + \theta C_2 = Z, \tag{21S-4}$$

where $\theta = (H_1 - F_1)/(F_2 - H_2)$ and $Z = W \times (H_1 F_2 - H_2 F_1)/(F_2 - H_2)$. Notice that because $H_1 > F_1$ and $H_2 < F_2$, both θ and Z are positive. Thus, equation (21S-4) looks like the budget line that appears in the usual analysis of consumer choice, with θ playing the role of a relative price and Z the role of income. This budget line is graphed in Figure 21S-1 as a straight line with slope $-\theta$ intersecting the vertical axis at Z.

Figure 21S-2 shows how the choices of C_1 and C_2—and, by implication, the choice of the portfolio share α—are determined. As usual, the investor picks the consumption levels given by point 1, where the budget line just touches the highest possible indifference curve. Given the optimal choices of C_1 and C_2, α can be calculated using equation (21S-1) or (21S-2).

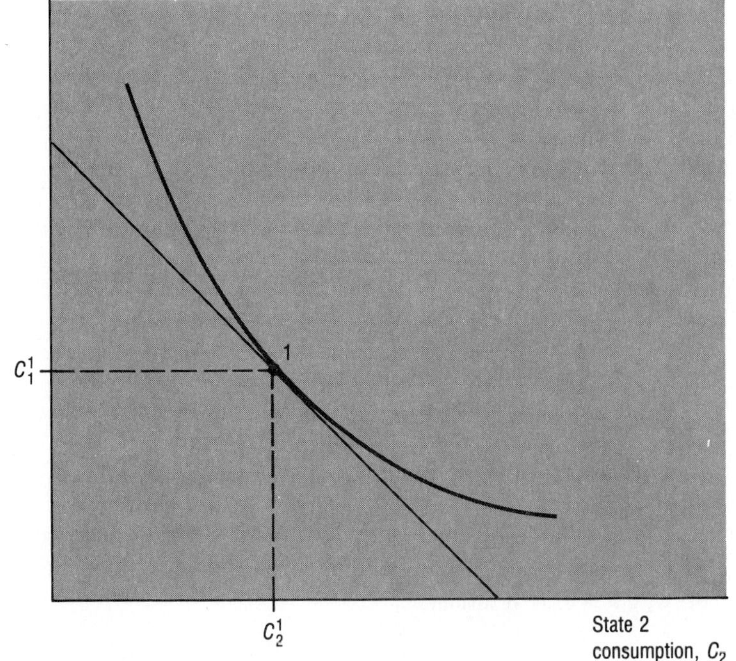

FIGURE 21S-2 Solving the investor's problem. To maximize expected utility, the investor makes the state-contingent consumption choices given by point 1, where the budget line is tangent to the highest attainable indifference curve. The optimal portfolio share, α, can be calculated as $(F_2 W - C_2^1) \div (F_2 W - H_2 W)$.

To interpret θ as the trade-off between state 2 and state 1 consumption (that is, as their relative price), suppose that the investor shifts one unit of her wealth from the Home to the Foreign asset. Because the Home asset has the higher payoff in state 1, her net loss of state 1 consumption is H_1 *less* the Foreign asset's state 1 payoff, F_1. Similarly, her net gain in state 2 consumption is $F_2 - H_2$. To obtain additional state 2 consumption of $F_2 - H_2$, she therefore must sacrifice $H_1 - F_1$ in state 1. The price of a unit of C_2 in terms of C_1 is therefore $H_1 - F_1$ divided by $F_2 - H_2$, which equals θ, the slope of budget line (21S-4).[1]

EFFECTS OF CHANGING RATES OF RETURN

The diagram can be used to illustrate the effect of changes in rates of return under risk aversion. Suppose, for example, that the Home asset's state 1 payoff rises while all other payoffs stay the same. The rise in H_1 raises θ, the relative price of state 2 consumption, and therefore steepens the budget line. (Intuitively, consumption in state 2 has now become more "scarce" relative to consumption in state 1.) This relative price change is not, however, the only change that occurs. Simultaneously, Z, the vertical intercept of the budget line, also rises.[2]

As usual, both "substitution" and "income" effects influence the shift of the investor's contingent consumption plan. The substitution effect is a tendency to demand more C_1, whose relative price has fallen, and to demand less C_2, whose relative price has risen. This substitution is accomplished by a shift from Foreign to Home assets, a move that raises the portfolio's state 1 payoff while lowering its state 2 payoff. In other words, a rise in H_1 raises the relative expected return on the Home asset, and the substitution effect is the resulting portfolio shift toward Home assets.

The income effect of the rise in H_1, however, pushes the budget line outward and tends to raise consumption in *both* states. Because the investor will be richer in state 1, she can afford to shift some of her wealth toward the Foreign asset (which has the higher payoff in state 2) and thereby even out her consumption in the two states of nature. C_1 definitely rises, but C_2 may rise or fall. Corresponding to this ambiguity is an ambiguity about the effect of the change on the portfolio share, α. If the investor is not too risk-averse, C_2 falls and a larger portfolio share is allocated to the Home asset, whose expected return has risen. In this case, α rises. If the investor is very risk-averse, however, she shifts her wealth toward the Foreign asset, whose relative expected return has fallen. By lowering α when H_1 rises, she raises C_2 and thus reduces the variability of her future consumption.

[1] For some values of C_1 and C_2, α may be negative or greater than 1. These possibilities raise no conceptual problems. A negative α, for example, means that the investor has "gone short" in the Home asset; that is, issued a state-contingent claim that promises to pay its holder H_1 units of output in state 1 and H_2 units in state 2. The proceeds of this borrowing are used to "go long" in the Foreign asset.

[2] The horizontal intercept of the budget line shifts inward. Notice, however, that the new budget line must pass through the pair of contingent consumption plans that would result if the investor did not change her portfolio's composition after the change in relative returns. This point lies vertically above C_2^1 if $\alpha > 0$, as we assume.

INDEX

Boldface page reference indicates definition.